T0114406

"A full and devastating history of lynching in America . . . much more than an accounting of the gory details connected with lynching . . . Dray places murderous vigilante justice (most though not all of it perpetrated by whites against blacks) within a much larger context."

—*The New York Times*

"*At the Hands of Persons Unknown* is the most comprehensive and thoughtful analysis I know of that most shameful concomitant of slavery and racism in America—the lynching of thousands of people of color. Philip Dray's book is an important contribution to our historical understanding. I hope it will be widely read."

—HOWARD ZINN

"Philip Dray's powerful new book . . . remind[s] us of the centrality of lynching in American history and of its wide acceptability as well."

—*Chicago Tribune*

"*At the Hands of Persons Unknown* is filled with history we need to know."

—*The New York Times Book Review*

"Riveting . . . My heart beat faster than normal as I read Philip Dray's *At the Hands of Persons Unknown.* . . . For hours at a stretch, I couldn't set it down, perhaps because Dray so skillfully and engagingly filled embarrassing gaps in my knowledge of the brutal practice."

—*Newsday*

"Dray has . . . made excellent use of recent work on the psychology and sociology of lynchings and has incorporated everything into a tight, cleanly written narrative."

—*The New Yorker*

"This is history most fundamental, the kind that forces us to ponder the very nature of humanity."

—*Kirkus Reviews*

AT THE HANDS
OF PERSONS
UNKNOWN

THE LYNCHING
OF BLACK AMERICA

PHILIP DRAY

THE MODERN LIBRARY

NEW YORK

2003 Modern Library Paperback Edition

Copyright © 2002 by Philip Dray

All rights reserved under International and Pan-American
Copyright Conventions. Published in the United States by
Modern Library, a division of Random House, Inc., New York, and
simultaneously in Canada by Random House of Canada Limited, Toronto.

MODERN LIBRARY and the TORCHBEARER Design are registered trademarks of Random House, Inc.

Library of Congress Cataloging-in-Publication Data
Dray, Philip.
At the hands of persons unknown : the lynching of black America / Philip Dray.
p.   cm.
Includes bibliographical references and index.
ISBN 978-0-375-75445-6 (pbk.)
1. Lynching—Southern States—History.   2. African Americans—Crimes
against—Southern States.   3. Southern States—Race relations.   I. Title.
HV6464 .D73   2002
364.1'34—dc21   2001040366

Modern Library website address: www.modernlibrary.com

Book design by Victoria Wong

So quietly they stole upon their prey
And dragged him out to death, so without flaw
Their black design, that they to whom the law
Gave him in keeping, in the broad bright day,
Were not aware when he was snatched away;
And when the people, with a shrinking awe,
The horror of that mangled body saw,
"By unknown hands!" was all that they could say.

So, too, my country, stealeth on apace
The soul-blight of a nation. Not with drums
Or trumpet blare is that corruption sown,
But quietly—now in the open face
Of day, now in the dark—and when it comes,
Stern truth will never write, "By hands unknown."

—from "So Quietly" by Leslie
Pinckney Hill (1921)

Preface

It's difficult for me to remember exactly what I thought about lynching before the day in 1986 when a librarian at the Tuskegee Institute introduced me to the school's lynching archives. Like most people, I was aware that lynching had been an aberrational form of racial violence in the Deep South, and a means by which cattle rustlers and card cheats had sometimes received rough frontier justice. The Tuskegee collection—its file cabinets, storage boxes, folders, and stacks of magazines and newspapers reaching toward the ceiling, containing records of the thousands of lynchings that had taken place in America over the past century—spoke of a far less sporadic phenomenon. "A holocaust!" I heard myself say, as I gazed upon the room's contents for the first time.

The lynching records at Tuskegee date from 1882, a year after Booker T. Washington established the school in the town of Tuskegee, Alabama. Several generations of Tuskegee librarians and students, guided by the example of Tuskegee's first Director of Records, sociologist Monroe Work, have carefully maintained a wide range of newspaper and magazine records of lynchings and other acts of racial violence in America, and until 1962 published a yearly tabulation that came to be considered a definitive tally—a kind of Dow Jones ticker of the nation's most vicious form of intolerance.

Although Booker T. Washington condemned lynching, for many years he was inclined to downplay it, or to suggest it befell mostly vagrants or lowlifes. The lynching records in Tuskegee's library, however, soon took on a life and an importance all their own. Lynch mobs rather pointedly do not keep accounts; in a sense, they seek to negate history itself. The Tuskegee files, silently accumulating during lynching's worst years, ultimately frustrated this result—simply by keeping track.

In the years 1882–85, the Tuskegee records show the number of whites lynched in America to have exceeded the number of blacks. After the year 1886, when the school recorded the lynching of 74 blacks and 64 whites, the number of blacks always exceeded whites. In 1892, the archive records 162 black Americans put to death outside the bounds of the law, chiefly in Alabama, Arkansas, Florida, Georgia, Louisiana, Mississippi, South Carolina, Tennessee, Texas, and Kentucky. Through 1944, when lynchings first began to decline strongly, Tuskegee recorded 3,417 lynchings of blacks and 1,291 of whites. Not until 1952 did a year pass without a single recorded lynching.

The term *lynching* has always been somewhat ambiguous. In the late eighteenth century it referred to nonlethal summary punishment such as flogging or tar-and-feathering. One hundred years later it meant the summary execution by a mob of an individual who had committed an alleged crime or a perceived transgression of social codes. In 1922 it was defined (in one version of proposed federal antilynching legislation) as "five or more persons acting in concert for the purpose of depriving any person of his life without authority of law" (in a final version the number of conspirators was changed to three). Twelve years later, a bill before Congress described a lynching as a "mob or riotous assemblage composed of three or more persons acting in concert, without authority of law, to kill or injure any person in the custody of any peace officer, with the purpose or consequence of depriving such person of due process of law or the equal protection of the laws." A federal criminal statute dating from Reconstruction that came to be used against lynch mobs in the mid-twentieth century cited two as the number required to constitute a conspiracy. Today, when lynchings are virtually nonexistent, the term is used primarily as a metaphor, the most well-known example being that of Supreme Court Justice Clarence Thomas who, in his televised confirmation hearing before the Senate Judiciary Committee in 1991, complained that he was the victim of "a high-tech lynching."

The lynching of black Americans was chiefly a Southern phenomenon, but it was not spread evenly across the South. From Tidewater Virginia to Alabama's piney woods, from New Orleans's French Quarter to the Texas ranchlands, the South has always held considerable topographical, social, and political diversity, and lynching statistics reflect it. The Deep South accounts for most lynchings, with Georgia, Mississippi, and Texas the dominant lynching states, followed closely by Louisiana, Alabama, and Arkansas. A majority of lynchings in Tennessee and Kentucky took place along those states' western borders; in Mississippi, in the densely black-populated area of the Delta. East Texas, more closely aligned in spirit with the Confederate South, saw more lynchings than the western reaches of the state. Generally, lynchings were more prevalent in low-lying agricultural lands than in the hills; indeed, they were rare among mountain folk in Kentucky and West Virginia. Despite this diversity, the South often tended to speak with one voice when it came to defending the practice or when threatened by federal antilynching laws.

Discerning who and what type of person took part in lynchings is made difficult by the fact that those who carried out extralegal punishments were pointedly anonymous. This was both practical—it protected lynchers from arrest and prosecution—and symbolic, in that the lynching was seen as a conservative act, a defense of the status quo. The coroner's inevitable verdict, "Death at the hands of persons unknown," affirmed the public's tacit complicity: no *persons* had committed a crime, because the lynching had been an expression of the community's will. Other protective euphemisms came into play. Lynchers, never identified by name, were "determined men," members of "Judge Lynch's Court," or men "agitated to a high degree"; and eyewitnesses, even law officers, invariably swore they hadn't recognized any of the mob's individual members.

Such efforts at concealment were largely successful, although participants generally fit into one of several categories. Because most lynchings were spontaneous events that required tremendous organization and purpose, a cell of highly motivated perpetrators was essential. These men and boys carried the rope or gasoline, fought with the sheriff's men, drove the automobiles, secured the victim; just beyond them was a ring of cheerleaders, men and women with a grudge or special interest in seeing "justice" done; present also might be a gentleman of some authority or social standing whose appearance lent the lynching a sense of legitimacy and whose words might be of some influence (for example, directing the mob to choose an appropriate location for the killing); then came the crowd of onlookers, passive, alternately frightened and fascinated; and lastly that much-referred-to but seldom-seen class, "the better people," who would not deign to show their faces at a lynching but whose complicity was essential; their weary comment the next morning, upon learning of a lynching ("Well, such things must be, mustn't they? Perhaps now we'll have some peace and quiet"), expressing the community's understanding and acceptance of what had occurred and bringing the affair to an end.

Although the most sensational and commonly repeated excuse for a lynching was a sexual assault by a black man against a white woman, the instigating reasons were actually wide-ranging. The black-owned Richmond *Planet* kept a running tabulation in a column entitled "The Reign of Lawlessness." Where possible, the paper gave the white accusation against the victim that led to the lynchings. In 1897, with two or three lynchings making news every week and a total of 123 black victims recorded for the year, the causes of the incidents ranged from murder, rape, and assault to wanting a drink of water and sassing a white lady. In a typical four-week period beginning June 14, 1897, Mrs. Jake Cebrose of Plano, Texas, was lynched for "nothing"; four men accused of murder—Solomon Jackson, Lewis Speir, Jesse Thompson, and Camp Reese—were lynched together in Wetumpka, Alabama; an eight-year-old black child identified only as "Parks" was lynched in South Carolina for "nothing"; Charlie Washington was lynched for "rape and robbery" in Alabama; William Street was burned at the stake for "assault" in Devline, Louisiana; Dan Ogg was put to death in Palestine, Texas, because he was "found in a white family's room"; and Alex Walker of Pleasant Hill, Alabama, had his life extinguished for "being troublesome." The National Association for the Advancement of Colored People (NAACP), working in the 1930s to combat the Southern argument that black men posed an inordinate sexual threat to white women, reviewed its own extensive case files for the actual causes of lynchings over several decades and produced a list that included such infractions as window peeping, making moonshine liquor, slapping a child, conjuring, stealing hogs, not turning out of the road for a white boy in an automobile, and disobeying ferry regulations.

The Tuskegee archives are widely respected and have been used by generations of scholars. But no one, not even the keepers of the archives themselves, regards its statistics as anywhere close to comprehensive. Prior to the turn of the century, newspapers were spotty in their coverage of race-related killings, often limiting themselves to the spectacle lynchings in which mobs tortured and burned victims to death as huge picnic-like gatherings of men, women, and children watched, and lynchings in which a mob removed someone by force from a jail or the custody of a sheriff. The nation's first antilynching advocate, Ida B. Wells-Barnett, estimated in the 1890s that as many as ten thousand black Americans had been put to death in the South since the Civil War; but other reformers and historians have ventured various other estimates.

Atrocities in isolated Southern backwaters often went completely unremarked upon, as did race-riot killings of blacks by mobs or police officers in cities. Almost every black American family has a story in its history of an ancestor who "come up missing," who vanished into that empty place—the rural crossroads or rail siding, the bayou or jail cell—where the white South at times sought to resolve its most intractable "problem." Regardless of any statistics, it is a living memory to most black Americans that their forebears were lynched and routinely subjected to violence and intimidation, and that they lived in almost constant fear of seeing a loved one lynched or of being targeted themselves. "I could not suppress the thought," James Baldwin would recall of seeing the red clay hills of Georgia from an airplane on his first visit to the South, "that this earth had acquired its color from the blood that had dripped down from these trees."

I was drawn to the story of lynching in part because I felt that in this pariah of a subject—what had long been known, almost officially, as the "Shame of America"—there must be some meaning, some message, to be derived. To an extent I was guided by the trend in historiography dating from the 1960s that has imparted new significance to violence as a social force. No longer ignored or viewed as merely an unfortunate disruption, outbreaks or sustained periods of violence have come to be evaluated as one of the primary ways in which societies evolve or seek change. Lynching proved overripe for just such an approach. Rather than viewing lynching as a frenzied abnormality, historians in recent years have sought to understand it as a tradition, a systematized reign of terror that was used to maintain the power whites had over blacks, a way to keep blacks fearful and to forestall black progress and miscegenation. The effect of the peculiar institution of slavery on black Americans is well documented, but the institution of lynching less so, yet it was for many decades an awesome destructive power, murderous to some, menacing to a great many, a constant source of intimidation to all black Southerners young and old and a daily reminder of their defenselessness. Is it possible for white America to really understand blacks' distrust of the legal system, their fears of racial profiling and the police, without understanding how cheap a black life was for so long a time in our nation's history?

Lynching, as everyone knows, has always had a special power to make us want to look the other way. This is because it possesses none of the ennobling features or redeeming sentiment that have popularized other aspects of America's violent past, such as the Civil War, Custer's Last Stand, Old West gunslingers and riverboat brawlers, or even the world of organized crime. There is much killing in American history, a great deal of it no doubt senseless and unnecessary, but lynching celebrates killing and makes of it a ritual, turning grisly and inhumane acts of cruelty into theater with the explicit intent that they be viewed and remembered. It is this ritualization, and the knowledge that victims were chosen for their race and put to death in specific defiance of reasonable values of fairness or decency, that makes the story of lynching so burdensome an American legacy to confront.

This task is mitigated somewhat by the example of the men and women who led the long and difficult fight to expose and eradicate the practice. Ida Wells, James Weldon Johnson, Walter White, and W.E.B. Du Bois were only a few of those who took great risks and, in some instances, devoted their lives to the antilynching crusade. They sustained their campaign with the ardent belief that their countrymen would, if adequately informed of the evil of lynching, join them in addressing so terrible an injustice; and they dreamed that from such a fundamental change in consciousness other improvements in racial understanding might flow. For all their tireless efforts—writing, speaking, riding Jim Crow all night on Southern trains to investigate a lynch site in the morning—most never lived to see a time when the report of a lynching was not somewhere in the day's news. If lynching, historically, is emblematic of what is worst about America—racism, intolerance, cruel and sadistic forms of violence—their fight may stand for what is best: the love of justice and fairness, and the conviction that one individual's sense of right can suffice to defy the gravest of wrongs. This book aspires to follow the trajectory of both these forces in American life, and to make the subject of lynching belong to us all.

Contents

AT THE HANDS
OF PERSONS
UNKNOWN

CHAPTER 1

"A Negro's Life Is a
Very Cheap Thing in Georgia"

Smartly dressed, with his walking cane in hand, W.E.B. Du Bois left his home in Atlanta on April 24, 1899, and began walking downtown along Mitchell Street. He was carrying a letter of introduction to Joel Chandler Harris, the white author of the Negro dialect tales known as the Uncle Remus stories and an editor at *The Atlanta Constitution*. At thirty-one, Du Bois was himself an acclaimed author, with degrees from Harvard and two years' study at a prestigious German university to his credit. In addition to his teaching duties as a professor of economics and history at Atlanta University, he also supervised an ambitious program of social research there.

Although he had lived in Atlanta since 1897, he had never bothered to seek out Harris, even though they had mutual friends; Du Bois rarely left the university to go into downtown Atlanta because he refused to ride the city's segregated streetcars. But a sensational rape and murder in rural Georgia in mid-April had caused an uproar, and a black farmhand, Sam Hose, said to have brutally killed his employer, Alfred Cranford, and to have "outraged" Cranford's wife, Mattie, had been lynched.

Du Bois had studied the lynching phenomenon and he knew that in such instances things usually weren't as they seemed. "It occurred to me," he said later, "that I might go down to the Atlanta *Constitution* and talk with

Joel Chandler Harris, and try to put before the South what happened in cases of this sort, and try to see if I couldn't start some sort of movement." In addition to his letter of introduction, Du Bois also carried a letter he'd written protesting the action of the lynch mob.

The crime that had "dethroned the reason of the people of western Georgia," as the *Constitution* put it, had occurred on Wednesday, April 12, 1899, in the small farming town of Palmetto, just southwest of Atlanta. The Cranfords, who were in their mid-twenties, were descendants of two of the area's most established families. Alfred's family owned extensive land, and Mattie (née McElroy) had been known before her marriage as "one of the belles of Newnan," the historic courthouse town that was the seat of Coweta County.

Alleged murderer Sam Hose, twenty-one, had grown up on a farm near Macon and had come to work for the Cranfords only six months earlier. The fact that he was unknown in Coweta may have enabled him to disappear more readily after the assault on the Cranfords, but it also made it more certain he would receive no quarter from the hundreds of lawmen and self-appointed guardians of the community's well-being tracking him along the back roads of west-central Georgia, in what was called the largest manhunt in the state's history. This "monster in human form," explained one much-reprinted account of the Cranford murder given by Georgia congressman James M. Griggs,

> . . . crept into that happy little home . . . with an ax knocked out the brains of that father, snatched the child from its mother, threw it across the room out of his way, and then by force accomplished his foul purpose. [He] carried her helpless body to another room, and there stripped her person of every thread and vestige of clothing, there keeping her till time enough had elapsed to permit him to accomplish his fiendish offence twice more and again!

Georgia governor Allen D. Candler, widely known to endorse lynching as a method of controlling black criminality, termed the Palmetto murder "the most diabolical in the annals of crime" and declared its details "too horrible for publication." In truth, the newspapers found them quite suitable for publication. Turn-of-the-century news accounts of incidents such as the Hose-Cranford case constituted a kind of "folk pornography" that made for welcome, titillating reading. Stories of sexual assault, insatiable black rapists, tender white virgins, and manhunts led by "determined men" that culminated in lynchings were the bodice rippers of their day, vying in the South's daily newspapers with exposés about black dives and gambling dens, drunkenness and cocaine addiction, and warnings about domestics who stole family heirlooms. The cumulative impression was of a world made precarious by Negroes.

The Sam Hose affair offered no end of lurid details—Hose, the "fiend incarnate," had crushed Alfred Cranford's skull with an ax "until the brains oozed out," then "snatched Mrs. Cranford's baby and dashed it to the floor," before forcing the poor woman "to submit to the most shameful outrage which one of her sex can suffer." And as it gave the public information about the case, the Georgia press also whipped up expectations that a huge spectacle lynching would be held when Hose was captured. As early as April 13, the day after the crime, the *Constitution*'s front-page headline read "Determined Mob After Hose; He Will Be Lynched if Caught," while a subhead suggested "Assailant of Mrs. Cranford May Be Brought to Palmetto and Burned at the Stake." On April 19, with Hose still at large, the *Constitution* assured readers: "When Hose is caught he will either be lynched and his body riddled with bullets or he will be burned at the stake . . . the mob which is in pursuit of him is composed of determined men . . . wrought up to an unusual degree."

Georgia authorities were cautioned not to attempt to interfere with "the people's will," because as the Newnan *Herald and Advertiser* pointed out, no punishment existed under law adequate to match the crime against the Cranfords. "The black brute, whose carnival of blood and lust has brought death and desolation to the home of one of our best and most worthy citizens," must be "run down and made to suffer the torments of the damned in expiation of his hellish crime." A few days later the paper couched the need for Hose's lynching in tones of civic necessity, insisting that Hose's punishment "be made summary enough to serve notice upon those who sympathize with him, that there is protection in Georgia for women and children."

"No community in Georgia has been more ready, at all times and in all circumstances, to show respect for the law or yield obedience to the mandates of the constituted authorities," an editorial in the Newnan paper said, "but in the present instance the provocation is so unbearably aggravating that the people cannot be expected to wait with patience on the laggard processes of the courts." The *Constitution* added that no law officer in his right mind would attempt to protect Hose from a mob. Even though he had not yet been apprehended, Sam Hose's fate was firmly sealed.

Born in 1868, William Edward Burghardt Du Bois was raised in Great Barrington, Massachusetts, in the foothills of the Berkshires, where, because of New England's relative leniency on matters involving race, the established, if modest, reputation in the town of his mother's family, and his own precociousness, he managed to participate fully in the life of the community and attend school with white children. As a result, he later wrote,

> I very early got the idea that what I was going to do was to prove that Negroes were just like other people. . . . [I]n the first place I was very much annoyed because nothing was ever said about Negroes in the textbooks, while, on the other hand, I, as a Negro in this school, seemed to be looked upon as unusual by everybody. Now, if I was unusual in this school, and a sort of curiosity, then the Negroes must be so in the world. And if I could easily keep up with and beat these students in the high school, why didn't the Negroes do it in the world?

Graduating from Fisk University in Nashville in 1888, he took a second bachelor's degree at Harvard in 1890 and an M.A. in history there in 1892, then went to Europe for two years' study at Friedrich-Wilhelm University in Berlin, concentrating on economics, history, and sociology. Returning to the United States in 1894, he taught at Wilberforce University in Ohio and the next year became the first black to be awarded a Ph.D. at Harvard. In 1896, when his Harvard doctoral dissertation on the suppression of the African slave trade was published to critical acclaim, Du Bois was at the University of Pennsylvania leading a comprehensive sociological study of Philadelphia's Negro population, the first such analysis ever made of an American black community.

In fall 1897, he joined the Atlanta University faculty and took charge of the "Atlanta Conferences," annual meetings designed to guide scientific research into the conditions affecting black Americans. Little if any data existed on this subject, sociology itself being a new discipline. Du Bois published the results of these conferences with the long-term goal of ultimately assembling a compendium of data and information about all facets of black life in America—urbanization, the black church, crime, health and physique, mortality, and the family, as well as black morals and manners. The Atlanta Conference papers were widely quoted and commented on, and Du Bois was increasingly seen as a respected authority on what was coming to be called the "Negro Problem," the question of how 8 million black Americans were to coexist with a white society that consistently rejected them as partners and obstructed their efforts at assimilation and self-improvement.

Just as Du Bois knew that the "problem" with black people was white people, he knew that the odds were good that Sam Hose had not raped Mattie Cranford. His doubts arose, to a degree, from some intelligence he had received about the case from black acquaintances—race relations in Coweta had been severely strained since January, when several blacks suspected of arson were herded into a warehouse roped together like cattle and shot to death—but also from his familiarity with the writings of Ida Wells-Barnett, the Chicago-based journalist who was the nation's preeminent antilynching crusader. In her many articles and lectures on the evil of lynching, Wells-Barnett had shown that in the majority of cases the charge of rape was untrue, and had either been added to a complaint about a black suspect in order to incense local whites or, in some instances, to obscure the fact that the black man's real sin had been to have consensual sex with a white woman. Du Bois, in his own informal study of the subject, had found that despite the generally held tenet that black men were lynched for assaults on white women, in only 25 percent of lynchings was that crime even alleged. He found that disputes related to wages and work conditions were more typically to blame in cases like Sam Hose's, where a black worker was accused of killing his white employer. Du Bois intuited that Hose was probably guilty at worst of committing an act of violence against a white in the course of defending his right to disagree, or in refusing to be physically intimidated. The rape charge, Du Bois believed, had been "trumped up to arouse the worst passions of the countryside." The scenario of the crime as presented by the newspapers—that Hose had first killed Cranford, then methodically raped his wife—sounded illogical. Du Bois later wrote:

> They started then to find Sam Hose and they couldn't find him. And then, suddenly, there was the accusation that Sam Hose had raped his wife. Now, everybody that read the facts of the case knew perfectly well what had happened. The man wouldn't pay him, so they got into a fight, and the man got killed—and then, in order to arouse the neighborhood to find this man, they brought in the charge of rape. Even from the newspapers you could see there was no foundation to it.

By definition, lynching denies a suspect due process under law, and so the kind of information that due process generates—lawyers' arguments, a judge's rulings, testimony, evidence—is not available to assist the historian in understanding the instigating deed. In the Hose case, there was no police investigation made of the crime scene, no evidence gathered, and Mattie Cranford was neither interviewed by any official or reporter nor examined by a physician. Most of the details were simply provided to the sheriff and to reporters by the Cranford family or their close friends.

According to the family's account, Alfred Cranford had reprimanded his hired hand for sloppy work habits shortly before the murder. Hose, in turn, had been heard to mutter threats against his boss, leading Cranford's father, G. E. Cranford, who lived on an adjacent property, to give his son a gun with which to defend himself. On the evening of Wednesday, April 12, Alfred and Mattie and their children were just sitting down to dinner when Sam Hose suddenly appeared outside, barefoot and wearing his work garb. Alfred called out to him—whether in greeting or to further discipline him is not known—at which Hose entered and immediately attacked Cranford with an ax, striking him before he could rise from his chair. The white man fell to the floor and Hose swung the ax again, this time with tremendous power, splitting Cranford's skull open to the level of his eyes.

Grabbing the terrified Mattie, the family's account continued, Hose then forced her to lead him through the house with a lantern, during which time he stole several small items, including a wad of Confederate money (a detail probably added as an insult to the killer, since it was a standing joke among Southern whites that blacks did not realize the currency was worthless). He then forced her back to the room where her husband lay dead or dying and, batting the Cranfords' four-year-old daughter and an eight-month-old boy out of the way, raped Mattie before making a hasty getaway.

Sobbing hysterically, Mattie then found her way to her father-in-law's house to raise the alarm. A round-the-clock search for Hose began almost immediately, inspired by the shocking details of the crime and, a short time later, by the generous reward monies offered for Hose's capture. In addition to the *Constitution*'s reward of $500, Governor Candler offered $500, Coweta County put up $250, the town of Palmetto $250, and a wealthy Atlantan, Mr. Jacob Haas, $100, for a total of $1,600—a small fortune in 1899. The *Constitution* described Hose in bold type on its front page as a mulatto with an unusual ginger-cake complexion, five feet eight inches, with two black teeth, close-cropped hair, a black mustache, and a habit of shaking his head while speaking.

As days passed without any sign of him, rumors circulated of the fugitive's invincibility. Hose, it was said, was in Florida, in Alabama, in Savannah, was hiding in a swamp, was heavily armed, was a superb marksman, had not eaten or slept in days, had vowed to kill more whites. *The New York Times* reported that most businesses in Palmetto had closed so proprietors could join the search parties, and that the three hundred or so men combing the area had such regard for the mulattoes (in an age that placed great faith in theories of racial determinism, mulattoes were thought to be more deviant than other Negroes) they could only "hope that he will be compelled to seek rest, and that they will be able to come upon him while asleep."

Seventy-five miles southeast of Palmetto, Sam Hose's mother lived and worked on a farm owned by two brothers, J. B. and J. L. Jones, near Marshallville. Sam had been employed there himself until 1896 or 1897, when he was accused of assaulting another worker, an older black woman, and instead of waiting around for his punishment had run away. Sometime after April 14, 1899, a black worker on the place informed the Jones brothers that Hose had returned and was lying low, taking meals in his mother's cabin. The white men at first assumed Sam was keeping out of sight due to his earlier trouble, but they became suspicious when they learned he had gone to the extent of disguising himself by darkening his face with lampblack. Aware that a man was being sought for a killing up in Coweta County, they double-checked the newspaper's description of the fugitive "ginger-colored Negro," then offered their informant a small amount of money to lure Hose out into the open. On the night of Saturday, April 22, Hose was persuaded by his acquaintance to attend a "frolic" at a nearby farm, and en route, at a prearranged signal, the Jones brothers leaped out of the bushes and took him prisoner. Hose offered no resistance.

Only upon turning Hose over to the law would the Joneses qualify to receive the reward money, and this meant somehow delivering him to the authorities in Atlanta without being intercepted by a lynch mob. The brothers decided it best to try to run the gauntlet early the next day by train. It would be a Sunday morning, and the manhunt, which was for the most part concentrating on the region's swamps, wooded places, and waterways, might be negligible on the railroads. After all, who would expect so wanted a criminal to buy a train ticket? They worked to improve Hose's disguise, powdering his face a shade darker, and forced him to wear an old raincoat so his bound hands would not be visible.

Their plan almost worked. Early in the morning they boarded an Atlanta-bound train at Powersville, just south of Macon, and by ten o'clock had safely reached Griffin, one of the last stops before Atlanta. But at the Griffin depot a fellow passenger became suspicious and alerted railroad workers. Shouts were heard—"The Palmetto murderer! The nigger's here in the cars!"—and men came running down the platform. In moments the Jones party was surrounded and taken off the train at gunpoint.

Excited telephone calls were made to Newnan and Atlanta. After complex negotiations involving the Jones brothers, the sheriffs of two counties, the railroad, and other interested parties, it was decided a special train would be assembled at Griffin to return Hose to Newnan. This train—it was really not much of a train at all, consisting only of a single coach car attached to a locomotive and coal car—was quickly loaded. In addition to Hose and the Joneses, numerous deputies and railroad officials got on board, as did about 150 unofficial "escorts," all armed, who crammed into the coach, hung on to the sides of the engine, and even crouched or stood precariously on the cowcatcher.

At Newnan, word of Hose's arrest had spread rapidly and dozens of men welcomed the train. A delegation came aboard and marched Hose and the Joneses through town to Sheriff Joseph L. Brown's jail, which within minutes was surrounded by curious townspeople. As they had arranged by phone from Griffin, the brothers agreed to surrender Hose to Sheriff Brown if they were given a receipt certifying that they had earned the right to the reward money. But a disagreement took place over what constituted the complete and satisfactory delivery of the fugitive to the authorities. The Joneses felt they had honored their part of the deal by bringing Hose to Newnan; Sheriff Brown said he could not consider himself to have custody of the prisoner so long as there was a mob in control of his jail. They finally agreed on a script in which the town jailer would lock Hose in a cell for a moment before handing him over to the mob. But the members of the mob grew alarmed when they saw the murderer being led into a lockup. They surrounded the jailer, held a pistol to his head, and took possession of Hose.

One of the leading residents of Newnan was William Gates Atkinson, a former governor of Georgia (1894–1898) who had supported a state antilynching law that had gone into effect in 1893. Under his administration an average of only fourteen lynchings a year occurred in the state, compared with twenty-eight per year under the prolynching Governor Candler, making Atkinson something of a progressive. Informed that a mob had Sam Hose and was about to lynch him, Atkinson came from his home near the courthouse square and, stepping up onto the seat of an open buggy, appealed to be heard. Out of deference the mob halted, although one man reportedly kept a pistol trained on the former governor as he made his remarks:

> My fellow citizens and friends, I beseech you to let this affair go no further. You are hurrying this Negro on to death without an identification. Mrs. Cranford, whom he is said to have assaulted, and whose husband he is said to have killed, is sick in bed and unable to be here to say whether this is her assailant. Let this Negro be returned to jail. The law will take its course, and I promise it will do so quickly and effectually. Do not stain the honor of this state with a crime such as you are about to perform.

Atkinson cautioned his neighbors that if a lynching occurred and an inquiry was later held concerning it, he would have no choice but to testify against the mob's leaders—a fairly empty threat, since everyone knew no such inquiry would ever take place. The governor received a respectful hearing, but when Judge Alvan D. Freeman followed Atkinson in pleading for Hose to be returned to jail, the mob stirred impatiently. "Think of his crime!" someone yelled, drowning Freeman out. "Burn him!" "On to Palmetto!"

Atkinson and Freeman were not the only Newnan citizens eager to avoid having their community associated with a lynching. Newnan was a relatively affluent town and enjoyed a certain historic cachet. Its antebellum mansions and tree-lined avenues had come through the Civil War virtually unscathed, and the town's demeanor seemed derived from a more genteel Old South past. It thus came as a relief to many onlookers when the crowd bearing Sam Hose, which had grown to more than a thousand, headed away from Newnan's courthouse square with their captive.

The one stop the mob was compelled to make was at the Newnan home of the McElroys, Mattie Cranford's parents, to allow Mattie, who was recuperating there, a chance to positively identify her attacker. This was a ritualized aspect of a Southern lynching. The woman who had been outraged was, when possible, asked to confront and identify her assailant and could, if she chose, participate in killing him, although in the actual bloodletting she was usually represented by a father, brother, husband, or other male relative, whose honor was deemed also to have been besmirched. That she be made to face her attacker and identify him was a somewhat curious tradition, considering that one of the frequent ratio-

nales for lynchings was that summary execution of rapists spared humiliated women the distress of having to answer questions in open court
about the outrage they'd suffered.

In Mattie Cranford's stead her mother came out to the road to tell the
lynch mob that her daughter was too ill to identify the accused man. Mattie, whose condition in the crime's aftermath had been variously described
as "crazed," "deranged," and "unbalanced," never did confront or identify
Sam Hose. (One later account even claimed she had been "unconscious"
for weeks after the traumatic assault on her family and person, a claim belied by her presence at her husband's funeral three days after his death.)
Her mother and a sister, however, did identify Sam Hose to the mob as
having been a hired hand on the Cranford place. News accounts of this
scene vary, although it appears Mrs. McElroy asked Hose why he had killed
Cranford. Hose replied that Cranford had threatened him and that he had
had no choice but to defend himself; he also denied raping Mattie. Someone in the crowd declared it would be fitting to lynch Hose on the spot, an
idea that was greeted with cheers. But the ladies asked that the lynching not
take place on their property, and as the mob was obliged by custom to respect such a request, it resumed pushing Hose along toward Palmetto.

The lynch mob hadn't traveled far, though, when word came that un-
scheduled trains from Atlanta were approaching Newnan. Concerned that
soldiers might be coming to separate them from their prize, the mob's leaders decided they could wait no longer. An area of scraggly farmland and
pinewoods alongside the Palmetto Road, known as the Old Troutman Field,
was accepted as a likely location for the execution. It had several large trees
set back off the road and would afford views to a large number of spectators.

Now that the lynching was at hand, men began carrying out prearranged duties. Those who had been toting kerosene and small pieces of
lumber began building the pyre, while others secured Hose to the trunk
of a pine tree. Young men and boys raced through the adjoining woods
seeking added kindling; old fence posts, railroad ties, and dead tree limbs
were piled around Hose's feet. The captive's clothes were cut or stripped
away. A heavy chain was wound around his upper and lower body, then
closed and locked in front of his chest. Word went out that the lynching
was about to commence, and the occupants of a column of buggies and
wagons stretching back almost to the Newnan courthouse abandoned
their vehicles and swarmed into the field.

The trains en route from Atlanta carried no soldiers but only more
spectators. Word of Hose's capture had arrived in the metropolis that Sun-

day morning just as many Atlantans were leaving church, and there had ensued a mad rush of worshippers to the train station seeking the swiftest possible passage. To cope with the demand, the Atlanta and West Point Railroad announced that a special excursion train for Newnan would depart at one o'clock. When the six coaches of the train appeared, pandemonium broke out. Passengers who had been unable to purchase tickets clambered on board and clung to every available part of the train. Friends helped one another climb in the windows, while vendors made quick profits stuffing sandwiches and coffee into outstretched hands. Police had to be called to clear those perched on the sides of the cars. In order to win the cooperation of those ejected, the railroad announced immediately that a second "special" was being assembled. This train, with ten coaches, was then drawn into the station and within moments it, too, was rushed and boarded, the railroad having by now abandoned all thought of selling or collecting tickets. Both trains sped south at full throttle.

Most press accounts concur that Hose evinced little fear during the march through Newnan. But whatever composure he was clinging to was lost completely when he glimpsed a flash of sunlight on a knife brandished by a member of the mob. He shrieked at the sight, it was reported, began "shaking like a leaf," and quietly urged his tormentors to kill him swiftly. This was a plea none was inclined to heed, as the mob's act of retribution would be considered something of a failure if Hose did not die a prolonged, painful death.

The torture of the victim lasted almost half an hour. It began when a man stepped forward and very matter-of-factly sliced off Hose's ears. Then several men grabbed Hose's arms and held them forward so his fingers could be severed one by one and shown to the crowd. Finally, a blade was passed between his thighs, Hose cried in agony, and a moment later his genitals were held aloft.

From the crude incisions he'd suffered, the bound, naked man was soon covered with bright crimson blood from head to foot, and must have appeared at last to be the "black devil" the newspapers had made him out to be all along. It was the last clear glimpse the crowd had of him, for with the command "Come on with the oil!" three men lifted the large can of kerosene and dumped its contents over Sam Hose's head, and the pyre was set ablaze.

"Sweet Jesus!" Hose was heard to exclaim, and these were believed to be his last words. As the flames began licking at his legs and smoke entered his nose, eyes, and mouth he turned his head desperately from side to side.

To the crowd's astonishment he somehow managed to reach back and, pushing with all his might against the tree to which he was chained, snapped the bonds around his chest, bursting a blood vessel in his neck with the strain of his exertions. For a moment it appeared this writhing, half-dead apparition might break free and stagger into the crowd, but the whites rushed forward and, using several large, heavy pieces of wood, pushed him back into the fire and pinned him down. One of these logs was near his head, and with a last desperate effort Hose grimaced and sank his teeth into it, then died.

The Atlanta trains had brought four thousand visitors to Newnan. Hundreds more had walked or hitched a ride over from Palmetto, where many had camped until the last moment, certain that Hose's execution would take place on the Cranford farm. Having missed the main event, the frustrated thrill seekers could only gather around those witnesses willing to narrate all that had occurred, or search for a suitable souvenir. Trophies of the occasion were instantly prizeworthy. When literally nothing remained of Sam Hose, the pine tree against which he'd died was chopped down and pieces of it were carried off. A man then came forward with a sledgehammer and separated the links of the chain that had been used to bind him, so that these, too, could be given out or sold.

"Overtaken by the wrath of an outraged community, burned at the stake, and his very ashes scattered to the winds, there is nothing to remind us that such a monster in human form ever had existence save the bitter recollection of his infamous career while on earth," *The Herald and Advertiser* noted with satisfaction the next day. It was the closest thing to a eulogy anyone cared to offer Sam Hose.

The *Constitution* reporter who had accompanied the crowds from Atlanta noted, "The excursionists returning tonight were loaded down with ghastly reminders of the affair . . . pieces of flesh and pieces of the wood placed at the negro's feet. . . . Persons were seen walking through the streets carrying bones in their hands."

Before W.E.B. Du Bois could reach the *Constitution* office to discuss the Sam Hose lynching with Joel Chandler Harris, he learned that Hose had been "barbecued" and that his knuckles were for sale in a grocer's window a few blocks ahead on the very street he was walking. Du Bois would allude to the moment numerous times during his long life as the shock that "pulled me off my feet." He stopped and slowly reversed his steps back toward the university. "I did not meet Joel Chandler Harris nor the editor of the *Constitution*," he later recalled, but walked home in a distracted state of mind, having had the sudden recognition that "one could not be a calm, cool, and detached scientist while Negroes were lynched, murdered and starved; and secondly, there was no such definite demand for scientific work of the sort that I was doing."

Previously, Du Bois had been inclined to believe that blacks were mistreated by a minority of coarser whites, and that if the majority of decent white people could be made aware of the injustice of black life in America they would—out of compassion, a sense of justice, even patriotism—act to alleviate the problem. But the manner and spectacle of Hose's death—the eleven days of hysterical, incendiary newspaper articles, the almost complete lack of responsible intervention from high officials, the crowds running pell-mell from houses of God so as not to miss seeing a human being turned into a heap of ashes, and, ultimately, a set of knuckles on display in a grocery store—showed him that lynching was not some twisted aberration in Southern life, but a symptom of a much larger malady. Lynching was simply the most sensational manifestation of an animosity for black people that resided at a deeper level among whites than he had previously thought, and was ingrained in all of white society, its objective nothing less than the continued subordination of blacks at any cost.

"I was very much disappointed at the results of my studies," Du Bois later reflected. "They had become important, they were known all over the world. . . . [B]ut it didn't have much effect upon what the people were doing and thinking in the South. And I began to realize that I had overworked a theory—that the cause of the problem was the ignorance of people. . . . [T]he cure wasn't simply telling people the truth, it was inducing them to act on the truth."

Du Bois's epiphany was coming to be shared by a growing number of black writers, editors, teachers, ministers, and other citizens. Some form of intense advocacy would be required if they were to make good on the guarantees made by the federal government during Reconstruction, including the promise of freedom from the fear of lynching. Moreover, it had become increasingly clear that blacks could no longer rely on whites for guidance, but must become the agents of their own destiny.

In the days following the lynching, several other black people in the Newnan-Atlanta area were killed or driven away for having either condemned the Hose execution or spoken ill of Mattie Cranford. This made it too dangerous for Ida Wells-Barnett, already a detested figure in the South, to undertake personally an investigation of the case. Wells-Barnett did convene a meeting in Chicago of concerned friends, and there raised funds sufficient to hire a white private investigator, Detective Louis P. LeVin, to venture into Coweta County.

The story that LeVin uncovered, after speaking with both blacks and whites, scarcely resembled that circulated in the Georgia newspapers (although, like the Cranford family's account, it probably contains only the partial truth of the incident). Hose, LeVin learned, had heard that his mother was ill, and had approached Alfred Cranford about receiving an advance on his wages so he could go visit her, but Cranford refused and the two had "hard words." Tempers flared and Cranford drew his gun. Hose defended himself with an ax. Cranford fell to the ground, mortally wounded, and Hose ran immediately to the woods. He did not see Mrs. Cranford at all. According to LeVin, Mattie did not initially report that Hose had assaulted her. This salacious accusation became attached to the charge of murder by others, including Cranford's father and E. D. Sharkey, a superintendent at the Atlanta Bagging Mills, who was a family friend and who claimed to have seen Mrs. Cranford in the period immediately following the killing. (Counter to LeVin's conclusion, a strong argument for the possibility of some kind of sexual assault is the fact that the Cranfords and McElroys were prominent Coweta families and would not have wished to stigmatize Mattie unnecessarily; the accusation that Hose had murdered Alfred Cranford would have been sufficient motivation for any lynch mob.)

LeVin indicted Sharkey and several other prominent citizens for advocating Hose's immolation, including W. A. Hemphill and Clark Howell, respectively the president and editor of *The Atlanta Constitution:* "Through the columns of their paper they exaggerated every detail of the killing, invented and published inflammatory descriptions of a crime that was never committed, and by glaring headlines continually suggested the burning of the man when caught." LeVin referred to the *Constitution's* five-hundred-dollar reward as "blood money" and pointed out that in all its extensive coverage of the crime and the search for the perpetrator, the newspaper had not once counseled its readership that the law should be allowed to take its course. In fact, the paper had declared proudly in presenting the five hundred dollars to the Jones brothers, "The *Constitution* never issued a check with greater pleasure."

"I made my way home," LeVin concluded in his report to his Chicago sponsors, "thoroughly convinced that a Negro's life is a very cheap thing in Georgia."

Judge Lynch's Law

In West Baton Rouge Parish, Louisiana, in 1899, Melby Dotson dozed off while riding on a train and had a terrifying dream: a mob of white people was after him, trying to kill him. Hands grabbed at his clothes, he was cursed, punched, and kicked, and, despite his pleas that he had done nothing wrong, his assailants slipped a noose around his neck.

The experience was so vivid, Dotson began to moan and twitch in his seat. When a white conductor approached and ordered him to be quiet, he awoke in a sudden fright and, seeing the uniformed figure looming over him, drew a pistol from his coat and fired. At the next stop, Port Allen, police placed Dotson under arrest. The following day he was assaulted in his cell by a white mob, dragged outside, and hanged from a telegraph pole.

For Melby Dotson, as for other black Americans at the turn of the century, lynching was a nightmare that had become all too real: "America's national crime," James E. Cutler, one of the first historians of lynching, termed it in 1905. "The practice whereby mobs capture individuals suspected of crime, or take them from the officers of the law, and execute them without any process at law, or break open jails and hang convicted criminals, with impunity, is to be found in no other country of a high degree of civilization," Cutler wrote. Lynching was an undeniable part of daily life, as distinctly American as baseball games and church suppers.

Men brought their wives and children along to the events, posed for commemorative photographs, and purchased souvenirs of the occasion as if they had been at a company picnic.

Through most of the early to mid-nineteenth century, lynching, where it occurred, was understood to exist in lieu of established systems of justice, and observers, even those who advocated the practice, believed that as a feature of frontier life it would be phased out by the advent of civilization—the coming of larger municipalities, courts, and a salaried constabulary. But beginning in the 1830s, when the abolitionist scare first hit the South, then again during Reconstruction, when the South resisted Northern interference and efforts at reform, a new lynching hybrid emerged—part rustic self-governance, part caste oppression. By the time Cutler's book *Lynch-Law* appeared in 1905, lynching had come almost exclusively to mean the summary execution of Southern black men.

Lynchings, even where they have been the accepted norm, have always disturbed many Americans. This is not simply because they are barbaric, inhumane acts, but because they inherently disavow a right Americans hold dear—the right to due process before the law. Since early in the eighteenth century, before the founding of the American republic, due process has been understood to include a clear accusation of charges stating what law the accused has violated, a court made up of competent authorities, the right to confront one's accuser in a trial held under proper proceedings, and the right to be freed unless found guilty. So fundamental is it to our notion of justice that the Founding Fathers embedded it squarely in the Fifth Amendment to the Constitution, which vows that "no persons . . . shall be deprived of life, liberty or property, without due process of law" by the federal government. In the Fourteenth Amendment, approved after the Civil War, Congress extended this same guarantee to the relationship between states and their citizens.

The framers of the Constitution were firm on this issue because, at the time of their work, due process was still a relatively new and fragile idea, the product chiefly of reforms in the English courts of the seventeenth century. One of the hallmarks of the Inquisitions of the Middle Ages and the Star Chamber of the Tudor period in England had been the inability of the accused to confront his accuser; until the mid-seventeenth century most English criminal defendants were not even told what they were being charged with, or who accused them, until the day of their trial. Public sensitivity to the innate unfairness of these prosecutorial methods was noted in 1603 during the trial of the British naval hero Sir Walter Ralegh, who was accused of treason for conspiring to establish Arabella Stuart as sovereign during the reign of James I. Ralegh asked the court to allow him to confront his accuser, Lord Cobham, or at the very least for the judges themselves to depose the accuser. They refused, and Ralegh was convicted and sentenced to death. There was so much support for the condemned, however, that the state was not eager to carry out his execution, and imprisoned him until 1616, during which time he wrote poetry and worked on his *History of the World*. He then led an expedition to the New World before the sentence was finally carried out in 1618—a full fifteen years later. Dissatisfaction with the courts' handling of the Ralegh case helped guide British jurists to an insistence on the creation of a judiciary independent of the Crown, and strengthened the idea that a trial should be a live contest over disputed facts between a defendant and his accuser.

Conditions on the American frontier often made due process seem unwieldy. Settlers living hundreds of miles beyond the limits of cities and towns, threatened by native tribes, horse thieves, cattle rustlers, and swindlers, felt themselves sufficiently vulnerable to take matters into their own hands. Even in locations where a traveling circuit judge periodically convened a court session, the public's zeal for retribution, compounded by the fear that local authorities would be unable to keep an outlaw's confederates from freeing him from jail before the circuit judge's arrival, made it popular and acceptable to enforce a swift, exacting "people's justice."

The administering of communal justice was frequently seen as a valued community service. The nineteenth-century historian Hubert H. Bancroft's thirty-nine-volume history of the West has two entire volumes devoted to "Popular Tribunals," chiefly the San Francisco Vigilante Committees of 1851 and 1856. These committees, led by the city's most prominent citizens, are credited with having "cleaned up" San Francisco in the rough-and-tumble period after the Gold Rush of 1848. Committee members believed that the gold mania had brought all sorts of unsavory characters to California, and that public apathy and official carelessness had made a concerted "people's" response necessary. Bancroft depicts vigilantism as an instinctual force for good, a demonstration of man's innate sense of civilization and his drive to establish it where it does not exist.

Such glorification of citizen justice from a noted scholar no doubt contributed to the American acceptance of the vigilante idea, as did literary treatments such as Nathaniel Pitt Langford's *Vigilante Days and Ways* (1890) and Owen Wister's *The Virginian* (1902). The term *vigilante* itself had entered common usage through the popularity of the celebrated 1866 book *The Vigilantes of Montana,* by Thomas Dimsdale. Two U.S. presidents, Andrew Jackson and Theodore Roosevelt, as well as numerous U.S. senators and governors, served at one time or another with vigilante forces.

If vigilantism has always been close to a mainstream idea in American life, it is in part because our origins as a nation are so firmly linked to the Revolution of 1775, a violent manifestation of the people's will to popular sovereignty—a vigilantes' war. Strong antiauthoritarian emotion was a persistent theme in Colonial America. The April 1775 outbreak of fighting in Lexington and Concord followed no fewer than eighteen previous insurrections in the Colonies, including Bacon's Rebellion in Virginia in 1676 and Culpepper's Rebellion in North Carolina in 1677. The Stamp Act riots of 1765 and the Boston Massacre of 1770 were in this tradition, as was one of the most celebrated vigilante actions in American history, the Boston Tea Party of 1773, in which colonists angered by the British import tax on tea disguised themselves as Indians, boarded British ships in Boston Harbor, and dumped hundreds of boxes of tea overboard. That Boston became the hotbed of revolutionary action it did in the 1770s was due in large part to the strength of the numerous local patriotic clubs and tavern-based vigilance associations, such as the Sons of Liberty, that had long operated in that city.

The Revolutionary era in America is remembered for its high-flown rhetoric of independence and liberty, but the nitty-gritty of the war was merciless, the fighting exceedingly violent, particularly in Virginia and the Carolinas, where rival gangs of Whigs and Tories gave each other no quarter. Soldiers on both sides of the conflict wasted away of starvation or died of disease or exposure, as at Valley Forge. The concept of popular sovereignty, glorified by the blood and mortal suffering of a long, costly insurrection, became an enshrined privilege in American life.

The Revolution helped foster two durable traditions in American life— *localism,* or Americans' belief that problems besetting a community are best addressed by those who live there, and *instrumentalism,* the uniquely American confidence that there are no societal functions off-limits to individuals; in a word, that anyone can do anything, including enforce the law. This did not mean that government would not be respected, but rather, as U.S. Supreme Court Justice Samuel Chase of Maryland once

explained, that the people's power "is like the light of the sun, native, original, inherent, and unlimited by human authority," while "power in the
rulers or governors of the people is like the reflected light of the moon,
and is only borrowed, delegated and limited by the grant of the people."

It was from this period of violent antiauthoritarian sentiment that "lynch
law" first emerged. Charles Lynch, a justice of the peace in the town of
Chestnut Hill, Virginia (neighboring Lynchburg is named for his
brother), was a Quaker who had served a term in the Virginia House of
Burgesses in the late 1760s. An ardent patriot with a fierce temper, Lynch
had been discouraged from attending Quaker meetings because of his inability to keep from swearing. During the Revolutionary War, because of
the great distances to established courts of law and the risk of travel for patriots in British-occupied areas, Lynch and some of his neighbors created
an informal court in Chestnut Hill to deal with suspected Tories and
horse thieves, horse stealing being an especially persistent problem due to
the shortage of good horses and the high prices the opposing forces would
pay for healthy animals. Thieves or other miscreants brought before Judge
Lynch and found guilty were tied to a walnut tree in his front yard and
given thirty-nine lashes. The hated Tories were likewise whipped and
made to shout "Liberty forever!" and to suffer additional humiliations.

When the British general Lord Charles Cornwallis, in charge of British
efforts in North Carolina, invaded Virginia in late 1780, Lynch responded
by ordering the incarceration of dozens of local British sympathizers in
order to keep them from abetting the enemy. After the war, however, the
men Lynch had jailed sued him on the grounds that, by imprisoning
them, his court had exceeded its localized powers. The matter wound up
in the Virginia legislature where, in a series of well-publicized hearings,
the plaintiffs lost their suit. It was ultimately agreed that "Lynch's Law"
had been appropriate given the stressful circumstances of the war, and in
this way the name for homegrown summary justice was coined.

The first widespread application of Lynch's Law, or "Lynch Law" as it
came to be known, was associated with the so-called Regulators of the
early nineteenth century. Operating in sparsely peopled areas of North
Carolina, Kentucky, and Indiana, the Regulators were informal bands of
citizens working to punish thieves, highwaymen, swindlers, and card
sharks. Usually the punishments meted out were nonlethal, such as tar-
and-feathering, beatings, and floggings. The Regulators did not limit
themselves to prosecuting traditional criminals, but were known to up-

braid those suspected of moral infringements such as wife beating, prostitution, and drunkenness. Special enmity was reserved for counterfeiters, who in an age before standardized currency often fleeced entire communities before being found out.

Tar-and-feathering, one of the best-known summary punishments, was widely used because it was humiliating as well as painful. The victim was seized, stripped of his clothes, then held to the ground as a coat of pitch tar, often used in the construction and repair of boats, was applied, followed by feathers or, in the South, cotton. Then the victim was made to scamper off with a posse of men, boys, and dogs in mock pursuit, or placed on a pole and carried to the outskirts of the community and dumped there, the origin of the expression "ridden out of town on a rail."

Nineteenth-century vigilantism came in many forms. Some towns maintained full-time "vigilance committees," associations made up of trusted men who monitored other citizens' behavior and intervened when required. Elsewhere, vigilantes or Regulators might come together on a short-term basis—for days or weeks, or until a specific threat, such as a gang of cattle rustlers, was removed. The actions of a lynch mob, a group of people coalescing spontaneously and then dispersing almost immediately after achieving their objective, represented what scholars of mob violence call "instant vigilantism."

The first widely publicized applications of lethal lynch law in America were two outbreaks of mob violence in Mississippi in the summer of 1835. During the previous year, a notorious highwayman and slave stealer named John A. Murel had been apprehended and jailed in Nashville. Murel had worked the Natchez Trace and the flatboat towns up and down the Mississippi River, specializing in enticing slaves away from their plantations with the offer to aid their escape, then selling them back to their owners. He was suspected of having murdered dozens of people, but had eluded arrest and often fooled his victims by disguising himself as an itinerant fire-and-brimstone preacher, a ruse that led to his being known as the "Reverend Devil."

Murel's capture had been arranged by one of his own confederates, a Georgian named Virgil A. Stewart, who proceeded to capitalize on his heroism by publishing a pamphlet bearing the sensational title "A History of the Detection, Conviction, Life and Designs of John A. Murel, the Great Western Land Pirate, Together with His System of Villainy, and Plan of Exciting a Negro Rebellion." The pamphlet warned that a massive slave uprising was being planned for Christmas Day 1835, and that Murel had orchestrated it with the help of a thousand or more associates across the South. So fearsome was the Reverend Devil's legend—he was reputed to dispose of some of his victims by disemboweling them, filling their remains with stones, and sinking them in the river—that his being behind bars apparently did little to assure anyone that his insurrection would not occur.

In late June 1835, whites in Madison County, Mississippi, became convinced that local slaves were planning an uprising based on the one suggested in Stewart's pamphlet. Several blacks were arrested and whipped. They admitted that a revolt had been planned for July Fourth, like Christmas a favorite date for suspected slave insurrections because the two holidays were, in many places, the only times slaves were allowed to congregate freely. The blacks also implicated two white men, Joshua Cotton and William Saunders, both "steam doctors," medical quacks who sold a then-popular cure involving the localized application of heat. Saunders maintained his innocence, but Cotton told his interrogators a wild tale of slaves preparing to seize control of central Mississippi, "murdering all the white men and ugly women—sparing the handsome ones [and] making wives of them—and plundering and burning as they went." Both Cotton and Saunders were hanged along with the blacks who had implicated them. A committee of plantation owners then sent posses into neighboring communities to capture new suspects, dozens of whom were interrogated and hanged on the spot. "I have not slept two hours in the twenty-four for six days and nights," wrote one of the committeemen of his exertions, "and have been on horseback more than four-fifths of the time."

Of course, neither the July Fourth nor the Christmas slave revolt occurred. But many years passed before a Mississippi politician felt secure venturing the opinion that the whole Murel conspiracy had been "one of the most extraordinary and lamentable hallucinations of our times," a pseudocrisis induced by public anxiety about the diminishing isolation of the region, as steamboats replaced flatboats on the rivers, bringing increasing numbers of strangers to the area, and the rise of abolitionist sentiment.

Lynching struck elsewhere in Mississippi that year in the frontier river town of Vicksburg. Like Natchez with its Under the Hill and Memphis its Pinch Gut, Vicksburg had its own "bad-man region" where rough flatboatmen drank, brawled, and gambled. Professional gamblers had taken over many of the hotels, saloons, and brothels, and because of their influence and ready cash swaggered about with little fear of the law.

On July 4, 1835, a notorious gambler named Cakler came uninvited to a picnic hosted by a local Vicksburg military company and proceeded to make a pest of himself. According to a contemporary account, "His conduct was wholly that of a ruffian and blackguard, under the influence of strong drink." He was escorted from the picnic and jailed. Released that evening, he angrily threatened those who had abused him and, after obtaining a gun, came to the square where the militia was engaged in exercises. The militiamen, by now fed up with Cakler's behavior, "determined to take him into the woods and lynch him, which is a mode of punishment provided for such as become obnoxious in a manner which the law cannot reach." The gambler was tied to a tree, whipped, tarred and feathered, and driven from town, approving citizens cheering and mocking him as he went skulking away up the road.

Emboldened by what they'd seen, the crowd then sought out another hated gambler named North, who took refuge with several cronies in the Kangaroo Saloon. What happened next is not clear, but North, apparently having learned of Cakler's humiliation and determined not to suffer his fate, either fired a gun from a window or shot as the mob burst in on him, killing a popular physician named Hugh S. Bodley. Shocked and infuriated to see Bodley fall, the people charged into the Kangaroo, seized North and four others, and took them to a makeshift gallows where they were "speedily launched into eternity." The bodies were left hanging for twenty-four hours as a warning to others.

Having lynched five men to death, Vicksburg's town fathers then saw fit to reassure the outside world that events in the town had resulted from the citizens' best intentions. A proclamation was published asserting that "the revolution has been conducted here by the most respectable citizens, heads of families, members of all classes and professions and pursuits. . . . None have been heard to utter a syllable of censure against either the act or the manner in which it was performed." The statement also asked that whatever "sickly sensibility or mawkish philanthropy may say against the course pursued by us, we hope that our citizens will not relax the code of punishment which they have enacted against this infamous, unprincipled, and baleful class of society."

The black uprising or slave insurrection was a central motif in whites' rationale for extralegal violence against blacks, and the rise of the Northern abolition movement exacerbated Southerners' fears that they stood at risk of a dreadful apocalypse. Their agitation grew sharply when the movement's tracts, and occasionally its representatives, began to appear in the South. Of profound concern was the 1829 pamphlet "Walker's Appeal," published by a Boston free Negro named David Walker, which advocated armed rebellion and the killing of whites. Walker advised slaves to "make sure [of your] work—do not trifle, for they will not trifle with you—they want us for their slaves, and think nothing of murdering us in order to subject us to that wretched condition—therefore, if there is an attempt made by us, kill or be killed." Also troubling was *The Liberator,* a periodical that was the brainchild of Boston abolitionist leader William Lloyd Garrison, which began distribution in 1831. Although Garrison, unlike Walker, did not advocate violence, the strength of his feeling was evident in the statement of purpose he printed in the first issue, of January 1, 1831:

> I am aware that many object to the severity of my language; but is there not cause for severity? I will be as harsh as truth, and as uncompromising as justice. On this subject, I do not wish to think, or speak, or write, with moderation. No! No! Tell a man whose house is on fire to give a moderate alarm; tell him to moderately rescue his wife from the hands of the ravisher; tell the mother to gradually extricate her babe from the fire into which it has fallen;—but urge me not to use moderation in a cause like the present. I am in earnest—I will not equivocate—I will not excuse—I will not retreat a single inch—and I will be heard.

The South resented the abolitionist cause for economic as well as emotional reasons. Recent technological advances in the cotton gin made it possible to clean as many as a thousand pounds of cotton in a day, accelerating the processing of cotton into salable fiber, but the picking of cotton remained a job that could be done only by hand, for removing the cotton required sufficient strength to tear it from the plant but also the dexterity to not injure it. Such work could be accomplished only by large numbers of cheap laborers.

With slaves more crucial than ever to the economy and self-esteem of the South, distribution of *The Liberator* and other incendiary tracts resulted in drastic punishments. Abolitionist sympathizers or free Negroes caught "tampering with the slaves" were summarily dealt with; antiabolitionist meetings raged into the night. A Charleston mob broke into that city's post office, seized hundreds of the tracts, and burned them in a huge bonfire. Townsmen of New Bern, North Carolina, got hold of an offending abolitionist pamphlet and "lynched" it, tar-and-feathering it before returning it along with a deadly warning to its Northern publisher. A Tuscaloosa County, Alabama, grand jury indicted New Yorker R. G. Williams in absentia for "distributing incendiary literature" because he had authored an abolitionist book, then went so far as to petition New York governor William L. Marcy to "extradite" him to Alabama for trial. (Marcy refused the request on the grounds that Williams was not a fugitive from justice.)

At the heart of the South's concern was an abject fear of the cataclysm that would surely ensue if slaves were emboldened to resist the status quo. No event brought this apprehension into greater focus than the antebellum slave insurrection, or rumors thereof. Scholar Herbert Aptheker estimates that there were as many as two hundred in America before the Civil War, although fears of insurrections usually far outpaced the number of actual events. As a Tennessee planter quipped in a letter to a friend in 1856, "We are trying our best in Davidson County to produce a Negro insurrection, without the slightest aid from the Negroes themselves."

That whites anywhere would react hysterically to such threats was clear as early as 1712, when New York City punished a failed slave insurrection by hanging thirteen blacks, burning three more at the stake, breaking one on the wheel, and starving another to death in manacles. So savage were these punishments, six remaining suspects opted to commit suicide. When in 1741 whites in New York discovered what they believed was a slave conspiracy to burn the city, numerous blacks and suspected white associates were hanged and immolated. The degree of violence in squelching the New York conspiracy may have been inspired by a notorious racial outbreak in South Carolina just two years earlier, in which captured slave insurrectionists were decapitated and their heads mounted on mileposts.

Better-known insurrections or attempted slave revolts stayed in slaveholders' minds for decades. Gabriel Prosser planned to topple Richmond in 1800 by seizing an arsenal and other official buildings, with the idea that slaves in surrounding communities would then rise up in support of the insurrection, much the same plan abolitionist John Brown tried to put into motion at Harpers Ferry in 1859. Before Prosser's insurrection could begin, however, an informer notified whites, and Prosser and thirty-four of his cohorts were executed. Denmark Vesey, a free black carpenter who raised a band to strike at Charleston in 1822, was similarly undone by informers and killed, along with numerous followers. Nat Turner's 1831 rebellion in Southampton County, Virginia, was the most successful slave uprising in U.S. history, as he and a band of coconspirators moved from plantation to plantation, killing sixty whites before being met by white militia with superior arms and numbers outside the revolt's planned objective, the town of Jerusalem (now Courtland). About one hundred of Turner's men were killed outright; another twenty were hanged after a trial. Turner himself evaded capture for a time but was apprehended, tried, and sent to the gallows, although not before giving the famous jailhouse "confession" that secured his legend.

From 1835 forward to the Civil War the issue of slavery was never absent from the political dialogue in America, and because the South was so sensitive to the North's intrusive interest in the matter, the region increasingly became a place insistent on and even proud of its own isolation. Strangers who ventured there, even business travelers, did so at risk of having their purpose and destination questioned; nonconformity of any kind tended to be challenged or suspected; and new restrictions were placed on the mobility of free Negroes, who, it was feared, might gossip and spread insurrectionary notions.

One of the South's precautionary responses was the creation of the patroller system. The patrollers—called "patterollers" or "paddy rollers" by the slaves—were armed committees of planters or, later, hired thugs whose purpose was to restrict slave movement, especially at night, inhibit slaves from congregating or visiting, and intimidate any who had designs on running away. Passes were used to establish and check identities, and black men and women unable to present appropriate passes to inquiring patrollers faced severe penalties. Whippings and other punishments were common. The system intensified in brutality and paranoia as abolitionist sentiment increased in the 1850s, firmly establishing the tradition of "night riding" that would return after the Civil War in the form of the Ku Klux Klan.

During these troubled antebellum years, the capacity for social intolerance and collective violence was on the rise elsewhere in America. It was seen not only in antiabolitionist disturbances and the suppression of imaginary slave revolts, but also in race riots in Northern cities, labor disorders, nativist demonstrations, and fistfights at polling places. In 1837 a young lawyer and politician from Illinois named Abraham Lincoln had given the phenomenon a name, calling it the "mobocratic spirit." Alluding to the 1835 Murel and Vicksburg lynchings in a lyceum speech delivered in Springfield, Illinois, Lincoln lamented "this process of hanging, from gamblers to Negroes, from Negroes to white citizens, and from these to strangers, till dead men were literally dangling from the boughs of trees by every roadside, and in numbers almost sufficient to rival the native Spanish moss of the country as a drapery of the forest."

A mob killing that particularly stung the nation was the 1837 murder of abolitionist minister and newspaper publisher Elijah P. Lovejoy. The chain of events leading to Lovejoy's death began in St. Louis in 1836, when a black man named McIntosh stabbed a deputy sheriff to death. Police took him into custody, but a crowd gathered at the jail and threatened to tear it down if he was not immediately handed over. The sheriff complied and the mob seized its victim, stringing McIntosh up in a tree and slowly roasting him to death over a huge bonfire. A grand jury convened by a magistrate with the improbable name of Judge Luke E. Lawless found that the mob had acted with justification and refused to indict its members. In his paper, *The Observer,* Elijah Lovejoy denounced the judge for his cowardice and for perpetuating an injustice. Soon after a group of whites, already angered by Lovejoy's views on abolition, broke into the paper's offices and destroyed the printing press and other equipment.

Lovejoy relocated twenty-five miles up the Mississippi River to Alton, Illinois, where he found his progressive sentiments no more welcome. His offices were trashed on three separate occasions, and he was forced to be constantly on guard, including taking the precaution of having a new printing press delivered by steamboat in the middle of the night. On November 7, 1837, Lovejoy and a group of his supporters were in a dockside warehouse guarding the new press when they were attacked by proslavery vigilantes. Shots were exchanged. The warehouse, being constructed of stone, was fairly impregnable, but someone in the crowd noticed that the roof was made of wood, and volunteers climbed onto the structure and set it on fire, intending to smoke the occupants out. Lovejoy himself ventured outside to challenge the arsonists, and was shot and killed from ambush.

By his violent death, Lovejoy was transformed into a hero, an all-purpose martyr for the abolitionist cause, for free speech and a free press. Many in the abolition movement thought his sacrifice as important as the "Shot Heard 'Round the World" at Lexington and Concord in 1775, and even some proslavery voices expressed disapproval that a minister engaged in as peaceful an enterprise as publishing a newspaper might have his life snuffed out for holding views contrary to those of his neighbors. Some later characterized Lovejoy's violent death as one of the first hints of the terrible Civil War to come—the unexpected blow, according to abolitionist Wendell Phillips, that "stunned a drunken people into sobriety"—in that it led both sides in the country's quarrel over slavery to acknowledge that the dispute would likely not be resolved without bloodshed.

One of the first recorded lynchings of a black American occurred in 1741. At Roxbury, Massachusetts, according to a fragmentary account, "A Negro was suspected of stealing some Money, was by divers Persons ty'd to a Tree and whip'd in order to bring him to confess the Fact; after which he was taken down and lying some Time upon the Grass was carried into his Master's House, but died soon after."

That a slave would be beaten to death for theft was in itself exceptional. Their value as property made the execution of slaves, summary or otherwise, rare except for major crimes such as murder. And because slavery so restricted blacks' freedom of mobility, there was less opportunity for individual slaves to perpetrate criminal acts and fewer reasons for whites to suspect them. When a slave did commit a serious offense, owners had a strong financial incentive to attempt to see that he or she was tried and sentenced in the legal sphere, and courts often let slaves off lightly if an owner could persuade a judge that the loss of the slave's labor would represent an economic hardship. Where a slave was sentenced to legal execution, most states offered owners partial compensation. But because of the widespread sentiment against destroying another man's property, slaves were often extended far more legal consideration than their free descendants, the nominal beneficiaries of emancipation and citizenship rights granted by the Thirteenth and Fourteenth Amendments.

In an insurrection scare, of course, all usual safeguards vanished, and, as in the Murel revolt, slaves were put to death. The abolitionist and former slave Frederick Douglass, who as a young man had been caught in an escape attempt on Maryland's Eastern Shore and hauled before a committee of inquiry, later recounted watching his owner skillfully guide the other whites away from the consideration that the escape had represented a slave insurrection, a finding that would have almost certainly resulted in Douglass's execution.

In cases of alleged rape, records suggest that antebellum courts, again because of the value of slave property, proceeded with relative restraint, and were even occasionally nuanced enough in their rulings to acknowledge that some black-white sexual relationships were consensual, a finding that would be unthinkable fifty years later. Indeed, due to the prevalent hypocrisy surrounding rape (antebellum laws against miscegenation were ubiquitous but routinely ignored by whites), such matters were frequently kept out of the courts entirely.

This is not to say brutal punishments were nonexistent. It is recorded that in 1827 a Georgia court sentenced a black man to castration and deportation for attempted rape (the Macon *Daily Telegraph* chided the court for its leniency) and that castration of slaves accused of rape was practiced in Missouri as late as the 1850s. Other punishments such as branding, eye gouging, and the cutting off of ears, all of which fell from official favor before the war, would reappear as part of late-nineteenth-century lynching ritual (or lynchcraft, as it was sometimes known), for the popularity of lynching may have been due in part to its preservation of some of the fiercer aspects of personal retribution that the conservative Southern mind associated with the simpler, more orderly antebellum world.

It is equally significant that the South, while emulating the development of the Northern penitentiary system in the years before the war, did not rush to create organized police departments or a multilayered, structured justice system. The region would long maintain its preference for more accessible, informal methods of justice based around the county courthouse, with its swaggering, all-powerful sheriff, his deputies, flask-sipping lawyers, patronage-system bureaucrats, and various hangers-on. Sheriff's office, county jail, and courtroom were often housed in one courthouse edifice, usually the largest and most impressive-looking structure in Southern towns. Due to the warm climate, the business of the law quite naturally spilled out into the benches of the courthouse square, where citizens gathered with local officialdom to smoke, spit, and talk politics. This convenient centralizing of the official functions of the justice system, as well as the constant intermingling of authorities and citizens, would prove important elements in many lynchings.

If law enforcement and the courts were often poorly developed, it was partly due to the extent to which crime of any kind in the South was regarded as personal, not civic business. An ingrained Southern code of honor made the extralegal settlement of disputes common, and tended to render much of the court's work unnecessary. In cases of rape, seduction, adultery, or slander of a woman, violence from a male relative of the victim would suffice to redress the wound. In lieu of dueling, which diminished after the war, perhaps because its gentlemanly aspect seemed absurd once the dignity of the South itself had been so thoroughly trampled, men simply shot one another down like dogs—in saloons, in the street, in one another's homes. And anyone who killed for the right reason was likely to be acquitted by the court. The Southern code of honor was defended proudly by its practitioners, who considered it morally superior to courtroom law since it derived from men's best instincts. In the North, the criminal was treated impersonally and answered to the state; in the South he answered directly to those he had abused.

W.E.B. Du Bois traced the origin of the Southern chivalric code to what he decried as the devastating psychological impact of slavery on the white planter class:

> The mere fact that a man could be, under the law, the actual master of the mind and body of human beings had to have disastrous effects. It tended to inflate the ego of most planters beyond all reason; they became arrogant, strutting, quarrelsome kinglets; they issued commands; they made laws; they shouted their orders; they expected deference and self-abasement; they were choleric and easily insulted. Their "honor" became a vast and awful thing, requiring wide and insistent deference.

A most flagrant application of the gentleman's code, and an incident that underscored the growing differences between the two sections of the country, occurred during the congressional debate over the introduction of slavery into Kansas. On May 19, 1856, Senator Charles Sumner of Massachusetts castigated a Southern rival, Senator Andrew Pickens Butler of South Carolina (who happened not to be present), as one who "has chosen a mistress to whom he has made his vows, and who, though ugly to others, is always lovely to him; though polluted in the sight of the world, is chaste in his sight . . . the harlot, Slavery." Sumner then moved on to lampoon Butler's state, observing, "Were the whole history of South Carolina blotted out of existence . . . civilization might lose, I do not say how little, but surely less than it has already gained by the example of Kansas, in its valiant struggle against oppression."

Sumner's speech in defense of a free Kansas was loudly applauded in the North, and thousands of copies of his comments were distributed. But a few days later, as he sat at his Senate desk writing after the body had adjourned for the day, he was approached by Preston Brooks, a South Carolina congressman and a son of Senator Butler's cousin, who told Sumner he had found his remarks slanderous of his relative and suddenly began whacking him with a gutta-percha cane. Sumner collapsed in a position between his desk and his chair from which he could not escape, and Brooks, younger and stronger than his victim, beat him mercilessly, stopping only when the cane splintered in half.

The Massachusetts statesman never completely recovered from his injuries (although he did return to the Senate), while Brooks, who was fined three hundred dollars for assault, became an overnight hero in the South, the *Richmond Enquirer* praising his deed as "a proper act, done at the proper time and in the proper place." One of the many new canes sent to Brooks from grateful Southerners bore the inscription "Hit him again!"

Reconstruction after the Civil War, the period lasting from 1865 to 1877, is one of the crucibles of race relations in America. It was in this era that black aspirations for economic independence and citizenship were both nurtured and thwarted, white resistance to the strivings of freed blacks began to assert itself, and a pattern of deadly violence as a means of repression emerged.

At the heart of the North's effort to reconstruct the South was the question of whether the defeated Confederacy was to be treated as a dysfunctional family member who had tragically lost his way, or a conquered and still-treacherous foe. Lincoln, in his second inaugural address of March 1865, just a month before General Robert E. Lee's surrender at Appomatox, vowed that the victorious North would act "with malice toward none, with charity for all." But powerful factions in the North were determined that prewar conditions would not be allowed to return to the South, and the status of black people was a key issue. The administration's position had changed dramatically over the course of the war, from not interfering with Southern "property" to considering captured slaves as "contraband," and ultimately to emancipation and the arming of black troops.

The majority of the people who emerged from bondage had a pronounced lack of skills and a tradition of performing only domestic or field labor. Slavery, after all, had not been a system that prepared its victims with an education or mechanical skills of any kind. It was left to the federal government to try to define the freedmen's status, and there were no guidelines or even jurisdiction for such a process. The states largely controlled citizens' legal and political rights, such as the franchise, and not even states had a say in so-called social rights, rules governing behavior toward individuals by businesses, factories, private schools, clubs, and associations. And in the South, because slavery had been protected by local and state, not federal, laws, there had come to be rooted a firm attachment to the idea of "states' rights" and a will to resist or negate the imposition of national laws.

Washington's answer was the Reconstruction amendments, which derived from a preceding half-century of moral and legal argumentation, best represented by the abolitionists, that suggested a national citizenship, equal enjoyment by black and white of certain national privileges and immunities, and the power of the federal government to enforce those ideals upon which the country had itself been founded. The Thirteenth Amendment abolished slavery; the Fourteenth nationalized the constitutional standards of freedom expressed in the Bill of Rights, granting all Americans, including blacks (but not Indians), equal rights and protection before the law, including the right to due process, and—in direct response to the *Dred Scott* decision of 1857, in which the Supreme Court had ruled that Negroes were not citizens of the United States—insisted on the national citizenship of all Americans; the Fifteenth attempted to protect the freedman by granting him the vote. The Congressional Reconstruction Acts of 1867 and the Enforcement Acts of the early 1870s expanded federal authority to protect citizens and uphold their constitutional rights.

The most ambitious effort on behalf of the freedmen was the Bureau of Refugees, Freedmen and Abandoned Lands, created by Congress in March 1865. The Freedmen's Bureau, as it was known, was the first public-assistance venture of its kind in American history, and in retrospect, given the vast issues it initially sought to address, impressive for its scope and optimism. The bureau's first job, under the leadership of the one-armed war hero Otis Oliver Howard, who, because of his piousness, was known as the Christian General, was to assist America's 4 million new black citizens, almost all of whom lived in the former states of the Confederacy. The bureau saw to the needs of those displaced by the war, providing food, medicine, and transport. It issued 21 million rations, created more than forty hospitals and treated 450,000 cases of illness, and helped as many as thirty thousand people resettle. Numerous freedmen's schools were opened, including the nation's first all-black colleges—Howard University, the Hampton Institute, Atlanta University, and Fisk University. As many as ten thousand teachers flooded into the South, drawn from Northern church groups, most prominently the American Missionary Association, and from Oberlin College, which had been founded by abolitionists in 1835. The bureau also established health and social services, a savings and loan, encouraged black voting and political involvement, and where possible served as an intermediary between former slaves and their former masters in negotiating labor or sharecropping contracts.

In its most controversial endeavor, and the one that meant the most to the landless ex-slaves, the bureau acted to seize former plantation lands and divide them among the freedmen in modest parcels of forty acres (the basis for the expression "forty acres and a mule," which had been first coined by General William T. Sherman in freedmen-resettlement efforts in the Georgia Sea Islands). As many Republicans favoring some form of land redistribution pointed out, land belonging to Tories had been confiscated at the close of the Revolutionary War; and in czarist Russia, where the serfs were emancipated during the years 1861–66, small parcels of land were also given away. But many of these ambitious reforms broke down under the weight of Southern resentment, the lack of commitment on the part of President Andrew Johnson, and ultimately the diminishing support of the Northern congressmen who had initiated them. By the end of 1865 Johnson had stripped away the land-redistribution program and was instead actively restoring lands to Southern planters. For blacks, the disappointment that attended the government's abandonment of the policy was overwhelming, for they saw the possession of property as "the consummation of their deliverance," according to Carl Schurz, a German immigrant and journalist who had served in the Union army and was dispatched by Johnson on a fact-finding tour of the conquered Confederacy.

The chief allure of land ownership for the freedmen was that it held the potential to separate them from the powerful grip of the planters. The former slaves were understandably mistrustful of their vanquished masters, fearing the whites would surely connive some means to reenslave them. Only one in ten freedmen was literate, so the rest had to take the word of white bureau agents for what the postwar labor contracts struck with the planters actually said, and, not surprisingly, these white-authored documents tended to emphasize the numerous labor obligations the black worker would assume, the deference to be paid to whites, and a strict adherence to rules and restrictions governing private behavior.

Some of these rules were reflected in the Black Codes, local ordinances drafted into law in many former states of the Confederacy. The codes restricted the movement of blacks, prohibited planters from attempting to lure black laborers away from existing jobs with promises of better pay and conditions, and allowed plantation owners to cheaply and arbitrarily hire black children who had no visible means of support. The codes also forbade blacks from having guns and from testifying against whites in court, outlawed intermarriage, and established fines or work punishments for public drunkenness. The most pernicious of the codes were the vagrancy laws, under which any person not lawfully employed could be arrested, hired out to the highest bidder, and kept in virtual bondage until he had "paid off" his fine.

Out of the powerful dissatisfaction with the Black Codes and the labor agreements, which too often resembled slavery, there evolved a new work relationship between white planter and former slave: sharecropping. Sharecroppers were given a piece of land to work, a modest house, seed, water, and other needs such as the use of wagons and furniture, and perhaps the right to tend a small vegetable patch for their own consumption. At year's end any cash payment from the sale of the cotton crop they had raised was divided between them and the planter, less the expenses incurred. Because the worker residing on the planter's land was likely to receive goods or services during the year that exceeded items stipulated in a work agreement, often the money eventually due him was already owed back to the planter before he got his hands on it. And because the white planter, not the sharecropper, sold the cotton at market, the sharecropper had only the employer's word as to what the final selling price had been. Thus the sharecropper, through a perennial cycle of debt, unpredictable crops, and an inconsistent cotton market, was kept, if not in perpetual servitude, in a weakened position from which he could advance only against great odds.

Freedmen's Bureau agents increasingly found themselves mediating between angry blacks and whites as misunderstandings developed over the signing of labor contracts and sharecropping agreements. The agents' work was complicated by the fact that, as army officers, few had any direct experience in dealing with farm management or the growing of cotton, or for that matter in working with black people.

It was extremely difficult for whites to engage in compromises with their former slaves. "In addition to the property loss to the upper- and middle-class whites occasioned by emancipation, there was a sharp narcissistic wound," sociologist John Dollard explains. "The Northern armies took more than property away; they changed in a fundamental manner the mastery-and-deference relations between the races." Many Southerners believed fervently that blacks would not work unless physically compelled, and had trouble coming to grips with a world in which they would not maintain some form of physical control over their labor. Some held out for years the hope that emancipation would be seen as wrongheaded, would be declared "unconstitutional" or otherwise revoked. Indeed, the bureau reported numerous instances in which federal troops had to be dispatched to plantations where blacks were being held in slavery by obstinate former owners.

That whites would resort to violence against their former chattel had never been much in doubt. "The number of murders and assaults perpetrated upon Negroes is very great," reported Schurz, adding, "It is a sad fact that the perpetration of these acts is not confined to the class of people which might be called the rabble. Several 'gentlemen of standing' have been tried before military commissions for such offenses."

The details of these offenses against the freedmen were often sketchy, but in hundreds of reports filed with the bureau in the year or two after the war, such as this surgeon's report from an army hospital in Montgomery, Alabama, there emerged a consistent pattern:

1. Nancy, colored woman, ears cut off by a man by the name of Ferguson, or Foster, an overseer.
2. Mary Steel, one side of her head scalped. Died. She was with Nancy.
3. Jacob Steel, both ears cut off.
4. Amanda Steel, ears cut off.
5. Washington Booth, shot in the back while returning from work by William Harris of Pine Level, without provocation.
6. Sutton Jones, beard and chin cut off.
7. Robert, servant of Colonel Hough, was stabbed while at his house by a man wearing in part the garb of a Confederate soldier, died on the 26th of June in this hospital.
8. Ida, was struck on the head with a club by an overseer, died of her wound at this hospital.
9. James Monroe, cut across the throat while engaged in saddling a horse.

Another report, from Assistant Superintendent of Freedmen W. A. Poillon, records the status of various outrages in his district of Alabama as of July 29, 1865:

1. Three Negroes were killed in the southern part of Dallas County, it is supposed by the Vaughn family. I tried twice to arrest them, but they escaped into the woods.

2. Mr. Dermott, Perry County, started with a Negro to Selma, having a rope around the Negro's neck. He was seen dragging him in that way, but returned home before he could have reached Selma. He did not report at Selma, and the Negro has never since been heard of.

3. A Negro was killed in the calaboose of the city of Selma, by being beaten with a heavy club, also by being tied up by the thumbs, clear of the floor, for three hours, and by further gross abuse, lasting more than a week.

4. At Bladen Springs, a freedman was chained to a pine tree and burned to death.

5. About two weeks later, and 15 miles from Bladen, another freedman was burned to death.

6. About the first of June, six miles west of Bladen, a freedman was hung. His body is still hanging.

7. About the last of May, a planter hung his servant (a woman) in presence of all the neighborhood. Said planter had killed this woman's husband about three weeks before.

8. About the last of April, two women were caught near a certain plantation in Clark County and hung. Their bodies are still suspended.

9. On the 19th of July, two freedmen were taken off the steamer *Commodore Ferrand,* tied and hung, then taken down, their heads cut off and their bodies thrown in the river.

10. July 11, two men took a woman off the same boat and threw her in the river. This woman had a coop, with some chickens. They threw all in together, and told her to go to the damned Yankees. The woman was drowned.

Following a format suggested by the bureau, field reports bearing the title "Complaints and Outrages" began arriving at headquarters in Washington. These listed some of the incidents' suspected causes, which ranged from "Not wanting to cut timber in the rain as per contract" and "Brutality to a mule" to "Killed because he did not take off his hat to Murphy" and "Not giving way in a buggy." Others dealt with trespass, unfair divisions of crops, and quarrels over hogs, cows, chickens, dogs, manure, shotguns, and, increasingly, politics. There was also the unspeakable—the familiar and romantic links between the races, affairs of the heart, jealousy, and unwanted pregnancies. Many disputes arose from blacks accusing whites of fathering children with their wives, sisters, or other relatives, or black men attempting to visit children who were being kept from them for various reasons. "A great outrage [was] perpetrated within 15 miles of this place a fortnight before," wrote one agent. "A freedman had returned to the plantation of a Mr. Fletcher to get his wife. Fletcher resisted the Negro, shot him, and afterwards cut off his head."

A lynching that reveals some of the attitudes at work was the March 15, 1865, killing of a Unionville, South Carolina, slave named Saxe Joiner. As pillaging Union troops raided nearby towns in the final days of the Confederacy, Joiner wrote notes to two white women in the household where he lived, offering to protect them if the federal soldiers entered Unionville. Joiner's devotion was not extraordinary—many slaves were moved to protect the families of their masters during this precarious time; but not many slaves were in the habit of penning notes to white people, particularly white women. Indeed, Joiner's literacy was exceptional, since in South Carolina it was against the law to teach a slave to read or write.

The notes somehow came into the possession of Joiner's owner, Dr. James E. Hix, who made them public. The first note, promising assistance and "a safe place" to Hix's wife, Martha, as Union forces marauded nearby, was not deemed troublesome because it could be construed as an expression of a slave's loyalty to his mistress; but the second note, addressed to an eighteen-year-old single woman who lived in the household, Susan Baldwin, with its suggestion that he knew a secret place where they would be secure, was offensive to local white sensibilities. Joiner was arrested, found guilty of a misdemeanor, and sentenced to immediate service with the Confederate forces, a judgment Dr. Hix probably requested as a means of sparing his slave from harsher punishment.

This sentence was seen as far too lenient by many local whites, and deemed disrespectful to Confederate soldiers at the front, including Susan Baldwin's brother. Claiming that Joiner had written "grossly insulting proposals" to Baldwin, a new trial was scheduled. When it was delayed because of the imminent threat of Union invasion, an impatient lynch mob swept into the jail, threatened the sheriff until he gave up the keys to Joiner's cell, then hanged the would-be protector of Martha Hix and Susan Baldwin from a tree across the street from the courthouse.

Saxe Joiner was lynched because at a historically disjunctive moment for the South, when white-black relations were in agitated transition, he offered succor to a respectable white woman. But as a Reconstruction killing in Haralson County, Georgia, demonstrated, a white woman's social standing could be immaterial. A black farmer named John Walthall had recently taken as his wife a black woman named Tilda, but he was suspected by whites of having previously frequented, or perhaps even lived in, a white brothel. Ku Klux Klansmen, garbed, according to Tilda, in "great big gowns, and great big, long sleeves," showed up at their farm in the middle of the night and immediately began chasing Walthall through the house. He tried to escape by raising a plank in the floor and slipping underneath the house, but he was shot, then dragged out into the yard and whipped. "I heard John holler when they commenced whipping him," a neighbor later recounted. "They said 'Don't holler, or we'll kill you in a minute.' I undertook to try and count, but they scared me so bad that I stopped counting; but I think they hit him about three hundred licks after they shot him."

The whites taunted Walthall as they struck him, demanding to know if he now felt like sleeping with any more white women. They then found Tilda cowering in the house, dragged her outside, and made her get down in the dirt next to her husband and put her arms around his neck, then beat them both senseless (he would soon die of his wounds). The Klansmen remained in the tiny black hamlet terrorizing other inhabitants and destroying property all night. "When they left," Tilda recalled, "chickens were crowing for day."

The Confederacy had lost the war, but it might still win the peace by thwarting in any way it could the Northern efforts to reconstruct the South. In early June 1866, six Confederate veterans living in Pulaski, Tennessee, formed the original chapter of the Ku Klux Klan. Tennessee was a "split state" during the Civil War, Unionist in the east, Confederate in the west, and the bitter rivalry between Unionist and ex-Confederate factions that would characterize Reconstruction was played out in the streets and town squares of numerous Tennessee communities such as Pulaski in 1865–66.

One persistent fiction, part of the larger myth that is the Southern version of Reconstruction, is that the Klan was originally intended as a social fraternity formed to help relieve the monotony of postwar life, and that its role as a terrorist cell came about almost accidentally. This notion is largely traceable to a slim book about the group's origins published in 1905 by two of the founders, J. C. Lester and D. L. Wilson, and reappears in numerous other partisan texts, including Claude Bowers's *The Tragic Era,* a bestselling account of Reconstruction published in 1929. It describes how a fraternity interested solely in diversion and play turned out, just by chance, to frighten the hell out of everybody, particularly former slaves. Bowers explains:

> Since the object was fun, why not costume and deepen the mystery? Agreed—and the young men joyously raided the linen closet and brought forth stiff linen sheets and pillow cases . . . And why not ride horses?—and disguise these, as well, with sheets. Yes, and ride out into the black night and call at the houses of parents and sweethearts in a silent serenade?

This ridiculous passage, describing the origins of the Klan as if it were some kind of pajama party, goes on to detail the Klansmen's "surprise" when it turns out that the freedmen are scared by the Klan's costumes, and explains that only after seeing this effect did it occur to the night riders what an effective tool of enforcement and intimidation they might have stumbled upon.

The idea that the Klan was meant to be a "fraternity" may have been inspired by the name's similarity to that of a popular antebellum college fraternity, Kuklos Adelphon, which had chapters throughout the South, the Greek word *kuklos* meaning "circle." But a more compelling suggestion as to the name's origin is made by folklorist Gladys-Marie Fry, who speculates that the name was derived from Clocletz, a phantom Indian chieftain who many slaves believed roamed the swamps and backwoods of northern Alabama at night with the ghostly remnants of his decimated tribe. The superstition was based on a historic Indian people who had once resided in the area, the Cocletz, who were known for their antipathy toward black people and who were often employed as slave hunters. It seems not unlikely that in choosing the name Ku Klux Klan the founders were selecting a term already known to inspire fear in their intended victims.

Ever since the first slave ship had unloaded its cargo in Virginia in the seventeenth century, whites had taken advantage of many Africans' beliefs in conjuring and hoodoo, preying on blacks' widely presumed fear of ghosts and haunted places. Slave narratives are replete with stories of roads not to be traveled or crossroads to be avoided after dark. Slave owners made use of such fears, promoting stories of supernatural occurrences and monsters to be encountered by those who rambled too freely after dark. The Klan renovated these time-honored methods. Each new member was required to provide for himself a white mask, a tall cardboard hat so constructed as to increase the wearer's height, a gown or robe, and a small whistle for use in signaling. Jefferson Huskins, a freedman visited by a

Klan posse, recalled, "Some had on these great horns, some had on false faces, and some had their coats turned wrong side outwards, and one had a handkerchief tied over his mouth." The Klan's pointed phallic hats and the horns, the use of white sheets, headless disguises, and stilts used to create the impression of ghosts walking in the air were devices that many freedmen knew from the patroller era before the war.

The Klan idea spread readily through towns filled with bitter veterans of the defeated Confederacy. Many continued to wear their faded soldiers' garb, and appeared ready at the slightest provocation to resume hostilities against the hated Yankees. Schurz observed:

> The incorrigibles . . . still indulge in the swagger which was so customary before and during the war, and still hope for a time when the Southern confederacy will achieve its independence. This class consists mostly of young men, and comprise the loiterers of the towns and the idlers of the country. They persecute Union men and Negroes whenever they can do so with impunity, insist clamorously upon their "rights" and are extremely impatient of the presence of the federal soldiers. This element is by no means unimportant; it is strong in numbers, deals in brave talk, addresses itself directly and incessantly to the passions and prejudices of the masses, and commands the admiration of the women.

A Union officer reported similar observations from Jackson, Mississippi:

> They boast of Jeff. Davis and President Johnson, try in every way to show their contempt for the Yankee, boast of the number they have killed, etc. They want it understood that they are not whipped—simply overpowered. The Negroes complain that these same "gallant young men" make a practice of robbing them of such trifles as knives, tobacco, combs, etc. If any resistance is made, death is pretty sure to be the result. . . . Negroes are often shot, as it appears, just out of wanton cruelty, for no reason at all that anyone can imagine. . . . In one day's travel I passed by different places where five colored men had been murdered in the five days just passed, and as many wounded.

Under names such as the Knights of the White Camellia, Knights of the Rising Sun, the '76 Association, the Council of Safety, the Pale Faces, the Constitutional Union Guards, and so on, Klansmen terrorized freedmen, Republicans, and Freedmen's Bureau agents. A special target was the detested Union League, a Northern white patriotic organization started during the Civil War that, after peace was declared, worked in the South to help the freedmen understand and exercise their new rights before the law. The destruction of black schools and churches was common, not solely because freedmen's education was frowned upon, but because these structures were sometimes used by blacks and their Northern white advocates for political meetings. White female schoolteachers, derisively known as "Oberlin girls," encountered frank hostility, as did a male teacher warned by the Klan in South Carolina: "You are a dern aberlition puppy and scoundrel if We hear of your name in the papers again we will burn your hellish house over your head cut your entrals out. The K Ks are on your track and you will be in hell in four days if you don't mind yourself."

The Reconstruction Klan was one of the more missive-happy terrorist organizations—specializing in descriptive messages illustrated with skulls and crossbones, moons, owls, serpents, and other imagery meant to evoke the group's "mysteriousness." A typical note sent to the Republican hiring chief on a section of the North and South Alabama Railroad in the early 1870s threatened a lynching:

Dam Your Soul. The Horrible Sepulchre and Bloody Moon has at last arrived. Some live to-day to-morrow "Die." We the undersigned understand through our Grand "Cyclops" that you have recommended a big Black Nigger for Male agent on our nu rode; wel, sir, Jest you understand in time if he gets on the rode you can make up your mind to pull roape. If you have anything to say in regard to the Matter, meet the Grand Cyclops and Conclave at Den No. 4 at 12 o'clock midnight, Oct. 1st, 1871.

When you are in Calera we warn you to hold your tounge and not speak so much with your mouth or otherwise you will be taken on surprise and led out by the Klan and learnt to stretch hemp. Beware. Beware. Beware. Beware.

Such auguries were best taken seriously. As early as 1866 the Freedmen's Bureau, in a dispatch from Georgia, was already reporting extensive Klanlike activity:

March—Manuel (colored), murdered by regulators (so-called), shot in bed by a party of white men (disguised).

June—Jordan Nelson, colored, of Harris County, murdered by parties unknown, was found in the woods hung by the neck.

July—Pike, Georgia, an unknown freed boy was murdered by a party of men (disguised). The boy was taken by force from the sheriff of this county and afterward found in the river with his throat cut from ear to ear.

Cato Tomlinson was most brutally beaten by parties unknown. Tomlinson was laid on his back and whipped through to his intestines.

Moses Hart was called out of his house at night by white men and shot in the face by parties unknown.

Freedmen Peter Smith and Robert Wiggins were beaten nearly to death by parties unknown who came on horseback dressed with sheets over them. No action by civil authorities.

Whipping, so long an essential element of slavery, was the Klan's preferred mode of punishment, as it most explicitly reminded blacks of their former status. "The habit is so inveterate with a great many persons," Schurz noted, "as to render, on the least provocation, the impulse to whip a Negro almost irresistible." Everyone in a house, including women, children, and even toddlers, was routinely flogged along with the primary victim the Klan had been seeking. No one, regardless of age or gender, was spared at least a few licks from the switch. Asked by a congressional investigator how many colored people had been whipped in her neighborhood, Harriet Hernandes of Spartanburg, South Carolina, responded: "It is all of them, mighty near . . . Ben Phillips and his wife and daughter; Sam Foster; and Moses Eaves, they killed him—I could not begin to tell all—Ann Bonner and her daughter, Manza Surratt and his wife and whole family, even the least child in the family, they took it out of bed and whipped it. They told them if they did that they would remember it."

A fresh switch cut from a hickory or gum tree was a favored weapon of discipline, but fishing rods, canes, or anything else that came to hand might also be used. Surprisingly, the available testimony suggests sexual molestation occurred only occasionally in such circumstances; whipping, prolonged and often ritualistic, and not rape, seemed the focus of the night riders' visits, although women were made to kneel on the ground and lower their garments around their waists, exposing their breasts and bare backs; occasionally they would be compelled to strip completely, a humiliation the victims referred to as "being made to show."

"They had a show of us all there," Caroline Benson of White County, Georgia, remembered. "They had us all lying in the road. Mary Brown, Mary Neal, and my next youngest daughter. They had us all stripped there, and laughed and made great sport. Some of them just squealed the same as if they were stable horses just brought out. You never saw such ill-behaved men."

Harriet Simril of Columbia, South Carolina, reported being raped. She said that one night the Klan simply walked right into her house. They were looking for her husband, and not finding him at home, they "ate all my pies up and took two pieces of meat," then "dragged me out in the road and ravished me out there. . . . Ches McCollum, Tom McCollum, and this big Jim Harper. . . . After they got done with me I had no sense for a long time. I laid there, I don't know how long. The next morning I went to my house and it was in ashes."

In spring 1867 Klan groups from several Southern states convened in Nashville to divide the Invisible Empire, as the Klan called itself, into realms, dominions, provinces, and dens. Former general Nathan Bedford Forrest, one of the Confederacy's most colorful heroes, was named grand wizard. Forrest was the ideal leader for a homegrown guerrilla operation such as the Klan for, unlike most Confederate officers, he had had no formal military education, but had risen through the ranks from private to general during the course of the war, the only soldier on either side of the conflict to do so. It was said he had had twenty-nine horses shot out from under him. "War means fightin', and fightin' means killin' " was his well-known philosophy, and his skillful application of it in several theaters of the war had made him one of the most feared of all Confederate cavalry leaders. Indeed, by war's end most Northerners considered him a war criminal. On April 12, 1864, when he led the capture of the Union garrison at Fort Pillow, Tennessee, troops under his command massacred dozens of black Union soldiers who had surrendered, as well as some white soldiers from a Tennessee Union regiment. Forrest denied wrongdoing at Fort Pillow and also never admitted to his role in the Klan, although in testimony to Congress he offered a rather damning view of how matters looked to him in the period 1865–66:

> There were a great many Northern men coming down there, forming [Union] Leagues all over the country. The Negroes were holding night meetings; were going about; were becoming very insolent; and the Southern people all over the State were very much alarmed. Ladies were ravished by some of these Negroes. . . . There was a great deal of insecurity in the country, and I think this [Ku Klux Klan] was got up to protect the weak, with no political intention at all.

Despite, or rather because of, Forrest's notoriety, interest in the Klan soared. In Nashville a children's baseball team took "Ku Klux Klan" as its name, as did a circus and purveyors of a range of useful products, from knives to tobacco and even a kind of paint. There also came into being several weekly news sheets dedicated exclusively to Klan activities, such as the *Daily Ku Klux Vedette, Ultra Ku Klux,* and the *Ku Klux Kaleidoscope.* Not even the Northern press could resist the Klan's allure. Much as first-person slave narratives intrigued Northern readers before the war, now the carryings-on of a mysterious masked brotherhood of avenging horsemen held strong appeal.

A bizarre manifestation of the Klan's emotional hold on the South occurred in Blount County, Alabama, in October 1870 when, during a religious revival taking place near Gum Grove, the white preacher's wife gave birth to a monstrous stillborn child that, according to those who saw it, looked exactly like a Ku Klux Klansman, its huge flat head, three times the size of an ordinary child's, covered by a "soft, spongy fungous growth." The eyes and mouth were smaller than an average child's, and "in a straight line from the crown of the head to the front of the forehead, commencing at each cheek bone, there was a sort of fringe flaring very little to near the top, and then full around the top. It was about an inch wide and about half an inch thick at the base; a gristly fringe, of a dark purple color." At the temples "were two grisly horns about an inch and a half long." Just before the birth, it was said, the mother had seen white-sheeted Klansmen in her dreams. The corpse of the tiny creature was so fantastic it was brought to the revival meeting and displayed to the approximately fifteen hundred people gathered there. There were other reported stillbirths of monstrous children resembling disguised Klansmen during this period.

When the Klan stepped up its activities with the intention of influencing the fall elections of 1868, it became glaringly apparent that the U.S. government would ultimately have to step in and confront the "masked Confederacy." General W. P. Carlin, Tennessee commander of the Freedmen's Bureau, reported to Washington in July of that year:

> Complaints are continually coming in of outrages committed by the Ku Klux Klan. The colored people are leaving their homes, and are fleeing to the towns and large cities for protection. They say that it is impossible for them to work during the day and keep watch during the night, which is necessary for them to do, in order to save their lives. Unless something is done immediately, by the Governor, to protect the colored citizens of the

country, the cities will be flooded by poor, helpless creatures, who will have to be supported by the State, or United States Government. The Ku Klux organization is so extensive, and so well organized and armed, that it is beyond the power of any one to exert any moral influence over them. Powder and ball is the only thing that will put them down.

Klan intimidation of would-be black voters increased, as it was believed the black vote had been instrumental in the close election victory of that despised Republican, General Ulysses S. Grant. By August 1869, a report from Georgia complained:

In many parts of the State there is practically no government. . . . There can be no doubt of the existence of numerous insurrectionary organizations known as "Ku Klux Klans," who, shielded by their disguises, by the secrecy of their movements, and by the terror which they inspire, perpetrate crime with impunity. There is great reason to believe that in some cases local magistrates are in sympathy with the members of these organizations.

The complete breakdown in civil authority in some areas resulted in the establishment by Congress in December 1870 of the Joint Select Committee to Inquire into the Condition of Affairs in the Late Insurrectionary States, while President Grant asked Congress to pass needed legislation to combat Klan operations.

The Joint Committee held extensive hearings in Washington and in three Southern towns for almost an entire year, from spring 1871 through February 1872. Most of the Southern white witnesses disavowed knowledge of the Klan but, like Nathan Bedford Forrest, often gave themselves away by making strong inimical remarks about freedmen, Yankees, or Republicans. Hundreds of black witnesses related stories of the whippings, lynchings, and other violence they'd endured, as well as the dangers from disease and starvation when their fear of the Klan drove them to "lay out" in the woods for weeks on end. The resulting thirteen-volume report was one of the most extensive ever made by Congress, and for the sheer quantity of compelling testimony it provides on Klan terrorism, and the disturbing snapshot it offers of Reconstruction at ground level in the rural South, it is a singular document in U.S. history.

Heeding President Grant's request, Congress on May 31, 1870, passed the First Enforcement Act, which promised federal action in instances where the rights of a voter were violated. The Second Enforcement Act, passed on February 28, 1871, dictated that federal supervisors should oversee elections, and made interference with elections a federal offense. The Third Enforcement Act, also known as the Ku Klux Klan Act, passed on April 20, 1871, declared that Klan activity constituted rebellion against the government of the United States. This act made it a crime to "go in disguise on a public highway to . . . deprive another person of equal protection," particularly "under color of law," as it had been seen that, in many cases, acts of terrorism against blacks were carried out in conjunction with local officials.

The Third Enforcement Act also gave the government the right to impose martial law if necessary, and on October 17, 1871, Grant suspended the writ of habeas corpus in nine South Carolina counties that had been particularly hard hit by Klan violence. In a roundup more than two hundred Klansmen were arrested, of whom about fifty were convicted and sent to federal penitentiaries. Trials were also held in Mississippi, under the new law, and in North Carolina hundreds of Klansmen were seized. The arrests, convictions, and sentencing were not significant in terms of numbers, but the overall federal effort, along with corresponding state condemnations—a few states passed laws making it permissible to shoot on sight anyone wearing a disguise—did seem to put a damper on Klan activity. Of course, one reason the Reconstruction-era Klan faded was that it had largely accomplished many of its goals; it had initiated the process of making full black participation in politics and in the mainstream of Southern life unattainable, and had established that intimidation and terror could be used to accomplish this end.

Although Southern spectacle lynching did not emerge as a significant phenomenon until the 1880s and 1890s, mob lynchings or summary executions were likely seen by the public earlier. Historian George C. Wright, examining the fragmentary lynching records for Kentucky in the years 1866–78, essentially the whole of Reconstruction, discovered 129 lynchings, of which 30 victims were white. As Kentucky was not even one of the eleven Confederate states—a slaveholding state, it had nonetheless remained loyal to the Union—it seems likely the numbers for Reconstruction lynchings in secessionist strongholds such as Georgia, South Carolina, Mississippi, and Louisiana would compare with or exceed Kentucky's total. Wright points out that about one third of all Kentucky lynchings ever recorded occurred during these thirteen years. What this suggests is that lynchings may well have been a common feature of Southern life during Reconstruction, even though historians have traditionally (and understandably) "started the clock" on the practice in the early 1880s, when it became a recorded public phenomenon.

By combing newspaper accounts of lynchings from the 1890s forward, Wright often found clues about earlier lynchings that had gone unrecorded. Such recollections were frequently associated in popular memory with a locally notorious "lynching tree" or other location used to deal with suspected black felons. For instance, when in December 1896 the local paper in Mayfield, Kentucky, reported the hanging of a black named Jim Stone, the article mentioned that it was the first lynching that had occurred in the county since 1870, when seven Negroes were hanged by masked mobs in and near the city: "One was lynched in Bullock's grove, one near the Primitive Baptist Church, one a short distance south of where Mr. Wm McDonald now lives, one at the old Conner orchard, two at Kess Creek on the Paris Road, and one in the same locality." In this way, Wright obtained information about historically "invisible" acts of lethal summary punishment.

Mass lynchings were not uncommon in the Reconstruction South. Ten blacks were taken from the local jail and shot and hanged in Union, South Carolina, in January 1871; that same year nine black prisoners were lynched together in Louisville, Georgia. In violence associated with the 1868 election in Louisiana, almost two hundred blacks were killed in a "skirmish" with a newly formed White League, and hundreds more perished at white hands in scattered incidents between April and November of that year. In Louisiana and Texas the anti-Republican forces were, for all intents and purposes, simply Confederate fighting units reconstituted, fifty to two hundred men riding together. Under such circumstances there was no need for masks or disguises; these were small armies intimidating or killing anything that got in their way. Reported *The New National Era* of one encounter between such quasi-vigilante forces and freedmen: "The butchery seems to have been prosecuted in the most shocking manner, men with their great knives stabbing and cutting right and left, walking upon the dead and with the stocks of their guns beating out the brains of those that were not yet dead." And in addition to well-known race riots in Memphis and New Orleans, more than two dozen other assaults were launched by whites against black urban populations during Reconstruction, almost always with black fatalities.

One of the rare lynchings to gain national press attention during this period took place in Kentucky in early November 1872, when a black Republican voter-registration leader, Samuel Hawkins, was killed along with his wife and daughter. *The New York Times* reported that Hawkins had been abducted with his family from their home in Fayette County and led in the direction of the Licking River, where the three were found the next day hanged from the same tree limb. The incident received notice because of its proximity to the reelection of President Grant over New York newspaper publisher Horace Greeley, and because the settling of a political grudge with the murder of an entire family was so unusual.

Richard Maxwell Brown's comprehensive study of vigilante violence in America estimates that in the four years 1868–71 there were more than four hundred Klan lynchings in the South. Union general Phil Sheridan calculated that 3,500 whites and blacks were killed between 1865 and 1875. Ida Wells-Barnett, writing in the 1890s, put the number of Negroes killed by whites since 1865 at 10,000, with only three white men executed for crimes against blacks in that period. Congress's report of 1872, based on the findings of the Joint Committee to Inquire into Conditions of the Late Insurrectionary States, speculated that as many as 2,000 blacks had been killed or wounded in Louisiana alone since the close of the Civil War. Author Dorothy Sterling, who combed through many thousands of documents and oral histories in her preparation of a noted compendium of the Reconstruction era, cited 20,000 as the number killed by the Klan just in the four years 1868–71. In the late 1890s, the influential back-to-Africa leader Bishop Henry McNeal Turner, eschewing numerical estimation, simply observed that enough black people had been lynched in America so that the victims would "reach a mile high if laid one upon the other."

Efforts to establish precise numbers are extremely useful but become, at a certain point, meaningless; whether people were being killed for an alleged criminal act, a transgression of social norms, or for holding minority political views, whether their number was 500, 5,000, or 25,000, by the time the antilynching movement got under way just before the turn of the century it was evident that the threshold for mob murder in America had long since been crossed.

In the North, the immediate postwar idealism and concern about the freedmen had given way to an era comparatively free of principled behavior in public life. It was a time of ambition, crassness, a joy in excess and the seeking of wealth—the "Great Barbecue," as it was known—as Democratic political machines looted Northern cities, and rapidly expanding railroad, mining, and manufacturing interests created sudden fortunes. Correspondingly, it was an age of waning public morality and growing relativism. Then, people residing in Northern cities soon had their own minority problem on which to focus, the entry into those cities of swelling numbers of European immigrants, a movement that was changing the very look and feel of America.

New understanding was extended to the Southern anxiety about black political domination. These fears were nowhere better crystallized than in an influential book, *The Prostrate State: South Carolina Under Negro Government* by James S. Pike, published in 1873. Pike had been an antislavery journalist and served as Lincoln's minister to the Netherlands, but was bothered by federal policies such as the declaring of martial law in parts of South Carolina. The book heaped scorn on the efforts at self-government engaged in by blacks, depicting South Carolina as a state where "300,000 white people . . . composing the intelligence and property-holders of the state, are put under the heel of 400,000 pauper blacks, fresh from a state of slavery and ignorance most dense." The white community, the author noted, "lies prostrate in the dust, ruled over by this strange conglomerate, gathered from the ranks of its own servile population." He termed the black efforts at rule "the most ignorant democracy that mankind ever saw." Pike's critique, which would become one of the touchstones of contemporary thinking on Reconstruction, was all the more damaging because it issued from the pen of a prominent Northerner.

A similar trajectory was that of the influential political cartoonist Thomas Nast, whose work during the Reconstruction era offers a literal illustration of the period's changing attitudes. Once sympathetic to the freedmen's plight, by 1874 Nast was lampooning their efforts at politics, depicting black legislators as apes and drunken buffoons, bare feet on their desks, hurling vegetables at one another—popular images that, perhaps more than the printed word, helped shape public views.

Such criticisms increasingly went unanswered, as the original Northern Republican brain trust—men such as Charles Sumner and fellow senator Thaddeus Stevens—either faded in stature or completely passed from the scene, Stevens with his last breath requesting burial in an integrated cemetery.

An incident revealing of the federal government's own growing indifference was its refusal in 1875 to send assistance to Mississippi when urgently requested by that state's Republican governor, Adelbert Ames, during intense antiblack election violence. President Grant, vacationing at

Long Branch, New Jersey, delegated the crisis to his attorney general, Edward Pierrepont, who informed Governor Ames, "The whole public are tired out with these annual autumnal outbreaks in the South, and the great majority are now ready to condemn any interference on the part of the government." A short time later Ames was chased from the governor's chair and made to flee Mississippi for his life.

As views toward black Americans hardened, attitudes toward the former Confederacy softened, and a powerful impulse toward reunion spread in the land. The South—defanged and shorn of slavery—began to seem appealingly exotic, for as life in the North became more complex, the simple charms of Southern life, its dominant Anglo-Saxon nature, its ruralness, its tradition of genteel aristocracy, came to possess new allure. If, as it was said, the Civil War had been a war between the future and the past, and the future had won, the past could still look awfully good at times.

Promoters of resorts in Virginia, North Carolina, northern Georgia, and elsewhere sold the idea of an Old South as an arcadia—an unhurried, unharried civilization peopled by gallant men, elegant women, and happy blacks. Pleasure travel, once a hobby pursued only by the elite, had given way to the nascent American tourism industry, and Yankees flocked to destinations such as White Sulphur Hot Springs from which they embarked on day trips to old plantations, battlefields, and settlements of picturesque darkies. White tourists attended black church services and were led to shacks where huge, charismatic "mammies" ladled up tasty suppers. Seeing the "natives"—the former slaves—in their habitat was regarded as the high point of the experience.

Reconstruction, clearly, had collapsed, a chief reason being the federal government's inability to promote a program of economic reform that would have included some redistribution of land. As a result, the plantation system, which was built on the doctrine of cheap labor, was essentially left intact. Propertyless, illiterate, without capital, ex-slaves remained highly vulnerable to political and labor-related abuses, and their resulting economic and social status left them more easily characterized as a restive group unable to fit into society.

The Freedmen's Bureau, chartered in 1865 for one year, renewed in 1866 for two more, was itself soon allowed to drift out of existence. Charles Sumner had once tried unsuccessfully to establish it as a permanent, separate cabinet post—elevating the challenge of reconciling the white and black races in America to the highest level of national concern, where it arguably belonged—but instead, as part of the War Department, its fate was linked inextricably with the increasingly unpopular U.S. military occupation of the South, and it sank along with the rest of the federal venture.

The abandonment of Reconstruction and of the freedmen by the North was probably inevitable, given the changes the North itself was undergoing, moving from rural to urban in its experience and outlook and becoming a more complex, industrialized society. On a fundamental level, Northern whites simply grew weary of the irremediable antipathy the South held for outside interference, and agreed to accept the argument that, burdened with a largely uneducated and occasionally troublesome racial minority, the region knew best how to cope with its singular predicament.

To Gather My Race in My Arms

Despite the federal government's withdrawal from the South and its eventual disavowal of the Reconstruction amendments, which formed the foundation of black people's new citizenship rights and were gutted by the Supreme Court by the early 1880s, what could not be taken away from the nation was an important idea that Reconstruction had set loose—that black people had a basic right to educate and improve themselves and to enter the mainstream of American society. In the face of tremendous obstacles, even harassment, many former slaves had moved swiftly to take advantage of these opportunities. Black literacy and mobility increased, black newspapers and political clubs sprang up, and many blacks voted and entered the political arena at the local and state level, several advancing to the U.S. Senate and House of Representatives.

The difficult if promising period of Reconstruction, the "glorious failure," as it came to be known, was perhaps most meaningful for those blacks fortunate enough to come of age during it, the first generation of black Americans to enjoy freedom and citizenship. Of all the extraordinary children this era begot, surely none was more remarkable than Ida B. Wells of Holly Springs, Mississippi. Born into slavery in 1862, she grew up believing fervently in the promise of black citizenship and accomplishment, and for the rest of her life chose to behave as though that promise had never been withdrawn. One of the first Americans to understand that lynching was a form of caste oppression and to recognize that it would have to be exposed to be destroyed, she was also one of the first to articulate its graphic horror. Wells undertook this work against such great odds, and with so sure a sense of purpose, that social activists in America have long strived to emulate her example.

Her life began in the midst of conflict, as the town of Holly Springs, forty miles southeast of Memphis, was captured and recaptured by Union and Confederate forces no fewer than fifty-nine times during the Civil War. Her father, James Wells, a carpenter, was named for his white master, who was also his father. During Reconstruction, when Ida was a girl, he was active in local freedmen's issues, and served on the first board of trustees of Rust College. James Wells's slave mother, Peggy, paid a price for her son's special status: when the senior James Wells died, his widow publicly stripped and beat Peggy, an assault from which she never recovered. Ida's mother, Elizabeth, also bore the markings from whippings she'd received as a slave. These visible scars on her mother and grandmother were reminders of the family's slave past and they became a touchstone to a young woman who willed herself to resist and challenge the white world's cruelty.

James and Elizabeth Wells took sick in the yellow fever epidemic that swept northern Mississippi in 1878, and both died on the same day. Though only a teenager, Ida refused her relatives' suggestions to break up the remnants of her immediate family, insisting that she could care for her four younger brothers and sisters. Lying about her age, she obtained work as a schoolteacher in Holly Springs. The following year, leaving two of her siblings behind, she moved to Memphis, from whence she commuted to a teaching job in a country school in nearby Woodstock, Tennessee.

As a black woman instructing black children Wells was unique, for due to the lack of qualified black educators the education of freedmen in the war's aftermath had been mostly performed by white missionaries; it was not until the 1880s that young people such as Wells began to fill the teaching ranks. Like many of her peers, she worked assiduously at self-improvement—taking elocution and drama courses in order to be able to speak properly, working constantly to improve her appearance. Only four and a half feet tall in a pillbox hat, but striking, with a strong, attractive face, she had an eye for clothes. She wore white gloves and dressed fashionably, and was a regular patron at Menken's Department Store. An avid reader of Shakespeare and romance and adventure novels, she drew sustenance from tales of individuals who cherish their independence and dare stand alone.

She endeavored to be, above all, a proper woman. In this, she shared the striving of utmost importance to women emerging from chattel slavery, a condition in which they had been promoted as breeders and subjected to whippings and other indignities, and who were justly sensitive to the lingering stigma of their degradation. "Our people, as a whole, are charged with immorality and vice," Wells wrote in an article in the late 1880s. "It depends largely on the woman of to-day to refute such charges by her stainless life."

While the diary she kept during her Memphis years reflects that she enjoyed her friendships with men, and even yearned for intimacy, she feared constraints on her freedom. Freedom to do what exactly was not always clear to her, as women's roles were then tightly proscribed, yet she sensed keenly that a life solely as wife and mother would be inadequate. As she wrote in an 1885 article, "What is, or should be woman? Not merely a bundle of flesh and bones, nor a fashion plate, a frivolous inanity, a soulless doll, a heartless coquette—but a strong, bright presence, thoroughly imbued with a sense of her mission on earth and a desire to fill it."

Wells's understanding of the importance of self-respect and personal esteem was at the heart of the incident that began her public life: a disturbance on a railroad train.

For black women, travel on Southern trains was often humiliating. They could purchase tickets to ride first class—sometimes a separate first-class "ladies' car" was available—but local laws or railroad regulations might force them to ride in a "colored car," which women in particular disdained because it was usually the train's smoking car and tended to attract rough characters of all types. "It stops out beyond the [platform] covering in the rain or sun or dust," W.E.B. Du Bois would recall. "Usually there is no step to help you climb on and . . . you must pass through the white smokers or else they pass through your part, with swagger and noise and stares . . . [T]he plush is caked with dirt, the floor is grimy, and the windows dirty. An impertinent white newsboy occupies two seats at the end of the car and importunes you to the point of rage to buy cheap candy, Coca-Cola, and worthless, if not vulgar, books." Black women, who were perhaps most inconvenienced by these conditions, played a leading role in fighting railroad segregation—surreptitiously, by dressing in finery so as to make their right to first-class travel seem unimpeachable, by passing as white, by pretending to be a nanny minding a white baby, or by impersonating a French woman (an innocent "*Je suis française*" having been known to deter officious train conductors), and directly, by challenging the segregation codes through lawsuits.

The situation on the trains worsened in 1883 when the Civil Rights Act of 1875, "Sumner's Law" (after Senator Charles Sumner), which sought to help the freedmen advance socially and economically by prohibiting individuals from discriminating against blacks in public places such as hotels and theaters, and on public conveyances, was repealed. Segregation on Southern railroads had until then been enforced inconsistently, but soon after the repeal the railroads instituted their own stricter rules separating passengers or firmed up their enforcement of state codes.

On May 4, 1884, Wells was en route from Memphis to her teaching job in Woodstock when she was ordered to leave a ladies' car and go to the "smoker" because of her race. She refused on the grounds that she'd purchased a first-class ticket. When a conductor remonstrated with her and attempted to grab her by the arm, she bit him. "I had braced my feet against the seat in front and was holding to the back," she recalled, "and as he had already been badly bitten he didn't try it again by himself. He went forward and got the baggageman and another man and of course they succeeded in dragging me out," as white passengers in the car stood and applauded.

Wells sued the Chesapeake & Ohio Railroad on the grounds that, having been sold a first-class ticket, she had the right to ride in a first-class car. A Memphis court found in her favor and awarded her two hundred dollars in damages. But the railroad successfully appealed the case. Soon after, Wells was kept from entering a ladies' car on the C&O and renewed her suit; in late December 1884 she was awarded five hundred dollars by the court, which ruled again that as the railroad had accepted her payment for a first-class ticket, it could not legally insist that she ride in a car that was inferior to a first-class coach. "A Darky Damsel Obtains a Verdict for Damages against the Chesapeake & Ohio Railroad—What It Cost to Put a Colored School Teacher in a Smoking Car—Verdict for $500," ran the headline in the Memphis *Daily Appeal,* December 25, 1884. This time the railroad appealed to the state supreme court, which reversed the lower court's ruling, declaring that Wells's chief objective had been to harass the railroad, not keep her seat on the train. Instead of receiving the five-hundred-dollar award, she was made to pay two hundred dollars in court costs. The case demonstrated what advocates of Sumner's Law had always feared: the states would not act to protect black citizens' access to public accommodations and conveyances. "I feel so disappointed because I had hoped for such great things from my suit for my people generally," Wells wrote in her diary. "I have firmly believed all along that the law was on our side and would, when we appealed to it, give us justice. I feel shorn of that belief and utterly discouraged, and just now, if it were possible, would gather my race in my arms and fly away with them."

Although she lost the case, its notoriety helped serve as a springboard to a new career when she described the suit in a series of weekly letters, signed "Iola," which she contributed to a regional church publication, *The Living Way*. Encouraged by reader response, she began to write short, helpful essays on everyday topics. In articles such as "Woman's Mission" and "The Model Woman: A Pen Picture of the Typical Southern Girl," she elaborated on her own example of what the upright Victorian black woman could and should be. Inevitably, her strong opinions on politics and race issues surfaced. At the suggestion of a mentor, William J. Simmons of the Negro Press Association, "Iola" began submitting articles to a wide range of black-owned periodicals such as Kansas City's *Gate City Press,* the Detroit *Plaindealer,* the Indianapolis *World,* and religious publications with broad distribution in the South, including the Louisville-based *American Baptist.*

In the 1880s, black newspapers and other periodicals were ubiquitous, a result of fast-growing literacy among blacks and a keen interest in the current events that affected their lives. The papers played an important role—emphasizing the achievements of the black community, bringing attention to accomplished individuals, providing advertising for black-owned goods and services, and allowing space for opinionated political discussion. Informative but emphatically practical, most featured a heavy social bent, with chatty columns such as "They Say," "Race Gleanings," or "Did You Know?" Above all, they offered an alternative to the white-controlled press, which tended to either marginalize or criminalize black people, or ignore them altogether.

Iola's measured advice, laced with her strong opinions, her intimate familiarity with the travails of both family and professional life, and the overriding novelty of a black woman writing in a traditionally male domain, made her an irresistible figure to readers as well as to the men who edited and published the nation's black press. "From a mere, insignificant country-bred lass she has developed into one of the foremost among the female thinkers of the race," the *Washington Bee* noted with admiration. T. Thomas Fortune, editor of the New York *Age,* wrote of Wells, "She has plenty of nerve, and is as sharp as a steel trap, and she has no sympathy with humbug."

The Age, probably the nation's leading black paper, reprinted several of Iola's columns, and she and Fortune struck up a casual correspondence, which led to his becoming and long remaining one of her great champions and friends. Fortune, as Wells knew, was more than a promising editorial contact, for he was active in the first stirrings of black organization and militancy that had come on the heels of the repeal of Sumner's Law. Fortune's writing had helped create an emerging consensus among "race men" that black-led initiatives, not those that relied on white Northern leadership, as in Reconstruction, would be necessary to win equal rights. It was time, Fortune and his colleagues believed, for blacks to begin making their own way. "There is no dodging the issue," he wrote. "We have got to take hold of this problem ourselves, and make so much noise that all the world shall know the wrongs we suffer and our determination to right these wrongs." The organization he founded in 1887, the National Afro-American League, brought together many of the nation's leading black activists and attacked, among other things, "the universal and lamentable reign of lynch and mob law." Wells thought Fortune's league "the grandest idea ever originated by colored men" for its "potential to protect citizenship, property, and lynch victims."

Wells's and Fortune's enthusiasm was not shared by all, however, particularly in the South, where many blacks feared that a national black organization clamoring for equality would only exacerbate their problems, perhaps even bring about a revival of the Ku Klux Klan. The editor of one black Alabama newspaper worried that Southern whites might respond to the National Afro-American League's existence by murdering all the black people they could get their hands on, "while T. Thomas Fortune sits in New York and collects money for complaining about what is happening."

Wells, in biting a railroad conductor, had already made clear the quality of her own regard for the feelings of white Southerners. She had little hesitation about confronting them, whether in print or in person, by herself or as part of an organization. Lynching in particular, which Fortune had editorialized against in *The Age,* troubled her, and in her columns she increasingly took up the cause—grieving over the report that "thirteen colored men" had been "shot down in cold blood" in Mississippi, or sharing her horror that "a colored woman accused of poisoning a white one was taken from the county jail and stripped naked and hung up in the courthouse yard and her body riddled with bullets and her body left exposed to view!"

In 1889, Wells purchased a one-third share in a black-owned Memphis newspaper, the *Free Speech and Headlight*. The paper's offices were in the Beale Street Baptist Church and theoretically under the editorial guidance of the Reverend Taylor Nightingale, but he was too busy with his congregation to have much involvement with the newspaper beyond selling it from his pulpit each Sunday morning. The actual editorship was in the hands of the other two owners, Wells and a man named J. L. Fleming who had fled to Memphis from antiblack violence in Arkansas the year before. In addition to her work as staff writer and editor, Wells personally took charge of increasing the paper's circulation, building it from 1,500 to 4,000 in less than a year by traveling extensively in northern Mississippi, western Tennessee, and Arkansas. It was her idea to have the *Free Speech* printed on pink paper so it could be easily recognized even by those who could not read its name.

The white-published Memphis newspapers made it a custom to reprint the more daring *Free Speech* editorials. In a piece written in 1889, most likely by Wells, and reprinted in the Memphis *Avalanche,* the *Free Speech* noted, "The dailies of our city say that the whites must rule this country. But that is an expression without a thought." As to the white alarm about the new generation of black people unwilling to coddle whites, the *Free Speech* explained:

> The old Southern voice that was once heard and made the Negroes jump and run like rats is "shut up," or might well be, for the Negro of today is not the same as Negroes were thirty years ago, and it can't be expected that the Negro of today will take what was forced upon him thirty years back. So it is no use to be talking now about Negroes ought to be kept at the bottom where God intended for them to stay; the Negro is not intended to stay at the bottom.

In fall 1891 the *Free Speech* defended black "desperadoes" who had stood up to white violence in Kentucky:

> Those Georgetown, Ky. Negroes who set fire to the town last week because a Negro named Dudley had been lynched, show some of the true spark of manhood by their resentment. Of one thing we may be assured, so long as we permit ourselves to be trampled upon, so long we will have

to endure it. Not until the Negro rises in his might and takes a hand resenting such cold-blooded murders, if he has to burn up whole towns, will a halt be called in wholesale lynching.

These were extremely provocative sentiments for their time and place, and a Jackson, Mississippi, paper responded to them by suggesting to "the people of Memphis" that the time had come to "muzzle the *Free Speech*"— a view many Memphians were beginning to share. Of course, it was not widely known among whites that the paper's sharp opinions were being written by a petite black woman. Instead, the *Free Speech's* enemies targeted its nominal helmsman, the innocent Reverend Nightingale, framed him on trumped-up assault charges, and sentenced him to eighty days in the county workhouse. Frightened, and unwilling to go to jail for a crime he had not committed, Nightingale departed for Oklahoma, leaving his newspaper in the hands of Fleming and Wells.

Underlying the growing concerns of people such as Ida Wells and T. Thomas Fortune in the 1880s was their sense that whites were determined to undermine black advances made during Reconstruction and maintain a strict racial caste system in the South at all costs. As Wells had pointed out in one of her columns, the old acquiescent Negro of slave days had been supplanted by his more assertive descendants, and whites, out of fear, had sought new ways to maintain their hegemony. Jim Crow laws, governing virtually every aspect of black people's lives, were instituted, while lynching increasingly was directed at those who posed a social, not just a political, threat. Most sensationally, lynching came to be associated with what was seen as the ultimate symbol of black autonomy, sexual access by black men to white women. Beyond this could only lie the nightmare of interbreeding and the blurring of caste lines. And because the idea of such an act drove Southern whites into a frenzy, the resulting punishments took on new, perverse forms of cruelty—the tortures and immolations of the spectacle lynching.

The anxiety over interracial sex was so great, it fostered the related notion that sex with white women was the real objective behind all black aspiration, that money, education, accomplishment of any kind were for black men mere stepping-stones en route to the bedroom and the ultimate nirvana of intimacy with white women. This, of course, was an expression of the whites' deeper concern about losing control of the status quo and of seeing their own position in society diminish if blacks were allowed to join the middle class; lynch mobs that sought to punish such strivers were often spurred into action by the idea that successful blacks represented just as keen a threat to Southern life as the black rapist.

Wells's involvement in the antilynching cause became deeply personal in 1892, when lynching claimed the lives of three black men of her acquaintance. Thomas Moss, Calvin McDowell, and Henry Stewart were partners in a new grocery store, the People's Grocery, situated in "the Curve," a predominantly black south Memphis neighborhood whose name derived from a sharp curve in the streetcar line. W. R. Barrett, a white grocer threatened by the new, black-owned operation, used the pretext of a falling-out among some boys in the neighborhood to stir up ill will against the blacks. A black teenager named Armour Harris was said to have thrashed a younger boy, the son of a white man named Cornelius Hurst, over a game of marbles. Cornelius Hurst chased down Harris to discipline him, and when several black men tried to intervene, Hurst clubbed one of them over the head. Barrett then went to the People's Grocery and accused coowner Calvin McDowell of hiding one of the blacks who had been in the brawl with Hurst; when McDowell denied it, Barrett struck him with a pistol. McDowell fought back, bloodying the white man. "Being the stronger, I got the best of that scrimmage," McDowell told a reporter who investigated.

Barrett sought revenge by convincing a Shelby County grand jury to indict the owners of the People's Grocery for maintaining a public nuisance. A rumor reached the store's owners that police, with the assistance of Barrett, Hurst, and other whites, planned to raid the store, and as they could not rely on police protection, the blacks arranged for men from the community to help them guard their business. On the night of Saturday, March 5, guards stationed in the rear of the store saw whites approaching and opened fire, wounding three. Next morning, outraged Memphis papers announced that the injured men, although they'd been wearing civilian clothes, were police officers.

The store owners—Moss, McDowell, and Stewart—as well as young Armour Harris, were all arrested, Harris's mother admonishing him as he was led away, "March on like a soldier, Armour. De Lawd's wid you an' agin de white folks." The People's Grocery was described in the papers as "a nest of turbulent and unruly Negroes." The *Appeal-Avalanche,* saluting authorities for carrying out the raid on the black grocery, praised them for their restraint in making peaceful arrests and not lynching anyone. With policemen shot, the paper averred, there was "justification for immediate personal reprisal," but the arresting officers had "remembered their functions." The article concluded, "Only in a community where the spirit of law and order is active and controlling would this have been the case. If we had an inefficient police, if the courts had not always been swift to punish law-breakers, we have no doubt that Judge Lynch would have appeared speedily on the scene."

But the newspaper's confidence was premature. A few nights later a posse of masked white men entered the jail in the middle of the night, held at bay the few jailers on duty, and removed the three store owners. Moss, McDowell, and Stewart were marched to an open field between Cubbins's Brickyard and the tracks of the Chesapeake & Ohio Railroad and shot dead at point-blank range.

"The affair was one of the most orderly of its kind ever conducted," observed the next day's paper. "There was no whooping, not even loud talking, no cursing, in fact nothing boisterous. Everything was done decently and in order. The vengeance was sharp, swift and sure, but administered with due regard to the fact that people were asleep all around." The local coverage seemed more impressed by the mob's discretion than concerned that a triple lynching had occurred.

A coroner's inquest found that Moss and Stewart had been murdered execution-style but that McDowell, singled out for having fought with the grocer Barrett, had been killed by multiple shotgun blasts to the face and upper body. "There were four holes in his face and neck, any one of them large enough to allow the insertion of a person's fist," it was reported. "The victims bled freely. Each of their heads was buried in a pool of blood so deep and so copious that at dusk last evening, notwithstanding the carmine fluid had lain on the absorbent clay and in the glaring heat of the sun all during the day, it still remained in a liquid state." The Shelby County coroner concluded that "the deceased were taken from the Shelby County Jail by a masked mob of men, the jailer overpowered, and taken to an open field and shot to death by parties unknown." Confronted with a lack of witnesses, a grand jury failed to produce any indictments.

The black community—enraged by the lynching of upright businessmen who were clearly not rapists or criminals—fought back in the only way it could: by following the example of the Reverend Nightingale and abandoning Memphis altogether. Tom Moss, before being put to death, had reputedly confided to one of his executioners, "Tell my people to go west—there is no justice for them here." The words of the martyred grocer, printed and seconded by the *Free Speech,* had a galvanizing impact, as the black population began leaving in large numbers—by train, wagon, and on foot—crossing the Mississippi and streaming west for lands in the Oklahoma Territory. About two thousand departed during the spring and summer of 1892.

"There is nothing we can do about the lynching now, as we are out-numbered and without arms," wrote Wells, who was godmother to Tom Moss's infant daughter. "There is therefore only one thing left we can do; save our money and leave a town which will neither protect our lives and property, nor give us a fair trial in the courts, but takes us out and murders us in cold blood when accused by white persons."

The westward exodus had a noticeable impact in Memphis, for white-owned stores began to miss their black customers, industry its laborers, homes their domestic help. In addition to these inconveniences, those blacks who remained staged a boycott of the city streetcar lines. The streetcar owners thought at first that blacks were staying away because the cars had recently been electrified and, at one point, two representatives of the company visited Wells to ask if she would write a piece reassuring Ne-groes that electricity on streetcars was safe. They retreated unhappily once she explained the reality of the situation.

In response to these two forms of black protest over the deaths of the three store owners, and concerned by the huge turnout for the three men's funerals, the town fathers called a meeting of leading white and black citizens in June 1892 at which resolutions were passed condemning lynching. But no action was ever taken to punish the lynchers of Moss, McDowell, and Stewart.

For Wells, the killing of so stalwart a member of the community as Tom Moss brought the cruelty of lynching home as had none of the other cases she had known. As she later wrote, she once had been willing to view lynching as "unreasoning anger over the terrible crime of rape" and accept that "perhaps the brute deserved to die anyhow and the mob was justified in taking his life." But the Memphis mob had been so brazen it hadn't even bothered to concoct a rape story. The lynching had simply been "an excuse to get rid of Negroes who were acquiring wealth and property and thus keep the race terrorized." For Ida Wells and other blacks who strove to improve themselves and gain respectability, it was disorienting that a man they knew to be good and decent could be murdered simply because he wanted to succeed.

Wells reacted by deepening her interest in the subject of lynching. She began culling articles from both black and white newspapers about lynch-ing incidents and keeping track of the reasons men were lynched. When possible, she visited towns in the Memphis vicinity where lynchings had occurred. Her research indicated that, despite the common belief that black men were lynched for rape, this crime was alleged in only two thirds of all cases, and where rape was charged the guilt of the man was often far from absolute. She also realized that, although real rapes did sometimes occur, consensual sexual relations between white women and black men, as well as small indiscretions such as glancing at, accidentally brushing against, or even talking about white women, were being trumped up as "rape." Whites could not countenance the idea of a white woman *desiring* sex with a Negro, thus any physical relationship between a white woman and a black man had, by definition, to be an unwanted assault. And as the *Appeal-Avalanche* assured readers, "When an unprotected woman is assaulted, whether the crime take place in New Hampshire, Oregon, or Texas, chivalrous men in the neighborhood forget there are such things as courts, and they at once seize a rope. This is human nature, and it is quite the same the world over."

Wells was one of the first people in America to perceive that the talk of chivalry and beastlike blacks ravishing white girls was largely fallacious, and that such ideas were being used to help maintain a permanent hysteria to legitimize lynching, as it reinforced the notion that the races must be kept separate at all costs. What was particularly insidious about this mythology was that, by using as taboo a subject as interracial sex and as ubiquitous a fear as "race pollution," it tended to push more moderate whites, even if they disapproved of lynching, to accept it as necessary.

Wells's personal investigations of lynchings convinced her that almost invariably the charge of rape concealed a more complex truth. The most egregious example Wells found was in Indianola, Mississippi, where, according to a newspaper report, a "big burly brute was lynched because he had raped the seven year old daughter of the sheriff." Wells traveled to Indianola and met the alleged rape victim, who was no girl but a grown woman in her late teens. The "brute," Wells learned, had worked on the sheriff's farm for a number of years and was acquainted with every member of the family. The woman had been found in her lover's cabin by her father, who led a lynch mob in order to save his daughter's reputation.

In late May 1892, Wells wrote in the *Free Speech:* "Nobody in this section believes the old thread-bare lie that Negro men assault white women. If Southern white men are not careful they will over-reach themselves and a conclusion will be reached which will be very damaging to the moral reputation of their women."

She knew she was courting disaster in publishing such an opinion. A few years earlier, in an incident that was well known among working members of the black press, Jesse Duke, editor of the *Montgomery Herald,* had been run out of Alabama for noting "the growing appreciation of white Juliets for colored Romeos."

Wells's unsigned column appeared on Saturday, May 25. The Memphis *Commercial* reproduced parts of it and, assuming her partner, *Free Speech* editor J. L. Fleming, had written the offending piece, called on the white men of Memphis to avenge this insult to the honor of their women. "The fact that a black scoundrel is allowed to live and utter such loathsome and repulsive calumnies," raged the *Commercial*'s editorial, "is a volume of evidence as to the wonderful patience of Southern whites. But we have had enough of it." The *Evening Scimitar* was even more forthright, noting, "Patience under such circumstances is not a virtue. If the Negroes themselves do not apply the remedy without delay it will be the duty of those he has attacked to tie the wretch who utters these calumnies to a stake at the intersection of Main and Madison Streets, brand him on the forehead with a hot iron and perform upon him a surgical operation with a pair of tailor's shears."

When Wells's authorship of the piece was made known, Memphis whites were outraged, accusing her in print of being a whore, an adventuress, a "saddle-colored Sapphira," and much worse. Fortunately she was in Philadelphia at the time, attending a conference of the A.M.E. Church, and had planned to go on to visit New York City at the invitation of T. Thomas Fortune. Unable to lay hands on either her or Fleming, who had wisely made himself scarce, thugs ransacked the *Free Speech* office. The *Scimitar,* meanwhile, not mincing any words, vowed that if and when Wells dared come back she should be brought into a public place, stripped of her clothing, and whipped in the manner of a slave. Deluged with telegrams from Memphis friends warning her not to return, Wells accepted Fortune's gallant offer that she relocate to New York and continue writing her antilynching pieces for the New York *Age.*

One of the avid readers of Wells's *Age* articles that summer of 1892 was Frederick Douglass, the former slave and abolitionist. Born in 1817 on the Eastern Shore of Maryland, Douglass had escaped to the North in September 1838 and become a prominent antislavery orator, as well as an author in 1845, when *The Narrative of the Life of Frederick Douglass* was published. From his home in Rochester, New York, he published his own newspaper, aided the Union effort in the Civil War, held various posts in business and the U.S. government, and was a confidant to many important figures of the mid-nineteenth century, from Abraham Lincoln to John Brown to Susan B. Anthony. Now, lionized and gray-headed, he enjoyed considerable respect from both black and white Americans.

Concerned with the lynching epidemic in the South—Tuskegee had reported 113 documented black deaths the previous year—he had recently prepared a piece on the subject for the July 1892 issue of the *North American Review*. Douglass astutely began by questioning the fundamental American respect for vigilantism, and wondered aloud if the praise and honor accorded the San Francisco Vigilance Committees of the 1850s had not, in a sense, created the reflexive use, and widespread acceptance, of lynch-mob justice in America. "It may now be fairly doubted whether even this example has not been an injury rather than a benefit to society," he wrote. Discussing the recent lynchings of the three Memphis grocers, Douglass, who often drew comparisons between Jews and blacks, noted that the "Jew is hated in Russia because he is thrifty," while in America the "Negro meets no resistance when on a downward course. It is only when he rises in wealth, intelligence and manly character that he brings upon himself the heavy hand of persecution." Then, tackling the rape issue head-on, he accused Southern lynch mobs of hypocrisy in their heated defense of womanhood:

> The crime which these usurpers of courts, laws and juries profess to punish is the most revolting and shocking of any this side of murder. This they know is their best excuse, and it appeals at once and promptly to a prejudice which prevails at the North as well as at the South. Hence we have with any act of lawless violence the same excuse, an outrage by a Negro upon some white woman. It is a notable fact, also, that it is not with them the immorality or the enormity of the crime itself that arouses popular wrath, but the emphasis is put upon the race and color of the parties to it. . . . The appeal is not to the moral sense, but to the well-known hatred of one class towards another. The device is used with skill and effect, and the question of guilt or innocence becomes unimportant in the fierce tumult of popular passion.

Douglass emphasized that the lynching of black rapists could not, in fact, possibly be about punishing the crime of rape, since any black man proven to be a rapist would be swiftly and most harshly punished within the law. "All the presumptions of law and society," he insisted, "are against the Negro." Finally, he called on the press and pulpit throughout the country to denounce the lynching evil because "[t]he sin against the Negro is both sectional and national, and until the voice of the North is heard in emphatic condemnation, it will remain equally involved with the South in this common crime."

While Douglass condemned lynching and the use of the charge of rape to hurry the accused to death without trial, he appeared willing to accept the notion that the black man was often "guilty of the peculiar crime so often imputed to him." When he read Wells's articles in *The Age,* however, he declared them "a revelation of existing conditions." She was, he believed, the first person to write with honesty and candor about Southern racial and sexual politics. He arranged to meet her, admitting that until he'd read her articles he "had begun to believe it true that there was increased lasciviousness on the part of Negroes."

For Wells, after the rigors of her spring exile from Memphis, it was a charmed and productive summer. She made the acquaintance of Douglass and worked on a booklet called "Southern Horrors: Lynch Law in All Its Phases," which she hoped to publish in the fall. She also prepared for her debut as a public speaker. On October 5, 1892, she addressed a large group of prominent New York black women known as the Woman's Loyal Legion. "I never believed I could speak in public," Wells later said. "But I finally wrote out a few of the outrages which my race was being subjected to and which I was familiar with, and read them from a platform." However inexperienced at the lectern, Wells effectively framed her antilynching activities in the context of her own compelling life story—the early loss of her parents, her struggles to hold her family together and to retain her dignity as a young black woman. Losing her composure midway through she broke down in tears, but the display of emotion only further endeared her to the audience, who gave her a warm ovation and took up a collection on the spot to finance the publication of "Southern Horrors."

"Brave Woman!" Douglass exclaimed in the book's preface:

> You have done your people and mine a service which can neither be weighed nor measured. If American conscience were only half alive, if the American church and clergy were only half christianized, if American moral sensibility were not hardened by persistent infliction of outrage and crime against colored people, a scream of horror, shame and indignation would rise to Heaven wherever your pamphlet shall be read.

The booklet summarized the statistics she had assembled, rued the gross injustice of lynching, and, as in her *Free Speech* articles, scolded the South for its pretense of virtue:

> The miscegenation laws of the South only operate against the legitimate union of the races; they leave the white man free to seduce all the colored girls he can, but it is death to the colored man who yields to the force and advances of a similar attraction in white women. . . . It is certain that lynching mobs have not only refused to give the Negro a chance to defend himself, but have killed their victim with a full knowledge that the relationship of the alleged assailant with the woman who accused him, was voluntary and clandestine.

To support her claim, Wells gave examples that exposed the ideal of the pure, virginal Southern woman as myth. She mentioned white women running away with their black coachmen; a white woman caught living with a black man who, when arrested for the offense, sought to protect her lover by claiming she herself was black; a white girl who, discovered by her family having sex with a mulatto, stole her father's money and ran away with her lover; a white woman who, discovered with her black lover in her bedroom, ingeniously stayed a lynch mob by explaining that she had hired him to hang the curtains. In Natchez, Wells reported, a woman of means who was having secret relations with a black servant gave birth to a child who seemed abnormally dark, but the child's complexion was "traced to some brunette ancestor." Soon another dusky child was born to this same woman. Her family suggested all kinds of "medical" explanations including "insufficient air in the womb." A physician, however, called in to clear up the mystery, stunned her loved ones with the announcement that the child was a Negro. The servant, it was discovered, had just left town, headed west.

Wells also took issue with the claim that blacks had of late developed a bestial sexual appetite, a calumny she declared "a falsehood of the deepest dye." If this was so, she asked, why did it not express itself before and during the Civil War, when white Southern men confidently left their women home alone with the slaves, or in Reconstruction, when hundreds of white "Oberlin girls" came south to work as teachers in the most heavily black districts? (Historian Ulrich B. Phillips, who investigated Virginia records covering the years 1783 to 1863, found only 105 convictions of blacks for sexual assault, 73 for rape and 32 for attempted rape. All but 2 were of white women.)

W.E.B. Du Bois remarked on the concern in his 1903 book of essays, *The Souls of Black Folk,* observing that the perceived increase in black crimes such as rape (and the attendant white alarm) had occurred largely because the white South was unprepared to deal with blacks as free men who would, on occasion, commit crimes. In slavery, blacks might be severely punished for the mildest transgression at the whim of virtually any white, while whites were not generally held accountable for their atrocities against blacks. In the postwar South there had not come into existence an adequate system to distinguish among various degrees of black crime or to instill notions of fairness into what had for so long been an entirely one-sided relationship. "[The South's] police system was arranged to deal with blacks alone, and tacitly assumed that every white man was ipso facto a member of that police," Du Bois wrote. "Thus grew up a double system of justice, which erred on the white side by undue leniency and the practical immunity of red-handed criminals, and erred on the black side by undue severity, injustice, and the lack of discrimination."

> [W]hen the Negroes were freed and the whole South was convinced of the impossibility of free Negro labor, the first and almost universal desire was to use the courts as a means of reenslaving the blacks. It was not then a question of crime, but of color, that settled a man's conviction on almost any charge. . . . When, now, the real Negro criminal appeared, and instead of petty stealing and vagrancy we began to have highway robbery, burglary, murder, and rape, there was a curious effect on both sides of the color-line: the Negroes refused to believe the evidence of white witnesses or the fairness of white juries, so that the greatest deterrent to crime, the public opinion of one's own social caste, was lost, and the criminal was looked upon as crucified rather than hanged. On the other hand, the whites, used to being careless as to the guilt or innocence of accused Negroes, were swept in moments of passion beyond law, reason, and decency.

Until more fundamental reforms might be brought, Ida Wells prescribed economic boycotts to protest indecent white-on-black violence, noting that whites in Memphis in 1892 had met to denounce lynching only after a black boycott of the streetcar lines and other white goods and services had taken effect. Whites, she wrote, could not be counted on to exercise their conscience but would respond to the power of black consumers. "The white man's dollar," Wells advised, "is his god." Finally, giving examples of lynchings that had been averted by self-defense, Wells—who carried a pistol and had vowed to take a few lynchers with her if she were ever attacked—suggested that "a Winchester rifle should have a place of honor in every black home."

At a time when Americans were keenly interested in the relative degrees of civilization among human "races," she cast lynchers as barbarians who trampled on law and defiled humanity, and their black victims as Christ-like sufferers, pointedly reversing the usual rhetoric. "The black shadow of lawlessness in the form of lynch law is spreading its wings over the whole country," Wells said, warning that the integrity of white civilization itself would soon be called into question if whites did not stand up to lynch law.

Ida Wells was one of the first reformers to exploit the fact that the bellicose pronouncements of Southern whites tended to sound obtuse to other Americans, and that they could be used without comment or adornment to create a most demeaning portrait. "Southern Horrors" reprinted the threat against the author that had appeared in the Memphis *Scimitar*—that she be stripped and whipped in public as would a slave woman—with the desired effect of shocking and angering most readers. Wells applied this tactic shrewdly in her public appearances as well, forcing her audiences to contrast the provincialism and cowardice of Southern lynch mobs and their apologists with her own quiet dignity and courage.

Wells understood that Southern whites, in their belief that black men were preoccupied with having intercourse with white women, were largely battling a monster of their own creation: the longstanding sexual access to black women that white men had enjoyed. To rationalize their continual subjugation of black women in slavery, their use of them as mammies and concubines, white men had come to believe in the fanciful idea that black women were highly sexed animals who encouraged, even welcomed, their own violation. In contrast, influenced by Romantic ideals and perhaps to adjust somehow for their animalistic lusting after black women, whites had placed their own women on a pedestal of virtue and purity—the polar opposite of the regard in which black women were held. "Exquisite, fine, beautiful; a creature of peach blossoms and snow, languid, delicate, saucy; now imperious, now melting, always bewitching," Thomas Nelson Page, an author of Negro dialect tales, had written in description of "that delicate, dainty, mischievous, tender, God-fearing, inexplicable Southern girl. . . . She was not versed in the ways of this world but she had no need to be."

As sociologist Trudier Harris has noted, the twisted arrangement that existed for decades among black women, white men, and white women in the region came with a heavy ultimate cost:

[T]he sexual usefulness of the [black] female and her role as a mammy could only have the effect of increasing the white man's fear of the Negro male, her rightful mate and legitimate possessor. This could not but help lead to the fantastic exaggeration in the white man's mind of the Negro's sexual prowess. And this, in turn, would necessitate more repressive measures against the Negro male—all caused by the white man's guilt and anxiety. The necessity to "protect" the white male against this fancied prowess of the male Negro thus became a fixed constellation in the ethos of the South.

Author Lillian Smith, in her memoir *Killers of the Dream,* notes:

The more trails the white man made to backyard cabins, the higher he raised his white wife on her pedestal when he returned to the big house. The higher txpedestal, the less he enjoyed her whom he had put there, for statues after all are only nice things to look at. More and more numerous became the little trails of escape from the statuary and more and more intricately they began to weave in and out of Southern life. Guilt, shame, fear, lust spiraled each other. Then a time came . . . when man's suspicion of white woman began to pull the spiral higher and higher. It was of course inevitable for him to suspect her of the sins he had committed so pleasantly and often. *What if,* he whispered, and the words were never finished. *What if . . .* Too often white woman could only smile bleakly in reply to the unasked question. But white man mistook this empty smile for one of cryptic satisfaction and in jealous panic began to project his own sins onto the Negro male. And when he did that, a madness seized our people.

In the postslavery South, with their own women placed at an emotional and sexual remove, and black women less and less available (one reason blacks preferred sharecropping to other labor arrangements was that it made black women less vulnerable to ravishment by white planters and overseers), frustrated white men developed a powerful fear of being overwhelmed by black men's alleged sexual insatiability. The black man's real "crime," no doubt, was that he was burdened with no historic guilt

about sex with either black or white women, and it was because he possessed this "freedom" that he was so feared and detested. The hypocrisy
of the situation couldn't have been more blatant, as Southern whites fever-
ishly held the line against insatiable "brute Negroes" and miscegenation—
a race-mingling they themselves had perpetrated, and whose result was
daily evident in the faces of the region's great number of mixed-race
children.

"In the Southern night everything seems possible, the most private, unspeakable longings," James Baldwin wrote in *Nobody Knows My Name,*
meditating on the region's collective sexual dysfunction.

> But then arrives the Southern day, as hard and brazen as the night was soft
> and dark. It brings what was done in the dark to light. It must have seemed
> something like this for those people who made the region what it is today.
> It must have caused them great pain. Perhaps the master who had coupled
> with his slave saw his guilt in his wife's pale eyes in the morning. And the
> wife saw his children in the slave quarters, saw the way his concubine, the
> sensual-looking black girl, looked at her—a woman, after all, and scarcely
> less sensual, but white.
>
> And the white man must have seen his guilt written somewhere else,
> seen it all the time, even if his sin was merely lust, even if his sin lay in
> nothing but his power: in the eyes of the black man. He may not have
> stolen his woman, but he had certainly stolen his freedom—this black
> man, who had a body like his, and passions like his, and a ruder, more
> erotic beauty. How many times has the Southern day come up to find that
> black man, sexless, hanging from a tree!

It was axiomatic that the rape of a white woman by a black man was deserving of the harshest imaginable punishment, for as historian Joel
Williamson suggests, "If black men were, in essence, having sex with an-
gels while white men abstained, then the punishment of black men must
be as awful as the white man's guilt in contemplating himself in the same
act, compounded by his frustration in abstaining."

The instant verdict of death for this black "crime" was accepted as a
kind of elemental truth, an immutable natural reaction. Lynch mobs were
compelled to act. "It would be as easy to check the rise and fall of the
ocean's tide as to stem the wrath of Southern men when the sacredness of
our firesides and the virtue of our women are ruthlessly trodden under
foot," stated one contemporary account.

The idea that lynchers were simply following nature's laws infiltrated the North as well. Yankees were to restrain judgment against Southerners, it was said, because they were largely exempt from the constant fear of sexual apocalypse. As the *New York Herald* lectured Northern whites, "[T]he difference between bad citizens who believe in lynch law, and good citizens who abhor lynch law, is largely in the fact that the good citizens live where their wives and daughters are perfectly safe." Texas journalist W. C. Brann reminded Northerners upset about lynching that he would gladly send them all the South's black people, but that they had better "put sheet-iron lingerie" on the Statue of Liberty or some morning they would "find the old girl with her head mashed in and bearing the marks of sexual violence."

Compounding the white man's certainty that black men desired white women was the gnawing possibility that white women desired black men. This made it necessary not only to despise and criminalize the black male but also to make him subhuman, a monkey man, to desexualize him and remove him altogether from the sphere of the white woman's potential sexual choices. "The white man's perception, more or less, of the Negro complex of sexual superiority," became, in James Weldon Johnson's words, a "mainspring for the rationalization of all the complexes of white racial superiority." Johnson, who himself narrowly escaped a lynching after being found in the company of a woman who looked white one afternoon in Jacksonville, Florida, in 1901, later said of that terrifying experience, "Through it all I discerned one clear and certain truth: in the core of the heart of the American race problem the sex factor is rooted; rooted so deeply that it is not always recognized when it shows at the surface."

When a sexual affair between a black man and a white woman was discovered, the punishment was swift and at times surreal. In "Southern Horrors," Wells relates the story of Edward Coy, who was roasted alive before a crowd of onlookers in Texarkana, Arkansas, on February 18, 1892. A white woman and Coy had been intimate for some time, and the mob compelled her to make charges of rape against him and even to participate in the lynching. When she was led to the pyre and confronted her former paramour, now trussed and bound, he affectionately called her name and asked plaintively how she could set him on fire after they had "been sweethearting" for so long.

In Florence, South Carolina, a black man named Ed had the misfortune to fall in love with a white woman who was unable to keep from putting her thoughts about their relationship on paper. A note intercepted by suspicious whites led to Ed's lynching:

Dearest Ed:

I thought of you all during the show last night, and wanted you with me. It is too bad that we cannot be together always. My love for you is greater than you can imagine. Sometimes I become so disgusted with conditions in Florence that I want to leave and go some place where people are sensible, where I can at least walk the streets with you in the daytime without danger and fear.

You often impress on me the fact that you are Colored and can't take chances. I know that, darling, but love is greater than color in my case, and we must do the best we can until both of us are in position to leave Florence.

I suppose you got the package I sent by mail to the barber shop for you. I have to be careful in buying things downtown because my little niece goes along with me and is so nosey. I had a beautiful shirt for you, but had to give it to my cousin because niece saw me purchase it.

Be a good boy and don't forget tomorrow. Yours, "DEVOTED"

Several other letters taken from the dead man's pockets after he was lynched gave further evidence that he and the white woman had been intimate. After learning of Ed's awful fate, "Devoted" ran away and spent a night hiding in a swamp, before crossing out of the county and requesting the protection of the sheriff in a neighboring town.

The depth of feeling on this subject in the South was no doubt a reaction to several other stimuli, including the generally intensified sexual anxiety of the Victorian era and its heightened concern with modesty and respectability. Another was clearly the coming of age of the first generation of black Americans who had no direct experience of slavery, and whose independence and seeming audacity unnerved whites and made them fear the loss of their race's automatic dominance. Whites were reminded daily of the change in atmosphere, for despite all manner of obstacles, including the advent of Jim Crow laws, black people were moving further from their former condition of servitude with each passing year, learning to read and write, buying land, operating small businesses and farms.

Not surprisingly, the era saw a flourishing of sentimental nostalgia among whites over the old days when "folks knew their place," out of which was born a powerful "cult of the mammy." Images of "Mammy" as a loving exemplar of stability, simultaneously the enforcer and nurturer of Southern custom, began to appear in newspaper advertisements and on billboards. Essayists penned serious tributes to her memory. In 1899 the

Newnan, Georgia, *Herald and Advertiser* celebrated her along with her male counterpart, the eunuchlike "Uncle Ned":

> As we stand on the verge of a new century and gaze down the dim vista of the past, we behold the decrepit and trembling figure of the old antebellum darkey as he slowly marches to the grave. No stronger love ever existed than that of old "Uncle Ned" for his master. No sweeter songs were ever sung than those which came from the lips of old black "mammy," by which we closed our weary eyes in sweet slumber with a confidence which she alone could inspire, never fearing for a moment the intrusion of some nocturnal marauder as long as old "mammy's" watchful eye was over us, and the faithful old darkey keeping a sleepless vigil over his "chillun," whom he loved and for whom he would consider death a small sacrifice.

"Mammy" and "Uncle Ned" were sorely missed, especially in comparison to their insolent descendants. But the old stereotypes, reflected in nineteenth-century America's long love affair with the minstrel show and its reliable cast of blackface characters, highlighted one of the chief paradoxes in American life: the paired aversion and adoration, even imitation, of black people by whites. The Negro was as helpless as a child; he was obsequious, loyal, lazy, afraid of the dark and of electrified streetcars. He was irresponsible, living one day at a time, and neither thrifty nor prudent. But he was also deceitful, at turns diabolical, waiting for his opportunity for revenge.

Whites said they "did not know the Negro anymore." The complaint was figurative, but was to an extent literally true, as increased mobility allowed blacks to move from town to town, from the country to the city. Whereas once black people were greatly limited in the scope of their movements, centered around a plantation or small town, blacks were now abroad in the land. The runaway slave or the rebellious maroon of antebellum times had become the "strange nigger"—the black vagrant of no fixed address, who had no master and answered to no one, and who represented the fear of racially deviant sexuality just as surely as brooding slaves had once connoted imminent insurrection.

Equally disturbing to whites as the wandering black man of the countryside was his urban counterpart—the slick character who lived by his wits, cut off from the structure, tradition, and religion of simple rural life. New to the city, shunned by white trade unions, unable to find work as readily as did black women (who were in perpetual demand as cooks and domestics), unskilled black men were left to survive as best they could, often slipping into hustling, card playing, pimping, and petty crime.

In addition to the fears about black encroachments on Southern society and white women, certainly the region's historic emphasis on protecting personal honor with violence played a role in the increased frequency of lynching, as did the lingering emotional connection to the Lost Cause and the warm memories of the vigilantism of the Reconstruction era. It's also impossible to discount the region's widespread religious fundamentalism, with its powerful emphasis on the forces of good and evil, or the economic depression of the early 1890s that sent cotton prices tumbling.

Economic factors were related to another likely influence, the dramatically changing roles for young white women in the South as the region began to turn away from its traditional dependence on agriculture. Whereas it had long been acceptable for black women to work outside their homes—indeed they commonly worked inside the homes of whites—it was a new trend for white women to do so. "For the first time in history," Jane Addams wrote in 1912, "multitudes of women are laboring without the direct stimulus of family interest or affection." Only a decade or two earlier such a thing would have been unheard of. But with hard times on the farms and steady wages offered in the South's burgeoning textile mills and other new industries, young Southern white women entered the workplace in great numbers. Of necessity, this meant that girls were spending time away from the controlling influences of their family and were physically more vulnerable, both to assault and to temptation. As Addams knew, "At the present moment no student of modern industrial conditions can possibly assert how far the superior chastity of woman, so rigidly maintained during the centuries, has been the result of her domestic surroundings." What was equally unsettling was that women often went to work in order to augment the relatively low earning power of their menfolk, thus reducing further the status of individuals already threatened by their loss of control of the region's black minority.

Like other emotionalized disturbances in American history, such as the New England witch trials of the late seventeenth century and the 1950s Red Scare, some of the reasons for the spread of lynching in the South appear straightforward and logical, while others remain unfathomable. In each of these historical instances, an overwhelming form of evil was thought to reside in individuals who were otherwise highly familiar—old women, young black men, one's next-door neighbors. *The New York Times* felt around the concept in an editorial following an 1899 lynching in Kentucky, terming it "an outrage so terrible and so shameful that it can only be explained as an outbreak of popular delirium." While acknowledging that the mob's "wild and uncontrollable thirst for vengeance" had been "aroused by the most infuriating of crimes," the paper noted: "Underlying these motives and rendering them more savage was the mysterious and subtle and venomous race hatred instilled in the days of slavery. These motives in combination produced what must be called temporary insanity."

On February 3, 1893, Ida Wells was in Washington, D.C., at Frederick Douglass's invitation, to deliver a speech to an integrated group of reformers, when news arrived of a major spectacle lynching at Paris, Texas. A young black man had been burned before a crowd of ten thousand people, one of the largest events of its kind to date.

Several days earlier, it was reported, three-year-old Myrtle Vance, the daughter of the local sheriff, had been "outraged with demoniacal cruelty and then taken by her heels and torn asunder in the mad wantonness of gorilla ferocity." The suspected killer, Henry Smith, was a retarded seventeen-year-old black man. His motive in killing the little girl, it was claimed, was vengeance against the father, who had arrested and harassed Smith on previous occasions.

As soon as the child's body was discovered, the community had swung into action, and for four days and nights two thousand men scoured the surrounding countryside of northeastern Texas, the railroads providing free passage to the search parties. Imbecile or not, Smith had had sense enough to disappear the moment he heard he was wanted in the case, and when law officers finally caught up with the fugitive, it was at Clow, a hamlet on the Arkansas & Louisiana Railroad about twenty miles north of Hope, Arkansas.

At Texarkana, en route back to Paris, thousands showed up at the depot to catch a glimpse of the man, and there was talk of lynching him on the spot. But speeches were made by leaders of the delegation from Paris, including the district attorney, asking the Texarkanans to resist taking action against Smith so that he could be delivered back to the rightful victims of his crimes. Only the year before, Texarkana had roasted Edward Coy before a crowd of fifteen thousand, and the men from Paris—whose plans for Henry Smith were no doubt inspired by Texarkana's example—were essentially warning their neighbors not to be so ill-mannered as to usurp another town's right to stage and enjoy its own lynching.

Back in Paris, word of Smith's capture quickly spread. Hundreds of spectators arrived from the countryside in open buckboards; others came from as far away as Dallas aboard special excursion trains. The townspeople clearly intended to maximize the event's theatricality and demonstrate that they were capable of putting on a grand show. They had brought to the Texas & Pacific depot a "cotton float," a large flat platform on wheels used for haulage, and placed a chair on top of it as if in anticipation of receiving a visiting dignitary. When Smith arrived the crowd led him from the train and made him sit on the chair, "in mockery of a king upon his throne." The float was then drawn by four white horses to the town square, which it circled numerous times "so that all might see the most inhuman monster known in current history," as men cursed and gave the rebel yell, women fluttered handkerchiefs, and excited children and dogs ran behind.

The parade then proceeded to an open prairie about three hundred yards from the depot, where a crude execution platform with steps had been constructed. The word JUSTICE had been painted in large white letters across the top. "Fathers, men of social and business standing, took their children to teach them how to dispose of negro criminals," a witness recounted of the large, expectant crowd. "Mothers were there, too, even women whose culture entitles them to be among the social and intellectual leaders of the town."

Smith was transferred from the float to the platform and bound securely, his shirt ripped open down the front. There was a small furnace on the platform with hot irons resting in it. By rights, the father of the murdered child was given the first opportunity to exact his revenge. Sheriff Vance, his brothers-in-law, and his fifteen-year-old son all in turn poked the captive black man with the irons, which seared the flesh to the bone.

"Smith screamed, prayed, begged and cursed his torturer," a newspaperman wrote. "When his face was reached, his tongue was silenced by fire, and henceforth he only moaned, or gave a cry that echoed over the prairie like the wail of a wild animal. Then his eyes were put out, and not a finger's breadth of his body being unscathed, his executioners gave way."

Once the Vance family had left the platform, the barely conscious Smith and the entire platform were soaked in oil and set on fire, and the flames rose up above the prairie in a fierce ball, JUSTICE faintly discernible in the inferno. Almost immediately afterward the scouring of the area for buttons, teeth, and other mementos began, and continued through the night. Paris had succeeded in mounting a more dramatic spectacle than Texarkana's; indeed, amply covered by the press and photographed, it became one of the most-talked-about spectacle lynchings of the day.

Wells used $150 of the $200 she had earned at her Washington speech to hire Pinkerton detectives to investigate the facts behind the Paris lynching. Based on her experience, Wells wondered if Myrtle Vance was really the innocent-looking child the newspapers depicted her to be, and she suspected that other details were perhaps not as they had been reported. For one thing, Smith seemed to have been a harmless person.

"The man died protesting his innocence," Wells later wrote. "He had no trial, no chance to defend himself, and to this day the world has only the word of his accusers that he committed that terrible crime . . . For that reason there will always be doubt as to his guilt. There is no doubt whatsoever as to the guilt of those who murdered and tortured and burned alive this victim of their blood lust." But Wells was disappointed by her inability to gather information about the affair. Instead of interviewing sources firsthand, the Pinkertons dispatched an agent from their Kansas City office who did little more than collect local newspaper accounts of the lynching.

Smith was one of 117 blacks whose lynchings were recorded that year. A few days after he was killed, a relative named William Butler was also lynched because whites believed he had known of Smith's whereabouts and had kept the information from the sheriff. Perhaps exhausted by their exertions in lynching Smith, the whites hanged Butler without ado, although some men stayed behind and used his body for target practice.

The high degree of ritual seen in the Smith lynching and many others—the use of fire, the sacredness of objects associated with the killing, the symbolic taking of trophies of the victim's remains, the sense of celebratory anticipation and then the lingering importance participants placed on such events—all suggest an anthropological basis for viewing lynching as a form of tribal sacrifice. Many observers commented on a lynching's ability to "clear the air," or described it as the kind of painful spasm a community "needed" in order to regain a feeling of normalcy, and many lynchings did occur in a climate of acute preexisting racial tensions—a fight between a black and a white, talk of insolence on the part of blacks, competition for jobs, an escalating exchange of insults, or the spread of damaging rumors.

Sociologist Orlando Patterson has explained the obsessive, ritualized killing of black males in the 1890s by suggesting that the South's dominant fundamentalist Christianity combined with its Lost Cause ideology to create a belief system in which the black man was perceived as an enemy within Southern society—the cause of a humiliating defeat in war and an ever-expanding threat, via miscegenation, to its perpetuity and survival. The black man of the 1890s, particularly one who was sexually, physically, or intellectually threatening, became a logical sacrificial scapegoat in a region mournful of its past and anxious about the future. Patterson writes, "After the trauma of Appomatox, the Southern community had to be restored in the most extreme compact of blood, and its God propitiated in the most extreme form of sacrifice known to man . . . It takes little imagination, and almost no feeling for the workings of the religious mind, to understand how, as the flames devoured the flesh and soul of each Afro-American victim, every participant in these heinous rituals of human sacrifice must have felt the deepest and most gratifying sense of expiation and atonement."

It was no coincidence that the South's triumph over Reconstruction was known as Redemption, and the leaders of this fight known as Redeemers. And Christianity was unique among the world's religions in promulgating the idea that Negroes—the children of Ham—were beings of darkness, as Ham and his children were cursed by Noah, who declared that a "servant of servants shall he be unto his people." Walter White, the longtime executive secretary of the National Association for the Advancement of Colored People (NAACP), wrote in 1929, "It is exceedingly doubtful if lynching could possibly exist under any other religion than Christianity. . . . No person who is familiar with the Bible-beating, acrobatic, fanatical preachers of hell-fire in the South, and who has seen the orgies of emotion created by them, can doubt for a moment that dangerous passions are released which contribute to emotional instability and play a part in lynching."

To antilynching reformers, Jesus Christ was the "first lynchee," the prototypical victim of mob violence borne to his fate by a cruel and uncomprehending society. The notion of the lynching as a ritual of sacrifice, specifically as a Christian offering for the sins of a sinful society, meanwhile, is a recurring motif in black poetry and literature, as in Claude McKay's "The Lynching":

> *His Spirit in smoke ascended to high heaven*
> *His father, by the cruelest way of pain*
> *Had bidden him to his bosom once again*

or in Countee Cullen's "The Black Christ":

Somewhere the Southland rears a tree
And many others there may be
Like unto it, that are unknown
Whereon as costly fruit are grown
It stands before a hut of wood
In which the Christ himself once stood
And those who pass it by may see
Nought growing there except a tree
But there are two to testify
Who hung on it . . . we saw Him die.

Patterson also stresses the suggestions of cannibalistic ritual in lynchings. It cannot be coincidence that the South's most popular outdoor entertainment, the barbecue, in which pigs, cows, or sheep were roasted and served picnic-style, was also the term commonly used for the spectacle lynchings of black people. As at a cookout, human victims were also butchered and roasted, often with members of the crowd offering suggestions on technique. The act of castration, a horrifying component of many lynchings, was at least mechanically familiar to most Southern participants, men accustomed to the slaughter of fowl and livestock and such practices as the gelding of horses. While attendees at lynchings did not take away a plate of food, the experience of having witnessed the event was thought by many incomplete if one did not go home with some piece of cooked human being; and there is much anecdotal evidence of lynch crowds either consuming food and drink while taking part in the execution, or retiring en masse immediately afterward for a meal or, in the case of a notorious immolation in Pennsylvania in 1911, ice cream sundaes. Even the victims seemed occasionally to join with the spirit of the occasion. "The negroes met their death with remarkable fortitude," noted a news account of a multiple execution in turn-of-the-century Georgia. "They sang and drank lemonade and joked with the sheriff."

Sometimes one festivity led naturally to another. In Greenville, Mississippi, in 1903, Henry Waring Ball reported:

A miserable negro beast attacked a telephone girl as she was going home at night, and choked her. She screamed and Harkins heard her and ran to her rescue. Bloodhounds were put on the trail, and a negro captured in bed. This morning the jail was stormed and the wretched creature carried down Washington Avenue to the telephone exchange, where he was hung up in front of it, while the girls looked on and applauded. Everything was very orderly, there was not a shot, but much laughing and hilarious excitement. . . . It was quite a gala occasion, and as soon as the corpse was cut down all the crowd betook themselves to the park to see a game of baseball.

Ball's account would seem to lend credence to *American Mercury* editor H. L. Mencken's mocking suggestion that the cure for lynchings might be to send brass bands to isolated Southern towns.

As Trudier Harris points out, lynchings—defended as actions necessary to combat sexual aggression—were themselves sexual events. The lynching of the alleged rapist is itself an act of rape, more specifically a gang rape, in that the victim is humiliated and degraded, stripped naked before a throng of people, then violated in the most intimate and personal way. Much of the extreme sadism and fury exhibited by whites against the black man's body was compelled by jealousy of his mythical sexual potency and larger genitalia. For reasons of delicacy, direct allusions to castration were left out of most contemporary lynching accounts, the general term *mutilation* being substituted, but there can be little doubt that it was often the centerpiece of the entire lynching ritual, and was accompanied by extensive comment, laughter, and debate about the size of the victim's organ, as well as appreciative touching, even stroking of the member. Afterward, it was the ultimate souvenir.

There was also a religious aspect to the taking of souvenirs from the remains of the punished victim. It was an old belief that the souls of monstrous criminals could be kept from rising on the Day of Judgment if their remains were burned or otherwise obliterated. Thus, lynch mobs that roasted their victims, chopped them into little pieces, and parceled out the remains were not simply rejecting a court of law's opportunity to pass judgment on the accused, but denying God the privilege as well. And these grisly souvenirs served to extend the intimidation of the act of lynching: a man's knuckles in a jar in a store window could serve for years as a quiet yet horrible warning to blacks of the consequences of stepping out of line.

As the mass exodus from Memphis following the People's Grocery lynching had made clear, the devastation of lynching extended far beyond the suffering of the unfortunate victim. The gore and intense emotion associated with the act itself was as a drop of arsenic in a pond, contaminating the thoughts and dreams of members of the victim's caste for miles around; the damage to individuals, particularly young people, was incalculable. Sociologist John Dollard, who studied black life in a Mississippi Delta town in the 1930s, found that the threat of lynching was in the minds of even very young children and that detailed memories of such events surfaced frequently in his talks with older blacks. Benjamin E. Mays, who later became president of Morehouse College, recalled the surge of lynching violence that visited rural South Carolina in 1898, when the violent white-rule gangs known as Red Shirts targeted and killed black Republicans in a wave of violence that prompted hundreds of local blacks to emigrate to other parts of the South: "[A] crowd of white men . . . rode up on horseback with rifles on their shoulders. I was with my father when they rode up, and I remember starting to cry. They cursed my father, drew their guns and made him salute, made him take off his hat and bow down to them several times. Then they rode away. I was not yet five years old, but I have never forgotten them."

As novelist Richard Wright recalls in *Black Boy*, the memoir of his childhood in Mississippi, "I had never in my life been abused by whites, but I had already become as conditioned to their existence as though I had been the victim of a thousand lynchings."

There was good reason for the sense of constant vulnerability. A lynching could seem like some finely tuned spring-release trap, its jaws wired open, ready to clamp shut. It required only a victim to step into the mechanism. Once set in motion it functioned automatically, simply, heedless of any surrounding doubt or complexity. Black parents learned to fear more for some sons than for others: those who were surly, rebellious, careless, who had not learned the art of appearing to know one's place, were in far greater danger. And, tragically, parents had no choice but to actively suppress those very qualities in their children—self-confidence, curiosity, ambitiousness—that might be misconstrued as insolence or arrogance by whites. However, there was only so much that foresight could do, for any set of ill-starred circumstances could instantly put a black man at deadly risk.

The near-lynching James Weldon Johnson narrowly survived in 1901 came about through a misunderstanding, but with a suddenness that he would never forget. As he sat on a park bench talking with a female colleague in the waning light of a Florida afternoon, Johnson recalled, "I became conscious of an uneasiness, an uneasiness that, no doubt, had been struggling the while to get up and through from my subconscious. I became aware of noises, of growing, alarming noises; of men halooing back and forth, and of dogs responding with the bay of a bloodhound."

As the sounds grew more disturbing, Johnson and his companion began walking back toward a streetcar stop, when they were suddenly confronted by a mob. "On the other side of the fence death was standing. Death turned and looked at me and I looked at death. . . . Quick as a flash of light the series of occurrences that had taken place ran through my mind: The conductor and motorman saw me leave the street car and join the woman; they saw us go back into the park; they rushed to the city with a maddening tale of a Negro and white woman meeting in the woods."

Johnson survived the misunderstanding, but barely, and remained deeply scarred by the impression of how the threat of total annihilation had risen so abruptly and from such seemingly ordinary events.

Not as fortunate was twenty-one-year-old William Denham, killed by a mob in Greensboro, Georgia, in spring 1894. Denham had stopped at a home near the railroad tracks and asked an eighteen-year-old white woman, a Miss Ida, for something to eat. She told him she would go inside the house and get him something, but once inside she quickly locked and bolted the door. Angry at being tricked, Denham pounded on the door and possibly broke into the house. The young woman began screaming and was "saved" when her brother-in-law suddenly appeared, scaring the intruder away. A while later, Denham asked for food from another white woman, a Mrs. Chambers, who was sitting outside her home, nursing her baby. According to Mrs. Chambers, Denham assaulted her and injured her infant before running away.

A posse had meanwhile been formed by Miss Ida's brother-in-law, but it had trouble finding Denham because no one knew what he looked like. Soon, however, a black man was located and placed under arrest. He was brought before Mrs. Chambers, who identified him.

There was no question a lynching would take place. Black vagrants had been pestering white residents for weeks, looking for handouts, and people had had enough of it. An armed mob broke into the jail, seized Denham, and dragged him screaming to a nearby pine tree. Hoisting him up on to a sturdy limb, they blazed away with rifles and six-shooters.

As historian Edward L. Ayers explains, "[N]o disinterested observer can help but note that much of what happened in this lynching might have resulted from mistakes, poor judgment, imagination, lies, and bad luck." Had Denham meant to attack Miss Ida, or was he simply looking for something to eat? Had he broken into her house or only frightened her by banging on the door? Was he the same person who asked Mrs. Chambers for food? And was he even the same person the posse eventually captured and the lynch mob executed?

Such lynchings would reverberate for years in small communities, their memory often continuing to taint relations between the races. This was particularly true in towns where a lynching attracted outside news coverage and earned the locale widespread condemnation, causing whites to become both defensive of their town and resentful of the blacks whose "fault" it all had been. To this day, a century after the fact, whites and blacks will still reiterate the conflicting sides of a story that set a lynching in motion in the first place, whites asserting that a particular black man was known for bothering white women, blacks insisting he was punished because he was "too successful" or that whites disliked his politics. Whites, while voicing "we're past all that" sentiments, remain sensitive about outsiders scrutinizing such matters and often will give an updated version of the "we were left a blighted, devastated region with all the country's blacks so what do you expect?" defense, or simply express a wish to change the subject. As the local historian in one Georgia town told a Northern visitor inquiring into a long-ago case, with no little vexation, "Wouldn't you rather see some of our antebellum homes?"

In spring 1893, Ida Wells received an offer to embark on a sponsored lecture tour of Britain. "Our English press has been getting hold of some of those Texas lynchings, and our people are beginning to feel that there is something very wrong somewhere," reformers Catherine Impey and Mrs. Isabelle Fyvie Mayo wrote to Wells. Impey was the editor of *Anti-Caste,* a magazine published by the Society for the Furtherance of the Brotherhood of Man. Mayo, an older woman known more commonly in Britain by her nom de plume, Edward Garrett, was a Scottish writer whose home was an asylum for Asian Indians. The *Anti-Caste* group had strong ties to the British temperance movement, and to Britain's small but militant "vegetarian cult." Wells's powerful booklet, "Southern Horrors," had been republished in Britain as "U.S. Atrocities," so her name was known in progressive circles, and Impey and Mayo considered it likely she would draw substantial numbers of interested listeners, much as had Brooklyn abolitionist minister Henry Ward Beecher and the American temperance crusader Mrs. Frances Willard. Impey had heard Wells speak in Philadelphia the year before and had been favorably impressed.

The tradition of traveling across the Atlantic to combat a homegrown problem such as lynching derived from a long history of British involvement in U.S. race issues. Americans had come relatively late to the abolition issue in comparison with the British, and had drawn considerable inspiration from their overseas counterparts. John Locke, Daniel Defoe, Alexander Pope, and others had denounced slavery in the British colonies as early as the mid-eighteenth century, and in 1784 the British Society of Friends petitioned Parliament to abolish the practice. William Wilberforce, an evangelical Christian, member of Parliament, and advocate for the rights of London's chimney sweeps, was a dynamic force in seeing slavery abolished in the British colonies in 1833, and also petitioned for its abolition in America. Prior to the Civil War, Frederick Douglass and other American antislavery speakers successfully toured the lecture circuit in Britain, where they found not only a willing public audience but also a sympathetic hearing in the British press.

To Wells, such exposure could be invaluable because the American press largely accepted the Southern fable that lynchings resulted from the actions of black rapists. But if the British press could be inspired to see this issue without the emotion that paralyzed so much American thought on the subject, then ultimately the United States might be shown the way. British and European opinion at the time exercised a strong influence on American thought.

As Wells battled seasickness on her first-ever Atlantic crossing, a London publication, *Society,* informed its readers, "A very interesting young lady is about to visit London in the hope of arousing sympathy for the Blacks, whose treatment in the United States is not seldom fiendishly cruel. Miss Ida Wells is an American Negro lady, who is fortunate enough to have secured as an ally Mrs. Isabella Fyvie Mayo, one of our cleverest writers of sound and useful literature."

Wells toured Britain from April through June of 1893. Traveling by train, boat, and carriage throughout England and Scotland with Miss Impey, stopping overnight at sympathetic households, Wells described the evils of lynching and her personal tribulations with much the same effectiveness as she had in the United States. She told how the inordinate fear of insurrection that had once alarmed slave owners had been joined, after the war, by the fear of black political power, and how onto that anxiety had now been added an obsession with the so-called threat of black sexual assaults on white women. Any contact between white women and black men was a potential offense, Wells explained; yet despite the South's laws against racial intermarriage, white men of that region had "so bleached the Afro-Americans that a race of mulattos, quadroons, and octoroons had grown up."

Wells alternated between shocking the British with accounts of American violence and flattering them with praise for their elevated standards of civilization. She found them somewhat naive about Jim Crow segregation, and they listened incredulously to her descriptions of some of its more farcical aspects, such as rules governing segregated hearses and cemeteries, and town ordinances that forbade "the playing of checkers with a Negro." Her descriptions of Southern lynchings were, however, entirely frank, and her audiences gasped, and occasionally fainted or left the room, as they heard for the first time the graphic details of American mobs that "are no longer content with shooting and hanging, but burn Negroes alive."

"The moral agencies at work in Great Britain did much for the final overthrow of chattel slavery," Wells reminded Britons in a letter to the Birmingham *Daily Post*. "They can in like manner pray, write, preach, talk and act against . . . the hanging, shooting and burning alive of a powerless race. America cannot and will not ignore the voice of a nation that is her superior in civilization."

The British returned her kindness. *The London Chronicle* described her as "very vivacious in manner, and decidedly good-looking . . . a woman of culture, a clear, effective platform speaker, and a dashing journalist of the American order." One reporter was moved to declare, "If her pleasant face is not an absolute guarantee of absolute truthfulness, there is no truth in existence."

Following successful appearances in London, Birmingham, and Manchester, Wells and her British hosts retreated to Edinburgh to plan a further phase of the visit when an unfortunate incident arose that caused a falling-out between Impey and Mayo and cast a pall on the remainder of the trip. Mayo had come into possession of a letter written by Impey to a Dr. George Ferdinands, an Indian, in which she professed her love and vowed to accept him as her husband despite societal norms that frowned on such relationships. Ferdinands had sent the letter to Mayo, complaining that he had in no way led Impey to think such thoughts. Furious, Mayo confronted Impey and pointed out that such an impropriety as writing to Ferdinands, if it became known, might compromise Wells's visit. At the height of the argument Mayo accused Impey of using her work with *Anti-Caste* as a way to meet foreign men, and called her a nymphomaniac, a term Ida Wells from Holly Springs, Mississippi, had never heard before, and which she had to ask Mayo to define.

This humiliating quarrel between Mayo and Impey, the two founders of the Society for the Furtherance of the Brotherhood of Man, was "the most painful scene in which I ever took part," Wells recalled. "I had never heard one woman talk to another as she did, nor the scorn and withering sarcasm with which [Mayo] characterized her." Mayo demanded that Wells break with Impey but Wells, after "a sleepless night praying for guidance," told Mayo she didn't feel the punishment warranted the crime and that she could not desert Impey. In a huff, Mayo immediately withdrew her support.

Wells tried to continue her tour with the sole assistance of Miss Impey, but Impey lacked the clout and organizational skills of Mayo, and the impact of Wells's appearances was greatly diminished. Wrapping up her remaining commitments, she decided to return to the United States and join Frederick Douglass at the world's fair in Chicago. The Chicago Exposition was a highly touted international gathering at which the host nation would show its best face, and she was determined that the world should know the extent to which that countenance still bore some unattractive features.

Situated along the scenic Lake Michigan waterfront, the Chicago World's Columbian Exposition of 1893, created to mark the four-hundredth anniversary of Columbus's discovery of America, was to be a vast panorama of the human experience. Modeled, like all world's fairs of the late nineteenth and early twentieth centuries, after the hugely successful Great Exhibition of 1851 at London's Crystal Palace, it sought to present an inspiring spectrum of human achievement, a synthesis of mankind's rich past and promising future. Recognized as a cultural watershed even before the first visitor passed through the turnstile, the Chicago fair went on to attract an estimated 27 million visitors during its six-month run, and introduced a number of major and minor innovations to American life—the Pledge of Allegiance, the hamburger, the Ferris wheel, Welch's grape juice, and a caramel-coated snack with the name Crackerjacks. It also acquainted most Americans for the first time with the term *anthropology*. The exposition was "one vast anthropological revelation," according to Otis T. Mason, curator of the Smithsonian Institution's Bureau of American Ethnology, which took the lead in orchestrating the exhibits along with Frederic Ward Putnam, director of the Peabody Museum at Harvard.

Black Americans who had hoped the fair would give them an opportunity to showcase their achievements were greatly disappointed. Reflecting the racial and cultural convictions of the day, the fair adopted an idea first used at the 1889 Paris Exposition, where "colonial villages" had been among the most popular amusements. In the Chicago fair's midway, known as "The Royal Road of Gaiety," living displays of Turks, North Africans, Samoans, and Chinese were arranged right alongside wild animals and other carnival displays. Visitors could wander from a "civilized" Teutonic city to a decidedly "uncivilized" Dahomey village where people dressed in animal skins.

"Sixty-nine of them are here in all their barbaric ugliness, blacker than buried midnight and as degraded as the animals which prowl the jungles of their dark land," read one description of the Dahomey exhibit. "Dancing around a pole on which is perched a human skull, or images of reptiles, lizards and other crawling things, their incantations make the night hideous. In these wild people we can easily detect many characteristics of the American negro."

Black Americans were entirely excluded from the fair's planning stages; indeed, in what one historian has termed "an all-too-powerful metaphor of the dominance of white people over those of color" at the fair, the national pavilions were gathered in an area known as "The White City." There was not a single Afro-American exhibit, with the possible exception of Frederick Douglass himself. At age seventy-six, the leonine white-haired abolitionist, author, and statesman was himself a living relic of the nation's formative struggles, a part of its history, and whites and blacks alike were drawn to see and speak to the great man who had known personally Lincoln, Sumner, Stevens, Grant, and so many now-legendary figures. But his presence had not been arranged by the United States. He was there as head of the Haitian national exhibit, having served as minister to the island country under President Benjamin Harrison between 1889 and 1891.

It was not Douglass's first rebuff at a U.S.-hosted world's fair. At the 1876 Philadelphia Exposition he had been invited to sit on the podium at the opening ceremonies, but had been denied entry to the VIP area by police. Only the intervention of New York senator Roscoe Conkling had saved the day, although Douglass was not allowed to address the crowd.

The Philadelphia fair's signal tribute to black life was a Southern theme restaurant where, according to the guidebook, "a band of old-time plantation 'darkies' . . . will sing their quaint melodies and strum the banjo." The Chicago fair, similarly, featured an idealized tableau of antebellum plantation life as part of the Georgia exhibit, complete with a live "Mammy," kindly "Uncle Ned," and other black extras.

Arriving in Chicago to join Douglass, Wells saw an opportunity to use the fair's obsession with "anthropology" and the popular fascination with the measurement of "civilized" and "barbaric" traits to promote her cause. With difficulty, but no doubt invigorated by her well-received tour of Britain, Wells raised five hundred dollars in order to print and distribute ten thousand copies of a new pamphlet she had provocatively titled "The Reason Why the Colored American Is Not in the World's Columbian Exposition." In the chapter of the booklet dealing with lynching, Wells cited *Chicago Tribune* statistics from 1882 through 1891 indicating that eight hundred persons had been lynched during that period. Douglass gave her a desk at the Haitian pavilion, where Wells stationed herself each day, handing out the booklets to visitors and accepting contributions.

"The Reason Why . . ." proved much in demand, partly because it contained Wells's full account of a recent sensational "scapegoat lynching" in western Kentucky. On July 5, 1893, two young white sisters, Mary and Ruby Ray, ages sixteen and twelve, had gone together to pick berries near their family's farm three miles north of the town of Bardwell. When the family dog, who had accompanied the girls, returned home alone and in an agitated state, the girls' mother became alarmed. A search of the area by neighbors and police discovered Mary and Ruby lying near each other, their throats slashed with a razor. Physicians who examined the bodies said both girls had been outraged.

According to a local newspaper, "People for miles around collected and began a search for the hell-fiend" who had committed the act. "So determined were the pursuers," the account added, "that it did not need any reflection to decide the fate of the scoundrel should he be apprehended and caught."

The initial suspect was an eccentric black man known as "Glass Eating Joe" for the bizarre street-corner entertainments he gave in Bardwell and the other towns of Carlisle County. But Joe was soon exonerated and a consensus grew that an outsider was to blame. Neighbors reported seeing a man they described as a light-skinned mulatto fleeing the area. Others believed they had seen a strange white man. A bloodhound borrowed from a nearby penitentiary to track the fugitive lost the scent nearby at the eastern bank of the Mississippi River, although a fisherman told searchers he had earlier rowed a large "yellow Negro" across the river's expanse. The trackers put the dog in the boat and ferried him across the river to the Missouri side but, upon landing, the hound immediately raced to the house of a white farmer and lay down, refusing to go farther.

The trail seemed to have gone cold until the next morning when a report arrived from Bird's Point, near Sikeston, Missouri. Officials there believed a young black arrested for hitching a ride on a freight train might be the Bardwell murderer. The man, who gave his name as C. J. Miller, wore a blue vest and pants that corresponded to a blue coat found near the crime scene. More damning, it was said, were two rings found in his possession with the names of the murdered girls on them, as well as a knife and razor caked with dried blood.

The girls' father, John Ray, went with the sheriff of Carlisle County and other interested parties to interrogate the suspect. They were disconcerted, however, when they finally encountered C. J. Miller. Instead of being light-skinned or "yellow," he was very dark complected, and two of the witnesses who claimed to have seen a man fleeing Bardwell, and who had accompanied John Ray to Sikeston, said they could not be sure Miller was the same man. The rings, meanwhile, turned out not to have any names inscribed on them at all, and after examining them John Ray said he did not think they had belonged to his daughters.

The sheriff then made the unfortunate decision to bring Miller, whose guilt now appeared uncertain, back to Bardwell, where a large mob was already assembling. All day and night, loaded buckboards had been arriving in the town bringing hundreds of men, women, and children from the surrounding countryside, while the steamboat *The Three States,* hastily chartered upriver at Cairo, Illinois, was en route carrying five hundred passengers to the scene.

The train bearing Miller arrived back in Bardwell at 11:00 A.M. on Friday, July 7. While deputies protected the prisoner, John Ray addressed the throng that had gathered for the lynching, and asked that the sheriff be allowed more time to investigate the suspect's alibi. "This is the man who killed my children," Ray said, "but let us keep quiet and at the proper time burn him." He said the authorities would take Miller to jail, and promised they would complete their investigation by three o'clock that afternoon.

As the aggrieved party in the affair, Ray's entreaty that Miller be spared, at least for a few hours, carried much weight with the crowd, which was armed and could have seized Miller at any time.

To the surprise of many, Miller himself then responded to the catcalls directed at him by making a direct appeal to the crowd. It was probably the most cogent set of remarks ever submitted to a lynch mob by its victim:

> My name is C.J. Miller, of Springfield, Illinois. My wife lives at 716 N. 2nd Street. I am here among you, a stranger; am looked on by you as the most brutal man that ever stood on God's green earth. I am standing here, an innocent man, among men excited, and who do not propose to let the law take its course. I have committed no crime, and certainly no crime gross enough to deprive me of my life or liberty to walk upon the green earth. I am not guilty. I got some rings, which I bought at Bismarck, Missouri, of a Jew peddler, and I gave him $4.50 for them. I left Springfield July 1. I came to Alton and from there to East St. Louis, and thence to St. Louis and to Jefferson Barracks. I came from Desoto to Bismarck, and from Bismarck to Piedmont, and then to Hoxie, Arkansas. From Hoxie I came to Jonesboro, Arkansas, and that was the day I came to Malden. I next came to Bird's Point.

The police attempted to verify Miller's story, and telegraphed to Springfield; but officials there replied that they had no record of a C. J. Miller at the address he had given. Meanwhile, the mob in Bardwell, growing impatient with the delay, demanded that the girls' father honor the 3:00 P.M. deadline he had earlier set and name the type of execution to be carried out. At 3:30 P.M. Miller was brought into the street from the jail to cheers and rebel yells from the crowd. Ray, apparently trying to balance his own uncertainty about Miller's guilt with the inevitability of violence, announced that he was still not convinced Miller was the culprit who had murdered his daughters, and for this reason he thought a burning would be inappropriate. But he allowed that, under the circumstances, a hanging would be acceptable.

With this basic assent from the chief mourner, the crowd rushed forward and seized Miller, stripping the clothes from his body and placing a heavy log chain around his neck. He was dragged through the streets to a crude platform of old barrel staves and other kindling. One end of the chain around Miller's neck was attached to a telegraph pole and he was raised several feet from the ground and let to fall. The first fall broke his neck, but the body was repeatedly raised and lowered while the crowd peppered it with small-arms fire. The corpse hung above the street for two hours, during which time it was repeatedly photographed, and the toes and fingers were cut off. Finally, it was cut down and allowed to sink onto the pyre, which was set aflame.

Ashes from the cremation of C. J. Miller flew around the streets and sidewalks of Bardwell for a couple of days after the burning. A visitor who inquired about the particles floating in the air was informed that they were all that remained of "a notorious character who lived by crime," a "black desperado, who had murdered two white girls."

The truth appeared to be far different. On further investigation, it was discovered that Miller did live in Springfield, where he was a law-abiding citizen. His full name was Charles Miller, and he and his wife had come to Springfield from Cairo in January because Miller believed he could get a job with the Illinois state government. This opportunity had not panned out, so he had briefly gone to work in a barbershop. He appeared to have been traveling in search of additional work when arrested.

Although these facts were not sufficient to acquit him in some minds— one newspaper continued to refer to him as "the Bardwell ravisher"—the murdered girls' father, John Ray, was troubled by what had occurred, and attempted to have the case reopened four years later when he came forward with evidence that the actual guilty party was a white man living in Missouri. There is no record of whether Ray ever developed his hunch any further, as the case was never officially reopened. What is certain is that no one ever produced any evidence that conclusively placed Miller at the scene of the crime or even in the state of Kentucky on the day it occurred. The false information about names on rings and bloody razors and knives provided by the police in Sikeston, the refusal to thoroughly look into Miller's alibi, the rush to punish a man who only marginally deserved to be a suspect, all showed the degree to which lynch mobs, once set in motion, and even when confronted with reasons their action was unsound or illogical, rarely reversed course.

Wells also included in "The Reason Why . . ." a description of a particularly gruesome lynching in Memphis, one whose details seemed certain to upset readers. In mid-July 1893 a black man named Lee Walker was reported to Memphis police by two white ladies, who complained he had aggressively approached them while they were driving in a buggy. Whether he intended to rob them or ask for a handout is not clear. Taken into custody, Walker became the target of a zealous mob so determined to lynch him it used a battering ram to break into the city jail, fought hand-to-hand with police guards, and in its impatience trampled one of its own leaders so severely he nearly died of his injuries. Walker defended himself vigorously, first with his fists and feet and then with his teeth, inflicting painful bites on the hands of his attackers, but he had no chance against a mob. He was carried from the jail and hoisted up the first available tele-graph pole, where he slowly strangled to death. It was reported that "a big fellow" cut off the dead man's penis. The crowd then engaged in the sport of swinging the corpse so that it bounced off the pole. A lone policeman tried to deter the mob from burning the remains, warning them they would disgrace all Memphis, but eager hands had already started a fire and the body was seized by the crowd and flung into it. According to Wells's booklet:

> The head was in plain view, as also were the limbs, and one arm which stood out high above the body, the elbow crooked, held in that position by a piece of wood. In a few moments the hands began to swell, then came great blisters over all the exposed parts of the body; then in places the flesh was burned away and the bones began to show through. . . . Two or three white women, accompanied by their escorts, pushed to the front to obtain an unobstructed view, and looked on with astonishing coolness and non-chalance. One man and woman brought a little girl, not over 12 years old, apparently their daughter, to view a scene which was calculated to drive sleep from the child's eyes for many nights, if not to produce a permanent injury to her nervous system.

After Walker's remains had been burned, the whites fought with one another for pieces of the rope that had been lashed tightly around his neck, while others reached into the still warm ashes to secure teeth, nails, and bits of burned flesh. The mob tied a cord around what was left of the corpse and dragged it down Main Street to the courthouse, where it was again suspended from a pole. Further excitement was attenuated when, in a bizarre occurrence, the rope suddenly snapped and, amid cries of horror, the charred object that had been Lee Walker came crashing down on the crowd's heads.

Some of the answers as to what had brought about lynching's hold on Americans at the turn of the century were to be found in prevailing late-nineteenth-century notions about race. While a majority of the whites who joined lynch mobs had probably never given much thought to Social Darwinism or read the theories of Harvard geology professor Nathaniel

Southgate Shaler in *The Atlantic Monthly*, such ideas filtered through all strata of society.

British naturalist Charles Darwin had triggered the era's avalanche of evolutionary and racial ideas with his seminal book, *The Origin of Species* (1859). Darwin both refuted the idea of the multiplicity of human species and included man in the same kingdom as other animals. As for races, Darwin believed that they differed from one another in certain ways, but he did not suggest that one was superior to another or that any occupied a more advanced position along evolution's path—ideas that were later wrongly attributed to him. By contrast, Robert Chambers, a Scottish predecessor of Darwin's, had contended in his *Vestiges of Creation*, published in 1843, that "evolution" was man's progressive journey over time through the various races, with the Negro race the lowest stage and the Caucasian race the highest and most perfect.

The term *Social Darwinism* was unfair to its namesake. Darwin wrote of natural selection, the adaptation of an organism to its environment, and pointedly avoided equating evolution with progress or drawing other social and political conclusions from his own thesis; it was a fellow Briton, philosopher Herbert Spencer, who applied Darwin's ideas about adaptation to the survival of particular species as opposed to others and hypothesized that a struggle for survival in which the strongest wins is natural and immutable—the concept that became known as "the survival of the fittest." And it was Spencer who picked up on Chambers's claim that humans pass through evolutionary stages, and then applied Darwin's conclusions about biological organisms to human society, claiming as he did so that European races were clearly "the fittest."

In America, the role of Social Darwinism in creating the national mood in the years before the turn of the century was significant, serving as a common prism for viewing the world and its peoples. If struggle for existence was competitive, with losers and winners, with some people winding up on the bottom and others on top, intervention in the process was plainly futile and notions of racial equality were, at best, "unscientific." The theory guided legal decisions, social behavior, and government policy. It encouraged laissez faire–ism, gave a pseudoscientific stamp of approval to Manifest Destiny, and helped Americans simplify and make sense of the confusing late-nineteenth-century influx of immigrant groups. The Irish were fond of saloons, firehouses, and ward politics; Italians were fruit vendors protected by secret criminal societies; Germans formed singing clubs and leaned toward socialism; Jews, as ever, were miserly and sly.

But these stereotypes and prejudices, while never completely abandoned, dissipated somewhat as members of these European groups
proved capable of assimilation into American life. More permanently out-
cast were Native Americans, admired for their courage and stoicism, yet
clearly savages and unfit for civilization; the dronelike coolie Chinese; and
blacks, who were cleverly imitative and capable of affection, but were
slow, dirty, and animalistic. The difference, of course, was that much more
than the other groups, blacks had already had a long and painful relationship with white Americans.

The question of who blacks were and what role, if any, they should play
in American life was at the heart of extensive experimentation carried out
in an attempt to "measure" and catalogue the races. One method was
physiognomy, the "science" of judging people's characters by their facial
features. (Darwin himself reported almost being rejected from joining the
expedition aboard H.M.S. *Beagle* because of his prominent nose which
suggested to the captain, a staunch believer in physiognomic methods,
that Darwin would not be up to the rigors of the long voyage.) A German
scientist, Peter Camper, measured Greek statues from antiquity and found
that on average they had facial angles of one hundred degrees, the most or-
thognathous, or straight, while Negroes had facial angles of seventy degrees, the most prognathous, or snoutlike, suggesting to Camper the
relative closeness of blacks to the lower animals. Camper's theories were
used in Congress by opponents of the Fifteenth Amendment.

A related method, also popular, was phrenology, which purported to
judge human faculty and character by the shape and protuberances of the
skull. Dr. Samuel George Morton of Philadelphia, one of America's leading phrenologists, boasted a collection of more than eight hundred crania
gathered from all over the world. In order to measure which had the
greatest intellectual capacity, Morton counted how many pieces of buckshot were needed to fill each skull, and in *Crania Americana,* published in
1839, shared his findings that human intelligence could be quantified by
correlating it to the size and capacity of the cranium, and that judging by
this criterion, blacks, Chinese, and Native Americans were at the bottom
of mankind's list. (Other researchers attempted similar determinations
based on men's hat sizes.)

A student of Morton's was Josiah Nott, an Alabama physician who fervently believed that whites and Negroes were two different species. In the
1840s, Nott produced the theory that without the guiding strictures of
slavery, blacks would soon revert to their original condition of barbarism,

an idea that would retain its currency in America for several decades. Morton's and Nott's views informed the action of the Supreme Court in the *Dred Scott* case of 1857. The case originally concerned the right of Scott, a freed slave, to sue a white person across state lines in federal court, but Chief Justice Roger B. Taney, under Morton's and Nott's influence, broadened the scope of the court's decision to declare that black Americans, whether slave or free, had no rights as citizens under the Constitution because blacks were so far below whites "in the scale of created beings."

The most significant mid-nineteenth-century scientist working in America in the area of race characteristics was probably Louis Agassiz, a Swiss paleontologist famous for his pioneering concept that large parts of the northern continents had been covered by ice in the geologically recent past. Agassiz came to America to join the faculty at Harvard in the late 1840s. After viewing Morton's huge crania collection and encountering an incompetent black waiter at a hotel in Philadelphia, Agassiz announced that Negroes were decidedly a separate species. Agassiz went on to head the nation's first school of anthropology at Harvard, and through his many influential students would have a major impact on anthropological thought in America.

Much as Morton and Nott had influenced *Dred Scott,* other pseudoscientific concepts about race would help guide the passage of numerous Jim Crow laws and affect court decisions, easing the South's creation of its edifice of blatantly racist law. These popular ideas also helped license a vicious character assassination of black Americans in journalism and literature.

"The Negro is a fellow of many natural defects and deformities," ran a typical passage in *Nojoque: A Question for a Continent,* a popular literary assault on blacks written by Hinton R. Helper and published in 1867. "Not only is he cursed with a black complexion, an apish aspect, and a wooly head; he is also rendered odious by an intolerable stench, a thick skull and a booby brain." Helper was a Unionist and had opposed slavery, but came to resent Northern efforts to turn Southern freedmen into citizens. Sections of his book bore titles such as "The Negro's Vile and Vomit-Provoking Stench" and "Black Nobodies." In the latter he provided exhaustive lists of accomplished people through all human history—statesmen, historians, philosophers, artists, explorers—and dared the reader to offer the name of even one Negro whose achievements would deserve inclusion. Another chapter contrasted the innate beauty of the color white to the negative connections with things black; yet another espoused putting all blacks and Chinese on reservations in Texas or Arizona, or if that proved too complicated, exterminating them. Helper concluded:

> As Americans, we must either soon recognize and accept the fact that, with reference to the world at large, Providence has ordained the sole and universal ascendancy of white men, and, at the same time, made equitable provision for the extinction of all the black and copper-colored races, or else we ourselves, as delinquent offshoots of the Caucasian type, are absolutely certain to be expunged from the earth, and will deserve to be so expunged, for our willful blindness and disobedience.

Helper was, even for his own time, a bit off-center, but his work accurately caught the rising indignation whites were beginning to feel toward America's colored minority, an abhorrence that would assert itself more broadly by the 1890s. Rayford Logan, who later surveyed many of the leading periodicals of the last decade of the nineteenth century, found ample evidence that no one was more mocked or treated with amused contempt than American blacks, routinely referred to in print as niggers, niggahs, darkies, coons, pickaninnies, mammies, bucks, uncles, aunts, high-yallers, and yaller hussies, and described invariably as having big feet, kinky or woolly hair, flat noses, and flappy ears. Writers and cartoonists condescendingly provided them with humorous titles such as colonel, senator, and sheriff, or highfalutin names such as Prince Orang Outan, Nuttin 'Tal, George Washington, Abraham Lincum, Napoleon Boneyfidey Waterloo, or Piddlekins. Most significantly, black characters were almost without exception given pronounced negative attributes, and were depicted as thieving, cowardly, lazy, stupid, or superstitious.

Like Helper, Nathaniel Southgate Shaler was a Unionist disenchanted with Reconstruction. A student of Agassiz's, he wrote articles for the day's leading magazines on a wide range of subjects—nature, science, history, travel sketches, and short fiction. Known for his ability to make sense of complex scientific ideas for a broad public, Shaler wrote at a time when magazines were proliferating in America. Cheaper to produce and to purchase than ever before, the magazine had become an important format via which ideas not treated in depth by daily newspapers were disseminated. Articles on race, immigrants, and "the Negro problem" flourished in publications such as *The Atlantic Monthly, The Nation, North Atlantic Review, Harper's,* and *Century.*

In 1884 Shaler came forward with a major piece in *The Atlantic Monthly* in which he reprised Nott's theory that blacks had survived slavery due to their powers of imitation and adaptation, but that without the civilizing effects of "the peculiar institution" would surely backslide to an earlier primitive state. A Kentucky gentleman–turned–Ivy League academic, Shaler was probably the worst enemy black America could have. Unlike a crude Southern belligerent or a rabid and thus dismissable commentator such as Helper, Shaler was a respected intellectual with impeccable credentials. Furthermore, on a personal level he seemed genuinely to like blacks; he had once ejected from his classroom a Southerner who refused to sit next to fellow student W.E.B. Du Bois.

Shaler saw the forced assimilation of the former slave population into American life as an unprecedented and potentially disastrous experiment in race mixing. He did not blame black people for the situation, but rather the cruel, avaricious slave traders who had created this monstrous dilemma, one that he warned future generations would have to grapple with. "The armies of the Old World, the inheritance of medievalisms in its governments, the chance evils of Ireland and Sicily, are all little burdens when compared with this load of African negro blood that an evil past has imposed upon us," Shaler wrote. He left no doubt as to his opinion of the probable outcomes of this unwieldy mingling of the races of Africa and of Europe on American ground. "They may be summed up in brief words—uniform hopeless failure."

Shaler reintroduced an idea that had originated in France in 1856 and had been a pet notion of Agassiz's, that the black person's problems coping with civilization had to do with the fact that his skull "closes" at an early, vulnerable age, around twelve or fourteen, gripping the brain tightly and halting its growth. This intellectual "clouding up," Shaler explained, inhibited blacks' ability to cooperate with others and made it hard for them to remain consistent in working toward a specific goal, or to maintain steady marital relations, for it left them unable to control "the lower passions." It followed that educating black people was pointless; they would only suffer from mental exhaustion if challenged in ways too intellectually taxing.

Edward Drinker Cope, of a prominent Philadelphia Quaker family, professor of zoology and comparative anatomy at the University of Pennsylvania, agreed with Shaler that the skulls of Negroes were not expandable enough to allow for significant mental development after age fourteen, and as a result, black people were in a permanent state of arrested development. Cope, worried that miscegenation would destroy "the finest race upon the Earth, the whites of the South," advised that the only solution was to deport all black people as soon as possible, no matter how much it cost.

Shaler saw deportation as impractical. He thought that America might better handle the problem of this inferior race in its midst by working to scatter blacks as widely as possible in the United States; this, at least, would hopefully prevent their becoming too much of a burden to any one region.

Shaler's concerns about blacks' inability to control "the lower passions" were reflected in a book of tremendous influence, *The Plantation Negro as Freeman,* written by Phillip Alexander Bruce, a Virginia historian, and published in 1889. Bruce believed that the rising incidence of black rape of white women was not only a sign of regressive apelike behavior, but also an expression of vengeance by black men against their former masters (an idea revived by Eldridge Cleaver and others in the 1960s). "[The Negro] is not content merely with the consummation of his purpose," Bruce explained, "but takes that fiendish delight in the degradation of his victim which he always shows when he can wreak his vengeance upon one whom he has hitherto been compelled to fear; and here, the white woman in his power is, for the time being, the representative of that race which has always over-awed him."

If blacks were a race in a downward spiral of regression, lashing out with lust and bitterness, then it followed that it was the duty of every white man to forcibly resist, for the invasion by sexually crazed blacks of the sacred white womb threatened nothing less than the future of the white race. "The protection of woman transcends all law, human and divine," Mississippi senator John Sharp Williams once observed, in a succinct statement of the creed.

Dangerously expanding on Bruce's interpretation was Lester Ward, professor of sociology at Brown University, who believed that members of a lower race instinctively acted on a desire to sexually interact with members of higher races because they understood on some level that the improvement of their own race would be the reward. A black man raping a white woman was simply responding to "the imperious voice of nature," a voice compelling him "to raise his race to a little higher level." But, Ward made clear, the fury of the white race in seeking to punish the interloper was equally motivated by the instinct of race preservation and was completely natural.

The importance of woman herself in safeguarding race was emphasized by Daniel G. Brinton, a professor of American archaeology and linguistics at the University of Pennsylvania, and author in 1890 of *Races and Peoples: Lectures on the Science of Ethnography*. Brinton concluded that, in terms of cranial capacity and facial angles, the black belonged "midway between the Orang-utang and the European white." Concerning the threat to white womanhood he was adamant:

> It cannot be too often repeated, too emphatically urged, that it is to the women alone of the highest race that we must look to preserve the purity of the type, and with it the claims of the race to be the highest. They have no holier duty, no more sacred mission, than that of transmitting in its integrity the heritage of ethnic endowment gained by the race throughout thousands of generations of struggle . . . That philanthropy is false, that religion is rotten, which would sanction a white woman enduring the embrace of a colored man.

Ten years later Brinton's view was rendered in more apocalyptic terms in the bestselling *The Negro a Beast, or "In the Image of God"* (1900) by Charles Carroll. A hodgepodge of dubious biblical interpretations and bogus science, it made the straightforward assertion that the Negro is not really a human being at all, not part of what Carroll called the "Adamic family" that originated in the Garden of Eden. The book was illustrated with provocative drawings, such as a virginal white bride standing at the altar with an apelike black groom in an awkward-fitting tuxedo, and a white Adam and Eve in the Garden of Eden with a kinky-haired black infant at their feet. One image, which depicted a fair maiden on a country lane resisting assault by a monstrous black vagrant, was captioned "Natural Results: The screams of the ravished daughters of the 'Sunny South' have placed the Negro in the lowest rank of the Beast Kingdom." Carroll applauded the fact that a process was already well under way by which the "pure Negro race" was being obliterated by the benign practice of white men taking black concubines, but that by no means should black men be permitted to cohabit with white women.

"Woman," according to Carroll, echoing Brinton, "is the great stronghold, the vital point, of the Adamic Creation. Hence, as long as the marriage relations of the pure Adamic females of a nation, or continent, is confined to pure Adamic males, the pure Adamic stock of that nation, or continent, cannot be absorbed and destroyed by amalgamation." The author, gathering steam, stated with certainty that the black's sluggishness is due to his being "in a state of partial sleep during the day," and that his "strong offensive odor" results from "the characteristic effluvium from the hold of a slave-ship [that] can never be got rid of."

While many worried about the sexual implications of the black's congenital immorality, Frederick L. Hoffman, a statistician with the Prudential Insurance Company of America, saw in it a sure indication of his physical decline. In *Race Traits and Tendencies of the American Negro* (1896), Hoffman shared his conviction that immorality was a racial trait, and that no education or economic improvement, even religion, could save the black man from his powerful lust. Because of this, Hoffman reasoned, blacks would ultimately contract so many sexual diseases—syphilis, gonorrhea, scrofula—as well as tuberculosis, that the result could only be the eventual extinction of the African race. Hoffman called on the government and philanthropies to disabuse themselves of notions of raising this inferior race to a higher level, for it was his belief that excessive fawning over the "poor Negro" would only exacerbate the problem. He wrote:

> All the facts brought together, prove that the colored population is gradually parting with the virtues and the moderate degree of economic efficiency developed under the regime of slavery. All the facts prove that a low standard of sexual morality is the main and underlying cause of the low and anti-social condition of the race at the present time. All the facts prove that education, philanthropy and religion have failed to develop a higher appreciation of the stern and uncompromising virtues of the Aryan race. . . . [I]t is merely a question of time when the actual downward course, that is, a decrease in the population, will take place.

Hoffman's extinction concept was given a wide currency, as was the perspective of William Graham Sumner, a Yale professor and disciple of Herbert Spencer who was known as the founder of American sociology, and who may have been the most influential synthesist of Social Darwinist thought in America. Progress, in Sumner's view, was brought about by allowing the unrestrained flow of "natural laws," what he called "folkways," with an absolute minimum of government interference. In his book *Folkways*, published in 1907, Sumner argued that laissez-faire economics, Social Darwinism, the work ethic, and a free market were the proper forces under which the fittest would succeed. The state's role was to stand aside and let these forces play out, and to defend the individual's rights to act freely and to compete. Programs aimed at equality and fairness only promoted mediocrity. Sumner's famous and much-quoted dictum, "stateways cannot make folkways," expressed what had become a reigning philosophy in America—that life was ruled by innate principles of human behavior and that laws, however eloquently worded or high-minded, could not alter them.

A prominent Liverpool clergyman, Reverend C. K. Aked, was one of the attendees of the 1893 Chicago fair most disturbed by the lynching accounts in Ida Wells's "The Reason Why the Colored American Is Not in the World's Columbian Exposition." On Wells's earlier visit to Britain, Aked had not bothered to hear her speak because he doubted that the stories she told of Southern lynchings could be true. But reading the disturbing news articles on the C. J. Miller lynching, as well as Wells's comprehensive description, had changed his mind. "I sat under the shadow of the Statue of Liberty in Jackson Park and read these accounts until I was wild," Aked would write. "I saw that 40,000,000 people read the same horrible story of the mob's hunt and openly expressed intention three days before the lynching, and nobody lifted a hand to prevent it."

Aked invited Wells to return to Britain for a speaking tour to commence in February 1894. As Wells sailed for England, Aked promoted her visit by attempting to shock others as he had been. He had obtained some of the photographic souvenirs of lynchings sold as postcards in the South. Until they were banned in 1908, these cards could be sent through the U.S. mail. Aked chose an 1891 postcard from Alabama showing a group of nine- and ten-year-old white boys standing beneath the corpse of a lynched black man. The card had been sent as a taunt to a "carpetbagger judge" by a "lynching committee." The message scrawled across the back read, "This fucking nigger was hung in Clanton, Alabama, Friday, August 21, 1891, for murdering a little white boy in cold blood for 35-cents cash."

When reproduced and circulated by Aked, it was widely denounced as a fraud; Britons refused to believe that a group of children would pose in this way or that such an image could be authentic. But when the card's authenticity was verified, some of even the most vehement skeptics joined Aked's ranks.

Wells herself was not immune to feelings of shock and revulsion. At a meeting in Manchester a speaker who took the podium after Wells read from a newspaper an account of the recent lynching of a black woman in San Antonio, Texas. The mob had displayed an evil ingenuity, sealing the victim in a barrel, driving long, sharp nails through the sides, and then rolling it up and down a hill until she was a bloody corpse. It was the first Wells had heard of the incident. "I sat there as if turned to stone," she later recalled, "with the tears rolling down my cheeks at this new evidence of outrage upon my people, and apathy of the American white people."

Aked and Wells achieved a breakthrough when elements of the British business community were moved to express the view that lynching had rendered the American South unattractive to investment. "I will not invest a farthing in States where these horrors occur," one executive was quoted as saying in a London newspaper. "I have no particular sympathy with [the British Anti-Lynching Committee, which Aked had helped create], but such outrages indicate to my mind that where life is held to be of such little value there is even less assurance that the laws will protect property." Richard H. Edmonds, editor of the influential *Manufacturers Record,* wrote, "A state of things in which the killing of Negroes by bloodthirsty mobs is an incident of not unfrequent occurrence is not conducive to success in industry." The article went on to worry about the demoralizing impact such terrorism must have on the black labor force, and to remind the American South that despite some "sneering" at the agitation of Aked and Wells, "the strongest sort of sentiment" by the British public was beginning to fall in behind the committee's work.

This reaction from the British, and the implied threat to the South's economic future, hit a nerve back home. Missouri governor W. J. Stone publicly denounced Wells for stirring up trouble abroad and trying "to keep capital and emigration [*sic*] from this section of our Republic." He also insisted that "Memphis is too high in the scale of civilization to be guilty of the crimes alleged by Miss Wells." The governor of Georgia, W. J. Northen, accused Wells in a letter to *The London Chronicle* of being allied with a group of Northern investors who wished to steer immigrants away from the Deep South, and of lying about the extent of lynchings there. But Northen's protest was undermined three days later when a cable brought news to Britain of a lynching in the governor's own state in which the victim had been skinned alive. South Carolina's governor, "Pitchfork" Ben Tillman, meanwhile, defended lynching itself, reminding his constituents that he "would lead a mob to lynch any man, white or black, who had ravished any woman, white or black."

When the Anti-Lynching Committee sent an open letter to American journalists about the need for greater U.S. press inquiry into lynching, a heated response was forthcoming from J. W. Jacks, head of the Missouri

Press Association: "The Negroes in this country are wholly devoid of morality. . . . They consider it no disgrace but rather an honor to be sent to prison and to wear striped clothes. The women are prostitutes and all are natural liars and thieves. . . . Out of 200 in this vicinity it is doubtful if there are a dozen virtuous women of that number who are not daily thieving from the white people."

Jacks's letter, copied and widely distributed, was so offensive to black women that it was credited with inspiring the founding of the National Association of Colored Women, which convened for the first time in Boston in July 1895 and set out to challenge degrading stereotypes of black women, lynch law, and other evils. An old Memphis acquaintance of Wells's, Mollie Church—now Mary Church Terrell, married to a prominent Washington, D.C., lawyer named Robert H. Terrell—became active as a leader in the organization and brought many Washington-based women's clubs into the fold, while Boston's Mrs. Josephine St. Pierre Ruffin marshaled support and interest from New England and elsewhere. At their inaugural gathering, the women hailed Ida Wells as the "Black Joan of Arc," although concern was expressed that the Jacks letter was one of "the natural results of the resentment provoked by the fierce denunciation of 'southern white women' that have been injudiciously indulged in by some of the 'mercurial persons' of the race," a clear allusion to the "mercurial" former editorialist from the Memphis *Free Speech.*

The Memphis press itself remained both chagrined and fascinated by its errant black daughter, whom they still identified on occasion as "that Wells wench." The city exported a significant amount of cotton to Britain's textile industry each year, and the town fathers surely blanched when the Memphis *Appeal-Avalanche* reprinted an item from the London *Sun* that read:

> Miss Ida B. Wells is a negress, a young lady of little more than twenty years of age, a graceful, sweet-faced, intelligent, courageous girl. She hails from Memphis, Tenn. She is not going back there just now, because the white people are anxious to hang her up by the neck in the market place, and burn the soles of her feet, and gouge her beautiful dark eyes out with red-hot irons. This is what the Southern American white man does with a Negro or negress for preference, when he wants a holiday sensation; and when he finds a charming victim, such as this sweet girl would make, the mayor of the town orders the schools to be closed, and the little scholars turn out in holiday ribbons, and their parents don the Sunday go-to-meeting best, and lead the youngsters out by the hand. They all go out to

see the fun, and have their photographs taken at the scene of martyrdom, and there is much rejoicing over the black sinner that repenteth not.

While Wells's tour made inroads for her cause at home, in Britain she had become enmeshed in a squabble with Mrs. Frances Willard, head of the Women's Christian Temperance Union (WCTU). The tension between Wells and Willard was a rift waiting to be exposed, for temperance crusaders tended to espouse the view that alcohol was an accelerant to black criminality, and to accept the premise that the latter was a problem requiring a strong cure. Trouble between the two women had been looming since Wells's first visit in 1893, when she'd publicly questioned Willard's position on lynching. Wells was convinced that Willard, in order not to endanger WCTU organizing efforts in the South, had made pandering statements to the effect that white Southerners' fears and prejudices regarding blacks were entirely understandable.

The charge underscored a growing contradiction in the turn-of-the-century reform movement, which viewed temperance as key to arresting the mounting vice and immorality of urban life. Since early in Reconstruction, temperance reform had targeted blacks as a special class, the thinking being that black people, like children, were behavioral problems waiting to happen. One prominent Georgian described the denial of whiskey to blacks as an act of benevolence, a discrimination to be sure but "a discrimination which a stronger race owed to a weaker race." Now that many blacks were becoming city dwellers, liquor, it was held, encouraged their weakness for card games, brothels, and saloons, and eased their quick "relapse into animalism."

The origin of Wells's quarrel with Willard was remarks the latter made to *The Voice,* a New York City temperance paper, in October 1890. After describing herself as a "true lover of the Southern people," Willard had complained:

> Alien illiterates . . . rule our cities today; the saloon is their palace, and the toddy stick their sceptre. It is not fair that they should vote, nor is it fair that a plantation Negro, who can neither read nor write, whose ideas are bounded by the fence of his own field and the price of his own mule, should be entrusted with the ballot. . . . The Anglo-Saxon race will never submit to be dominated by the Negro so long as his altitude reaches no higher than the personal liberty of the saloon, and the power of appreciating the amount of liquor that dollar will buy.

I pity the southerners, and I believe the great mass of them are as conscientious and kindly-intentioned toward the colored man as an equal number of white church-members of the North, [but] the problem on their hands is immeasurable. The colored race multiplies like the locusts of Egypt. The grog-shop is its center of power. The safety of women, of childhood, of the home is menaced in a thousand localities at this moment, so that men dare not go beyond the sight of their own roof-tree.

When Wells returned to Britain in 1894 she brought a copy of the offending article, and not only read from it in her lectures but gave it to the editor of the British periodical *Fraternity* for excerption. Wells lamented that Willard was "no better or no worse than the great bulk of white Americans on the Negro question," and that this kind of acquiescence represented the attitude of so-called Christian reformers. She mocked the WCTU's fierce opposition to such social "evils" as card playing, sports, and "promiscuous" dancing, when "during all the years prior to the agitation begun against Lynch Law, in which years men, women and children were scourged, hanged, shot and burned, the WCTU had no word, either of pity or protest. Its great heart, which concerns itself about humanity the world over was, toward our cause, pulseless as a stone."

Lady Henry Somerset, a power in the British temperance movement and Willard's host and confidante, got wind of Wells's efforts to have the piece republished and blocked it by threatening to use her considerable influence to ensure that Wells never mounted a speaking dais in Great Britain again.

In truth, Wells could have caught many white progressives out on the lynching issue. Part of the problem was that the rift between nineteenth-century feminists and Afro-American rights crusaders had never fully healed. Women who had lent brave support to the abolitionist cause felt betrayed when Reconstruction brought black male enfranchisement but excluded women's suffrage. Even Susan B. Anthony, whom Wells greatly admired, admitted that she had sought to distance herself from the efforts of black women to join the suffrage movement for the greater expediency of winning the sympathy and support of Southern white women.

Despite her bickering with Willard, which would continue for years, Wells's second British tour was a sensational success. She appeared in more than one hundred engagements, from lecture halls to churches to ladies' parlors, as well as weekly events in London sponsored by the Pleasant Sunday Afternoon Society aimed at middle- and lower-class Britons.

She also came away with dozens of resolutions from church groups and civic organizations denouncing lynching. Most valuably, the British Anti-Lynching Committee succeeded in creating news about her back home. Members of the committee gathered each morning to clip articles about Wells from the British press and sent them immediately to America—to the White House, senators and congressmen, other elected officials, and U.S. editors of both white- and black-operated newspapers.

"A year ago the South derided and resented Northern protests. To-day it listens, explains and apologizes for its uncovered cruelties," wrote William Lloyd Garrison II, son of the famed abolitionist, of Wells's success in using a British platform to thrust the issue of lynching into the press and pulpit here at home. "Surely a great triumph for a little woman to accomplish! It is the power of truth simply and unreservedly spoken."

Wells had completed a spectacular arc from her humble Mississippi beginnings. She had endured great hardship and risk, taken on immense struggles, yet had managed through her own diligence to serve as messenger for a most vital cause. In an age when blacks were written about almost exclusively as a problem, she had established lynching as a practice in which whites were the problem and blacks those in need of compassion and justice. If for the time being no white person in America was writing or thinking overly much about the injustices of Jim Crow segregation, lynching was an injustice so egregious that it could no longer be ignored. It was surely not the most favorable reason for whites to contemplate and discuss their feelings toward black Americans, but it was something, and Ida Wells had almost single-handedly started the dialogue.

The Compromise

Lynching was only the most depraved and fearsome element in the broad assault under way on black Americans by the 1890s. U.S. Supreme Court decisions between 1875 and 1883 had essentially severed the federal government's involvement with the postwar South, the repeal of the Civil Rights Law of 1875 being just one of several blows suffered by Reconstruction-era legislation. Where Congress had sought in the Reconstruction amendments to expand federal authority over the states and to honor a national obligation to safeguard equal protection under the law—a gesture aimed specifically at protecting the newly freed slaves and easing their transition to citizens—the federal judiciary set out to undo all that had been done. In the 1873 *Slaughterhouse* cases, the Supreme Court ruled that the states, not the federal government, were primarily responsible for safeguarding the protections of citizenship, and that individuals could not turn to the federal government for relief when they believed their rights were being abused. This decision was buttressed in 1876 in another case originating in Louisiana, *United States v. Cruikshank,* which derived from the infamous Colfax Massacre of 1873, in which whites had murdered more than a hundred blacks while breaking up a political meeting. Initially, three whites were found guilty of violating the Enforcement Act of 1870, but the Supreme Court ruled that the federal government could legislate against states but not against individuals, and that as a result the three convicted men were beyond the Enforcement Act's reach. The cumulative result of these decisions was to put the Fourteenth Amendment, with its guarantees of national citizenship, equal protection under law, and the right to due process, into a deep sleep.

Next it was the Fifteenth Amendment's turn. In the 1876 case of *Reese v. United States* the court held that the amendment did not grant suffrage to individuals so much as it sought to prevent states from discriminating against voters. The court drew a distinction between the federal government's ability to confer the right of suffrage and its power to prohibit the exclusion of voters on racial grounds. This opened the way for clever Southern legislatures and county clerks to keep blacks off the voting rolls by devising various tests and measures that, while not explicitly racial in content, had the effect of limiting blacks' access to the vote.

Then, in 1894, Congress repealed those sections of the first two Enforcement Acts that guaranteed equal voting qualifications, federal supervision of elections, and punishments for those who interfered with voters' rights. Southern legislatures began grinding away at black voting rights, rewriting state laws and constitutions to discourage or eliminate black voting, essentially making official the de facto disenfranchisement that had existed in many places since late Reconstruction. In 1890 Mississippi set a model for the rest of the South by having its citizens affirm a revision to the state constitution that established a poll tax and literacy qualifications for prospective voters. As James Kimble Vardaman, editor of a daily newspaper in the central Mississippi Delta town of Greenwood, a member of the state's House of Representatives, and later governor and U.S. senator, notoriously warned: "I am just as opposed to Booker Washington as a voter, with all his Anglo-Saxon reinforcements, as I am to the coconut-headed, chocolate-colored, typical little coon who blacks my shoes every morning. Neither is fit to perform the supreme function of citizenship."

Another significant reversal was the 1896 U.S. Supreme Court ruling in *Plessy v. Ferguson.* Homer Plessy was a Louisianan who had been ejected from a railroad car because he was an octoroon, one-eighth Negro. In a devastating ruling, the high court in *Plessy v. Ferguson* handed down a decision echoing the "folkways" argument of the Social Darwinists. The majority opinion centered around the idea that the Fourteenth Amendment concept of "equal protection of the laws" could be satisfied by the separate but equal doctrine used in an 1890 Louisiana statute. "Legislation is powerless to eradicate racial instincts, or to abolish distinctions based upon physical differences," wrote Associate Justice Henry Billings Brown, "and the attempt to do so can only result in accentuating the difficulties of the present situation. . . . If one race be inferior to the other socially, the Constitution of the United States cannot put them on the same plane." Despite a valiant dissent from Justice John Harlan—"Our Constitution is color blind, and neither knows nor tolerates classes among citizens. . . . The thin disguise of 'equal' accommodations for passengers in railroad coaches will not mislead any one, nor atone for the wrong this day done"—the doctrine of "separate but equal" was established, installing racial segregation as the law of the land.

Ingenious methods of eliminating black votes proliferated across the former Confederacy. These included, in addition to the creation of poll taxes and literacy tests, the "understanding clause," which called on applicants to explain, to the satisfaction of the registrar, certain sections of state constitutions or other legal or legislative documents. Although black literacy had climbed impressively since Emancipation—from 18.6 percent in 1870 to 42.9 percent in 1890—black people's inability to read, and the fear of having to demonstrate one's intellectual skills before a hostile white registrar, had the intended effect of decreasing Negro balloting. Another tactic, the "grandfather clause," probably first employed in Louisiana, was a means of exempting illiterate whites from the literacy qualification. They needed only to prove that an ancestor had been registered to vote on January 1, 1866. Of course, this loophole was closed to black citizens since their forebears had, at that date, still not been granted the franchise. Other devious obstacles to black voting were improvised, such as South Carolina's "Eight Box" law. Poll workers set up eight different boxes into which voters were to place their ballots, each labeled with the name of a corresponding office, such as "senator," "governor," or "representative." Any ballot placed in an incorrect box was discounted, ensuring that the ballots of blacks who couldn't read the signs would be disqualified. To thwart efforts to memorize their positions, the boxes were shuffled periodically.

Still another weapon was the white primary system, in which a state's Democratic party declared itself a private entity and limited membership to whites only. Since in the South of that era Republican opposition was often of token strength, the Democratic primary *was* for all intents and purposes the final election, and as blacks were not allowed to participate in it, their rights as voters were essentially meaningless.

The cumulative impact of these deterrents to black voting was soon visible. In Louisiana, for example, there were 130,334 registered black voters in 1896, a number that by 1904 had plummeted to only 1,342. And while in 1896 blacks held an electoral majority in twenty-six Louisiana parishes, by 1900 they led in none.

The threat of black voting had consumed Southern politics since the Redemption of the South by Democrats in the late 1870s. It had animated some of its most vicious outrages and verbal belligerence, and helped to create the swaggering style of Southern demagoguery associated with the period. Most colorful of the Southern demagogues was undoubtedly "Pitchfork" Ben Tillman, governor of South Carolina in the 1890s and later a U.S. senator. (He had received his nickname after once threatening to "prod" President Grover Cleveland with the implement "in his old fat ribs.")

Tillman was always famously unapologetic for his leading role in the Red Shirt movement that attacked black Republicans and redeemed South Carolina from Reconstruction: "We took the government away. We stuffed ballot boxes. We shot them. We are not ashamed of it." This kind of defiance and bluster, coupled with his sobriquet, made him into a somewhat cartoonish and one-dimensional national figure—loved by lower-class Southern whites, despised or barely tolerated by everyone else.

He took the Southern demagogue routine further than most, going to the extreme of appearing before black audiences that booed and catcalled him while he stood defiantly center stage and recited his version of Southern history, informing his enraged auditors that slavery was the best thing that had ever happened to blacks and reminding them of what he considered their ancestral proximity to the baboon. To Northern whites he detailed the daily horror of life in a region populated with black people, chided them for their abolitionist sentiment and their handy opinions about a subject with which they had no experience, and warned, "Keep your long Yankee noses out of the Negro question." Not surprisingly, he supported lynching as a needed defense against black crime, and vowed he would personally lead a lynch mob if necessary to avenge the lost honor of a white woman. In the U.S. Senate in the early years of the twentieth century he was a powerful voice for Dixie, a puffed-up living legend who went to his grave warning of an apocalyptic race war if unruly Southern Negroes were not adequately suppressed.

The federal government ultimately lost its fight with the states over the issue of black disenfranchisement. James A. Garfield of Ohio, a U.S. representative, had introduced resolutions in 1869, 1871, and 1875 favoring enforcement of the second part of the Fourteenth Amendment, which stipulated that states which disenfranchised voters would lose representation in the House and the electoral college. Ascending to the presidency in 1880, he called for enhanced education for blacks and again assaulted disenfranchisement, stating that "there was no middle ground for the negro between slavery and equal citizenship," and cautioning that "there can be no permanent disenfranchised peasantry in the United States." More blacks than whites purchased tickets to his inaugural ball and many marched in the inaugural parade. Garfield in turn made several appointments of blacks, including Frederick Douglass as recorder of deeds of the District of Columbia.

The administration of Benjamin Harrison, elected in 1888, was potentially of great help to blacks, for with his election the Republicans controlled the White House and both houses of Congress for the first time since Reconstruction. Harrison stressed to Southerners the link between regional prosperity and the demonstration of respect for law and order, and was one of the first high public officials to prophesy accurately that the continued exercise of lynch law and mob activity in the South would ultimately darken the region's image and inhibit its commercial and industrial growth. Sadly, Harrison's sentiments and the flagrant Republican hegemony in Washington only served to help alarm the cotton South, revitalizing Southern antagonism toward federal involvement in its affairs, particularly when Congress pursued two pieces of legislation—the so-called Force Bill, which would grant the federal government stronger powers in regulating elections, and the Blair Bill, aimed at promoting greater opportunities in education for all citizens. Southerners defeated both bills with the traditional defense that such legislation represented a return to Reconstruction and unwanted federal intervention in the South's affairs. The Force Bill in particular was denounced as a naked attempt to create black pluralities at the polls and steal the governing authority from whites.

As Garfield had come to recognize, the federal ability to guarantee voting rights in the South was, for the foreseeable future, nearly impossible. "Time is the only cure for the Southern difficulties," he confided to a friend shortly before his assassination in the summer of 1881. "In what shape it will come, if it come at all, is not clear."

The most significant public statement made by a black leader during this vexing era of lynching, black disenfranchisement, and Jim Crow segregation—what Rayford Logan calls the "nadir" of the black experience in post–Civil War America—was the September 1895 address of Booker T. Washington to the Cotton States and International Exposition in Atlanta.

The exposition was in the tradition of other world's fairs, but with special emphasis on the South's heritage, progress, and dynamic future. Black Americans were relegated to less than a supporting role, with only insulting stereotypes to represent them and numerous restrictions on where they could eat, ride, and relieve themselves. The only noticeable black presence was the convict laborers who toiled to build the fairgrounds, and the black minstrels and waiters at "The Old Plantation," a midway attraction that attained instant fame when President Cleveland, who came to officially open the fair, made it the sole attraction he bothered to visit. "Many people have written, asking whether the exposition is worth coming to see," a black Atlanta newspaper, *The People's Advocate,* commented. "If they wish to feel that they are inferior to other American citizens, if they want to pay double fare on the surface cars and also be insulted, if they want to see on all sides 'For Whites Only' or 'No Niggers or dogs allowed,' if they want to be humiliated and have their man and womanhood crushed out, then come."

Such disillusionment was at odds with the accommodationist stance of Washington's speech. In place of rancor, Washington prescribed patience and hard work; instead of unruly demands for what would not be given to black people anyway, he counseled a steady effort to slowly earn wealth, citizenship rights, and white people's respect. The chief of the exposition's "Negro Department," Richard C. Hill, seemed to paraphrase the educator's wisdom when he advised black fairgoers, "Do not indulge in the pastime of throwing stones at the stars."

With the death of Frederick Douglass in February 1895, Washington had become black America's most visible spokesman. Born in 1856, the son of a slave woman and her white owner, he had through great determination obtained "book learning" as a youngster and then won acceptance to the Hampton Normal and Agricultural Institute in Virginia. Entering Hampton in 1872, he excelled under the tutelage of General Samuel Armstrong, a progressive white educator, and in 1881 was appointed head of Alabama's newly opened Tuskegee Institute, which was based on the Hampton model. Washington proved an adept principal, fund-raiser, and promoter at Tuskegee, and traveled extensively in the North, where he made numerous influential white contacts, including steel-industry millionaire and philanthropist Andrew Carnegie. He won praise for his "realistic" accentuation on black resourcefulness and hard work, and for minimizing the importance of advanced education, political rights, and social equality for blacks.

Washington began his Atlanta address by reminding his audience that one third of the South was black, and that if the region expected to progress economically it would have to come to terms with its minority populace. To blacks who dreamed of a return to Africa or emigration elsewhere, he said, "cast down your bucket where you are," and counseled them to build a respectable life in the region that had always been their home. He urged them to learn the honor of common labor, and not to expect to begin at the top. "No race," he declared, "can prosper till it learns that there is as much dignity in tilling a field as in writing a poem." In turn, he asked whites to utilize the South's own black, English-speaking labor, rather than rely on immigrant manpower, and to trust those who had already contributed so much to their homeland without the disruptive threat of strikes or other labor conflicts. Promising that Southern blacks were the "most patient, faithful, law-abiding and unresentful people that the world has seen," Washington proposed: "In all things that are purely social we can be as separate as the fingers, yet one as the hand in all things essential to mutual progress." True social equality would come not through agitation, but through hard work; it would be the "result of severe constant struggle rather than of artificial forcing," admonished Washington. "The opportunity to earn a dollar in a factory just now, is worth infinitely more than the opportunity to spend a dollar in an opera house." Such loyalty, obedience to law, and hard work as he described would "bring into our beloved South a new heaven and a new earth."

A thunderous ovation greeted his address. So taken with his remarks were some of the whites on the dais they momentarily forgot the taboo against shaking hands with a black man. Newspapers across the country applauded with equal enthusiasm. Washington's had been a brilliant and economical proclamation, addressing the South's number-one phobia by cogently explaining who the blacks of the postslavery South were and who they aspired to be—a talented native work force, loyal even in times of strife, now poised to embark on a program of industrial training to take their rightful place in society.

Washington's address, which came to be known as the "Atlanta Compromise," echoed Frederick Douglass in some respects—the disavowal of emigration, the reliance on hard work and industry, the need for economic independence, the denigration of foreign labor. Like Douglass,

Washington professed an admiration for the Jews—a group that, though disliked and excluded, had by dint of thrift and dedicated effort managed to gain a solid foothold in America. Where he differed from Douglass was in the "compromise" he proffered to whites—that in exchange for being given the chance to work and prove themselves, blacks would relinquish immediate demands for political and social equality.

The speech helped make Washington famous and enhanced Tuskegee's stature, but of course the words of the Wizard of Tuskegee, as Washington was known, were less a prescription for action than an acknowledgment of the current reality. And his concept of blacks earning their citizenship rights through hard work and obedience to the law was put to a hard test in early 1898, when the victims in a sensational South Carolina lynching proved to be a dedicated federal employee and his family.

At the time, rural farm delivery was still in its infancy, meaning that farm people and rural dwellers still came to their local post office at least two or three times a week to pick up and send their mail. This made the post office in rural communities an important gathering place, and the character and nature of the postmaster of great significance to the towns-people who relied on him. Republican officials had long used employ-ment in the post office as patronage to reward black party members. In 1888, President Harrison chose James S. Clarkson, an old cohort of aboli-tionist John Brown, as postmaster general. In turn, Clarkson appointed sixteen thousand blacks to federal positions in the post office. The admin-istration of William McKinley continued this tradition by handing out dozens of postmaster jobs to blacks for their support in the election of 1896. New jobs opened up frequently, for in the twenty years between 1870 and 1890 the number of post offices in the United States had more than doubled, from 28,000 to 62,000.

The very thing that made such appointments advantageous for South-ern blacks—the federal government's ability to reach in and anoint a black individual to an otherwise unattainable position of prominence in a Southern community—was deeply offensive to local whites. Post offices, in whites' view, became informal gathering places for black acquaintances of the postmaster and for Republican political caucusing. Even more dis-tressing, white women using the post office had no choice but to interact with a black man, as an equal, and on a regular basis.

In fall 1897, when Frazier B. Baker, a forty-year-old schoolteacher and Republican from Florence, South Carolina, was made postmaster of nearby Lake City, local whites immediately launched a vigorous campaign to dislodge him. At first, they boycotted Baker's post office by carting their mail to the village of Scranton, three miles away. Next, they circulated a petition which they sent to J. L. Bristow, fourth assistant postmaster general in Washington, pointing out that Baker was lazy, incompetent, and "impolite to ladies." In Washington, Senator Ben Tillman and other South Carolina officials called on U.S. Postmaster General James A. Gary, a recent McKinley appointee, for Baker's immediate removal. Things took a more sinister turn in December when shots were fired at Frazier and his assistant, James Braveboy, and again in January 1898, when the Lake City post office mysteriously burned to the ground. Refusing to abandon his assignment, Baker moved the post office into his own home on the outskirts of town, further infuriating and inconveniencing whites.

At shortly after one in the morning on February 22, a mob of three hundred or more people surrounded Baker's house, set it on fire, and shot at the occupants as they fled the blaze. Baker, the first to reach the door of the burning dwelling, was immediately hit and fell back into the house. His wife, Lavania, and three of his children were wounded as they attempted to flee, and an infant girl being carried by Mrs. Baker was struck in the head and killed instantly. Lavania, shot in the forearm, collapsed near the house and would have burned to death if neighbors hadn't pulled her clear of the flames. Investigators the next day discovered the partly burned bodies of Postmaster Baker and his baby daughter and counted more than a hundred bullet holes in the walls of the home. The Charleston *News and Courier,* loyal to local white sentiment, offered that the "authorities in Washington had been notified of their mistake and error in appointing this man, they knew of his incompetency. And the people of the whole United States ought to be made acquainted with the fact that the post office authorities in Washington are largely responsible for the death of Frazier B. Baker."

The federal government reacted by withdrawing postal service from Lake City and offering rewards for information about those responsible for the assault. Because only the state of South Carolina could bring murder charges, Postmaster Gary stated that he doubted the perpetrators of the crime would ever be convicted by a jury in that state because any such jury would most likely be composed of some of the members of the lynch mob itself. And although some whites in Lake City disapproved of the attack, chiefly because it had included an assault on a woman and children, it was expected they would be of little help in any prosecution because "it would be hazardous for them to attempt to make that section their home after testifying against the mob."

The crime resonated with the nation in ways other lynchings had not. Lynch mobs might be granted a wide latitude when it came to dealing with "black beast" rapists, but massacring a postman and his family was excessive, and made moderate Southerners uncomfortable while infuriating most other Americans. Ida Wells—now Ida Wells-Barnett upon her 1895 marriage to Chicago attorney Ferdinand Barnett—was among those deeply outraged. Having organized a mass meeting in Chicago where heated declarations were heard and resolutions drafted, she went to Washington and, along with several legislators, met with President McKinley to appeal for federal action. She pointed out to the president that Baker's death "was a federal matter, pure and simple. He died at his post of duty in defense of his country's honor, as truly as did ever a soldier on the field of battle." McKinley assured her that a federal investigation of the Baker case was already under way.

The lynching of Postmaster Baker, the first since Reconstruction to warrant a federal response, occurred in the midst of another, larger national crisis—the destruction of the U.S. battleship *Maine* by a mysterious explosion in Havana harbor on February 15, 1898. With great loss of life and rumors of Spanish sabotage abounding, egged on by the relentless jingoism of the Hearst press, the United States seized on the event to declare war against Spain. American troops quickly routed the demoralized Spanish garrison at Santiago de Cuba, while on the other side of the world American battleships won a decisive naval victory over Spanish forces in the Philippines.

The nation's black press, juxtaposing the Baker case with the larger issues of the day, criticized an administration that thought itself fit to bring democracy to peoples in foreign lands but cared little about injustice in South Carolina. One Kentucky newspaper suggested that blacks should abandon the popular war slogan "Remember the *Maine*" and substitute "Remember Postmaster Baker." Indeed, many blacks took heart at the prospect of an energized federal government, one that would assign troops to battle Spanish soldiers and Filipino rebels, or to settle domestic labor disputes. If federal troops could be dispatched halfway around the world and, at home, sent to shoot at American workers, as they did during the 1894 Pullman strike outside Chicago, why could not the federal government deal harshly with Southern lynch mobs? Of course, the spontaneity and speed with which most lynch mobs acted did not generally allow for the possibility of a military show of force. And the government's best approach, through the federal courts, had yet to be much tried, let alone proved.

The conclusion of the Baker case delineated the limits of even the best federal intentions. For although in June 1898 the federal government made arrests in the case, the defense successfully scuttled the U.S. offensive at trial in federal district court in Charleston in April 1899 by exposing the fact that one of the two members of the mob who had turned state's evidence, Early P. Lee, had a prior larceny conviction for stealing a saw, thus casting doubt on his credibility. Prosecutors also faced a wall of silence and noncooperation from Lake City residents, and as a result several of the accused were acquitted for lack of evidence. A hung jury set the rest free. The sole prize the prosecution came away with was the report that a South Carolina federal judge involved in the case had become tearful at the verdict. They were "not effeminate tears," a Georgia newspaper reported, "but tears shed by a strong man in sorrow for the shame which lynchers have brought upon his beloved state."

The Baker case opened a minor rift in the nation's black leadership when Wells-Barnett, citing the murdered postmaster, stated publicly that Booker T. Washington was wrong if he thought learning a trade would save the Southern black from mob violence. This was an audacious jibe at the now-powerful Washington, whose views were widely quoted in the white press as representing the views of black Americans. But it was a point on which the Wizard of Tuskegee was vulnerable, and Wells-Barnett knew it. At the time of his 1895 Atlanta Compromise speech there had been 1,600 recorded lynchings in the preceding decade, and 113 already that year, yet in 1897 Washington felt comfortable stating, "The men who are lynched are invariably vagrants, men without property or standing." Asked by reporters whether lynching was pushing blacks toward insurrection, he replied, "No, not at all. God did not put very much combativeness into our race. Perhaps it would have been better for us if we had not gone licking the hand that had beaten us. But that is the way of our race." Such sentiments were anathema to Wells-Barnett and even to Washington loyalist T. Thomas Fortune, who had joined her in calling for black self-defense in the face of lynchings. Her questioning of Washington's reasoning in the aftermath of the Baker case would prove an augury of a far more massive assault on the Wizard that would take shape in the years to come.

The Baker lynching was prominent enough to attract one of the first white antilynching crusaders to the cause, although her career would be brief and controversial. Lillian Clayton Jewett, a twenty-four-year-old aspiring novelist, seemingly burst from nowhere when, on July 16, 1899, she rose to address a black audience at Boston's St. Paul's Baptist Church with the offer to travel to South Carolina and bring the surviving members of the Baker family to safety in Boston. Reverend Benjamin W. Farris of St. Paul's, a Mississippi native educated in Canada and a leading activist in black Boston, encouraged Jewett's involvement, pronouncing her "the new Harriet Beecher Stowe." Citing her familiarity with the South from her college days in Virginia—she said she had attended Hollins College before being forced to suspend her studies on account of illness—Jewett assured her St. Paul's listeners that Southerners were good people who secretly detested lynching and who could be motivated to join the antilynching cause. Following Farris's lead, Jewett worked to link her cause to the splendid tradition of New England abolitionism, emphasizing that the antilynching movement should begin in Boston, "where all great movements for right and justice have had their birth." Bringing the family of Postmaster Baker north, she said, would not only provide desperately needed help—the Bakers, stranded in Charleston, had been threatened and were in dire economic traits—but would also help galvanize antilynching support.

Reverend Farris and other black Bostonians embraced a young white woman barely known to them out of their desperation to do something to combat lynching, but some immediately suspected that they had too reflexively accepted the likelihood that white leadership of any kind would be more effective than their own, and a rift developed over the propriety of placing so much responsibility in Jewett's hands. Mrs. Josephine St. Pierre Ruffin of the National Association of Colored Women announced that her organization had already been working toward bringing the Bakers to Boston, and didn't see why the project should be handed to "some chit of a white girl who sprang up overnight." Reverend Farris and lawyer Isaac B. F. Allen defended Jewett. Over the next few weeks, Ruffin continued to argue that Jewett could not be trusted, even charging that she was trying to make money off the Bakers' plight. She also unearthed evidence that the "illness" that had forced Jewett to leave college had been no physical malady, but psychological problems that had led to her being put in a mental asylum, a charge Jewett denied. At one raucous Boston meeting, Isaac Allen scandalized everyone present by warning all "colored journalists" who had written unflattering accounts of their efforts that "lynching is good enough here in Massachusetts." The remark brought gasps and shouts of outrage. Insults were heard from all sides. Reverend J. Allan Kirk had to pound the gavel for order, saying, "Mr. Allen . . . You are going too far. We are not going to have lynching here in Massachusetts." But Allen persisted. "I tell you, if we are going to have such Negroes around here contaminating the minds of the white people it is better to lynch them." Reverend Farris tried to set the meeting back on track by announcing that he had received invitations from several groups in Georgia asking him to go South and explain the antilynching cause, but when he stated, "They want to see me, and I am going," someone shouted, "You won't come back!," again throwing the meeting into turmoil. At this point, the Reverend Alfred W. Adams, secretary of the group, stood and announced his resignation, saying, "The organization, if it continue[s] in frivolity and not in seriousness regarding lynching, is apt to run overboard."

On August 4, unable to gain a consensus from the fractured Boston group, Lillian Jewett took matters into her own hands, departing alone for South Carolina. The Bakers had indeed had a rough time since the trial of their attackers had ended, and Jewett found them living in poverty and poor health. The federal government had never provided them with anything more than witness fees of a few dollars for appearing in court, and finding work was difficult, as they had attracted much unkind attention by testifying against the lynch mob. Rosa, the eldest daughter, had worked as a chambermaid for a month in the home of a local physician, only to be paid a grand total of twenty-five cents for her labors. In addition, the Bakers complained of having been exploited by a Southern black cleric named Reverend John Dart, who had traveled through black communities selling photographs of the Baker family and a written account of the trial, all the while collecting donations and assuring contributors the family was under his care. From this fund the Bakers claimed they had received less than thirty dollars. Given their circumstances, Lillian Jewett, with her money for train fare and expenses and her promise of a new life in the North, must have seemed heaven-sent.

The trip to Boston felt triumphant. Jewett introduced the Bakers to a warm ovation at a rally in a Providence, Rhode Island, auditorium once used for abolitionist meetings. The high point of the evening came when George Downing, an elderly black veteran of the Underground Railroad, clasped Jewett's hands in his and told her he had been the last person to shake the hand of that great friend of the Negro, Charles Sumner, and that now, in shaking her hand, he was passing on the conscience and leadership of that venerable old abolitionist and statesman. "Go on with your great work," he urged her, "for you are the needed woman of the hour."

Jewett did make good on her promise and helped the Bakers resettle in Boston, although following an initial burst of interest and support from both white and black New Englanders, she found it difficult to maintain a steady flow of donations. There were six people in the Baker family, they were largely unable to work and generate their own income, and several had lingering health problems. Soon, Boston's black leaders renewed their carping about Jewett, the Bakers and Jewett fell out and parted ways, and William Lloyd Garrison II had to step in to raise funds to settle the family in a home in Chelsea, Massachusetts.

White determination to stem all black political participation in Southern life, joined with the conviction that black men must be lynched to preserve white womanhood, led to a violent conflagration in 1898 in the eastern counties of North Carolina. This was a region where, with dense black populations and effective black political organizations, the "Negro control" that filled so many whites with dread had come close to being a reality. At Wilmington, a historic port city on the Cape Fear River, blacks had not only achieved access to positions of civic authority—there were black aldermen, black lawyers and editors, a black county treasurer, a black assistant sheriff, and a black coroner—they had also established themselves in small businesses, amassed property, and were among the city's most prominent artisans.

As one letter to the editor in a Wilmington paper vowed in the run-up to the November 1898 gubernatorial election, "North Carolina is a white man's state and white men will rule it, and they will crush the party of negro domination beneath a majority so overwhelming that no other party will ever again dare attempt to establish negro rule here." The ensuing campaign would become one of the low points in the history of American electoral politics—a coup, for all intents and purposes, in which antidemocratic forces used violence and intimidation to influence an election and to remove legitimate officeholders.

The immediate source of whites' agitation was that, after "redeeming" North Carolina from Republican rule in the 1870s, they had lost the state back to Republicans and Populists in the elections of 1894 and 1896. The victorious Republicans had installed as governor Daniel L. Russell, who was white, the first man of his party to hold the job since Reconstruction. Democrats made the familiar claim that blacks had become outrageous in their behavior under Russell, that they were corrupt and embezzled and committed fraud, although there is little historical evidence that black elected officials were any more corrupt than whites. Still, public opinion was easily led around to the conviction held by *The Washington Post* that "[t]he negro has proved to the satisfaction of the entire country that he is incapable of conducting a civilized and wholesome government."

One of the ringleaders of the antiblack campaign was former Democratic congressman Alfred M. Waddell who, it was said, had become enraged at a recent report that a black attorney had told a white attorney over a dispute in court, "Young man, you have got to go to school again. You are now talking to a lawyer." Subsequently, Waddell was heard to complain that "nigger lawyers are sassing white men in our courts," and swore, "We will not live under these intolerable conditions. No society can stand it. We intend to change it, if we have to choke the current of Cape Fear River with negro carcasses."

To keep blacks from voting in the 1898 election, white Democrats donned the garb of the South Carolina Red Shirt movement of the 1870s, the white supremacist Democrats who were proud of having helped "redeem" the South from Reconstruction. The Red Shirts had caused a calamitous episode on the Georgia–South Carolina border in July 1876, in an incident known as the Hamburg Massacre (after the South Carolina town where it occurred), when they filed trumped-up charges against members of a black militia and, after a bloody confrontation, executed several of the blacks in cold blood. The Grant administration's feeble response to the outrage was thought by many to signal the beginning of the North's disconnection from Southern affairs that would characterize the end of Reconstruction. North Carolina's version of the Red Shirts appeared ready to replicate their neighbors' misdeeds, and went about heavily armed, vowing to win back the state "peaceably if we can, forcibly if we must." South Carolina's Ben Tillman, who had been present at Hamburg as a young Red Shirt militia captain, came over personally to bless the North Carolina undertaking. One unit of North Carolina Red Shirts took the name of Teddy Roosevelt's Rough Riders. The name was more than fanciful. Just as it was necessary to stand up to Spanish interlopers in our hemisphere, it was deemed essential to save North Carolina from Negro "domination."

Blacks, although threatened with violence if they attempted to vote, largely remained defiant, insisting they would not forfeit the franchise. In response, whites raided their enemies' offices, threw eggs at Republican speakers, and shot off cannon in close proximity to Republican rallies—a form of intimidation known as "Democratic Thunder." The environment became so volatile, Governor Russell could not even appear in public to make a campaign speech. There were several threats to assassinate him, and at least one actual attempt. At a railroad depot in Laurinburg shortly before the election, Red Shirts on horseback surrounded Russell's train and demanded his "surrender." The governor avoided detection, and probably saved his own life, by hiding behind a trunk in the baggage car.

In support of their own candidate, Charles B. Aycock, the Democrats staged massive rallies such as one at Burlington, where town fathers shut down the cotton mills for the day so employees could attend. A throng of humanity entered a parade ground to the music of a brass band thrumming "Dixie" and other favorites, as dignitaries rode past on a float filled with women in flowing crinolines sitting beneath a banner that read WHITE SUPREMACY—PROTECT US. The crowd heard a sampling of strident Democrat oratory, then sat down to what must have been one of the largest picnics in American history—142 lambs and pigs roasted and served on a single table 516 feet long and 4 feet wide.

"Winchesters, Colts and Smith & Wessons were everywhere in evidence," said a newspaper account of one North Carolina Democratic rally. "In the parade beside the humble laborers could be seen the banker, merchant, lawyer, and others in every sphere of life, all animated and enthused over the same spirit purpose [sic]—the supremacy of the Anglo-Saxons." Fiery anti-Republican speeches were cheered, including one particularly well-received address calling for the lynching of Governor Russell. A broadside distributed at the event by the Democratic state chairman lamented the fact that parts of North Carolina had come to be run by "a negro congressman, negro solicitors, negro revenue officers, negro collectors of customs . . . negroes in charge of white schools, negroes holding inquests over the white dead . . . negro constables arresting white women and white men." It went on to complain that white and black convicts on road crews were now chained together.

In the middle of this already inflamed environment, a chain of events occurred that led to a paroxysm of incendiary rhetoric about miscegenation and the sexual prowess of black men, with tragic results. The trigger was a controversial remark made the previous summer by an outspoken Georgia reformer named Rebecca Felton. Born in 1835, Felton was the daughter of an affluent Georgia family; her husband, Dr. William H. Felton, was for many years a Democratic representative in the U.S. Congress.

Beginning in 1885 she and her husband published a newspaper, *The Courant,* in Cartersville, and for twenty years she wrote a column about rural affairs for *The Atlanta Journal.* Felton would become increasingly obsessed by the perceived dangers to white women posed by black men, particularly the vulnerability of white farm wives who lived in isolation among large numbers of blacks in rural districts. Asked to address the Georgia State Agricultural Society at its convention on Tybee Island on August 12, 1897, she titled her talk "Woman on the Farm." One of her chief tenets for improving life for farm women was the need for men to provide more security, since black men with unlimited access to liquor were now permitted to roam freely. "If it takes lynching to protect woman's dearest possession from drunken, ravening human beasts," she told the gathered farmers, "then I say lynch a thousand a week if it becomes necessary."

Her remarks, reprinted nationally, caused an uproar. She responded to an onslaught from the Northern press with her usual vinegar, assuring the editor of the *Boston Transcript* in a widely quoted response, "The black fiend who lays unholy and lustful hands on a white woman in the state of Georgia shall surely die!"

The controversy she'd stirred lingered into the summer of 1898 when, with the tumult of the upcoming November election already causing North Carolina blacks to double-bolt their doors, Alex L. Manly, editor of a black Wilmington paper, the *Daily Record,* made the suicidal decision to respond to Felton's remarks. In an editorial published on August 18, 1898, Manly took on the rape myth point-blank, noting that what whites were quick to call "rape" was often simply an exposed liaison:

> Our experiences among poor white people in the country teach us that the women of that race are not any more particular in the matter of clandestine meetings with colored men, than are the white men with colored women. . . . Meetings of this kind go on for some time until the white women's infatuation or the man's boldness brings attention to them and the man is lynched for rape. Every Negro lynched is called a "big burly black brute" when in fact many of these . . . had white men for their fathers and were not only not "black and burly" but were sufficiently attractive for white girls to fall in love with them. . . . Mrs. Felton must begin at the fountain head, if she wishes to purify the stream.

Manly then addressed the white men of North Carolina directly: "You set yourselves down as a lot of carping hypocrites; in fact, you cry aloud for the virtue of your women, while you seek to destroy the morality of ours. Don't think ever that your women will remain pure while you are debauching ours. You sow the seed—the harvest will come in good time."

Seemingly inspired by Manly, fellow black Wilmington newspaperman John Campbell Dancy chimed in, escalating the rhetoric in yet another article: "Why should it be considered low or unseemly for a negro man of culture and respectability to marry a white woman of character and refinement, or why should it be considered a disgrace to such a white lady to marry the colored gentleman if she loves him?"

In North Carolina in 1898 these were about as far from routine editorial-page observations as one could get. When, as expected, local Democrats succeeded in "Red Shirting" the November election and ousting Governor Russell and numerous other Republican officeholders, they set out to deliver a more lasting blow to the black community, with Manly the chief target. On November 10, a mob of four hundred led by Alfred Waddell invaded Wilmington's black neighborhood, located the building that housed the *Record,* and burned it to the ground. Some witnesses said the mob appeared resentful that no violence had occurred on election day, and were eager to make up for lost time. Manly had prudently left town, but unable to find him, the mob turned on other blacks and their property. In the confusion, a white Democrat was shot, at which point the "Rough Riders" went berserk, chasing people up and down the streets, attacking black people at random and killing as many as twenty-five. Black families fled en masse to the surrounding woods. Thousands were said to have left the city.

Despite the endless Democratic proclamations about wanting to rid Wilmington of "ignorant negroes," it was actually the successful, educated blacks who were most carefully chosen for immediate exile. Black "objectionable characters"—officials, professionals, and successful black businessmen—were rounded up and marched to the train depot under escort and sent toward Richmond, Virginia, with the admonition never to return, as were a handful of prominent white Republicans, including G. Z. French, the white Republican deputy sheriff, and J. R. Melton, the ex–chief of police. French had a noose put around his neck and was hoisted up a telegraph pole, choking and pleading for help, before the mob allowed him to dash onto a train, where he hid under a coach seat until the train pulled away from the station.

As the mayhem continued, Governor Russell, in hopes of quelling the bloodshed, telegraphed from Raleigh his assurance that all black officials in Wilmington would immediately resign their positions, an offer the Democrats must have found immensely humorous. Most blacks had already "resigned their positions"; they had been chased away or had fled for their lives. A white mob now ruled Wilmington, and its leader, Alfred Waddell, had just appointed himself mayor.

What had occurred in Wilmington would later be cited as a kind of model by other Southern communities eager to rid themselves of black citizens. Whites agitated by growing black political hegemony, work-related disputes, and fears of black criminality and immorality, or beset by other difficulties related to their black populations, forced the exodus of thousands of blacks from Southern precincts during the early years of the twentieth century. Known as "clearances," they frequently would involve lynchings or other racial violence either as a precipitating factor or as a means of facilitating blacks' immediate departure. Blacks would not soon forget Wilmington either. It is a matter of historical debate whether Waddell's threat to "choke the current of Cape Fear River with negro carcasses" was ever actually carried out, but that disturbing image was one that lived on for years in the memories of black North Carolinians.

In the summer of 1900, Ida Wells-Barnett's well-known exhortation that a Winchester rifle should enjoy "a place of honor" in every black household in America was acted upon most catastrophically by a black resident of New Orleans. Robert Charles, thirty-four, a convert to a back-to-Africa movement and a man known to be agitated by recent reports of lynchings, chose to fight back when harassed by police and surrounded, ultimately, by a white mob. By the time Charles was finally cornered with his Winchester on the top floor of a burning building, he had caused days of violent upheaval in the city, shot twenty-seven whites, killing seven, including four policemen, and was front-page news in almost every newspaper in the United States.

There is scant information about Robert Charles's early life. It is known he grew up in a large family in rural Copiah County, Mississippi, and probably attended school, for he was literate. In 1896 he moved to New Orleans, where he held a series of unskilled and semiskilled jobs. It was there he came under the influence of the International Migration Society, a group led by Daniel J. Flummer of Birmingham, Alabama, a back-to-Africa disciple of Bishop Henry M. Turner of the African Methodist Episcopal Church in Atlanta. On behalf of the society, Robert Charles gave out pamphlets and sold magazines, and through the mail put down a small payment toward his own emigration to Liberia.

The dream of emigration to Mother Africa had been a constant in black American life since early in the nineteenth century. The white-sponsored American Colonization Society (ACS) was founded in 1816 with the blessing of President James Monroe, and Congress gave funds in 1820 to enable the ACS to found the nation of Liberia on the northwest coast of Africa. In gratitude, early settlers named the new nation's capital Monrovia. Probably no more than a few thousand black Americans ever went there, but the emigration ideal never completely disappeared from the black American imagination, and many prominent Americans, not least among them Abraham Lincoln, lent support at one time or another to the proposal that repatriating American blacks to Africa was the most sensible way to address the nation's race dilemma. (The notion would resurface in grandiose form in the 1920s with Marcus Garvey's plan for his Black Star Line, a fleet of steamships that would transport black passengers "back" across the Atlantic.)

After the explosion of the cotton market in the 1820s and the unrelenting demand for slave labor, Southern planters began to strongly resist the repatriation idea, and there never arose a groundswell of enthusiasm among blacks themselves for it, nor the practical means to move large numbers of indigent people to a different continent. For many people, however, including Robert Charles, who detested their status as noncitizens in white America, emigration remained a sustaining hope.

Charles was, as historian William Ivy Hair has written, "trapped by a problem that neither he nor the world around him was capable of solving," an individual who felt deeply and personally the constant animosity aimed at black people, particularly now that all restraints on white opposition had been abandoned. People who knew Robert Charles related after he had made himself infamous that several recent events had distressed him, notably the official disenfranchisement of blacks in Louisiana in 1898 and the Sam Hose lynching in Georgia in April 1899. The Newnan lynching, friends said, drove Charles "beside himself with fury."

It was shortly after the death of Hose that Charles stepped up his emigrationist activities and began corresponding directly with Bishop Turner in Atlanta, becoming a sales agent for Turner's monthly magazine, *Voice of Missions*. Turner was, in 1900, perhaps the most prominent American advocate of emigration to an African homeland. A chaplain in the Union army and a Republican legislator in Georgia during Reconstruction, he believed simply and fervently that no future existed for black people in the United States. Turner conceded that slavery may have been God's plan of introducing blacks to Christianity, but held that whites had reneged on their part of the "plan" by not permitting ex-slaves to become full-fledged citizens and human beings; thus, blacks had to pursue the next phase of God's intentions by repatriating themselves to Africa. Turner had not overlooked the practical challenges involved: by his calculation, the United States owed the former slaves $40 billion for their two and a half centuries of unpaid labor; he asked only $500 million of it for the purpose of colonization, and readily pointed out that this would in the long term be more affordable for white America than the cost of continuing to suppress several million black people.

He did not advocate violence against whites; indeed, he thought it demonstrated far superior dignity to behave civilly toward them. But he held resolutely that blacks had the right to self-defense if attacked, and lynching he considered an abomination. "Until we are free from menace by lynchers," Turner assured Robert Charles and his other followers, "we are destined to be a dwarfed people."

On the warm and muggy night of Monday, July 23, 1900, Charles, who had recently been laid off from his job at a sawmill, and his roommate, Lenard Pierce, went to call on two women of Charles's acquaintance. Not finding them at home—or perhaps waiting for their white employers to turn out their light so they could visit the women surreptitiously—the two men sat down on a nearby stoop. Their presence attracted the curiosity of a detail of New Orleans police, who approached and asked them their business. Charles, apparently resenting the question, stood up as if to leave, at which point Sergeant August T. Mora reached for his billy club to restrain him. Charles and Mora began to struggle, and both men simultaneously drew pistols. Mora fired first, his bullet hitting Charles in the leg; Charles, as he fled down the street, returned Mora's fire, wounding the officer.

Charles half-ran, half-limped to his home, where he dressed his wound and hurriedly gathered some belongings. He also took down his Winchester. At this point, surrendering to the police was not much of an option, nor could he allow himself to be captured. He had shot a white policeman. If he was not killed outright, Charles feared, he would either be hanged or, at the least, sent for life to the chain gang.

Meanwhile, police had placed Lenard Pierce under arrest and learned from him where Charles lived. Captain John T. Day, who had won promotion from sergeant just the year before for rescuing people from a burning hotel, led three other patrolmen to Charles's apartment, which lay at the end of a small alleyway, and approached, carrying a lantern to illuminate the narrow passageway to the door. Day hollered, "Open up there!" and demanded Charles's surrender. The door swung open slightly and Charles, seeing the policemen's silhouettes clearly in the lantern light, twice squeezed the trigger on the Winchester. The captain, shot in the heart, made a soft cry and fell over dead. Patrolman Peter J. Lamb collapsed, shot in the head and mortally wounded. The other two policeman scattered, while Charles took advantage of the confusion to flee.

By dawn, the local newspapers had hold of the story, and morning commuters on the city's streetcars read of "one of the most formidable monsters that has ever been loose upon the community . . . a ravisher and a daredevil . . . a fiend in human form." (Charles, of course, had not ravished anyone, but it was by now an almost obligatory accusation.)

The incident had occurred at a precarious time, for race relations in New Orleans were already at the tinderbox stage. White laborers were upset because several local steamship firms and municipal work projects had begun hiring large numbers of blacks in order to lower payrolls. Indeed, whites had to contend not only with an influx of "plantation negroes"—rural blacks like Robert Charles—who effectively competed for low-paying manual jobs, but also a burgeoning Italian population, which had made strong inroads into the labor market as dockworkers and produce handlers and sellers. One of the city's leading newspapers, *The Times-Democrat,* had recently published a provocative series of articles on "The Negro Problem" and prophesied "we are on the threshold of a race war." The paper, in making recommendations as to how to address that inevitability, prescribed forced deportation of blacks and quoted medical experts who thought it advisable to begin reducing the overall number of black people through "asexualization, a measure which should be practiced at the earliest possible period of life."

New Orleans was already thoroughly associated with lynching in the minds of many Americans, for it had been the scene in 1891 of the nation's most notorious summary execution, one that involved eleven white victims. This had come in retribution for the October 15, 1890, killing of Police Superintendent David C. Hennessy, shot from ambush as he walked alone at night near his home on Girod Street. At thirty-two, Hennessy was one of America's youngest police chiefs, famous in the nation's tabloid press as an expert on the "stiletto" or "vendetta" societies, Italian criminal groups that had built a substantial presence in several large cities, including New Orleans, where they held sway over the dockworkers and the city's lucrative fruit and produce trade. Asked to name his assassins as he lay mortally wounded on the cobblestones, Hennessy was reputed to have uttered a single word: "Dagoes."

Mayor Joseph A. Shakespeare, under pressure to act, ordered a police roundup of Italian suspects. Two hundred were netted in the initial sweep of the city's Sicilian neighborhood, Little Palermo, although charges in the Hennessy slaying were leveled ultimately at only nineteen men. Several were tried and acquitted early the next year and others were still waiting to come to trial when rumors circulated that the jury in the initial case had been bought off by Italian underworld figures. A vigilance committee that included some well-known citizens met and issued a "call" in the city's newspapers:

MASS MEETING!
All good citizens are invited to attend a mass meeting on Saturday, March 14, at ten o'clock a.m., at Clay statue, to take steps to remedy the failure of justice in the Hennessy case. Come prepared for action.
John C. Wickliffe,
W.S. Parkerson

In response, on March 14, 1891, a crowd gathered at the parish prison where the suspects were being held. Egged on by District Attorney William S. Parkerson, who declared, "When the law is powerless, the rights delegated by the people are relegated back to the people, and they are justified in doing what the law has failed to do," a mob surged into the prison, chased down the Italians, and dragged them from their hiding places. Nine were executed at point-blank range inside the jail, while two were spared so they could be handed over as a "courtesy" to the crowd waiting outside. These two were seized and flailed at by the throng, then suspended from lampposts and shot to death.

Characterizing the incident as "a spontaneous uprising of the people," a grand jury refused to bring charges against any of the lynchers, and local papers endorsed the mob's action. So celebrated was the affair that District Attorney Parkerson embarked on a national lecture tour to promote the cause of restricting immigration. Parkerson's message appealed to the most raw nativist sentiment, the worker and employer who feared the impact of immigrant labor, as well as the high-minded reformer concerned about vice, crime, and corruption in the big cities. "If there is one thing more hateful to Americans . . . it is secret, oath-bound societies which employ assassination as a recognized means of carrying out their objects," commented Massachusetts congressman Henry Cabot Lodge, seeming to speak in defense of the lynch mob that had avenged Hennessy's death.

After some of the initial euphoria surrounding the New Orleans affair had dissipated, voices of concern and condemnation began to be heard. Additional facts came out about the killings that cast doubt on the guilt of the lynch victims, while it emerged that numerous city officials had known of the planned executions in advance. The argument that Italians were members of an inferior "race" bent on thuggery and vice proved to lack the emotional staying power of the myth that black men were the ha-bitual ravishers of white women; and the New Orleans lynchings, after a few months, began to sit far less comfortably on the public's conscience. As a result, the U.S. House of Representatives took up the subject of lynching, albeit briefly, and, for the first time, a number of states, includ-ing Alabama, adopted official remedies for lynching, enacting legislation to punish collusion and the dereliction of duty on the part of sheriffs, jail-ers, and other officers of the law. Few of these laws were actually used, and it was disheartening that an injustice suffered regularly by black people had received attention only when it had occurred to whites, but the ques-tion of whether lynching was acceptable had been "officially" raised for the first time, and powerful men made to ponder the answer.

Nine years later, Mayor Paul Capdevielle no doubt had the Italian lynch-ings of 1891 in mind as he struggled to diminish the possibility of violence during the search for Robert Charles. Capdevielle took several precau-tionary steps—enlisting five hundred special deputies, ordering a citywide curfew, and requesting militia to stand by at the state capitol in nearby Baton Rouge—while publicly declaring his intention to prevent a lynch-ing at all costs. A mob had already threatened the jail where Lenard Pierce was being held, but the mayor was closely monitoring the situation and the jail's warden had assured him that nothing short of dynamite would get his prisoner out.

Despite such bravado, the New Orleans police were in reality ill-prepared to control the roving bands of riotous whites who had taken to the streets. The force had only about three hundred policemen, a modest number given the city's population of 310,000, and its makeup reflected the persistent influence of cronyism, as there were many older police who had little business even being in uniform. (One of the patrolmen sent in Captain Day's detail to apprehend Robert Charles was sixty-six years old.) Like most city police forces at the time, the New Orleans police had no formal training in handling large groups of people, particularly unruly mobs (tear gas had not yet been invented), and unlike a fixed standoff between an angry crowd and authorities, as in a labor strike, the armed mobs roaming the city, nominally looking for Robert Charles but taking satisfaction in tormenting any black they could lay their hands on, were mobile and able to quickly disperse and reform somewhere else.

The city got little help from its newspapers. The editor of *The States,* Major Henry J. Hearsey, an unreconstructed Confederate, had made himself muse and mentor to the rabble in the street. In Robert Charles, Hearsey insisted, whites were confronting nothing less than the face of imminent race insurrection:

> Under the dark, seething mass of humanity that surrounds us and is in our midst, all appears peaceful and delightful; we know not, it seems, what hellish dreams are arising underneath; we know not what schemes of hate, of arson, of murder and rape are being hatched in the dark depths. We are, and we should recognize it, under the regime of the free negro, in the midst of a dangerous element of servile uprising, not for any real cause, but from the native race hatred of the negro, inflamed continually by our Northern philanthropists.

Of course, the potential horrors Hearsey feared were as nothing compared to the real havoc white citizens were already bringing to the city streets. In a representative incident, a group of whites descended on a crowded streetcar, Car 98 on the Villiere Line, at the corner of Canal and Villiere. "Here's a Negro!" someone shouted, at which members of the mob started firing their weapons. A black man, later identified as August Thomas, managed to lose himself momentarily in the crowd, but then he was spotted. He ran "with the speed of a deer" to Customhouse Street, the mob at his heels.

"A burly fellow, grabbing him with one hand, dealt him a terrible blow on the head with the other," recounted a witness. A kick to the head forced Thomas's upper body down under some water running in the gutter. The crowd waited to see if he would drown, and when he did not, they pulled him out and resumed beating him. After a few minutes someone struck a match and, holding it to his face, pronounced him dead. "He ain't dead!" another insisted. Someone finally offered to "fix the damn nigger," and squeezed a shot from a revolver into Thomas's head. Then the streetcar motorman clanged the bell, the passengers reboarded, and the car disappeared around the corner, leaving the corpse facedown in the street.

At a loss, or perhaps unwilling, to prevent such random attacks, the police were even more frustrated in their attempts to locate the source of all the trouble. Robert Charles was the kind of black man who "attracted little notice from white people until the last week of his life," as one historian of the incident has noted. Police and reporters who tore apart his room searching for clues discovered a bullet mold for the home manufacture of ammunition, numerous copies of the *Police Gazette* and tracts from African emigration societies, some diary entries, and a bottle of cocaine. His clothing, it was noted, "was little more than rags," an assessment that came as a surprise to the one white person with whom Charles was known to have regular contact, Hyman Levy, the proprietor of a men's clothing store on Poydras Street. Charles was, according to Levy, nothing if not a sharp dresser; and it would later be remembered that from his first exchange of gunshots with Police Sergeant Mora until the very moment of his death, Charles kept a bowler hat neatly in place on his head.

On Thursday, July 26, police received a solid tip that Charles had taken refuge in a house near the corner of Saratoga and Erato. Sergeant Gabriel Porteous, known within the police force for having a good rapport with blacks, was dispatched to check out the information along with three patrolmen. After speaking with several black residents, Porteous and his men moved on to a residence at 1208 Saratoga. They placed a man they encountered in the yard, Silas Jackson, under arrest, then forced him to lead them to a rear building where they believed Charles might be hiding. Peering inside, Porteous saw nothing suspicious. He did, however, see a water bucket with a dipper on top of it, and decided he wanted a drink.

Secluded in a closet, watching Porteous approach, was Robert Charles, who raised his gun just as Porteous lifted the dipper to his lips, and fired, killing him with a single shot. He also managed to mortally wound Patrolman John F. Lally, who had followed Porteous into the room.

At the sound of gunfire the entire neighborhood sprang into motion, police and other whites running in, black people quickly making themselves scarce. Charles, recognizing that the moment had come to make his last stand, took advantage of the chaos to run upstairs to a top-floor room, where he kicked out a partition so that he and his rifle could command a wide view of the area.

The first whites to arrive in the yard directly below Charles's perch made the mistake of assuming the gunman had fled; they crowded around as a priest bent over to give the last rites to Patrolman Lally. Charles calmly took aim and fired at a nineteen-year-old white man named Arthur Brumfield. Hit in the hip, Brumfield staggered a few feet, looked up to the window where the barrel of Charles's weapon was visible, and cried, "Oh, God! For God's sake, don't shoot!" just as Charles fired another round that tore into Brumfield's chest, killing him.

It was the last clear shot Charles would have. In minutes, the area was jammed with young men and boys with guns, as well as police, and the slopes of all the adjacent roofs filled quickly with snipers who poured concentrated fire onto Charles's position. Charles would appear for a split second, long enough to get off a round, then disappear. In the exchange he killed two additional men—Andrew Van Kuren, an employee of the city jail, and Howell H. Batte, a civilian from Mississippi; he also wounded nineteen others, including two policemen.

Unaccustomed to dealing with blacks who offered armed resistance, the police had up to this point been careless about exposing themselves to Charles's accurate fire. Now, having at last developed a healthy regard for his marksmanship, they turned away from the strategy of picking him off with a well-placed shot and decided to smoke him out. A fire chief and several volunteers managed to sneak into the ground floor of the dwelling, where they doused an old mattress with kerosene, set it afire, and then dribbled water on it, producing thick clouds of black smoke that carried up to Charles's hideaway. The fugitive, forced out by the smoke and heat, made a dash into the backyard and almost reached an outbuilding there but, unbeknownst to him, police and volunteers were hiding inside; Charles was struck by a slug fired by a young medical student named Charles A. Noiret. Wounded, he staggered into the room; Noiret fired again at close range, killing Robert Charles with three direct shots.

The body was dragged out into a yard and the crowd pressed in and began shooting into it, with relatives of slain policemen granted priority. After the initial exultation, there was anger that Charles had died so swiftly, and a cry went up to incinerate him. Another part of the mob, unable to get near the corpse, acted on its frustration by breaking away into an adjacent block and murdering the first two black people it encountered.

Police eventually got the body away. It was tossed into a police wagon haphazardly, Charles's mangled head dangling over the back end, and a mob of children followed the wagon for blocks striking at the head with sticks and knives. Made aware of this awful spectacle, the mayor ordered the city to do everything possible to keep the public from seizing the body or carrying out any other ghoulish pranks. Charles's remains were buried secretly in a potter's field, to the particular distress of a carnival owner who had offered a large sum for the cadaver with the promise that he would pickle and display it as "The Archfiend of the Century."

In the wake of so unprecedented a killing spree by a black criminal, the people of New Orleans, indeed of all the South, were left to evaluate what the outburst had meant and what, if anything, it portended for the future. Some guessed Charles's rampage had been fueled by desperation at the black man's plight. Others wondered if he hadn't been at least part white, since it seemed unbelievable a black individual could carry out so focused a program of malevolence. A few experts weighed in with the view that Charles's actions had been fueled by cocaine. The drug was abundant in the city at the time, and young blacks liked to drink a cocktail of it mixed with claret and water, a pint of which, noted a local paper, had the capacity to turn "a stupid, good natured negro into a howling maniac." One account conceded that Charles had shown incredible courage taking on the entire city of New Orleans, but emphasized that his was "the courage of the beast of the jungle," not to be confused with "ordinary" concepts of heroism. Still others blamed Northern propaganda. Charles, said *The Times-Democrat,* "knew nothing of grievances or oppression until it was drummed into his head by the exaggerated and sentimental writers on the wrongs of the negroes." Finally, in the only characterization that appeared indisputable, it was concluded that Charles had simply been "the boldest, most desperate and dangerous negro ever known in Louisiana."

Among blacks there was far less mystery about what had driven Robert Charles to act as he had. Ida Wells-Barnett recognized in him the inherent tragedy of black manhood in turn-of-the-century America, for it had been his best qualities—his intelligence, courage, and self-respect—that had led him to rebel and that had made his death inevitable. "Men who knew him say that he was a law abiding, quiet, industrious, peaceable man," she wrote. "So he lived and so he would have died had not he raised his hand to prevent unprovoked assault and unlawful arrest. . . . That made him an outlaw, and being a man of courage he decided to die with his face to the foe. The white people of this county may charge that he is a desperado, but to the people of his own race Robert Charles will always be regarded as the hero of New Orleans."

No one was foolish enough to celebrate his deeds too conspicuously. A song about his exploits enjoyed a brief underground vogue in black New Orleans, although as local jazz pioneer Jelly Roll Morton reflected many years later, "I once knew the Robert Charles song but I found out it was best for me to forget it, and that I did in order to go along with the world on the peaceful side."

"Let the Eagle Scream!"

In the early years of the twentieth century most people considered the "Negro capital" of America to be located in the small north Alabama town of Tuskegee. Booker T. Washington, who oversaw the Tuskegee Institute, had with his Atlanta Compromise address and the passing of Frederick Douglass in 1895 become the nation's most influential black man. His accommodationist view of black Americans as a labor force, not a political force, striving for betterment within the caste system, was an ideology perfectly suited to the times, and for espousing it in a variety of lectures, articles, and meetings with prominent whites in business and government, Washington won wide recognition and approval. In 1901 his autobiography, *Up from Slavery,* an inspiring account of his ascent from dirt-floor slave cabin to the world's corridors of power, was a bestseller, and in 1903 steel magnate and philanthropist Andrew Carnegie gave Tuskegee $600,000—a staggering endowment that secured the institute's future.

Feted by Queen Victoria, consulted by presidents, Washington became the anointed referee of all federal appointments involving black Americans, and his opinion was sought by the heads of government for policy decisions regarding the South as a whole. As white Northern philanthropists and businessmen flocked to Tuskegee to observe Washington's experiment in black education and training in action, he came to influence not only the charitable contributions to his own school, but the flow of funds generally to black educational institutions in the United States. And through his eventual domination of many of the nation's leading black newspapers, the Wizard of Tuskegee seemed more often than not to actually control all of black life in America.

Quietly, however, Washington's guiding vision of blacks' role in America, while remaining popular with whites, began to wear thin under the weight of grandfather clauses and literacy tests, incidents such as the Wilmington riot in which even the most assimilated blacks were targeted by whites, and the steady stream of lynchings in the South. Living in constant dread that their son, father, or brother might be shot down in cold blood, or even roasted alive, it was difficult for Southern blacks to believe they were gaining from the famous compromise Washington had proffered on their behalf.

Lynching presented one of the fundamental problems with Washington's philosophy. Hard work, diligence, and thrift, rather than winning white people's respect, instead often brought the worst forms of retribution. But Washington, according to historian Donald T. Grant, "did not view lynching as a tool maintaining the caste system of the South, but as an aberration of that society.... He thought it was the work of poor whites venting their frustrations rather than the final resort of a society determined to preserve the caste oppression of blacks at all costs."

This was only one of several "discrepancies and paradoxes" in Washington's leadership, W.E.B. Du Bois believed. "It did not seem fair," Du Bois later recalled, "that on the one hand Mr. Washington should decry political activities among Negroes, and on the other hand dictate Negro political objectives from Tuskegee. At a time when Negro civil rights called for organized and aggressive defense, he broke down that defense by advising acquiescence or at least no open agitation." A deeper problem, as Du Bois saw it, was that Washington put "the chief onus for his condition on the Negro himself," even as he excused or ignored Southern actions to disenfranchise black voters and put strong Jim Crow laws in place.

"When Washington made his first speech at Atlanta, in which he said we could be as separate as the fingers, socially, and yet united as one hand, and so forth—I rather agreed with him," Du Bois said, tracing the development of his concern. "I thought it was a good general statement. It was a compromise, of course, but if the South accepted it, I thought that was going to be a great step ahead, and lead away from any physical violence and lawlessness."

Du Bois's private doubts about Washington may have begun in 1899, when the Wizard offered him a position at Tuskegee and proceeded to behave in a somewhat overbearing manner about the terms and conditions of employment, while appearing to sabotage Du Bois's chances for another job as assistant superintendent of colored schools of the District of Columbia. Du Bois ultimately turned down the Tuskegee appointment and came away from the experience with new apprehension about Washington's methods and values. The great educator's views of the race's prospects, Du Bois began to see, were strongly guided by cynicism and suspicion. "He was a man who believed that we should get what we could get," Du Bois recalled. "It wasn't a matter of ideals or anything of the sort. He had no faith in white people, not the slightest."

In 1903, Du Bois and black activist and editor William Monroe Trotter both challenged, in distinctly different ways, the Wizard's national dominance over black thought and action. Du Bois's came in a sage critique of Washington included in his elegant book of essays published that year, *The Souls of Black Folk*.

"Herein lie buried many things which if read with patience may show the strange meaning of being black here at the dawning of the Twentieth Century," Du Bois wrote by way of introduction. "This meaning is not without interest to you, Gentle Reader; for the problem of the Twentieth Century is the problem of the color-line." The book's diverse yet complementary parts made for an engaging, well-rounded reflection on the black experience in America, sensible yet also bravely sentimental. As Henry Louis Gates, Jr., has pointed out, *The Souls of Black Folk* was the first book to give narrative voice to black nationhood, a nation-within-a-nation "of eight million descendants of both the African past and human bondage, flung together from hundreds of cultures and geographical locations, from Senegambia and the Gold Coast to Angola and the Congo, and forged into a new people, *sui generis,* in the harsh cauldron of chattel, race-based slavery in the New World."

The essay "Of Mr. Booker T. Washington and Others" is one of the book's best known. Du Bois began it by saluting Washington's efforts, emphasizing how remarkable it was that a black man born a slave was now the most famous Southerner since Jefferson Davis, and acknowledging the value of the Wizard's efforts to negotiate with the South. "Mr. Wash-

ington came, with a single definite programme, at the psychological moment when the nation was a little ashamed of having bestowed so much
sentiment on Negroes, and was concentrating its energies on Dollars."
However, Du Bois asserted, the price of Jim Crow degradation and other
restrictions on full political equality was too high to pay: "So far as Mr.
Washington preaches Thrift, Patience, and Industrial Training for the
masses, we must hold up his hands and strive with him. . . . But so far as
Mr. Washington apologizes for injustice, North or South, does not rightly
value the privilege and duty of voting, belittles the emasculating effects of
caste distinctions, and opposes the higher training and ambition of our
brighter minds . . . we must unceasingly and firmly oppose them."

While not affixing blame to Washington personally, Du Bois reminded
the reader that since 1895 and the Atlanta Compromise, the South had
formally disenfranchised blacks, created a legal status for them as inferi-
ors, and had withdrawn almost completely from the task of educating
black children. The obvious conclusion was that the repression in the
South was abetted by the Wizard's attitudes: "[Washington's] doctrine has
tended to make the whites, North and South, shift the burden of the
Negro problem to the Negro's shoulders and stand aside as critical and
rather pessimistic spectators; when in fact the burden belongs to the nation, and the hands of none of us are clean if we bend not our energies to
righting these great wrongs."

Du Bois's cogent arguments offered blacks who'd grown discontented
with Washington their first well-articulated brief. The book went through
numerous printings in the next few years, and helped establish Du Bois as
one of the leading "race men" of his day, in the intellectual tradition of
Frederick Douglass.

Washington—angered by his inability to muzzle Du Bois by bringing
him into the Tuskegee fold, and stung by Du Bois's criticisms—flatly condemned Du Bois and the Atlanta University project, warning in 1903 in a
public letter: "If Atlanta University intends to stand for Dr. Du Bois' out-
givings, if it means to seek to destroy Tuskegee Institute, so that its own
work can have success, it is engaged in poor business . . . Tuskegee will go
on. It will succeed . . . not withstanding the petty annoyances of Du Bois
and his ilk." Criticizing the Wizard was not without its real dangers, for
Du Bois knew only too well that Washington could create serious fund-
raising problems for Atlanta University, and that he, Du Bois, would soon
wear out his welcome at any academic institution if he remained a target
for Washington's ire.

Editor and publisher of the fiercely independent black weekly the Boston *Guardian,* William Monroe Trotter was a Harvard acquaintance of Du Bois's who had become a successful real estate broker. His wife, Geraldine "Deenie" Pindell, the daughter of a prominent black Boston family, was *The Guardian*'s associate editor. Perhaps more than any other black spokesman of the period, Trotter was unrestrained in expressing his anger at the dismal condition of black Americans, and openly contemptuous of those such as the Wizard who appeared accepting of the status quo, charging Washington with being in essence a political boss posing as an educator. *The Guardian* was every inch a vehicle for Trotter's vehement opinions, down to the advertising section, where he barred promotions for alcohol and products he deemed offensive to his race, such as those that promised to straighten black people's hair or lighten their complexion.

Trotter was not content to criticize Washington in print, but sought to confront him directly. On July 30, 1903, when the Wizard visited Boston to address a branch of the National Negro Business League, an organization he had founded, Trotter and his followers laid an ambush. As T. Thomas Fortune tried to introduce the guest of honor, Trotter's forces threw cayenne pepper on the stage and the audience hissed whenever Washington's name was mentioned. Washington himself then appeared to loud hooting and catcalls, and tried to talk over the noise, strangely—given the audience's apparent hostility—by telling one of the self-deprecating tales about country Negroes his critics most detested. In the rising confusion, Trotter stood up in the audience and tried to ask Washington a number of prepared questions intended to reveal the weaknesses in the great educator's philosophy, but a squad of police, tipped off ahead of time by the Washingtonians, suddenly appeared, blowing their whistles. Pandemonium broke out. Trotter, now standing on a chair, continued to shout his questions to a flummoxed Washington. In the audience, punches were thrown, chairs overturned. Trotter's sister, Maude Stewart, stuck a policeman with a hat pin. Both Maude and her brother were arrested.

Du Bois thought Trotter's language and tactics too strident, but had too much respect for the truth plainly spoken not to admire Trotter's pluck, and he was upset that the editor had been put in jail. Indeed, in the end Trotter's "Boston Riot" proved quite successful from the point of view of its chief conspirator, for the incident and its attendant notoriety served as a rallying cry for other blacks who'd grown weary of Washington's gradualism. Du Bois for one now stepped up his criticism of Washington, making the point that the Wizard unfairly controlled the nation's black press through subtle and not-so-subtle threats to withhold favors or money. (Fortune, one of the leading black editors loyal to Washington, responded by calling Du Bois a "professor of hysterics.")

A more significant result of the "insurrection" against Washington was a national call to black leaders—issued by Du Bois—to convene for the purpose of discussing expanded black rights. The Niagara Movement, gathering for the first time in 1905, was very much the non–Booker T. Washington movement, expressly distancing itself from the great educator's accommodationist positions and explicitly demanding equal employment, aid for education, and other rights from the federal government. "We will not be satisfied to take one jot or tittle less than our full manhood rights," Du Bois wrote in the group's founding charter. "We claim for ourselves every single right that belongs to a free American, political, civil and social; and until we get these rights we will never cease to protest and assail the ears of America."

While Ida Wells-Barnett, W.E.B. Du Bois, and others worked to awaken the country to the barbarism of lynching, some Americans were beginning to look at the problem from the other side of the glass—asking what failings within society, and specifically the legal system, prompted citizens to join lynch mobs. What inadequacies in the ways police maintained law and order and the courts administered justice drove people to take the law into their own hands? Was lynch law a legitimate response to citizens' sense of vulnerability? Was the law itself too slow to punish criminals, and too caring of the rights of the accused?

Recorded lynchings of blacks had decreased in the first years of the new century, from 105 in 1901 to 57 in 1905, but at an average of more than one a week the practice remained an unwelcome fixture of American life. Also of concern were reported acts of vigilantism in Montana, Texas, and other western locales in the 1880s and 1890s that claimed between 150 and 200 lives, and the advent of a new breed of regulators, calling themselves White Caps, who began to appear—first in Indiana, then as far east as New Jersey and New York State, in the years 1887 to 1900. Unlike the Reconstruction-era "whitecappers" of Mississippi and the Deep South, who used violence to force blacks off desirable land, White Caps rode in order to enforce moral codes—punishing wife beaters, adulterers, drunkards, and petty thieves. Influenced by the original Klan, White Caps wore masks, and like the Klan disciplined with nonlethal but painful floggings.

Public approval of this trend was so widespread, efforts were made in several communities to legalize whippings as court-ordered punishments. Several advantages of the practice were apparent—the harshness and immediacy of the punishment satisfied people's desire that the repression of crime be firm and unmistakable; the shame attached to the experience would discourage recidivism; and where miscreants could be dealt with summarily the costs of incarceration would diminish, allowing municipalities to use precious public funds for more worthwhile projects. In dealing with blacks, it was thought by some that a return to routine flogging would render lynching obsolete. "Why kill out the race by lynching when subordinancy through fear of the lash will stop it all?" a letter to the editor of the Newnan *Herald and Advertiser* proposed.

Judge Simeon E. Baldwin, who served on the Connecticut Supreme Court and occupied that state's governor's mansion for two terms, was so taken with the White Cap example he recommended in 1899 the legalization of both whipping and castration. Baldwin promoted legalized castration as a civic reform that might halt lynching, since if angry mobs knew castration of a convicted rapist would be swift and certain, they might be more inclined to allow the accused his right to stand trial. Castration thus became, in Baldwin's formula, a humanitarian policy that would save lives and spare society the shame of lynching. This idea—the legal "unsexing" of rapists and those who commited assault with intent to rape—was endorsed by many periodicals and civic groups. According to Clarence Poe, editor of the Raleigh, North Carolina, *Progressive Farmer,* writing in *The Atlantic Monthly* in February 1904, the "surgeon's remedy" would give absolute protection to society against the repetition of the rapist's offense. "The Wilmington, Delaware negro who was lynched last spring had once been in prison for attempted assault," Poe reminded readers. "Set free with the same lustful mania, a wolf in human form, he brought death to himself and to a pure-hearted victim, and shame to a great state. . . . The proposed legal remedy may be objected to as a reversion to barbaric custom, but . . . we must recognize the fact that we have a peculiar crime, to be dealt with in a peculiar manner."

When John Temple Graves, editor of the Atlanta *Georgian,* published a series of articles discussing the restoration of such antebellum punishments as branding and castration to curb black crimes that led to lynchings, the flood of incoming letters to the editor was overwhelmingly supportive. Some readers went so far as to suggest that rather than apply such punishments only to convicted felons, all black men should be immediately castrated, and that black women might also be "unsexed" so they could not give birth to any more rapists. Graves's own concern with lynching was that the practice, if it must exist, be put to better use to educate the black community about the consequences of their criminal inclinations. Black people usually made themselves scarce when lynchings occurred. Graves suggested that they be coerced to watch the events, although he allowed as how it might be best if the actual moment of death come in some secluded spot, since blacks, who were thought highly superstitious, would be more inclined to fear something they knew to be dreadful but had never seen with their own eyes.

Author Thomas Nelson Page suggested in 1904 that Southern blacks be made to form their own special "Negro police force," much as the British had done successfully with the natives in India and their other colonies, and that once an outrage of a white woman was reported, black leaders take responsibility for turning in the rapist. Page repeated what had become a mantra for lynching apologists—that "if papers and men, remote from them, said as much to the negro concerning the enormity of rape as they say to the white people concerning the enormity of lynching, raping would become less common."

In fact, black leaders and intellectuals did take black criminality seriously. From W.E.B. Du Bois to Booker T. Washington, most of those concerned with the situation of African Americans did focus attention at some point on the problem of black crime, Du Bois in *The Souls of Black Folk* noting:

> There can be no doubt that crime among Negroes has sensibly increased in the last thirty years, and that there has appeared in the slums of great cities a distinct criminal class among the blacks. . . . So great an economic and social revolution as swept the South in '63 meant a weeding out among the Negroes of the incompetents and vicious, the beginning of a differentiation of social grades. Now a rising group of people are not lifted bodily from the ground like an inert solid mass, but rather stretch upward like a living plant with its roots still clinging to the mold. The appearance, therefore, of the Negro criminal was a phenomenon to be awaited; and while it causes anxiety, it should not occasion surprise.

And, in the aftermath of lynchings, black communities often did, through their civic and religious leaders, express regret over the crime that had sparked the mob's action, and even voiced appreciation that the fiend had been properly dealt with. This was particularly true in cases where the crime was horrific and the suspect could be readily ostracized and condemned. When, for instance, a South Carolina black man named Bob Davis was lynched in 1906 after assaulting a white shopgirl and, later, a black teenager, local blacks took part in the lynching and their community leaders issued a statement approving of the affair. The mother of the black girl who had been assaulted was given the privilege of firing the first shot at Davis, who had been bound to a tree. With a crowd of armed white men behind her offering advice and encouragement, the mother stood several paces from the prisoner, took aim at his midsection, and squeezed the trigger. The crowd then joined in, its fusillade blowing Davis into pieces.

Of course, in small, isolated towns, agreeing after the fact that a lynching had been good and proper was also a sound survival strategy—best to allow the lynch mob's fury to end with its original victim than spread to the whole black community, as too often happened.

Many observers agreed that the reason lynch law and vigilantism were so hard to eradicate was that they were ingrained in society as legitimate expressions of popular sentiment. As Southern newspapers frequently pointed out, those members of a community who took part in a lynching were the same individuals who would most likely form its grand and petit juries; mob seizures and summary executions of "known" criminals were thus simply expeditious. The end result was the same, without the bother and expense of the trial sequence. And with a lynching, shared values and community bonds were reinforced. Citizens got to participate in ridding their community of something unwanted, be it by pulling a rope, throwing a stone at the victim, taking home a souvenir, or simply yelling encouragement. This question—whether the pursuit of justice can exist as a separate and objective entity apart from the passions of the people, and what degree of personal involvement the people will have in punishing those who have wronged them—has never entirely disappeared from American life.

The concern that the legal process had the capacity to drag on, thus sparing a monstrous criminal for weeks, months, or longer from meeting his just deserts, was also repeatedly cited as a factor in motivating mob violence. "Society, as well as criminals, has its rights," the mayor of a small Mississippi town once wrote to that state's governor. "One of these rights is the enforcement of its laws without needless, vexatious and asinine delay. If the courts of this country and the law of the land are to be perverted into a sanctuary where criminals may abide indefinitely with impunity, the administrations of justice will become a farce."

American criminal courts, it was said, too often conducted their affairs as if their highest objective was the avoidance of technical error, instead of the meting out of justice. A 1906 article in the *Southern Atlantic Quarterly* complained of the inordinate amount of time granted for appeals, changes of venue, peremptory challenges to prospective jurymen, pleas, and other technicalities that served to stall the justice system. "The conviction is rapidly growing that the administration of the criminal law in most American communities operates in practice more to protect the criminal than the public," wrote James W. Garner, professor of political science at the University of Illinois. Garner quoted recently-retired U.S. Supreme Court Justice Henry Billings Brown, who had compared the sluggish pace of American criminal law with that of England, where testimony and lawyerly oratory were sharply limited and new trials were rare. "One is irresistibly impelled," Brown stated, "to ask himself why it is that with the reputations of Americans for doing everything from the building of bridges over the Nile or battleships for Russia or Japan, to harvesting, reaping, plowing and even making butter by machinery, faster than other people, a court in conservative old England will dispose of a half dozen jury cases in the time that would be required here in dispatching one."

Of course, the people's forbearance with the justice system could be relative. It is revealing that in 1892, a year in which 162 black men—at the very least—were lynched without trial, Lizzie Borden, a proper white woman in Fall River, Massachusetts, accused of murdering her father and mother with an ax, was accorded such generous due process she was acquitted of a crime many historians agree she probably committed. Among other things, by disallowing compromising testimony the defendant had given at a coroner's inquest on the grounds that she had not had counsel present, the judge in effect extended to Borden her Miranda rights, a legal protection the U.S. Supreme Court would not put on the books for another seventy-four years. Borden walked free because America in the 1890s reserved special regard for upper-middle-class white women, and judge and jury could not bring themselves to ascribe to her the will and capacity to commit so brutal a crime. Had she gone for a stroll in rural Georgia, any black man suspected of leering at her might well have been accused, captured, and immolated all on the same afternoon.

In a climate in which "due process" took a backseat to "crime control" by popular consensus, defenders of lynching were unfortunately only speaking the truth when they made the point, as Louisiana attorney Thomas J. Kernan did in 1906, that the spirit of vigilantism already existed in various shapes and forms within the law itself. Police, Kernan pointed out, often acted like vigilantes, zealously pursuing an individual perpetrator, bending or breaking procedural rules, perhaps "sweating" or brutalizing informants for information. Elected officials frequently egged on police and sought to appease citizens by declaring a "war on crime." Kernan also reminded his readers that the courts were almost never truly objective, usually showing more interest in combating crime than in upholding standards of due process. And popular presumptions about certain crimes and the people accused of perpetrating them could not but influence judicial behavior at trials or patterns of conviction and sentencing. A wronged husband, someone protecting their honor from slander, or a participant in a fair fight stood superior chances of acquittal or light sentencing; cattle rustlers, horse thieves, adulterers, counterfeiters, or those suspected of violence against children were often presumed guilty as charged; corporations were usually considered guilty in suits brought by aggrieved individuals. Thus, vigilantism and due process were at times amorphous, overlapping concepts, highly relative in their meaning.

Another influential voice was that of jurist and educator Roscoe Pound, a native of Nebraska and later dean of Harvard Law School, who as a young man had personally seen vigilante squads in action. Pound was a leading advocate of "sociological jurisprudence," a movement in the legal community that called for the law's administration to reflect actual social conditions and human nature, rather than adhere to long-established rules and precedents. His lengthy essay "The Causes of Popular Dissatisfaction with the Administration of Justice," published in 1906, described a legal system in disrepair, overly consumed with etiquette, reliance on fine points, technicalities, and smothering niceties, all of which threatened to make criminal law an anachronism for its inability to serve people's needs. No apologist for lynching, Pound nonetheless was willing to understand it as a shortcut to justice that citizens, out of frustration, sometimes felt compelled to take. He compared it to the routine evasion by men of commerce of statutes that they believed interfered with their ability to conduct business, although lynching, Pound emphasized, represented a "disrespect for law at the bottom of the social scale, where it takes cruder, more direct, and less subtle forms."

The inherent dilemma Pound confronted involved the ambivalent relationship between Americans and their government, the inconsistency of a nation that promises noninterference in individual matters yet seeks to exercise control over certain collective endeavors. As Pound observed, the early colonists' insistence on religious freedom in the New World, the American Revolution, the drafting of our Constitution, all had fostered an emphasis on "liberty as contrasted with order, on rights as contrasted with duties, on checks upon government as contrasted with efficient government, on the dangers of governmental oppression as contrasted with the menace of anti-social individual action." The founders themselves had been impressed enough with this raw American spirit to worry that men might choose, for a finite purpose or period of time, to hold themselves above and apart from the law. "I can think of no threat more evil for our democracy . . . [than] the spirit of independence gone drunk," wrote Thomas Jefferson.

In 1899, Charles J. Bonaparte, later attorney general under President Theodore Roosevelt, conceded that lynching was an expression of the "people's wisdom," suggesting that although in a lynching "the law is violated in form," it is "vindicated in substance." While he regretted that inevitably some errors would be made and innocent men killed, he pointed out that blunders were also made, and made routinely, in the other direction, allowing many dangerous criminals to go free. Bonaparte suggested a number of reforms to address the people's wish for stronger redress against criminals and the delivery of swifter punishments, such as abandoning pardons and grand juries, limiting the number of peremptory challenges allowed the defense during jury selection, and executing criminals after conviction for their third serious offense.

To expedite the period between trial and punishment, a contemporary of Bonaparte's, U.S. Supreme Court Justice David J. Brewer, suggested abolishing the appeals system. Another popular reform idea was to abolish the unanimity requirement in jury trials. Most European countries, it was pointed out, were in the practice of accepting majority verdicts.

Historian Richard Maxwell Brown suggests that the retreat from concepts of due process urged by distinguished jurists such as Bonaparte, Brewer, and Simeon Baldwin indicates how fully lynch law and vigilante values had permeated American legal culture by the turn of the century. However, their thinking on lynching did not extend very far if at all into an appreciation of lynching as a social and racial phenomenon. The real issue was not simply one of whether criminals deserved due process or people's justice, but why black men were more likely to be judged criminals in the first place and why they were predominantly the ones singled out for lynching. The NAACP, which began a campaign against lynching shortly after its founding in 1909–10, attacked directly the suggestion that lynching could be eliminated by more expeditious forms of justice. Lynching and mob violence were not simply expressions of frustration with the slow grinding of the wheels of justice, but rather the result of race hatred and the compulsion on the part of whites to control and place limits on the lives of black Americans. The organization was understandably impatient with arguments that courts could put lynch mobs out of business by emulating them. This would simply mean bringing Judge Lynch indoors and garbing him in a black robe.

Lynching's validity as a means of redressing public grievances, the South's resistance to outside meddling in its dealings with its black minority, and the federal government's impotence in the region were issues brought to a head by a noteworthy 1906 case in Chattanooga in which a lawman gave to a mob a prisoner who was under the protection of the U.S. Supreme Court.

Situated in a picturesque valley of the Tennessee River, Chattanooga was at the turn of the century an important rail hub and a major industrial crossroads of the South, with its own Coca-Cola bottling facility, numerous mills and shipping concerns, and multiple daily newspapers. Because of the city's longtime industrial emphasis (the "Dynamo of Dixie," boosters called it), it had never had a large slave population, and was a Unionist stronghold during the Civil War. But like all the burgeoning cities of the New South it was plagued by simmering racial problems. In July 1905 blacks in Chattanooga attempted a boycott of the city's segregated streetcar line. A black taxi company was formed and with three horse-drawn carriages provided scheduled service between downtown and Churchville, the black neighborhood. The protest succeeded so well, officials had to concoct phony health violations such as "working old worn-out animals from early morning until late at night and only half feeding them" to shut down the carriage service.

Far more seriously, in late 1905 the local newspapers began fanning white fears about an alleged black crime wave. On December 11, a fifteen-year-old orphan was reported to have been raped by a black man; on December 19, a white teenager surprised a black intruder in her home, who stabbed her as he made his escape; on December 20, a white schoolgirl was attacked; December 24 saw a white policeman shot and wounded by a notorious black gambler; and on Christmas Day police received no fewer than eight reports of assaults and robberies carried out by blacks, leading the *Chattanooga Times* to produce the banner headline: "Desperadoes Run Rampant in Chattanooga: Negro Thugs Reach Climax of Boldness."

Such black "crime waves" were often exaggerated by white newspapers, but anxiety turned to public outrage on January 23, 1906, when a twenty-one-year-old white woman named Nevada Taylor reported that she had been attacked and raped by a black man. Taylor, a popular young woman, worked as a bookkeeper and secretary in a large grocery business, and lived with her father and siblings in a district known as St. Elmo, at the foot of the tramway that rose to the heights of Lookout Mountain. Returning home from work in the cold winter twilight, Taylor recounted, she had been grabbed from behind; her assailant, muttering soft assurances that he would not harm her, pulled a leather strap tightly around her neck and forced her into an abandoned marble yard adjacent to a cemetery.

Hamilton County sheriff Joseph Shipp immediately began the search for Taylor's attacker. He had little to go on. It had been almost dark at the time of the assault, the attacker had come upon her from behind, and she had never seen him clearly. She wasn't even certain at first whether her attacker was black or white, although ultimately she said he had been black.

The local papers let it be known that so savage a crime would not go unpunished. Indeed, there could be only one response to an outrage that, according to the *Chattanooga News,* was "a sample of the crimes which heat Southern blood to the boiling point and prompt law-abiding men to take the law into their own hands." Even the more moderate *Chattanooga Times,* which had been founded and was managed by the Ochs family, publishers of *The New York Times,* noted that Chattanooga was so angry over the assault on Taylor that many otherwise calm citizens had expressed the "desire to aid in meting out punishment to this Negro whenever caught" and to "help in pulling the rope or wielding the weapon that would send such a brute into eternity at the earliest possible moment."

With a rapist on the loose, the public up in arms, but no witnesses to the crime and Taylor herself unable to give many details, Sheriff Shipp realized he was in difficult straits: his own reelection was approaching in a few months. "Captain Shipp," as the sheriff was known, was a colorful official, a Confederate veteran who frequently regaled hushed groups of listeners with his tale of the legendary battle of the ironclad battleships *Monitor* and *Merrimac* on March 9, 1862, off Hampton Roads, Virginia, which he claimed to have witnessed. But he knew his reputation as a raconteur would not save his job if he failed to capture the "Negro ravisher" who'd had his way with Nevada Taylor.

Shipp decided to employ a method he had used before, offering a $50 reward for information leading to the arrest of the guilty party. Taylor's employer put up another $50, Tennessee governor William Cox added $200, Forest Hills Cemetery, where William Taylor, Nevada's father, worked, raised $50, and a citizen's committee in St. Elmo added $25, for a total of $375. The response was immediate. A tipster came forward to provide information and on January 26, the third day after the assault, Shipp arrested Edward Johnson, a twenty-three-year-old black carpenter who did odd jobs at the Last Chance Saloon. Johnson had been seen by the informant walking with a leather strap in his hand near the St. Elmo tram station at about six o'clock on the evening of the assault. Johnson declared his innocence to Shipp, explaining that he couldn't have been in St. Elmo because he'd been working at the saloon.

So great was the call for Taylor's assailant to be lynched that the very day of Johnson's arrest Sheriff Shipp bundled his prisoner onto a train and moved him halfway across the state to Nashville. He'd acted none too soon. That very night a lynch mob besieged the Chattanooga city jail, demanding the rapist. Deputies, unable to convince the mob that Johnson was not present, and concerned other inmates would be hauled out and lynched in his stead, defused the threat by allowing a delegation to tour the jail and look for itself.

By the time Johnson was returned to Chattanooga on February 6 to stand trial, Shipp had discussed with Judge Samuel McReynolds and District Attorney Matt Whitaker the dangers posed by citizens eager for a lynching, and the three men concurred that the public's interest and safety would be best served by a speedy verdict of guilty. Tennessee law, however, mandated that anyone facing the death penalty was entitled to legal representation, even if, as in Johnson's case, they could not afford it. Judge McReynolds, seeking to appoint defense counsel, had little to choose from. All the established lawyers in town shunned involvement in the case, and of the three local attorneys he eventually selected—Robert Cameron, W.G.M. Thomas, and Lewis Shepherd—only one, Shepherd, had any experience in criminal trials. Cameron was particularly unqualified, having served as little more than a paralegal.

The chief problem facing Johnson and his defenders—in addition to the lawyers having received little time to meet with their client or interview potential witnesses—was that his alibi relied on the word of employees and customers of the Last Chance Saloon. Given the era's strong feelings about race and intemperance, such witnesses were unlikely to be seen as credible by the jury. At trial, District Attorney Whitaker dismissed the alibi witnesses as "Thugs, thieves and sots—the off-scourings of hell." One, a man named John Jackson, was described in the official court records as "a Negro of the fun-making variety."

There were other questionable practices. Whitaker made public remarks to the effect that only brave jurors could put a stop to Chattanooga's crime wave. The accused, Ed Johnson, was made to don a cap and stand before Nevada Taylor to see if he resembled her assailant, a clear violation of his Fifth Amendment rights. At one point a juror stood up and declared that if Taylor would swear then and there that Johnson had assaulted her he would "get down out of the jury box and cut his heart out," a display of Southern chivalry averted only when Taylor admitted that she merely "believed" Johnson was the culprit. In his closing argument defense counsel Shepherd accused the prosecution's chief witness of fingering Johnson for the reward money and told the court Sheriff Shipp was ramming a conviction through on flimsy evidence in order to safeguard his own reelection. He also charged that jury tampering had taken place. The jury heard Shepherd's plea, then lost no time in convicting Johnson, who was given the death sentence.

Through both extensive police interrogation and his trial Johnson had steadfastly maintained his innocence. His own lawyers believed he was being railroaded. But in the end they concluded that, given the sure threat of a lynching or a race riot, it would be best not to appeal his conviction. This left Johnson with a rather bleak set of options. As the defense lawyers told their client, "Ed, there are two choices here. You can accept the verdict of the court and die in an orderly, lawful manner. Or you can die horribly by the hands of the mob. Do you want to die at the hands of the mob? Do you want to die in an orderly fashion or do you want a lynch mob to take you from your cell, drag you into the streets, beat you, and hang you in front of everyone, leaving your body there for all to see?"

"No, sir," Johnson replied. His execution was set for March 13, and he was quickly whisked away to Knoxville for safekeeping as work began on constructing a gallows in the basement of the Chattanooga jail. While the choices Johnson's attorneys outlined seem unduly cruel, particularly since they believed him innocent, there were several well-known precedents of accused men (whose guilt may or may not have been proven) requesting official execution for fear of being turned over to a mob.

Concerned that his son was being sped to his death and that the defense attorneys were not sufficiently committed to saving his life, Ed Johnson's father, who was known as "Skinbone," sought out Chattanooga's most prominent black lawyer, Noah Parden, to ask if he would mount an appeal of his son's conviction. Parden was skeptical. He was intimate with the case already, having done some of the legwork for Shepherd in tracking down alibi witnesses for Johnson, but he had stipulated that Shepherd not reveal his involvement because as a black attorney in a Southern metropolis his business was precarious enough. Only the poorest clients used black lawyers, because it was believed white judges did not take them seriously.

Parden, who was acquainted with W.E.B. Du Bois, telephoned him in Atlanta for advice. Du Bois told him that white lawyers should be allowed to carry Johnson's case, but Parden, perhaps because he was more familiar with the situation than Du Bois and knew that the only white attorneys available had served Johnson poorly, assured Skinbone he would see what he could do.

On March 3 Parden, accompanied by his law partner, Style Hutchins, filed a petition for a writ of habeas corpus in the Johnson case in the U.S. Circuit Court for the Northern Division of the Eastern District of Tennessee. Parden argued that Johnson's speedy trial in Hamilton County court had been rushed and unfair. Blacks had been excluded from the grand and petit juries; defense counsel had failed to request a change of venue or a continuance to allow the lynch-mob atmosphere surrounding the case to subside; and defense counsel had clearly been intimidated—afraid to raise objections, enter a plea, or take any meaningful action on the defendant's behalf for fear of inciting the mob. Finally, the defense was willing to let its client be executed rather than appeal the trial's glaring procedural errors.

On March 10 federal circuit court judge Charles D. Clark denied Parden and Hutchins's petition, although Clark granted Johnson a stay of execution until March 23 (changed by Governor Cox to March 20) so Parden and Hutchins would have time to take their appeal to the U.S. Supreme Court.

Although a fair trial is guaranteed to citizens by the Sixth Amendment, in 1906 the federal judiciary had still never inserted itself to try to enforce that guarantee in a state criminal case. Thus, while the Hamilton County court had violated several of Ed Johnson's constitutional rights, there was no precedent of federal courts acting to insist that such rights were observed on the state level. There had been recent scuttlebutt in the legal community, however, that the Supreme Court might be ready to act to ex-

pand federal guarantees of due process because several of the sitting justices had become frustrated with the poor quality of criminal justice in
state and county courtrooms. The one area where Parden thought he
might get somewhere with the high court involved the question of jury
selection. In 1886 the Supreme Court had ruled that states and counties
had to include blacks in jury pools, and in the Johnson case this stipulation
had been clearly violated.

On Saturday, March 17, Parden traveled to Washington to appeal the
circuit court's denial of his petition. In the effort to see if the Supreme
Court would take on the appeal, he was assisted by a well-known Washington black attorney, E. M. Hewlett. After a long wait, Parden and
Hewlett were ushered in to meet with Justice John Harlan, whose lone
stand in *Plessy v. Ferguson* in 1896 had won him the nickname "The Great
Dissenter." Harlan was thought to be sympathetic to the injustices black
Americans suffered but he was also known for suffering fools badly and
for sharply chastising lawyers who came before him with half-baked petitions. He appeared gruff and noncommittal as Parden presented the facts
about the sham trial Ed Johnson had received in Chattanooga, although
he agreed to read the trial transcript that Parden and Hutchins had paid for
out of their own pockets. In parting, Parden respectfully told Harlan that
equal protection meant more than arranging for blacks to get a lawyer and
a trial. It meant giving them the same rights and respect as whites charged
with crimes, and the same presumption of innocence. Harlan nodded and
promised to consider the case carefully. There was then nothing for Parden to do but return to Chattanooga and hope the high court's intervention came in time to spare Ed Johnson's life.

Johnson, in the meantime, had been doing some preparation of his
own. He had become deeply devout as he awaited execution, and his last
request to Sheriff Shipp was that he be allowed to be baptized before he
died. By county law, Shipp had no choice but to honor the request in some
way. For his own peace of mind, perhaps because he himself knew or suspected that Johnson had been framed, he hoped the conversion might lead
Johnson to confess his guilt, something Johnson, even facing imminent
execution, had refused to do. Shipp, of course, couldn't allow Johnson to
leave the jail to go to a church, so he invited the Reverend W. B. Fleming
from St. James Baptist Church, and some of the church's congregants,
into the jail to witness the baptism.

Johnson, since he had embraced God, had been in a near-euphoric
state, more like a man about to depart on a well-earned vacation than as-

cend a scaffold. He ate hearty breakfasts of grits, biscuits, and gravy, and spent his days agreeably posing and chatting with white people who came to the jail to have their photos taken with him. In exchange for these macabre souvenirs, the whites left him chocolates and pieces of fruit.

The press in Chattanooga, in the meantime, had become impatient with the delay. "People here are definitely anxious as to whether Johnson is to suffer death for his crime next Monday or escape for an indefinite period by reason of intervention of the court at Washington," noted the *Times,* while the *News* vowed that "if by legal technicality the case is prolonged and the culprit finally escapes, there will be no use to plead with a mob here if another such crime is committed. Such delays are largely responsible for mob violence all over the country."

On Sunday, March 18, two days before Johnson was to be hanged, deputies put the finishing touches on the gallows and stretched out the rope by dropping a hundred-pound weight on it so it wouldn't "kink up" during the hanging. Directly upstairs, Reverend Fleming preached a stormy sermon on Johnson's behalf, punctuated by hallelujahs and cries for mercy from his congregation members, then baptized Johnson in a bathtub that had been set up outside his cell. "Johnson emerged from the water in an ecstatic paroxysm," reported *The New York Times.* "He ran down the corridor clapping his hands and staring upward. This excited the women, some of whom shouted and sang, while others fell prostrate on their faces."

On Monday, March 19, Justice Harlan responded to Parden's appeal. Upon reviewing the transcript, Harlan had become convinced that Johnson had received little more than a trial by mob law. That afternoon, Tennessee circuit court judge Clark received a telegram from Washington advising him of the high court's decision to hear Johnson's appeal and announcing that as of that moment Johnson should be considered under federal protection. The message was given to Sheriff Shipp and was published in the late edition of the *Chattanooga News.* Harlan emphasized in separate telegrams to both Shipp and Clark that with the court's act Johnson had in essence become a federal prisoner, and that the state's officers (Shipp and his deputies) were now responsible to the federal government for his safety.

Harlan's decision struck at the very core of the lynch-mob ethos, for the aversion to allowing a suspect to enter the criminal justice system in the first place was related to the fear that he might through just this kind of unpredictable legal chicanery evade retribution, or receive it so long after the commission of the crime as to render it meaningless.

That night the mob struck back. Shortly before eight o'clock an angry horde stormed the jail, where Sheriff Shipp had left on duty only one guard, Jeremiah Gibson, a man in his early seventies. Attempting to telephone for help, Gibson found the wires had been cut. The mob located the iron gate that led to the corridor where Johnson's cell was located and began working to break the bolts on the door. About this time Judge McReynolds notified Shipp by telephone that a mob was in the jail. Shipp, who lived only a few blocks away, arrived, only to be immediately seized and locked in a bathroom. After a few minutes he was released, but made no effort to intervene or get help, even though a full hour was required for the mob to break through the iron door, and only a few blocks away a full company of the local militia was practicing parade maneuvers in the armory.

Finally breaking through to the passageway to Johnson's cell, a dozen men dragged him out of the jail and hustled him to the nearby Walnut Street Bridge over the Tennessee River, followed by about two hundred boisterous spectators. The last lynching in Chattanooga had occurred in 1893, when a black man named Alfred Blount was hanged from the bridge's first span. It was decided to lynch Johnson from the second span.

Slipping a rope around his neck, the mob demanded that Johnson confess, assuring him he had nothing to lose now by telling the truth. "I am ready to die," Johnson replied, adding,

> But I never done it. I am going to tell the truth. I am not guilty. I am not guilty. I have said all the time that I did not do it and it is true. I was not there. I know I am going to die and I have no fear to die and I have no fear at all. I was not at St. Elmo that night. Nobody saw me with a strap. They were mistaken and saw somebody else. I was at the Last Chance Saloon just as I said. I am not guilty and that is all I have to say. God bless you all. I am innocent.

Someone fired a pistol, then a spray of bullets struck him. One shot split the rope and Johnson fell to the ground, where his body was fired into hundreds of times as it lay motionless on the ground. The mob then departed, leaving a note pinned on the corpse:

"To Justice Harlan. Come get your nigger now."

Harlan was incensed when told what had occurred. "The mandate of the Supreme Court," he declared, "has for the first time in the history of the country been openly defied by a community." Sheriff Shipp, who quite clearly had permitted the lynching to take place, apparently decided that public sentiment was running too strongly in favor of summary punishment for him to abide by the Supreme Court's intervention. Describing the court's behavior as "the most unfortunate thing in the history of Tennessee," he told a reporter: "The Supreme Court of the United States was responsible for this lynching. . . . The people of Hamilton County were willing to let the law take its course until it became known that the case would not probably be disposed of for four or five years by the Supreme Court. . . . The people would not submit to this and I do not wonder at it."

That Chattanoogans agreed with Shipp on the matter became clear that summer, when he was soundly returned to office in an election whose main issues were the need to keep local racial problems in check and the vulnerability of white women, many of whom worked as volunteers in his campaign. According to *The New York Times,* the women of Hamilton County set about "beseeching the men of the county to reelect him as a vindication of the stand he took in the Johnson case." It was said that Shipp's margin of victory was the largest ever given a Democrat in the county's history. Only black people, it appeared, had voted against him.

Shipp understood Hamilton County well enough, but he had not appreciated how seriously the Supreme Court would take his defiance of its order. What particularly galled Justice Harlan and his colleagues was that the militia was close by and could easily have been activated to guard the jail. Local authorities had had no difficulty activating the same company in January, when Johnson was first arrested, and also on March 21, after the lynching, when black Chattanoogans outraged at Johnson's death stormed into downtown streets, throwing bricks and stones at whites and police. Shipp, the Supreme Court alleged, had come to the jail when the mob had gathered and had "showed his contempt and utter disregard for the order of the Supreme Court" by displaying sympathy for the mob and doing nothing to check its actions, including standing around for the better part of an hour while the mob broke through the last door protecting Johnson.

One of the interesting aspects of the Shipp case was its demonstration of how much could be learned about a lynching if proper law enforcement and investigative techniques were applied, something that was rarely if ever done. Immediately following Johnson's death the court dispatched to Chattanooga a team of Secret Service agents who identified by name a long list of participants, witnesses, and newspaper reporters who had seen the lynching. The evidence gathered was sufficient to charge Shipp, eight of his deputies, and sixteen other citizens with contempt of court. In *United States v. Shipp,* the sheriff and five others were ultimately found guilty and given modest sentences in federal prison, marking the first time the Supreme Court had chosen to become involved in a state criminal case because of procedural error. It would be the first of a number of federal judicial actions in the twentieth century aimed at better protecting prisoners and broadening guarantees of due process at the state and county level.

The legal breakthrough the case represented did nothing for Ed Johnson. He had been buried at a small cemetery for indigent blacks, "a resting place for Negroes" on Missionary Ridge outside Chattanooga, beneath a modest epitaph that reprised his last words to the mob that lynched him: "God bless you all. I am a innocent man."

Progress on a federal response to lynching was almost always inconsistent, the judiciary generally moving forward with very slow and deliberate caution while Congress and the executive branch flailed indecisively. If 1906 brought hope in the Ed Johnson case, another incident later in the summer at an army base in Texas suggested how far the federal government had yet to go.

That summer the all-black Twenty-fifth U.S. Army Infantry Regiment was relocated from its longtime base camp in Nebraska to Fort Brown in Brownsville, Texas, on the U.S.-Mexican border. One of four black regiments created by Congress during Reconstruction, the Twenty-fifth had served with distinction on the Western plains, in Cuba, and in the Philippines. Fort Brown was the oldest federal garrison in the area, dating from 1846. While an army presence in the community had long been routine, the posting of black soldiers there was new, and the welcome the white and Mexican-American townspeople gave the black soldiers was far from cordial: citizens insulted them to their faces; saloons either banned them outright or "Jim Crowed" them into separate areas; and a freshly painted sign appeared at the entrance to a city park, reading, NO NIGGERS OR DOGS ALLOWED.

The already tense situation deteriorated rapidly when a resident, Mrs. Lon Evans, reported that she had been outraged by a black soldier. She said he had come up behind her as she sat on her porch, threw her to the ground, and tried to molest her, but her screams had driven him away.

The next day's Brownsville *Daily Herald* carried a front-page story head-lined "INFAMOUS OUTRAGE: Negro Soldier Invaded Private Property Last Night and Attempted to Seize a White Lady."

Most of the men of the Twenty-fifth believed the story had been fabricated to demean their reputation and serve as an excuse for a lynching. Even their white commanding officer doubted the likeliness of such a sexually motivated attack by one of his men, particularly in a town full of affordable Mexican prostitutes, but the regiment's officers felt they had no choice but to conduct a full barracks search and investigation and cancel all leaves and passes.

Around midnight on August 13 shooting broke out in the streets near the fort. White citizens later charged that the black troops had come rampaging out of the fort and attacked them, although it's never been entirely clear if this was true or whether the whites had instigated an assault. What was indisputable was that Frank Natus, a white bartender who had been particularly rude to the troops, was killed and several other whites were hurt, including the chief of police. In the aftermath, the blacks were restricted to barracks and a "citizens' guard" of 150 armed white men took up a position between the fort and the town to make sure the soldiers did not reenter Brownsville.

Local whites appealed by telegram to President Theodore Roosevelt, urging him to remove the soldiers immediately from Brownsville. As a stanza in a poem printed in *The Daily Herald* characterized the situation:

> *Our daughters murdered and defiled,*
> *Black fingers crooked about fair throat,*
> *The leering fiend—the tortured breath,*
> *Where's time for laggard red tape now,*
> *When moments may mean life or death?*

Roosevelt, a hero of the Spanish-American War, had never had much use for black soldiers, whom he referred to as "smoked Yankees." Black troops had been used prominently in the war (known as "Immunes," they were thought to be less susceptible to tropical diseases), but Roosevelt thought they made unreliable soldiers who would fight only at the point of an officer's sword. Ironically, his legendary charge up San Juan Hill with the Rough Riders had been supported by black soldiers from the Twenty-fifth Infantry, some of the very men now condemned in Brownsville.

He also had his public image to worry about, never having fully vindicated himself in the eyes of the South for having had Booker T. Washington to dinner at the White House in 1901. Roosevelt had not anticipated how deeply the specter of social equality alarmed Southern whites. "It means the President is willing that Negroes shall mingle freely with whites in the social circle," the Richmond *Times* worried of the Washington dinner, "[and] that white women may receive attentions from Negro men," while South Carolina's bellicose Senator Tillman thought the meal would "necessitate our killing a thousand niggers in the South before they will learn their place again." Roosevelt was stung by the criticism, as he admired and felt a kinship with the South and its traditions, and afterward he was far more circumspect in his dealings with blacks, although Washington continued to serve as an unofficial adviser.

The president had publicly criticized lynching as a "loosening of the bonds of civilization," but he'd also given voice to two of the most common and erroneous myths about the practice—that it was caused by the black man's runaway sexual appetite, and that the "better element" of blacks could help abolish lynching by relinquishing colored criminals to the authorities. This latter idea, often put forth by "concerned whites," was ludicrous and particularly insulting—demanding that the "better element" of blacks turn members of their race over to police who would in turn give them up to lynch mobs, while the "better element" of whites refused to testify against such mobs. Roosevelt, it must be added, had long been sympathetic to vigilante-style justice. During a *Wanderjahr* in North Dakota in the mid-1880s he had even attempted to enlist in a vigilante movement forming to eradicate local cattle rustlers. The vigilantes refused Roosevelt's services, then embarked on a lynching spree in which thirty-five people were summarily executed.

In the Brownsville case, Roosevelt decided that the white citizens' accusations merited an inquiry by the inspector general of the army, Brigadier General Ernest A. Garlington. The troops of the Twenty-fifth, however, offended at being treated as criminals and afraid they would be made to inform on one another, refused to cooperate with the investigation, while continuing to maintain their innocence. Garlington's report, submitted to the White House in late October, concluded that "beyond a reasonable doubt" soldiers had fired "into the houses of the city of Brownsville" and had refused "to tell all that it is reasonable to believe they know concerning the shooting." Garlington urged the harshest punishment.

Roosevelt accepted Garlington's advice and in November 1906—without subjecting the accused to any formal hearing, trial, court martial, or other form of due process—dishonorably discharged 167 soldiers of the regiment, removing from them all military benefits, pensions, and other allowances. In this group were some troops with twenty-five years of service in uniform, and six who had won medals for valor in combat. In essence, as the nation's black press vehemently complained at the time, the men of the Twenty-fifth were punished for daring to be black U.S. soldiers in Brownsville, Texas, in 1906. The insult to black America couldn't have been more severe, as black men in uniform were particularly admired, their individual achievements noted regularly in newspapers and church newsletters. The concern over the mistreatment of the Brownsville soldiers would serve as a kind of augury for the great outcry that would be heard twelve years later, when black troops who had fought in Europe returned to the South to be beaten, humiliated, and lynched.

As the 1890s had brought the spectacle lynching to prominence, with the Paris, Texas, lynching of Henry Smith and the Georgia immolation of Sam Hose two of the best-known incidents, the Brownsville episode pointed to the kinds of assaults on black communities that would occur in concentrated urban areas in the first decade of the new century. Race riots of course were nothing new, but the tendency for rumors of sexual outrage to stir masses to riot, to create lynchings writ large, was distinctly of that age. Two major urban race riots of the period, Atlanta in 1906 and Springfield, Illinois, in 1908, grew from similar origins—a rash of news articles about black sexual assaults on white women—and both deeply disturbed white Americans, thrusting the subject of lynching, and race relations generally, onto the nation's editorial pages. While isolated lynchings were shameful and troubling, the wholesale destruction of property in civic areas, the total breakdown in law and order, struck at the very heart of Americans' concept of their civilization.

The Atlanta riot of September 1906 pointed up the problems that could result from the rapid socioeconomic changes the region was experiencing. The influx of many apparently rootless young black men into the Decatur Street area, and the ravishment crisis drummed up by Atlanta's newspapers, preyed on whites' powerful anxiety that the earth was shifting beneath their feet. With the decline of Southern agriculture, and with industry becoming consolidated in large textile mills, two powerful forces were at work—the relocating of rural blacks into urban areas of the South and the entry of white women into the work force and into public life generally.

At the same time, established black businessmen of Atlanta were growing more prosperous, there was an expanding class of black urban laborers, and the newly arrived blacks off the farm were creating an urban demimonde of saloons, pawnshops, billiard halls, and brothels along Decatur Street. Whites tended to find this worrisome and despicable—a neighborhood seemingly given over to the strutting to and fro of "biggety" Negroes and the pursuit of immoral behavior. It was said that young blacks there drank gin from bottles with pictures of scantily clad white women on the labels. The Decatur Street zone also produced almost daily stories of vicious knife fights and shootings. The fullest and most convenient expression of resistance a white man could make toward these twin specters of emboldened black men and freewheeling white girls was to insist on a heightened need for his own services in defending women from black ravishers, real or imaginary, and in maintaining however he could his version of the status quo.

Added to and exacerbating this already volatile situation was a tightly fought Georgia gubernatorial campaign that summer that pitted Hoke Smith, a former U.S. secretary of the interior and coowner of *The Atlanta Journal,* against Clark Howell, editor of *The Atlanta Constitution.* Their papers, abetted by John Temple Graves of the Atlanta *Georgian,* had for months been working to top each other's reports of racial and sexual deviancy, describing an epidemic of sexual assaults with the objective of stirring up a white-black confrontation that would frighten black voters away from the polls in the fall election. Smith had publicly declared his willingness to "imitate Wilmington" if necessary, an allusion to the North Carolina riot of 1898 that had driven blacks from power. He also introduced the novel argument that disenfranchisement was in black Georgians' best interests, since by attempting to exercise equality, blacks would only hasten the day when they would have to be either deported or exterminated.

In August 1906, just a month before the riot, one Atlanta paper had interrupted its steady flow of "Negro Beast" and "Big Black Brute" articles to remind readers that "it is the duty of all men who appreciate a noble, innocent, true woman, of all men who love their homes, their mothers, their wives, their daughters, and their sweethearts, their friends and companions, to bend every effort and every energy, and every means of running down and capturing, and punishing to the fullest extent" any black man believed to have assaulted a white woman. Other articles and letters to the editors exhorted white men not to allow their commercial interests in using cheap black labor to blind them to the criminal sexual appetites of black men. As ever, the subtext was that all of the black man's palaver about equality and citizenship rights was merely an effort to gain intimacy with white women, and that it was a biological necessity that this brutish intruder, this would-be mongrelizer, be stopped at the gates of heaven. No set of circumstances was too innocuous for extra caution. One paper took issue with "progressive white women" who chose to sit next to the drivers of their carriages: "To see a big black Negro sitting alongside of or touching the body of a white woman makes the blood in every white man's veins boil . . . [for] it is utterly impossible for the women to keep from touching the body of the Negro. This is a horrible sight for white people to witness."

An editorial in the *Journal* warned:

> Political equality being preached to the negro in the ring papers and on the stump, what wonder that he makes no distinction between political and social equality. He grows more bumptious on the street, more impudent in his dealings with white men; and then, when he cannot achieve social equality as he wishes, with the instinct of the barbarian to destroy what he cannot attain to, he lies in wait, as that dastardly brute did yesterday near this city, and assaults the fair young girlhood of the South.

When stories of actual sexual assaults were unavailable, editors didn't hesitate to fabricate them. "Negro, Seen in Dream, Causes Death of Girl," ran a headline above an article in the *Constitution* on September 6: "Crazed with a frenzy of fright at the dream that a negro was trying to kill her, Miss Annie Morgan was overcome with an attack of heart trouble and died within a few minutes. Crying out in her fright, Miss Morgan ran out of her room shouting, 'A big negro is standing over my bed trying to kill me with a knife,' then she sank to the floor, unconscious."

By mid-September Atlanta was in a pique of sexual and racial hysteria whipped up by the newspapers' claims of "an intolerable epidemic of rape." This included a dozen reported assaults through the month of September, and then four fresh ones on Friday the twenty-first and Saturday the twenty-second. Most of these were either wholly concocted or else were minor incidents blown out of proportion: in one, a woman had seen a strange black man in her neighborhood and notified police; another involved a botched suicide.

On Saturday, September 22, a large number of whites from greater Atlanta had come downtown to hear a speech by Democratic presidential candidate William Jennings Bryan. Many of these men mingled with a roving lynch mob that had gathered the night before in an effort to seize "a sinister looking negro" named Lucius Frazier, who'd been arrested for attacking Orrie Bryan, eighteen, at her home. "Miss Orrie," as the papers identified her, said Frazier had stalked about in front of her house for several minutes and then boldly entered it and attempted to strike her with "a heavy shoe." She escaped by locking herself in a closet, "thus frustrating the fiend's purpose," but told reporters that as Frazier was led away by police he had sheepishly said, "I wouldn't hurt you, honey, for I love you." She concluded her account by telling a reporter, "I hope they will kill him, for he was the most terrible-looking object I ever saw." Orrie's father, Thomas, who was not home at the time of the alleged assault but learned of it upon his return, immediately grabbed an ax and tried to get into the police van where Frazier was being held, dozens of neighbors supporting his demand.

Frustrated in their efforts to get satisfaction, this mob had never really dispersed. By the next evening, with a day's growth of stubble and full of cheap liquor, it was big enough and bold enough to brush off the personal pleas of Atlanta mayor James Woodward to go home. "Oh, go home yourself, Jim," someone told him. "We're after niggers."

On Saturday evening, the embers the press had been fanning so long finally exploded into flame. The lynch mob, combining with agitated Democrats emerging from the Bryan address and by now numbering several thousand, swept into the Decatur Street area, smashing black-owned businesses and chasing black individuals down while police held back. Blacks tried to flee for their lives or cowered under streetcar seats as whites stoned the trolleys and then boarded, dragging people off to be beaten, kicked, and spit upon. One woman and her daughter, part of a family that owned a restaurant, were beaten with wagon-wheel spokes as a mob broke the establishment's dishes and furniture, and then shot the woman's young grandson. Two people were stabbed in the main entrance of the Piedmont Hotel before hundreds of witnesses. Another victim fell to the pavement and was then killed by numerous white people smashing bottles over his head. After he was dead an attacker stood triumphantly over the corpse displaying a late newspaper headline about an alleged black sexual assault on a white woman.

The riot soon spread to almost every part of the city. As blacks disappeared from the streets the mob became even more obsessed, destroying windows, storefronts, numerous streetcars, and part of an intercity passenger train. The search for victims was so intense, even people who'd found refuge in their own homes or businesses were hauled out and beaten. Some of the corpses of the dead were carried to the base of the monument to Henry W. Grady, the former *Constitution* editor and New South champion, as a kind of macabre offering to the Southern orator who had warned his fellow citizens so frequently about the dangers posed by the Negro. Seeing a white man whom the mob believed to be a Northerner standing by and observing, they seized him and forced him at gunpoint to say he approved of their actions.

For blacks, the sense of abandonment during the riot was virtually complete. The police were distinctly unhelpful, and state militia and federal soldiers stationed at nearby Fort McPherson arrived only after several hours, and then primarily with the goal of halting black retaliation. Some whites were injured, as blacks did return stones, bricks, and, occasionally, gunfire, but it was the damage to Atlanta's black community that was most devastating—thirty killed, hundreds injured, thousands forced to abandon their homes and places of work.

With the city reeling, the very papers that had incited the disorder now called for its end—"To Every Atlantian: Obey the Law and Get Back to Your Business," read a banner headline—and laid the blame for the riot squarely on the monstrous assaults on white women. "Atlanta has had its race riot and it was one of the most terrible since the days of Reconstruction," summarized the *Constitution,* adding, "The causes that led up to it were the recent criminal assaults made by brutal negroes on defenseless white women. For months past there has been on an average of one woman assaulted a week. The climax came yesterday when it was reported that there were four white women who had been attacked at their homes by negroes. The news . . . inflamed the people beyond endurance."

One of the most prominent victims of the Atlanta disturbance was someone who was not even there. Shortly before the riot, Booker T. Washington's National Negro Business League had met in Atlanta and, at the urging of John Temple Graves, the Wizard had issued statements encouraging local blacks to turn away from crime and cooperate with white authorities in bringing black hoodlums to justice. The league also passed resolutions to this effect, the wording of which now appeared immensely foolish in light of what had occurred. Washington was revealed as being rather hopelessly out of touch with the reality of blacks' troubled coexistence with whites in large cities, and with a problem that black Atlantans now intimately understood—the rape myth could be used to foment not just isolated lynchings, but outbreaks of mass rioting as well.

The 1906 riot brought Atlanta a great deal of unwanted notoriety, although because it was one of the capitals of the former Confederacy what had transpired there seemed somewhat predictable. Far more disturbing to the nation was a near reprise of the incident two years later in Springfield, the capital of Illinois and in spirit one of the most "Northern" towns in America, for it had been the home and was the final resting place of Abraham Lincoln. In his memory Springfield had become a national shrine, visited each year by tens of thousands; when rioting broke out in August 1908, Springfield was in the midst of preparing for the February 1909 centenary celebration of the birth of the Great Emancipator. On account of the Lincoln heritage, the Springfield riot would help make the nation's persistent racial problems more clearly discernible, and inspire the creation of the NAACP.

The riot's underlying cause was white anxiety over an influx of Southern blacks into two Springfield neighborhoods, Badlands and the Levee. The violence began on August 14, when a lynch mob surrounded the city jail and demanded two black men—one accused of assaulting a married white woman, the other of murdering a white man who'd tried to stop him from outraging his daughter. The sheriff asked the fire department to race its trucks up and down the street to distract the crowd while he spirited the two out of town in an automobile owned by Harry Loper, proprietor of Springfield's best-known restaurant. When the mob realized it had been fooled, it surged toward Loper's restaurant and inflicted considerable damage. Cursing the town's most famous son and his Emancipation Proclamation, and uttering such oaths as "Lincoln brought them to Springfield and we will run them out!," the crowd then moved on to the Levee and Badlands and began setting homes and stores on fire. They also burned shops run by Jews and other known "nigger lovers."

The state militia, summoned from Decatur, thirty-nine miles away, did not arrive until the middle of the night, and so for several hours the crowd roamed virtually unrestrained—smashing windows, looting and burning black-owned homes and businesses to their foundations. After much destruction of property, the mob targeted the home of a black barber named Scott Burton, who, fearing for his life, fired on the rioters with a shotgun. Whites tackled Burton when he attempted to slip out a side door, grabbed a clothesline from an adjacent backyard, and strung him up in a tree. With flames illuminating the scene the mob filled Burton's suspended body with bullets before perpetrating "fiendish cruelties" upon it with pocket-knives and shards of glass.

While the lynchers were preoccupied with fighting over the souvenirs from the Burton lynching, a line of militia approached. When an order to leave the area was ignored, the soldiers fired into the crowd, wounding several people. Only after this confrontation did the crowd disperse.

The chaos resumed the next evening, when bands of rioters stormed those black residential areas that had been left unprotected by the militia. In one such district lived eighty-year-old William Donnegan, targeted by the mob because he owned property and was married to a white woman. As one rioter waved an American flag, Donnegan was dragged from his home and pounded with bricks the crowd had pried loose from the sidewalk. An attempt to hang him was interrupted by the sudden arrival of the militia, but Donnegan's throat had been slashed, and he died in the hospital the next day.

Once again the militia restored order, although by the morning of the sixteenth, after two consecutive nights of street violence and arson, Springfield was a smoking shambles. Whole blocks had been leveled. Citizens who'd lost their homes wandered the streets like refugees in a time of war, along with curiosity seekers from Chicago and St. Louis who'd come to view the damage. Many of the visitors went first to the spot where Burton had been lynched, and by noon the tree on which he'd died had disappeared, torn apart by souvenir hunters. Postcard views of the damaged buildings and a photograph of one of the alleged rape victims were selling briskly. Meanwhile, the city's newspapers reminded readers that the trouble had been ignited by the "hellish assault" that had been perpetrated by a "Negro fiend," thus arousing a feeling of righteous indignation among the people of the city. The articles defended the necessity of the riot's violence and praised the "good citizens" who, due to the conditions present in the city, "could find no other remedy" in dealing with black "misconduct, general inferiority [and] unfitness for free institutions."

In addition to the two blacks lynched, four whites had been killed and hundreds of people of both races had been injured, and the costs of the damage were staggering. Much of the worst violence had taken place close to Lincoln's home and his tomb. And although the riot was over, feelings of racial animosity had hardly cooled. A white boycott of black businesses was under way, and black people had been threatened with further violence if they dared retaliate for the riot. In a neighboring hamlet, a sign posted at an interurban stop read: ALL NIGGERS ARE WARNED OUT OF TOWN BY MONDAY, 12 P.M. SHARP. (SIGNED) BUFFALO SHARP SHOOTERS.

Springfield touched Americans in ways the Atlanta riot had not— emotionally because of the Lincoln connection, but also by clearly demonstrating that race issues were no longer solely a regional concern. Southern editors could barely conceal their satisfaction that, with whole blocks of "Lincoln's town" in ruins, Northern hypocrisy had at last been fully exposed.

Author, social activist, and philanthropist William English Walling, who had come down from Chicago to view the wreckage of Springfield and was much disturbed, knew that the Southern commentators were to a great degree correct. The race issue was a national problem, and to Walling that meant it was time to fight back, not against the South, but against race hatred itself. "Either the spirit of the abolitionists, of Lincoln and of Love-joy, must be revived and we must come to treat the Negro on a plane of absolute political and social equality, or Vardaman and Tillman will soon have transferred the race war to the North," Walling wrote in an indignant piece in *The Independent*. "Yet who realizes the seriousness of the situation, and what large and powerful body of citizens is ready to come to their aid?"

"Drums beat in my heart," recalled New York reformer Mary White Ovington of her reaction upon reading Walling's words. What Walling was proposing was the rejuvenation of the old abolitionist coalition—whites and blacks working together for far-reaching goals of equality—an idea that aligned closely with Ovington's own sensibility. A friend and disciple of Du Bois, she had helped pioneer the expansion of the New York settle-ment-house movement to serve the needs of some of the city's black res-idents, and had at Du Bois's invitation joined the Niagara Movement and attended its 1906 meeting at Harpers Ferry. Ovington contacted Walling and invited him to join her and a friend, Dr. Henry Moscowitz, for a meeting in New York in January 1909 to discuss the implications of Walling's article.

The three gained an influential ally in Oswald Garrison Villard, owner of the *New York Post* and a grandson of William Lloyd Garrison. On Lin-coln's Birthday, February 12, 1909, the small committee acted, sending out a national "call" written by Villard and signed by Jane Addams, Lin-coln Steffens, William Dean Howells, Ida Wells-Barnett, Lillian Wald, and other progressives, calling for a concerted effort to deal head-on with the country's racial problems. The appeal pointedly avoided the familiar kind of Tuskegee rhetoric about the black American pulling himself up the economic ladder and instead sought to revive the spirit of 1863:

> If Mr. Lincoln could revisit this country in the flesh, he would be disheartened and discouraged. [He] would see black men and women, for whose freedom a hundred thousand soldiers gave their lives, set apart in trains in which they pay first-class fares for third-class service; he would observe that state after state declines to do its elementary duty in preparing the Negro through education for the best exercise of citizenship. Added to this, the spread of lawless attacks upon the Negro, North, South and West—even in the Springfield made famous by Lincoln . . . could but shock the author of the sentiment that "government of the people, by the people, for the people, should not perish from the earth."

The organizers laid plans for the conclave to be held in New York City in late May 1909 that would found the NAACP, uniting settlement-house workers, muckrakers, labor progressives, and "race scientists," as well as Niagara Movement veterans. Ovington was perhaps the key figure in bringing the conference to fruition, for she straddled two worlds as a veteran New York reformer and the sole white member of the Niagara Movement. Just the year before, her promotion of interracial discussions in New York had produced an unexpectedly sensational result. In April 1908 she arranged for the Cosmopolitan Club, an interracial group, to have a dinner at a Manhattan restaurant with speeches by prominent socialists, educators, and journalists. The Southern papers, tipped off to the affair (some suspected by Booker T. Washington), seized on the evening as "an orgy with drinking and lovemaking between voluptuous white women and smirking black men," an "equality love feast." The Savannah *News* observed that the "high priestess, Miss Ovington, whose father is rich and who affiliates five days in every week with Negro men and dines with them at her home in Brooklyn . . . could have had a hundred thousand Negroes at the Bacchanal feast had she waved the bread tray." The dinner's notoriety led it to be denounced on the floor of the U.S. Senate.

This time, Villard took it upon himself to manage skillfully the noninvolvement of the Wizard. Remaining on at least civil terms with him would be essential if the new organization hoped to tap into the powerful white benefactors whose loyalty Washington controlled. Fund-raising had always been a problem for the Niagara Movement, a failure that some thought partly attributable to Washington's obstructions. Villard courteously invited him to the May 1909 gathering and respectfully promised that the new organization would not be aligned with anti-Tuskegee factions, but at the same time made sure Washington knew that something radical was afoot, something with which he might not wish to be publicly identified. Washington seemed to get the hint, and to the relief of all, replied that pressing work in the South would keep him from attending.

The two-day conference, held in the historic Great Hall at Cooper Union where Lincoln had won acclaim for his first 1860 presidential candidacy with his famous "Right Makes Might" lecture, reflected the broad spectrum of the day's thinking and concern about the race issue. The first day involved a talk by Du Bois about the importance of blacks achieving political status in order to advance economically (a gentle assault on Washington's philosophy), as well as anthropological presentations meant to put to rest the question of whether black people were like other human beings. In one of these presentations, the brains of a white, a Negro, and an ape were exhibited in order to allow delegates and reporters to note the identical appearance of the white and black brains.

The second day took on a more spirited, less academic tone, as Ida Wells-Barnett, speaking on the topic "Lynching: Our National Crime," recounted for the assembly the lynching statistics of the past decade. "No other nation, civilized or savage, burns its criminals," Wells-Barnett stated. "Only under the Stars and Stripes is the human holocaust possible." Discussions intensified as it came time to choose a steering committee and to word resolutions stating the group's aims. Generally, the people in control of the conference—Ovington, Villard, and to a lesser degree Du Bois—attempted to guide a middle course, both in the selection of committee members and in shaping the message of unity that would emanate from them; individuals not known for their ability to compromise, such as Wells-Barnett and William Monroe Trotter, were shunted to the side. Wells-Barnett seethed quietly, but Trotter misbehaved, raising his voice to speak over others' comments and fighting every small change in the language of the resolutions. Trotter, as ever, was the antithesis of an organization man, unless it was an organization he happened to be running, and in any case he probably would never have thrived in the NAACP because of his distrust of whites. At one point a black woman in the audience jumped up and exclaimed, "They are betraying us again—these white friends of ours!" It was true that the whites, in their planning, had made certain judgments in advance of hearing the blacks' views. "I find myself still occasionally forgetting that the Negroes aren't poor people for whom I must kindly do something," Ovington later admitted, "and then comes a gathering such as that last evening and I learn they are men with most forceful opinions of their own."

The final resolutions struck a balance between conservative and radical notions, acknowledging the Tuskegee line that "the transformation of the unskilled colored laborers in industry and agriculture into skilled workers is of vital importance," but demanding access to education at all levels and the enforcement of the Fourteenth and Fifteenth Amendments, while characterizing the right to vote as central to blacks' economic betterment.

The New York Times gave the Cooper Union gathering a relatively benign write-up, although not without alluding to two of the more incendiary views expressed at the meeting, both of which it took out of context—attorney Clarence Darrow's suggestion that blacks stage a work stoppage to protest harsh conditions in the South, and anthropologist Franz Boas's observation that the "Negro Problem" would ultimately be solved through the "amalgamation" of the races. *The World* headlined its coverage "Whites and Negroes Mix at Conference," then inserted the obnoxious subhead "Absence of Young White Women Is Deplored by One Colored Delegate." As could be expected, the Southern press took a dim view of the proceedings, the Raleigh *Observer* heading its story "More Fool Negroes" and expressing mocking regret that, instead of plotting a social revolution, some of the "loud-talking agitators could not be forced to make connection with a plow and a mule."

In denying Ida Wells-Barnett a leadership role with the NAACP, Mary White Ovington later said, organizers had been acting on their conviction that Wells-Barnett "had to play a lone hand." Wells-Barnett would have very little to do with the new organization, even when it launched an extensive antilynching crusade, although she continued to play her "lone hand" admirably: in 1909 she managed to force the state of Illinois for the first time to punish a sheriff who had allowed a lynch mob to remove a prisoner from his custody.

Ever since the New Orleans lynchings of eleven Italian Americans in 1891, several states had moved to curb collusion between mobs and law officers. By the early years of the new century Alabama and Indiana had instituted a system of fines for sheriffs who lost prisoners to mobs, and Ohio had made counties liable for as much as five thousand dollars to the families of mob victims. States such as Ohio and Illinois had modest lynching problems compared with Alabama and other Southern locales, and then most often in their own southernmost rural counties, which often contained a high percentage of citizens who had emigrated from Southern states. There had been thirty lynchings in Illinois since 1882, half of the victims white. In 1905, Edward Green, the lone black representative in the Illinois legislature, succeeded in producing a law stating that a sheriff or deputy who had a prisoner taken from his custody would be presumed unfit for his office and made to resign. The lynching of a person under police protection, the law decreed, was "conclusive evidence of the failure on the part of such sheriff to do his duty."

Green's law received its first test after a lynching in downstate Cairo. On November 8, 1909, a white woman named Anna Pelly, twenty-four, was found raped and murdered in an alley, strangled to death. There was more than the usual outpouring of sympathy for the victim, for Pelly, a well-liked salesgirl at Pupkin's Dry Goods, was recently orphaned and resided with a married sister. She had been on her way home from Pupkin's about suppertime when, disembarking from a trolley car in a light drizzle, she had apparently been forced into an alley, gagged with a piece of cloth, and assaulted. In addition to the blue marks on her throat where she had been strangled, her face was swollen on one side; police surmised that she had been struck one fierce, overwhelming blow in an attempt to render her unconscious. Her parasol had been found broken off at the handle, evidence that she had struggled with her attacker.

Bloodhounds traced the scent on the piece of cloth used to gag Pelly to the home of William "Froggie" James. A teamster for the Cairo Ice and Coal Company, James was a large, powerful black man, his strength developed from his occupation of shoveling coal and lifting heavy blocks of ice; he would have had no problem, the newspaper noted, subduing Anna Pelly. It was also reported that he appeared "nervous and uneasy" when the hounds barked and snapped at him, and his answers to questions about his whereabouts on the night of the crime struck his interrogators as vague. James emphatically denied killing anyone, and said he'd gone directly home from work that evening because he felt unwell, a story confirmed by his sister. Police had found a damaging piece of evidence at James's home, however—a handkerchief matching the cloth used on the murdered woman.

A lynch mob had already begun to form, so Alexander County sheriff Frank Davis spirited James out of town on a northbound train. About twenty-five miles north of Cairo, however, the sheriff and his deputy, Tom Fuller, learned that a mob was waiting to seize James at an upcoming station. The lawmen and their prisoner hastily disembarked and spent the night walking through the woods. Davis's plan was to head overland in an easterly direction to the town of Mill Creek and there attempt to board another northbound train.

In the morning, in order not to arouse suspicion, the officers took the handcuffs off James, and at one point the three walked along a railroad track in single file in an effort to look like hobos. But when Sheriff Davis entered a store at the town of Karnak to buy food, he was recognized. Word got back to Cairo and an armed posse came in pursuit. Davis's party was discovered late in the afternoon lying in some weeds near the railroad tracks outside Belknap, waiting to jump a freight train under cover of darkness. The sheriff fired his gun in the air as a warning, but the posse was not intimidated and he was quickly disarmed. People emerged from their doorways to hiss and spit at the bound prisoner as Davis, Deputy Fuller, and Froggie James were marched through the town of Belknap to the train depot.

When their train came to a halt at Cairo's Union Station, Davis made one more effort to persuade the crowd not to stage a lynching, but his plea was ignored. James was dragged into town and hanged from the steel arch over Eighth and Commercial, the town's main intersection. Someone had the ingenious idea to turn on the electric lights that illuminated the arch, and for a moment the crowd was treated to a surreal tableau of a large, slowly strangulating black man profiled against the dusk sky and the festive bulbs of the arch. As the crowd shouted "Burn him! Burn him!" Anna Pelly's sister and several other women suddenly seized the rope and pulled hard, until James's boot heels were spinning high above. Everyone took this as the signal to open fire.

It was later estimated that no fewer than five hundred bullets entered James's body, introducing enough lead weight to cause it to come crashing to the ground. Cheering, the mob then dragged the body up Washington Street and, reaching the place where Pelly had been found raped and murdered, cut off James's head and stuck it on a fence post. A huge bonfire was built and the rest of the corpse was burned, once the heart and other organs were removed to be sold as keepsakes.

The mob was by now in such a frenzied state it set off in search of other black "suspects." The town's entire black population having, for the moment, vanished, a pack of shouting men and boys invaded the jail, seized a white man named Henry Salzner awaiting trial for murdering his wife, and hanged him in a courtyard.

———

Hearing of the events downstate, Wells-Barnett and other prominent Chicago blacks telegrammed Governor Charles S. Deneen, citing Illinois's antilynching law and demanding that Frank Davis be ousted from his position as sheriff of Alexander County. It was ironic that Davis would wind up the target of this effort, as he had clearly made strenuous efforts to save Froggie James, and had hardly been complicit with the mob, as sheriffs were in many lynchings, but Wells-Barnett believed it important to attempt to exercise the state's new antilynching statute. Davis's critics pointed out that his adventures hiding in the countryside with Froggie James would not have been necessary in the first place if he and his men hadn't allowed themselves to become preoccupied with solving Miss Pelly's murder and had paid closer attention to the emotions being whipped up over the case. Davis had requested the help of the state militia only when the lynching was already under way, and had surrendered to the posse when it had found him, rather than shoot to protect his prisoner. After some hesitation, Governor Deneen acted on the request and fired the sheriff.

The 1905 law stipulated that an officer removed from his post had the right to a hearing at which he could offer reasons for his reinstatement. Friends of the sheriff's had already canvassed the black community in Cairo, securing signatures on a petition on behalf of Davis. Wells-Barnett traveled to Cairo and found that many blacks were willing to assume that, since Froggie James had a reputation as a rough character, he was probably guilty and deserved his fate. Others supported Davis because he was a Republican and had appointed a few black deputies. Learning that many of the signatures had been obtained by posting the petitions at the town's two black barbershops, Wells visited both and attempted to convince those who had signed to reconsider. "There were only a few signers present when I was there," she later said, "but to the few who happened to be standing around I gave the most blistering talk that I could lay my tongue to." She also managed, with local assistance, to arrange emergency meetings with Cairo's black citizens and a group of black clergymen. At both she persuaded people to help word and sign a resolution that would counter Davis's petition.

At the hearing in Springfield, Wells-Barnett and the lone black attorney who had volunteered to assist her faced a committee of highly respected whites who'd agreed to support Davis's reinstatement, including a U.S. land commissioner and a state senator. The sheriff had also gathered statements of endorsement from many other prominent individuals—priests, businessmen, bankers, and merchants, as well as the mayor of Cairo.

Wells-Barnett's chief argument was that were Davis to be returned to his post and the punishment established by the 1905 law disregarded, the state would miss an opportunity to show convincingly that mob violence would not be tolerated. Ultimately, Governor Deneen—no doubt with the recent shame of Springfield on his mind—allowed himself to be swayed by her contention that what had happened in Cairo could not be swept under the rug just because Davis had influential friends. On December 6 he announced that Davis would not be reinstated, saying, "Mob violence has no place in Illinois. It is denounced in every line of the Constitution and in every statute . . . our legislature has spoken in no uncertain terms."

Given that Sheriff Davis and other Alexander County Republicans had supported him in the previous election, Deneen's was a politically courageous act, although some were willing to credit Wells-Barnett's role in forcing the issue. As the Chicago *Defender* exclaimed, "If we only had a few men with the backbone of Mrs. Barnett, lynching would soon come to a halt in America." Indeed, after the 1909 killings of Froggie James and Henry Salzner, there was never another lynching recorded in the state of Illinois.

Not that people gave up trying. The very next spring a mob attempted to abduct two alleged black pickpockets from the Alexander County jail. This time, Sheriff Nelis, the man who had replaced Davis, bolstered his guard and issued orders to shoot the first would-be lynchers who dared cross the threshold. When the charge came, Nelis's men opened fire, killing John Halliday, son of a former mayor of Cairo, and injuring several others. The mob retreated, carrying its wounded, and did not return.

Wells-Barnett had convincingly shown that antilynching laws had the potential to reform officers' behavior, for the fate of his predecessor had clearly been on Sheriff Nelis's mind. What remained unknown was whether lawmen in those parts of the country that had more entrenched lynching traditions could also be educated to stop relinquishing prisoners to mobs.

In the history of the resistance to lynching, few events would prove more auspicious than the founding of the NAACP. With its twin convictions that basic rights were unjustly denied black citizens and that agitation was required to secure them, the organization represented a spirit of resolve that had been sorely missing from the lives of black and white Americans. Aligning the humanistic spirit of the abolitionists with the militant race consciousness of the Niagara Movement, drawing on the spirit of T. Thomas Fortune's Afro-American Council (formerly the Afro-American League) and the progressive impulse of Socialists and settlement-house workers, it was the long-awaited response to the systematic stripping away of human rights that had afflicted America since the end of Reconstruction. Lynching—the complete disavowal of a black person's humanity and rights—was an obvious target for the NAACP's radicalism, and the group initiated a pitched campaign against the practice almost as soon as its operations began in 1910–11.

Du Bois and the NAACP understood, as had Wells-Barnett, that the war on lynching would to a great extent be a contest of language. Inflammatory newspaper articles and political demagoguery propped up lynching ideology, both goading mobs into action and helping to define their deeds in positive terms, while the thick use of euphemism in newspaper articles about "determined men" seeking to give "black brutes" a hearing in "Judge Lynch's Court" too often succeeded in skewing or obscuring the reality of such crimes. The NAACP set out to reverse the very language of lynching by emphasizing the criminality of lynchers and those who protected them, and to rub America's face in the gritty business of hanging, shooting, and roasting defenseless human beings. "I can think of no more nauseating work for a kindly set of people than this task of setting forth brutality," Ovington later wrote. "But it was necessary to shake the nation out of its complacency and to superimpose on the picture of the black brute . . . the picture of the white brute, taking his pleasure in a bestiality that we now understand only too well, and that we have learned to fear as we fear nothing else."

It came as a kind of strange gift to the NAACP propagandists that one of the first lynchings they publicized was also one of the more bizarre incidents of civic violence in American history. During a barroom brawl in Livermore, Kentucky, in April 1911, a black man named Will Porter allegedly shot a white man named Frank Mitchell. Porter was immediately placed under arrest. The sheriff, knowing that a lynch mob was forming and not wanting his jail violated, had the clever idea to hide Porter in the basement of the local opera house. The mob discovered the sheriff's scheme, however, and stormed the building. Quickly locating Porter in the basement, they bound him hand and foot and dragged him upstairs.

The mob's leaders then acted on a perverse inspiration. Kicking aside some scenery, they tied Porter to a pole at center stage and informed the crowd waiting for the culprit to be carried outside and put to death that the lynching would take place inside the theater. Two different kinds of seats would be sold for the "performance." An orchestra seat would allow the patron to empty a six-shooter at Porter, while those in the balcony would be limited to one shot, with all proceeds going to the family of Frank Mitchell, who was not expected to recover from his wounds.

Fifty men paid the admission and quickly found seats. The mob was unsure how to turn the stage lights on, so the event took place in an eerie semidarkness, Porter's silhouette barely illuminated from behind. The sound of fifty weapons blazing in an empty theater was so earsplitting, dozens of frightened rats went scurrying across the stage as Porter's body was perforated by gunfire.

"Of about 200 shots fired," reported *The New York Times,* "nearly half entered the body of the black man and the remainder tore to shreds the woodland scenery arranged for the presentation of a much milder drama.

"In the residents of Livermore," the paper concluded, "the dramatic sense is strongly developed . . . it is quite certain that the Negro who made in the Livermore opera house his first and last appearance on any stage will never again offend the delicate and tender sensibilities of his fellow townsmen."

The NAACP investigated and publicized the Porter killing, and sent resolutions denouncing the crime to members of Congress and the governor of Kentucky, as well as releasing information about the affair to the Associated Press and a number of newspapers. A delegation of citizens from Washington, D.C., was allowed to present President William Howard Taft with a copy of the resolution, although he demurred that lynching was not a federal matter. The NAACP's agitation did help arouse condemnation in Kentucky, where eighteen men were arrested for their role in the opera-house lynching. All were rapidly acquitted, but the fledgling civil rights organization could claim a small victory in that the lynchers had been publicly identified and detained, however briefly.

The Livermore lynching so thoroughly epitomized the unenlightened backwardness associated with the rural South, it was almost laughable. It was certainly the kind of grotesque occurrence from which most Americans could feel comfortable distancing themselves. But the comforting sense of distance from hideous Southern customs would be strained four months later when a disgraceful spectacle lynching occurred in eastern Pennsylvania, within a half-day's travel of New York and Washington,

D.C. The incident raised the distinct and troubling question of whether Northern whites would be able to adapt to the influx of Southern blacks into their communities without adopting the lynching tradition.

Coatesville, forty miles west of Philadelphia, was a burgeoning steel-mill town in a lush valley on the Brandywine Creek. Since 1900 the town's population had more than doubled, from 4,500 to 12,000, thanks to the presence of the town's two booming industries, the Worth Brothers Steel Company and the Lukens Iron Works, and the aggressive recruitment of Southern and immigrant labor. Agents who toured the South glowingly described to blacks and their families Coatesville's ample work opportunities, its electrically lit Main Street, the mills' average pay of $1.50 per day, and the absence of Jim Crow segregation.

On Saturday night, August 12, 1911, Zachariah Walker, a recent arrival from Virginia, emerged from a Coatesville saloon and began shooting a revolver into the air. He was immediately intercepted by Edgar Rice, a former town policeman now employed as a special police officer for the Worth Brothers mill. Rice had a reputation for reasonableness and for discreetly steering drunks home before they could get into trouble with their wives or the police. He was also a respected family man and a member of the local volunteer fire company.

Walker, who was drunk, resisted Rice's efforts to restrain him. "Quit leaning against me," Rice told Walker. "If you don't come with me I'll hit you over the head with this club."

"Hit me and I will kill you!" shouted Walker.

The two men began to tussle, Walker holding his gun in one hand and throwing punches with the other. Rice struck Walker with his nightstick in an attempt to subdue him, but then dropped it or had it knocked from his hands, and immediately drew his gun. Walker, seeing the officer's weapon, fired three times into Rice, who staggered a few paces and fell to the ground, dead.

Walker fled into the pitch-black countryside, pursued by Chief of Police Charles E. Umsted and a posse that included Rice's fellow volunteer firemen, police colleagues, some mill workers, and Captain Al Berry, an itinerant hot air balloonist who had performed just the day before at a local harvest festival. Even the Worth brothers themselves, William and Sharpless, drove out in their big touring car to see if they could be of help.

The fugitive eluded the searchers all night by hiding in a barn. In a farmer's orchard early the next morning he climbed a cherry tree, put his gun to his ear, and pulled the trigger in an attempt to take his own life, succeeding only in fracturing his jaw. Surrounded and taken into custody, he was driven to the police station—known, on account of Chief Umsted's girth, as "Fort Jumbo"—then on to the Coatesville Hospital, where his wound was dressed. Out of fear he would try to kill himself again, attendants placed Walker in a straitjacket with his legs chained to the footboard of his bed.

There was no doubt that Walker had murdered Rice. He was found in possession of Rice's gun and later, when Chief Umsted visited him in the hospital, he made a full confession. "I was too quick for him," said Walker. "I killed him easy." But he explained he had fired only because the officer had drawn a gun on him.

In town there was talk of little else. "For hours groups on the sidewalk discussed the worthlessness of Walker and the value of Rice," recalled a local historian. Rumors about the black murderer were rampant all day in the town—that he'd been taken away to Philadelphia, that he'd shot himself, that he was dead—until someone ascertained that he was still very much alive and convalescing in the local hospital. At a little after eight o'clock that night a mob of workmen and teenage boys surged up the street toward the institution, situated on a steep hill overlooking one part of the town. On the front lawn the crowd held back; then a ringleader strode up onto the hospital portico and addressed the throng: "Men of Coatesville, will you let a drunken Negro do up such a man as Rice?"

"No!" came the reply, and the crowd stormed into the building past frightened doctors, nurses, and patients.

Chief Umsted, it was later revealed, spent much of Sunday evening walking up and down Main Street, telling groups of listeners about his role in the exciting capture of the fugitive. At one point the balloonist, Al Berry, pleaded with Umsted to drive to the other side of town because there was talk of a lynching. When Umsted waved away the suggestion, dismissing the mob as "a lot of young fellows and some of them don't know how to carry a gun," Berry became impatient, reminding the chief that he personally had dissuaded the men who arrested Walker from lynching him earlier that day in the orchard. Umsted turned on him, bellowing, "You are God damned popular for a man that has only been in town a few days. You might be able to run a hot air balloon, but you cannot run me."

Back at the hospital, the mob found itself unable to disentangle Walker completely from the bed, so he was dragged from the building with his legs still attached to the footboard. They carried him up the hill from the hospital along a winding road that led to open farmland. "For God's sake, give a man a chance," Walker begged, as his captors lashed him to a fence post. "I killed Rice in self-defense. Don't give me a crooked death because I'm not white." It had rained the night before so finding the fuel for a bonfire proved difficult, but volunteers who entered a nearby barn found and removed armloads of hay and straw, and added it to some dry chestnut fence rails they'd come upon. The wood and other flammable materials were stacked around Walker's feet and oil was poured over him.

By now word of Walker's abduction had reached the townspeople back at the bottom of the hill, and a crowd surged uphill to the site of the burning. According to the West Chester *Daily Local News,* "5,000 men, women and children stood by and watched the proceedings as though it were a ball game or another variety of outdoor sport." The Coatesville *Record* noted: "Everything was quiet and orderly around the fire, if such a thing can be said of a lynching. There was no loud talking, no profanity, and the utmost deference shown to the hundreds of women who came to the scene. Men stepped back as the women came forward and led them to points of vantage where they could obtain the best view of the burning Negro."

When Walker, in supreme agony, tried to escape the flames, the mob drove him back with pitchforks and fence rails. As in Southern lynchings, many participants remained in the area waiting for the fire to cool, then advanced with pliers, knives, and other implements to secure fingers and toes as souvenirs. Another large contingent adjourned back down the hill for soft drinks and dessert at the Coatesville Candy Company. Concluded the next day's newspaper: "Not in the history of the town has there been so much excitement in Coatesville."

Outside the town, the lynching was an immediate scandal, the stuff of countless editorials and sermons. Pennsylvania had long been regarded as a bastion of Republican-style patriotism, the home of Thaddeus Stevens, Benjamin Franklin, the Liberty Bell, and the hallowed ground of Gettysburg. The area around Coatesville itself had been a stop on the Underground Railroad, and there were still towns nearby that were considered Quaker enclaves. That such an event could occur where it had was deeply shocking, and residents were further stunned when a photograph of Walker's remains—a blackened and twisted form that was barely recognizable as having once been a human being—was circulated and published along with some of the more outrageous articles.

What distressed people beyond the horror of the lynching itself was a

fear that what had happened in Coatesville meant that lynching as a prac-
tice might be ready to establish itself outside the backwoods South. The
real lesson of Coatesville, William Monroe Trotter wrote in the Boston
Guardian, was that in "not pulling the South up to the standards of the
North in race relations, the North has allowed the South to pull it down
to their level." *The Guardian* carried a photo of the portly president of the
United States over the caption, "Wm Howard Taft—Silent as Citizens are
Burned Alive." The NAACP's monthly magazine, *The Crisis,* ran a car-
toon of a lynching victim in the process of being consumed by fire point-
ing accusingly and in vain toward an apathetic figure of Justice, while Du
Bois's editorial, entitled "Triumph," was as biting as it was lyrical:

> Let the eagle scream! Again the burden of upholding the best traditions of
> Anglo-Saxon civilization has fallen on the sturdy shoulders of the Ameri-
> can republic. Once more a howling mob of the best citizens in a foremost
> State of the Union has vindicated the self-evident superiority of the white
> race. . . .
>   Ah, the splendor of that Sunday night dance. The flames beat and curled
> against the moonlit sky. The church bells chimed. The scorched and
> crooked thing, self-wounded and chained to his cot, crawled to the edge of
> the ash with a stifled groan, but the brave and sturdy farmers pricked him
> back with the bloody pitchforks until the deed was done. Let the eagle
> scream! Civilization is again safe. . . .
>   But let every black American gird up his loins. The great day is coming.
> We have crawled and pleaded for justice and we have been cheerfully spit
> upon and murdered and burned. We will not endure it forever. If we are to
> die, in God's name let us perish like men and not like bales of hay.

The killing was condemned by Coatesville's church and civic groups,
but the town's deeper hurt was finding its name, after generations of quiet
anonymity in the placid hills of eastern Pennsylvania, attached to headlines bearing the likes of "burned alive," "shameful outrage," and
"fiendish barbarism." The question Coatesville had to answer now, as *The
Nation* stated it, was "What would her representative men have to say;
more, what would they do, when they realized the stigma which a lawless
mob had brought upon the place they called home?" Observers seized on
the hope that, if lynching could occur in Pennsylvania as in the South, at
least here in the North it would be shown that lynch mobs could be
brought to justice.

Governor John K. Tener appeared to take seriously the need for a concerted response. He issued a proclamation denouncing the affair and exhorted a grand jury to remove the blot of lynching from the state by indicting the guilty parties, ordering his subordinates to spare neither time nor expense in prosecuting the case.

On August 16, eight defendants were indicted, including Chief of Police Umsted, Deputy Stanley Howe, and several mill employees, including George Stoll, sixteen, Joseph Swartz, eighteen, and Norman Price, twenty-one. Talk of a lynching had spread throughout Coatesville in the hours before it took place, the grand jury stated, and Umsted had ample opportunity to take steps to protect Walker. It was also said the chief wasted precious time investigating Walker's abduction from the hospital even as the mob was up the road lynching him. Umsted was clearly either negligent or complicit in the affair.

The trials began with a full head of steam but one by one juries found reasons to acquit the mostly young defendants. There appeared to be strong local resentment that the state was going after mere boys, and offense was taken at the arrest of Chief Umsted and Deputy Howe, precisely because, like the martyred Edgar Rice, they were perceived to be law officers simply doing their jobs. Judge William Butler later said the jurymen did not even appear to seriously consider the evidence. They consistently ignored testimony from mob members who had turned state's evidence and handed back verdicts in minutes rather than the hours that would have been necessary to sift through and evaluate all the relevant information. They were, in the end, farmers who wanted to get back to their harvesting and who clearly thought jury service, particularly as it concerned the death of a "no-count nigger" such as Zach Walker, an utter waste of time.

After the acquittals, District Attorney Robert Gwathney asked the state's supreme court for a change of venue, which was at first denied. But even when the case was moved elsewhere the result was the same, as witnesses from Coatesville experienced lapses of memory, told intentionally confusing versions of what had occurred, or simply lied. Judge Butler concluded: "For some reason that I am entirely unable to understand, a sentiment in this county . . . is utterly opposed to the prosecution and conviction of anybody and of everybody who took part in this horrible affair." As a writer in the West Chester paper observed, the legal proceedings had made as much a mockery of justice as had the original lynching. Ultimately, prosecutors and judges alike concluded that a fair trial would not be possible, and that, as historian William Ziglar has observed, "to continue would only further stain the pursuit of justice."

This result was supremely embarrassing. Many people in the North had smugly anticipated that, though nothing could be done to undo the ghoulish lynching itself, Pennsylvania would certainly show its ethical and moral superiority to the South by swiftly bringing the guilty parties to justice. Events had made a mockery of that confidence, and Governor Tener, taking a last swipe at the lynch mob and the environment that protected it, took the extraordinary step of threatening to revoke the charter of the Borough of Coatesville, accusing the town itself of "consorting with and shielding murderers." But this idea was strongly criticized and never pursued.

The governor's threat against Coatesville likely resulted from the pressure brought by the NAACP. The organization had followed the case closely, dispatching field secretary Mary Maclean to investigate. She returned with the view that District Attorney Gwathney himself was in on the plot to thwart prosecution, perhaps out of fear, since it was known he had received death threats. As a result, in the summer of 1912 the NAACP hired the William J. Burns Detective Agency to attempt to gather evidence against the lynchers. The Burns operatives opened a hot dog stand in Coatesville as a screen for their activities, detectives posing as vendors. As everyone in town knew who the lynchers were, it didn't take long for the Burns men, making chitchat with their customers, to learn what had happened and who was to blame. In September, Villard, Burns, NAACP legal counsel William Wherry, and journalist Albert Jay Nock went to the Pennsylvania capitol in Harrisburg to present their findings to the governor. Tener admitted the Walker lynching was the thing he was most ashamed of during his administration and vowed to resume the prosecution, but the case was allowed to fade away. "People are largely addicted to a number of curious delusions about statutory law," Nock wrote soon after in *American Magazine.* "One of which is that it works by some kind of natural inherent force residing in itself. Really, it does nothing of the kind."

"As the agitation which culminated in the abolition of African slavery in this country covered a period of fifty years," T. Thomas Fortune noted in the early years of the twentieth century, "so may we expect that before the rights conferred upon us by the war amendments are fully conceded, a full century will have passed away. We have undertaken no child's play. We have undertaken a serious work which will tax and exhaust the best intelligence of the race for the next century." Fortune's estimate of an entrenched campaign was echoed by a general NAACP statement of purpose that Du Bois wrote for the organization's annual report in 1915. The NAACP, Du Bois wrote, "conceives its mission to be the completion of the work which the great Emancipator began. It proposes to make a group of ten million Americans free from the lingering shackles of past slavery, physically free from peonage, mentally free from ignorance, politically free from disenfranchisement, and socially free from insult."

One of the quiet miracles of the early NAACP was that Du Bois, often haughty and remote (he was notorious for failing to remember other people's names), managed to successfully bridge the differences between the white organizers and the other black participants to emerge as the group's only black officer, director of publications and research, a job that included the editorship of *The Crisis*. The position, in Du Bois's hands, would become a far more influential one than Villard and others imagined at the time, for it was *The Crisis* that gave the organization its initial profile and public voice.

The journal's name was inspired by the James Russell Lowell poem "The Present Crisis," with its lines seemingly addressed directly to Du Bois and his colleagues:

> *Once to every man and nation*
> *comes the moment to decide.*
> *In the strife of Truth with Falsehood,*
> *on the good or evil side;*
> *Some great cause, God's new Messiah,*
> *offering each the bloom or blight,*
> *Parts the goats upon the left hand,*
> *and the sheep upon the right,*
> *And the choice goes by forever*
> *'twixt that darkness and that light.*

The Crisis, which first appeared in November 1910, was guided by the same sensibility that had illuminated Du Bois's *The Souls of Black Folk*— enlightened political and social criticism blended with a profound love of black people and a deeply rooted faith in their pride and originality. Du Bois shaped *The Crisis* to reflect in unprecedented ways the whole gamut of the black American experience. Features included such regular columns as "The Colored College Athlete," "Men of the Month," and

"What To Read," as well as Du Bois's aphoristic editorials and coverage of lynchings and other racial conflicts. More innovative was Du Bois's internationalist orientation, giving news and perspective on racial affairs in foreign lands, such as South Africa, and affirming the connection between the lives of black Americans and all the world's people of color, an editorial perception that was unique in the black press of the period.

The first issue of *The Crisis* sold 1,000 copies. By 1912 more than 16,000 copies of each issue were reaching readers, by 1913 30,000, and by 1918 100,000. "In an era of rampant illiteracy," historian David Levering Lewis notes, "when hard labor left Afro-Americans with little time or inclination for reading Harvard-accented editorials, the magazine found its way into kerosene-lit sharecroppers' cabins and cramped factory workers' tenements. In middle-class families it lay next to the Bible." *The Crisis* quickly became America's leading black publication, and would remain an integral part of black cultural life until the 1950s.

The white founders of the NAACP had not foreseen to how great an extent the editor of the publication would come to represent the organization itself, and Du Bois stood apart from the whites naturally in that he could speak to issues of blackness with an authority with which others could not begin to compete. The tension this caused ultimately led to a break between Du Bois and Villard, who felt Du Bois had put too much of his own personality into the publication, making *The Crisis* too much a reflection of his own strong opinions rather than a mouthpiece for the NAACP. (It couldn't have helped matters much that Villard was prohibited by his Georgia-born wife from bringing any black people, including Du Bois, into their home.) Du Bois had a staunch defender in Ovington, who admitted to Villard that she simply believed too much in Du Bois's genius not to defer to him, despite the more prickly side of his personality. She later told NAACP board director Joel Spingarn, who accused her of idolizing Du Bois, that she did indeed "worship genius," and that she believed sincerely that Du Bois was "the master builder, whose work will speak to men as long as there is an oppressed race on earth."

That Du Bois had a genius for the work was never much in doubt. Ovington had been convinced of it upon reading *The Philadelphia Negro* and *The Souls of Black Folk,* and was reminded of it almost daily. She often spoke of a dramatic slide show Du Bois presented at the close of the 1912 NAACP meeting in Chicago. The audience sat in darkness watching projected silent images of the country's grandest museums, libraries, opera houses, and theaters; only after a dozen or more of these images had been illuminated did it slowly dawn on viewers that their common theme was that they were all off-limits to black people. Next appeared pictures of schools black children could not attend and playgrounds where they could not play, houses where whites lived and blacks could not, and so on, until the projections ended with slides contrasting the different kinds of cemeteries where black and white folk ended up, separated in death as in life. It was a poignant, moving presentation, Ovington reflected, one that could only have been assembled by a poet.

The NAACP, however, had discovered the problem within a problem that has historically plagued integrated activism in America. "I am sick at heart over it," Ovington confided about the tension between Villard and Du Bois. "It means a confession to the world that we cannot work with colored people unless they are our subordinates." She worried that "when we demand that some colored man be put in office . . . we shall be told, 'You can't give a nigger a big job. Haven't you found it out yourselves?' "

At 9:30 P.M. on March 19, 1911, a well-dressed black gentleman was seen walking up and down in front of an apartment building at 11½ West Sixty-third Street in New York City. Every few minutes he entered the vestibule to examine the names on the doorbells. Suddenly a white man, a thirty-four-year-old carpenter named Albert Ulrich who lived in the building and had been observing the stranger, rushed out and assaulted him, accusing him of having said "Hello, sweetheart" to his wife as she had passed by. After pounding him with his fists, Ulrich obtained a cane from a passerby and began bludgeoning the black man, who hardly fought back, and who then attempted a clumsy, desperate escape in the direction of Central Park, a half-block away. Ulrich pursued him to the edge of the park, where several other whites joined in beating and kicking the man, who repeatedly fell to the ground, only to rise and be knocked flat again. He would possibly have been beaten to death if a policeman patrolling in the park had not seen the melee and intervened.

At the Sixty-eighth Street police station, to everyone's astonishment, the bleeding, rumpled victim identified himself as Booker T. Washington of the Tuskegee Institute. He proceeded to file assault charges against Ulrich, who in turn told police that Washington had been lurking around the house, peeping in keyholes, and had made a sexually explicit remark to his wife. Washington, regaining his dignity, denied these charges as ludicrous. He said he had been seeking Daniel C. Smith, the auditor of Tuskegee, who had written to him saying he was staying at that address with friends.

Expressions of support and concern for Washington arrived from across the country. Injured in the head and ear, he had required a trip to the hospital and sixteen stitches to close a wound in his scalp. Andrew Carnegie and President Taft sent telegrams, and the white and black press alike grieved that a benevolent figure such as the Wizard had been subjected to such brutality. Du Bois was also sympathetic, although he heard rumors that the dwelling Washington had visited was not entirely respectable, that it housed high-class prostitutes, and that Washington had visited it before. The Wizard's own explanation of what had happened did sound somewhat half-baked. It was found that Smith, the auditor, maintained an office at 32 Broadway and resided in Montclair, New Jersey, and that both locations were equipped with telephones, suggesting there was no need for Washington to be fumbling around in anyone's doorway at 9:30 at night. When asked to produce Smith's letter instructing him to go to the West Sixty-third Street address, Washington reported that it had mysteriously disappeared.

The Tuskegeean ordered his attorneys to find out all they could about Ulrich, and their efforts were well rewarded: the carpenter, it turned out, had deserted his real wife, who resided in New Jersey. He was living at the Sixty-third Street house with another woman. It also emerged that Ulrich had a somewhat shady reputation as a "dealer in animals," and had been arrested earlier that year and charged with the theft of a prizewinning Pomeranian.

Southern newspapers, of course, made hay with the incident. "It all goes to show that human nature is pretty much the same the world over," noted *The Atlanta Constitution*. "Red blood boils at the same affront—whether real or imaginary—in every part of the civilized world." Southern demagogues such as Tillman, Vardaman, and Tom Watson agreed that Washington should have been killed for his offense, and even the black-published Richmond *Planet* had to concede: "Down here this woman's word would have lifted a less prominent person than Mr. Washington to the limb of a tree." A Southern campaign was launched to help pay Albert Ulrich's legal fees, the donations described as going to serve "the protection of white womanhood."

Although many Northern friends suspected that Washington had not been entirely candid about what had occurred, almost all stood by him, either out of personal regard for his accomplishments or because it was easy to see how damaging the truth would be to the cause of equal rights. Some people may have felt a bit sorry for him. His influence had waned somewhat recently as it became evident the NAACP would stand on its own feet and that the new group intended to fight the very political and moral battles from which he had long shied away. He no doubt also benefited from the fact that a local news story of far greater significance, the March 25 fire at the Triangle Shirtwaist Company in lower Manhattan, in which 146 young garment workers died as a result of employer negligence, soon claimed New York's and the nation's headlines and helped distract public attention from his predicament.

At court, other witnesses seconded Ulrich's contention that Washington had been skulking around the building on the night in question, and Ulrich was acquitted of the assault charge after convincing the judge he had had every reason to believe Washington was either a prowler or a rogue. Washington had to be satisfied with watching Ulrich get taken into custody on the charge of abandoning his wife.

The complete truth of what Washington was doing in front of 11½ West Sixty-third Street that spring night in 1911 was never known. But there was no glossing over the fact that the most respected black man in America had been accused of insulting a white woman and had been beaten by a white mob, nor could Washington erase the impression that he, too, was susceptible to the "brute instinct" so frequently ascribed to his race. His reputation and powerful friends, and the seediness of Ulrich's background, spared him further embarrassment, but there can be little doubt he came away with a more deeply felt understanding of a black man's vulnerability in the white man's world.

Writing History with Lightning

The year 1915 brought two events that showed a country still strug-gling to reconcile itself to the breach represented by the Civil War and Reconstruction. One was the release of America's first major narra-tive film, D. W. Griffith's *The Birth of a Nation,* which combined technical and artistic brilliance with a controversial rendering of Reconstruction that rehashed many of the most enduring and painful Southern myths about black Americans. The other was the lynching in Georgia of Leo Frank, the Jewish manager of a pencil factory, convicted of murdering a thirteen-year-old female employee. This bitterly divisive case pitted Southerners outraged over the defilement of an innocent girl against Northern liberals and Jews who saw in Frank's horrendous fate the tragedy of a good, literate man caught in the unforgiving snare of South-ern lynch-mob justice.

With the lingering effects of the turndown in the Southern economy of the 1890s, the mass migration of blacks to Northern cities, the advance of the women's suffrage movement, and the growing uneasiness that the United States would be drawn into the war in Europe, the stage was set for *The Birth of a Nation*—a masterful and unprecedented "entertainment" that carried Americans back to what now appeared as a simpler, heroic time when a divided America had reunited, and rediscovered its purpose, by suppressing the unruly minority populace in its midst. But black people and organizations such as the NAACP could only stand aghast as thousands flocked to see a spectacular historical melodrama that, while technologically fascinating, deliberately evoked the nation's most disturbing racial themes in ways both offensive and morally reprehensible. It was as if all America had vicariously joined a lynch mob.

The film script was based on two novels by a white North Carolina preacher named Thomas Dixon, who set out in 1901 to write a novel to counter Harriet Beecher Stowe's unflattering depiction of Southern life in *Uncle Tom's Cabin.* The result, *The Leopard's Spots,* set against a backdrop of Reconstruction-era North Carolina where a heroic Ku Klux Klan is driving out Republican corruption, relates the story of a Harvard-educated black who is rebuffed after asking his white benefactor for his daughter's hand in marriage. The novel sold an unheard-of 1 million copies. Dixon's follow-up effort, *The Clansman,* which also sold briskly, is set in the years 1865–70 and tells the story of a Thaddeus Stevens–like character named Austin Stoneman and the romantic liaisons that spring up between Stoneman's family and a South Carolina clan, the Camerons—relationships that become threatened by the wiles of promiscuous blacks, until the Klan rides to the rescue. In one of the most-talked-about sequences in the book, a doctor examining a dead white woman, who leaped from a cliff rather than submit to a black man, identifies the attacker through a microscope when he sees an image of the "brute" imprinted upon her retina.

Dixon was inspired to capitalize on the success of *The Clansman* by turning it into a drama. Trounced by critics, the play nonetheless proved a favorite with audiences, who were particularly thrilled by the use of live horses on stage. Because its subject was so inflammatory, however, many cities banned local productions. Some Atlantans blamed a popular run of the melodrama for helping to spark the destructive 1906 riot.

Seeking a filmmaker who would consider adapting his play for motion pictures, Dixon found little interest until he encountered director David Wark Griffith, who had written and directed numerous one-reel photoplays for Biograph beginning in 1908, but longed for the opportunity to make longer, more substantive films. When in 1913 the Mutual Film Company offered him that chance, he left Biograph, taking with him the studio's talented cameraman G. W. "Billy" Bitzer and one of its most promising stars, Lillian Gish. Griffith, a Kentuckian and the son of a Confederate officer nicknamed "Roaring Jake," believed *The Clansman* provided sufficient drama and sweep for the kind of large-scale movie he wished to create. Eleven of the one-reelers he had made for Biograph were Civil War melodramas, and Griffith was aware that he had already helped kindle the public's fascination with the idea of the Civil War as a metaphor for the rededication of America as an enlightened, unified nation. Interest in the subject was particularly keen, Griffith knew, as the country prepared to observe the fiftieth anniversary of Appomattox and Lincoln's assassination.

The movie, filmed in the suburbs of Los Angeles between July and October 1914, was the longest American motion picture ever made—two and a half hours, twelve reels, in an era when four or five reels was considered exceptional. Like many later Hollywood spectaculars, the film was over budget—the actors worked on deferred salaries and sewed their own costumes; Griffith and Bitzer were forced to put up their life savings to keep production going—and before filming ended there were rumors that the director had lost his mind. But if the ambitious project had an ad hoc working spirit, it was one that led Griffith and Bitzer to pioneer innovations that would soon become staples of the new art form—the close-up, the long vista shot, the montage, the fade-out, the iris dissolve, the chase, and the climactic action sequence.

When the film, at that point still titled *The Clansman,* was screened in Los Angeles in February 1915, that city's branch of the NAACP alerted Villard, Du Bois, and the New York office that "every resource of a magnificent new art" was being employed "to picture Negroes in the worst possible light." Immediately, the NAACP's opposition to the film was announced by Villard and Moorfield Storey, the Boston attorney who had once clerked for Charles Sumner and who served as president of the NAACP. The film's creators were not in the least surprised. They had anticipated their work would come under attack, as had Dixon's novels and play. Yet they were also confident they had manufactured something grand and unprecedented—perhaps they'd even made history. At the end of one screening prior to the film's release, Dixon admitted to Griffith that he now felt his original title, *The Clansman,* was far too modest for so sweeping and triumphant a film. What if it were called *The Birth of a Nation?*

The stage for the controversy that would engulf *The Birth of a Nation* had been set a few years earlier by a very different kind of motion picture—the fight films of the charismatic black boxer Jack Johnson, the world heavyweight champion during the years 1908–15. Fight films were among the most popular of all the early motion pictures exhibited, shown in saloons or in special theatrical venues or tacked on to the end of vaudeville shows. Black fighters appeared from time to time in these films, usually seen in defeat or behaving as cheats or cowards.

Johnson, however, beginning with his 1908 defeat of Tommy Burns in Sydney, Australia, demonstrated that he was a new kind of black pugilist; he was not only a magnificent-looking man who won handily, he was said to laugh at his hapless white opponents, and his life out of the ring only seemed to enlarge on his daring inside it, for he liked to drive fast cars, extravagantly entertain his friends, and date white women. When the film of Johnson besting Burns was exhibited in the United States in 1909, many white fight fans were exasperated. As the legendary fighter "Gentleman" Jim Corbett sadly remarked, "The white man has succumbed to a type which in the past was conceded to be his inferior in physical and mental prowess."

Calls went out for Jim Jeffries, a former white champion who had retired from the ring because there were no suitable opponents left for him to fight, to return and redeem the world boxing stage from the "Ethiopian Colossus." Before Jeffries, whom the sports pages instantly dubbed the "Great White Hope," could encounter Johnson, a previously scheduled bout took place between Johnson and Stanley Ketchel on October 16, 1909. Australian authorities had had the good taste to clip the actual ending of the film showing Johnson beating Burns, but the film of the Johnson-Ketchel fight left little to the imagination. In the last sequence, Ketchel knocked Johnson to the mat, but the black man rose and connected hard to Ketchel's face, sending him sprawling to the canvas, where he lay unconscious. Worse, Johnson then stood by nonchalantly, hand on hip, looking down at his prostrate opponent as the referee counted Ketchel out. This image went around the world like a shot. As one scholar of the Johnson-Ketchel film has noted, "The movies, along with the widely reprinted still photos of Johnson standing over an unconscious white hope, confronted white viewers with an historically unprecedented image of black power."

When Johnson and Jeffries finally met in Reno on July 4, 1910, the fight was more evenly matched, but Johnson's conditioning gave him an edge, and in the fifteenth round he twice sent Jeffries reeling to the mat. Rising the second time, Jeffries appeared disoriented, so the referee stopped the fight and declared Johnson the winner.

Clearly unhappy about Johnson's staying power as champ, a chorus of voices in the United States called for the film of the Johnson-Jeffries bout to be suppressed. A number of religious and temperance groups were already opposed to fight films of any kind, and seized on the popular disgust with Jack Johnson to attack them anew, as did several prominent editorial writers. A point of view most frequently heard in the South was that it was wrong to delude the Negro race by showing such falsely encouraging images. Congress, responding to this outburst of concern, passed legislation banning the interstate transportation of prizefight films, a law clearly intended to halt their exhibition entirely since virtually all fight films, many of which originated abroad, had to be shipped across state lines.

Once authorities had established a method to suppress Johnson's movies, they geared up to go after the man himself, for his not-so-private private life was to many even more disturbing than his successes in the ring. The White Slave Traffic Act of 1910, better known as the Mann Act after its author, Representative James R. Mann of Illinois, forbade the transportation of women in interstate or foreign commerce "for the purpose of prostitution or debauchery, or for any other immoral purpose." The law was nominally aimed at commercialized vice, but was written broadly enough to make it applicable to virtually any woman other than one's lawfully wedded spouse. In 1912 the government used the newly minted statute to prosecute Johnson after a Minneapolis woman alleged that her daughter, eighteen-year-old Lucille Cameron, had been taken by Johnson to Chicago for "immoral purposes."

By the time of his arrest, most whites and even some blacks had come to hold a disapproving view of a celebrity who so flagrantly defied convention and pushed the boundaries of acceptable good taste. "It goes to prove my contention that all men should be educated along mental and spiritual lines," Booker T. Washington said of the trouble Johnson now found himself in, "[for] a man with muscle minus brains is a useless creature." But it was also clear that the government was out to get Johnson as certainly as any lynch mob seeks its victim. He was burned in effigy in white neighborhoods, and cries of "Lynch him! Lynch the nigger!" were heard whenever he appeared. Southern newspapers made no secret of their belief that the boxer should, as one put it, be "given the hemp." His "obnoxious stunts," commented the Beaumont, Texas, *Journal,* "are not only worthy of but demand an overgrown dose of Southern 'hospitality.' "

Johnson seemed unfazed by the ridicule; indeed, he was probably the first black man in America with the power and stature to consciously goad whites with behavior deemed "lynchable." Confronted with his legal difficulties, he stood defiant: "I want to say that I am not a slave and that I have the right to choose who my mate shall be without the dictation of any man. I have eyes and I have a heart, and when they fail to tell me who I shall have for mine I want to be put away in a lunatic asylum." Of Washington's arrogant remarks, Johnson deftly countered, "I never got caught in the wrong flat. I never got beat up because I looked in the wrong keyhole."

The government's case against Johnson was transparently designed to convict a black man for having white girlfriends, so to forestall prosecution, Johnson married Lucille Cameron. But government agents then dug up one of Johnson's earlier white paramours, a woman named Belle Schreiber with whom he had had a long relationship and who was willing to testify against him. Johnson was charged with transporting her from Pittsburgh to Chicago on August 10, 1910, one month after the Mann Act had gone into effect. Johnson's defense was that he had indeed traveled with Schreiber across state lines, but that he had enjoyed an ongoing relationship with her and was not guilty under the Mann Act of transporting her solely for the purpose of engaging in commercial sex.

Despite the speciousness of the government's case, Johnson was doomed from the start, for he had become a symbol of the country's obsession with the sin of miscegenation, the fear, as Georgia congressman Seaborn A. Rodenberry told the House of Representatives, that if "sombre-hued, black-skinned, thick-lipped, bull-necked, brutal-hearted African" men could marry white women, war between the races would be unavoidable. Convicted in the summer of 1913, Johnson went into self-imposed exile in Europe rather than serve time for a crime he and everyone else in America knew he had not committed.

Johnson, even as a fugitive from justice, did not lose the affection of black Americans, indeed of people of color the world over who learned of his exploits. In a sense, by his very example of physically dominating white men, enjoying the company of white women, and refusing to be intimidated by those who didn't like his behavior, his life was a powerful rebuff to the lynching ethos, casting those who threatened lynching as cowards. His tormentors, it was apparent, were unable to acknowledge that an individual black man might in some ways be superior to them, and could beat them in fair competition. In retrospect, Johnson's ordeal was partly a result of the fact that he had come along a decade before his time. After World War I and the tremendous growth of black pride the war era produced, the so-called New Negro would emerge, a type for which Johnson had clearly been an outrider. The NAACP would be in the vanguard of the New Negro movement—no longer content to merely expose lynchings in the hope exposure would lead to their eradication, but challenging the practice directly in a concerted effort to make it a federal crime.

Thomas Dixon, like Jack Johnson, knew what it was to be targeted. He didn't much mind what black critics said of him—he had no respect for the "Negro Intermarriage Society," as he disparaged the fledgling NAACP (in fact he suspected their hostility might be useful for promotion)—but what was of real concern was the possibility that censors or other public officials might be moved to block exhibition of his and Griffith's masterwork.

Film censorship has always been an ambiguous affair in America due to the nation's reluctance to place governmental restraints on freedom of expression. Yet Americans have always expressed concern about the power of film to inspire behavior deemed unacceptable. The new medium of film seemed to spring on America suddenly in the early years of the century, emerging as a full-blown art form wedded to technology in a manner that made it instantly powerful and irresistible. Even in its infancy, as an attraction in nickelodeons, concern had been raised about questionable material; in 1907, the Children's Society of New York had a theater manager arrested for exhibiting a movie called *The Great Thaw Trial,* about the Harry Thaw–Evelyn Nesbit–Stanford White sex-murder scandal, and two years later that city's mayor, George B. McClellan, ordered all movie houses closed, a ban lifted only when a group of prominent New Yorkers offered to examine all films before they were shown. The movie companies responded to the threat of municipal censorship by creating an entity known as the National Board of Review, a three-person committee that was politically appointed and that tried to navigate a middle ground—protecting film moguls from undue meddling while safeguarding the public, particularly children, from the most egregious images of immorality. Many states and cities established similar bodies. Of course, most of the delicate issues confronting these film boards had to do with suggestive living arrangements and starlets in negligees, not the inappropriate portrayal of a race of Americans.

What made the censorship concept so unsteady, and what put the NAACP at a disadvantage in its desire to scotch the film, was that no one yet felt comfortable saying how significant or powerful a societal force film really was. Audience members seated in the front rows of a theater in 1915 still tended to jump out of their seats when a locomotive came toward the camera; it was not clear how and to what extent viewers related what they saw on screen to real life. The leaders of the NAACP were no more or less sophisticated than anyone else about the new medium; their concern was not merely that the portrayal of blacks in *The Birth of a Nation* was unflattering, but that the film would somehow conjure a literal return to Reconstruction-era night riding and terrorism (a fear borne out when the film encouraged a Ku Klux Klan revival in Georgia).

In late January 1915 Dixon hit upon an idea of how he could safeguard his and Griffith's masterwork. He and President Woodrow Wilson had known each other as students at Johns Hopkins University and Dixon, years before, had nominated Wilson for an honorary degree at Wake Forest College in North Carolina. Now Dixon wrote to request an audience with the president and Wilson agreed to receive his old friend.

After assuring the president that he had not come seeking an appointed office, Dixon told him about a motion picture he felt Wilson should see, "not because it was the greatest ever produced or because his classmate had written the story . . . but because this picture made clear for the first time that a new universal language had been invented. That in fact it was a new process of reasoning by which the will could be overwhelmed with conviction." Wilson was intrigued but explained that, for security reasons, it would be impossible for him to go to a movie theater. Having anticipated this obstacle, Dixon immediately offered to bring the film to the White House.

On February 18, 1915, with the president, his daughters, his cabinet, Dixon, and Griffith present, *The Birth of a Nation* was screened in the East Room of the White House. Wilson was no doubt flattered to find that a series of title cards used early in the film to explain Reconstruction quoted his own 1902 book, *A History of the American People:*

> Adventurers swarmed out of the North, as much the enemies of the one race as of the other, to cozen, beguile, and use the Negroes. . . . In the villages the Negroes were the office holders, men who knew nothing of the uses of authority, except its insolences. . . . The policy of the Congressional leaders wrought . . . a veritable overthrow of civilization in the South . . . in their determination to put the white South under the heel of the black South.

Wilson sat spellbound through the entire two-and-a-half-hour spectacle, at the conclusion of which he rose and warmly pumped Dixon's hand.

"It is like writing history with lightning," exclaimed the president. "And my only regret is that it is all so terribly true."

The NAACP did not enjoy like access to people in high places. In fact, relations between President Wilson and black America could not have been at a lower ebb. When Wilson first ran for the office in 1912, blacks and Northern liberals placed great hope in him, believing that because he was an intellectual and a Southerner, his word would carry more weight with his Southern brethren. But his actions once he was installed in the White House were hardly in keeping with the expansive campaign sentiments he'd voiced about justice for black Americans. Soon after his 1912 election, Wilson allowed three of his Southern appointees, Secretary of the Treasury William G. McAdoo, Secretary of the Navy Josephus Daniels, and Postmaster General Albert S. Burleson, to begin segregating federal employees in certain Washington agencies, while also downgrading or eliminating a number of black officeholders appointed during the Roosevelt and Taft administrations. Cafeterias in some departments were placed off-limits to blacks, and Jim Crow bathrooms were installed in government buildings. "Deserving white girls in this City," wrote the National Democratic Fair Play Association, a group active in the segregation effort, "have appealed to us from nearly every Government Department where they are compelled to work alongside of a greasy, ill-smelling Negro man or woman; that sometimes, where a Negro is in charge or control . . . those poor girls are forced to take dictation from, be subservient to, bear the ignominy and carry the disgrace of the taunts, sneers or insults of such Negroes." The association publicized a letter supposedly written by a white woman who worked in the Department of the Interior who complained of having to take dictation from drunken black men, and mentioned: "I also worked for a dark-skinned, wool-headed Negro. I then felt if a human would ever be justified in ever ending his existence I would then, for I was a Southern woman, my father a distinguished officer during the Civil War."

With segregation the rule in lunchrooms and seating galleries throughout Washington, as well as in the Treasury and Post Office departments, the nation's capital seemed firmly in the hands of racist white Southerners. No executive order had been issued, but the federal government for the first time was itself enforcing a policy of Jim Crow segregation.

"Mr. Wilson, do you know these things?" Du Bois fumed in *The Crisis*. "Are you responsible for them? Did you advise them? Do you not know that no other group of American citizens has ever been treated in this way and that no President of the United States ever dared to propose such treatment? Here is a plain, flat disgraceful spitting in the face of people whose darkened countenances are already dark with the slime of insult."

Even Booker T. Washington criticized Wilson and the segregation program. Never before had the federal government discriminated against its own employees based on color. For activists accustomed to looking to the federal government for hopeful, if undelivered, relief from such onerous policies on the state and community level, the federal government's adoption of such a program for its nineteen thousand black workers was appalling.

If blacks could get no action from the president, they at least derived some pleasure from a sideshow on November 12, 1914, when Boston's enfant terrible William Monroe Trotter arrived at the White House. Trotter had gone with a delegation to visit Wilson in 1913 and had complained about the segregation policies, bearing a petition with twenty-one thousand names; Wilson had promised to investigate the matter, but had done nothing. Now, when Trotter raised the issue again during a visit, Wilson replied that he had looked into it and found that segregation was needed in government departments to alleviate friction between white and colored employees. Trotter responded that Wilson's explanation was "not in accord with the known facts," because black and white federal employees had worked side by side "in peace and harmony and friendliness" for fifty years. Wilson suddenly cut him off, saying Trotter's manner offended him.

"In what way?" Trotter asked.

"Your tone, with its background of passion."

"But I have no passion in me, Mr. President, you are entirely mistaken," Trotter replied. "You misinterpret my earnestness for passion."

The interview rapidly deteriorated. On the way out Trotter stopped to explain to reporters the gist of the conversation and to clarify that the president was wrong in asserting that friction between black and white federal workers necessitated segregation. In 1914 for anyone to quote the president to the press, particularly in a way that appeared to question his judgment, was seen as the height of effrontery. The McComb, Mississippi, *City Enterprise* was one of many Southern papers to complain of the "recent episode in which a Nigger leader of a delegation of Niggers practically insulted the President of the United States at the White House in Washington."

As in his Boston confrontation with Booker T. Washington in 1903, Trotter had with his usual candor managed to speak the sentiments others had been too reserved to express. Villard observed that perhaps "one has to be rude to get into the press and do good with a just cause," while former Massachusetts attorney general Albert E. Pillsbury, of the NAACP's Boston chapter, noted, "Trotter, by accident, has . . . accomplished more by insulting the President . . . than all the polite words ever uttered on segregation could or will accomplish."

For his part, Wilson instructed his aides and secretaries to never allow "that unspeakable man, Tucker [sic]" to come anywhere near him again.

Dixon's public-relations strategy was paying off. In New York the National Board of Censorship of Motion Pictures heard out representatives from the New York *Age* and the NAACP, but agreed to ask Griffith to make only a few minor edits of objectionable scenes. The truth was that probably no amount of cutting could obliterate the racist content of *The Birth of a Nation,* as offensive elements were so thoroughly embedded in it. In the film, black legislators pass a law legalizing intermarriage, signs at a campaign rally demand EQUAL RIGHTS, EQUAL MARRIAGE, and the black characters depicted—most of whom are whites in blackface—vary hardly at all from the stereotypes of obsequious darky, smothering mammy, and treacherous mulatto. Even when blacks in the film take up arms, they are shown as herdlike and cowardly. It would have to be all or nothing, and the board essentially chose the latter—insisting on cuts in a chase sequence and in a scene showing black legislators behaving like monkeys, but passing the film and clearing the way for its scheduled March 3 New York premiere. The board then issued two tickets to the NAACP for a preview screening with the stipulation that only white members of the organization were welcome to attend.

The March 3 premiere at New York's Liberty Theater was, by anyone's account, a magnificent affair, with gallant-looking ushers in Civil War uniforms of blue and gray, ladies dressed in antebellum crinolines, and the stirring music of a forty-piece orchestra. As soon as the lights went down the audience was enthralled. Many were seeing a motion picture for the first time, and the experience of watching history animated—"a Mathew Brady photograph come to life," one film historian later termed it—must have been exhilarating. Here, after all, were many of the nation's most formative, traumatic experiences—slavery, the Civil War, the assassination of Lincoln, the utter demise and glorious redemption of the South and its reunion with the North—all lucidly, tragically, "alive" on-screen. Prior to *The Birth of a Nation,* even the most highly regarded films were little more than a series of long shots and static tableaux, featuring stage acting and a camera that remained in one location until a particular scene had resolved itself in real time. But in filming his epic, Griffith moved the camera along different planes, cut scenes short, dissolved from tearful close-up to panoramic battle scene—in essence, took control of the narrative film medium in a way no one had before.

The film opens by stating its sympathies directly. "The bringing of the Africans to America planted the first seeds of disunion," reads a caption. It then moves to its story of the brothers Phil and Tod Stoneman of Pennsylvania visiting their school friends, the Camerons of South Carolina, in the days before the Civil War. Phil falls for Margaret Cameron, while Ben Cameron dreams of Phil's sister, Elise, whose photograph he has seen. War erupts and two younger Cameron brothers and Tod Stoneman are killed. Ben Cameron is wounded and taken prisoner in a Yankee hospital, where he is nursed by Elise Stoneman.

At war's end, the Stonemans' father, Austin, is a Radical Republican out to punish the South and empower the black politician Silas Lynch. But the Union occupation of the region creates so much lawlessness, Ben Cameron is moved to become head of a Klan unit. His youngest sister, Flora, meanwhile, is stalked by the black vagrant Gus, whom the titles introduce as "a renegade, a product of the vicious doctrines spread by the carpetbaggers." Caught between submitting to his attentions and death, Flora hurls herself off a cliff. "For her who had learned the stern lesson of honor," reads the title, "we should not grieve that she found sweeter the opal gates of death." Elise Stoneman then approaches Silas Lynch to ask him to save her brother Phil from the black militia who have him surrounded in a log cabin. Silas insists he'll help only if Elise will marry him. Ben Cameron, at the head of a Klan legion, then descends—saving Phil from the armed blacks and Elise from the debauched Silas Lynch, and killing the renegade, Gus. At the end Phil, a Northerner, weds Margaret, a Southerner, while Ben, a Southerner, marries Elise, a Northerner. Thus, the blacks are denied their attempted usurpation of white women and power, and with overlapping bonds of family and region, as the music swells, the two halves of the nation are doubly reunified. In the film's incredible last image, Jesus Christ himself appears, sanctioning the characters' attainment of sectional reunion and their safeguarding of racial purity.

"It is spiritual assassination," wrote Francis Hackett of the film in *The New Republic* at the time of the film's release. "It degrades the censors that passed it and the white race that endures it." Edward T. Ware, president of Atlanta University, called its technical innovations "sugar-coating for a dose of black poison," and Soviet director Sergei Eisenstein found the film's racism "disgraceful propaganda" that "cannot be redeemed by purely cinematographic effects." But crowds overwhelmingly favored the film. Advertisements in New York papers boasted of its sky-high production cost of half a million dollars, its "18,000 people and 3,000 horses," and quoted a critic who had raved, "The mind falters and the typewriter balks before an attempt to describe Griffith's crowning achievement." Giant, white-sheeted Klansmen reared their horses over Times Square, part of a massive billboard that promised a "red-blooded tale of the true American spirit."

Having failed to block the film's opening in New York, the NAACP set its sights on Boston, where the film was scheduled to open on April 10. Dixon and Griffith knew Boston would be the toughest place to secure a showing for the film because of that city's long history of liberalism and abolitionist sentiment. Ohio had already banned the film, as had Pennsylvania on the grounds that it insulted the memory of Thaddeus Stevens, a favorite son. There was reason to fear something similar might happen in Massachusetts, for a decade earlier Boston mayor John "Honey Fitz" Fitzgerald had banned Dixon's play, *The Clansman.*

To discuss the matter, Ovington and Storey of the NAACP met with Boston mayor James M. Curley and Griffith. Curley said he had the right to censor parts of the film but could probably not keep it out of the theaters. Ovington, probably one of the few Americans who had actually read the lengthy 1872 congressional report on the Ku Klux Klan and knew how thoroughly fraudulent the movie was, succeeded in convincing Curley to excise the chase sequence of Gus the rapist and the death of Flora. Peeved, Griffith said he would donate ten thousand dollars to charity if anyone in the room could name a single scene in the film that was not true. Storey asked if a black lieutenant governor of South Carolina had ever locked a white woman in a closet and refused to release her unless she agreed to marry him. Griffith did not answer directly, nor did he make any such contribution. At the meeting's close, Storey refused to shake hands with Griffith. It was the first time anyone could remember that a white man had refused to shake the hand of another white man over the rights of black people, and it won Storey great praise from his NAACP colleagues.

Griffith was on solid ground defending his film as merely reflective of the prevailing understanding of Reconstruction—the prostrate South preyed upon by carpetbaggers and saddled with 5 million burdensome, corrupt Negroes egged on by a pack of vengeful Radical Republicans in Washington, with the heroic Klan the understandable response. He could cite works by no less than the president of the United States, Woodrow Wilson, whose *History of the American People* was serialized by the *Chicago Daily News* after the movie provoked reader interest; William A. Dunning, professor of history and political philosophy at Columbia University and president of the American Historical Association; and E. M. Coulter, whose ten-volume *The South During Reconstruction: 1865–1877* was considered an authoritative source. This traditional view of Reconstruction, which ignored the humanitarian aspects of the era, such as the transitional problems encountered by newly freed, landless, illiterate slaves, and the work of the Freedmen's Bureau, was assaulted periodically by black American writers, most notably W.E.B. Du Bois in his masterful *Black Reconstruction*, published in 1935, but the traditional interpretation would hold sway into the 1960s.

Trotter had been away from Boston, stump-speaking about the evils of the Wilson administration's segregation policy, when the flap over the film began. But upon returning he plunged into the controversy with his usual zeal. On the night of April 17, Trotter led a protest of five hundred blacks at the Tremont Theater. When he and some of his supporters refused to leave the lobby, they were attacked by police with billy clubs. Trotter was knocked down and arrested, along with several others.

"It is a rebel play," Trotter declared, "[and] an incentive to great racial hatred here in Boston. It will make white women afraid of Negroes and will have white men all stirred up on their account. If there is any lynching here in Boston, Mayor Curley will be responsible." At a meeting in Faneuil Hall the next day Trotter charged that if the movie maligned Irish people as it did blacks, Mayor Curley would find a way to stop it.

Trotter's crowd moved on from Faneuil Hall to the Massachusetts State House, where as many as twenty-five thousand gathered opposite the statue of Colonel Robert Gould Shaw, the white commander of the Fifty-fourth Massachusetts Colored Regiment in the Civil War. Inside the capitol, Governor David Walsh met with the state attorney general, Mayor Curley, and police officials to discuss banning the film. Curley said he could not stop the movie's exhibition because it was not obscene. Walsh set in motion an effort to get a special bill through the legislature to ban films "that raised the race question," but it was deemed unconstitutional. He did succeed, however, at getting a stricter censorship law passed, although Boston's censors refused to play along, still insisting they would not revoke the film. The NAACP issued a statement expressing "profound regret" that the censors "in disregard of the plain intent of the legislature" had refused to ban *The Birth of a Nation.* "We deplore this decision," the association wrote, "as a rejection of the just claims of our colored citizens to be protected against a malicious misrepresentation of their race in a play involving a perversion of our national history and a glorification of lynching."

Trotter continued his protest rallies on Boston Common and in front of the theater, and criticism of the film continued to roll in from all parts of American society, even as it played to packed houses. To many people's surprise, one of the leading supporters of Trotter's militant tactics was none other than his old nemesis Booker T. Washington. With the coming to office of Woodrow Wilson, with whom, unlike his predecessors Roosevelt and Taft, Washington had little rapport, the Wizard's power over the nation's black populace had effectively ended. In frail health, sensing the conclusion of his long, active life drawing near, Washington was newly willing to speak out about racial injustice, a development that his biographer Louis Harlan links to the traumatic 1911 assault he'd suffered in New York City. While Harlan acknowledges there were other causes of the evolution in Washington's thinking, he asserts that "surely the most vivid and recurrent was his self-recognition as he ran bleeding through the New York streets, that in the atmosphere of American racism even Booker T. Washington was lynchable."

At the Los Angeles preview of *The Birth of a Nation,* actors made up as Klansmen had ridden by on horses as a promotional stunt. By the time the film premiered in Atlanta in fall 1915, real-life horsemen in full regalia from a newly revived Klan paraded up and down Peachtree Street before the theater. "Ku Klux Fever" gripped the South, and Klan hats and other souvenirs were sold. Watching the movie, Southern audiences whooped the rebel yell and, at one showing, emptied their revolvers into the screen. In rural areas, *The Birth of a Nation* swept through almost as if it were a traveling circus, with extras dressed in period garb hawking the movie on village streets. Where no movie theater existed, special excursion trains were arranged to bring country people en masse into urban areas to take

part in this national rite of passage. Feeding on the excitement, Klan re-
cruiters worked the theater lobbies.

The NAACP had known from the start that it had the weak hand in the
fight with Dixon and Griffith's creation. Censorship was not much of a
strategy for social change, especially in the hands of otherwise freethink-
ing progressives, and downright pitiful against a film touted as the "Eighth
Wonder of the World." And while many sympathized with the association's fundamental objection to the film as offensive and historically inac-
curate, the NAACP found that few took seriously its warning that the film
would cause race riots. The NAACP was correct in the larger sense that
the film encouraged racial animosity—as the reinvigoration of the Klan in
Georgia showed—but there had been periodic race riots in U.S. cities for
years, and aside from some boos and catcalls, eggs thrown at the screen,
and a few random gunshots, moviegoers remained relatively well behaved. The only consolation, perhaps, was that the film's over-the-top
racism fostered a new militancy among black Americans, and the chief
beneficiary of this aroused race consciousness was the NAACP.

The Birth of a Nation was if nothing else a forceful demonstration of the
power of film—even Du Bois admitted he liked some of the battle sequences—and it was only logical that those who questioned the film's
message would consider responding by using the medium themselves.
The first person to whom this seems to have occurred was D. W. Griffith
himself, who in the face of rancorous charges from his black critics offered
to film an epilogue to be added to *The Birth of a Nation* that would show
black Americans' progress since Emancipation. The idea was warmly seconded by public officials, who saw in it a possible way out of the vexing
censorship squabble. For positive images of black Americans Griffith's
team turned first to the Tuskegee Institute, and when Booker T. Washington refused to have anything to do with the project, to the Hampton Institute. Somewhere along the line Griffith himself obviously lost interest
in the idea, or didn't have time to pursue it, since the five- or six-minute
epilogue, titled *The New Era,* consisted solely of contributed film footage
of "young colored men and women who are fitting themselves for high
places in the industrial world" that Hampton had already made for promotional purposes. This epilogue was attached to *The Birth of a Nation* as
early as the film's exhibition in Boston in mid-April 1915, and was shown
with the film in numerous other cities, although the few published comments about it suggest that, tacked on to Griffith's sweeping Reconstruc-

tion melodrama, it was a nonsequitur and practically meaningless. No prints of the epilogue survive.

A more ambitious corrective film project was launched by an NAACP officer named May Childs Nerney, who had been centrally involved in the censorship fight and lobbied the NAACP leadership to respond to Griffith by making a film of its own. There was discussion of basing it on "The White Brute," a short story Ovington had published in *The Masses* in October 1915, in which black newlyweds waiting for their train at a Southern whistle-stop are bullied by two local white men, one the son of the sheriff. Although the husband is physically powerful, his memory of seeing another black man lynched paralyzes him, and he can do nothing as the white men take his wife away and rape her. Booker T. Washington suggested his own stirring autobiography, *Up from Slavery,* as a fitting response to the work of Dixon and Griffith, an idea pursued by Washington's aide-de-camp, Emmett J. Scott, after Washington's death in November 1915. Neither Ovington's disturbing tale nor Washington's memoir were selected, and instead the NAACP embarked on a stumbling "art-by-committee" endeavor that would prove an embarrassment.

The NAACP engaged a writer, Elaine Sterne, who began working with a premise she called "Lincoln's Dream." Almost immediately different opinions arose among Ovington, Du Bois, and others as to what form the story might take. Through Emmett Scott's efforts, the film attracted preproduction endorsements from former president Taft and Julius Rosenwald, the president of Sears & Roebuck, and financial support from Carl Laemmle, head of Hollywood's Universal Studio. The resulting film, three years in the making and plagued by distractions related to the country's entry into the war, was a surreal historical hodgepodge—Lincoln freeing the slaves, Columbus discovering America, Paul Revere's ride, the Jews fleeing Egypt, and finally, black and white farmers exchanging their overalls for uniforms and marching off together to defend America from the kaiser. Titled *The Birth of a Race,* the film had the ill fortune to open in November 1918, the month of the Armistice, when its allusions to patriotism and the U.S. entry into the war were deprived of most of their resonance. Described as "grotesque" and "tangled" by even the kindest critics, the film toured the lower tier of the nation's movie houses, then fell into obscurity.

In the end, the best response to *The Birth of a Nation* was probably that hit upon informally by several theater owners in Chicago, who simply attached to the end of showings of the Griffith twelve-reel spectacular an old print of the Johnson-Jeffries fight film of 1910. How better to counter an epic of white supremacy than with footage of the "Ethiopian Colossus" flattening the "Great White Hope"?

The most disturbing story in *The Birth of a Nation,* that of the virgin Flora who takes her own life rather than surrender to the evil Gus, had special meaning for viewers in Georgia. A sensational murder case involving the sexual predation and death of a young Southern girl had riveted the region for two years, and had only been "resolved" in August 1915 when a determined mob had abducted the convicted killer, Jewish factory manager Leo Frank, and lynched him near his victim's grave. The Frank case is one of the great national criminal dramas, on a par with the Lizzie Borden trial, the Lindbergh kidnapping, and the O. J. Simpson case. From spring 1913, when the murder occurred, until 1915, when Frank "paid" for his crime, it was like a powerful searchlight illuminating several themes then current in the life of the South—the resistance to change as represented by a Northern capitalist, a strain of anti-Semitism that had evolved out of the Populist distrust of the urban North and was inflamed in the Frank case by former Populist leader Tom Watson, and the continuing will to rely on sensationalism and mob intimidation, including lynching, to enforce regional codes of justice.

The victim of Frank's alleged crime was Mary Phagan, a thirteen-year-old employee of the National Pencil Company in Atlanta, who was discovered murdered in the basement of the factory by a night watchman on April 27, 1913. She had been strangled and hit on the head with a blunt object, and appeared to have been killed while fending off a sexual assault. After interviewing several suspects, police arrested Frank, the plant manager, a New Yorker who had come south in 1907 to manage his uncle's business. "Frank is a small, wiry man, wearing eyeglasses of high lens power," *The Atlanta Constitution* noted. "He is nervous and apparently high-strung. He smokes incessantly and stuffed a pocket with cigars upon leaving for police headquarters. . . . His dress is neat, and he is a fluent talker, polite and suave."

Frank, who held a degree in mechanical engineering from Cornell, was married to Lucille Selig, the daughter of a prominent Atlanta Jewish family, and was president of the local B'nai B'rith. He had cooperated fully with the police as they examined the crime scene and arrested a few early suspects, readily admitting he had been in the factory on Saturday, the day Phagan had been killed. He reported that he had given her the $1.20 in pay she had come to collect. He was incredulous when it became apparent the police suspected him of the killing. "I am not guilty," he averred. "Such an atrocious crime has never entered my mind. I am a man of good character and I have a wife. I am a home-loving and God-fearing man. They will discover that. It is useless to detain me, unless for investigation and for information I might be able to give."

The environment in which the trial of Leo Frank took place was both emotional and intimidating. Spectators in the courtroom were allowed to retain their weapons, and mobs outside shouted threats up through the windows at judge and jury, warning them against bringing in anything but a guilty verdict. In a strange twist on the usual course of Southern justice, the other leading suspect in the case, Jim Conley, the factory's black janitor, managed to convince the court of his own innocence, while successfully casting guilt on Frank. Conley had changed his alibi so many times that the story he finally settled on—that he had abetted Frank in a string of sexual dalliances with young female employees, and that Frank had murdered Phagan and asked Conley to help him burn the body and write a pair of misleading notes about the crime—struck many people as the truth simply because it seemed too complicated a lie for a black person to make up. Conley cleverly played to the jury's twin prejudices—that Frank, as a Yankee Jew, would be unable to resist taking sexual advantage of the factory's vulnerable young female workers, many of whom, like Phagan, were adolescents; and that a black person would be incapable of devising so sinister a plot without a white man's guidance. It seemed to register not at all that Frank was an upstanding member of the community and Conley had a police record for theft and disorderly conduct. When Frank's defense team, led by Luther Rosser, one of the most respected criminal attorneys in the state, was unable to poke holes in Conley's story, the failure served to bolster the sense that the humble black man had spoken the truth.

Southern fears about the increasing industrialism of the region and the social changes it boded, concerns about immigrants, foreign ideologies, and the encroachments of Yankee capitalists—all came to be represented by the fate of a young Southern girl forced by circumstances to take a low-paying job in a factory owned by a New York Jew. Invoking these anxieties, Frank's attackers insisted that Phagan had died defending her honor and chastity. Even though medical evidence indicated the girl had not been raped, she was partially undressed when found, suggesting a sexual assault had been attempted. Much testimony was allowed to the effect that

Frank was overly familiar with female workers at the factory, spied on them in their changing room, and even performed cunnilingus with his oversized "Jewish" nose. Meanwhile, carefully retouched photos of the victim appeared, showing a virginal working-class daughter of the South, an avid churchgoer, a pretty, self-possessed young woman who, after picking up her $1.20 in pay that fateful Saturday, intended to hurry to the annual Confederate Memorial Day Parade to catch a glimpse of the widow of Stonewall Jackson riding by. "Little Mary Phagan was Southern, white, and an innocent virgin," historian Joel Williamson writes. "She was born in the country and killed in the city, in a Yankee-owned factory, fighting to preserve her purity against a bestial Jew. Such was the menace to the South at large."

One newspaper article encouraged women and girls to view Phagan's corpse as a lesson in what awaited those who were not adequately on guard against perverted, oversexed Jews. "Every woman in Atlanta, every working girl, every school girl, ought to see that little girl in there," one woman said outside the funeral home where the dead girl lay in state. "They ought to take a good look at her. They ought to see what perils and dangers they have to face." Ten thousand people—"the largest crowd that ever viewed a body in Atlanta"—responded to such admonitions and lined up for hours to file past her open coffin.

Throughout the Frank trial, Georgians' interest in the case had been cynically manipulated by Tom Watson. The 1890s Populist and "friend of the common man," who had once vowed that "the accident of color can make no difference in the interests of farmers, 'croppers and laborers," had by 1913 become an unabashed racist, anti-Semite, and anti-Catholic, whose obsessions ranged from the Northern Jews who he believed controlled the nation's financial fortunes to the deadbeat priests and nuns who rode free on Atlanta's streetcars. As though ashamed of his own earlier idealism, Watson turned against Southern blacks with a vindictiveness so severe it may have contributed, some observers feared, to his becoming slightly deranged. Watson published two influential periodicals—the weekly *Jeffersonian* and *Watson's Monthly*—both of which took up the cause of Mary Phagan with a vengeance. He described Phagan as "a daughter of the people, of the common clay, of the blouse and the overall . . . who, in so many instances, are the chattel slaves of a sordid Commercialism that has no milk of human kindness in its heart of stone," and Frank as a Jewish pervert who had tried to rape and had murdered a poor Christian girl. Frank was a "typical young libertine Jew" with "a ravenous appetite for the forbidden fruit—a lustful eagerness enhanced by the racial novelty of a girl of the uncircumcised." Publishing a particularly ethnic-looking photograph of Frank, Watson encouraged his subscribers to "study the lips, nose, and averted gaze." Despite such rampant anti-Semitism—some have called Leo Frank the "American Dreyfus"—in the end it was more likely the depiction of him as the abusive employer and despoiler of young girls "forced" into factory jobs that motivated such extreme feelings of animosity toward him, and that made his demise inevitable.

Many Southerners also became irritated by the determination of Frank's supporters, who rallied Northern opinion against the "closed-minded South," and by such high-handed tactics as hiring the self-important William J. Burns, known as "America's Sherlock Holmes," to clear Frank's name through private investigation. The Atlanta police had clearly botched several opportunities to gather crucial evidence. They had neglected to take fingerprints before the crime scene had been disturbed, and the two "murder notes" that Conley claimed Frank had told him to write had been set aside and ignored during an early phase of the police investigation. Any serious analysis of the notes tended to incriminate Conley, not Frank. Burns managed to establish that much of the testimony coloring Frank as a sexual pervert was of dubious origin, that some witnesses for the prosecution had been coerced, and that the police had not thoroughly examined Conley's criminal past or his modus operandi in other crimes that bore resemblance to his actions in the Phagan case. He also suggested that the fact that Phagan's purse and money were never found tended to exonerate Frank, who as a prosperous factory manager would hardly need to steal the nickels and pennies of a thirteen-year-old. On May 1, 1914, the *Constitution* ran a banner headline: "A HORRIBLE MISTAKE, SAYS BURNS."

> "In driving Leo Frank to his death without a fair trial, you are making the most horrible, the most awful mistake I have ever heard of . . . I have absolutely cleared Frank of charges of perversion which were wholly responsible for the conviction and have shown beyond a shadow of a doubt that Conley is a pervert and murderer."

Burns's potential influence was quickly smothered, however. The Atlanta police did not take kindly to being second-guessed, particularly by a Yankee celebrity detective, and they responded by closing the Atlanta office of the Burns agency, arresting many of its investigators, and issuing a warrant for Burns himself. Ultimately, Burns departed Georgia with a lynch mob at his heels, after being chased out of Marietta, Mary Phagan's hometown, by angry citizens.

As for Northern liberals who rallied to Frank's support, the cause proved far more compelling than the usual lynching of a black man, for just as Mary Phagan was a familiar and highly sympathetic persona to Southerners, Frank was clearly a man whom most Northern urbanites could relate to and take pity on—a hardworking member of the middle class, a respectable family man, who had through a tragic coincidence found himself an outsider accused of having violated a region's most significant taboo, while possessing traits and an ethnic identification threatening to those who were to judge him.

For this reason the Frank case was the source of some confusion to many blacks. While the determined prosecution and lynch-mob atmosphere of the case were painfully familiar, they resented the ease with which the cause of an unjustly accused white man marshaled such tremendous public sympathy and concern. And many were offended by those portions of Frank's defense, aimed at Jim Conley, that appeared eager to remind people of where public indignation rightfully belonged in a case of a young white girl's murder.

When Frank was convicted and sentenced to death (Conley received a one-year sentence for his role as accomplice), Frank's lawyers launched a series of appeals over the unfavorable conditions of his trial, leading to their seeking a writ of habeas corpus in federal court. Frank's trial, they claimed, had been held virtually in the midst of a lynch mob, as people in the courthouse square below the open windows of the stifling courtroom shouted up such slogans as "Hang the Jew, or we'll hang you!" The mob had created such a dangerous environment, the judge had ordered that the defendant and his attorney not be present when the verdict was read. As a result, claimed Frank's appeal, his due-process rights had been compromised. The appeal went to the U.S. Supreme Court, which in April 1915 ruled in *Frank v. Mangum* (C. Wheeler Mangum was the Fulton County sheriff) that "as long as a state court observed the form of a trial the federal government had no right to go beyond the form and inquire into the spirit which animated the trial," a decision that was extremely discouraging to legal and civil rights reformers, including the NAACP.

The Supreme Court also refused to revoke Frank's sentence, so his supporters turned their efforts to obtaining executive clemency from the governor, John M. Slaton. From outside Georgia the plea for commutation, if not a complete pardon, was almost deafening. The governors of several states and numerous state legislatures sent resolutions to Slaton, their concern echoed by editorials in newspapers from every part of the country. Pro-Frank petitions bearing more than 1 million signatures arrived at the Georgia statehouse.

The target of this massive effort, Governor Slaton, was a former speaker of the Georgia House of Representatives who had been swept into office as governor in 1913 by an overwhelming majority. Only in his late forties, he was believed to have a promising career ahead of him, one that might lead to the U.S. Senate. Faced with the unenviable choice of disappointing his own constituents or ignoring the overwhelming national sentiment, aware that his political future was riding on the decision, Slaton, an experienced attorney, determined to review the entire case by himself. After devoting long hours to a meticulous reevaluation of all the evidence, the trial transcript, and the considerable newspaper coverage, Slaton produced several reasons Frank's guilt was doubtful, none of which had previously received adequate consideration. The "murder notes" that Conley contended Frank had dictated to him upstairs after killing Phagan were written on outdated company forms kept in the basement, making it unlikely they had come from Frank's desk; and the coroner's report indicated that Phagan's mouth and nostrils were coated with sawdust, clearly showing she had taken her last desperate breaths in the basement, not upstairs in Frank's office as Conley maintained.

Slaton also called attention to revealing evidence the police and even William Burns had apparently overlooked. When detectives first arrived in the factory basement they came by way of the stairs, and while investigating the crime scene they noted a fully formed human stool at the bottom of the elevator shaft. Conley had admitted to defecating at the bottom of the basement elevator shaft on the morning of the day of the murder. But he also said that he and Frank used the elevator to bring Phagan's body down to the basement. Later, when police used the elevator to descend during their investigation, the stool was crushed and a dreadful odor was released in the basement. Thus, Slaton deduced, Conley's contention that he and Frank brought the girl's body to the basement on the elevator could not be true.

On June 21, with Slaton's wife assuring him that "I would rather be the widow of a brave and honorable man than the wife of a coward," Slaton commuted Frank's sentence to life imprisonment.

The outcry in Georgia was vociferous. Tom Watson assured his readers that a Jewish conspiracy had arranged it so that "no aristocrat of their race should die for the death of a working-class Gentile." Prosecutor Hugh Dorsey and other officials also denounced Slaton's action. A mob quickly formed outside the governor's residence in suburban Buckhead, heaving bottles and brickbats and threatening to lynch Slaton if he dared show himself. One incensed citizen sprinted into the mansion with a loaded revolver, to be tackled only at the last moment by guards. Twenty-six men and boys were arrested in connection with the disturbance, and Slaton became the first governor in American history to declare martial law for his own protection.

On the night of August 16, 1915, a group calling itself the Knights of Mary Phagan set out to exact the "people's justice" on Leo Frank. Shortly before midnight, a group of about thirty-five men in eight automobiles descended on the prison farm at Milledgeville. They held guns on the warden, J. T. Smith, and the superintendent, J. M. Burke, then overpowered two guards sleeping on the porch of Frank's dormitory. Smith, Burke, and the two guards were placed in handcuffs as Frank was hustled outside. The Knights—the first lynch mob in history known to travel by automobile—set out to drive their captive a hundred miles northwest to Marietta, where they intended to execute Frank on Mary Phagan's grave. They cut the telephone lines at Milledgeville to hinder any attempt at pursuit, and as a distraction, one carload of lynchers split off from the others and began firing their guns in the air. "The minuteness of detail with which the tragedy was executed indicated a master mind at lynchcraft," noted one account of the flawless getaway.

The original plan to kill Frank on Mary Phagan's grave had to be scrapped when daybreak came and the caravan was only on the outskirts of Marietta; the mob quickly detoured to a wooded park near a cotton gin and hanged Frank from a tree. Frank had sustained a serious throat wound in a knife attack by another inmate at Milledgeville, and now it reopened and he quickly bled to death.

The Frank lynching was sternly criticized by the nation's editorial pages. The *Chicago Tribune* felt there was nothing else to conclude but that "the South is half educated. It is a region of illiteracy, blatant self-righteousness, cruelty and violence. Until it is improved by the infusion of new blood and better ideas it will remain a reproach and a danger to the American republic." The Pittsburgh *Dispatch* said that "Georgia is reaping what she sowed. For years she had tolerated mob violence against one race. . . . The mob that is allowed to set its belief above the law in one case, will not hesitate to arrogate to itself the same power in another." The Milwaukee *Leader* called the lynching "a dastardly crime" and suggested: "After attempting to murder an innocent man by judicial procedure and being frustrated, the cowardly lynching was perpetrated. . . . Instead of sending troops to Mexico, the Federal Government should send an army to Georgia. Nothing so barbarous has been recorded in Mexico."

The two immediate beneficiaries of the Frank case were undoubtedly Tom Watson and Hugh Dorsey. "The Voice of the People," Watson wrote in high satisfaction at the conclusion of the Frank affair, "Is the Voice of God." Watson's publications enjoyed tremendous sales and his long-troubled political career was revived, culminating in his election to the U.S. Senate in 1920. Dorsey, who had been carried from the courtroom on supporters' shoulders after the original Frank verdict and who had defended the verdict against Frank's numerous appeals, used his celebrity—which brightened considerably next to the dark example of Governor Slaton—to win election to the governor's chair in 1916. As for Slaton, the once-popular governor fell completely from public grace. He remained in Georgia but never again held elected office.

The other visible result of the Frank lynching, in conjunction with the popularity of *The Birth of a Nation,* was the resurrection of the Ku Klux Klan. In fall 1915, William J. Simmons, a circuit-riding preacher, garter salesman, and part-time history teacher, gathered the remnants of the Knights of Mary Phagan along with two elderly Reconstruction-era Klansmen and several other gallants to establish the Knights of the Ku Klux Klan, naming himself Imperial Wizard. In addition to its presence at the Atlanta premiere of *The Birth of a Nation,* for which Simmons garbed the Knights in bedsheets and had them ride up and down Peachtree Street firing rifle salutes, the Klan dramatically announced its resurgence by scaling Stone Mountain, a rocky eighteen-hundred-foot height east of Atlanta, and lighting a cross that was plainly visible from the city. The idea for the cross-burning had come not from Klan lore—the Reconstruction Klan never burned crosses—but from the fictional world of Thomas Dixon.

CHAPTER 7

The Wisest and Best Response

The Supreme Court's unwillingness in *Frank v. Mangum* to consider the rampant denial of due process at the state level to be within its jurisdiction—this despite the view of many in the legal community, including the presiding judge, that the Frank trial had been procedurally flawed and erroneous in its verdict—was a disheartening blow, although not entirely unexpected, since the federal government had no track record of interfering in state criminal proceedings. Still, if states and municipalities were allowed to conduct criminal trials in which blatant irregularities occurred, locally tried, mob-influenced criminal cases would amount to little more than legal lynchings. The proceeding might possess all the trappings of a bona fide trial, but ultimately the accused's rights were as worthless as if he'd been taken out and summarily shot. Reversing *Frank v. Mangum* would become an overriding concern of the NAACP's legal division in the years to come.

The association was energized by the national outcry against the Frank lynching, and when the following year the sham trial of a black murder suspect in Waco, Texas, led to a particularly gruesome lynching, the NAACP mobilized quickly. It investigated and then successfully publicized the incident by producing, under Du Bois's supervision, one of the nation's most comprehensive and disturbing accounts of a lynching.

Situated on the Brazos River midway between Dallas and Austin, Waco saw itself as an up-and-coming city of the New South. Home to Baylor University and several other colleges, with a population of more than thirty thousand and over two hundred manufacturing concerns, including the world's first Dr Pepper bottling plant, the town was in 1916 a flourishing regional capital, with a Business Men's Club and a Young Businessmen's League, "the cleanest and best-sprinkled streets of any city in the state," and even one of Texas's first skyscrapers, the Amicable Life Insurance Building.

Much to the ultimate regret of Waco's hometown boosters, some ugly traditions had not been entirely left behind in the city's determined march into the twentieth century. This became clear in the days after May 8, 1916, when Lucy Fryer, fifty-three, was found bludgeoned to death at the door of her family's seed shed near Robinson, six miles away. Suspicion immediately fell on Jesse Washington, a seventeen-year-old black neighbor who worked as a hired hand for the Fryers. Sheriff Samuel Fleming drove to Washington's home, where he found the suspect sitting on the front porch distractedly whittling a piece of wood, and saw what looked like blood on the boy's clothes. Taken into custody, Washington, who was illiterate and known for being "slow," offered several conflicting statements, but emphatically denied hurting Lucy Fryer.

Later that day, however, after a more extensive interrogation, Washington allegedly confessed to the murder and told police where they could find the murder weapon, a blacksmith's hammer he had stashed under some brush. The attack, according to an NAACP account, had occurred when Mrs. Fryer scolded Washington for beating a team of mules. Sometime after Washington's initial arrest, it was announced that the black teenager had raped Mrs. Fryer as well as murdered her. As in the Sam Hose case, it's likely this charge was attached more as the result of rumor than of evidence, as the description of the murder suggests an enraged employee striking out in anger at an overbearing boss.

Word of the crime spread quickly through the small farming towns near Waco, including Robinson, where the Fryers lived. Soon after, a mob of farmers and village merchants arrived at the jail and demanded that Sheriff Fleming give Washington up. When Fleming explained that the prisoner had been taken elsewhere for his own safety, the posse insisted on being allowed to search the premises. Fleming readily agreed. Eleven years before, in 1905, a crowd denied access to the jail after making a similar request had become infuriated and smashed its way in using sledgehammers, causing extensive damage before removing a black suspect named Sank Majors and lynching him from a river bridge. This time Fleming allowed the mob to comb the jail carefully and peer into the faces of several terrified black prisoners. It then departed peacefully, with the sheriff's promise that Washington would soon be brought before a judge and jury.

The sheriff was true to his word. The trial began the following Monday, May 15, with a throng of "interested parties" in attendance. Judge Richard Irby Monroe had permitted fifteen hundred people to crowd into a courtroom that ordinarily held five hundred, and the folly of trying to appease the mob by letting it have such a huge presence in the room was immediately apparent. When the judge remarked that everyone would have to behave or "There won't be any court today," someone replied curtly, "We don't need no court!" The moment Washington appeared, a man was heard to mutter, "Might as well get him now," and pulled a large revolver from his coat. He was overpowered and disarmed, his friends assuring him, "Let them have the trial. We'll get him before sundown." Judge Monroe, sensing that normal standards of decorum would have to be relaxed, sighed and requested merely that all "gentlemen" remove their hats.

The trial moved swiftly, attorneys and judge alike clearly impressed with the need to expedite the proceedings by the bulging outlines of firearms visible in the spectators' clothing. Washington's defense was nonexistent. His court-appointed attorney failed to exploit the most glaring weakness in the prosecution's case—that the physician who had examined the body of Mrs. Fryer, in his brief testimony, made no mention whatsoever of any evidence of a sexual assault. After the simulation of a legal hearing had continued a few minutes more, the prosecutor rose to declare, "The prisoner has been given a fair trial, as fair as any ever given in this courtroom," to which the packed room responded with the rebel yell. The jury spent four minutes in deliberation before pronouncing Washington guilty.

At the announcement of the verdict, the mob swept over the officers of the court and seized Washington. They forced him out a back door and down a flight of stairs to an alley, where other men were waiting with a heavy chain, and the mob and its captive headed toward the steel suspension bridge over the Brazos. En route to the bridge, however, word came that another group had already begun building a bonfire next to the city hall. The crowd's greater enthusiasm for immolation helped swing the procession in that direction.

As he was prodded and dragged along, Washington was kicked, stabbed, hit with bricks and shovels, and had most of his clothes torn off, then was forced naked onto the pyre. The chain around his neck was looped over a tree limb, and he was jerked into the air. His body was sprinkled with coal oil, as were the boxes and scraps of wood below. There was a momentary delay when it was discerned that the tree itself, which adorned the city hall square, would be destroyed by the fire, but by now the crowd was huge and pressing in from all sides—students from Waco High on their lunch hour, secretaries, and businessmen had wandered over to take in the event—and there was no stopping what was about to occur.

Washington was lowered down one last time so that participants could cut off his fingers, ears, toes, and finally his penis, then with the crowd's delirious roar of approval the oil-soaked boxes were lit and Washington's body began to be consumed by the flames. "Such a demonstration as of people gone mad was never heard before," recorded the *Waco Times-Herald.* When Washington was dead, a man on a horse lassooed the charred remains and dragged them through town, followed by a group of young boys. The skull eventually bounced loose and was captured by some of the boys, who pried the teeth out and offered them for sale.

A local professional photographer, Fred A. Gildersleeve, had documented the lynching for the inevitable souvenir postcards. Gildersleeve's skill wound up contributing to the ensuing national outrage over the lynching, for the images he captured are among the most compelling lynching photographs ever made, detailed enough to capture the wafts of smoke rising from the immolation, harsh in their compositional juxtaposition of young straw-hatted onlookers and Washington's blistered remains.

Elizabeth Freeman, a white suffragist who went to Waco on the NAACP's behalf to investigate, found that the local press and townspeople endorsed the lynching, but disapproved of the mutilation and mistreatment of the corpse. "If only they had just hung him," she wrote, paraphrasing opinions she'd heard expressed, "they felt that would have been all right, but the burning—the dragging of the charred torso through the streets is so much worse than his crime." The town's business leaders, alarmed at the countless news articles and copies of Gildersleeve's stark photographs that had begun showing up across the country, fretted over the tarnishing of Waco's reputation. Gildersleeve told Freeman: "We have quit selling the mob photos. This step was taken because our 'City dads' objected on the grounds of 'bad publicity.' As we wanted to be boosters and not knockers, we agreed to stop all sale."

Freeman wrote a lengthy article for *The Crisis* about her investigation, which the NAACP titled "The Waco Horror" and published as a special eight-page supplement to the magazine, along with Gildersleeve's disturbing photographs. Even the NAACP board members expressed doubt about Du Bois's idea to put one of Gildersleeve's images of Washington's burnt corpse on the cover, but Du Bois was adamant and got his way. The organization distributed copies to seven hundred newspapers, all members of both houses of Congress, five hundred "prominent" individuals in the arts and political life, as well as *The Crisis*'s own forty-two thousand subscribers, and dispatched Freeman on a national lecture tour. "The Waco Horror" was undoubtedly the largest and most concerted effort made up to that time to acquaint Americans with the reality of a Southern lynching, and the killing of Jesse Washington contained all the classic ingredients—a farcical judicial process, feeble law enforcement, burning and mutilation, and a refusal by authorities to hold anyone responsible despite Freeman's discovery of the names of six of the mob's leaders. Texas had no antilynching law that might have enabled a case to be made to dismiss Sheriff Fleming and other officials. In this instance, not only had Fleming been derelict in refusing to call in the militia to protect Washington, Judge Monroe had shown weak judgment in allowing a trial to proceed while his courtroom was in the possession of an armed mob.

The Waco case was a vivid example of why the Supreme Court's decision in *Frank v. Mangum* had been shortsighted: in Waco, the form of a trial had been enacted, but only as a kind of frontier burlesque; there'd been no real justice for Jesse Washington. The sheriff and other authorities had had as their top priority the keeping of a lynch mob at bay. But in staving off a lynching by promising a swift trial, the trial had become a lynching itself.

"The idea of *you* lynching anybody! It's amusing," says Colonel Sherburn in *The Adventures of Huckleberry Finn* as he faces down a mob. "Why, a man's safe in the hands of ten thousand of your kind—as long as it's day-time and you're not behind him. . . . But if only *half* a man—like Buck Harkness, there—shouts 'Lynch him, lynch him!' you're afraid to back down—afraid you'll be found out to be what you are—*cowards*—and so you raise a yell, and hang yourselves onto that half-a-man's coat tail, and come raging up here, swearing what big things you're going to do."

Real-life Colonel Sherburns did appear from time to time in the early years of the century, facing down lynch mobs and safeguarding their prisoners. They were inspired by the antilynching publicity of the NAACP, concerns by commercial interests that the "modern" image of their community not be dragged down, local antilynching laws, and even anxiety about mass desertions by frightened black laborers. The NAACP actively encouraged such brave stands, serving as boosters for courageous public officials and even giving them awards.

One of the first to come to the NAACP's attention was Alabaman Emmett O'Neal who, as U.S. district attorney for northern Alabama, had been instrumental in establishing a law giving the governor of that state the power to remove from office any sheriff who through cowardice, connivance, or neglect allowed a prisoner to be taken from custody and killed. In 1911, when O'Neal himself became governor, he had a chance to test it. On April 2, Aberdeen Johnson was arrested for "criminally assaulting" Mrs. Archie Butt in the small town of Goshen in the southeast part of the state. "The circumstances of his crime had been revolting, arousing Bullock and adjoining counties to a fever heat of wrath," O'Neal later said, "but that did not, to my mind, at all excuse [a] summary, lawless procedure." When "determined men" descended on the Bullock County jail in Union Springs, where Johnson was being held, Sheriff P. W. Jinwright told the mob that as the attack on Mrs. Butt had occurred in Goshen, which lay on the boundary between neighboring Pike and Crenshaw counties, the sheriff of Crenshaw County would be arriving on the 6:30 P.M. train to take custody of the prisoner. The mob understood this to mean that the transfer would provide an ideal opportunity to intercept Johnson and lynch him, so it withdrew, leaving their guns with Sheriff Jinwright at his request, and adjourned to a local restaurant for lunch.

In the meantime Jinwright contacted Governor O'Neal in Montgomery by phone and explained the situation, saying that at dark there was likely to be a lynching and that he would be unable to stop it. O'Neal instructed him to deputize as many men as needed and guard the jail closely. The governor then, by telegraph, notified Jinwright that he was sending a unit of state militia by train the forty miles from Montgomery to Union Springs, and that they would arrive by four o'clock. An employee in the Union Springs telegraph office who handled the incoming telegram tipped the mob off as to the anticipated arrival of troops. The mob stormed immediately back to the courthouse, took Jinwright prisoner and placed handcuffs on his wrists, then broke into the jail and lynched Aberdeen Johnson.

Governor O'Neal ordered an official investigation, but at the same time discreetly dispatched E. V. O'Connor, a Mobile newspaperman, to Union Springs as his secret agent. Pretending to be a reporter sympathetic to the mob, O'Connor dug up incriminating evidence against Sheriff Jinwright. It turned out that, despite Governor O'Neal's order, Jinwright had not deputized anyone; he had instead sent the few deputies he had home for lunch, then merely locked the jail and gone next door to the courthouse. When the mob caught up with him, Jinwright "placidly permitted himself to be bound and witnessed the breaking down of the jail doors and the taking away of the negro."

O'Neal moved to have Jinwright impeached under the state law, sending the intelligence he had gathered to the Alabama Supreme Court. Supporters of Jinwright gathered almost three thousand names on a petition to have the case against the sheriff dropped, but the court voted unanimously to evict Jinwright from office, explaining:

> The Governor had given him positive orders to place a guard at the jail and protect the prisoner at all hazards. . . . Yet he did not organize [deputies], did not give them any order what to do, let them all go off to their dinners at the same time, without any instructions or agreement as to when they were to return, left the jail without a single man in it . . . left the arms of the mob in his office with the door open, and suffered himself to be completely surprised and overcome by the mob. . . . It seems evident that the Sheriff, with three or four resolute men, armed, could have prevented the entrance of the mob into the jail.

The 1910 Cairo, Illinois, lynching of Froggie James had been the first instance of a sheriff losing his job over a lynching, although the Jinwright case was the first in which this had occurred in the South. A week after Jinwright's downfall, O'Neal later reported, another Alabama sheriff contacted the governor about a black prisoner in his custody, vowing to do his utmost to safeguard the man and mentioning that he knew he would lose his job if he did not. "The fact that [Jinwright's] impeachment prevented other lynchings was proof positive that such affairs can be prevented," O'Neal later said. "The sooner they are . . . the better it will be for the whole South and the whole country." O'Neal was such a welcome figure to reformers, the NAACP later brought him to New York to address an antilynching symposium.

The rights organization found another hero in late summer 1916, when Sheriff Sherman Ely of Lima, Ohio, stood his ground between a lynch mob and a black prisoner, and almost paid with his life. On August 30, Ely had arrested Charles Daniels for an alleged assault on Mrs. John Barber, a white woman. Daniels was accused of slashing Mrs. Barber and beating her. Hearing that a mob had gathered and was heading for the jail, Sheriff Ely hurried his prisoner into a car and sped off toward the State Hospital for the Criminally Insane in Ottawa, eighteen miles away.

In his absence, the mob descended on the Lima jail and forced the sheriff's wife to open all the cells. Furious to discover that Ely had spirited Daniels away, the mob waited in ambush for his return, then chased him on foot through his own house and into a nearby Elks Club, where he was seized and dragged outside to be hanged. The fire department attempted to disperse the mob with hoses, and the chief of police tried to convince a group of citizens to join his men in an attempt to free the sheriff, but the mob was too large. After the lynchers had hoisted Ely up a pole with a noose around his neck, the sheriff broke down and agreed to take the mob to Daniels.

More than fifty automobiles roared into Ottawa, demanding the black prisoner. The hospital staff had wisely already removed Daniels to another refuge, and during the confusion Ely, with two broken ribs from the beating he'd sustained and his clothes in shreds, escaped from his captors and hid in a hotel.

The black-published Cleveland *Advocate* spared no feeling in praising the courageous lawman:

> Here in our own Ohio, one of the greatest states of the Union, a frenzied mob makes a desperate attempt to besmirch the name of the Buckeye State—to class it with Georgia, Texas, and the rest of "lynch-law abodes." But, luckily, in the town of Lima there was a MAN WHO DARED TO DO HIS DUTY AS HE SAW IT. . . . In the midst of the maelstrom of frenzy which had engulfed the citizens of Lima stood a pillar of manhood, Sheriff Sherman Ely, the hero of the hour. . . . Think of it! This was surely HEROISM if there ever was such. . . . IN ALL TIMES LIKE THESE, GOD GIVE US MEN LIKE ELY.

The NAACP, seizing on the promotional value of a lawman who would put his own life on the line to deny a lynch mob its victim, arranged a gathering in Columbus to present Sheriff Ely with an award. The governor, Frank B. Willis, assured the honoree that the world appreciates a man "who stands squarely with a heart unafraid and his face to the front at times of stress." Sheriff Ely, as modest in speech as he was heroic in deed, thanked people for all the attention but said he had only been doing his job.

An important motivation for Southern officials to work against lynchings in the years before the First World War was the continuing exodus of black workers from counties where acts of summary violence occurred. An estimated 1.5 million black people migrated from South to North between 1900 and the mid-1920s, with many more to come in the decades following, and during the years 1914–17 the northward movement accelerated to between five thousand and ten thousand people per month. Often blacks simply "voted with their feet," as Du Bois put it, abandoning particularly hostile communities; in clearances, whites acted aggressively to chase blacks away, coveting their land and property and deeming their necessity as laborers to have diminished with the turndown in the cotton market and the increased mechanization of the cotton farm. Several other stimuli were responsible—the crop-destroying boll weevil, which struck with particular severity in the years 1915–17; floods that annually ravaged the Mississippi Delta; and a general weariness with the region's unjust and dangerous conditions.

While insects and floods were a major nuisance, it was influences created by human beings that most strongly spurred departure—the sharecropping system that made it virtually impossible for black farmers to get ahead, the lack of sanitary conditions and decent streets, the day-to-day insults blacks endured when they rode the streetcar or attempted to shop in a store, and the constant threat of physical assault that hung over every family. Hovering just beyond all the other daily indignities of life in the region was lynching, and even where a lynching never occurred it sat, a brooding possibility, over all aspirations Southern blacks might have. Running afoul of any one of a number of Southern racial codes could instantly put one's children, husband, or other relatives in lethal jeopardy. "There is scarcely a Negro mother who does not live in dread and fear that her husband or son may come in unfriendly contact with some white person so as to bring the lynchers," a Savannah newspaper related, "which may result in the wiping out of her entire family." A 1919 black religious conclave in Atlanta concluded that it was "lynching and mob violence" that "have sent from the South in the last three or four years more than a million . . . and they continue to go."

Even the race riots that occasionally hit northern communities did not dissuade Southern blacks from the view that life in the North was preferable. Many would have agreed with poet Langston Hughes: "At least, if trouble comes, I will have my own window to shoot from."

One notable influence on the migration was the black-owned and published Chicago *Defender,* which was widely read in the South. Started in 1905 by an ex-Georgian named Robert S. Abbott, the paper regularly printed atrocity stories about Southern lynch mobs, poems, cartoons, and advice encouraging Southern blacks to leave. *The Defender* saw itself performing a heroic role, on par with that of the abolitionists, in encouraging northward migration, and willingly served as a kind of clearinghouse for appeals from black Southerners eager to depart. "After twenty years of seeing my people lynched for any offense from spitting on the sidewalk to stealing a mule," one man wrote to *The Defender,* "I made up my mind that I would turn the prow of my ship toward the part of the country where the people at least made a pretense at being civilized." Many enclosed newspaper clippings about recent lynchings to lend impetus to their appeal for help. "I was just reading in the morning Beaumont *Enterprise* Paper where thay Burn one of the Race to Stake," wrote a correspondent from Texas. "For God sack please help to get me out of the South."

In 1915 it started countless families on the trek north by printing a shocking photograph of a black Texas farmer and his three sons hanging dead from the same tree; their so-called crime, a caption explained, was to have brought in their district's first cotton harvest. Perhaps the paper's most popular feature was the editorial-page cartoon. One printed in August 1916 showed a poor black man who had fallen asleep atop a bale of cotton slowly awakening. The caption read: "After 50 years of sound napping, depending on the white Southerner and his cotton crop, the members of the Race are migrating into [the] northland, where every kind of labor is being thrown open to them, where decent houses are obtainable for him to house his family and better schools to educate his children."

Another featured a drawing of a black man scrambling up an embankment, atop which waited a Northern industrialist in a large touring car with the motor running and the door open, as hounds labeled "Lynchers" bounded after him, nipping at his heels.

The Defender frequently took license with the facts, and didn't mind exaggerating the details of a lynching or other injustice, but in a sense the publication was merely keeping faith with its readers in adhering to its central message: lynching and other Southern violence toward blacks was an abhorrence, and out-migration the wisest and best response. The paper's circulation was nearly a quarter of a million copies by 1916 when authorities in Georgia and Mississippi banned its sale.

At times the slow trickle of northward migration became a roaring stream, when sensational lynchings and campaigns of Ku Kluxing drove masses of Southern blacks out of specific areas. One of the better-known disruptions of this kind occurred in 1904 in Bulloch County, Georgia. On July 29, a white family named Hodges was ruthlessly murdered and two turpentine workers, Paul Reed and Will Cato, were arrested. After days of moving the prisoners around the state, a mob overwhelmed a group of state militia guarding the blacks in Statesboro, and Reed and Cato were burned to death in front of a large crowd.

The community's wrath had been only partially vented by the lynching, partly because it was believed Reed and Cato had had accomplices. A committee of white planters formed and agreed that an undesirable class of insolent blacks existed in Bulloch County and was to be driven away. Unlike the Red Shirt assaults in South Carolina, the objective was not the breaking of black or Republican political hegemony but rather dealing with a minority group that seemed to have grown newly resistant to white authority. The next day Handy Bell, a suspect in the family's murder who had been released by the court, was followed by whites until he was outside of the city and was then "shot to pieces," while an elderly black man named Albert Roberts, identified by the newspaper as "one of the old-time darkies," was shot and wounded as he sat in his cabin. Several blacks found buggy whips propped against their cabin doors, a sign that they must vacate. Many took to the woods and hid out there for weeks or, if possible, boarded trains leaving the district. "The lynching of Cato and Reed has made a profound impression on the negroes," a Statesboro paper observed, although *The Atlanta Constitution* pointed out that the planters' fears of insurrection were probably exaggerated: "The danger to the whites of Bulloch County now lies more in the large deportation of labor and consequent effect on the cotton picking season than from any other cause."

Such clearances often had the long-term impact of effectively making certain Southern counties black-free. After a spate of lynchings in Forsyth County, Georgia, in 1912, more than a thousand blacks left the vicinity. By the time of the 1920 census there were only thirty black people residing in the county; in 1960 the number was four. By 1980 there was officially one, but no one knew for certain where that individual could be found.

In 1916, the NAACP monitored a dramatic case in which South Carolina governor Richard I. Manning helped fight a clearance in Abbeville County after a much-publicized lynching. A bustling cotton town located on the main North-South rail line between Atlanta and points north, the county seat, also named Abbeville, boasted a famous opera house and luxury hotel on its leafy town square. The hotel had figured in one of the darkest chapters of Southern history when Jefferson Davis and his cabinet, on the run from Union troops after the fall of Richmond in spring 1865, had met there to formally dissolve the Confederacy.

Born just before Davis's historic visit, Anthony Crawford was one of the black children of Reconstruction allowed to grow up imagining that hard work and thrift might secure him a place in the emancipated South. Immediately after the war, Crawford's father came into possession of a modest cotton spread, which Anthony inherited and which by 1916 had grown to a sizable holding of 427 acres. Many of his own sons and daughters had settled on land adjoining their father's house.

"He was getting rich, for a negro, and he was insolent along with it," the Charleston *News and Courier* would later comment. Though the newspaper's remark was hostile and misplaced, it was true that, as a self-made man, worth about twenty thousand dollars and undoubtedly one of the richest individuals in Abbeville County, Crawford was known to brook little disrespect from others, even white people. His children had often heard him say, "The day a white man hits me is the day I die."

On Saturday morning, October 21, 1916, Crawford drove a wagonload of cotton into Abbeville to be baled, and quarreled with white store owner W. D. Barksdale over the price of cottonseed. Barksdale at one point called Crawford a liar, at which Crawford cursed at Barksdale and strode out of his store. One of Barksdale's clerks followed and struck him on the head with an ax handle. Reeling from the blow, Crawford shouted for help, bringing policeman T. H. Botts to the scene. Botts separated the two men and arrested Crawford, probably for his own protection, as a white mob had already begun to form.

After being detained briefly, Crawford was released on fifteen dollars bail and let out a side door of the jail, but was spotted by the mob and chased into a nearby cotton gin, where he hid in the boiler room. A hammer was lying nearby and when a member of the mob, a buggy salesman named McKinny Cann, approached, Crawford knocked him senseless.

Sheriff R. M. Burts arrived and rearrested Crawford against the wishes of the infuriated whites. Burts convinced them to allow him to lock

Crawford up, although he had to promise Cann's brothers that he would not attempt to spirit Crawford out of town before the extent of Cann's injury was known. The latter, it turned out, was not badly injured, but in the afternoon a rumor went around that Sheriff Burts was "fixing to take the nigger away on the four o'clock train." At three P.M. a crowd of about two hundred men came to the lockup, overwhelmed and disarmed Burts, and removed Crawford from his cell. They dragged him through the town's black quarter with a rope around his neck, then chased a young black man out of the lumber wagon he was driving, commandeered it, and used it to carry Crawford to the entrance of a nearby fairground, where they suspended him from a pine tree and used his body for target practice. "Negro Strung Up and Shot to Pieces" read the next day's headline. At sunset, Coroner F.W.R. Nance led a jury to the spot and cut the remains down, recording that Crawford had died "at the hands of parties unknown."

Crawford's murder brought a swift denunciation from Governor Manning, who ordered Sheriff Burts and State Solicitor R. A. Cooper to conduct a full investigation that would lead to the mob's indictment. Numerous men were detained, including three brothers of McKinny Cann. It soon became clear, however, that absolutely no one in Abbeville would testify against them and that an impartial jury would never be assembled. At Manning's urging, there was talk of moving the case to another county. In the interim, an extraordinary document came to light—a statement purportedly written by men from the Abbeville lynch mob itself, and published in the Abbeville *Scimitar:*

> We are ALL responsible for the conditions that caused Crawford's death. Those involved might have gone too far, but they are white men and Crawford was black. The black must submit to the white or the white will destroy [him] . . .
>
> There were several hundred who participated in this lynching, and nearly ALL the others were well-wishers, therefore to pick out a few to satisfy a newly imported mawkish sentiment, is pitiful and cowardly. Men of Abbeville, the eyes of all white men are upon you. Acquit yourselves as white men. The conditions made by US ALL, make us all responsible, so let's not ask only eight to shoulder the whole burden. Answer a mawkish sentiment generated by hypocrisy and craven fear with the ringing verdict, Not guilty.

The *Scimitar* continued to ridicule Governor Manning's efforts, finally advising in an editorial that Crawford's death was "inevitable and

RACIALLY JUSTIFIABLE" and attributable to "his own reckless course, due to chest inflation from wealth."

> It does not matter . . . whether the cause of killing [Anthony Crawford] was insufficient, IT WILL NEVER DO TO CONVICT WHITE MEN FOR THE ACT, FOR WE WILL HAVE MORE NEGROES TO KILL BECAUSE OF IT. IT MUST BE NOT GUILTY ON ALL COUNTS.

The town's other newspaper, the *Press and Banner,* took a more enlightened view, pointing out that the boll weevil infestation that had ravaged crops elsewhere in the region was only "one hundred miles from Abbeville," and that its imminent arrival would require a full and healthy labor force not demoralized by the fear of lynch mobs. Dealing with lynching as a matter of morals was probably useless, the paper conceded, but suggested "it may be as well to get down on the lower level of the pocketbook."

> By permitting a negro to be lynched for assault and battery and by declaring that a mob may kill a negro for that offense, do white people wish to accelerate the movement northward of the negro population? Shall the negroes be driven out of South Carolina? Shall the farms be depopulated? Shall the mob go into partnership with the boll weevil to drive away the labor from the farms and bankrupt this Southern country?

The Crawford lynching, by prompting evaluation of these questions, exposed a growing rift in Southern communities. The "newly imported mawkish sentiment"—the growing disapproval of lynching—was beginning to influence middle- and upper-class whites. When NAACP investigator Roy Nash wrote an article about the Crawford case for *The New Republic,* criticizing the Abbeville lynching and putting forth the idea that lynch mobs were "an expensive luxury" the South could no longer afford, the piece was widely reprinted in the region's newspapers, a remarkable development considering its origin.

The rupture among whites in Abbeville broke into the open at a meeting at the courthouse on Monday, August 23, when the remnants of the lynch mob and many other lower-class whites voted to clear the entire Crawford clan out of South Carolina and seize their extensive landholdings, and to immediately close up all the black-owned stores in Abbeville. An opposing group of white businessmen, fearing the impact such an exodus would have on the area, acted to deter the more radical faction.

When the meeting took a recess, a handful of businessmen rode out to the Crawford place and explained the situation to the dead man's family. They then returned to the courthouse and reported that the Crawfords had been suitably obsequious, had removed their hats "like good niggers," and had quietly agreed to leave the county by mid-November, abandoning their father's property.

Satisfied, the roughnecks went away, but the elite really were just buying time. Although many Crawfords did leave Abbeville, the white leaders managed to build a consensus to oppose the rabble, and at a meeting on November 6 attended by virtually every businessman in the town, "war" was declared on the faction that had voted to run the Crawfords out. The businessmen passed resolutions denouncing lawlessness, suggested the creation of a local militia, promised protection to citizens of all colors, and moved to form a permanent "conciliation committee" of local residents. They even went so far as to resolve that, where the constitutional rights of an Abbeville citizen of any color were threatened, the town would welcome state and federal involvement to see to it those rights were protected. The idea that a town in the great secessionist state of South Carolina would invite federal intervention in its racial affairs was an audacious one, but as an editorial in the Columbia *State* noted, it was a sentiment increasingly shared by communities grown weary of the mob's harmful influence on black workers and sharecroppers.

NAACP field secretaries and other officials often put their lives on the line to investigate lynchings. Not all were as fortunate as Roy Nash, who investigated the South Carolina murder of Anthony Crawford and several other lynchings under the pretense of being a timber speculator, at a time when Southerners were still too sure of themselves to be on guard against white strangers asking leading questions about lynchings. The risks for NAACP representatives would increase as the organization itself achieved greater visibility and blacks took over its leadership. Two black field secretaries—James Weldon Johnson and Walter White, who joined the group in 1916 and 1918 respectively—represented the vanguard of blacks who would play an expanded role in the coming antilynching crusade. Both were initiated into the cause by undertaking dangerous investigative assignments in the wake of mob lynchings in the South.

One of the hallmarks of the early NAACP was that many of its officers had widely varied literary and artistic interests—Du Bois was a poet and author of several noteworthy books, Villard a journalist and publisher, Joel

Spingarn a poet and literary critic, Mary White Ovington a novelist and playwright. James Weldon Johnson perhaps best epitomized this trend: he was an educator, attorney, U.S. envoy, musician, lyricist, novelist, and editor. As a small child he had, out of a sense of inner destiny, walked up to President Grant in the Jacksonville, Florida, train station and extended his hand, and the famous man, surprised by the youngster's forwardness, had appreciatively taken it. It was an appropriate beginning. After training as a lawyer and serving as a high school principal in his native Jacksonville, he came north in the 1890s and made his reputation as a lyricist, cowriting vaudeville and Broadway show tunes with his brother J. Rosamond Johnson. It was a fruitful time for black musical theater in New York. Blacks were beginning to create their own full-scale musicals, departing from the long-standing minstrel "variety show" format. The first complete black musical, *A Trip to Coontown,* was a success in 1898, quickly followed by *Clorindy—the Origin of the Cakewalk* and *Jes Lak White Folks.* Also emerging at about this time were the first real stars of black theater—Bob Cole, Bert Williams, George Walker—with whom the Johnson brothers worked and collaborated. While still in Florida James had written "Lift Every Voice and Sing," with music by Rosamond, for the state's black schoolchildren, a song later to gain renown as the "Negro National Anthem."

Johnson was profoundly moved by an outbreak of racial violence in New York City in August 1900, when police-abetted mobs rampaged through the West Side just south of the Theater District, beating black men and women at will in reprisal for the death of a white police officer. The street violence continued for three days, with some of Johnson's vaudeville acquaintances specifically targeted by rioters. While the city's investigation was a whitewash, the incident forged a coalition of local black editors, activists, and churchmen under the leadership of T. Thomas Fortune that for the first time mounted a united black challenge to white authority in the city.

With the help of Booker T. Washington, Johnson received a U.S. consular appointment to Venezuela in 1906, and served admirably there and in Nicaragua before being passed over for reassignment by the incoming Wilson administration in 1912. That same year he published a novel, *The Autobiography of an Ex-Colored Man,* which contains a vivid account of a young black man's disillusionment and abandonment of the South after he has witnessed a lynching. Upon his return to New York he edited Fortune's New York *Age* before joining the NAACP as a field secretary in 1916.

Du Bois, who famously believed that an echelon of educated, refined black Americans might well lead their less-sophisticated brethren forward, saw in the multifaceted Johnson the personification of his ideal, and vigorously seconded Joel Spingarn's offer to Johnson to join the NAACP leadership. "At first I was afraid that this would not be in accordance with your real life work of literature," Du Bois wrote Johnson in fall 1915, "but I am inclined to think that contact with human beings will be an incentive rather than a drawback to your literary work."

Johnson embraced the NAACP's antilynching crusade. He had not only witnessed the 1900 street violence in New York City, he had also been fairly traumatized by his own brush with a lynch mob in Florida in 1901. Despite having defied the odds, the incident haunted him:

> For weeks and months the episode with all its implications preyed on my mind and disturbed me in my sleep. I would wake often in the night-time, after living through again those few frightful seconds, exhausted by the nightmare of a struggle with a band of murderous, bloodthirsty men in khaki, with loaded rifles and fixed bayonets. It was not until twenty years after, through work I was engaged in, that I was able to liberate myself completely from this horror complex.

One of Johnson's first major assignments for the NAACP came in spring 1917, when he was asked to investigate the lynching of a Memphis black named Ell Persons. The Persons lynching was notable for the inventiveness of the Memphis newspapers in trying to strike new middle ground on the lynching issue by redefining the practice as one that could be socially useful and acceptable—if only it was carried out in a clean, dignified manner.

The instigating event occurred on April 30 when Antoinette Rappel, a sixteen-year-old white girl, was found outraged and murdered near the Macon Road Bridge over the Wolf River, south of the Memphis city limits. She had been decapitated, apparently by a blow from an ax. A black deaf-mute named Dewitt Ford, who was known throughout the neighborhood as "The Dummy," was immediately suspected, but quickly exonerated. Suspicion fell on Persons, a farmer whose small plot of land was near the murder site. Twice arrested, interrogated, and released, Persons was picked up a third time, beaten by police, and then "broke down and confessed," according to a Memphis paper.

Local authorities shuttled the prisoner back and forth between Mem-

phis and Nashville in an effort to keep him from the mob, but when word
spread that he would be moved back to Memphis for his arraignment,
armed members of a "lynching committee" calling themselves the Shelby
Avengers established roadblocks and began keeping watch at the railroad
station. Acting on a tip, they tracked Persons to a Memphis-bound train
from which the prisoner was virtually handed over to the mob. The police
may have considered it best to let the Avengers have Persons before he arrived in Memphis, as public anger over the crime was so great a riot would
have likely occurred if the law had been forced to protect him. Indeed,
even if he'd made it safely to court a technical problem would have arisen,
for not a single local attorney was willing to assume his defense.

The next morning's papers announced the intention of the mob to
lynch Persons at the scene of the crime. Scores of men, women, and children had been camped out at the site for more than twenty-four hours,
and the press coverage brought still more, some parents sending notes to
school asking that their children be excused to attend. "Conspicuous
among the mob were several vendors of sandwiches and chewing gum,"
noted a reporter who mingled with a crowd he estimated at three thousand.

At about nine in the morning Mrs. Wood, the mother of the murdered
child, reached the place, at which time a signal was given to the mob to
bring in the car bearing Persons. A "master of ceremonies" raised his hand
for quiet so Mrs. Wood could make a statement. "I want to thank all my
friends who have worked so hard in my behalf," she said, then added, to a
roar of approval from the crowd: "Let the Negro suffer as my little girl
suffered, only ten times worse!"

"We'll burn him!" someone yelled back.

"Yes," said Mrs. Wood. "Burn him on the spot where he killed my little
girl."

The men in charge, however, explained to her that instead of using the
exact spot, they had selected a cleared space on the opposite side of the
levee to burn Persons, as it would afford more people a view. Mrs. Wood
assented to the site chosen, then pleaded with the heavily armed crowd
not to shoot at Persons, thus potentially shortening his suffering.

To everyone's astonishment, it was then announced that Ell Persons
himself wanted to make a statement. The crowd, hushed, pressed in on all
sides as Persons was allowed to stand up in the car. Bearing a pained expression, he stared out at the sea of white faces. For a moment it appeared

he might speak, but then he frowned and looked downward, unable to bring himself to make any remarks.

"Burn him!" screamed a woman.

"And burn him slow!"

Still in shackles, Persons was hoisted out of the car and half-marched, half-dragged to the place of execution in a narrow hollow. As several jugs of gasoline were poured over him and the fire slowly burned at his feet, two white men quickly stepped up and sliced off the victim's ears, although others who tried to come forward and take souvenirs were kept back. One spectator, a woman, became concerned that too much fuel had been used for the pyre. "He'll burn too fast!" she shouted. This concern was shared by others, who became agitated and pushed toward the fire with such force that the Avengers had to use the rope they'd brought to hang Persons with to keep the crowd from surging into the flames.

"Persons went to his death terrified beyond the power of expression," according to the Memphis *Commercial Appeal*. "His animal eyes rolled and shifted unceasingly, and he frequently moistened his parched lips. . . . His death was almost instantaneous. The Negro drank deep of the first sheet of flame and smoke, and relaxed upon his hellish couch."

Attendees had difficulty returning to Memphis because so many people were still arriving at the site. Asked by the late arrivals to describe the killing, those who had seen Persons roasted to death generally praised the affair, although some complained that too much gasoline had been used and as a result he had been incinerated too fast. Several spectators had become ill from the nauseating smell of burning flesh, and were vomiting in a gully by the road.

Persons's corpse soon cooled sufficiently to be dismembered. His head was briefly placed on a post near the bridge, then was taken down and driven in an automobile to the corner of Rayburn Boulevard and Beale Street in downtown Memphis, where whites flung it onto the sidewalk at the feet of a group of black pedestrians, shouting, "Take this with our compliments." Photographs of the head, with ears, nose, and lower lip severed, were available for twenty-five cents throughout Memphis, and the head itself was briefly displayed in a barbershop before being taken into custody by authorities.

What distinguished the Persons lynching in the estimation of the Southern press was not its overwhelming cruelty, but the admirable officiousness with which it had been performed. "[T]hroughout the entire proceedings there was perfect order," said the *Commercial Appeal*. "The crowd was dominated completely by the committee which had planned and executed the capture of the black slayer from the state authorities, and none offered violence not countenanced by the summary court." The execution, orchestrated with the use of automobiles and telephones, had been a model of exemplary lynchcraft, a "civilized lynching" showing taste and flair. The Avengers had even elected a treasurer so as to compensate those men who had lost wages from their regular jobs while participating in the search.

When James Weldon Johnson arrived at the location of the lynching, Persons's ashes still marked the place of execution. After interviewing the sheriff, reporters, and white and black residents, and scrutinizing the local newspaper coverage, Johnson found no solid evidence indicating that Persons had been guilty. Struck by eyewitness descriptions he'd gathered of the lynching, which emphasized the packlike behavior of the crowd, Johnson had a sudden insight, one that would guide the rest of his long battle against lynching:

> I reassembled the picture in my mind: a lone Negro in the hands of his accusers, who for the time being are no longer human; he is chained to a stake, wood is piled under and around him, and five thousand men and women, women with babies in their arms and babies in their wombs, look on with pitiless anticipation, with sadistic satisfaction while he is baptized with gasoline and set afire. . . . I tried to balance the sufferings of the miserable victim against the moral degradation of Memphis, and the truth flashed over me that in large measure the race question involves the saving of black America's body and white America's soul.

Johnson had only just returned to New York and written up his account of the Persons lynching when a terrible outbreak of racially motivated violence took place in East St. Louis, Illinois, on July 2, 1917. A major industrial town with huge meatpacking and manufacturing concerns, East St. Louis had become something of a way station in the great migration northward of Southern blacks. The availability of cheaper black labor was responsible, it was said, for undermining civic stability; the blacks' presence drove wages down generally, and during the previous summer they had been used as strikebreakers at three large packing plants. Disturbances occurred sporadically in East St. Louis through the spring of 1917. On the night of Sunday, July 1, white toughs driving through the black district around Market Street began shooting into homes and were themselves fired upon. Then an unmarked police car sent into the area to investigate was mistakenly shot at by black residents, with the result that both detectives inside were killed. The next day furious whites went on a rampage, setting houses on fire, shooting at blacks, and beating people to death. Men were lynched from streetlamps. Even children were considered fair game. This massacre, which resembled a European pogrom for its targeting of an entire community, took the lives of thirty-nine black people and displaced as many as six thousand. There were eight white fatalities. A congressional committee investigating the fracas reported that some of the police and Illinois National Guardsmen called in as peacekeepers wound up joining the white rioters.

"Just as America was speeding up its noble and ideal effort to promote the world drift toward democracy," one Northern paper observed, "out walked the national skeleton from its closet and paraded before all the world the special weakness that our democracy has developed." A substantial amount of the national press coverage compared events in East St. Louis to stories of German atrocities in Belgium, revealing an emerging slant on America's race crimes created by the war in Europe. One leading daily conceded:

> We have been inclined to disbelieve some of the tales of atrocities committed by the German troops . . . because they were so shocking that we could hardly believe it possible that civilized beings could be guilty of such conduct. But when we read that a mob of white men and women tore the clothes from an 18-year old colored girl . . . struck her on the mouth with a club . . . and chased her half naked and bleeding through the streets of an American city, we confess that we are . . . ashamed.

The NAACP distinguished itself by stepping in and offering social and legal services to the refugees. Du Bois himself went to East St. Louis along with NAACP staff member Martha Gruening to investigate, and *The Crisis* ran a lengthy article that included shocking testimonials from the victims.

James Weldon Johnson, sitting in on a meeting of the NAACP's Harlem branch, heard discussion of a plan to stage a protest gathering at Carnegie Hall over the East St. Louis violence and other indignities. On his return from Memphis a few weeks before, he had organized a rally in Harlem to protest the Ell Persons killing, and had been impressed by the turnout. Now he suggested that instead of an indoor public meeting, the New York black community stage a much larger protest, a "silent march" down Fifth Avenue right through the center of Manhattan that would be certain to capture the nation's attention. The idea was immediately accepted and Johnson and his colleagues quickly went into action, aware that the protest they envisioned would be one of the first, and certainly one of the largest, organized demonstrations by black Americans in the nation's history.

With the horrors of the Ell Persons lynching and the East St. Louis violence fresh in their minds, an estimated ten thousand black adults and children marched down Fifth Avenue from Fifty-ninth Street to Madison Square on July 28, 1917, in the Negro Silent Protest Parade. More than twice that number of blacks, joined by sympathetic or curious whites, lined the street. By design, no one in the parade spoke a word, nor, where possible, did any of the spectators—the only sound came from a unit keeping time on muffled drums—but the march's message was clearly articulated on dozens of signs:

INDIA IS ABOLISHING CASTE, AMERICA IS ADOPTING IT

MEMPHIS-WACO, CENTRES OF AMERICAN CULTURE

WE ARE MALIGNED AS LAZY AND MURDERED WHEN WE WORK

MOTHER, DO LYNCHERS GO TO HEAVEN?

MR. PRESIDENT, WHY NOT MAKE *AMERICA* SAFE FOR DEMOCRACY?

The parade was led by three hundred children, followed by nearly five thousand women dressed entirely in white, then by a large group of men in military uniform bearing a sign that read: WE WERE FIRST IN FRANCE— ASK PERSHING. As the march passed down Fifth Avenue, black Boy Scouts handed out copies of a leaflet, probably written by Johnson, titled "Why Do We March?"

We march because by the Grace of God and the force of truth, the dangerous, hampering walls of prejudice and inhuman injustices must fall.

We march because we want to make impossible a repetition of Waco, Memphis and East St. Louis by arousing the conscience of the country, and to bring the murderers of our brothers, sisters and innocent children to justice.

We march because we deem it a crime to be silent in the face of such barbaric acts.

We march because we are thoroughly opposed to Jim-Crow Cars, Segregation, Discrimination, Disenfranchisement, LYNCHING and the host
of evils that are forced on us.

The event succeeded on numerous levels. By calling on the coordinating powers of almost one hundred churches, fraternal lodges, and civil
rights organizations—most prominently the NAACP—it helped create a
basis for future combined action. By adopting what was known as the
"silent sentinel" method of public demonstration, an approach borrowed
from the suffragettes, it greatly impressed the nation's editorial writers,
who gave the parade largely supportive reviews. At a time when the
United States had just entered the war in Europe and patriotic feeling as
well as uncertainty over the war's outcome were running high, the restrained example of the Negro Silent Protest Parade seemed a model of
reasonableness, its cause highly laudable. "No arguing about economic
conflict and individual negro provocation," noted the *New York Post,* "will
do away with the responsibility which lies on the nation and the duty imposed on its official leaders to prevent by word and deed the recurrence of
crimes such as those called forth by last Saturday's procession of mourn-
ing." The NAACP's leading role in such a celebrated and well-received
protest helped affirm the organization's preeminence as the representative
advocate for black Americans, positioning it to take on more difficult and
dangerous fights in the days to come.

In the rural counties of eastern Arkansas in 1919 sharecroppers attempted
to reform a local agricultural economy in which they for decades had occupied the bottom tier. The NAACP's involvement in the clash led by
Walter White, whom James Weldon Johnson had recruited for the
NAACP while on a trip to Atlanta in 1918, would illuminate the economic issues that plagued the sharecroppers, and encourage the federal
judiciary to act forcefully to suppress the power of the mob. White was a
recent Atlanta University graduate active in local civil rights efforts and
had worked as a traveling life insurance salesman, a position that gave him
the familiarity with hundreds of small Southern communities he would
soon put to good use as an investigator of lynchings.

White was only of marginal Negro ancestry—he was five thirty-seconds
black and looked like and regularly passed for a white man—but a childhood brush with a mob during the Atlanta riot of 1906 had, by his own account, forced him to recognize and accept his identity. When a roving

band of armed whites had entered their neighborhood during the disorder, White's father, a postman, sent the rest of the family into hiding, while he and his eldest son took up positions with rifles at the front of the house. Twelve-year-old Walter, who had never fired a weapon before, was instructed by his father to shoot the first intruder to set foot on their property. As he crouched by the front window with the loaded rifle in his hands, White saw the mob flow toward him in the flickering light of a streetlamp and heard voices curse and vow to "get the nigger mailman." As he later recalled:

> [I]n that instant there opened up within me a great awareness; I knew then who I was. I was a Negro, a human being with an invisible pigmentation which marked me a person to be hunted, hanged, abused, discriminated against, kept in poverty and ignorance, in order that those whose skin was white would have readily at hand a proof of their superiority. . . . It made no difference how intelligent or talented my millions of brothers and I were, or how virtuously we lived. A curse like that of Judas was upon us, a mark of degradation fashioned with heavenly authority.

The mob became distracted and went elsewhere, an act of fate for which White was always grateful, since in the next moment he and his father would have opened fire, with what consequences he feared to imagine.

Like Walter White and his father cowering in a darkened living room in Atlanta in 1906, black farmers in Arkansas's rural Phillips County thirteen years later were also trapped—hostages in a system in which there was no chance of betterment or escape. The sharecropping system, a half-century after its development, remained inherently despotic and unjust. Theoretically, the owner contributed the land, the farmer contributed the labor, and at year's end they divided the profits from sale of the cotton crop, less those expenses that could be charged to the sharecropper such as seed, equipment, and other overhead. However, it was the practice that the white owner controlled the division of the profits, and thus the farmer could be paid based on a lower price per pound than what the white owner had received for the cotton. Many sharecroppers in Phillips County had not received a settlement on their fall 1918 cotton harvest until July 1919, and most believed they had been cheated. That year, the sharecroppers had learned, cotton was worth thirty or forty cents per pound, yet many of their landlords settled with them at a rate of only fifteen cents per pound.

Because individual rebellion against the system so often in the past had led to violence and lynchings, seven hundred farmers in Phillips County united in 1919 in hopes of attaining some relief through their strength in numbers. Under the leadership of a charismatic black farmer, Robert L. Hill, they named themselves the Progressive Farmers and Householders Union of America and sought the help of white Little Rock attorney U. S. Bratton to challenge the accounting methods used by the plantation owners. The goal was to gain the right to sell their own cotton crop on the open market before settling with their landlord. To make their point, the group's entire membership was prepared to withhold its fall cotton harvest from the planters. The involvement of Bratton, a veteran attorney who'd successfully prosecuted a number of individual peonage cases in Arkansas, sometimes asserting that planters were violating the Thirteenth Amendment, gave Phillips County whites cause for concern.

Union meetings were held throughout the spring and summer of 1919 in the small towns of Ratio, Elaine, and Hoop Spur. The organization, emulating the national craze for lodges and fraternities, had a fanciful side, with an elaborate system of secret greetings and handshakes, a password (*"We've just begun!"*), and a rallying song. Robert Hill, described in a contemporary account as "a short, thin, very black man wearing a frock coat," used the preposterous title "United States and Foreign Detective," and at the top of many of the group's broadsheets appeared the highfalutin words "Orders of Washington, D.C. The Great Torch of Liberty," which were meaningless, since the union had no connection to the federal government.

Phillips County was a sparsely populated place, with vast marshy areas and long, lonely stretches of unpaved road dotted with brooding stands of trees. Across the Mississippi River from Memphis and forty-five miles to the southwest, it had the feel of a land seemingly cut off from the rest of the world, and so when word of the sharecroppers' union got around during the summer of 1919, talk of a black insurrection also spread. In such remote country, where blacks outnumbered whites four to one, the spirit of Nat Turner was alive and well—at least in the fears of white landlords after dark.

On the night of September 30, two white lawmen and a black jail trusty were driving in the vicinity of Hoop Spur when their car broke down near a church where a union meeting was in progress. The whites' presence alarmed the meeting's guards, who thought the whites had come to spy on them (which may well have been the case). It has never been established who fired first, but in an exchange of gunfire one of the whites, Special

Agent W. A. Adkins of the Missouri Pacific Railroad, was killed, and the other, Deputy Charles Pratt, was wounded.

Word quickly spread among whites that the long-awaited rebellion had started, and when a posse of white men arrived in nearby Elaine, seeking to confiscate blacks' weapons, general shooting broke out. As guns boomed across town, blacks fled into the woods and canebrakes while whites hastened to get their families to safety aboard any train headed for Helena, the nearest city. Aware they were outnumbered, local whites put out the call for assistance to neighboring Arkansas counties and even Mississippi. Over the next few days armed whites poured into the area, engaging in what the NAACP termed "indiscriminate hunting, shooting and killing" of blacks. Combatants and noncombatants alike were treated as fair game. The NAACP estimated that as many as two hundred or three hundred blacks were killed (the actual number was probably closer to a hundred), and whites took dozens of black men prisoner and marched them with hands over their heads into a lockup in Elaine. The town had been placed under martial law by Governor Charles Brough, who arrived with five hundred state militiamen who in turn eagerly joined in the sport of hunting down black "rebels." Reported the Helena *Daily World:* "In the vicinity of Elaine last night four Negroes, discovered making their way toward the River, were commanded to stop. They declined to halt and were fired upon with machine guns. Two of them were killed, a third wounded, and the fourth taken prisoner."

In the most excessive violence, four brothers named Johnson from the Helena area who had been out squirrel hunting and were not even aware of the "uprising" were surrounded by a posse of whites just south of Elaine. One, Elihu Johnson, was a dentist from Helena; another, D. A. Johnson, was a pharmacist; a third was a physician home on a visit from Oklahoma. All four were disarmed and placed in the back of a deputy's car for the trip to Helena. Phillips County treasurer Amos Jarman later explained that they had no handcuffs, but used cord to bind the Johnson brothers' feet. When the car stopped to aid another vehicle that appeared to be having mechanical problems, one of the brothers reportedly grabbed the gun worn by Helena city councilman O. R. Lilly and shot him, causing the whites from both vehicles to fire on the blacks, killing all four brothers at once.

With all that is known about black men in the custody of white posses on lonely rural roads, this story seems doubtful. It's more likely that the two cars of whites decided to murder the Johnsons and that Lilly was killed in the chaos, or that he was killed elsewhere and his death so angered his friends that they massacred the Johnsons in retaliation. Even if one of the Johnson brothers did lunge for a weapon, the execution of all four men would seem unnecessary. Witnesses said later that the entire rear of the car was sprayed with bullets, as if from a machine gun.

Those blacks taken captive in Elaine were held incommunicado, denied access to legal counsel, and subjected to kangaroo trials held by a "Committee of Seven," appointed by Governor Brough and composed of three white planters, the sheriff, the county judge, the mayor of Helena, and the president of the Helena Business Man's League. The committee issued a statement describing the sharecroppers' union as "a deliberate insurrection of the negroes against whites . . . for the purpose of banding negroes together for the killing of white people." It charged that a general uprising had been scheduled for the first week in October, in which "black Paul Reveres" would ride through the countryside spreading their password, which was a signal for whites to be killed. The committee also charged the Progressive Farmers with telling members that the federal government would come to their aid in seizing white men's lands. And in an echo of the infamous Murel Rebellion of the 1830s, the committee stated that Robert Hill, who had vanished at the time of the outbreak, was not a farmer or labor organizer but a swindler who played upon the "ignorance and superstition of a race of children."

The trial of nearly a hundred arrested sharecroppers was held in Elaine on November 3 under highly questionable conditions. Most of the defendants had never been formally charged with anything, their court-appointed defense counsel did not consult with them before the trial, no witnesses were called by the defense, and the defendants were not allowed to testify. "Confessions" had been taken from some men, almost all of whom had been tortured. Some had been flogged, others had foreign objects inserted in their mouths and nostrils, and a few had been interrogated while strapped into an electric chair. Perhaps most critically, no motion was made for a dismissal or a change of venue even though the court and town of Elaine were crowded with "determined men" swearing terrible harm to anyone who interfered with the desired result of the trial. As the U.S. Supreme Court later concluded when it examined the circumstances of the trial: "No juryman could have voted for an acquittal and continued to live in Phillips County."

The trial itself, with a lively mob hooting and milling about outside the courtroom, lasted all of forty-five minutes, after which the jury convened for a mere five minutes before announcing its verdict. Twelve of the defendants were given death sentences for their roles in the "insurrection," and sixty-seven others received sentences of up to twenty years.

Taking advantage of his ability to pass as white, Walter White obtained phony press credentials from an acquaintance on a Chicago newspaper and presented himself in Arkansas as a reporter researching an article about the trouble in Phillips County. White gained an audience in Little Rock with Governor Brough, who expressed his gratitude that an objective newsman from a big-city paper was willing to come all the way down to Arkansas and approach the story with an open mind, particularly since the Chicago *Defender* and the NAACP had been spreading "foul lies . . . about the good white people of Arkansas." Brough assured his visitor that the problems in Phillips County had, for the most part, been stirred up by Northern agitators, and that the whites in authority there had done a good and fair job of containing the crisis. In parting, he gave White a letter of introduction for use in Phillips County that described White as "one of the most brilliant newspapermen [I] have ever met."

The letter proved invaluable as White made his way through the rural area, interviewing whites connected with the case. He pointedly avoided speaking with blacks, as he knew they would become the victims of reprisals when he returned north and wrote his account, but he did travel to Helena, where the jailed men were then being held, in the hope of visiting them.

White never did see any of the prisoners. Walking down a street in Helena, a black stranger sidled alongside and whispered that he had something to impart to him. White followed him into a wooded area, where the man warned the NAACP field secretary that the white folks had discovered who he really was and were laying to "fix" him. Hurrying to the train depot, White learned there was a train leaving Helena for Memphis in just a few minutes, and not another until later that night. As the train pulled in, White discreetly crossed the tracks and boarded from the side opposite the platform. When he offered cash for his ticket, the conductor looked at him strangely. White thought it was because of the method of payment he was offering, and began explaining that he was in a rush to get to Memphis and hadn't had time to buy a ticket. The conductor assured him that was no problem, adding: "But you're leaving, mister, just when the fun is going to start. There's a damned yellow nigger down here passing for white and the boys are going to get him."

"What'll they do with him?" White asked.

Professor, author, and sociologist W.E.B. Du Bois would often refer to the moment he learned of Georgia lynch victim Sam Hose's fate in April 1899 as the shock "that pulled me off my feet." He concluded that "one could not be a calm, cool, and detached scientist while Negroes were lynched, murdered and starved." (Schomburg Center for Research in Black Culture, New York Public Library)

WHIPPING A NEGRO GIRL IN NORTH CAROLINA BY "UNCONSTRUCTED" JOHNSONIANS.

Whipping was the Klan's preferred mode of punishment in the Reconstruction South, explicitly reminding blacks of their former status. "The habit is so inveterate among a great many persons," noted Carl Schurz, "as to render, on the least provocation, the impulse to whip a Negro almost irresistible." (Culver Pictures)

Forced to flee the South in 1892 for challenging the hypocrisy of its lynching ethos, journalist Ida B. Wells crusaded to awaken American concern. "What is, or should be woman?" she asked. "Not merely a bundle of flesh and bones, nor a fashion plate . . . but a strong, bright presence, thoroughly imbued with a sense of her mission on earth and a desire to fill it." (Schomburg Center for Research in Black Culture, New York Public Library)

The 1909 nighttime lynching of William "Froggie" James in Cairo, Illinois, occurred after a mob caught the sheriff and his deputy attempting to spirit the alleged murderer north to safety. An illuminated arch in the city's shopping district helped lend a festive air to the event. (Allen-Littlefield Collection, Robert W. Woodruff Library, Emory University)

Wrongly convicted of murdering a thirteen-year-old female employee, factory manager Leo Frank was abducted from prison and lynched in Marietta, Georgia, in August 1915. His trial, sensationalized by anti-Semitism and claims of sexual perversion, led to a national outcry and an appeal to the U.S. Supreme Court challenging the lynch mob atmosphere of the proceedings. (© Bettmann/Corbis)

The avenging Ku Klux Klan assaults freedmen loyal to the corrupt black politician Silas Lynch in D. W. Griffith's controversial 1915 film spectacular, *The Birth of a Nation*. Spellbinding in its technical virtuosity, the film was labeled a historical distortion by the NAACP. (Culver Pictures)

His investigation of the gruesome lynching of Ell Persons in 1917 led the NAACP's James Weldon Johnson to conclude "that in large measure the race question involves the saving of black America's body and white America's soul." (Schomburg Center for Research in Black Culture, New York Public Library)

In a lynching that was announced to the nation by newspapers and radio before it had occurred, farmworker Claude Neal was put to death in October 1934 near Marianna, Florida, for the rape and murder of nineteen-year-old Lola Cannidy. When authorities removed Neal's corpse from this tree outside the Jackson County courthouse, late arrivals demanded it be replaced. (© Bettmann/Corbis)

An NAACP flyer about the July 19, 1935, killing of Rubin Stacy in Florida decried lynching's horrific impact on the young. (Schomburg Center for Research in Black Culture, New York Public Library)

Do not look at the Negro.

His earthly problems are ended.

Instead, look at the seven WHITE children who gaze at this gruesom spectacle.

Is it horror or gloating on the face of the neatly dressed seven-year-ol girl on the right?

Is the tiny four-year-old on the left old enough, one wonders, to comprehen the barbarism her elders have perpetrated?

Rubin Stacy, the Negro, who was lynched at Fort Lauderdale, Florida, o July 19, 1935, for "threatening and frightening a white woman," suffere PHYSICAL torture for a few short hours. But what psychological havoc being wrought in the minds of the white children? Into what kinds of citizen

The case of Isaac Woodward, a veteran of the Second World War who had been blinded in a racist attack in South Carolina in 1946, was one of many injustices challenged by the NAACP's indefatigable Walter White (third from right). (Schomburg Center for Research in Black Culture, New York Public Library)

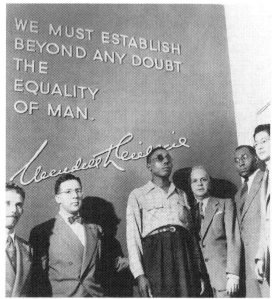

WE MUST ESTABLISH BEYOND ANY DOUBT THE EQUALITY OF MAN.

"Lynch Robeson! Give us Robeson!" Lax security by state police and other authorities encouraged jeering and violence at two scheduled Paul Robeson concerts in Peekskill, New York, in August and September 1949. (AP/Wide World Photos)

A defiant Paul Robeson at a press conference following the Peekskill violence. "This means from now on out we take the offensive. *We* take it," he assured his supporters. "I want my friends to know, in the South, in Mississippi, all over the United States, that I'll be there with my concerts. . . ." (Culver Pictures)

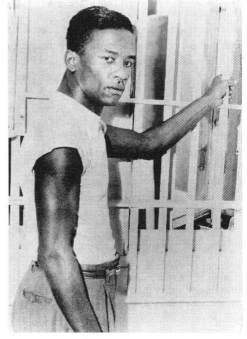

The plight of Willie McGee, convicted and sentenced to death after being accused of rape by his white lover, spawned an international outcry in the late 1940s and early 1950s. Mississippi's highest court ultimately refused to consider the notion that consensual sexual relations were possible between a black man and a white woman. McGee was electrocuted in May 1951. (Schomburg Center for Research in Black Culture, New York Public Library)

Carolyn Bryant, a key figure in the 1955 "wolf-whistle" lynching of Emmett Till, fourteen, following their encounter at a crossroads grocery store in Money, Mississippi. Bryant's husband and brother-in-law were acquitted of the crime by an all-white Mississippi jury but later sold their "confession" to a national magazine, explaining, "When a nigger even gets close to mentioning sex with a white woman, he's tired o' livin'." (AP/Wide World Photos)

Friends restrain a grief-stricken Mamie Till Bradley (left) as the body of her son, Emmett Till, is lowered into the grave on September 6, 1955, in Chicago, Illinois. (© Bettmann/Corbis)

The conductor laughed. "When they get through with him he won't pass for white no more."

Safely back home, White wrote articles for *The Nation* and other publications that told a fuller story of the Phillips County upheaval than had been aired in the mainstream press. He carefully explained the injustices of the sharecropping system and scolded Governor Brough, who had been a professor of economics for seventeen years, for remaining blind to how unfair the system was to Arkansas blacks. He also questioned the famous chivalric code of proud Southern white men who clearly did not mind stooping so low as to cheat hardworking poor black farmers out of their fair share of the profits from a cotton crop. In conclusion, White pointed out that had insurrection really been on the minds of the nearly 27,000 blacks in Phillips County, they would have conceivably done much worse damage to the county's 7,176 whites than they had.

Prior to White's exposé, a conspiracy of silence and willful ignorance about the incidents, fostered by the biased coverage of the *Arkansas Gazette* and the physical remoteness of Phillips County, had combined to conceal and whitewash the real story. Even *The New York Times* had been fooled into passing on the bogus tale of black insurrection. And Arkansas authorities had succeeded in stopping copies of *The Crisis* and *The Defender*, in which Wells-Barnett had written of the Phillips County violence, from circulating in the state.

Wells-Barnett had thrown herself into the case in typical confrontational mode. Attending a Chicago meeting of concerned blacks at which the Arkansas situation was being discussed, she inquired about specific strategies. When assured that a host of actions were under consideration, she snapped, "But, Mr. President, what have you *done* about it?" With a small amount of money she'd raised, she traveled alone to Arkansas—her first trip back to the South since the sacking of the Memphis *Free Speech* office in 1892—and met with the mothers, wives, and other relatives of the condemned men. Taking advantage of the fact that, to most white men, all middle-aged black women looked pretty much alike, Wells-Barnett slipped in to visit with the jailed men along with a group of their female relatives, and surreptitiously took down statements from them. When visiting hours were ending, the imprisoned men entertained their loved ones with spirituals. Wells-Barnett listened appreciatively, but encouraged the men to stop singing about dying, the Lord's plan, and that "great gettin' up mornin' " and start vocalizing about life, freedom, and vindication. She then quietly left the state.

The point of White's and Wells-Barnett's writings was that Phillips County had, at the least, erred in mistaking the formation of a sharecroppers' union for armed rebellion. The Arkansas Supreme Court nonetheless upheld the executions of six of the twelve men originally sentenced and Governor Brough insisted that the executions go forward, as did the American Legion and various other Arkansas civic groups. On several occasions the men came within seventy-two hours of being put to death as the NAACP forced the cases all the way to the U.S. Supreme Court. Moorfield Storey told the nation's high court in 1923 that a white conspiracy of state courts, newspapers, elected officials, as well as organizations like the Rotary Club and the American Legion, had all worked to unjustly rush the condemned men to execution, that cruel tortures had been used to extract confessions, and that the presence of a crowd outside the courthouse whose mood resembled that of a lynch mob had rendered the trials a travesty of justice. "We have the whole community inflamed against the defendants, prepared . . . to lynch them, only refraining from doing so because they are assured by leading citizens that the trial would accomplish the same purposes," Storey told the high court.

The Supreme Court ruling in the case, *Moore v. Dempsey,* handed down on February 19, 1923, was a major victory for the NAACP. The majority opinion, written by Justice Oliver Wendell Holmes, Jr., who'd penned the dissent in the Leo Frank case, concurred with the association that in the Elaine cases "the proceeding of the state court, although a trial in form, were only a form, and . . . the appellants were hurried to convictions under the pressure of a mob without any regard for their rights and without according them due process of law." The ruling essentially countered the court's 1914 decision in *Frank v. Mangum,* which had acknowledged that a mob atmosphere had probably influenced the outcome of the Atlanta trial of Leo Frank but that it was up to the state's appeals system to address the problem. *Moore* departed from *Frank* by stipulating that any denial of due process was the concern of the federal government. By offering an important new interpretation of the due-process clause of the Fourteenth Amendment, asserting that it must be applied to state and county trials, *Moore* became the first of several decisions in the twentieth century that would provide stronger federal standards for what constituted a legitimate criminal trial. It also represented a serious blow to the power of mobs; no longer would it be legally acceptable for a boisterous crowd to sway a judicial hearing or threaten its participants. A criminal trial was to be immune from such overt emotionalism, and was not to be viewed by the public as a means of exacting revenge or dealing with social ills.

The war years and their aftermath proved to be a time of tremendous growth for the NAACP. At least some of the credit for this transformation was due to the leadership of John Shillady, a social worker and specialist in the administration and fiscal management of social-service organizations, who became executive secretary in January 1918 and, taking over the group's membership appeals, oversaw in only six months a phenomenal rise in membership from ten thousand to almost thirty-six thousand. Shillady emphasized the development of chapters nationwide, and conceived of and directed the assembly of the NAACP's first book, *Thirty Years of Lynchings in the United States, 1889–1918.*

By now the NAACP had established something of a routine for investigating and exposing lynchings. Where possible, whites or blacks who could pass for white entered communities to investigate; then, armed with as much firsthand information as could be safely gathered, the organization sent telegrams and letters of protest to officials, shared intelligence with news organizations, and in some instances published reports on specific lynchings or ran special supplements in *The Crisis.* Frequently the NAACP accounts of acts of mob violence varied from and were much more in-depth than official or press versions of the same events. If for no other reason than that NAACP investigators had greater access to and made a more concerted effort to get the black community's side of any lynching story, the organization's write-ups tended to be definitive, and gradually came to be viewed as such by lawmakers and editors.

The NAACP's lynching book, by Martha Gruening and Helen Boardman, strived to be compelling and informative, but also aimed to discomfort the reader, recounting 100 of the most disturbing lynchings (out of a total of 3,224) that had occurred over the three decades. The book told of blacks being roasted alive who addressed their tormentors even as their limbs burned through to the bone; a mob so bloodthirsty it forced its way into a Georgia jail and lynched seven men, only one of whom had actually been convicted of a crime; a black farmer and his two daughters in Tennessee ambushed as they drove to a cotton gin, all three hanged from the same tree and their load of cotton then set afire beneath them.

One of the stories intended to sear readers' sensibilities was that of Haynes and Mary Turner of Valdosta, Georgia, and their former boss, white planter Hampton Smith, who had been killed on May 16, 1918, by someone shooting into his home. His terrified wife, who was wounded, ran into the woods and wandered around for hours before being taken in by neighbors. She accused a black man named Sidney Johnson of having carried out her husband's murder, but he disappeared and could not be found, despite the best efforts of a hastily formed lynch mob. Irritated at not being able to lay hands on their primary suspect, the lynchers exacted summary revenge on several other black men, including Haynes Turner, who was known to have disliked Smith.

Mary Turner, who was eight months pregnant, was infuriated by her husband's death. She declared him innocent and vowed to seek justice, although, as *The Atlanta Constitution* reported, she protested what had occurred too vehemently and "made unwise remarks . . . the people were angered by her remarks, as well as her attitude." The sheriff placed her under arrest, possibly for her own protection, but then gave her up to a mob that took her away into the woods near the Little River at a place called Folsom's Bridge. There, before a crowd that included women and children, Mary was stripped, hung upside down by the ankles, soaked with gasoline, and roasted to death. In the midst of this torment, a white man opened her swollen belly with a hunting knife and her infant fell to the ground, gave a cry, and was stomped to death. The *Constitution*'s coverage of the killing was subheadlined: "Fury of People Is Unrestrained."

"Mister, you ought to've heard the nigger wench howl!," Walter White, in Georgia to investigate the case, was told by a helpful white man who took him to the site of the lynching. Turner and her infant had been buried directly beneath the tree on which she'd died, and someone had set up an empty whiskey bottle with a half-smoked cigar in its neck as a "tombstone." White sent Governor Hugh Dorsey the names of seventeen members of the mob that had killed Mary Turner, but Dorsey's office sent back what seemed to be almost a form letter saying that all efforts to bring the guilty to justice had been futile.

The horrific details of the mob killing of Mary Turner shocked even hardened antilynching activists. The atrocity was described in numerous articles and editorials, was discussed in Congress, and became an instant rallying point for further agitation. Such barbarism was getting some distance away from any hoary notions of honorable men defending women's chastity. It introduced a new low in the level of degradation associated with lynching.

It also was a bracing reminder of the horror and callousness that made antilynching work so depressing and always difficult. The campaign could at times center around dry legalisms and considerations of the right to due process and other constitutional guarantees, but it always returned to the kind of details that, James Weldon Johnson observed, "were enough to make the devil gasp in astonishment"—babies spilling out of people's stomachs, charred torsos dragged down Main Street, severed heads skewered on poles. NAACP workers were, in Ovington's words, "a kindly set of people" performing "nauseating work," who saw themselves engaged in a Manichaean struggle: the most educated and genteel people in America—artists, poets, civil rights lawyers—versus the worst the primordial backwoods of the nation had to offer, thugs and ignoramuses capable of posing with the "trophy" of a human being they had murdered at their feet. How could one even begin to understand such behavior, let alone persuade its practitioners to cease and desist?

In the NAACP office in New York, far from the bayous and isolated courthouse squares where such things took place, news of the latest feral act of a Southern mob could still cause goosebumps to break out along one's arm, and cause a thoughtful person to reflect on the possibility that pure evil existed in the world and that the lynch mob must be its chief mode of expression. Perhaps, as a character in James Weldon Johnson's novel *The Autobiography of an Ex-Colored Man* philosophized, America had been naive to think its ultimate evil—slavery—could ever be fully dissipated. Perhaps what had happened instead was that this powerful force of dark energy had never really gone away at all, but had simply atomized into smaller fragments, such as lynching, the original dose of evil wholly intact. For even the most stalwart reformer there was always the nagging fear that, despite the hundreds of articles, petitions, resolutions, and speeches generated in opposition, lynching would never be dislodged from American life.

Particularly distressing was the treatment of black soldiers home from the war in Europe. Black participation in the war had been advocated by many leaders of the race, including Du Bois, and was seen as a source of pride. But the appearance of black veterans in uniform in the South set off a reaction as strong as that which had greeted black Union troops in 1865, or had led to the dismissals of the Brownsville soldiers in 1906. Of seventy-six reported lynchings of blacks nationwide in 1919, many were of returning soldiers. Whites, it seems, were afraid that having learned "social equality," that is, the privilege of sleeping with white women, as was vividly rumored, in France, returning blacks would surely expect the same kind of rights here and would be uncontrollable. Veterans were attacked with baseball bats, arrested on trumped-up charges, assaulted for even discussing their wartime service. In Blakely, Georgia, a gang of whites intercepted returning black veteran Wilbur Little at the train depot and forced him to take off his uniform and walk through town to his family's home in his underwear. A few days later Little defied the mob's warning not to appear in the uniform again and was killed.

Near the end of 1919 it was the turn of one of the NAACP's highest officers to experience this degeneracy firsthand. The Austin, Texas, branch had come under unfriendly scrutiny by state officials after *The Crisis,* which was sold on some newsstands in Texas and reached seven thousand NAACP members in the state by mail, carried statements from an NAACP conference in Cleveland calling for the abolition of Jim Crow laws on buses and trains. Such published remarks, Texas authorities feared, might stir up discontent among blacks. In August 1919 the Austin chapter informed the New York office that the attorney general of Texas had demanded to see the local group's account books and was threatening to shut the chapter down.

The threat held significant ramifications because Texas was a big field of NAACP operations, with thirty-one active chapters. Ovington suggested that the executive secretary, John Shillady, go to Austin himself to meet with state officials, explain that the NAACP was a national educational organization, and describe its peaceful aims and purpose. She believed that a miscomprehension of the organization's nature must lie at the heart of the Austin dilemma, and Shillady, who had devoted so much energy to expanding the network of local chapters, had much at stake in resolving this kind of challenge before it was replicated and used to disrupt NAACP growth elsewhere. When he asked Ovington if she thought such a trip would be dangerous, she assured him that what the situation required was the leadership of just such a gentle diplomat as himself. "There might be danger to someone else," she told him, "but not to you."

Shillady telegraphed Governor William P. Hobby and the state's attorney general, expressing the desire to meet with them, but when he arrived in a stifling hot Austin in mid-August both men were out of town. Shillady met with the acting attorney general, who hardly made the visitor feel at ease, repeatedly using the word *nigger* and warning Shillady that Texas blacks were preparing to rise up and attack white people. Shillady tried to convince him that the NAACP was not in the business of scheduling Negro uprisings, and showed him an NAACP antilynching petition signed by many prominent Americans, including several governors and the attorney general of the United States, but the Texan still seemed un-convinced of the organization's respectability.

The interview with the acting attorney general was cordial compared with what followed. On his way to his next appointment, Shillady was stopped on the street by a policeman, served a subpoena, and brought be-fore a so-called court of inquiry. A county judge by the name of Dave Pickle, along with other local officials, accused him and the NAACP of vi-olating the laws of Texas by trying to abolish Jim Crow ordinances. The legitimacy of this court of inquiry was dubious, but Shillady cooperated in the hopes of quelling the Texans' distrust, explaining that while the NAACP might advocate for social change, only the federal government could actually take such steps.

The next morning Shillady was on his way to meet with the head of the Austin chapter when he was jumped by a group of men and beaten up. He recognized two of his assailants as Dave Pickle and a constable who had participated in the hearing the night before. The roughing-up was more than physically painful: it breached the sense of personal security Shillady had felt on account of his white skin. Now that it was broken, a creeping awareness that he had been suppressing since his arrival in Austin burst upon him. He was all alone here, and the once-remote concern that he and Ovington had discussed in the safety of the New York office—that the head of a national civil rights organization fighting mob violence could himself be lynched in Texas—began to seem palpably less remote, indeed like a distinct possibility. It was far from reassuring when the clerk at his hotel said by way of greeting and without cracking a smile, "I wouldn't have your job for a thousand dollars."

From his hotel room Shillady called for a doctor to come and stitch up the wounds in his face, then contacted the mayor by telephone, explained who he was, and demanded that the city provide him protection to the train station. With a police escort that the mayor only begrudgingly pro-vided, he arrived at the train depot to find a group of rough-looking men on hand, who appeared to be watching him. Shillady made it onto the train but remained nervously vigilant. The train wouldn't cross out of Texas for twenty-four hours, and he knew his lynching lore well enough to be aware that victims were often taken off trains at lonely whistle-stops. An Associated Press reporter happened to be on the train, however, and hearing of Shillady's misadventure, wrote it up and put it on the AP wire. By the time Shillady reached New York's Penn Station two days later he was a hero, and the entire staff of the NAACP's New York office turned out to applaud him, along with the station redcaps, as he stepped down from the coach.

The NAACP considered bringing charges against the authorities in Austin for Shillady's mistreatment, perhaps to force a kind of show trial in which the duplicity and intolerance of the officials would be exposed. What was especially damning, from the NAACP's perspective, was that it appeared likely that both the abduction of the executive secretary and the roughing-up he'd received had been authorized by state officials. The NAACP appealed to Governor Hobby to find and punish Shillady's attackers, although Hobby replied by telegram that Shillady had essentially only got what he had coming, and an Austin deputy sheriff who exchanged communications with Ovington explained that Shillady had simply been "received by red-blooded white men" who would act similarly toward any "Negro-loving white men" who entered the precinct. As Ovington later recorded, she could find not a single public official in Austin who would admit that "it was wrong to beat up a visitor who had come to the city to make a courteous inquiry."

The chief reason plans to pursue Texas officials never materialized was that Shillady himself had no interest in returning there as a witness, even if the case might prove politically valuable. His wife had been extremely upset about what had befallen her husband while he was on a "business trip" for the NAACP, and she was adamant that he not be exploited for the sake of an organizational objective. Incredibly, no NAACP staff member had ever been physically assaulted in the organization's ten-year history, and the psychological effect on Shillady was pronounced. Ovington thought his condition resembled that of a soldier who'd endured too much shelling. As Walter White recounted: "His great gaiety and warm smile disappeared. The superb efficiency which had been his was replaced by an indecisiveness as though he were paralyzed." The organization gave him a six-week vacation and paid for many of his medical expenses, but Shillady soon announced his resignation, writing to his colleagues: "I am less confident than heretofore of the speedy success of the Association's full program and of the probability of overcoming, within a reasonable period, the forces opposed to Negro equality by the means and methods which are within the Association's power to employ." This highly capable white man who had helped guide the group's struggle against America's most shameful evil, White concluded, was, in the end, himself "a victim of lynching, as surely as any Negro who had been strung up to a tree or burned at the stake."

The fear among Texans that the NAACP might try to change laws affecting race relations, the very anxiety Shillady had gone to Austin to address, proved to have actually been somewhat prescient. Shillady's replacement as executive secretary, James Weldon Johnson, would launch a broad effort in the early 1920s to try to attain federal antilynching legislation, a fight that would ultimately sweep Congress, the White House, the press, and the entire nation into a debate over the deadly practice the NAACP called "The Shame of America."

CHAPTER 8

The Shame of America

The movement toward social reform that characterized American life in the early 1900s was slowed dramatically by the country's involvement in the First World War. The impetus behind America's participation in the war in Europe—the concern for the defense of France and the patriotic summoning of men and materiel for the U.S. effort—had principally been a moral crusade, nurtured by President Wilson but based on existing progressive attitudes. Disillusionment with the war and American internationalism quickly set in, however, seen in the vociferous criticism of Wilson's peace negotiations at Paris, Congress's refusal to rubber-stamp American participation in the League of Nations, and, finally, the ouster of the Democrats from the White House in the election of 1920.

One of the results of the nation's spiritual fatigue in the war's aftermath was the rise of a powerful new conservatism. It took the form of an intensified contempt for immigrant minorities, a dislike of Catholics and Jews, suspicion of "Bolsheviks" and "Reds," and anxiety about the moral implications of automobiles, big cities, and expanded freedoms for women. The trend had perhaps its clearest expression in the rise of the new Ku Klux Klan, which from its prosaic origins in Atlanta in the fall of 1915 became a national phenomenon boasting several million members by the early 1920s.

The 1920s saw a new term—*fundamentalism*—become popular to describe the pervasive religious mood of the Christian South, where an increasing number of people believed that salvation lay in the acceptance of a literal reading of the Bible, and church and conservative forces busied themselves with the enforcement of prohibition and the control of private morality. This fundamentalist trend, and the attendant rift between urban and rural America, was memorably dramatized by the 1925 Scopes "Monkey Trial" in Tennessee over the teaching of the theory of evolution.

The animosity did not all flow in one direction. As America lost its rural orientation and became a predominantly urban nation, city dwellers became more openly dismissive of their country cousins, particularly those residing in the states of the former Confederacy. Such derision informed H. L. Mencken's 1920 essay "The Sahara of the Bozart," in which he took delight in mocking the artistic and intellectual aridness of a region given over to Bible-thumping preachers, pellagra, and catfish suppers. He compared the present-day South unfavorably with the grandeur and promise of its rich Colonial period, depicting a blighted place that, having lost its soul in the Civil War and never recovered it, was now sinking into the further idiocy of revival religion and Ku Klux Klanism. But it was perhaps the South's failure to develop any group of deep thinkers, any modern intellectual tradition of any kind, that most troubled Mencken:

> It is, indeed, amazing to contemplate so vast a vacuity. One thinks of the interstellar spaces, of the colossal reaches of the now mythical ether. Nearly the whole of Europe could be lost in that stupendous region of fat farms, shoddy cities and paralyzed cerebrums: one could throw in France, Germany and Italy, and still have room for the British Isles. . . . [F]or all its size and all its wealth and all the "progress" it babbles of, it is almost as sterile, artistically, intellectually, culturally, as the Sahara Desert. . . . It would be impossible in all history to match so complete a drying-up of a civilization.

Of course, the suspicion of that which was foreign, of change itself, and the willingness to act on irrational fears was not confined to the Cotton South. In these same postwar years, the federal government hounded and deported numerous "radicals"; two Italian anarchists, Nicola Sacco and Bartolomeo Vanzetti, were executed in Massachusetts on circumstantial evidence linking them to the killing of a bank guard, over the strenuous objections of a worldwide clemency movement; and Socialist presidential candidate Eugene Debs was arrested for sedition and locked away in a federal penitentiary. Faith in the government itself was rocked in 1922 when President Warren Harding's secretary of the interior, Albert Fall, was found to have accepted bribes to lease oil rights to the navy's Teapot Dome, Wyoming, oil reserve.

The country's drift into reactionism augured poorly for progress in addressing serious social ills or race-related issues such as lynching. "[I]f American intelligence could be measured by the Scopes trial, American justice by the Sacco-Vanzetti case, American tolerance by the Klan, and American political morals by the Prohibition farce and Teapot Dome," historian Richard Hofstadter observes of the 1920s, "it seemed simpler to catch the first liner to Europe or to retire to the library with [H. L. Mencken's] *American Mercury* than to engage oneself seriously with proposals to reform American life."

It was nonetheless in this era of reduced expectations that the NAACP prepared to build on its longstanding publicity campaign against lynching with a concerted effort to secure federal antilynching legislation. The NAACP's decade of education and publicity on the subject had helped bring about an encouraging diminution of sensational Southern news stories of "big black brutes" and insatiable black rapists, even if the number of recorded lynchings held steady at fifty-three in 1920, fifty-nine in 1921, and fifty-one in 1922; and a generation of northward migration had concentrated large numbers of blacks in major cities, making them potentially a political force that would influence legislation.

This very migration had also helped fuel what James Weldon Johnson dubbed the "Red Summer" of 1919, a season of unprecedented racial violence that, in the NAACP's view, put great urgency on the task of winning federal action against lynching and mob violence. Even President Wilson, whose fondness for the ways of the Old South was no secret, had been moved to declare that any American "who takes part in the action of a mob . . . is no true son of this great democracy, but its betrayer." The 1917 riot in East St. Louis over jobs and housing proved a kind of template for the increasing number of clashes during the next twenty-four months, as the advance of blacks out of the cotton fields of the South and into the assembly lines of the North created new demands for economic equality and pressures for a fair share of accommodations and services.

In 1919 race riots broke out in more than twenty cities, including Chicago, Omaha, Tulsa, Washington, D.C., Charleston, and Knoxville. There also occurred seventy-six recorded lynchings of blacks that year as well as the deadly "sharecroppers' war" in Phillips County, Arkansas. In

Washington, D.C., the rioting included the shameful spectacle of hundreds of uniformed U.S. sailors and soldiers, enraged by a false report of a sexual assault on an officer's wife, chasing and beating black men and women within view of the Capitol dome. During the Omaha violence, when authorities tried unsuccessfully to halt the abduction and burning of a black suspect, a mob turned on the city's mayor, tying a noose around his neck and hoisting him to a lamppost before police could intervene.

Most upsetting of the era's racial disturbances was the summer 1919 race riot in Chicago, the metropolis that only a generation before had hosted that grand celebration of American achievement, the Columbian Exposition of 1893. In the quarter-century since the popular Chicago fair, large numbers of Southern blacks, drawn northward from Mississippi, Arkansas, and Louisiana on the rails of the Illinois Central, had moved into the city's South Side and were now beginning to encroach on other neighborhoods. Chicago had always been a city of fiercely guarded ethnic turf and contested boundaries, and as the war in Europe ended and the labor boom it had created came to an abrupt halt, competition for jobs and housing increasingly took on racial overtones.

The violence was sparked on a hot day in late July over an incident at a bathing beach on Lake Michigan. Black and white youths had been throwing stones at one another all afternoon at the beach between Twenty-sixth and Twenty-ninth streets when Eugene Williams, a black youngster apparently not engaged in the rock throwing, was struck on the head and drowned. Blacks pointed out the white man who had thrown the stone to a white policeman, Officer Daniel Callahan, but Callahan refused to arrest him, instead taking into custody one of the complaining blacks. At this blatant injustice months of long-stored-up resentment erupted.

For more than a week sporadic violence broke out over the sprawling city. White mobs, many attached to territorial Irish neighborhood "athletic clubs" with such names as the Ragen Colts, the Hamburgers, Our Flag, the Dirty Dozen, and the Sparklers, roamed the South Side, dragging black victims off trolleys, ganging up on individuals as they went to work, and assaulting small businesses. Wielding bricks, stones, baseball bats, and iron bars, the whites had the upper hand, as police either stood by or in some instances participated in the attacks. Blacks did fight back defiantly, alone and in groups, against white mobs and police. In the end, 23 blacks and 15 whites were killed, and 537 people were wounded in beatings, stonings, and stabbings. More than a thousand families, mostly black, were made homeless.

Although America was disheartened that such an incident could occur in a city that many viewed as a haven from Southern bigotry, a number of blacks heralded the 1919 Chicago riot as an important turning point: unlike the one-sided massacres of the nineteenth century, in which blacks were mowed down like sheep or simply fled for their lives, many in Chicago's black community had stood their ground and resisted. In some neighborhoods they had given almost as good as they got. Leaders could not help speculate that perhaps the long search for a corrective to the nation's race troubles had at last been found. Some predicted that relations between whites and blacks might actually improve once whites understood that abuse would no longer be tolerated without an equally devastating response. That same month, the young black poet Claude McKay created a stirring hymn to the new militancy:

> If we must die, let it be not like hogs
> Hunted and penned in an inglorious spot,
> While round us bark the mad and hungry dogs,
> Making their mock at our accursed lot.
>
> If we must die, O let us nobly die,
> So that our precious blood may not be shed
> In vain; then even the monsters we defy
> Shall be constrained to honor us though dead!
>
> O kinsman! We must meet the common foe!
> Though far outnumbered, let us show us brave
> And for their thousand blows deal one death-blow!
> What though before us lies the open grave?
>
> Like men we'll face the murderous, cowardly pack,
> Pressed to the wall, dying, but fighting back!

Despite the courage shown by Chicago blacks in resisting white mobs, their Southern kin remained highly vulnerable. During 1919, lynch mobs operating below the Mason-Dixon Line summarily executed blacks at the rate of approximately one every five days. In early January, one Bragg Williams was burned at the stake in Hillsboro, Texas; on February 6, John Daniels was hanged in New Bern, North Carolina; on March 13, Cicero Cage was lynched and his body cut to pieces in Tuscaloosa, Alabama; that same day, Joe Walker was shot to death in Greenville, Florida; and on and on it went throughout the year.

On June 26, in a case the NAACP would cite as an example of why the federal government must become involved in the battle against lynching, John Hartfield of Ellisville, Mississippi, was accused of assaulting a white woman, a Miss Meek, as she walked along a railroad track. Hartfield was hunted down by the sheriff and a citizens' posse. The sheriff held Hartfield briefly for investigation before handing him over to the mob, who announced their intention to put him to death at the railroad siding where he had accosted Miss Meek, although there was disagreement as to whether his crime warranted hanging or immolation. While the locals debated the fine points, three thousand strangers began pouring into the town from New Orleans and Jackson to witness the killing, which had been announced in the region's newspapers alongside a provocative comment from Mississippi governor Theodore Bilbo:

> I am utterly powerless. The State has no troops, and if the civil authorities at Ellisville are helpless, the State is equally so. Furthermore, excitement is at such a high pitch throughout south Mississippi that any armed attempt to interfere with the mob would doubtless result in the death of hundreds of persons. The negro has confessed, says he is ready to die, and nobody can keep the inevitable from happening.

The NAACP, gearing up to take its antilynching fight to Congress, cited Bilbo's callous remarks as the maddening proof of the unwillingness of states to stand up to lynch mobs.

It also prepared to mobilize its large membership. Due to the rise of a black urban class, the agitation of the 1919 riots, and the promotional skills of the departed John Shillady, the organization's membership had soared tenfold, from nine thousand in 50 branches in 1916 to ninety thousand in 356 branches by 1920. In direct response to the Red Summer violence, the group had sponsored more than two thousand public meetings across the country, in churches, lodge halls, and school basements, at which twelve thousand dollars had been raised in nickel and quarter contributions for the antilynching campaign. Virtually every staff member was involved, Du Bois himself unfurling from the windows of the new NAACP offices on Fifth Avenue a banner that read: "A Man Was Lynched Yesterday."

The centerpiece of this effort was the NAACP's May 1919 National Conference on Lynching in New York City, a two-day gathering addressed by Charles Evans Hughes, former New York governor and Republican presidential candidate, who told an audience at Carnegie Hall:

"We have not destroyed the menace of force because we have licked the Kaiser; the menace of force resides in every community." Former governor Emmett O'Neal of Alabama, renowned for his brave stance as a Southern elected official who opposed lynching, received an effusive ovation for urging the removal from office of sheriffs who failed in their duty to protect prisoners in custody.

In his remarks to the gathering, James Weldon Johnson, who was to lead the NAACP's legislative effort, predicted—accurately, it was to turn out—that resistance to a federal antilynching law would center in part on the resilient myth that lynching was necessary to deter black men from raping white women. "The veil of self-satisfaction has got to be torn away from the face of this nation, and it must be made to look at itself as it is," Johnson urged. "The raw, naked brutal facts of lynching must be held up before the eyes of this country until the heart of this nation becomes sick, until we get a reaction of righteous indignation that will not stop until we have swept away lynching as a national crime."

The conference ended with praise for New York's 369th Colored Infantry, which had served with distinction in Europe, and strongly worded resolutions calling on Congress to investigate lynching. "By the God of Heaven," Du Bois exhorted readers of *The Crisis,* "we are cowards and jackasses if now that that war is over, we do not marshal every ounce of our brain and brawn to fight a sterner, longer, more unbending battle against the forces of hell in our own land. . . . Make way for Democracy! We saved it in France, and by the Great Jehovah, we will save it in the United States of America, or know the reason why."

The time seemed auspicious for obtaining federal action. The atrocities of the just-concluded war had thrown America's own brand of barbarism into unflattering relief, and after the violence of the Red Summer, mobs appeared to be an authentic threat to law and stability. Furthermore, the NAACP could not help but be inspired by the successful results achieved recently by two other long-standing reform movements, the fight by the Women's Christian Temperance Union and the Anti-Saloon League to win the Eighteenth Amendment (Prohibition) in 1918, and the suffragist victory resulting in the Nineteenth Amendment (women's suffrage) in 1920. "If the American people can stop long enough to change the Constitution to decide whether the American people shall drink or not, or 6,000,000 people shall vote," the NAACP noted, "they can at least stop long enough to change the Constitution to say whether 12,000,000 people can live in safety." Another aspect of the political climate the antilynching forces found encouraging, even as many disapproved of it, was the zeal with which the federal government pursued suspected Communists and anarchists. If such concern could be directed toward those whose threat to society was largely abstract, how long could the government remain nonchalant about anarchy in one of its purest forms, the lynch mob?

On a purely tactical level, the prospects also appeared good. Republicans held a majority in both houses of Congress, and the sitting Republican president, Warren Harding, supported the idea of antilynching legislation, having described lynching as a "very sore spot on our boast of civilization." A 1921 address by Harding to the nation's lawmakers had included the admonition: "Congress ought to wipe the stain of barbaric lynching from the banners of a free and orderly, representative democracy."

The NAACP's "man of the hour" in Congress was white Missouri representative Leonidas C. Dyer, who represented a largely black constituency in St. Louis. Dyer, elected to the House in 1910, had introduced an antilynching bill as early as 1911, and had subsequently proposed several variations, most of which never made it out of committee. Dyer had redoubled his efforts, however, after the East St. Louis riot of 1917. Many of the victims of that disturbance had found refuge across the Mississippi River in his district, and he had listened to their stories of mob brutality firsthand. When he appeared before a congressional committee investigating the violence, he referred to the East St. Louis assaults on innocent black men, women, and children as "the most dastardly and most criminal outrages ever perpetrated in this country," and estimated that there had been five hundred black fatalities, a number well above any other estimate, including that of the NAACP.

Another impetus to a national antilynching law was the gnawing fear in the upper states of the Union that the practice of lynching would follow the black migration north, that lynch mobs might become as prevalent in New York, Oregon, or Maine as they were in Georgia or Louisiana. A June 1920 multiple lynching in Duluth, Minnesota, one of the northernmost cities in the United States, had shown this concern to be completely warranted.

The atmosphere in the hilly iron-ore capital on the southwest shore of Lake Superior had grown racially tense in the years after the war. U.S. Steel, Duluth's largest employer, imported Southern blacks as cheap labor and then used them as strikebreakers when labor relations with whites went sour. Many young whites, just released from service in the wartime army, were angry not to find the local labor scene more hospitable upon their return, and the police, understanding their restlessness and respectful of their status as veterans, tended to cut them a great deal of slack, even when some joined a Klan chapter and crosses were burned on the heights overlooking the city.

On June 14 a traveling circus arrived in town from Indiana, bringing a large complement of young black men who served as roustabouts, haulers, and unskilled workers. That night a teenage Duluth couple who'd gone necking in a field near the circus site claimed they had been attacked by "circus niggers," and that they had been held at gunpoint while the girl was raped. What actually happened between the two parties was never determined. A doctor's report indicated the girl had not been raped, and other elements of the story were contradictory. Identifying the men responsible for the alleged assault proved nearly impossible. There were more than a hundred blacks with the circus, most of them thin, muscular youths in their late teens or early twenties, all of whom looked virtually identical to the Duluth police. The young victims of the alleged crime, however, identified thirteen of the blacks, all of whom were immediately arrested.

The next night, a story made the rounds that the girl had died from the injuries she'd sustained. (Later, it was found that the rumor had originated with a man who had asked the girl's mother from a passing car how the girl was doing. The mother replied, "She's in bed," but he heard the words *she's dead*.) A few nights later, with several leading Duluth police officials away interviewing additional suspects who had moved on with the circus to a neighboring town, a frenzied mob bullied past a smaller and thoroughly intimidated group of police holding the jail. They seized three of the blacks—Elias Clayton, nineteen; Elmer Jackson, nineteen; and Isaac McGhie, twenty—all of whom had repeatedly declared their innocence, and hanged them from a lamppost in downtown Duluth before a crowd of several thousand men, women, and children.

The Dyer antilynching measure considered by Congress in the early 1920s was not the first federal antilynching bill to be debated in that body. George H. White of North Carolina, the lone black representative in the House at the turn of the century (and the last for several decades), had introduced one in 1900. In doing so he argued that the so-called fear white women had of black men was based on a myth, and that white men actually outraged black women at a much higher rate. The bill had virtually no support, even from White's constituents, and his remarks about the Southern sexual double standard earned him only scorn from his fellow North Carolinians. The indignant Raleigh *News & Observer* noted, "[I]t is bad enough that North Carolina should have the only nigger Congressman," let alone one who would introduce such unkind legislation. White's antilynching bill languished in the House Judiciary Committee and was quickly forgotten. When he left the House in 1901 both bodies of the North Carolina legislature passed resolutions of thanksgiving, and back in his native state White found the elimination of blacks from politics so complete, he and others who tried to attend a state Republican convention were chased away by men armed with clubs.

The world had changed much in the intervening twenty years, of course, and Dyer's NAACP-backed legislation, introduced in the House on April 11, 1921, had not only a white author but also the support of numerous liberal voices. The Dyer Bill defined a lynching as a murder of any citizen of the United States by a mob of three or more people. A sheriff or other state officer who failed to make a reasonable effort to keep a prisoner in his custody from being lynched, or to catch and prosecute members of a lynch mob, was guilty of a felony and could be sentenced to as many as five years in prison and fined five thousand dollars. If the sheriff was found to have actively aided the mob he could be imprisoned for between five years and life. Under another of the bill's terms, the federal government could prosecute lynchers if the state failed to do so, and any county or counties in which a lynching occurred was to pay ten thousand dollars to the victim's survivors.

The proposed legislation acknowledged the power of the Southern sheriff, and was based on the recognition that at the county or local level only the sheriff and his deputies had the power, if they chose, to stop a lynching. Generally, the sheriff had immense control of the county he ruled, dispensing law and order on a first-name basis and often personally administering the county's fee system. In some areas, a thriving black market in liquor manufacture and smuggling existed, with the sheriff receiving lucrative payoffs for his silence or cooperation. While there were, to be sure, many decent Southern lawmen, it has been suggested that a significant number were for all intents and purposes not so much law-enforcement professionals as benevolently corrupt businessmen. As businessmen, it was in sheriffs' interest to maintain the local status quo, and this naturally included an adherence to local caste and racial barriers and a resistance to outside influences that threatened stability. Sheriffs often ran for and held office based on their explicit promise that nothing would ever change—come labor organizers, Communists, or other busy-bodies—and, most important, that the local black people would not get out of line.

Antilynching laws, where they were supported at all, usually had as their backers those officials, such as governors, U.S. senators, and congressmen, who remained above the fray of local and county politics. They, along with some large city newspapers and business leaders, were more inclined to see lynching as a stain on a state's reputation, and mob violence as hurtful to the desire to attract outside investment and retain a steady labor force. Laws to punish lynchers and the sheriffs who allowed lynching had been enacted in North Carolina and Georgia in 1893, South Carolina in 1896, Texas and Ohio in 1897, Tennessee in 1898, Alabama in 1891 and again in 1901, and Illinois in 1908 in the wake of the Springfield riot. Some had been enacted by Democratic officials as a sop to the Populist sentiment of the mid-1890s. At the county and local level these laws were unpopular and their impact slight, and more often than not they were completely ignored.

If authoritative laws against lynching were hard to enforce at the state level, the traditional bias in the South against federal intervention of any kind made the passage of a federal law such as the Dyer Bill daunting in the extreme. An illustrative lesson for antilynching forces in the 1920s was the trajectory of Governor Hugh Dorsey of Georgia. As the state's solicitor general he had been the zealous prosecutor of Leo Frank, and had won public acclaim and the political support of Tom Watson, who labeled Dorsey "fearless, incorruptible," the man "who won the great fight for LAW AND ORDER, and the PROTECTION OF WOMANHOOD." Watson provided the backing that enabled Dorsey to win two terms as governor. During his second term, however, Dorsey began to express concern about lynching and other racial injustices. His administration published a widely respected report entitled *The Negro in Georgia,* in which numerous instances of lynching and peonage across the state were cited, and which, in its conclusion, asked the reader to consider whether Georgia should continue to be humiliated by such obvious wrongs. The NAACP hailed the publication and cited Dorsey's shift as a sign of the regional sea change in attitudes about lynching among Southern moderates. But his candor and introspection cost him dearly. Watson angrily withdrew his support and then in 1920 returned to politics himself to successfully oppose Dorsey for a U.S. Senate seat.

At the core of the antilynching campaign in Congress was also a constitutional tug-of-war that was as old as the republic itself—the question of the relationship between the states and the federal government. Was it constitutional for the federal government to hold direct prosecutorial powers over citizens? This issue troubled congressmen on both sides of the aisle. Opponents pointed out that several Supreme Court decisions of the 1870s and 1880s, most notably the *Slaughterhouse* cases, had limited the Fourteenth Amendment guarantee of equal justice under law to checking actions by states, not individuals. Some cited the rights reserved to the states under the Tenth Amendment, and made the time-honored argument that the federal government itself was the creation of the various states and had no powers other than those the states ceded to it.

The NAACP's legal expert on the issue, Albert Pillsbury, warned James Weldon Johnson that the constitutional basis for a federal antilynching law was shaky, and that the NAACP could expect the bill to become stuck in congressional judiciary committees. Dyer argued that there were federal laws on the books to protect federal judges and prisoners in federal custody, and cited the precedent of the Reconstruction statutes that made it a federal crime to deny any citizen "the free exercise or enjoyment of any privilege secured to him by the Constitution." In 1883, however, the Supreme Court, in *United States v. Harris,* had refused to uphold Reconstruction-era anti-Klan statutes that had been designed to penalize conspiracies aimed at depriving federal citizens of equal rights under state law.

"You have two horns of the dilemma," NAACP vice president Arthur B. Spingarn told the House Judiciary Committee, which held hearings on the Dyer Bill in January 1920. "The states are either powerless to prevent lynchings or they do not choose to prevent lynchings. If they are powerless to prevent lynchings, then we have mob rule in the States, 'mobocracy' and the violation of the [Tenth Amendment to the] Constitution itself. If they can do it and they do not prevent it, you have a violation of the Fourteenth Amendment in that we do not give equal protection." Spingarn and other supporters of the Dyer Bill readily admitted that there were complex constitutional issues at stake, but suggested that it was the duty of Congress to pass the best bill possible to remedy a problem, and leave the question of constitutionality to the courts. After all, the constitutionality of the two recently adopted amendments, the Eighteenth and the Nineteenth, had been much debated before their passage. "It is the proud boast of our law that wherever there is a wrong there is a remedy," Spingarn concluded. "It is quite evident the States either can not or will not remedy [lynching]. The only power left to act is the legislative power, this body . . . the Congress of the United States. The Government of this country is very wisely divided into the executive, the judicial and the legislative body and it is not for the legislative body to determine, ultimately, whether a bill is constitutional or not."

Indeed, as Dyer Bill advocates pointed out, in addition to the Volstead Act, which established prohibition, other legislation such as the Mann Act of 1910, the 1914 Harrison Narcotics Act, the Espionage Act of 1917, and its successor, the Sedition Act of 1918, all showed the willingness of Congress to assert strong control over Americans' private conduct. If Congress was able to dictate whether someone in New Hampshire could or couldn't have a glass of whiskey, shouldn't it also be able to stop men in Georgia from burning human beings at the stake?

As it turned out, Spingarn and his colleagues would be fortunate if Congress got around to focusing on the bill's constitutional nuances at all, for the South's main line of counterattack was far more emotional. After the bill was favorably reported out of the Judiciary Committee, Representative Hatton Sumners of Texas opened the floor battle with a harangue that could have been lifted from the *Congressional Record* of sixty years earlier. The South, it seemed, had been unfairly burdened with Negroes. "Only a short time ago," declared Sumners, "their ancestors roamed the jungles of Africa in absolute savagery. . . . Now we have them here." Extreme measures may be called on from time to time to protect white women from ravishment, he explained, because "you do not know where the beast is among them. Somewhere in that black mass of people is the man who would outrage your wife or your child, and every man who lives out in the country knows it." Sumners defended lynching as an expression of whites' "racial instinct" to defend the God-given boundaries of racial distinction. "When men respond to that call, they respond to a law that is higher than the law of self-preservation. It is the call to the preservation of the race. When that call comes every man who is not a racial degenerate has to answer it."

By the early 1920s, talk of the vulnerability of white women in their lonely farmhouses had lost much of its former resonance—one Northern legislator said he found Sumners's remarks "as much out of place in this day and generation as a sod house on Fifth Avenue"—but the tone of the debate had been set. Northern legislators could only sit and roll their eyes heavenward as their Southern colleagues boomed that the Dyer measure was surely a "bill to encourage rape," worried that "the ignorant negroes of the South would interpret the bill as a federal license to commit the foulest of outrages," and that such a law would surely mean the "lynching of the Constitution." Some of the Southerners worried aloud that federal intervention would retard the evolution of democratic processes at the state and local level. "How can a State be a sovereign unit of government when you hold over it the uplifted lash of the Federal Congress," one congressman pleaded, "telling its officers and people what they must do, and, if they fail, sending them to the penitentiary?" The Macon *Daily News* termed the Dyer Bill a "monstrous attempt to federalize the police powers of the State," while disparaging the NAACP as "pharisaical intermeddlers" and "sociological imbeciles" who "derive their knowledge of the negro from hearing jazz orchestras recruited from the West Indies in the rancid cafes of Paris . . ."

Congressman Edgar C. Ellis of Missouri rose to the defense of the bill, challenging "the old, pestiferous bugaboo of states' rights" raised by Sumners and demanding "to be shown that my national government has not the inherent right and power to protect its citizens from mobs and to preserve its very life and conserve its civilization." He said that what the bill's opponents really feared was that a national remedy for lynching would "deprive southern communities of a recognized and tolerated instrumentality for dealing with their Negro population." And proponents of the bill pointed out that it did not impose any federal action against municipalities or states that would not be warranted by their disregard for constitutional guarantees of due process. A county that accorded its prisoners the right to a fair trial and whose officers did their duty by repelling lynch mobs would not be interfered with. "A cynic might deduce from the bitterness of the opposition manifested in Congress to the passage of the antilynching law that thus a precious privilege would be taken away," a Northern newspaper editorialized, "[but] no state or town where lynching was prevented by efficient and timely action ever would have to pay any penalties. . . . Only those doubtful of their own powers or intentions can be afraid of it."

The Dyer Bill had a rancorous passage through the House, although that body's Republican majority, with the bill's author himself working the floor and the corridors, appeared ready to push it through. Southerners responded by strategically vacating their places so as to leave the body without a quorum. On December 19 and 20, 1921, it was necessary to lock the doors of the House and issue warrants for the truant members. James Weldon Johnson was by now working Capitol Hill vigorously. "I am pouring into them as much of our dope as they will hold," he confided to Walter White of his lobbying of House members.

When the House took the matter up again on January 25, 1922, the exchange soon turned ugly and personal. The Democrats began by characterizing the antilynching effort as runaway black activism on the part of the NAACP and denounced it as a sly maneuver by Dyer to win reelection in his predominantly black district. Then, Mississippi's Thomas Sisson stated that lynching was needed to safeguard women, at which point Wisconsin's Henry Cooper rose from his seat to charge that Sisson's remarks "openly advocated" mob violence. Sisson in turn called Cooper "idiotic," at which several hundred black spectators who were crowded into the gallery began noisily cheering Cooper on. As the chair desperately gaveled for order, Southern legislators shook their fists at the black faces upstairs. Someone yelled, "Sit down, niggers," at which the demonstrators shouted back, "We are not niggers, you liars." The blacks were "silenced with difficulty," reported *The New York Times.* The next day, with House Republicans proudly honoring their party's historic dedication to the cause of equal rights, and Democrats smug in the knowledge that their Senate brethren could be counted on to derail so noxious a piece of legislation, the House passed the Dyer Bill by a vote of 231 to 119.

James Weldon Johnson and the NAACP knew the South's resistance would harden considerably in the Senate. To succeed there would require the strong advocacy of a senator who would fight as vigorously for its passage as had Congressman Dyer in the House. They saw their best hope in longtime Massachusetts senator Henry Cabot Lodge, the Republican majority leader. The Harvard-educated Lodge was one of the most powerful men in Congress, although somewhat unpredictable and known for being prickly toward those with whom he disagreed. A Mugwump—a Northern Republican who espoused reactionary, Populist-like sentiments on issues such as immigration and foreign affairs—he had favored U.S. internationalism and entry into the Spanish-American War, then vehemently opposed the country's membership in the League of Nations. He had helped draft the Sherman Anti-Trust Law of 1890, and then—shocked, like countless Americans, by the revelations about slaughterhouses and the packaged-food industry in Upton Sinclair's novel *The Jungle*—sponsored the Pure Food and Drug Act of 1906. But he had vehemently opposed women's suffrage.

Lodge had often tangled with the Southern bloc in the Senate, dating back to his cosponsorship in 1891 of the so-called Force Bill that would have provided direct federal supervision of national elections—a bill that determined Southern lawmakers filibustered to its grave. He had worked diligently for the election of Warren Harding in 1920, and he remained close to the president. The NAACP believed that Lodge was the kind of political warrior who, if he put his mind to it, and with a Republican Senate and president behind him, might carry the antilynching bill to victory.

The association made certain that Lodge, as one of the leaders of the Republican party, understood that after six decades of unflagging loyalty to the so-called Party of Lincoln, black Americans expected something in return. The group had not been coy about letting its membership know that, if the Republicans could not deliver on the Dyer measure, no self-respecting black should vote Republican in the upcoming midterm congressional elections of 1922. And in an extremely rare and provocative move by a junior member of the party, Dyer himself traveled to Massachusetts, Lodge's home state, to tell a gathering that should Lodge fail to get the lynching bill passed, they should work to defeat him in his bid for reelection.

The NAACP had a sympathizer but not necessarily an ally in another important Senate personage—Judiciary Committee chair William E. Borah of Idaho, known to his colleagues as the "Big Potato." Like Lodge, Borah was capable of gifted advocacy in the name of progressive causes, but also held passionately conservative, isolationist views. He explained to Johnson that while he saw lynching as an abomination that should be abolished, he was not sure he could support the Dyer Bill on constitutional grounds. Borah typified a problem the NAACP encountered with numerous legislators: most were attorneys and considered themselves experts on constitutional issues, and were unwilling to leave the constitutionality question to the courts, where the NAACP believed it rightly belonged.

Appearing before Borah's committee, Johnson argued for a federal role in suppressing mob violence. If lynching was simply murder, he explained, the federal government would have no business attempting to prosecute. However, he said:

> The analogy between murder and lynching is not a true one. Lynching is murder, but it is also more than murder. In murder, one or more individuals take life, generally, for some personal reason. In lynching, a mob sets itself up in place of the state and acts in place of due process of law to mete

out death as a punishment to a person accused of crime. It is not only against the act of killing that the federal government seeks to exercise its power through the proposed law, but against the act of the mob in arrogating to itself the functions of the state and substituting its actions for . . . the law guaranteed by the Constitution. . . . The Dyer Anti-Lynching Bill is aimed against lynching not only as murder, but as anarchy—anarchy which the states have proven themselves powerless to cope with.

Johnson used the word *anarchy* deliberately, for it had a powerful resonance in America at the time. Walter White, in one letter to NAACP supporters of the bill, had suggested that if Americans could be made to think of the thousands of people who participated in lynchings as "anarchists," there would be no question of resisting federal intervention.

The Dyer Bill made it through the Senate Judiciary Committee by a narrow vote of eight to six, with Borah voting against the measure. Thankful to have passed that hurdle, but knowing no one could satisfactorily put the constitutional issues to rest, Johnson hammered away at the legislators' emotions, trying to arouse a sense of patriotic outrage about lynching. On June 1, 1922, he sent a letter to each senator calling attention to the fact that in just the past month a dozen black Americans had been lynched, including three who had been burned alive in a single afternoon in Kirvin, Texas.

The Kirvin lynchings superbly illustrated the practice's callousness and idiocy. They had occurred after a seventeen-year-old white girl, Eula Ausley, went missing and was found murdered in a forest clearing, her throat slashed from ear to ear. The girl's grandfather John King, one of the area's most prosperous ranchers, concluded upon learning of the killing that such an act must have been motivated by vengeance. He immediately suspected a neighboring white family, the Powells, with whom the Kings had a long-running feud, and for this reason expressly cautioned Sheriff H. M. Mayo not to allow the lynching of any blacks, who he knew would be the natural suspects. Despite King's warning, Mayo soon arrested "Shap" Curry, Mose Jones, and John Cornish, black laborers on the King ranch. The three men, loudly maintaining their innocence, were easily taken from Mayo's custody by a lynch mob, roped together and tied to a cultivator, then led through the streets of Kirvin before being taken to a secluded spot where they were gruesomely put to death by a mob of five hundred indignant whites. "No organ of the Negroes was allowed to remain protruding," read a newspaper's euphemistic account of the castration and mutilation of the three. Curry, saturated with oil and set ablaze, was heard to call, "O Lord, I'm a'comin.' " The other suspects met similar fates, their bodies burned to parchment as the bonfire was kept glowing for six hours by enthusiastic participants, including many boys under the age of ten.

The next day, Sheriff Mayo arrested two white brothers, Cliff and Arnie Powell, and accused them of being the real murderers of Eula Ausley, based on a set of footprints he had found leading away from the murder site. Both brothers were released by Sheriff Mayo, however, after they convinced him that they had been in the vicinity of the murder only because they kept a still there. The two soon moved away from Kirvin.

When the Dyer Bill was introduced on the Senate floor on September 21, Johnson and the NAACP had immediate concerns about the commitment of their Republican allies. The task of introducing the bill had been given to a novice Republican senator from California, Samuel Shortridge, and at a time when several key supporters were not even in their seats. The Democrats, some of whose members had intentionally left the chamber, quickly seized a parliamentary angle and called for a quorum. There being none, the bill was assigned to be held over until the next congressional session, scheduled to convene in late November. As this would come after the midterm elections, it had the effect of diminishing important NAACP leverage. Republicans who relied on black votes in their states could now breathe much easier.

The NAACP smelled a rat. "My heart sank as I thought of the gap between a Borah and a Shortridge," Johnson later said. Shortridge was a new senator with great ambition—he fancied himself in the tradition of the great orators of the Senate such as Charles Sumner and Daniel Webster, and stood with his right hand in his coat while addressing the body—but he had little experience with procedural tricks such as quorum calls and filibustering, tactics the Southern representatives would certainly employ. It occurred to Johnson that Shortridge had been chosen to be the sacrificial lamb for the Republican bill.

The NAACP delivered on its long-standing promise that it could provide a massive show of public support for the measure. It submitted to Congress a huge petition signed by twenty-four governors, thirty-nine mayors of large cities, forty-seven renowned lawyers and judges, eighty-eight bishops, twenty-nine college presidents, and dozens of writers, editors, artists, and other prominent people. The association had worked closely with a national coalition of black women, the Anti-Lynching Crusaders, led by Mary B. Talbert, president of the National Association of Colored Women. Talbert, who had traveled throughout the country selling war bonds and was well known in black communities, had helped found the Crusaders in response to a remark by Congressman Dyer that his bill would pass if 1 million people would unite behind it. The Crusaders concentrated exclusively on generating publicity and raising donations to support the passage of the bill. One important aim was to raise money for newspaper ads so that "not a single person who reads the daily newspapers shall be ignorant of the fact that we are the only country that burns human beings at the stake." The Crusaders' fund-raising missives, bearing the twin slogans "A Million Women United to Suppress Lynching" and "To Your Knees and Don't Stop Praying," raised almost seventy thousand dollars for the antilynching cause, some of which was used by the NAACP to publish full-page ads on November 22 and 23, 1922, in eight major newspapers, including *The New York Times,* the *Washington Star,* the *Chicago Daily News,* and *The Atlanta Constitution.* Beneath the bold headline "THE SHAME OF AMERICA" the ad inquired:

> Do you know that the <u>United States</u> is
> the <u>Only Land on Earth</u> where human
> beings are <u>BURNED AT THE STAKE</u>?

It went on to denounce through statistics the oft-repeated tenet that rape was the cause of lynching, and offered as the "remedy" for the problem the Senate's passage of the Dyer Bill, listing the measure's numerous endorsers. Placing such highly visible notices about America's darkest secret had its intended effect, as the ads were much remarked upon.

When the Dyer measure was once again brought up in the Senate on November 27, 1922, a group of Southern senators immediately seized the floor. In their filibuster, led by Minority Leader Oscar W. Underwood of Alabama and Byron P. Harrison of Mississippi, the Southerners demanded that the clerk read the entire contents of the previous day's "Journal of the Proceedings of the Senate," including the chaplain's prayer, suggested superfluous edits and changes to the journal, offered pointless procedural motions and objections, and otherwise demonstrated that they could bring the Senate to a dead halt.

"It must be apparent to the Senate as well as to the country that this effort is to defeat a certain bill, namely the so-called Dyer Anti-Lynching

Bill," Underwood told the New York *Evening Globe.* "I now inform you that this Bill is not going to become a law at this session of Congress."

In the face of such insolence, the Republicans caucused and at first appeared willing to fight it out, one senator assuring reporters that the "battle has just begun." But the Republicans failed to make any meaningful attempt to combat the filibuster. They might have adopted a rule against the body's daily adjournment, thus forcing the Southerners to continue the filibuster around the clock, instead of permitting them to go home each evening, prepare the next day's filibustering obstructions, and return in the morning refreshed and ready to cause more mischief. As it was, Shortridge, Lodge, and the other Republicans did not seem able to find a way to break through the blockade. Observers and legislators on both sides agreed that the Democratic senators had conducted their campaign in a "scientific way," and even the veteran Republican whip, Charles Curtis of Kansas, admitted he had not seen a filibuster so complete and well managed since the Force Bill was talked to death in 1891.

After what appeared to some like a halfhearted Republican feint at combating the filibuster, the party folded its efforts. On December 2, after the Southerners had made a sufficient-enough spectacle that blame for the bill's failure would primarily be affixed to them, the Republican leadership agreed to withdraw it. Lodge assured Underwood that the Republicans would not raise the bill again in the Sixty-seventh Congress, thus completely destroying its chances, since to be reintroduced in the Sixty-eighth it would have to start all over again in the House and win approval there.

"We cannot pass the bill in this Congress," Lodge told reporters, "and, therefore, we had to choose between giving up the whole session to a protracted filibuster or going ahead with the regular business of the session, which includes the farm legislation, the shipping and the appropriation bills. The [Republican] conference decided very reluctantly that it was our duty to set aside the Dyer Bill and go on with the business of the session."

The New York Times, which had thrown its influential support behind the bill, scored Lodge's obvious humiliation for allowing the minority Democrats to tell him, his fellow Republicans, the Harding administration, and the American people what issues could and could not be addressed in the nation's highest legislative body. In an editorial entitled "The Senate's Surrender," the paper grieved, "The leader of a party having twenty-four majority . . . was obliged to confess that he was powerless in the face of a determined filibuster. Never before has the Senate so openly advertised the impotence to which it is reduced by its antiquated rules of procedure. . . . Seldom can the leader of a proud party have had to make so mortifying a confession as that of Mr. Lodge."

Once the Dyer Bill had been smothered in its cradle, it seemed clear that, aside from a few devoted souls, the Republicans had merely been going through the motions all along, chiefly with the aim of not displeasing the emerging blocs of black voters in the urban North. While there was still some hope of the bill's passage, Johnson had continued working diligently and kept his creeping suspicions about the Republicans to himself. Now that all was lost, he did not disguise his anger and frustration. Johnson had believed, and thought that Lodge understood, that when the anticipated Southern filibuster arose, the Republicans would face it down with the help of clamorous public backing orchestrated by the NAACP. The association had drummed up an unprecedented volume of support; it seemed a tragic waste not to have put it to use.

Lodge was incensed to be the target of so much criticism. When he received a telegram from Johnson asserting, "You said to me bill would not be abandoned on terms laid down by filibusters," Lodge replied angrily: "I said nothing whatever about terms because nothing of that sort arose, and the words you attribute to me were never uttered by me. Nothing of that sort was said."

On December 13 Johnson dashed off an "Open Letter to Every Senator of the United States" in which he insisted they take note of the fact that since December 4, the day the Senate had abandoned the Dyer Bill, there had been four lynchings in America. One victim was tortured and burned at the stake. "This outbreak of barbarism, anarchy and degenerate bestiality and the blood of the victims rest upon the heads of those Southern senators who have obstructed even discussion of the measure designed to remedy this very condition," he wrote. "And the responsibility rests equally with the Republican majority who surrendered with hardly a struggle to the lynching tactics of the Democrats."

Republican legislators attempted to cheer Johnson by vowing to work to change the Senate rules by which factions could use the filibuster to thwart legislative action, and the NAACP received assurances from the White House that President Harding shared their disappointment. But Johnson and the NAACP were inconsolable.

———

Although the Dyer Bill's failure in Congress was a decided setback, the effort surrounding the NAACP fight and the accompanying press coverage had actually accomplished more than the antilynching forces could at first know. They had widely promoted the idea that lynching was an act deserving of fierce condemnation, and there was evidence that, in some Southern states where lynchers had once acted freely, sentiment was turning against the practice. Governor Dorsey's report criticizing lynching and other conditions of black life in Georgia had been a step in this direction. Another was the concerted action of law officers in Lexington, Kentucky, to use lethal violence to repel a lynch mob—one of the first well-publicized incidents of this kind.

On February 4, 1920, a ten-year-old girl named Geneva Hardman was found murdered at South Elkhorn, Kentucky, in southern Fayette County. She had been abducted while walking to a country school not far from her home, dragged into a cornfield, and sexually assaulted. Will Lockett, a black army veteran, was quickly arrested and under interrogation confessed to the crime. The local newspapers guaranteed a speedy trial and a guilty verdict. To ensure this result, on the day of Lockett's trial a large mob of mill hands, farmers, and packinghouse workers gathered outside the Fayette County courthouse in Lexington. Inside, after pleading guilty, Lockett had his court-appointed counsel read a note he had written: "I know I do not deserve mercy, but I am sorry I committed the crime and I would give anything if the little girl could be brought back to life."

In exchange for his plea and words of contrition, Lockett requested life in prison instead of the death penalty, but the jury—which, in an unusual procedure, was allowed to conduct its deliberations right in the courtroom, before the defendant—ignored Lockett's appeal and sentenced him to die in the electric chair. The entire trial, including the jury deliberations, had lasted twenty-five minutes.

That the gathering outside had been relatively well-mannered was due to the presence of a squad of militiamen ordered into service by the newly elected governor, Edwin P. Morrow, who had vowed to prevent lynchings. Morrow, it was later reported, had given the head of the militia unit unequivocal orders: "Do as much as you have to do to keep that negro in the hands of the law. If he falls into the hands of the mob I do not expect to see you alive."

Shortly after the verdict and death sentence were announced to cheers outside the courthouse, a newsreel cameraman encouraged some of those assembled to shout and make a commotion for the camera. The abrupt sound and movement caused people who couldn't see what was taking place to assume the mob was assaulting the jail, and suddenly the whole crowd surged forward. The militia, at a shouted command from an officer, opened fire, and within moments there were dead and wounded sprawled on the courthouse steps. Five mob members were killed immediately, another died later, and as many as fifty were hurt.

The townspeople, furious with the militia for daring to shoot at citizens, descended on local pawnshops, looted all the pistols and other firearms, and let it be known they would return to the courthouse. The militia, taking the threat seriously, dug in, preparing for a pitched battle. But the townsmen delayed their attack to await the delivery of some dynamite, and before they could mount their assault a contingent of heavily armed federal troops arrived by train and paraded through town, squelching the uprising before it could begin.

To many people's astonishment, the national reaction to the news that troops had fired into a mob was overwhelmingly favorable. There almost seemed to be a sense of relief, as if an old taboo had finally been shattered. It had long been apparent that lynch mobs were at heart cowardly enterprises and that their much-vaunted "determination" might crumble if authorities were willing to resist them with lethal force. As the police in Duluth and countless other locales had found to their discredit, and as Sheriff Nelis at Cairo had shown in 1910, a mob could not really ever be deterred unless authorities were willing to fire into it. "We need sheriffs and jailers who are not afraid to shoot," the *Houston Post* had editorialized on the subject in 1915. This was the crux of the matter—whether local police or militia could summon the will to use deadly force against neighbors and friends opposing them in the ranks of an unruly mob. Du Bois in *The Crisis* applauded the stand the Kentucky militiamen had made, dubbing it "The Second Battle of Lexington." He hoped that, like the first, it would signal a new resolve to resist tyranny.

Kentucky had a harder time reconciling itself to what had occurred, since several of its citizens had been killed. When six years later Lexington was again tested by a lynch mob—a black farmhand named Ed Harris had been accused of murdering his employer's family—the state acted with overwhelming determination to deny a repeat of the courthouse bloodshed in the Lockett case. Governor W. J. Fields ordered to the Fayette County courthouse no fewer than eight infantry companies, four troops of mounted cavalry, two machine-gun squads with thirty machine guns, three .37-millimeter guns, and, for good measure, a tank battalion. To disabuse any would-be lynchers of the notion that the soldiers on hand were good ol' boys who might wink and smile at a mob's antics, the authorities planted stories in newspapers describing the troops as hardened combat veterans of the World War, and emphasized they had been ordered to shoot to kill. "Any sullenness, disobedience of orders or 'back talk' from persons ordered to move on [will] bring swift punishment with gun butts, bayonets or gas bombs," it was advised, "with a certainty of rifle and machine gun fire in the event any attempt is made to assault the troops."

In addition to these precautions, the sheriff of Fayette County and the mayor of Lexington agreed to close the local tobacco warehouses and stockyard, the town's chief places of employment, on the day of Harris's trial, while the streetcar company promised not to transport anyone into the area around the courthouse. With all these elaborate steps taken, the trial was mob-free, and transpired with unprecedented swiftness—only sixteen minutes from opening gavel to final verdict—and with the usual outcome for the accused, who was sentenced to death.

There was reason to be encouraged by the two Lexington cases. Lynch mobs had been rebuffed by the use of actual or threatened force. The defendants had been legally tried. Yet Will Lockett's and Ed Harris's convictions had been announced in the newspaper before the trial, no substantive defense had been attempted, and other procedural safeguards had clearly been abused. Anyone sincerely interested in the principle of equal treatment under law would have to be concerned.

The 1920s in the South may be generally understood as a period of indecision and stress as the region somewhat awkwardly entered the modern age. It can also be viewed as a time of opposition between two groups, both headquartered in Atlanta, each led by Southerners, designed to address the spiritual and communal needs of the South. One of course was the revived Ku Klux Klan, the other a new type of organization known as the Commission on Interracial Cooperation (CIC).

The Klan that had organized in 1915 bore little relation to its historic Reconstruction-era ancestor. It was more a Christian fraternal order than a vigilante group, intimidating by its mere presence and its use of Klan rituals and garb rather than through actual vigilante action. In its propaganda, and where it did employ violence, the new Klan's agenda was also far broader, targeting not only blacks but also Jews, Catholics, immigrants, suspected radicals and labor organizers, as well as drunkards, wife beaters, and other morally delinquent whites. Klan leaders, while never hesitating to invoke the organization's more portentous symbolism, liked to portray themselves as more akin to the Knights of Columbus or the B'nai B'rith, addressing the social and spiritual needs of their followers as a spiritual crisis roiled America. The Klan, historian Wyn Wade writes, saw itself confronting myriad social ills:

> The mass production of the Model T, which ministers denounced as a "bawdyhouse on wheels," permitted earlier sexual experimentation by young people. Movies and radio brought worldly ideas and attitudes to rural communities that otherwise would have remained unthreatened. The drive of youngsters to savor the new age resisted traditional restraints, and concerned citizens despaired over the "disappearance of strict parental discipline."

Marketed like any other business or lodge association, the Klan was eventually franchised in twenty-seven states and varied its purpose to confront a wide palette of enemies. To a town inundated with unemployed blacks, one historian has pointed out, it was the Klan of the Griffith film; if bootleggers ran amok, the Klan was an auxiliary police outfit; in the face of labor activism, Klan members became corporate thugs and enforcers; where immigrants threatened to overwhelm a city, the Klan stood ready to publicize 100-percent Americanism. As the organization served as a kind of enforcement group for godly values, many clergymen became Klan members or boosters. Jesus Christ himself, it was said, would have been a Klansman.

One significant difference between the '20s Klan and its Reconstruction predecessor was that the original Klan did not have to reckon with a nemesis as equally Southern as itself, the CIC. Formed in 1919, the Commission was the brainchild of two Southern moderate churchmen—Will W. Alexander, a Methodist minister from Nashville, and Willis D. Weatherford, a Texan with a divinity degree from Vanderbilt who had served since 1901 as the international youth secretary of the YMCA. The YMCA, a nondenominational organization founded in England and long active in the South in the areas of youth programs and Christian education, was an ideal place for young Southerners of conscience to meet and share their concerns, for as an entity of Southern Christians it was largely immune from charges of extremism. This protection was absolutely vital, since it is difficult in retrospect to appreciate the degree to which progressive ideas on race placed an individual not only outside the Southern mainstream, but also possibly in harm's way.

Weatherford had won the esteem of many black people at a meeting of the Southern Sociological Congress, an annual conference of teachers and church leaders held in Memphis, in 1914, when the white owner of the Orpheum Theater threatened to evict the group for allowing black and white delegates to sit together. After the blacks walked out, Weatherford arranged to move the meeting to a more hospitable local church, over the objections of many whites; then, at the 1916 meeting of the congress, held in New Orleans, he gave a speech denouncing both lynching and the black rapist myth. The NAACP, impressed by the daring of this young Southerner who was willing to acknowledge the truth before a Southern white audience, distributed fifty thousand copies of Weatherford's address.

Weatherford crisscrossed the South by train during the war years, building a grassroots confederacy of moderates and progressives—white society women, schoolteachers, hillbilly radicals, and churchmen such as the minister Will Alexander, who served as a chaplain at Southern army bases. Helping young Southern boys off the farm adjust to life in the U.S. Army, Alexander gained an understanding of the challenges the South itself would face, with its native conservatism and its intractable race problems, as the modern world overtook the region. A large, bespectacled, unassuming-looking man who spoke with a slight stammer, Alexander, or "Dr. Will" as he was known, was famous for being able to put people at their ease, whether boot-camp recruits, academic sociologists, or illiterate sharecroppers, a style that was emulated by a generation of college-trained men and women who worked under the auspices of the CIC in the rural South in the 1920s and during the Depression.

With the Armistice in 1918, Alexander shared with Weatherford his desire to put the work he had been doing among the troops into the form of a more permanent organization. Weatherford tapped the YMCA for a small amount of funding, and in January 1919 they called the first meeting of the CIC to order in Atlanta with six people in attendance.

Motivating both of these young Southern Christians was a powerful sentiment known as the Social Gospel, a nineteenth-century response to Social Darwinism. Whether one read Social Darwinism to mean that some human beings would always remain inferior to others, or that the lower orders of humanity were in a state of upward striving, the Social Gospel was an attempt to give comfort to the less fortunate and encourage social betterment. The Gospel intersected with and helped foment a number of the era's progressive endeavors—the settlement-house movement, labor reform, biracial brotherhood, temperance, the antilynching crusade, and the proliferation of the concept that the finding of lasting solutions to social problems is enabled by sociological analysis.

Weatherford's most fundamental insight, as he expressed it his influential *Negro Life in the South,* published in 1910, was that the South's future was linked inextricably to its ability and willingness to deal realistically with its racial issues. With the continuing out-migration of black laborers and the violence of the Red Summer of 1919, it was clear to both Weatherford and Alexander that most Southerners, despite their patented boasting to the contrary, did not "know the Negro" at all, and perhaps never had. Whites and blacks interacted as equals only at the lowest levels of society, while a huge gap existed among educated people of both races. Compounding the problem was Southerners' long reliance on codes of honor and retributive violence, practices that had left the region with no substantial tradition of using dialogue and reason to settle differences. But if the gap could be closed even a little bit, Weatherford and Alexander believed, huge benefits might result for the South as a whole, for it seemed to them that there was a natural reservoir of familiarity between Southern whites and their longtime black neighbors that had only to be animated and given a chance to thrive.

Calling on press, church, and men of business to unite, the CIC emphasized its own Southern roots and spoke in hopeful, at times almost boosterish terms of an enlightened South in which backward institutions such as lynching would not be tolerated. Appeals to bankers, real estate developers, and other "money men" to back biracial progress were in no way incidental. By throwing in the face of capitalists the clear evidence that lynching was bad for business, the CIC was attempting to incite the inevitable showdown between New South moneyed interests and the lynching scourge that had long been prophesied: "Commerce has no social illusions," Walter Nelson Page had written as early as 1890. "It has the knack of rooting up vested social interests that stand in its way; and it has been left for commerce, by infusing its influence into the body of local public sentiment in the South, to rid us at last of this historic, red-handed, deformed and swaggering villain."

The CIC did not hesitate to identify the Klan as a supremely negative force, dangerous not only to Southerners' physical well-being but also to their intellectual maturity. In 1921 the CIC urged a congressional investigation of the group, and when this failed to develop, it provided its considerable file on the Klan and acts of Klan terrorism to the New York

World. The World's editors used the CIC material to create one of the most sweeping newspaper exposés in American history, a series of articles that ran for twenty-eight days. The series, which simultaneously belittled and sensationalized the Klan, was widely syndicated in the nation's newspapers and brought about the congressional investigation the CIC had sought in the first place, although turning the national spotlight on the organization created an effect opposite to that which the CIC had sought.

Klan founder William Simmons, summoned before a House committee, gave two full days of emotional testimony in which he described the Klan as an army of misunderstood do-gooders, a benevolent group that spoke for the forgotten American, repudiated the violence of its past, and sought only to help right a society in moral turbulence. When, near the end of his long recitation, the eccentric Simmons, who was suffering from a debilitating illness, collapsed out of his chair onto the carpet, the hearing room stood in ovation. Before he left town a newly minted hero, Simmons met privately with President Harding, whom he inducted into the Klan.

Thanks in part to the sudden notoriety of the *World* articles and the scrutiny of Congress, the Klan grew steadily between 1921 and 1924, the year the organization's leader, Hiram Evans (who had replaced the ailing Simmons), appeared on the cover of *Time* magazine and the Klan claimed a national membership of 4 million. During these years the Klan became a way of life for many—there were Klan picnics, sermons, women's groups, even Klan weddings; it was also active as a conservative political force, electing a number of men to public office, including sixteen U.S. senators. In 1925 legions of Klansmen met for a grand "Klonclave" in Washington, D.C., and paraded up Pennsylvania Avenue, creating the unforgettable image of cone-hatted imperial wizards and exalted cyclops marching beneath the nation's Capitol.

The public's disenchantment with the Klan, however, came as suddenly as had its initial infatuation. One of the first signs of the Klan's receding influence arrived in May 1924 when an Indiana chapter attempting to rally in South Bend was attacked by a combined force of local Catholics, police, and students from Notre Dame, who tore off their disguises and chased the defrocked Klansmen up and down the streets. The following year brought financial difficulties and a sex-murder scandal involving the head of the Indiana Klan, and membership dwindled as revelations of political payoffs and other chicanery exposed the organization's hypocrisy in violating its own ethos of Christian righteousness.

———

Like the NAACP, the CIC understood that reversing common perceptions about black people and helping to humanize them in whites' eyes was key to fighting prejudice and deterring racial violence. To combat the stereotypical images of blacks that abounded, the CIC made a practice of feeding to Southern newspapers a steady stream of positive stories about blacks—boys saving people from burning buildings, kindly railroad porters accepting awards for courteous service, breakthroughs by blacks in education, science, or the military. To implement its progressive ideas on the community level, the CIC used a method it called the "biracial conference." A team of two people—one white, one black—would work together in their community to help local citizens resolve racial differences. In the near term, such minimal cooperation might at least enable Southern towns to head off riots and lynchings, and who knew what other positive results might develop. A typical effort was that of a CIC biracial committee in Louisville, Kentucky. Black children, long excluded from the main public pools, were forced to swim in the Ohio River, where each summer, inevitably, a few drowned. Whereas an exclusively black effort to convince the local park commissioners to build a pool for black children would probably have gone nowhere, these same officials acceded to the demands of a CIC-backed biracial coalition that cited the project's clear humanitarian necessity. The group also contributed to racial stability simply by squelching dangerous rumors. When "insurrectionary" black men were seen drilling with firearms in a North Carolina town, the CIC investigated and publicized the fact that they were actually members of a lodge rehearsing for a funeral.

In a related effort in 1926, the CIC instituted a public-relations program of awarding medals to law-enforcement officers who showed valor in protecting prisoners from lynch mobs. "Careful study has convinced us that the sheriff is the key to the situation," Will Alexander wrote in a letter to Southern governors announcing the plan. "Whenever a sheriff anywhere in the South shows particular courage and intelligence in outwitting a mob or defending a prisoner it is the purpose of the Commission to confer one of these medals upon him in the name of the people in the South."

One of the first to be honored was Schuyler Marshall, Jr., sheriff of Dallas County, Texas, who on May 21, 1925, led a spirited defense of his jail when a mob of three hundred men and women arrived to abduct two black prisoners. The presence of women in a lynch mob could be disarming, often serving to intimidate police or militia from using aggressive measures. Marshall, knowing his deputies would be disinclined to shoot in any case, but particularly at women, ordered his men to douse the mob with fire hoses. The tactic caught the crowd by surprise and drove them back. Wounded by flying glass in the melee, the sheriff nonetheless managed to telephone for reinforcements and even placed one of the women under arrest.

Another honoree was Sheriff John C. Sanders of Harrison County, Texas, who prevented a lynching later that year. A mob came to his jail to deal with three blacks suspected of shooting a white farmer and his son. Aware that he lacked the manpower to fight off the group, Sanders welcomed the posse and pretended to allow them into the part of the jail where the suspects were being held, then abruptly locked the doors behind them.

One of the more celebrated recipients of the CIC medal was Mrs. J. C. Butler, wife of the sheriff of Carroll County, Tennessee, who in April 1931 single-handedly defied a lynch mob that had arrived when her husband was away, demanding a black prisoner accused of shooting a policeman. Mrs. Butler at first told the visitors the man was not there, but when the mob insisted on entering she took down a shotgun and barred the way, telling them, "If you come in here it will be over my dead body. You can shoot me down if you will, but you can't have my prisoner."

Alexander, Weatherford, and their colleagues were not starry-eyed. While they dreamed of revolutionizing Southern life, they assumed that certain changes in the region would be slow in coming. The CIC did not challenge the status quo of segregation, which Alexander was convinced would have to wait to be resolved "by the wisdom and justice of oncoming generations." The strongest recommendation it put forth was that the South "tilt up the color line," in effect honor the "equal" in the "separate but equal" doctrine of racial segregation. "Up to this time we have made the color line horizontal, the white man above it, the Negro below," read a CIC brochure entitled "America's Obligation to the Negro." "If we are to be even Christian about this business of separation, we must 'tilt up the color line' to a vertical position, with equal rights and opportunities extended to those on either side of it, living racially separate but with mutual respect and confidence." In the beginning the organization had segregated its own members. Weatherford led the whites in training workshops at a YMCA retreat in North Carolina, and Alexander held forth to the blacks at a seminary in Atlanta. Although many regionally prominent blacks such as Robert R. Moton, who had succeeded Booker T. Washington as head of Tuskegee Institute, and John Hope, president of Morehouse College, soon joined the CIC leadership, no black people ever worked in the CIC's Atlanta headquarters; and some Southern black leaders never entirely got over their suspicion that the CIC was at heart a white man's program to orchestrate mild appeasements to blacks in order keep cheap labor from leaving the South.

Significantly, as an organization of Southerners, the CIC did not support the Dyer Bill. Lynching, in the CIC's view, was not so much a betrayal of law and due process as it was a failure of the human spirit; it would end not when federal laws tightened the screws on Southern misbehavior but when Southern whites learned to treat the black minority in its midst with greater respect. But if the CIC was willing to eschew Washington's intervention on lynching, it did insist on taking at their word those Southern legislators who had stood up in Congress and denounced the Dyer Bill on the grounds that the South could handle its own problems. The CIC chose to hear the lawmakers' loud abhorrence of Yankee meddling as a sincere expression of the South's new willingness to deal with mob violence. "It is distinctly up to the States to make good the promises and professions of their senators and representatives, which is that the States themselves will settle this problem, settle it right and for all time," read a quote from the Atlanta *Georgian* that the CIC reprinted. "Here is a chance to vindicate 'State rights' and to preserve the great principle involved therein, so long cherished as a vital thing in the South." The quote was featured in a 1923 CIC broadside entitled "It's Up to Us."

The idea of pacifist clergymen representing the 1920s' most radical assault on the Southern status quo seems, in retrospect, extraordinary, although at the time this gentle effort to ease the South into the modern age was decidedly cutting edge, effective—where it was effective—because it genuinely appeared to come from inside Southern society. This strategy of having social reform flow from a relatively stable and unknockable Southern source would be reprised in the 1930s by the CIC-inspired Association of Southern Women for the Prevention of Lynching (ASWPL), in the late 1940s by the biracial Southern Regional Council (SRC), and to a degree in the 1950s by Martin Luther King, Jr.'s Southern Christian Leadership Conference (SCLC), all of whom relied greatly on their inherently Southern character and composition.

In the mid-1920s, as the CIC stressed that the backward tradition of lynching was a harmful evil that could be best abolished through self-awareness and self-reflection on the part of Southern whites, an important legal case in faraway Detroit was demonstrating how fully whites were willing to acknowledge the psychological impact lynching had had on all black Americans. The Detroit case, which arose from a bloody confrontation over a black family's right to choose where it would own a home, would have lasting meaning for the question of whether black and white Americans could live side by side, and represented one of the first times that whites would publicly debate the effects of their own prejudices.

"Negro Family Leaves City When Ordered," read a headline in a local paper after the Springfield, Illinois, riot of 1908:

> The first negro family routed from Springfield by a mob was the Harvey family, residing at 1144 North Seventh Street, who were told Sunday morning to "hike" and carried out the orders yesterday afternoon. The family proved themselves obnoxious in many ways. They were the one negro family in the block and their presence was distasteful to all other citizens in that vicinity.

In that small news story lay a problem that had plagued black Americans since Emancipation and had led to countless lynchings and race riots—black people's freedom to own property and to live where they chose. It was also an issue the NAACP had made a primary concern from its earliest days as an organization.

In 1917 the association won a major legal victory against forced segregation in housing when Moorfield Storey appeared before the Supreme Court in the case of *Buchanan v. Warley*. The dispute had originated in Louisville, Kentucky, where municipal authorities were in the practice of designating certain residential city blocks as "white" or "black." The attorneys for the city argued that the designations were intended to inhibit possible antagonism between the races, but Storey countered that a mere street or alleyway was insufficient to stop racial animosity, and called into question the notion of racial purity that such distinctions relied on. *Buchanan v. Warley* ruled against Louisville's block-designation system and abolished the practice of municipalities establishing segregated housing zones.

In Detroit in May 1925, a black physician named Ossian Sweet and his wife, Gladys, bought a home on the corner of Garland and Charlevoix avenues in a predominantly white neighborhood. When they moved in on

September 8 they immediately began receiving threatening phone calls. The next night Dr. Sweet took his two-year-old daughter to stay with Gladys's mother, while he and his wife, his two brothers—Otis, a dentist, and Henry, a student at Wilberforce—and several friends attempted to have supper in the house. Early in the evening a white crowd gathered outside, catcalling, cursing, and occasionally pelting the residence with rocks. Police on hand made no attempt to intervene. Suddenly shots were fired from a window in the house. Two whites were struck; one, Leon E. Breiner, was shot in the back, mortally wounded. Police rushed into the house, arrested everyone present, and charged them with murder.

Black attorneys hired by Gladys Sweet's mother were allowed to speak with the prisoners only after they had been held incommunicado for two days, and one of the lawyers contacted NAACP headquarters in New York to explain the unique circumstances of the case. Walter White, recognizing the situation's importance, was soon on a train for Detroit. "A group of five thousand Nordic gentleman have been demonstrating their biological and mental superiority by attacking the home of a colored physician who was too prosperous 'for a Negro,' " he telegrammed his NAACP colleagues from the train. "The police force kept their hands off and the mob got the surprise of its life when the colored doctor opened fire."

The attack on the Sweets had come after months of growing racial tension in Detroit. The availability of jobs in the automobile industry (some paying seven dollars per day) had swelled the city's black population from eight thousand in 1911 to eighty-two thousand in 1925, in what seemed to many whites to be an overwhelming and unacceptable black influx. One Ford Motor plant alone employed nearly eleven thousand black workers. Many of the new arrivals lived in east Detroit in an area known as "Paradise Valley," but as the neighborhood filled in some residents began to push into "white" areas. The local Ku Klux Klan reprinted and distributed an inflammatory article that had appeared in a Birmingham, Alabama, newspaper claiming that Southern blacks considered Detroit "the Mecca of the Colored Race," and that Mayor John W. Smith, a Catholic who was a moderate on race issues, had vowed to welcome and protect all blacks. The Detroit Klan, which was well represented in the city's police department, had recently burned a cross on Smith's front lawn, and Charles Bowles, a Klan-backed candidate, was expected to give the mayor a tough fight in the upcoming election, with the city's exploding black population a key issue. During the summer of 1925, the Klan had mounted a rally in a public park that had drawn several thousand people.

The Sweets had waited for the summer to end before moving into their new house, in hopes the tense atmosphere would abate. That past June a professional acquaintance of Dr. Sweet, a black physician named Alexander L. Turner, had received a cruel rebuff when he and his wife attempted to move into a home they had purchased on Spokane Avenue. So fierce was the local resistance to the Turners' imminent arrival that even some white housepainters Turner had hired were chased away amid a hail of rocks and brickbats. When Turner and his wife actually tried to move in, a Klan-led mob hurled stones, broke every window in the house, and even removed all the tiles from the roof. Three policemen inside the house with the Turners did nothing to stop the barrage. After the assault had relented, a group of men arrived, saying they were a "delegation from the mayor's office," but once inside identified themselves as a "citizens' committee" from a neighborhood "improvement association." They had brought papers for Turner to sign that would relinquish his ownership of the house. With the police looking on, Turner was coerced into signing them. When the moving van pulled up with the Turners' furniture, the police authorized the "improvement association" to deliver the belongings back to the couple's former house, and Turner and his wife were then marched outside to their Lincoln automobile, which had been badly damaged, and made to drive away behind their departing furniture. "Had Turner stood firm, he would have won and thereby scotched the wave of mobbism against colored property owners," Walter White reported to the New York office. "However, Turner quit cold."

White, meeting with the Sweets and their black lawyers, convinced them that public sentiment against them for killing a white man was too strong to be met solely by black counsel. The key to winning so pivotal a case, he believed, was to hire a prominent white attorney. Clarence Darrow, the most celebrated defense attorney in America, was a member of one of the NAACP's governing boards, and had an interest in such cases. After the 1919 Chicago riot, Darrow had urged the NAACP to use one or more of the instances in which blacks stood accused of assaulting whites to prove that such cases could be defended on the grounds that blacks were entitled to present an "aggressive self-defense" during a race riot because they were outnumbered by whites and poorly defended by police. But Darrow's legal strategy was a bit too radical for the NAACP at that time, and the specific case he had selected on which to test his strategy was discharged for lack of evidence.

Darrow had a deep personal connection to the fight for black equality.

He had grown up in an abolitionist household and liked to tell the tale of how when he'd been a small child the legendary abolitionist John Brown stopped at the Darrow house in rural Ohio to visit his parents, and had placed his hand on young Clarence's head, telling him, "The Negro has too few friends; you and I must never desert him." The story is unlikely— Darrow was born in 1857 and Brown was executed in late 1859—but now, as the NAACP appealed to Darrow to take the Sweets' case, it seemed like "the Negro" was calling on the famous attorney to make good on that long-ago vow. Almost sixty-nine years old, Darrow was due for a rest—he had only recently returned north following his defense of teacher John Scopes over the freedom to teach the theory of evolution in the Tennessee "Monkey Trial"—but allowed himself to be convinced by the NAACP that the Sweet trial would be an essential undertaking.

The Sweet case lacked the outsize emotion of the Scopes trial, but as White wrote to James Weldon Johnson, it was without a doubt the "dramatic high point of the nationwide issue of housing segregation," and would make a fitting climax to the NAACP's work in this area. When the Sweet case first emerged in 1925, Storey and the NAACP were in the midst of an effort to build on their victory in *Buchanan v. Warley* by taking on a more insidious form of housing segregation—the private agreements between property owners known as restrictive covenants, legally binding arrangements between buyers and sellers of real estate that property could not be sold to specified groups of prospective buyers, such as black people. A case in which this issue was central, *Corrigan v. Curtis,* dealt with the contested sale of a home in Washington, D.C., to a black woman, and Storey intended to argue before the Supreme Court that the federal government could not prohibit residential segregation by municipal fiat in *Buchanan v. Warley* but then allow it through judicially enforceable private agreements in the form of restrictive covenants. *Corrigan v. Curtis* was scheduled on the high court's calendar for 1926.

The NAACP thus saw the Sweet case as the third piece of a trifecta. A successful defense of the Sweets in Detroit, along with the 1917 win in *Buchanan v. Warley* and the hoped-for victory in *Corrigan v. Curtis,* would put the final nail in the coffin lid of segregated housing. Such harmful prejudice—by law, by private contract, by mob—could be abolished forever. Indeed, all these issues were unified in the Sweet case, for a Michigan court had only recently reaffirmed the right of property owners to establish restrictive covenants, providing a kind of judicial "approval" to those whites who, in attempting to intimidate black homeowners by throwing rocks, saw themselves as acting in faith with the highest laws of the state.

On October 12, 1925, Darrow arrived in Detroit to interview his new clients, accompanied by his friend Arthur Garfield Hays, chairman of the American Civil Liberties Union, who would assist him. The strategy Darrow suggested to Dr. Sweet and the others was to admit they had fired the shots at the white mob, but had done so because they were afraid. Conditioned their whole lives by lynchings and mob violence, their reaction had been a simple matter of self-preservation.

The Sweets and their friends had come to savor their standing as heroes in the eyes of the local black community, and were at first reluctant to take Darrow's advice if it meant they would have to admit they had acted out of fear. To convince them, Darrow outlined the other quite incriminating facts of the case. First, it was clear that Dr. Sweet and his family had not only anticipated trouble but had armed themselves to respond to it. They had moved very little furniture into the house, but had instead brought in provisions to last several days, six pistols, two rifles, one shotgun, and two thousand rounds of ammunition. It was also known that Sweet intended to make a point of not succumbing to the mob, as had his friend Dr. Turner. He had assured the police beforehand that he would not go quietly, but would "die a man or live a coward." If the Sweets did not concede that such actions had been inspired by fear, Darrow explained, a jury might well conclude that it was they who had picked the fight and started the violence.

When the trial got under way, the prosecution produced seventy-one witnesses who testified that the group gathered outside the Sweet house on the night of September 9 had not constituted a threatening mob. Sweet initially said there were about two thousand people outside his house; some of the prosecution witnesses stated there were as few as fifteen or twenty. This was a key point because, as Judge Frank Murphy told the jury, under Michigan law twelve or more persons armed with clubs or thirty unarmed persons were considered to constitute an unlawfully gathered mob. The prosecutors tried to paint a picture of a quiet evening along Garland Avenue in which neighbors sat on their porches discussing the weather and friends stopped to chat on their way home from the grocery store, while a few mischievous boys threw stones at the Sweet house; into this relatively innocuous scene, the state contended, the blacks had, without provocation, opened fire. Based on the varying accounts, Darrow believed that approximately five hundred people were present in the dark outside the Sweet home and, through cross-examination, he was able to show that many of the witnesses had been coached by a police detective to use the word *few* in describing the number of people on hand. His most effective witness was Philip Adler, a white reporter from the *Detroit Free Press,* who said that there were so many people he could barely force his way across the street, and that when he did he was told by someone in the crowd, "A Negro family has moved in here and we're going to get them out."

Darrow and Hays cited an 1860 Michigan case that had established that a man "assaulted in his dwelling is not obliged to retreat," and may use any means, including killing an attacker, if the latter is engaged in "a felonious assault." Hays said of the Sweets in his opening remarks: "These people had in their minds the persecution to which their people had been subject for generations. They knew of lynchings, sometimes of innocent victims in various parts of the country; of negroes taken from policemen said to be guarding them, and burned at the stake by slow fire; even of women mistreated by mobs." Darrow then told the court that a gathering of an "improvement association" had taken place in a high school directly across the street from the Sweet residence on July 12, and that the idea of resisting the Sweets' arrival at the Garland and Charlevoix house had been the main topic of discussion. A man who had been a leader in the effort to dislodge the Turners from Spokane Avenue spoke at the July 12 gathering, and offered to assist the Garland Avenue group. Police were present but made no move to arrest or identify any of the speakers, even though several had urged the gathering to use violent means to scare off the neighborhood's newest residents. At a subsequent meeting of the Garland improvement association, a well-known local realtor told the assembly, "We'll load this nigger's goods on the same van that brings them out and send them back where they came from."

Following Hays's description of the 1860 law, Darrow picked up the theme of the Sweets' psychological state. "The question is not what a white man in a city of whites would do under certain circumstances," he told the jury. "The question is what a colored man, a reasonable colored man, with his knowledge of the prejudice against him because of his color . . . with his knowledge that there was a society of men (a so-called improvement association) formed for the purpose of ejecting him from his home; with his knowledge of what mobs do and have done to colored people when they have the power."

Darrow explained why Dr. Sweet, of all black Americans, had certainly earned the right to live where he chose. The son of a Florida minister, Sweet had left home at fourteen, worked his way through Wilberforce Academy in Ohio by working summers as a waiter and bellhop on Great Lakes steamers, and later attended Howard University Medical School. He had practiced medicine in Detroit for a number of years, married Gladys Mitchell, the daughter of a well-to-do black family, then gone abroad to study gynecology and pediatrics in Vienna and at the Curie Institute in Paris.

Despite these accomplishments, Darrow emphasized, Dr. Sweet like all black men could not escape the tragedy and difficulties that plagued his race. Growing up near Orlando, Sweet often passed a tree that was filled with lead from the time a black man had been strung up there and shot to death. On another occasion, he came upon a small group of people gathered around the ashes of a black man who had been immolated. His most searing childhood experience was when he saw a mob of several thousand whites pour kerosene over a black youth and set him afire. Terrified by the victim's shrieks, Sweet hid nearby as the crowd remained around the area getting drunk, snapping photographs of the corpse, and sifting through the remains.

Like many people of achievement who have had to face down social obstacles and prejudice, Sweet was supremely conscious of himself as one of his race's representatives. A sense of responsibility—to himself, to his family, and to his people—had made him feel he had no choice but to stand his ground when attacked.

Darrow put Sweet on the stand to relate the events of the night of September 9. The doctor described how he and his friends had been playing cards—his wife was cooking a dinner of ham, baked sweet potatoes, and greens—when a mob gathered outside. Despite promises from the dozen or so police who were on hand to protect them, the mob grew and insults were heard, then one rock hit the roof, then another. A window shattered. Suddenly a torrent of rocks, bricks, and pieces of coal landed on the house. Inside it was "pandemonium," Sweet testified, as people ducked and scrambled from place to place to avoid flying glass. At that moment a taxi pulled up to the house carrying Otis Sweet and a friend, William Davis. When Dr. Sweet opened the door the mob—"it looked like a human sea," he recalled—surged toward the house. "When I opened the door to let them in, I realized that for the first time in my life I stood face to face with the same mob that has haunted my people throughout its entire history," Sweet later said. "I knew that my back was against the wall, that I was black, and that because I was black and had found the courage to buy a home, they were ready to wreak their vengeance on me."

Shots came from an upstairs window. A moment later Police Inspector Norton N. Schuknecht burst in, demanding, "What in hell are you fellows shooting about?," to which Sweet anxiously replied, "They are destroying my house." Schuknecht left, promising to stop the rock throwing. In a minute other policemen entered and arrested all the occupants, although no one told the Sweets until they were in jail that a man had been killed. Police who confiscated the guns and ammunition stockpiled in the house noted that chairs had been put near upstairs windows to serve as defensive positions for the shooters.

At Darrow's urging, Sweet talked on the stand of his direct experiences with racial injustice. The doctor said that while studying in Paris he had donated three hundred francs to the American Hospital, yet when his wife was about to give birth to their daughter he could not gain admittance for her there. He mentioned his strong reaction to the Red Summer of 1919—he had been in Washington, D.C., during that city's race riot—and the killings in the sharecroppers' war in Phillips County, Arkansas. He also cited a story he'd once read about a prominent doctor in Tulsa, A. C. Jackson, considered the country's top black surgeon, who was given a police guarantee of safety and protection when a mob attacked his home, and had on that basis surrendered his weapons, only to be immediately killed. These incidents, and thousands of other incidents of lynchings and riots, ran through his mind as the stones rained down on his home, he said, and he had determined to write a different ending to all those other horrible stories. He would never be able to respect himself, he said, if he allowed a "gang of hoodlums" to put him out of his own house.

The Nation described Darrow's questioning of Sweet's state of mind as "one of the most remarkable direct examinations to be found in all the records of criminal cases: a vivid picture of the fear-ridden mind of a black man, terrified by a crowd of hostile whites outside his home." The prosecutors objected to Darrow's putting such testimony before the jury, but Darrow emphasized that just as the white people in the mob had been driven by their backgrounds to act as they had, so it was crucial to understand the psychological motivations of the black people involved. Judge Murphy, who was an admirer of Darrow's, and politically ambitious—he would later be the mayor of Detroit, governor of Michigan, and a U.S. Supreme Court justice—overruled most of the prosecution's objections.

When the case went to the jury, no agreement about the defendants' guilt could be reached, so the case was set for retrial. This time, however, Darrow asked that the defendants be tried separately. Henry Sweet, the only person who admitted firing a gun, would go first. His was the strongest case the prosecution had, and Darrow knew that if this case could be won the rest would be thrown out.

The case against Henry Sweet proceeded much as the first had, until the end. Darrow, feeling a historic victory close at hand, decided to allow himself a bit of the grandstanding that had so engaged the public during the Scopes trial. As his closing address he gave an eight-hour oration on the condition of blacks in America:

> I insist that there is nothing but prejudice in this case; that if it was reversed and eleven white men had shot and killed a black while protecting their home and their lives against a mob of blacks, nobody would have dreamed of having them indicted. I know what I am talking about, and so do you. They would have been given medals instead.

It was a Darrow performance, and everyone in the courtroom listened and watched in awe as he alternately paced, stomped on the floor, struck the table with his fist, whispered, prayed, and thundered at his listeners.

> There isn't a man in Detroit who doesn't know that the defendant did his duty, and that this case is an attempt to send him and his companions to prison because they defended their constitutional rights. It is a wicked attempt, and you are asked to be party to it. . . . Now, that is the case, gentlemen, and that is all there is to this case. Take the hatred away, and you have nothing left.

He asked that the jury and all America awaken to the reality of the Negro's harsh existence:

> Eleven persons with black skins, eleven people, gentlemen, whose ancestors did not come to America because they wanted to, but were brought here in slave ships, to toil for nothing, for the whites, [and] whose lives have been taken in nearly every state in the Union . . . food for the flames, and the ropes, and the knives, and the guns . . . regardless of law and liberty, and the common sentiments of justice that should move men.

Finally, he turned to what seemed the inevitable conclusion:

I believe the life of the Negro race has been a life of tragedy, of injustice, of
oppression. The law has made him equal—but man has not. And after all,
the last analysis is what man has done. Gentlemen . . . I ask you on behalf
of the defendant, on behalf of this great state and this great city which must
face this problem and face it squarely, I ask you in the name of progress and
of the human race to return a verdict of not guilty.

The speech had its intended effect. Many in the courtroom, including
James Weldon Johnson, openly wept. Afterward the prosecution made its
closing argument, but it was, in the words of one observer, like "the clatter of folding chairs after a symphony concert." Henry Sweet was declared
not guilty and all the other cases were dropped. After the final ruling,
Judge Murphy told an interviewer he thought Darrow "the most Christ-
like man I have ever known."

The NAACP reprinted thousands of copies of Darrow's address, which
Langston Hughes termed "one of the greatest in the history of American
jurisprudence," and basked in the acclaim of the country's largely approving editorials on the verdict, many of which specifically applauded Darrow and the NAACP. The significance of the Sweet case was enormous,
particularly for the NAACP, which had set out to prove that a black man
could be acquitted of murder in defending his life and property when
countless others had been put to death for attempting to exercise that basic
right. *The Nation* declared, no doubt correctly, that the trial had been
"probably the fairest ever accorded a Negro in this country."

Unfortunately, the corresponding victory the NAACP had hoped for in
its related housing rights case, *Corrigan v. Curtis,* suffered a defeat in the
Supreme Court in early 1926. The court ruled that it had no jurisdiction
to challenge restrictive covenants, so for the time being the rights of property owners to affix such restrictions to their holdings remained intact.

Despite such rewarding outcomes as the Sweet acquittal, the granting of
the CIC medals to brave sheriffs, and Kentucky's forceful protection of
prisoners Willie Lockett and Ed Harris, lynchings continued to occur at a
consistent level throughout the 1920s, and at times in disturbing new
places. The CIC and the NAACP were always steeled for news of gruesome deaths at rural crossroads and courthouses in backward Southern
counties, but in April 1923 came the disheartening news of a lynching on,

of all places, a college campus, when students at the University of Missouri demonstrated convincingly that mobbing a fellow citizen to death was not the sole privilege of the uneducated.

The incident began with a rumor that James T. Scott, a black janitor at the university's main campus in Columbia, had made an amorous pass at Regina Almstedt, the fourteen-year-old daughter of the chairman of the German department. Scott was arrested, and that night a crowd of several hundred students, assisted by other Columbia residents, broke into the city jail. After a halfhearted effort to stave off the mob, the sheriff and police gave way, standing by helplessly for nearly two hours while the intruders used an acetylene torch to cut through the bars of Scott's cell. Thoroughly petrified after being made to view this lengthy operation with his own eyes, Scott was dragged from the building before a huge cheering crowd that had gathered outside, a throng that included many young couples who had just left a nearby dance hall. He was bound with rope, marched through the streets of Columbia to a bridge that traversed a ravine just off campus, and made to climb onto a railing with a rope tied securely around his neck.

The father of the victimized girl, Professor H. B. Almstedt, rushed to the scene and pleaded with the students to release Scott immediately back to the custody of the law, but was shouted down. When he persevered he was warned that he would "swing along with the nigger" if he didn't leave the mob to its business. He eventually gave up and went home. A few city officials who tried to get the crowd to listen to reason were likewise abused and threatened. "Over with him!" the crowd roared. "Over with him!"

Scott appeared to be praying throughout the ordeal, but having heard the pleas on his behalf fall on deaf ears, he ventured to speak in his own defense. He reminded the mob that Almstedt's daughter, in reporting the incident, had said that the black man who had bothered her had spoken of having a troubled marriage. Scott told the crowd that this fact should certainly exonerate him, for he had a perfectly good marriage, and he encouraged the students to go and check with his wife about it if they disbelieved him. "Before God," he cried, "I swear I am innocent." A young man holding the rope around Scott's neck appeared to be affected by the condemned man's words, but the next moment an older man grabbed the rope and in one swift movement lashed it taut to the bridge and pushed Scott over the railing. Scott fell for a few seconds, then his neck snapped. He would have died instantly.

The identities of the mob's leaders were never established. The Boone County district attorney described them as "roughneck men from out of Columbia," and Dr. Isidore Loeb, president of the university, assured reporters that no student had taken part in the affair. Nonetheless, the school came in for a drubbing from the nation's press, which was uniform in its view that a lynching at a college campus was somehow more unforgivable than one in the remote outback of the Cotton South. "We are glad to note that the University of Missouri has opened a course in Applied Lynching," Du Bois reported in *The Crisis*. "Many of our American universities have long defended the institution, but they have not been frank or brave enough actually to arrange a mob murder so that the students might see it in detail. . . . We are very much in favor of this method."

If universities were no more immune to racial violence than the rest of America, they were also the fountainhead for the new ideas necessary to attack lynching's racist ideology at its roots. One of the heroes in this effort was Franz Boas, a Columbia University anthropologist whose work provided desperately needed illumination to the ongoing American debate about the significance of race.

Many of the theories about race and ethnicity that had come forth in the 1880s had received extensive discussion; but in the early 1920s, as European emigration to America, interrupted by the war, stirred again, often with several thousand immigrants arriving each day, the subject erupted onto the pages of the nation's magazines and daily newspapers. A major stimulus was a book by Madison Grant called *The Passing of the Great Race,* a warning that Americans were in danger of being overwhelmed by immigrant hordes. Grant argued that the history of civilization was made up of three basic races—Nordic, Alpine, and Mediterranean—and that the majority of history's adventurers, soldiers, sailors, and explorers were Nordic types. The Nordic man was threatened, the book warned: not only were his blond genes recessive, he was unfit for living in urban settings or performing industrial work. He was by nature an outdoors man. He was undone by his own goodness and devotion to democracy. Not only did he allow non-Nordic types to infiltrate and destabilize the body politic, he also routinely marched off to battle and died a hero's death, leaving "the little dark man" as "the final winner." Nordic man's chivalry, courage, and virtue had become his fatal flaws.

Although published in 1916, the impact of Grant's book was not felt until after the war, when many of his ideas surfaced in *The Saturday*

Evening Post in a series of articles by Kenneth Roberts, later collected in a book, *Why Europe Leaves Home.* Roberts had gone to Europe after the war, conducted research, and returned to the United States convinced that the influx of southern European and Semitic peoples to America would render Americans among the most worthless and ineffectual human beings on the planet. Another writer influenced by Grant was Lothrop Stoddard, a Massachusetts attorney whose *The Rising Tide of Color* expressed the fear that the brown and yellow peoples, to whom he referred collectively as the "Under Man," would now seize the opportunity created by the self-destructive "civil war" recently fought in Europe between the white elites of the world to advance and ultimately overwhelm them.

The confidence of such polemics was belied by the fact that science had never offered evidence to support such ideas. There had been abundant measuring of crania, hairlines, noses, and facial features, even hat sizes, yet ethnologists had never agreed on a foolproof means of categorizing races, let alone a way of measuring those physical qualities that distinguished the "most civilized" from the "least civilized" peoples.

This resurgent conviction that history was largely determined by factors of race and social caste excited interest during the 1920s in the emerging field of eugenics, founded and named in the 1870s by Francis Galton, a cousin of Charles Darwin. Galton's theory that intelligence and leadership skills were essentially inherited traits, and that an individual's potential was more or less defined by, and could be controlled by, one's genetic makeup, had attracted scant attention until it rose to meet the concerns of the postwar period. Eugenics was, in a sense, a proactive response to the dangers publicized by the Madison Grants of the world: rather than sit back and allow the Nordic and other "superior" races to fade away, the eugenicists encouraged the propagation of "better" people through the control of biological factors. In this era, eugenics societies and associations proliferated, as did books with such apocalyptic titles as *Mankind at the Crossroads* by Edward East or *The Mongol in Our Midst* by F. G. Crookshank, while the American Museum of Natural History in New York and other prestigious institutions opened their doors to international eugenics conferences. A favorite argument put forth by eugenicists was that, as controlled breeding had become thoroughly accepted in the manipulation of livestock and other animals, and with good results, it made sense to apply the same sort of skillful planning to our own species.

Such ideas were not merely discussed at the high reaches of academia but spread widely, repackaged and consumed through sermons, magazines, and Sunday newspaper supplements; they influenced social policy and bolstered the creation of quotas for various arriving ethnic groups, while fueling the rise of anti-Semitism in the United States and the activities of the Ku Klux Klan and other nativist organizations. On the West Coast the concern manifested itself with new restrictions on Japanese immigrants and in revived fears about Italian "Black Hand" societies. It also stoked the strident anti-Semitism of America's leading industrialist, Henry Ford, who gullibly, and maliciously, published sections of the fabricated tract "The Protocols of the Elders of Zion" in *The Dearborn Independent,* a periodical he distributed free through his automobile dealerships.

Franz Boas disdained the sweeping generalizations about race and ethnicity made by reckless authors and ethnologists. He had pioneered the concept of cultural relativism, the idea that cultures, even those that appear primitive, cannot be judged as "civilized" or "uncivilized" from the outside. Each had its own rationale, its own logical or illogical reasons for beliefs and rituals that could be understood only on their own terms. To even begin to comprehend other people, Boas urged, a scientist needed to go and perform fieldwork among them, learn their language and customs, and look at the world through their eyes—an approach that has been at the heart of all anthropological inquiry since Boas's time, and would be advanced by a generation of American anthropologists he trained at Columbia including Ruth Benedict, Ashley Montagu, Margaret Mead, Melville Herskovits, and Zora Neale Hurston.

In the 1920s, Boas directly challenged the anti-immigrant ravings of Madison Grant, Henry Fairfield Osborn, and Lothrop Stoddard, using the results of a 1912 study he had made in which the heads of 17,821 immigrants and their children were measured. His data showed that within even one generation the head shapes and characteristics of the immigrants' children had changed from those of their parents, suggesting the powerful influence of environment and showing that the concept of firm ethnic types so central to much anti-immigrant opinion was not supportable. Indeed, Boas stressed, what was remarkable was how quickly most immigrant families shed their native physiological characteristics and began the process of becoming Americans.

Boas had developed a concern for the plight of black Americans as soon as he arrived on these shores. The pseudoscientific attacks made upon blacks offended him professionally, for he believed that "every classification of mankind must be more or less artificial," and that such views, irresponsibly couched in phony anthropological terms and carelessly disseminated, could not be supported with data. He also reacted morally, as a liberal and a Jew—he still bore a facial scar from a duel he'd fought as a student in Europe over an anti-Semitic insult—and quietly despaired as black rights were eroded by judicial and legislative edict, and by mob violence. His efforts to dispel misconceptions about black Americans proceeded along two basic paths—he questioned whether "inferior" traits ascribed to blacks as innate were actually the result of social and economic forces, and pointed out the high degree of development and achievement in African civilizations, suggesting that black Americans could not be judged fairly by their experience in the New World.

In 1904 Boas published a groundbreaking article entitled "What the Negro Has Done in Africa." It described American blacks not as a problem, nor in terms of their innate inferiority, nor as former slaves, but in terms of their rich cultural heritage as Africans. At Du Bois's invitation, Boas repeated many of these ideas in May 1906 in a commencement address at Atlanta University. Du Bois was delighted by Boas's account of the accomplishments of African civilizations—the advanced commercial and judicial system of the Sudanese, the regimented armies of the Zulus, the creativity in bronze casting demonstrated by the natives of Benin. "At a time when the European was still satisfied with rude stone tools," Boas told the graduates, "the African had invented or adopted the art of smelting iron." He added, "If, therefore, it is claimed that your race is doomed to economic inferiority, you may confidently look to the home of your ancestors and say that you have set out to recover for the colored people the strength that was their own before they set foot on the shores of this continent."

One of the most dangerous shortcomings in American society, Boas believed, was the sheer popular ignorance about black people. In order to combat the lies and half-truths that characterized most writing on the subject, he attempted to obtain funding for an in-depth "study of the Negro."

"It seems plausible that the whole attitude of our people in regard to the Negro might be materially modified if we had a better knowledge of what the Negro has really done and accomplished in his own native country," Boas said of his ambition. But this plan, like his aspiration to collect exhibits for a projected "Museum of Negro History," failed to attract the backing of philanthropists.

In his address to the 1910 meeting of the NAACP, Boas continued his fight against many of the prevailing theories of racial superiority. He explained that simply because blacks and whites showed different kinds of physical development, this did not mean that one was superior to the other. Addressing the 1906 contention of Johns Hopkins anatomy professor Robert B. Bean that the Negro brain was smaller than that of whites in critical areas (thus giving blacks greater proclivity for activities such as singing and dancing but less willpower and self-control), Boas asserted that even if some brains were smaller than others, such data was meaningless. There was a wide range of variance in such measurements even within the same race, and in any case brain weight did not appear to correlate to levels of individual achievement or intelligence. Boas also challenged the common theory about arrested development in black children, saying it was not shown to be hereditary, but rather social and environmental. The same slowing of development had been seen in whites of lower classes.

Picking up the theme of his 1906 address at Atlanta University, Boas insisted that whites' impressions of black people were based overly much on slavery and its legacy in this country, and he assaulted the popular notion that mulattoes were a particularly dangerous half-breed race, pointing out that the process of mixing populations had gone on for millennia in the animal kingdom without evidence of any intrinsic degradation of a species. In his most influential writing, *The Mind of Primitive Man* (1911), Boas argued that there is no such thing as a racially pure group and that the inherent differences among races are minor compared to their similarities.

Boas's impact on the intellectualization of race and racial issues began to flow more assuredly in the postwar years, as the activities of the Ku Klux Klan and the eugenicists lent his theories new urgency. The so-called Negro Problem, Boas insisted, was not blacks' innate inferiority and inability to fit into American society, as was commonly believed, but rather an American environment that had shaped and continued to oppress them. Black people had no inherent "problem"; it was perhaps white people who did. This simple idea represented a huge conceptual leap, but once made, had the potential to powerfully transform the ongoing dilemma of race relations and render the relevant issues freshly comprehensible.

By stressing the inherent integrity of any group, Boas helped trigger a seismic shift in the way Americans thought about race, a receptiveness reinforced by the country's fundamental egalitarianism and seen in a plethora of articles appearing in magazines of the early '20s, with such titles as "We Take Off Our Hats to Negroes Who Have Made Good" and

"Black Is a Perfectly Beautiful Shade" (*World Outlook*); "Americanization of the Negro" (*Catholic World*); "Negro Race Not Dying Out" (*Literary Digest*); and "Our Diminishing Tide of Color" (*Current Opinion*). "If my view is correct," Boas wrote in 1921, "it is clear that the only fundamental remedy for the situation is the recognition that Negroes have the right to be treated as individuals, not as members of a class." In 1924 he publicly challenged the findings of the paleontologist Henry Fairfield Osborn, director of the American Museum of Natural History, who had claimed the superiority of the "Nordic race," and four years later concluded in his book *Anthropology and Modern Life,* "[S]ome of the most firmly rooted opinions of our times appear from a wider point of view as prejudices." Boas's debunking of the false philosophy of race took on even greater impetus during the 1930s, as eugenics and notions of racial purity assumed central roles in the ideology of European fascism, the latter a movement Boas most passionately resisted.

"It is possible," according to historian Thomas F. Gossett, "that Boas did more to combat race prejudice than any other person in history." Anthropological quarrels about the relative strengths and weaknesses of different races have never completely disappeared, but since Boas—and the world's subsequent horror at the Nazis' abhorrent misuse of eugenics and ideas of genetic determinism—their power to persuade has severely diminished. Few theories of innate racial or ethnic inferiority surface today that are not immediately challenged and placed under sharp scrutiny.

The years 1900–1920 had been for black Americans a period of tremendous growth and change, as the Tuskegee ideal receded and a new black identity emerged—represented by such developments as the NAACP, the Urban League, the back-to-Africa militancy of the Jamaican-born visionary Marcus Garvey, the Great Migration, and the flowering of arts and literature by blacks. If the representative black American of 1900 had been a tenant farmer scratching out a living in rural Georgia, drawing inspiration from Sunday-morning sermons and the declarations of Booker T. Washington, by the end of the war he was a seven-dollar-a-day automobile assembly-line worker in Detroit, an NAACP member, and an avid reader of *The Crisis.*

This new man, who worked and lived increasingly in cities, voted, perhaps had served and fought in the war, was known as the New Negro, and belonged to a movement that had its most vivid expression in the artistry of the Harlem Renaissance. The Renaissance and the New Negro movement formed a logical response to the white efforts of the past sixty years to disenfranchise, ignore, and obliterate blacks from American life, for this upsurge was nothing if not an insistence on identity and belonging. Blacks appeared more ready to assert their Americanism, to mourn and celebrate their past and proclaim the importance and singularity of their role in this nation, and were newly interested in recognizing their African heritage and connection to other nonwhite peoples around the globe. This latter impulse was perhaps best represented by Garveyism and the continuing promotion of an international consciousness of color by Du Bois in *The Crisis,* as it was embodied by Du Bois's leadership at international conclaves such as the Pan-African Congress.

The Renaissance featured the literary talents of Jean Toomer, Langston Hughes, Countee Cullen, Claude McKay, and Arna Bontemps; musicians Duke Ellington, Eubie Blake, Fats Waller, Count Basie, and Bessie Smith; anthropologists Zora Neale Hurston, E. Franklin Frazier, and Kelly Miller; historians Rayford Logan, Carter G. Woodson, and Arthur A. Schomburg; and folklorists such as Arthur Fauset. Critic Alain Locke's seminal 1925 book, *The New Negro,* offered a portfolio of many of these emerging activists and intellectuals, galleries and critics attached new importance to black artists and writers, and *The Crisis* and *Opportunity,* the Urban League's periodical, encouraged artistic and intellectual endeavor both in Harlem and elsewhere by offering publication and cash prizes for excellence.

Lynching was a motif in many works of fiction and poetry of the period, and it was characteristic of the close relationship between the arts and issues in the Renaissance that antilynching reformers such as Du Bois, James Weldon Johnson, and Walter White all took time to give artistic expression to their beliefs.

The most well-known literary effort about lynching during the Renaissance was Walter White's novel *The Fire in the Flint,* which caused a sensation upon its appearance in 1924. White was one of the more fascinating figures active in the antilynching cause—a man who had an early brush with a lynch mob and went on to personally investigate forty-one separate lynchings and lead the nation's fight against the practice. His experiences, many of which were both traumatic and dangerous, served him well when in 1923 he produced his novel on the subject.

The idea that White should write a novel originated with *American Mercury* editor H. L. Mencken, who made it a point to encourage writing by Southerners about the South. Mencken admired and was a bit in awe of

White's obsession with lynching, and shared his understanding that it represented the supreme example of human intolerance and race hatred. White had never entertained ideas of being a novelist, but was enough of an egotist to take seriously Mencken's flattering suggestion that he could certainly write a better novel about the South than some recently produced. Mary White Ovington offered him the use of her country house in Great Barrington for the purpose and White dutifully churned out the novel in only twelve days.

The Fire in the Flint centers on the story of black physician Kenneth Harper. The Southern-born Harper attains a medical degree at a Northern university and serves honorably in the First World War, but passes up an opportunity to work in the North in order to return to his hometown in Georgia, where he wants to help provide quality medical care to his own people. He knows that to succeed as a black man in the small-town South he will have to steer clear of local politics, much as had his father, a carpenter who had built many of the homes in town.

Amateurish in its literary stylings, White's book has a compelling momentum, or as a critic for the New York *Tribune* noted, it "lives and breathes by the terrible truth and reality of its own substance." On one level the book is a kind of catalogue of the many facts of racial violence White knew firsthand—brutality toward returning black war veterans, victimization of upwardly striving black men, sexual exploitation of black women, the Klan's revival, peonage, a sharecroppers' revolt, and a lynching.

Reality intrudes in White's novel in the form of a headstrong younger brother, Bob, who warns Kenneth that times have changed, and that the delicate balance their father managed to maintain in the town may no longer be possible. Indeed, some of the town's black inhabitants are considering action to assert their rights as tenant farmers, and at the behest of a young woman for whom he has romantic feelings Kenneth agrees, against his better judgment, to get involved with the group, where his education and worldly experience soon thrust him into a position of prominence.

Younger brother Bob—who represents the New Negro—knows that he is destined to suffocate or come to a bad end in the claustrophobic world of the town, and is determined to go north for an education. He is about to depart when the cruelest kind of fate intervenes: his and Kenneth's sister, Mamie, is gang-raped by white men. Bob, in a rage, shoots and kills two of the whites he suspects of raping Mamie, and is himself then hunted down and killed by a lynch mob.

Kenneth, distraught at his sister's ruin and furious over his brother's death, tries to fight against his own urge for revenge. Before he can act he is called to minister to a sick white woman whose life he had earlier saved. Struggling with his powerful feelings of personal loss and hatred for whites, he arrives in time to help the patient, but his visit to her household is misunderstood by Klansmen who watch him enter and leave, and he is also killed by a mob. The novel ends with the ironic use of the kind of bland news item that often described lynchings in the white press:

ANOTHER NEGRO LYNCHED IN GEORGIA

CENTRAL CITY, Ga., Sept. 15.—"Doc" Harper, a negro, was lynched here to-night, charged with attempted criminal assault on a white woman, the wife of a prominent citizen of this city. . . . Harper evidently became frightened before accomplishing his purpose and was caught as he ran from the house. He is said to have confessed before being put to death by a mob which numbered 5,000. He was burned at the stake.

This is the second lynching in Central City this week. On Thursday morning Bob Harper, a brother of the Negro lynched to-day, was killed by a posse after he had run amuck and killed two young white men. . . . It is thought the Negro had become temporarily insane.

In a telegram to the Governor to-day, Sheriff Parker reported that all was quiet in the city and he anticipated no further trouble.

White's subsequent attempts at fiction fell far short of his initial success, and when he returned to the subject of lynching again in 1929 it was with a nonfiction account, *Rope and Faggot: A Biography of Judge Lynch.* The book was an insightful summing-up of numerous issues related to the phenomenon, and although he outlined some reasons for optimism, White sadly concluded that lynching had become so ingrained a part of American life it might never be completely erased. "Mobbism," he wrote, "has inevitably degenerated to the point where an uncomfortably large percentage of American citizens can read in their newspapers of the slow roasting alive of a human being in Mississippi and turn, promptly and with little thought, to the comic strip or sporting page. Thus has lynching become an almost integral part of our national folkways."

The Tragedy of Lynching

Only eleven recorded lynchings occurred in the South in 1929, but that number doubled to twenty-two in just the first eight months of 1930. It was a demoralizing development, for lynching deaths had been seen to decrease consistently throughout the 1920s, and many reformers engaged in monitoring the statistics had dared to assume that the curve would never again turn upward. "It is hard to tell just what is the reason back of this recrudescence of lynching," Walter White wrote to James Weldon Johnson. "I am inclined to believe that the unemployment and the financial depression play a part—lynchings usually go up in number when the price of cotton goes down." He complained of the Depression's effect on race relations, adding, "They are trying to bully again into submission Negroes generally. Unhappily, the brother is still asleep, and the vast majority of them don't care how many lynchings take place as long as they themselves are not incinerated."

The Depression, hard on virtually all Americans, was particularly devastating in the rural South. Remote agricultural areas still climbing out of the nineteenth century were the first to feel the effects of economic disaster. Some regions fell back to a sense of isolation and deprivation not known since Reconstruction, and in this atmosphere old animosities and ways of life stirred anew. For antilynching advocates, the uptick in lynchings was distressing precisely because they had derived significant strength from the idea that they were winning their fight, or at least having an impact. And although it was obvious the Depression was having an effect on lynching, the new data nonetheless was a troubling reminder of the practice's staying power. It thus barely seemed surprising that the early 1930s saw a new participant in the black rights and antilynching cause, a legal rights group known as the International Labor Defense (ILD) that was identified with the American Communist party, and which linked lynching and racial injustice to economic oppression and a global struggle for minority rights.

Sharing the ILD's concern with economic and social factors, the CIC in 1930 created the Commission on the Study of Lynching, an effort to offer the first "scientific" analysis of lynching as a social phenomenon. The newly formed commission had among its board members Dr. Howard W. Odum, of the Institute of Research in Social Sciences at the University of North Carolina in Chapel Hill, and Julian Harris, the son of Joel Chandler Harris, to whom Du Bois was going to deliver the antilynching editorial during the Sam Hose affair. Along with his wife and coeditor of the Columbus, Georgia, *Enquirer-Sun,* Julian Harris had won a Pulitzer Prize in 1926 for the paper's stand against lynching and the Klan.

The new endeavor was different from lynching investigations that had come before in that it sought to examine not just details of the alleged crime and the lynching that followed, but all aspects of a case, including relevant social and economic factors, and it employed trained sociologists to perform this work side by side with local people of both races. The CIC's case-study idea was in keeping with its overall approach to fixing what troubled the South—joining sociological understanding with biracial cooperation and treating lynching not as a problem requiring federal laws, but as one that could be comprehended, and hopefully dealt with, as the result of solvable community tensions.

Under the direction of Arthur F. Raper, the commission was prodigious in its work, and within a few years had published and distributed to the South's editors, ministers, educators, and elected officials numerous antilynching handbooks, case studies, and brochures. Many of its findings were assembled in *The Tragedy of Lynching,* published in 1933, which argued and provided data to support the point that economic issues, politics, and the envy of black advancement were at the heart of most lynchings.

One of the lynchings the commission investigated and wrote up was the July 29, 1930, murder of S. S. Mincey, seventy, a black political leader in Montgomery County, Georgia. The details of his death could almost have been drawn from the annals of the Reconstruction-era Klan of sixty years earlier. Mincey had headed the local Republican organization for twenty-five years, was active in the state Republican party, and had gone four times as a Georgia delegate to the Republican National Convention. He was also a prosperous farmer who owned forty acres of good land and a substantial house, was the patriarch of a large family, and belonged to numerous local fraternal lodges. But while working to expand his political operations in Montgomery County in spring 1930, he fell out with some of the so-called lily whites—white Republicans who resented and worked against black domination of the party. At issue were the patronage positions Mincey controlled, as well as a verbal slight he had tossed at the whites at a party conclave on April 5, when he had compared them unfavorably to Democrats, essentially calling them "white trash," an affront that, coming from the lips of even a prominent black man, was an unbearable provocation.

In a nighttime raid, Mincey was abducted from his home by masked intruders, beaten over the head and hustled into a waiting truck, then driven into the countryside and brutally flogged. When he was found crawling by the roadside the next morning his clothes were in tatters, the skin on his back hanging in bloody strips. He lived for a few hours, long enough to partially describe his ordeal.

Many in Montgomery County reacted with astonishment to the news that one of its leading citizens had been lynched by masked men as in the glory days of the Klan. The anachronistic nature of Mincey's murder—that he had been whipped and "tortured to death in an unmerciful and heinous manner," according to a community resolution denouncing the crime—fueled his neighbors' disgust and anger. Local newspapers were unanimous in condemning the incident, and mass meetings were held where anarchy and mobbism were assailed.

The CIC investigation showed that despite the universal concern expressed, no one was willing to testify against the mob, even though many circumstantial facts, some provided by Mincey before he died, pointed to the truck used in the abduction and even the identities of some of his assailants. In the end, though the community knew the murderers and disapproved of their act, residents chose to continue living peaceably among them rather than risk coming forward to tell what they knew.

The Mincey lynching and other acts of racial violence that year were devastating news to the CIC; instead of discovering that a decade of antilynching advocacy had begun to bend the sympathies of Southern moderates, the group was left to conclude by their investigation that most whites still accepted the practice. Voices in a community might be raised against lynching, but most people were unlikely to speak out against it except in the broadest generalities, and none was willing to risk testifying against the guilty parties.

Other incidents suggested this continuing tacit approval from Southern communities. The people of Maryville, Missouri, on a clear, crisp day in January 1931 chained a young black man to the roof of a colored schoolhouse, doused the entire building with an accelerant, and set it on fire, creating a conflagration visible ten miles away. The victim, an accused murderer, died silhouetted against the pale winter sky, howling like a banshee and struggling uselessly against the chain that held him taut. "A strong wind was blowing," reported the *Literary Digest,* "and the little schoolhouse, with the Negro bound on the ridge-pole, and plentifully soaked with gasoline, made a spectacular blaze." The dead man, it was rumored, had not been quite right in the head.

Although it was reported that every one of Maryville's three thousand residents witnessed the execution, the event appeared to make little dent in the town's moral life. An investigator from the Federal Council of Churches who visited the following Sunday heard no mention of the grotesque human sacrifice and destruction of the school in any of three church services he attended: one minister preached the evils of drunkenness, another asked for donations to support missionary work among the heathens in faraway lands, and a third encouraged his flock to "look for the little signs of God's presence" in their daily lives.

In addition to the recognition by those studying the phenomenon that mob murder might be more entrenched than they had assumed, the early 1930s brought other important conceptual changes in the way Americans thought about lynching. With the rise of fascism abroad, mob violence in the United States came increasingly to be viewed as a parallel to the European model. Perceptive commentators did not hesitate to identify lynch mobs as being of a piece with the newsreel images Americans saw frequently of goose-stepping Nazi phalanxes and book burnings off the Unter den Linden. Even a lynching in such an undeniably American locale as Tampa, Florida, was now likely to be seen as less a regional depravity than the manifestation of a dark, universal impulse mankind could not control. In a sense this was good news, for it was where the debate over lynching had always belonged—liberated from the rhetoric of section and chivalry in which it too frequently took refuge.

Another development was a deepening concern with the legal lynching. The Leo Frank case, the Arkansas sharecroppers' war, and the efforts in Lexington, Kentucky, to defeat a lynch mob by rushing through criminal hearings had raised the specter of a judiciary too eager to satisfy a mob's thirst for blood by appropriating, or appearing to appropriate, some of the mob's interests. Legal lynching attracted worldwide notoriety in the 1930s as the result of a case involving nine young black hobos, dubbed the Scottsboro Boys, who were accused of rape and subjected to three intense and controversial trials, all of which were contested as unfair by civil rights and legal-reform organizations.

Finally, the spirit of federal activism that attended the New Deal—the broadening acceptance of the idea that the federal government had an important role to play in addressing the economic, social, and legal problems besetting the country—would be reflected in the U.S. Supreme Court's issuing of several decisions during the 1930s that sought to impose federal concepts of due process on state courts.

The Scottsboro affair began on the afternoon of March 25, 1931, at the height of the Depression, as young people rode a freight train bound from Chattanooga to Memphis in search of work. The train was making its way slowly through the verdant country of northeastern Alabama when, between the towns of Stevenson and Scottsboro, a white man hitching a ride on the train told a stationmaster that there had been a fight aboard, and that black youths had attacked a group of whites, forcing them to jump off. A phone call to the train's next stop, Paint Rock, alerted the sheriff, who instructed his deputy to intercept the train and arrest any blacks on board. The deputy quickly rounded up several helpers and, armed with shotguns and pistols, they boarded the train as it entered Paint Rock and made a rapid search of its forty-two cars, evicting nine black men, one white man, and two white women dressed as men.

The nine blacks, who had not all been traveling companions, were tied together with a piece of rope, while the two women sat to one side. After about twenty minutes one of the women, Ruby Bates, informed the deputy that she and her companion, Victoria Price, had been raped aboard the train. Bates and Price related that they had been looking for work among the textile mills in Chattanooga and, having had no luck, were hoboing back to Huntsville, Alabama. They said a fight had erupted on the train, with the blacks forcing the whites to "unload," and that the gondola car in which they had been riding had been suddenly overrun with blacks, who gang-raped them.

The women were sent to be examined by two local physicians while the black youths, who ranged in age from thirteen to twenty, were taken into custody in nearby Scottsboro, the seat of Jackson County. Word spread quickly, and a throng of citizens formed at the courthouse. The large number of suspects doubtless would have made lynching a daunting task even for the most zealous mob, although what probably saved the boys from prompt annihilation was the fact that Bates and Price were not local residents.

On Monday, April 6, the boys went on trial at the Jackson County courthouse. A huge crowd was on hand, inside and outside, some visitors coming by buckboard and automobile from as far as fifty miles away. The defendants—Haywood Patterson, Olen Montgomery, Clarence Norris, Willie Roberson, Andrew Wright, Roy Wright, Ozie Powell, Eugene Williams, and Charley Weems—all pleaded not guilty.

The trial was, in legal expert Randall Kennedy's phrase, "a parody of due process." The original court-appointed attorneys for the defendants quit shortly before the trial was to start, giving the two new defense lawyers only thirty minutes to acquaint themselves with the boys and design a strategy. Neither of the attorneys had any significant expertise in criminal law. One was drunk throughout most of the trial and the other was a kindly but doddering former state legislator, nearly seventy years of age, who was considered more a mascot around the courthouse than a practicing attorney. They did, at least, have the presence of mind to request a change of venue, citing the fact that a mob surrounded the building, making the atmosphere dangerous for any juror who dared vote for acquittal. The judge denied this motion and ordered the trial to proceed.

Under Alabama law a jury decided not only guilt but also punishment. For rape, the sentence could be anything between ten years' imprisonment and death. Within two days of trials and jury deliberations, all nine boys had been found guilty and eight had been sentenced to death. The jury hung on the punishment for Roy Wright, the thirteen-year-old. On account of his age, prosecutors had requested only life imprisonment; one juror agreed this was sufficient, but the others believed he deserved the electric chair.

This travesty of justice would ordinarily have continued on to its accustomed denouement, with the boys sent speedily to their deaths, but the large number of defendants, their youth, and the severe penalties handed down had attracted outside interest and concern. Among the groups that went into action to protest the arrests and sentences was the Communist Party of the United States of America (CPUSA), which had covered the case in its publication, *The Daily Worker.* The CPUSA had increasingly immersed itself in the issue of race relations as a result of policies disseminated at a 1928 international Communist gathering in Moscow. Blacks, the meeting emphasized, were an oppressed people trapped inside the American system, and their liberation was a priority. *The Daily Worker's* correspondent, who was in Scottsboro to observe the proceedings, wired to New York his strong concern about the sham trials that had transpired. He also shared his view that what was unfolding in the sleepy Alabama town had the potential to be another legal cause on par with that of Sacco and Vanzetti, the anarchists executed in Massachusetts in 1927.

The NAACP, to its detriment, proceeded with greater caution. It had monitored the Scottsboro case through its members in Chattanooga, and while there was concern about mob influence on the trials, the NAACP failed initially to see clear-cut evidence that the boys' constitutional rights were being abused. It seems curious that someone as knowledgeable about the usual dynamics of such situations as Walter White, who with the departure of James Weldon Johnson for a teaching post at Fisk University had become executive secretary, would not have been more suspicious of the charges in the case, or concerned that the defendants were being denied their due-process rights. But the NAACP may have simply been taking a wait-and-see approach. White patiently waited for copies of the trial transcript to arrive, a step that was inexorably delayed due to Jackson County's byzantine system of recording its legal proceedings and producing transcripts. Meanwhile, his office phone began to ring off the hook as NAACP members and reporters demanded to know what response the nation's leading civil rights organization would have to the miscarriage of justice in Alabama.

The International Labor Defense was already jumping in with both feet to rescue the Scottsboro Boys. Founded in 1925, it had fought long and hard for Sacco and Vanzetti and had worked for leniency in the case of West Coast union organizer Tom Mooney, who'd been framed for the bombing of a patriotic Preparedness Day parade in San Francisco in 1916 and sent to prison. The ILD was more than a legal-aid society; it mounted mass protests to call attention to the class prejudices of the justice system and the plight of those prisoners it represented, and provided financial support to the families of jailed individuals. Although its critics consistently strove to denigrate ILD activities because of the group's links to the Communist party, it enjoyed an independent reputation and high regard among civil libertarians for its dogged efforts on behalf of the accused.

As word of the Scottsboro convictions reached New York, ILD operatives were already in the South securing the permissions of the boys' parents to represent them in an appeal. Once the NAACP got wind of what was taking place and realized they'd been caught napping, angry insults were exchanged—the NAACP accused the Communists of exploiting the boys' plight for propaganda purposes, and the ILD castigated the NAACP as "bourgeois reformers" not sufficiently devoted to revolutionary change or true racial equality. The rift exposed a classic breach on the left—the NAACP worked within the framework of the Constitution with the goal of having constitutional guarantees enforced, while the Communists challenged the entire American system. The difference was most loudly trumpeted by the Communists who, until the rise of fascism forged the creation of the left-wing Popular Front in 1935, made it a point to draw a sharp distinction between their own commitment to a global workers' revolution and those whose reform efforts were seen as compromised or inadequate.

American blacks were largely skeptical of Communist dogma. The party leadership at this point was exclusively white, and it tended to dote in a somewhat patronizing fashion on its black members. More significantly, most black Americans did not share the view that their predicament was a result of class oppression; their own experience told them something different. And the CPUSA failed to appreciate the powerful emotional and even patriotic connection many black people felt toward the United States. As Paul Robeson once forcefully replied to a House Un-American Activities Committee (HUAC) inquisitor who asked why he didn't go live in Russia, "Because my father was a slave, and my people died to build this country, and I am going to stay here and have a part of it just like you."

Thus, while W.E.B. Du Bois and others in the NAACP brain trust might admire a Marxist analysis of the economic forces affecting racism, and understand the link between the struggle of U.S. blacks and anticolonialism elsewhere in the world, they did not necessarily agree that black Americans were potential foot soldiers in a worldwide revolutionary vanguard. The NAACP—associated with a tradition of abolition and democracy consonant with the founding traditions of the nation—acted out of the belief that what black people wanted was equal rights and equal access to American society, not a revolution to topple it.

What worried Clarence Darrow was that the ILD's involvement in Scottsboro, however well-intentioned, might compromise the boys' chances of acquittal. It would do this by forcing Alabama into a political cul-de-sac where state officials would refuse to admit the defendants' innocence in order to prove that they would stand up to Communists. Subsequent events, both in the Scottsboro case and in other incidents in which Southern blacks were defended by the ILD, would reveal the prescience of this concern.

While many were disappointed that the NAACP had not acted more swiftly to take a major role in the case, most civil rights supporters came to feel that the ILD did perform heroically in making the boys' plight an international cause. It organized numerous rallies for the Scottsboro defendants, raised a million dollars toward their defense fund, and in the end probably saved their lives. "The only party that comes out squarely for giving the Negro every right that would be his under the Constitution if his skin were white is the Communist Party," the NAACP's own Oswald Villard observed, "and that is a fact that the older parties had better take note of." But neither the CPUSA nor the NAACP could be proud of the bad blood spilled between them. At its most irresponsible the CPUSA attacked the NAACP as an organization of "gradualist preachers" who were indifferent toward or even in league with lynch mobs, a ridiculous and wholly undeserved accusation. For its part, NAACP leaders were not above occasional Red-baiting, frightening moderate whites with the prospect of an increased Communist influence on U.S. blacks if the NAACP's own remedies for curing racial injustice were not supported.

The April 1931 convictions of the Scottsboro Boys were appealed by the ILD all the way to the U.S. Supreme Court, resulting in the landmark decision in *Powell v. Alabama* in November 1932, which found that the right to adequate counsel was not a dispensable element of due process. Of the Scottsboro trials the high court noted, "It is perfectly apparent that the proceedings, from beginning to end, took place in an atmosphere of tense, hostile and excited public sentiment." The defendants, the court ruled, had been represented by two inexperienced attorneys with no time to prepare the defense; and the prosecution's case, riven with perjured testimony and supported by dubious evidence, could likely have been successfully opposed if qualified counsel had been present. "The failure of the trial court to give them reasonable time and opportunity to secure counsel was a clear denial of due process," the court ruled. "A defendant, charged with a serious crime, must not be stripped of his right to have sufficient time to advise with counsel and prepare his defense. To do that is not to proceed promptly in the calm spirit of regulated justice but to go forward with the haste of the mob."

For the March 1933 retrials, which were moved from Scottsboro to the nearby town of Decatur, in Morgan County, the ILD engaged top New York criminal lawyer Samuel Leibowitz, who agreed to defend the Scottsboro Boys without fee. Leibowitz, who was not a Communist, asserted that the case "touches no controversial theory of economy or government, but the basic rights of man." The trial judge was James E. Horton, a respected jurist from an old Alabama family. Radiating an aura of confidence and openness, Horton welcomed the press to Decatur and impressed Northern observers by unself-consciously shaking hands with the black reporters covering the trial.

Leibowitz opened the defense by proving that local blacks had been excluded from the jury pool. Indeed, he showed through testimony from several witnesses who were lifelong residents of Morgan County that no black person in living memory had ever served on a jury. Since the qualifications for jurors in the county specified only that they be "honest and intelligent men" of "good character and sound judgment" who understood English and had never been convicted of "any offense involving moral turpitude," blacks meeting these qualifications, Leibowitz asserted, would by law have to be included in the pool. To deflect the anticipated argument that no such blacks existed in the county, he put numerous black men on the stand who were property owners, teachers, members of school boards—upstanding citizens all and clearly qualified under the county's rules. It did not win him the mistrial he requested, but it laid the foundation for an appeal if the case ended in conviction.

Leibowitz also brought far more intense scrutiny on the testimony of the state's key witnesses—Victoria Price and Ruby Bates—than had been seen in the earlier trials. He demonstrated that Price was probably lying about having spent the night before the Scottsboro incident in a respectable boardinghouse in Chattanooga, as she had claimed, and asserted that she most likely had sexual intercourse in a Chattanooga hobo camp shortly before the fateful train ride. The medical evidence gathered the afternoon of the alleged attack on the train, Leibowitz stated, indicated recent intercourse, but was inconsistent with her claim that she had been gang-raped by six men. He also showed that she had been previously convicted for adultery.

At the time, courts did not embrace the idea that the past sexual behavior of a rape victim should be off-limits as evidence, and Leibowitz and others attorneys who defended the Scottsboro Boys did not hesitate to rake over the checkered pasts of both women, whom Leibowitz at one point referred to as "cut-rate prostitutes."

The defense's star witness was Bates, who had recanted her earlier testimony and declared that neither she nor Victoria Price had been raped aboard the train. For reasons that Bates did not clarify they had concocted the rape scenario—possibly because the young women feared they would be prosecuted as vagrants after being caught in the roundup at Paint Rock. On cross-examination, however, prosecutors had some success depicting Bates as an opportunist who had been coopted by influential people from New York (the ILD), who had given her money and fancy new clothes in exchange for her change of heart. In his closing statement, one of the prosecutors, Morgan County solicitor Wade Wright, exhorted the jury: "Show them that Alabama justice cannot be bought and sold with Jew money from New York!"—a remark that despite Leibowitz's strenuous objection failed to gain a mistrial.

When the jury found the first defendant, Haywood Patterson, guilty, supporters of the Scottsboro Boys staged marches and demonstrations in New York and Washington, and editorials nationwide criticized the verdict. Even some Alabama newsmen had begun to feel uncomfortable, suspecting that Victoria Price was not telling the truth and that the boys had most likely been framed. In June 1933, Judge Horton threw out the jury's verdict and set aside Patterson's conviction on the grounds that the testimony of Victoria Price was simply unbelievable. He cited the historic tendency of women of low repute to "make false accusations upon any occasion whereby their selfish ends may be gained."

The defense's attempt to convince judge and jury that Price fell short of being an exemplar of Southern womanhood had been both essential and risky—essential because impeaching her character was crucial to destroying her version of events, risky because it could be perceived as an assault on white womanhood, forcing Alabamans to come to her defense. To an extent, it appeared the latter had occurred, which explained the jury's verdict. As one local man explained, Victoria Price "might be a fallen woman, but by God she is a white woman." All the defense's evidence, asserted another, "don't count a mite with the jury" once it heard Price say "that nigger raped her."

Judge Horton's dismissal of Patterson's conviction in a case where the tainted honor of Southern womanhood was concerned was, like Governor Slaton's commutation of Leo Frank's death sentence in Georgia in 1915, a brave act of conscience, and like Slaton, Horton paid for his candor, losing his job in the next election. For, despite the fact that public opinion had largely come around to the belief that the boys were probably innocent, Alabama authorities could not bring themselves to drop the charges and set them free. As Clarence Darrow had foreseen, they were not about to hand victory to an outfit such as the ILD and make heroes of a bunch of Communists.

Alabama's third attempt to convict the boys was such a sham it would have been comical if nine people's lives weren't dependent on the outcome. This time Leibowitz was faced not with the wise and congenial Judge Horton but his direct opposite, a hostile jurist named William Callahan who seemed determined to secure a guilty verdict. He refused to allow Leibowitz to present key testimony that might explain Price and Bates's behavior, as well as medical evidence that threw further doubt on Price's story. At one point Callahan told the jury to bear in mind that sex between a black man and a white woman, by definition, constituted rape, regardless of the white woman's social standing. Then, in his charge to the jury, he neglected to explain what to do in case they found the defendants innocent.

Given the widespread sentiment about the case, the third round of trials was the most cynical of all—a repulsive exercise aimed at reaching a desired conclusion, the conviction and execution of innocent young men in order that Alabama might avoid freeing blacks, accused of a sexual assault on a white woman, who happened to be represented by Communists. "It is doubtful if a single person in the United States, including the judge and jury in Alabama," Du Bois wrote, "has any thought that the black victims who are being tried in Scottsboro have committed any crime that deserves punishment. Nevertheless, they . . . are going to be punished because an uncivilized community and a brutal judicial system cannot do anything else."

As expected, the Callahan jury voted for convictions, although Leibowitz successfully appealed on the grounds, as he'd established in the second trial, that the jury pool had not included any black people. In

March 1935, the Supreme Court ruling in *Norris v. Alabama* reversed the third Scottsboro convictions. To protest the exclusion of blacks from the jury, as well as the long tradition of such exclusion, the justices invoked the Fourteenth Amendment's guarantee of equal protection under the law. The state's already weak position was diminished further when it was found that, made aware of Leibowitz's intended challenge, someone in Alabama had hastily written several names of black people onto the bottom of the jury rolls in an attempt to fool the Supreme Court.

As the decade progressed, the assumption that the boys were innocent became fairly universal, but political factors continued to make it difficult for Alabama to countenance "surrender" to Communists. When Democrat Bibb Graves became Alabama's governor in 1935, there was hope he would pardon the defendants, for he had publicly upheld the two Supreme Court decisions that had grown out of the case. In 1937 four of the boys were released, but in 1938 Graves reneged on his vow to release the others, despite a personal appeal from President Franklin Roosevelt. Indeed, the last Scottsboro defendant was not released from jail until 1950, and only in 1977, forty-six years after they were taken from a freight train in Paint Rock, did the state of Alabama acknowledge their innocence with a full official pardon issued by Governor George Wallace. By then only one of the "boys," Clarence Norris, remained alive to hear the news.

Of a piece with the trend in Supreme Court decisions, exemplified by the Scottsboro appeals, aimed at filling the legal vacuum created by ineffective state criminal procedure, was a ruling in a bizarre 1934 case in Mississippi. On March 30 of that year Raymond Stewart, a white planter in Kemper County, was slain, and three black farm laborers—Ed Brown, Arthur Ellington, and Henry Shields—were charged with his murder. Their trial began on the morning of April 5 and by the next afternoon all three were convicted and sentenced to death based on statements they had made to a deputy sheriff. No other physical or circumstantial evidence was provided.

During the brief trial, however, the defendants informed the judge that their confessions had been coerced by the use of torture. Ellington showed the court the rope marks on his neck where he had been noosed and hung from a tree. He said he had been removed from his own home by a deputy sheriff named Dial and taken to the home of the murdered man, where a group of angry whites awaited him. They accused him of the crime and when he vehemently denied it, grabbed him and suspended him from a tree with a rope around his neck, then took turns whipping him. He continued to insist upon his innocence and was finally taken home, but Deputy Dial returned two days later and drove Ellington across the state line into Alabama, then pulled him from the car and began flogging him, telling the prisoner that this time he would not stop until he confessed to killing Stewart. Finally, Ellington broke down and agreed to confess in a statement the deputy would dictate.

Brown and Shields told a similar story. They were arrested and held in the Kemper County jail where, on the night of April 1, they were visited by a large number of white men who made them undress and lie across chairs; the whites, including Deputy Dial, another officer, and the jailer, then beat the prisoners with a belt with metal buckles until their "confessions" matched that given by Ellington.

So confident were the police in their actions that when Deputy Dial followed the accused to the witness stand he did not dispute their testimony. Asked by the judge how seriously the men had been beaten, the deputy replied, "Not too much for a negro; not as much as I would have done if it were left to me." Despite having heard the accused complain of torture and Dial admit that the confessions had been extracted by force, the jury voted to convict.

The case was appealed to the Mississippi State Supreme Court, which upheld the convictions on the grounds that the Fifth Amendment protection against self-incrimination—as in a coerced confession—did not apply in state courts, and that the treatment the defendants had suffered was uniform for all criminal suspects in Kemper County; in seeking relief on appeal, the appellants were requesting special treatment under the law. In a dissent, Justice V. A. Griffith described the parts of the trial transcript in which the tortures were detailed as resembling something out of the Middle Ages, and characterized the trial overall as having been little else than "a fictitious continuation of the mob."

The U.S. Supreme Court, in reviewing the case, shared Griffith's concern. Indeed, the transgressions against law and common decency were so egregious they made the judicial failings in the Scottsboro case seem like petty misdemeanors. The high court's opinion in its February 1936 decision, *Brown v. Mississippi,* noted that the original trial transcript "in pertinent respects . . . reads more like pages torn from some medieval account, than a record made within the confines of a modern civilization which aspires to an enlightened constitutional government." While acknowledging that a state was "free to regulate the procedure of its courts in accordance with its own conceptions of policy," it could not "substitute trial by ordeal." The opinion averred that "The rack and torture chamber may not be substituted for the witness stand," and concluded: "It would be difficult to conceive of methods more revolting to the sense of justice than those taken to procure the confessions of these petitioners, and the use of the confessions thus obtained as the basis for conviction and sentence was a clear denial of due process."

The Brown case, like *Moore v. Dempsey, Powell v. Alabama,* and *Norris v. Alabama* before it, was a stepping-stone in the slow march toward expanding federal guarantees of the rights of accused citizens, what legal historians would later call "the due-process revolution." But, in *Brown,* the court's reprieve did not end the defendants' predicament. Despite a favorable ruling from the highest court in the land, anger in Kemper County about Stewart's murder had not abated, and no other likely suspects had ever been identified. This meant that even if the three defendants, on retrial, managed to win acquittal, they would almost certainly be put to death by a lynch mob. To avoid that eventuality, as well as the risk that they might again be convicted and sentenced to death despite the lack of any evidence, they agreed to plead guilty to a lesser charge. Though innocent of the murder of Raymond Stewart, Brown, Shields, and Ellington accepted prison terms of ten, five, and three years, respectively.

"The majority of the victims of lynching mobs are friendless, penniless individuals, wholly without political or other influence which might aid them in escaping swift punishment," Walter White told a U.S. Senate committee in early 1934. White was addressing one of lynching's oldest rationalizations—that criminal cases left in the fumbling hands of the courts might be unduly prolonged. "I challenge any reputable and honest person to assert that there is any lack of speed whatsoever in apprehending, indicting, trying and convicting Negroes charged with crime."

White's views were legitimate, but if the Scottsboro case had taught Southerners anything it was that outside legal professionals were quite capable of impeding justice on behalf of supposedly "friendless" prisoners, and of utterly frustrating the people's will. When these outsiders happened to be Communists their presence only further upset local sentiment, as residents of two disparate Southern regions—central Alabama and Maryland's Eastern Shore—demonstrated in 1933.

In Tuscaloosa in August of that year, ILD lawyers had themselves almost been lynched, and the three black men they were defending had been promptly delivered into the hands of a mob, when Tuscaloosa whites learned of the "communistic" lawyers' determination to protract the case and clear the accused. The defendants—A. T. Harden, sixteen, Dan Pippen, eighteen, and Elmore Clark, eighteen—were charged with the June 1933 rape and murder of a young white woman named Vaudine Maddox. In something of a reversal of the usual relationship between victim and perpetrator in such crimes, Harden and Pippen were devout churchgoers and members of the choir, while the murdered woman's family was so poor and dissolute it had moved into a black settlement, where they were shunned because the father was a moonshiner and his daughters were rumored to be prostitutes. CIC field investigator Arthur Raper, who interviewed numerous individuals in both the white and black communities in the aftermath of the lynching, discovered that Vaudine Maddox cohabited with a shady older white man named Powell who claimed to be her cousin, and that many blacks quietly suspected Powell of having killed her. A source of general agitation to both the white and black communities was the fact that several young white women in the area, with few if any options for earning a living, were thought to have begun charging money to have sex with black men. This was apparently a lucrative endeavor, since it was considered high status for a black man to sleep with a white woman, regardless if she was a prostitute. "A certain type of Negro will work his head off to get the money to go see a white woman where it is relatively safe," an Alabama friend assured Will Alexander in a letter to the CIC.

Raper also learned that whites had been particularly upset by the description of Maddox's body when it was found in a field days after she had gone missing. "We had to put her in a canvas," a member of the search party told Raper. "The buzzards had eaten a hole in her side, and the dogs ate one arm off. The skin slipped when we tried to pick her up; we had to hold her by the head and by the shoes—it was awful." Raper learned from the black community that one of the black suspects, Elmore Clark, was known to whites and blacks as a troublemaker, "a mean nigger" who "ought to be killed on general principle."

August 1, the day the trial of Harden, Pippin, and Clark began, a mob of several hundred gathered outside the Tuscaloosa County courthouse while inside Judge Henry B. Foster ruled that attorneys Allan Taub and Irving Schwab, ILD lawyers who had traveled south to defend the accused, and their Birmingham cocounsel, Frank B. Irwin, had no jurisdiction in the case. Only the presence of a National Guard unit lobbing tear-gas grenades and holding the crowd back with fixed bayonets got the lawyers safely onto a northbound train. An hour later, as the train approached Birmingham, it was halted near the small town of Blocton by a group of vigilantes demanding that the three lawyers be handed over. A lynching was averted only when the posse was informed that the men were traveling "under the protection" of Judge Foster.

The trial had been held over for several days when word arrived that the ILD lawyers intended to return and resume their defense of the three accused. On the night of August 13, Sheriff R. L. Shamblin, apparently with the approval of Judge Foster, tried to relocate the prisoners from Tuscaloosa to Birmingham for their own safety; however, in an episode that reeked of official complicity, the midnight transfer was intercepted by two cars of masked men on a back road about twenty miles from Tuscaloosa. Harden, Pippin, and Clark were removed from the police cruiser, lined up before a firing squad, and shot. Pippin and Harden were killed outright; Clark, shot in the arm and the thigh and left for dead, managed to break his handcuffs off with a brick and drag himself to a black family's shanty. Ultimately returned to jail, where National Guard troops were needed to protect him from yet another mob, the dazed and gravely wounded Clark "voluntarily" signed a statement that he could not recognize any of the men who had stopped the sheriff's car and murdered his codefendants. Raper's informants told him that one of the police ringleaders of the shootings, an officer named Murray Pate, was a notorious "nigger-killer" who boasted of having taken the lives of eleven blacks "in the line of duty."

The Tuscaloosa incident brought strong condemnation of the ILD for prompting the lynch mob's action, as many in the Alabama town said they equated the outsiders' involvement with the likelihood that the prosecution of Vaudine Maddox's killers might go on indefinitely. Judge Foster remarked, "Tuscaloosa County was willing to see the Negroes tried and was willing to give them a fair trial, but some were not willing to have us go through another Scottsboro case." A news item reporting that the ILD attorney in the Scottsboro trials, Samuel Leibowitz, had, from the safety of New York, described Alabamans as "lantern-jawed morons" certainly could not have helped to endear his ILD colleagues to the residents of Tuscaloosa.

A waitress in a Tuscaloosa restaurant told the CIC's Raper, "Everybody knows it was them New York lawyers that caused it. They were going to let the negroes have a fair trial and go to the chair until the Jews butted in."

Another townsman confided: "For New York Jews to butt in and spread communistic ideas is too much." Raper heard enough similar remarks to conclude:

> All the emotion stirred by the crime and its vivid description reiterated time and again by the papers, and even more vividly described by those who saw the body, would not have lasted long due to the fact that the [Maddoxes] had no friends in the community, and no status. But when the papers and gossipers began saying "New York lawyers" are entering the case to "clear the niggers," that they are "Jew lawyers," that "they are holding meetings, spreading communistic literature, telling niggers they are as good as whites," sending "threatening telegrams," going to return to defend the niggers and will be protected by troops sent by the governor—this increased the tension. Soon the alleged criminals were practically forgotten and the whole reaction "transferred" over to the ILD.

A sham investigation of the lynching led by Alabama attorney general Thomas Knight, Jr., who had helped prosecute the Scottsboro Boys, failed to find anyone accountable, and the U.S. Justice Department turned away pleas from the ILD and others to open a federal investigation. Under existing federal law, only a potential prosecution of Sheriff Shamblin, his deputies, and Judge Foster might be feasible, and the federal government would need to prove that these officials had acted "under color of law" to deny Pippen, Harden, and Clark a constitutional right. In the 1930s the Justice Department was not actively pursuing such cases, and there was no solid evidence linking Shamblin to the mysterious masked mob. There was, in fact, little physical evidence of any kind. When the bodies of Pippin and Harden were exhumed as part of the state's inquiry, it was discovered that someone had meticulously carved the bullets from their corpses, possibly to eliminate evidence, more likely for souvenirs, in any case hopelessly dooming any chance of establishing culpability.

An even more sensational example of ILD "provocation" was a dramatic lynching and riot on Maryland's Eastern Shore that, like the Coatesville, Pennsylvania, lynching of 1911, garnered extensive coverage because of its proximity to New York and Washington. In October 1931, a sixty-three-year-old Eastern Shore black named Euel Lee had been arrested and charged with the brutal killing of a white farmer and his wife and two daughters, all found murdered in their beds. Lee, with the help of ILD attorneys Bernard Ades and David Levinson, managed to escape execution for two years. His first conviction was successfully appealed on the grounds that a mob spirit had prevailed; a second was voided on the grounds that blacks had been excluded from the jury pool. Throughout this process, authorities moved Lee off the Eastern Shore several times to a secure jail in Baltimore because of the continuing threat that he would be lynched.

The Eastern Shore, never prosperous in the first place, had been particularly hard hit by the Depression. Asking the region to endure the further humiliation of a black mass murderer avoiding execution through the help of "Communist" lawyers proved too much. When another racially explosive crime occurred in October 1933, the impatience and simmering resentment of the residents finally boiled over. The new case centered around twenty-eight-year-old George Armwood, arrested and charged with raping Mrs. Mary Denston, a white woman in her late seventies. In the process of attacking Denston, Armwood was said to have chewed off one of her breasts. The black community told a different story. Reporter Rose Bradley was told that the idea that Armwood would rape an old lady like Mrs. Denston was ludicrous. The accused had worked for a white man named John Richardson, and it was thought that the two men had hatched a plan to rob the older woman because she was known to carry large sums of cash on her person. The robbery, conducted by Armwood, went awry when Denston resisted. Richardson at first tried to hide his accomplice, but as the search intensified he gave him up to the police. Most blacks conceded that Armwood had probably tried to rob Mrs. Denston, but the rape story, and the detail about Armwood's chewing his victim's breasts, it was held, were "pure gossip."

Like Euel Lee, Armwood was removed to Baltimore for his own safety. But then, inexplicably, with his trial not scheduled to begin for another week, he was returned to jail in the Eastern Shore town of Princess Anne despite widespread knowledge that a mob was waiting for him. On the night of October 18, more than two thousand people, including the twenty-year-old granddaughter of Mrs. Denston, gathered in front of the jail and taunted the handful of state police on guard. They jeered the nervous young troopers as "traffic cops" and reminded them they had no business interfering in the town's affairs. Robert F. Duer, a local judge who had been involved in both the Euel Lee and Armwood cases, came from his dinner table to attempt to calm the mob, but was shouted down, one spectator hollering emphatically: "We don't want any 'Euel Lees' in Somerset County."

The mob used a crude battering ram, possibly a discarded railroad tie, to collapse in the front door of the jail. The state troopers fought hand to hand with some of the intruders and hurled tear-gas bombs, although the gas proved largely ineffective because many in the crowd, having anticipated its use, had brought along their protective army gas masks from the First World War. Breaking through three sets of interior doors with the ram, the mob seized Armwood, tied a rope around his neck, and dragged him through the streets.

Unlike mobs in Deep South towns, who might be more likely to have a traditional sturdy "lynching tree" to turn to, the Maryland group was forced to improvise. Seeing some promising large trees in the yard of a man named James Stirling, the mob halted, but Stirling dashed out and pleaded with them to pass by. "I have children in there. Please don't do it here," he said. "I don't want them to see it." The procession continued on, stopping numerous times so new arrivals could have a chance to beat the captive. A teenage boy unsheathed a knife and came away with one of Armwood's ears. Finally locating a suitable tree in the yard of ninety-two-year-old Mrs. Thomas Bock, who was confined to bed with a severe illness, the mob suspended Armwood by rope and committed further mutilations on his body; then he was cut down, most likely already dead, stomped on, and dragged to the intersection of Main and Prince William streets, where he was hurled into a bonfire.

Several reporters from nearby Baltimore and Washington, D.C., having been given ample reason to expect a lynching that night, had been present, and their graphic firsthand coverage helped put an incident the *Washington Herald* called "the wildest lynching orgy that Maryland has ever seen, reminiscent of a Salem witch-hanging" in the national headlines. Most eyewitnesses, even hardened crime reporters, remarked on the extreme animal frenzy of the crowd.

"I saw 3,000 men go mad with the blood lust tonight. I saw them take a human being and make of his body a holocaust of revenge," one woman told a reporter. "I saw men whose faces were grotesque masks of barbarity, turn into fearsome creatures with one overpowering motive in their lives—Revenge. . . . I saw men throw gasoline, oil and pitch on their victim. I saw a match struck. I saw flames, and I saw the end of George Armwood, Negro."

"I can't tell you how it made me feel," admitted a man from Baltimore. "I know I looked up there and saw the Negro hanging from the rope in the darkness and I said to myself, 'Are you living in the year 1933?' "

In the wake of the Armwood lynching, no one was more furious than

Governor Albert C. Ritchie, particularly since many blamed the violence on the state's fumbling and procrastination in the Euel Lee case (Lee himself was finally executed by hanging at the Maryland Penitentiary on October 27). Ritchie had not authorized Armwood's return from Baltimore to Princess Anne, and when told of it he had demanded and received assurances of the prisoner's safety from Captain E. M. Johnson of the state police. But Johnson himself had been struck over the head with a heavy object and knocked unconscious in the attack on the jail, as his troopers were overwhelmed.

With the nation's editorial pages lambasting Maryland for delivering a man into the hands of a lynch mob, the state's attorney general, William P. Lane, informed Ritchie that investigators had identified nine leaders of the lynch mob. When authorities on the Shore ignored the state's order to take the men into custody, the governor dispatched a special battalion of National Guardsmen to make the arrests. The soldiers captured four of the suspects, although Guard officers then made a dreadful misjudgment in deciding that the detachment and its prisoners would spend the night at the Salisbury armory on the Eastern Shore before continuing on to Baltimore in the morning. That night, a mob assaulted the armory, training high-pressure hoses on the building and hurling bricks. The troops retaliated with tear gas, and gunshots were exchanged in a running battle that carried on for hours.

By daybreak the battalion fought its way out and escaped to Baltimore with the prisoners, but an Eastern Shore sheriff traveled to Baltimore soon after with a writ of habeas corpus issued by Judge Duer, and the four suspects were released and returned home to a hero's welcome (no one was ever prosecuted for the Armwood lynching).

In the state capitol at Annapolis, Governor Ritchie found himself assailed from all sides. Legislators representing the Eastern Shore were demanding his impeachment for meddling in their region's affairs (some were threatening to secede from Maryland altogether), while civil liberties groups and editorial-page writers up and down the East Coast railed at him for allowing justice to have been so thoroughly disgraced. It would be Ritchie's unhappy fate to hear his state's name, and his own, frequently mentioned in a forthcoming antilynching debate in Congress as an example of all that could go wrong when states were left on their own to combat lynch law.

States' Rights, States' Wrongs

L ynching was a conspicuous enough evil to energize resistance from numerous sectors of society—black organizations, church groups, Communists, society folk, and even some Southern officials grown weary of having their reputations dragged through the mud. Soon, however, a distinct and powerful new player in the antilynching battle would emerge—the Southern white woman. The putative beneficiary of the creed long dedicated to safeguarding her chastity, she had always occupied a position at the very heart of the South's lynching ideology.

When the dramatic upsurge in lynchings occurred in 1930—the development that spurred the CIC's creation of its own lynching commission—Florida black educator Mary McLeod Bethune told Will Alexander that she was going to issue a statement calling on Southern white women to do something to halt the rise in violence. Originally, the CIC had studiously avoided bringing white women into its fold because the prospect of white women working side by side with black men seemed too provocative a notion. "She was supposed to have ideals but no ideas," historians Wilma Dykeman and James Stokely have said of the limited reform work a proper Southern white woman of the 1920s might be allowed to pursue. "She might talk as long as she had nothing to say, and she might belong to social groups as long as the meaning of 'society' was bounded on one side by a teacup and on the other by a basket of fruit for shut-ins." Most Southerners' idea of an acceptable women's organization was the United Daughters of the Confederacy, which undertook such projects as introducing bills in Congress to fund the construction of a "Mammy Monument" in Washington, D.C., and having the name of the conflict that had engulfed the country in the 1860s changed officially from the Civil War to the War Between the States. (The "mammy" idea was vehemently opposed by Mary Church Terrell and many others, who suggested that a more fitting remembrance would be meaningful legislation to protect black people from lynching.)

Will Alexander, however, knew that Southern women were, especially regarding the fight against lynching, a great untapped resource—perhaps the ultimate weapon. He believed that if they applied themselves as forcefully as many women had in the recent suffrage victory, their impact might be enormous, because they themselves were one of the cornerstones of the South's racial caste system. It was they who were adored and protected and used by the system to maintain white supremacy, and in whose name so much racial violence took place. Were they to speak, they would do so with a singular legitimacy.

Alexander's idea went beyond empowering white women to speak out. He wanted them to join with black women in order to do so. He had been instrumental in bringing about a historic meeting in 1920 between representatives of the CIC Women's Division and the National Council of Negro Women's Clubs. The whites who went to Tuskegee Institute for the gathering hosted by Margaret M. Washington, the great educator's widow, had almost exclusively known black women as maids and cooks. They had no experience dealing with black women as equals or hearing intelligent black women speak on serious subjects, and they stumbled when it was necessary to pronounce a black woman's name with a prefix of "Miss" or "Mrs." For their part, the black women feared that the whites' underlying interest in "improvement" in the black woman's condition was really just a desire to produce a better class of maids and nannies. But much of the awkwardness was soon dispelled by a spirit of frankness. "We have just emerged from a world war that cost the lives of thousands of our boys fighting to make the world safe for democracy," a black delegate, Lugenia Hope, told the visitors. "For whom? Women, we can achieve nothing today unless you . . . who have met us are willing to help us find a place in American life where we can be unashamed and unafraid." Before leaving Tuskegee, the whites asked the blacks to draw up a list of ways the CIC Women's Division might help their cause, and invited them to send delegates to an upcoming CIC conference in Memphis.

For the whites the Tuskegee meeting had been a novel experience. They used words such as *revelation* and *breakthrough* to describe the gathering, and praised the blacks' frankness of speech and confidence that was clearly derived from the "Christian spirit." Most important, the whites sensed that they had made an important connection that would enhance their future work. Sara Estelle Haskin and Carrie Parks Johnson told Will Alexander that after Tuskegee they believed that "the men might as well hang their harps on a willow tree, as to try and settle the race problem in the South without the aid of the Southern white woman." The black women had been no less impressed. Educator Charlotte Hawkins Brown returned from the Tuskegee gathering hailing the CIC as the "greatest step forward . . . since Emancipation."

The romance continued to bloom at the CIC Women's Division conclave in Memphis where, in what Alexander later termed "the most beautiful act of courtesy I ever saw," one hundred white women rose to their feet as the four black delegates entered the room. There was an awkward moment of silence until one voice, that of Belle Bennett, daughter of a Confederate general, began to sing.

> *Blest be the tie that binds*
> *our hearts in Christian love;*
> *the fellowship of kindred minds*
> *is like to that above.*

Slowly the others, white and black, joined in:

> *We share each other's woes,*
> *and mutual burdens bear;*
> *and often for each other flows*
> *the sympathizing tear.*

The moment of recognition and acceptance was to become legendary in the annals of biracial cooperation in the South.

The black women had brought the list of recommendations for action the whites had requested at Tuskegee. They saw great room for improvement in the most common relationship white and black women shared, that of employer and domestic, and respectfully asked whites to improve working conditions and give greater consideration to the fact that maids had children and households of their own to care for. Margaret Washington spoke about the dismal education provided to the children of share-croppers, who were often kept from school in order to work. Others addressed the need for improved child welfare, better and more sanitary arrangements for colored women's travel, and an end to lynching.

"The continuance of lynching," the blacks had written, "is the gravest menace to good will between the races, and a constant factor in undermining respect for all law and order. Toward the suppression of this evil we suggest that white women (a) raise their voices in immediate protest when lynching or mob violence is threatened; (b) encourage every effort to detect and punish the leaders and participants in mobs and riots, and (c) encourage the white pulpit and press in creating a sentiment among law-abiding citizens for outspoken condemnation of these forms of lawlessness."

"We all feel that you can control your men," Charlotte Hawkins Brown emphasized, "that, if the white women would take hold of the situation, that lynching would be stopped, mob violence stamped out and yet the guilty would have justice meted out by due courses of law and would be punished accordingly." Addressing the excuse that lynching was needed to protect white women, Brown added: "I want to say to you, when you read in the paper where a colored man has insulted a white woman, just multiply that by one thousand and you have some idea of the number of colored women insulted by white men."

On the second day Brown riveted the white women's attention by relating how, on her way to this very conference, she had been nearly taken from a train and lynched by white men angry because she had managed to secure a Pullman berth. Only by agreeing to abandon the berth was she saved from rough treatment at the hands of these men, she explained, and then concluded her remarks with scorching emotion:

> I am one of the Negroes that is not entirely subservient, and one that believes in knocking at the conscience of the white men. I believe in knocking, knocking, knocking, and then I believe sometime in the Spirit of the Lord Jesus Christ in speaking, speaking, speaking, and I believe that is the purpose of this conference. . . . If I have to sit up all night traveling . . . to

carry the message God has given me to carry, and cannot get a berth in a Pullman car; and when I have seen the diagram and have been told that they were sold out; when over the telephone, where you don't talk like a Negro, you have asked for a berth, and you have given your name as "Mrs. Brown" and you have been assigned berth No. 5 in car No. 24; and when calling at the station you are told that they are sold out or you cannot have it; or if I have to make believe sometime that I am traveling with a white baby in order to get a good night's sleep; or if you go a step further and make one of the light members of your race pose as a white man and you pass as a maid, and then I come and look you in the face and tell you that I love you, although you permit that; then you can get some idea of the desire of my people. It is a very serious thing with me, and I go from such an experience, and falling upon my knees with tears in my eyes I cry, "How long, O Lord, how long?"

The Tuskegee and Memphis meetings were the painful beginnings of a difficult and awkward unification between black and white women reformers in the modern South. As one white delegate tearfully assured the black women, "We are humiliated. We are ashamed. But we are determined that this is not the end." The groundwork had clearly been laid for Bethune's call in 1930 for Southern white women to follow up on their now decade-old promise to take the lynching issue in hand. A most willing respondent was Jessie Daniel Ames, an experienced white reformer from Texas who had recently become director of the CIC Women's Division. Already beginning to tire of what at times seemed the CIC's overly studious approach to the resolving of the South's problems, Ames took Bethune's words to heart. She understood intuitively that perhaps no group of Southerners could have as intense an effect on the lynching issue as the South's "God-like pure snow white angelic American Women." And the idea of a single-issue advocacy organization—Southern women opposing lynching—no doubt appealed to Ames because it would re-create some of the intensity she'd known in the crusade for women's suffrage.

The widowed mother of three children and part owner of a local telephone company in rural Texas, Ames once described her instinct for reform work as an "abnormal sense of justice." This impulse drew her first to the suffrage movement, then to the state legislature, to three national Democratic conventions as delegate-at-large from Texas, and finally, in 1922, to her state's branch of the Women's Division of the CIC. Like Will

Alexander and Willis Weatherford, she knew that meaningful social progress in the region would come only when the South began to deal honestly with its race problem. She had been haunted by a statement she'd heard a black woman make at an interracial meeting in Texas—that so long as white men lynched black men, black Americans would never have any faith in white people—and she'd been infuriated to hear white officials in Dallas explain that improvements in local social welfare services must be denied for the sole reason that "nigger wenches" would be among the beneficiaries.

An incident that helped convince Ames of the potential importance of an antilynching organization was the May 1930 execution of George Hughes in Sherman, Texas. In an echo of the Sam Hose case, the killing stemmed from an accusation that Hughes, a farm laborer and newcomer to Sherman, had savagely raped his white boss's wife, although it was held by many blacks in town that there had been no rape at all and that Hughes had simply fallen out with his employer over wages. A mob spirit was fed by intense antiblack feeling that had existed in the area for some years, and exacerbated by the Depression's effect on the local economy. When Texas Rangers and local police managed to keep a mob bent on seizing Hughes from entering the Grayson County courthouse, where Hughes was being held, the crowd retaliated by torching the entire building, destroying Hughes and a sixty-thousand-dollar public edifice in the process. The mob then entered the smoldering ruins of the building and removed Hughes's corpse, chained it to an automobile, and dragged it through the streets of Sherman. The celebration spilled over into a general assault on the black business area. Stores were looted and three entire blocks were laid to waste, as virtually the whole black populace fled to the outskirts of town.

Anarchy, murder, and the destruction of the courthouse, the structure that was the town's embodiment of law and order, all set in motion by the dubious story of a white woman's violation—in the ashes of the Sherman riot Ames said she saw the future of the entire South, if courageous voices failed to make themselves heard.

"Distressed by the recent upsurge of lynchings," read the founding resolution of the group Ames headed, the Association of Southern Women for the Prevention of Lynching (ASWPL), which convened for the first time in Atlanta on November 1, 1930, "and noting that people still condone such crimes on the ground that they are necessary to the protection of womanhood, we, a group of white women representing eight Southern

States, desire publicly to repudiate and condemn such defense of lynching, and to put ourselves definitely on record as opposed to this crime in every form and under all circumstances."

The women, as Southern author Lillian Smith later remembered appreciatively, "went forth to commit treason against a Southern tradition set up by men which had betrayed their mothers, sometimes themselves, and many of the South's children, white and mixed, for three long centuries. It was truly a subversive affair. . . . The lady insurrectionists . . . said calmly that they were not afraid of being raped; as for their sacredness, they could take care of it themselves; they did not need the chivalry of a lynching to protect them and did not want it.

"They had more power than they knew," Smith wrote. "They had the power of spiritual blackmail over a large part of the white South."

Within months of its founding it was evident the group's program had hit a nerve. When Senator Cole Blease of South Carolina roared to his followers, "Whenever the Constitution comes between me and the virtue of the white women of the South, I say to hell with the Constitution," the ASWPL's Kate Davis fired back: "Hundreds of thousands of white women in the South feel that the law . . . is their honorable protection and avenger. The women of the South are not afraid to stand by the Constitution." A newspaper in Georgia averred that the coming of the ASWPL meant that "rope-and-faggot courtesy" from men was no longer welcome, while a reporter for a Mississippi journal, taking note of the ASWPL's chastisement of Cole Blease, observed that the day had come when white women would not allow lynchers to "hide behind their skirts."

Like the CIC, the ASWPL was broken down into state operations. A director in each state oversaw the organization's many areas of activity, including gaining recruits by speaking to women's groups, lobbying elected officials (particularly county sheriffs), investigating the truth behind accusations of interracial rape, and asking authorities and citizens to sign an ASWPL pledge to oppose lynching. Both at the state and regional levels, master lists of women's names and communities were kept on file, so that when word of an impending lynching arrived, the ASWPL could activate women close to the scene to intervene.

Ames's experience running a rural telephone company gave her an appreciation for the power of rapid communication to influence events. One of the first pamphlets the ASWPL published, meant to be posted by a member's telephone, carefully outlined the steps to take when a lynching threatened. Monitoring of a potential lynching meant putting the sheriff on notice that the situation over which he had control was being closely watched by a national organization, one that was prepared to alert governors' offices and newspapers. Less formally, and probably more effectively, ASWPL women in rural counties were also quite willing to dial up a few of the sheriff's friends and relatives, maybe even his wife, to remind them that the lawman held the community's fate in his hands: he could do his job, or he could allow the town to be tainted by a lynching. Ames's blunt style, a product of her upbringing in the frontier atmosphere of Texas, probably served as an encouraging example to her colleagues, women raised in the more genteel culture of the Old South.

The ASWPL grew steadily. By 1935 most big Southern lynching states, including Mississippi, Georgia, Texas, and Florida, were organized, and as of 1936 almost thirty thousand women had signed the ASWPL's antilynching pledge. By the early 1940s more than a hundred national women's groups had endorsed the ASWPL's mission, giving Ames and her staff the backing of nearly 4 million people. The association also gathered signatures of county sheriffs on a pledge to protect their prisoners from mobs, and succeeded in getting more than 1,300 by 1941. When sheriffs would not cooperate, the ASWPL did not hesitate to identify them to news organizations and to list the names of prisoners who had died on their watch in widely distributed ASWPL publications.

Even though white women enjoyed a status in the South that allowed them to be outspoken in ways their husbands could not, the ASWPL women suffered their fellow citizens' indignation, and many were threatened. Several women reported that local authorities would not allow them to address public groups. Some officials insisted on reviewing any speech a member intended to give and examining any materials that would be distributed. Some members hid their ASWPL activities from their loved ones, both out of fear of disapproval and out of concern that they would endanger them, and Ames received a steady stream of hate mail.

Although the image of well-heeled ASWPL women racing to the scene of an impending lynching to personally confront mobs is more myth than reality, members did save lives. When in May 1933 a black man assaulted a white woman in Apalachicola, Florida, ASWPL state chairman Jane Cornell sounded the alarm, alerting the sheriff, the local judge, and the governor to the high risk of a lynching, mentioning that the national press had also been informed of the situation. No lynching occurred and the accused was given a trial for which defense counsel requested and received a change of venue. In a case in southern Mississippi, ASWPL member

Bessie Alford was unable to reach the sheriff in a neighboring town where a lynching was rumored, but had numerous kin in that county, so she raised several of her relatives by phone and ordered them to their local jail, where they helped protect a prisoner until a highway patrolman from Jackson could arrive.

Lynchings that it could not stop the ASWPL nonetheless made a point of investigating. Frequently the story uncovered by the ASWPL completely contradicted that spread by whites and printed in newspapers. A striking example occurred in Bolton, Mississippi, in the mid 1930s, where Alford went to investigate the lynching of a twenty-six-year-old black handyman named James Sanders. He and another man, John Henry Williams, were rivals for the affections of a woman named Pinky Burnes. Sanders hit upon the villainous idea of getting rid of the competition by sending a "love letter" in Williams's name to Mary Lancaster, a pretty twenty-three-year-old white woman, in the hope of getting Williams lynched, or at least run out of the county. The plan backfired, however, when Sanders's authorship of the letter became known. Lancaster's male relatives, whose umbrage Sanders had been counting on, did not disappoint; they immediately took Sanders out into the country, pushed him down into a ditch, and shot him to death.

The trials of the Scottsboro Boys challenged Ames and the ASWPL in two distinct ways. The group refused to expand its criticism of lawless lynching to include "legal lynchings," for despite much internal consideration of the question, the organization's essential message remained that the protection of prisoners and the conducting of formal criminal proceedings were a far superior alternative to mob violence. The ASWPL, like the CIC, also made clear its patriotism and regional loyalty by deploring the involvement of the "Communist" ILD in Southern lynching cases, and by stubbornly refusing to endorse any form of federal antilynching law.

One of the high points of Ames's career came in 1936, when she was invited to address the all-male Southern Newspaper Publishers Association. It was a fitting honor because the ASWPL's greatest impact had been on the Southern press. Overheated news accounts of virginal white girls ravished by black brutes had diminished, although coverage of such incidents remained highly sensationalized. Ames told the editors that Southern papers still lacked a comprehensive editorial take on lynching. Many published five-paragraph editorials condemning lynching as a blot on the South, yet—as she pointed out—disapproving editorials deep inside the newspapers' pages did little to adjust public attitudes when front-page headlines read "Hunt Negro After Child Is Attacked" and "Feeling Is Intense as Posse Scours Woods." Such sensationalism overrode any good achieved by the occasional editorial urging moderation, and went a long way toward creating the atmosphere that exacerbated the lynching mood. Ames told the newspapermen that as a Southerner she had been "brought up on this theory" that black men were sexual predators and white women their prey, but that she had become convinced by the evidence that this was a myth. She encouraged the journalists to follow the example of anti-lynching activists, and to take the time necessary to learn the real truth about lynchings.

On November 9, 1933, Brooke Hart, twenty-two, a junior executive at a San Francisco department store owned by his family, was kidnapped when he went to retrieve his automobile from a downtown parking lot. Two strange men jumped in alongside him and, saying they had a gun, forced the young man to drive with them out of the city. Here they transferred Hart to a second car, drove onto the San Mateo–Hayward Bridge and bludgeoned him numerous times over the head with a brick. They then bound his arms and legs tightly with wire, put a pillow slip over his head, and threw him over the side into the water. The men then raced back to the Hotel Whitcomb in San Francisco and made a telephone call to the Hart family, assuring them their son was safe and demanding forty thousand dollars for his return.

A week later, ransom negotiations had still failed to progress because Brooke's father, Alexander J. Hart, had demanded proof that his son was still alive, and on November 16, the kidnappers—Thomas Thurmond and J. M. Holmes, both thirty—were caught in the act of phoning the Hart home. Thurmond and Holmes, once in custody, confessed to police that they had murdered young Hart immediately upon abducting him because they were uncertain what they would do with him during their effort to make the family deliver the ransom.

A police search of the waters under the bridge located Hart's decomposed body, the kidnappers' restraints still around his wrists and ankles. The newspapers' horrific descriptions of the corpse, juxtaposed with photographs of the handsome, clean-cut young man Brooke Hart had been in life, infuriated Californians. That night a mob laid siege to the Santa Clara County jail in San Jose where Thurmond and Holmes were being held. Smashing down the front door with a battering ram, the crowd poured in, beat up the sheriff and his deputy, and removed the two kidnappers. Crying and pleading for their lives, the two men were carried into a city park across the street, where a crowd of several thousand had gathered, and hanged from low-lying tree limbs. "Like angry dogs, men of the mob leaped up and tore off the trousers from Thurmond's body," explained one eyewitness account. "Some one made a torch of a newspaper, poured cigarette lighter fluid on it and burned the bottoms of Thurmond's feet, then fired his coat and shirt." Holmes's corpse was found in a similar condition, naked but for one sock and one shoe.

More shocking for America than the lynching itself was the strong support it received from California governor James Rolph, Jr. Rolph defended the lynching as "a fine lesson for the whole nation" and warned criminals to take note of how rapidly an aroused citizenry had become an effective mob. "They'll learn they can't kidnap in this state," he vowed. "If any one is arrested for the good job I'll pardon them all." Rolph added that he was tempted to release all San Quentin and Folsom penitentiary inmates then serving time for kidnapping into the custody of "those fine, patriotic San Jose citizens who know how to handle such a situation."

Such prolynching statements from the governor of one of the most populous states in America struck people throughout the country as undignified and offensive. The outrage grew when Rolph revealed he had actually had a hand in the executions. Notified that an assault on the Santa Clara County jail was likely, he had postponed a scheduled trip to a governors' conference out of state for fear that in his absence some underling would be sentimental enough to call out the National Guard to protect Thurmond and Holmes. When contacted during the mob assault by the frantic sheriff, he had blatantly refused to send help to Santa Clara County.

"The people make the laws, don't they?" he demanded, completely unrepentant in the face of national concern over his opinions. "Well, if the people have confidence that troops will not be called out to mow them down when they seek to protect themselves against kidnappers, there is liable to be swifter justice and fewer kidnappings." The San Jose lynchers, he pointed out, were guided by the same patriotic spirit and love of community that had inspired the legendary San Francisco vigilante committees of the 1850s. Rolph was not alone in his views. Clarence Morrill, chief of California's Bureau of Criminal Investigation, noted that "The people have shown that they are weary of the technicalities of law and in favor of speedy action rather than the slow procedure of courts." Another state official defended lynching as "a sincere demand for law enforcement." Across the country, a group of citizens in Princess Anne, Maryland, site of the George Armwood lynching, went so far as to telegraph Rolph their regards and suggest he run for president.

Criticism of Rolph was loud and sustained and came from a great number of organizations, including the NAACP, the CIC, the ILD, and the ASWPL, as well as numerous church and civil liberties groups; his remarks became fodder for almost every sermonist and newspaper editorialist in the country. "People react strongly to Rolph," wrote Walter Lippmann, "because his acceptance of lynching is an admittance that government cannot function to halt criminality, and this does not sit well with the American public." Walter White cited Rolph's inflammatory statements as "the most brazen approval of lynching . . . the country has ever seen," while a New York minister told his congregation, "The violence of the California mob turns back the clock to the days of the jungle."

The late fall of 1933 did seem like one of those disquieting moments when the moorings of civilization have shaken loose. Lynching dominated the headlines as at no other time in American history. In addition to the San Jose example and public concern about "Rolphism," National Guardsmen in an armory in Salisbury, Maryland, were just then fighting a pitched battle to repel a mob attempting to free the four suspected lynchers arrested in the Armwood case. News photos of the Salisbury violence resembled nothing if not scenes of First World War trench warfare, with steel-helmeted soldiers holding their position behind sandbags as tear gas swirled in the air. Skipping a column or two away from the California and Maryland stories, one could read about nineteen-year-old Lloyd Warner, a St. Joseph, Missouri, man who, accused of assaulting a white woman, had been dragged from his cell and hanged on the lawn of a county courthouse. When a unit of forty state troopers moved in to disperse the mob, citizens counterattacked, driving the soldiers away and capturing a National Guard tank.

The sense that lynchings were suddenly rampant, that soldiers were powerless to stop them, and that even elected officials sanctioned acts in which the public took the law into its own hands, fed a whiplash public reaction—denunciations of Rolphism and strengthened demands for some form of federal antilynching legislation. Commentators asked whether President Roosevelt would speak out on the subject. Former president Herbert Hoover had lost no time censuring Rolph, while Socialist leader Norman Thomas had already called on the people of California to consider impeachment. On December 6, FDR finally lent his voice to the cause. In a nationally broadcast address Roosevelt challenged Americans to confront and defeat the "pagan ethics" of lynching that had no place in "our boasted modern civilization." Seeming to rebuke Governor Rolph directly he warned: "We do not excuse those in high places or in low who condone lynch law." Then, raising the hopes of those eager for federal antilynching legislation, he observed that a "new generation" of Americans "seeks action"—action by government and individuals working together to end mob violence. "This new generation," the president vowed, "is not content with preaching against that vile form of collective murder—lynch law—which has broken out in our midst anew."

Inherent in the Southern rejection of the Dyer antilynching bill in 1922 had been the claim that the South itself could handle mob violence and did not require federal intervention. The CIC had willfully transformed this idea into something more akin to an honorable and hopeful commitment, as expressed in the title of its January 1923 press release "It's Up to Us." For years following the Dyer Bill's defeat, the CIC had reason to believe its antilynching work was having an effect, as annual recorded lynchings tracked by the Tuskegee Institute fell to a low of sixteen in 1927, eleven in 1928, and ten in 1929. But in 1930 the total had leapt back up to twenty-one, prompting the CIC to inaugurate its commission on Southern lynching and later to sound an alarm with its pamphlet "The Mob Still Rides." Lynching's persistence, historian Herbert Shapiro has written, constituted a problem that "decent opinion could not ignore," and by 1934, with highly publicized cases such as those of Maryland and San Jose, legislators in Washington were once again examining a possible federal solution.

Several other factors pointed to the likelihood that antilynching legislation might play better this time around. For one thing, reformers could show that, in the dozen years 1922–34, since the failure of Congress to enact the Dyer Bill, a total of 277 recorded lynchings had occurred. During this same period only six states had enacted or strengthened their own antilynching laws, only one of which, Alabama, was in the Deep South. More significantly, the exigencies of the Depression had made the consideration of federal remedies to local problems far more palatable, and the South's traditional "state's rights" argument sounded distinctly off-key at a time when the region welcomed massive financial aid from Washington in the form of public works and other relief.

Another influential change in the intervening years had been the national crusade to end Prohibition. This federal law had had the exact opposite of its intended effect: rather than rid America of drunkenness and low "saloon culture," it had fostered a vast criminal underworld to serve the undiminished public appetite for alcohol, and in so doing had created a nation of citizen outlaws—rumrunners, smugglers, operators of home breweries and secret distilling operations, "blind pig" owners, and the hundreds of thousands of Americans who patronized this illicit industry. In 1932 alone the federal government arrested almost 75,000 people, seized 12,000 automobiles, confiscated 3.5 million gallons of beer, and shut down more than 40,000 illegal manufacturing operations—from full-scale underworld breweries to backyard stills.

While the public had come to detest Prohibition, it had gained a greater appreciation of the role the federal government had to play in combating the kind of organized underworld crime Prohibition had brought into being. Crime in the years since the war had come to seem more frightening because it was now more mobile and random, hence the obsession with kidnapping, while mob violence, thanks in large part to the efforts of the CIC and NAACP, was increasingly seen as a dangerous atavism totally inappropriate to modern life, shorn almost completely of its onetime status as an accepted element of the Southern code.

This heightened level of public acceptance of the federal role in fighting crime seemed to augur well for the passage of antilynching legislation. At the time, a record number of new federal criminal laws were either in place or in the process of being put on the books. In addition to kidnapping, it had now become a federal crime to practice extortion over the telephone or by telegraph or radio, to transport stolen goods across state lines, or to flee across state lines to avoid prosecution or to avoid testifying in a criminal proceeding. The federal courts were already prosecuting cases of motor vehicle theft, postal law violations, violations of the immigration act, illicit sale of liquor and narcotics, and acts of forgery and counterfeiting. Such prosecutions would reach an average of fifty thousand per year by the end of the decade. In conjunction with this national campaign against lawlessness, a broader use of federal investigatory powers to combat crime had also come to be accepted. Thus it seemed a natural leap from fighting underworld mobsters to combating lynch mobs. "National Disgrace No. 1 should have the same treatment by all the authorities, local, state and federal, as Public Enemy No. 1," one newspaper declared. "Lynching could not long survive . . . if there were the same cooperation against it . . . that there was against Al Capone, [John] Dillinger, [Bruno] Hauptmann and 'Pretty Boy' Floyd."

A profound influence on Americans' view of the lynching evil was the rise of fascism in Europe. Concern in this country over what was happening across the Atlantic began as early as Hitler's ascension to power in 1933. A steady stream of articles appeared in U.S. magazines with such titles as "Germany's Revolt Against Civilization," "Germany Sinks into Slavery," "Germany's Lowest Depths," "Hitler and His Gang," and "Goodbye to Germany." That same year anti-Nazi protests began to appear in U.S. cities, particularly New York, where fifteen hundred Jews rallied at a Lower East Side school to denounce German anti-Semitism and Columbia University students booed and hooted at the German ambassador when he arrived at the campus to give a lecture. The Nazis themselves did not hesitate to exploit the hypocrisy that lynching illustrated in the land where "all men are created equal." The infamous pictures of Jesse Washington's charred body in Waco, and later an image of several young girls gazing upward at the corpse of 1935 Florida lynching victim Rubin Stacy, were published in Germany and disseminated throughout Europe.

The NAACP connected the dots as well. When Senator William H. King of Utah denounced conditions in Germany and asked for the formation of a committee to investigate Nazi persecution of Jews and Catholics, the NAACP publicly insisted that King explain "how America can, with good grace, protest against what is happening in Germany or anywhere else outside of the United States, as long as we do nothing about lynchings in our own country?" As awful as things had become in Germany, the NAACP reminded Senator King, the Nazis have "not yet sunk to our own level of burning human beings at the stake."

As if in tandem with the rise of European fascism, the Klan came roaring back to life in parts of the Deep South, a renewal spawned by the outrage over the intrusion of Communist party operatives, Socialists, and labor organizers in the region. It was a slimmed-down, less pageantlike Klan than a decade before, for as the Memphis *Commercial Appeal* observed, with people struggling just to keep food on the table, "Not many persons have $10 to throw away on an oversized nightshirt." But unlike the 1920s' "businessman's Klan," there was now a greater proclivity for violence. Norman Thomas was roughed up in Arkansas in 1937 after going to the town of Tyzonga to speak to a biracial sharecroppers' union, and the activist and sometime NAACP lynchings investigator Howard "Buck" Kester was himself almost lynched while working for the same effort.

Party workers in Dallas were ambushed and brutalized, and in Tampa, the owners of the citrus groves, cigar factories, and turpentine stills worked hand in glove with the police and the Klan to squelch labor unrest.

The Klan was thought responsible for the 1934 murder of Lakeland, Florida, citrus-industry labor organizer Frank Norman. Three men who claimed to be sheriff's deputies came to Norman's house at night and said his help was needed to identify a black man found lynched on the outskirts of town. Sensing a trap, Norman asked a friend, Ben Surrency, to come along, but after a few blocks Surrency was forced out of the car at gunpoint, and the three "deputies" rode on with Norman, who was never heard from again. The killing was effectively hushed up—Norman's body was never found—but a far more publicized incident soon brought national attention to the local Klan-police despotism. In November 1935 Tampa police raided a meeting of a labor-based political group known as the Modern Democrats and arrested founder Joseph Shoemaker and two other leaders, Eugene Poulnot and Sam Rogers. Shoemaker had attempted to organize citrus workers around such goals as a thirty-hour workweek and unemployment insurance, and had initiated an assault on the local Democratic political machine by running an independent candidate for mayor. After booking the men at the station house, police forced or tricked them into waiting cars—Poulnot resisted and had to be dragged (police explained to passing shoppers that they were taking a lunatic to a mental institution)—then drove them to a warehouse district down by the docks and turned them over to a group of Klansmen. Their new captors took them deep into the woods outside town, formed a circle around them with headlights from a dozen automobiles, and ordered the men to undress, then flogged them with chains and burned their flesh with hot tar. Poulnot and Rogers survived, badly scarred, but Shoemaker, who was singled out for the harshest treatment—he was mutilated and had one foot plunged into a bucket of boiling tar—later died of his injuries in a Tampa hospital. To his brother, who kept a bedside vigil, he confided, "I didn't think that people could be so mean."

Pressure from outside Florida led to a state investigation that found extensive evidence of Klan infiltration of the city government and police. Chief of Police R. G. Tittsworth, a police sergeant, and several other officers who were Klansmen or in league with the Klan were arrested, charged, and convicted of Shoemaker's murder. The convictions were later overturned by the Florida Supreme Court and Tittsworth and the others went free, stirring a national outcry from influential groups such as the American Federation of Labor, which in protest canceled a convention scheduled to take place in Tampa.

The NAACP's resolve to try once again to shepherd antilynching legislation through Congress did not come without some internal strife at the organization. There had long existed differences in personal style and political orientation between Walter White and W.E.B. Du Bois, and with the departure of James Weldon Johnson in 1929 to take a teaching position at Fisk, the other two main spokesmen for the NAACP were left alone, without benefit of Johnson's skilled diplomacy, to sort out their disagreements. White wanted the group to carry on the antilynching fight as an assault on the most repugnant manifestation of white supremacy; Du Bois believed the era's singular economic malaise and its harsh toll on black people required the NAACP to work in more fundamental economic areas—interracial unionism, buying cooperatives, and consumer boycotts. At the height of their disagreement, Du Bois accused White of favoring a fight against lynching solely because, as a highly sensational cause, it more reliably generated contributions from whites.

The dispute between the two men abruptly intensified in early 1934 when Du Bois, in two back-to-back articles in the January and February editions of *The Crisis,* launched a polemic stating that he no longer opposed segregation, only the discrimination that accompanied it, and that segregation in some aspects of American life might be preferable to integration. He defended his views, and angered many NAACP supporters, by insisting that, despite the public perception of the NAACP as an integrationist group, it had never formally opposed segregation. A flurry of letters and countering opinions flowed into the New York office, some accusing Du Bois of transporting the campaign for black equal rights backward in time to the discredited theories of Booker T. Washington. That spring, after nearly a quarter-century of enormously consequential service, Du Bois resigned from *The Crisis* and the NAACP, sounding weary and bitter in a final editorial about the absurd threat of execution still hanging over the heads of the Scottsboro Boys. "The South," Du Bois wrote, "[has] built [its] prosperity and private fortunes upon a treatment of the unfortunate which is contemptible, and in addition to this they have tried through their treatment of Negroes to satisfy the blood lust of a sadistic people. . . . They are going to continue it until the South becomes civilized and no one living is going to see that day."

White, shaking off Du Bois's cynicism, told his colleagues that he believed the new Southern liberalism represented by such groups as the CIC and ASWPL, and the rising concern for fascism and violence in Europe, had created a ripe opportunity for antilynching reform. He considered the Maryland lynching of George Armwood to have shown overwhelmingly that lynching was an evil even well-intentioned state authorities were not able to deter. Maryland had admitted its inability to prosecute the guilty and it had failed even briefly to hold suspected mob leaders under arrest without turning parts of the Eastern Shore into a combat zone.

White had an ally in Colorado's progressive Senator Edward Costigan, who had been infuriated by the double lynching of the Hart kidnappers in San Jose and the subsequent behavior of Governor Rolph. Costigan agreed to lead a fight to secure the legislation, and Senator Robert F. Wagner of New York cosponsored the bill. Costigan and Wagner were two of the best legal minds in the Senate, and they set out to design legislation that would preempt many of the objections that Southerners had raised to the Dyer Bill in 1922.

Introduced in January 1934, the Wagner-Costigan Bill defined a mob as three or more persons, imposed five years' imprisonment and a five-thousand-dollar fine on any state officer who through neglect allowed a prisoner to be taken from him by a mob, and proposed a potential sentence of between five and twenty-five years for anyone who cooperated with or was in collusion with a lynch mob. Any county where a lynching occurred would be fined two thousand to ten thousand dollars, the funds going to the lynching victim's family or, if no family existed, to the federal government. The financial punishments aimed at counties were meant to undercut what had long been an argument used in support of lynching: that summary execution saved the public money on trials and imprisonment. In South Carolina, where an 1896 antilynching law levied fines against counties, no county that had been once fined for such an abuse ever had another recorded lynching.

The most important aspect of the Wagner-Costigan Bill lay in the fact that it did not criminalize lynching per se. What it did criminalize was negligence or collusion by state officials, essentially sheriffs and their deputies. And the perceived federal usurpation of state powers so off-putting to the South would be minimized under the bill, because all convictions would have to be arrived at by local juries near to where the lynching had occurred, although perhaps not in the same county. In any case, state officials were given thirty days to act on their own; only after this period had elapsed would the federal government step in if no state response had occurred. This was intended to eliminate or at least minimize the notion that the federal government would automatically supplant the state's authority or "take over" responsibility for law enforcement in the South.

Some critics of the bill pointed out that lynch mobs might be tempted to skirt such a law by simply not involving sheriffs and their jails. This was a prescient concern; in the coming years, as law enforcement and media coverage became larger factors in formerly isolated areas of the South, a distinct trend would emerge toward more secretive lynchings. However, in most locales where lynchings occurred it was very difficult for a sheriff or his deputies to be completely ignorant of incipient mob activity. Mobs were known to form swiftly, but generally it would be hard for a sensational or "lynchable" offense such as a rape or murder to occur, and for a mob to form, without local officials having some knowledge of what was about to take place.

Much as James Weldon Johnson had linked himself to the fate of the Dyer Bill, Walter White worked assiduously to drum up support for Wagner-Costigan, a bill he thought was very well crafted and stood a good chance of becoming law. He obtained endorsements from a myriad of organizations, including the American Civil Liberties Union, the National Urban League, and the National Council of Jewish Women—in all, organizations whose memberships represented roughly 40 million Americans. The legislatures of numerous states and the city councils of several large cities passed resolutions in support of the bill, as did church, labor, fraternal, and professional groups. Southern newspapers from Roanoke to Houston, including the *Richmond News Leader,* the *Chattanooga Times,* and the *Birmingham Post,* gave at least measured support for some kind of federal-state cooperation and, significantly, no major Southern paper expressed vehement opposition. "There are States' rights, undeniably," the Lynchburg, Virginia, *News* admitted. "But what about States' wrongs?"

Still, White knew that convincing Southern legislators that lynching was not a "states' right" would be a formidable task. His best hope lay in somehow keeping a Southern filibuster from ever getting started, for once it did, Southern representatives would rally round and support it—either because they believed that was what their constituents would want them to do, or on account of pressure from conservative Southern voices in Congress and in the press. White's strategy for defeating the filibuster before it could begin was twofold—convince the Southern representatives in Washington that the people of the South were ready to accept antilynching legislation, and reassure them that the president himself supported the measure.

It was true that, unlike in 1922, the Southern press was sympathetic to the idea of some kind of federal antilynching penalty. "Twenty years ago the mere thought of such legislation would have caused Southern colonels to tear their mustachios with rage and Southerners of lesser rank to implore the deity to save Dixie," Virginius Dabney, editor of the Richmond *Times-Dispatch,* wrote in *The Nation.* "Fortunately such hysteria is no longer widely prevalent. . . . The diehards are distinctly in the minority." In addition to press clips to circulate, there were the many endorsements. Even Will Alexander and the CIC, under pressure from black CIC members, rang in with an endorsement in 1935, after years of refusing to support a federal law. The CIC's statement linked the overall decline in lynchings to Southern lawmen taking their responsibilities more seriously, but shared its discouragement that the successful prosecution of lynchers still seemed well beyond the states' capability.

White knew that the president's support would be critical. White had befriended both the Roosevelts in New York during the late 1920s and early 1930s, as FDR had been that state's governor and Eleanor Roosevelt was active in the same reform circles that White and other NAACP leaders frequented. White was greater friends with Eleanor. Their relationship was formal—even after years of acquaintance and extensive correspondence they continued to address each other as Mrs. Roosevelt and Mr. White, and he was more or less permanently cast in the role of supplicant, repeatedly requesting appointments with the First Lady and generally meeting with her at her convenience. But she was consistently attentive to his needs and frequently shared his correspondence and suggestions with the president. Charming, highly intelligent, forceful but not threatening, White was, in a sense, black America's representative to the White House during the 1930s, accepted and "accredited" by the Roosevelts even as he and many of his demands were kept at arm's length.

When it came to addressing the evil of lynching, Eleanor favored federal intervention but the president largely withheld his direct support, fearing it would alienate Southern congressmen on whom he was reliant for the passage of New Deal legislation. Eleanor was left to juggle her loyalty to her husband, and her sympathy for his role as chief executive during one of the country's most difficult times, with her own keen sense of racial injustice and her greater willingness to commit to needed reforms. For her open concern for black Americans, Eleanor Roosevelt herself was denigrated and viewed with suspicion by many whites. A popular rumor in the South was that black women were organizing into so-called Eleanor Clubs to leave their jobs as cooks and domestics and to engage in mild terrorism such as pushing white women off the sidewalk; later, black soldiers returning from the Second World War would be referred to derisively as "Eleanor's Chosen Children."

Despite her well-publicized efforts on behalf of black Americans during the New Deal era, there existed a persistent resentment among blacks that not enough of the government's social and economic benefits were directed at them. These grievances were seldom brought into the open. Antilynching legislation, on the other hand, because it was a high-profile issue and an emotional one as well, served as a distinct rallying point, and provided a more immediate measure to blacks of where prominent whites stood. FDR's condemnation of Governor Rolph had won him sustained applause, but blacks were largely disappointed a year later when, in an address to Congress on January 5, 1935, he made absolutely no mention of lynching or the Wagner-Costigan Bill. As Eleanor explained to White, her husband's position most closely resembled that of the 1920s CIC. "The President feels that lynching is a question of education in the states, rallying good citizens, and creating public opinion so that the localities themselves will wipe it out. However, if it were done by a Northerner, it will have an antagonistic effect." The country's black leadership and editors were not swayed. The *New York Amsterdam News,* in a gesture that was much remarked upon, printed on its front page a huge, entirely blank space, almost as if there'd been a printer's error, with the small, devastating caption:

"Here's Mr. Roosevelt's message on lynching."

An incident that largely helped define and inspire much of the agitation to end lynching in the 1930s was the mob killing of Claude Neal in rural Jackson County, Florida, in October 1934. The last of the big American spectacle lynchings, the event was advertised almost nationwide in advance, thanks to the Associated Press and commercial radio stations, and involved a motorized lynch mob crossing a state boundary to seize its victim. Like the Sam Hose murder of 1899, it engaged and fascinated the public because it combined sex and murder and its ensuing drama of pursuit, abduction, and execution was spread over several days. The NAACP, having learned a bitter lesson in the Scottsboro case, had become involved almost immediately; not only was Walter White an important player in the lynching as it unfolded, but the association's investigator on the scene, Buck Kester, compiled a detailed, stomach-turning account that White made sure went into the hands of every news editor and public official in the nation.

Jackson County, located in the Panhandle, was a place of abandoned sharecroppers' shacks, a flat, verdant land of palm trees and peanut farms, of dirt roads that led bullet-straight to the horizon. In 1934, in the depth of the Depression, it had staggering unemployment, no public libraries, and the highest illiteracy rate of any county in the state. Its most popular local entertainments were the huge religious rallies held frequently on the outskirts of the county seat, Marianna. The self-proclaimed Peanut Capital of Florida, Marianna was a deeply Southern town, one where blacks scraped and bowed before whites and even white children felt free to insult and demean black adults. Race relations worsened in the early 1930s as competition intensified for available jobs. At the exceedingly low rates for which they could be hired (between two and four dollars a week), blacks were much in demand for unskilled positions such as porter, maid, and house servant. But many whites resented the fact that blacks should hold jobs while whites were out of work, and employers who routinely hired blacks were often threatened by a local Klanlike group known as the Purification League, which was also active in efforts to push blacks off the relief rolls. "There are too many niggers and too many white people looking for the same job," said one resident of the county's dilemma.

Into this racial powder keg there suddenly flew a blazing spark. Shortly after noon on Thursday, October 18, 1934, nineteen-year-old Lola Cannidy went to a water pump in a field on her family's farm. Also in the field was Claude Neal, a twenty-three-year-old black farmhand who, along with his mother, Annie Smith, who was known as "Kitten," worked for the Cannidys and lived directly across the road. Neal was descended from slaves who'd belonged to Daniel Odum Neal, one of the pioneers of Jackson County; the Cannidys, whose spread was located near the hamlet of Greenwood, several miles northeast of Marianna, were also old Jackson County stock. Claude and Lola had known each other all their lives.

When Lola didn't return home that evening, her family began looking for her in the vicinity and telephoning friends who might know her whereabouts. The next morning there was still no word from her, so her father, George, rang Jackson County sheriff W. F. Chambliss in Marianna. The sun was barely up when Chambliss drove out to the Cannidy farm and, after a short search through the still-dewy grass, he came upon Lola's body in a woods a half-mile from the house, covered by pine boughs and partly submerged in a pond. She was fully clothed, and had been strangled. One side of her face was slightly crushed in, suggesting she had also been dealt a blow to the head.

At the sheriff's behest, Lola's body was examined by a local doctor, who quickly announced that she had been raped. Aware of what such a finding would mean, Chambliss had the remains examined by a second physician, who concluded that the dead woman had had sexual intercourse shortly before her death, but had probably not been raped. Meanwhile, Chambliss's deputies discovered two sets of footprints indicating that a man and woman had walked together to the site of the murder. Someone, probably another farmhand, said that the last time Lola had been seen alive she had been standing in the field talking with Claude Neal.

Chambliss immediately tracked Neal to a neighbor's peanut farm, where the young black man also worked, and placed him under arrest. He also took into custody Neal's mother, Kitten, and his aunt, Sallie Smith, because it appeared the women had helped Neal wash blood out of his clothes. The sheriff had other physical evidence of Neal's guilt—a part of a watch and a piece of fabric from his shirt found with Lola's body, suggesting that killer and victim had struggled.

The sheriff's quick work in taking the young man into custody no doubt spared Neal's life, for knowing that a lynch mob was sure to form, Chambliss bypassed his own lockup in the Jackson County courthouse in Marianna and took Neal and his female relatives directly to the neighboring town of Chipley, in Washington County. Later that day, when rumors of a lynching party began to buzz in Marianna, Chambliss ordered Neal moved even farther away, to Panama City, fifty miles south on the Gulf Coast.

That night, Chambliss received word that a posse of Marianna cars were on the highway in the vicinity of Chipley, looking for Neal. He immediately phoned Panama City and ordered that the prisoner be moved yet again, this time to Pensacola, farther to the west. At Chipley, where the two women had remained, Washington County sheriff John Harrell faced an angry mob armed with guns, an acetylene torch, and (it was claimed by the men besieging the jail) dynamite. The mob threatened to blow the jail to bits if necessary. According to Harrell, most of the men had been drinking, and some were so overcome with rage and frustration that they began to weep, pleading like children for the sheriff to hand over his prisoners.

Fearful that an assault on his jail was imminent, Harrell had his deputies distract the mob while he slipped the two women out of town by having them lie on the floor of his automobile. En route to Pensacola, Kitten Smith admitted to Harrell that she had washed blood from her son's clothes.

By then, Neal himself was being transported again, this time all the way to a jail in the town of Brewton, Alabama, more than a hundred miles from Marianna. The choice of Brewton was a curious one, since Tallahassee and Mobile were both nearby, and as larger cities would have offered "mob-proof jails"—facilities far superior to the vulnerable small-town lockups from which lynching victims were usually plucked. Chambliss apparently thought Brewton was so obscure a destination that no one would think to look for Neal there.

According to the report written by Kester for the NAACP, "a prominent business man of Marianna arranged with friends in Pensacola to notify him the moment Neal was removed," and in this way the mob soon learned of Neal's transfer to Brewton. In the middle of the night, a small caravan from Marianna stole quietly into the Alabama town and confronted jailer Mike Shanholster and the two deputies on duty, saying, "We'll tear your jail up and let all the prisoners out if you don't turn him over to us." Guns were held on Shanholster and the others as the Florida men escorted the terrified Neal from his cell. The lynch mob seemed "professional," Shanholster remembered, and worked fast. They explained they'd come to return Neal to the father of the girl he had killed. Neal cried as he was put into the lead vehicle. The mob then disappeared with its captive up a two-lane road into the deep woods of southeast Alabama.

The next day, when reporters arrived in Brewton to report on the abduction, Escambia County sheriff G. S. Byrne told them that while in the lockup Neal had confessed to murdering Lola Cannidy. Byrne quoted Neal as having said he had not meant to harm Lola, but that after he had struck her, "I got to thinking I had done played the devil and she was half dead anyhow, so I went back and killed her."

For two days the mob held Neal for "interrogation" in an undisclosed location, while allowing it to be known that they would deliver him to the Cannidy family for execution. A newspaper in Dothan, Alabama, carried news of Neal's impending lynching, and word of it was broadcast on a local radio station. Newspapers in Jacksonville, Tampa, and Montgomery began to cover the story—"Officers at Loss on Means to Prevent Lynching of Slayer," read one headline; "Florida to Burn Negro at Stake," vowed another—and the Associated Press, after being notified by Jane Cornell, Florida state chairman of the ASWPL, reported it up and down the East Coast. Radio listeners in Washington, D.C., Boston, and New York City, unaccustomed to such a news item, were horrified to learn that authorities were powerless to stop a lynching that had not even occurred yet. Walter White at the NAACP in New York and Jessie Daniel Ames at the ASWPL in Atlanta sprang into action, firing off urgent telegrams to Sheriff Chambliss, Florida governor David Sholtz, and President Roosevelt.

White's wire to Sholtz implored intervention:

Associated Press just informed us that . . . tonight between eight and nine o'clock a mob will take Claude Neal charged with murder tie him to stake near Greenwood and permit father of dead girl to light fire to burn Neal to death. Every decent person North and South looks to you to take every possible step to avoid this disgrace upon the state of Florida. Dothan Alabama *Eagle* also announces that Negro is being held four miles from scene where he is to be burned at stake. We urge upon you to take immediate steps to rescue Negro from mob and place him in safe custody.

Will Alexander of the CIC dashed off a similar message to Sholtz:

We are informed Negro abducted this morning from Brewton Alabama is to be lynched at Greenwood Florida at eight o'clock this evening. You are urgently requested to take all possible steps to avert this threatened crime.

Governor Sholtz had reason to be concerned, for Florida had endured much derision in recent years from the ASWPL and the NAACP over its seeming inability to control mob and police-sanctioned violence against blacks. Earlier that year a black Tampa resident named Robert Johnson, arrested for stealing chickens, had been removed from jail in the middle of the night by a man who was not even a policeman, driven out onto a lonely country road, and shot dead. Despite extensive ballistics evidence and the charge by a city attorney that the visitor had been "wholly without legal authority in transferring the negro from the city jail," no charges were ever brought. In the wake of the "chicken thief lynching," Sholtz promised the ASWPL that, given two hours' warning, he would have troops present anywhere in Florida to protect a potential lynch victim. The Claude Neal abduction presented a perfect opportunity to call Sholtz on his vow, and the ASWPL's Jane Cornell immediately reminded the governor of his pledge, ending her telegram with the ringing admonition: COLD BLOODED PROSPECTIVE LYNCHING OF NEGRO IN JACKSON COUNTY TONIGHT TOO HORRIBLE TO CONTEMPLATE.

Sholtz spoke with Sheriff Chambliss several times and accepted his word that the situation in Jackson County was under control, although Chambliss's reluctance to request backup is particularly incomprehensible because, in addition to the hysteria over what was about to happen to Claude Neal, a separate deadly crisis had just struck Marianna. On the evening of Thursday, October 25, two convicted bank robbers were being driven from the Jackson County courthouse in Marianna to the jail in Chipley when one, Buford Mears, pulled out a pistol and shot Deputy Dave Hamm. The deputy, as he collapsed, drew his own weapon and fired, killing the other bank robber, Harrison McKinney. Deputy Hamm died later that day of his wounds, and there was angry talk about stringing up Mears for the murder of the officer. Chambliss had not one but two potential lynchings on his hands.

The day after the Mears shooting, October 26, a crowd formed at the Cannidy farm. Word had come from the men holding Neal that they would produce him that afternoon. While waiting, a few of the three thousand on hand went to Neal's home across the road and burned it to the ground. No one said much about it; the deed seemed meaningless, almost reflexive. Everyone's attention was on the dirt road leading into the farm, and also on a large white man in patched overalls, George Cannidy, Lola's sixty-year-old father, who stood by the road clutching a black-handled .45. The mob had promised George Cannidy that he would have first crack at Claude Neal, to which Cannidy had vowed solemnly: "When I get my hands on that nigger, there isn't any telling what I'll do."

Much to the father's and the crowd's disappointment, however, the mob holding Neal had decided to kill him in a nearby woods, purportedly because they worried that the mass of people on the Cannidy farm, drinking and armed to the hilt, were too riled up and "the nigger was too low for anybody to be hurt on his account." There were a number of precedents of "innocent" members of lynch mobs, often young boys, getting shot during the frenzy of a lynching. But it's also possible the mob, far from being altruistic, was afraid the law would attempt to snatch Neal back into custody if he was produced alive.

The men holding Neal had beaten him severely, castrated him and forced him to eat his own genitals, then finished him off with a blast from a 12-gauge shotgun. Still intent on observing tradition, however, the men rode into the Cannidy place dragging Neal's corpse behind a truck, in order to "present" it to George Cannidy who, as the crowd pressed in behind him, cursed at and shot repeatedly into the lifeless body. Mrs. Cannidy, who had remained behind closed doors most of the day, emerged from the house with a steak knife and plunged it into the dead man's heart. When the family was finished, others stomped and urinated on the body and hacked at it with knives. One young man in a jalopy roadster drove his car over it. Then a triumphant caravan dragged the remains through the streets of Marianna and hung them from a tree on the courthouse plaza not far from a statue honoring the Confederate dead.

Early the next morning, hundreds of whites from the surrounding area arrived in Marianna in hopes of seeing a lynching. Upset that the much-heralded event had already taken place, the whites lashed out at a few blacks unfortunate or unwise enough to be in the vicinity. One black man, Bud Gammons, retaliated by striking a white over the head with a pop bottle. Police intervened, bringing Gammons into the courthouse for his own protection. He almost certainly would have been lynched on the spot. The crowd, agitated at missing out on the Neal lynching and now denied access to Gammons, turned west from the courthouse and began randomly assaulting blacks in the town's main business district.

"The mob apparently started from the west side of the Plaza and began driving Negroes from the streets and stores," Buck Kester later reported. "An observer stated that 'the mob attacked men, women and children and that several blind persons were ruthlessly beaten.' A man who watched the riot from several blocks away said: 'They (the blacks) came from the town in droves, some driving, some running, some crying, all scared to death.' " Within an hour, hundreds of black men, women, and children were huddled for safety in the fields west of town.

Back at the courthouse plaza entrepreneurs were conducting a profitable business selling photographs of Neal's mutilated body. But as many whites had arrived after Neal's remains had been removed, they insisted that Sheriff Chambliss rehang the corpse, saying they would burn the whole town and even attack the police if he refused. Chambliss, after consulting by phone with the governor, managed to strike a compromise with the whites: he could not put the body back in the tree, but he would have the remains laid out in the lobby of the courthouse for their inspection, if they would pass by quietly and without violence. That way, everyone would have a chance to see the nigger who'd started all this trouble.

———

Even with the complete breakdown of order in Marianna, Sheriff Chamblis still would not acknowledge the desperate need for troops. They arrived only after the mayor of the city, John Burton, contacted Governor Sholtz directly to request help. The militia's first assignment upon reaching Marianna—at the mayor's order—was to form a personal guard around Chambliss, whose life had been threatened because of his protection of the bank robber Buford Mears and the black rioter, Bud Gammons. The soldiers also set up machine-gun nests on each corner of the courthouse plaza, the sight of which did much to dampen thoughts of further rioting.

Governor Sholtz, put on the spot by Northern editorialists and civil liberties groups in the wake of the disorder, claimed that he was not aware of the threatened lynching until 6:30 in the evening of Friday, October 26, the day Neal was killed. An angry Walter White wrote to the governor on October 30:

> It is most surprising to us to learn that the proposed lynching of Neal was not called to your attention until 6:30 in the evening. New York City is some twelve hundred miles from Marianna but the Associated Press telephoned us at three o'clock in the afternoon to read us dispatches . . . giving full details. Are we to understand . . . that it was impossible for the State of Florida and its Governor to dispatch troops a distance of only fifty miles from Tallahassee to Marianna?

With the winter tourist season about to begin, Sholtz also heard from some angry seasonal visitors. "I am not coming to Florida this year," a woman wrote. "Charleston will see me and many of my friends. . . . Your lynchings are abhorrent to civilized people."

Criticism also came from within Florida. *The Tampa Tribune* depicted the eight hundred carloads of whites who reportedly descended on the Cannidy farm as sick individuals "hungry for the kill," and termed the exhibition of Neal's body in the courthouse square "a gory spectacle to satisfy . . . crowds that . . . had to be content with post-mortem gloating." (The paper noted that the lynch mob itself had acted with greater decorum, killing Neal in private rather than indulging the blood lust of the huge crowd.)

Kester, meanwhile, had managed to make the acquaintance of one of the men who had been in the woods with the posse that tortured and murdered Claude Neal. He wrote to White:

He described the scene in all of its horror, down to the minutest detail. I was quite nauseated by the things which apparently gave this man the greatest delight to relate. I am doing my best to discover the leaders but I am already under suspicion and I have to move with the greatest care possible.

There is little room for doubt that Neal actually killed Lola Cannidy but no evidence at all that there was any rape. Of course there could be no rape since they had been having sexual relations for some time.

This relationship has extended over a period of months and possibly years. Recently Lola became engaged to a white man and she wanted to break off her relations with Neal. She asked him to meet her so that she could talk everything over with him. Lola told Neal not to speak to her again and if he did that she would tell the white men of the community on him. When she told Neal that she wanted to "quit" and "would tell on him," he "got mad" and killed her. . . . This is straight. I got it from prime sources.

White sent a copy of Kester's write-up to Eleanor Roosevelt, explaining to the First Lady, "I have investigated some 41 lynchings and eight race riots and thought I was almost immune to these tortures, but this case has made me more ill and disheartened than any of the lynchings which have occurred in my memory."

A grand jury considering the case reported to the Circuit Court of Jackson County in November 1934, "We have not been able to get much direct or positive evidence with reference to this matter; practically all of our evidence and information being in the nature of hearsay and rumors." Some of the latter information came from Kester, who gave the grand jury the names Bowen Griffin, Bruce Carter, and "Peg-Leg" Brown as alleged members of the lynch party. Kester also reported that he believed a man named "Red" who worked at a Shell Oil station in Marianna had had something to do with it. These leads were either not followed up or ignored, for the grand jury soon offered its conclusion:

Miss Lola Cannidy was brutally raped and murdered in this county on the 18th day of October, 1934, by Claude Neal, a negro, and that Claude Neal came to his death in this county on the 26th day of October, 1934, at the hands of a small group of persons unknown to us; after being forcibly removed from the jail at Brewton, Alabama, about 175 miles from here, by persons unknown to us.

White attempted to interest the federal government in the Neal case by citing the recently enacted Lindbergh Law, which arose out of the kidnapping and murder of aviator Charles Lindbergh's infant son in 1932. This crime against the family of a renowned American hero had led Congress to establish a federal statute against it. The law's original emphasis was on abductions in which kidnappers held an individual for ransom or reward, but in 1934 the law was amended to include the words "for ransom or reward or otherwise." The NAACP and many other liberal voices in the wake of the Neal case demanded that the United States act on the term *otherwise* to allow for the federal prosecution of lynching. More than most lynchings, in which mobs made relatively quick work of their victims, Neal's abduction, lasting several days and involving the crossing of state lines, certainly had the features of a kidnapping. The federal government refused to act, however. "Otherwise" apparently meant many possible things—child custody disputes, enslavement, sexual assaults—but these were personal trespasses; what distinguished lynching, White sadly concluded, was that it was understood to stand for something much larger than one person; it represented the will of a community.

"I am trying delicately to effect a union of art and propaganda," Walter White wrote to a friend in fall 1934, describing his effort, in the wake of the Neal lynching, to promote an art show based on the theme of lynching. White got the idea from a September 1934 *New Yorker* magazine cartoon by the artist Reginald Marsh entitled *This Is Her First Lynching.* In the drawing, a mother holds up her child so the little girl can see over the heads of a crowd watching a mob execution. White was so struck by the cartoon that he requested and received the original drawing from the artist. He knew of other cartoons and art works dealing with the theme, including the George Bellows drawing *The Law Is Too Slow,* which had graced the cover of White's own book *Rope and Faggot,* as well as two striking works just acquired by the Whitney Museum in New York—John Stuart Curry's *The Fugitive* and Julius Bloch's *The Lynching.*

"This, of course, seems and is morbid," White wrote to a potential sponsor about his determination to stage an exhibit. "But even a morbid subject can be made popular if a sufficiently distinguished list of patronesses will sponsor the exhibit."

With the national shame of the Neal lynching fresh in people's minds, White's timing was right. To make sure no one missed the relevance, he sent out copies of the NAACP report on the Marianna lynching along with letters promoting the show. With its frank discussion of castration and self-cannibalization, the report must have made startling reading for the uninitiated. Sponsors quickly signed on, including such notables as Sherwood Anderson, Robert Benchley, Stephen Vincent Benét, Charles Beard, and Max Eastman.

The show opened on February 15, 1935, at the Arthur U. Newton Galleries on East Fifty-seventh Street, featuring forty-nine lithographs, paintings, and drawings, including two strong new works by William Chase, the black cartoonist of the *Amsterdam News,* one with the disturbing title *Son, derned if that nigger ain't made us late for prayer meeting.* Other artists represented were Thomas Hart Benton, Rollin Kirby, Paul Cadmus, Isamu Noguchi, José Clemente Orozco, and the black artist Alan Freelon, whose *Barbecue—American Style* was one of the most commented-upon pieces. In *I Passed Along This Way,* by E. Sims Campbell, Christ carrying the cross was seen with his hand over his face, trudging up a hill alongside a black man being pulled by a rope around his neck. Another important work, titled *Southern Holiday,* by Harry Sternberg, dealt with the subject of mutilation and was captioned "Pass by quickly, nice people. Retain your fixed smile. This is not something that happened only once, somewhere, when a maniac got loose."

The New York Times referred to the exhibit, which was seen by three thousand people between February 15 and March 2, 1935, as "one of the most macabre art shows ever scheduled for this city." One patron at the opening clearly agreed, keeling over in a dead faint. Others, it was noted, walked about the room gingerly. "The large crowd," said the *Times,* "was more like one going to some sacred shrine, to some high and holy place of atonement, than to just 'another' exhibit." Eleanor Roosevelt, who attended at White's invitation, advised strongly against his plan to try to tour the exhibit in the South.

As White had anticipated, the exhibit was highly effective because of the recent publicity lynching had received; many Northern whites who attended were interested in deepening their awareness of the issue, while others were coming to the subject for the first time. "When I look at these dreadful walls and see these pictures, which I know to my despair are true pictures, I cannot tell you what I feel," novelist Pearl Buck remarked at the exhibit's opening. "Two years ago, when I came to know people outside the white race, I realized that potentially they all stand in danger of this experience of lynching."

Evenly spaced above Jessie Daniel Ames's desk in the ASWPL's Atlanta headquarters were portraits of two American heroes rarely found side by side, Abraham Lincoln and Robert E. Lee. But her associates believed the odd pairing perfectly symbolized her strong views on the South's relationship to the rest of the United States. She had joined Walter White and others in calling for federal intervention in the Claude Neal lynching on the basis of the Lindbergh Law, and even wrote to federal officials quoting from the law's text. In early 1935, however, Ames rejected White's request that she speak out and bring Southern women into line behind the Wagner-Costigan bill, and also turned down the NAACP's invitation to come to Washington and testify in support of the bill at the Senate Judiciary Committee hearings.

Unlike many of her fellow Southerners, Ames did not resent outside criticism of a region she knew to have serious problems; what she refused to accept was the need for outside intervention. She remained firm in her stance that the South needed to police itself, a position White and the NAACP saw as particularly regrettable since the power of the ASWPL to influence and reassure Southern legislators would have been considerable. The CIC had come around to supporting a federal antilynching law, but the difference between the CIC and the ASWPL on the Wagner-Costigan Bill may have come down to the organization's leaders. Will Alexander, it was believed, had bowed to the feelings of black CIC members, whereas the more autocratic Ames beat back or ignored such sentiments when expressed by her subordinates.

The truth was that federal antilynching laws were antithetical to both the CIC and the ASWPL for reasons that went beyond their immediate feelings about mob violence. Both groups envisioned change in Southern life coming about as the result of a deliberate process that would have the general consent of all parties, and which would be excruciatingly painful to none. This expectation was built on two rather precarious ideals—that whites would work visibly and responsibly, with some prodding, toward the goal of better interracial relations and enhanced black opportunity, and that blacks would remain acquiescent and accept gradual improvement out of deference to the emotional needs of whites, who were not to be, could not be, rushed. But their optimism that the decent white folks of the South would eventually "come around" on their own typified a faith that was a holdover from the Progressive Era, and which already seemed outdated in light of the New Deal's activist approach to social problem-solving.

It was clear that despite an enormous number of endorsements, petitions, resolutions, and telegrams supporting Wagner-Costigan, not to mention the best efforts of Walter White and Costigan himself, who roared on the Senate floor, "No man can be permitted to usurp the combined functions of judge, jury and executioner of his fellow men," the South was prepared to use its traditional blunt weapon of choice, the filibuster, to tie up the legislative process for weeks, months if necessary. It meant to kill the antilynching bill by threatening to thwart other legislation before the Senate, including the extension of the National Recovery Act, as well as bills affecting Social Security and transportation reforms. The Southerners felt comfortable that the public would soon see that it was not they but rather those insisting on locking horns over an antilynching bill who were selfish and obstructionist, who stood in the way of the legislation the country really needed. The Wagner-Costigan bill "hangs over the calendar and the President's program like a poised avalanche, with destruction its promise," New York Times reporter Arthur Krock observed.

Supporters of the bill resented pressure brought by editorials that for the good of the nation and FDR's legislative program the lynching measure be dropped. The bill had already waited a full year to come up for consideration, had been approved out of the Senate Judiciary Committee, and had too many organizations and individuals voicing support for it to fail to come up for consideration. Costigan, declaring that "National problems demand national remedies," estimated that 53.7 million Americans supported his bill. Unimpressed, a Southern colleague assured him, "We'll be here until Christmas before this thing comes to a vote."

Senator Josiah W. Bailey of North Carolina described the pending bill as "not the camel's nose, but the camel itself," and warned the Senate, "It shall not pass. . . . We'll speak night and day if necessary. And as to the responsibility for delaying other important legislation, we'll place as much of it as possible on those who insist on this bill, but such as they will not take, we'll gladly assume ourselves."

The filibuster began on April 26. White, through Eleanor Roosevelt, obtained an interview with the president in the hope his intervention might break the filibuster. They met on the White House portico on a Sunday afternoon, where they were joined by Eleanor and the president's mother, Sara Delano Roosevelt. As White reported the encounter, FDR began by telling several amusing stories, which was his custom and which visitors believed he used to avoid getting around to the real reason for a conversation. When the filibuster was finally mentioned, the president found White so well armed to take issue with all of his arguments that he accused him, accurately it turned out, of having been prepared for the interview by Eleanor. Feigning hurt, Roosevelt turned to his mother and said, "Well, at least I know you'll be on my side," at which the older woman shook her head vigorously and said she agreed with Mr. White. The president laughed at finding himself so completely betrayed, but later, in a more serious moment, confided to White:

> I did not choose the tools with which I must work. Had I been permitted to choose them I would have selected quite different ones. But I've got to get legislation passed by Congress to save America. The Southerners by reason of the seniority rule in Congress are chairmen or occupy strategic places on most of the Senate and House committees. If I come out for the anti-lynching bill now, they will block every bill I ask Congress to pass to keep America from collapsing. I just can't take that risk.

On April 29 FDR went on the radio in one of his "Fireside Chats" and complained that his programs were stuck behind the filibuster. Supporters of the bill voted narrowly to oppose adjournment, which would have given the Southerners a chance to seize the floor and introduce other legislation. By May 1 the fight was over, however, and the bill was dropped.

Like his predecessor James Weldon Johnson thirteen years before, White made no secret of his frustration. He understood the president's explanation of the imperatives facing the country, but still thought that he had been overcautious. Even the Southern press had appeared ready to accept the new law. For Roosevelt to have spoken out much more forcefully against the filibuster would not have involved great political risk and might have helped weaken the Southern blockade.

"It is a matter of great disappointment that you as president did not see your way clear to make a public pronouncement," White wrote to FDR, "giving your open endorsement to the anti-lynching bill and your condemnation of the shameless filibuster led by a willful group of obstructionists who, under the antiquated rules of the Senate, were able to thwart the desire of three times their number of senators to vote for the bill and many millions of Americans, North and South, and of all races and creeds, who insisted upon passage of a bill to end lynching. It is my belief that the utterly shameless filibuster could not have withstood the pressure of public opinion had you spoken out against it." In protest, White resigned from the Virgin Islands Commission, which he had joined at the president's request the year before.

Roosevelt's reluctance may have been partly attributable to a view that would have been awkward for him to try to explain at the time, for it was very much a white man's view of a black man's problem. It was that while lynching was understandably an emotional issue deserving of all the contempt it aroused, and all the petitions and pledges arrayed in opposition, it was not necessarily a problem requiring a dramatic federal remedy. Progress was being made in race relations, lynching deaths were generally declining and were nowadays almost always condemned—it could only be a matter of time before this most anachronistic custom simply withered and died. Ideally, a national antilynching statute might have been voted into law a half-century earlier, when lynchings were occurring every two or three days, but of course at that time such legislation would have been inconceivable. The widest support for the law had thus come at a time when the provocation itself seemed to be diminishing of its own accord.

White soon had an opportunity to address himself directly to one of the filibuster's leaders, Senator Bailey of North Carolina. On July 20, 1935, a cruel lynching of a retarded black man occurred in the town of Louisburg, in the senator's home state. Govan "Sweat" Ward, notorious for his irrational outbursts, had decapitated a white farmer named C. J. Stokes with an ax. When authorities came to arrest him he was seated in the yard of his home playing with the severed head, which he had wrapped in bedclothes. A mob of twenty-five or thirty persons that included several city and county officials swarmed into the yard and easily captured Ward. Instead of taking him to jail, they hoisted him by rope into a nearby tree and took turns shooting into his body. A member of a National Guard unit sent in to help deter the lynchers was seen cutting off one of the dead man's toes as a souvenir. Although many in the lynch mob were known, no state action was taken, even after the NAACP investigated the case and provided North Carolina officials with the names of nine men involved.

White wrote to Bailey and pointedly raised the facts of the Ward lynching, asking the senator if he now wished to reconsider the recent statement he had made on the Senate floor that in punishing lynchers Southerners "need no incentive to do our duty." Bailey, clearly annoyed, wrote back to demand that he not be bothered again by any communications from White or the NAACP. In closing, he advised the leader of the country's largest organization of black Americans to "go out and make an honest living instead of trying to attend to other people's business."

The NAACP took one final run at winning federal legislation in spring 1937, when a bill proposed by Representative Joseph A. Gavagan of New York came up for debate in the House. The timing of Gavagan's effort seemed uncanny, for just as the bill came under discussion, news arrived of a horrific double lynching on the eastern edge of the Mississippi Delta. The incident, which occurred in tiny Duck Hill, near Winona, would haunt the sleep of black residents of the Delta for decades. In the short term it helped propel the Gavagan measure out of the House and into the Senate.

The trouble in Duck Hill began in December 1936 when George Windham, the white owner of a "crossroads store," was killed by a shotgun blast through the front window of his establishment. At first no one could be linked to the crime. All that appeared certain was that robbery had been the motive, as the cash drawer and Windham's wallet were missing. Suspicion soon fell on two black men—Roosevelt Townes and "Bootjack" McDaniels—who had recently made themselves unpopular by peddling moonshine, traditionally considered a "white man's business." Townes and McDaniels had already been whipped and warned they might die of "sudden pneumonia" if they didn't make themselves scarce.

Sheriff E. E. Wright arrested Townes and McDaniels in early April 1937 for the Windham murder and whisked them away to Jackson for safekeeping, but a week later, on April 13, he returned them to Winona, the seat of Montgomery County, for arraignment. Windham's friends and family had been notified of the schedule for bringing the prisoners in and out of court, and as Townes and McDaniels were exiting the courthouse under police guard, a mob of about one hundred men muscled the guards aside and seized the prisoners. The two men, who had pleaded not guilty in the case, were put aboard an empty school bus that had been allowed to park directly in front of the courthouse. The bus then roared away, leading a caravan of cars and pickup trucks down the twelve miles of dusty roads to Duck Hill. Sheriff Wright later said he had not recognized anyone in the mob that relieved him of his prisoners.

In a woods close to the scene of the original crime, three or four hundred men, women, and children gathered to await the mob's arrival. Sobbing and begging for mercy, the prisoners were dragged from the bus and tied between two pine trees, then whipped with a chain and tortured with the flame from a blowtorch. Both men continued to swear their innocence, but McDaniels ultimately broke down, his screams sending children scurrying to their mothers' sides. Once he'd confessed to the crime, he was shot to death. Townes had his eyes gouged out with an ice pick and was then slowly roasted with the torch until he, too, agreed to confess. When he finally uttered the words the mob wanted to hear, he was doused with gasoline and set afire.

Part of the agitated mob then spotted a black farmer named Everett "Shorty" Dorroh, who had wandered too close to the scene, and chased him down. On the spot, despite his earnest denials, Dorroh was named an "accomplice" in Windham's murder. He miraculously survived the mob, although he was whipped, forced to confess his "guilt," and was let go only on the condition that he would leave the state of Mississippi. As he hurried away the mob opened fire at him, buckshot lodging in the back of his leg, but Dorroh kept running until he had crossed into a neighboring county.

Legislators winced at the details as an account of the assault on Townes, McDaniels, and Dorroh was read on the House floor in Washington. Proponents immediately pointed to the outrage as evidence of the bill's necessity, reminding the Southerners in the chamber that the honor of Southern womanhood could not be used as an excuse in this barbaric killing. The Southerners stirred uncomfortably in their seats when photographs of the Duck Hill victims were displayed, prompting a Mississippi Democrat to angrily demand of a New York colleague whether the Gavagan law would also apply to the "gang murder for which your state is known." The next day's New York *Daily News,* in response to the Southern legislator's "sarcastic remarks," noted that "This Southern attitude [toward lynch mobs] is markedly different from the Northern attitude toward gangster killings. . . . Up North, we deplore gang killings and hire men like Thomas E. Dewey [a New York special prosecutor] to try to break up rackets; we don't defend them with flowery speeches about Northern womanhood or insults to our dignity."

To the chagrin of leading Southerners in Washington, outbreaks of vicious mob activity back home continued to complicate their own efforts to stave off federal interference. Just a few weeks after Duck Hill, an angry crowd consisting in part of women and teenaged girls forced its way into a funeral home in Bainbridge, Georgia, and seized the dead body of a twenty-four-year-old black man, Willie Reid, an alleged murderer and rapist who had been killed by police. The corpse was dumped into the trunk of a car and carried in a horn-blowing motorcade through central

Bainbridge and around the town square. While decent people closed their windows and pulled down the shades, teenagers in jalopy convertibles shouted to their friends, "We got the nigger, we got the nigger!" The procession—by now grown to seventy-five automobiles containing men, women, and children—then headed to a local colored baseball field where a huge fire in which to cremate Reid was made by tearing wooden planks from the outfield fence.

On the heels of the Duck Hill incident in April and the Bainbridge outrage in May, the Gavagan Bill was approved in the House and moved into the Senate, where it was combined with a Senate antilynching proposal known as the Wagner–Van Nuys Bill then under consideration. The prolegislation forces were ready this time to combat a prolonged filibuster, but the Southerners gave them more than they bargained for, tying up the Senate for thirty working days. This filibuster included the setting of a new Senate record for continuous holding of the floor when Allen J. Ellender of Louisiana lectured his colleagues for twenty-seven hours and forty-five minutes on the inevitable "mongrelization" of the white race that would occur if blacks were ever granted full social equality.

President Roosevelt, despite having been told by his attorney general, Hugh Cummings, that the Wagner–Van Nuys measure was the best antilynching bill ever written, again chose not to weigh in on the filibuster. Curiously, the antilynching forces counted seventy senators on their side, and thus, in theory, could have forced closure on the filibuster and a vote on the bill. But there were some senators who refused to move for closure, perhaps because the president was not willing to take the lead in standing up to the Southern bloc. Senators also were well aware that the Southerners, by virtue of the seniority system, controlled many of the body's leading committees, and to provoke them was to run the risk of diminishing one's legislative objectives and possibly one's career. The supporters of the lynching bill were forced to concede, and the Gavagan–Wagner–Van Nuys bill went the way of its predecessors.

The 1937 attempt had the strongest support across the board of any antilynching measure to date. As James Weldon Johnson told a disconsolate Walter White, "You certainly know my sentiments about the splendid fight you put up. . . . [W]e didn't secure passage . . . but we certainly made a dent in the national conscience." A poll conducted in January 1937 showed that 70 percent of the national population and 65 percent of Southerners thought the government should pass legislation making lynching a federal crime. White was awarded the NAACP's annual Spingarn Medal for his antilynching work, over his own strenuous objections because he felt he had failed in his work.

The downfall of the 1937 effort seemed to sap finally the optimism and will of those who had supported antilynching efforts throughout the 1930s. After the president's refusal to intercede on behalf of Gavagan–Wagner–Van Nuys, there arose a sense among blacks that they had come to see the limits of Franklin D. Roosevelt's sympathies. When they approached him again in 1941 it would not be with another bid at legislation, but with a far more militant brand of activism.

CHAPTER 11

It Can Happen Here

The Second World War could not help but transform the way Americans viewed their own society. It had been waged, at tremendous sacrifice and deprivation, as a crusade to save the world from evil. Once committed to that fight, moral choices toward tolerance, democracy, and equality took on new and profound importance, as the postwar world adjusted to the dawning of the atomic age and learned the full horror of the European wartime genocide.

"The defense of our democracy against the forces that threaten it from without has made some of its failures to function at home glaringly apparent," Wendell Willkie observed during the war. "Our very proclamations of what we are fighting for have rendered our own inequities self-evident. When we talk of freedom and opportunity for all nations the mocking paradoxes in our own society become so clear they can no longer be ignored."

Confronted with this heightened sense of moral concern, the South's ideology of lynching finally collapsed in on itself. Horrific forms of domestic racial violence, except in the minds of the most stubborn Southern Neanderthals, became clearly unacceptable as the issue of segregation itself moved front and center in the nation's troubled racial dialogue. Lynching was so apparent an anachronism by the late 1940s that it slipped quietly off the radar of civil rights groups such as the NAACP as they began increasingly to focus on the brewing desegregation fight.

The war years had also seen the very methods of agitation become more confrontational. In 1941, Asa Philip Randolph, head of the Brotherhood of Sleeping Car Porters, had protested the exclusion of blacks from defense industries as the economy rapidly expanded to meet the anticipated demands of war. He had pressured President Roosevelt into signing an executive order banning such discrimination by threatening a massive march by black workers and the unemployed on Washington. Randolph believed he was simply acting on the lessons of history. At the time of the First World War, as the editor of a socialist weekly, *The Messenger,* he had advised black Americans not to fight for a country that would expect them to lay down their lives equally with whites but would not grant them equal rights. Randolph's position stood in marked contrast to that of W.E.B. Du Bois, who in a July 1917 editorial in *The Crisis* entitled "Close Ranks" had argued that blacks would gain in self-respect and stature by participating in the American war effort. "Let us while this war lasts forget our special grievances and close our ranks shoulder to shoulder with our own white fellow citizens and the allied nations that are fighting for democracy," Du Bois counseled. Many black Americans had "closed ranks," had fought and otherwise served, and had come away with nothing. Homecoming black veterans were beaten and killed in the Red Summer of 1919, and had found white society neither grateful nor newly generous in terms of lessening the crippling restraints of Jim Crow. Therefore, Randolph asserted, if the United States expected its black citizens to fall in line in support of this new war, it would have to acknowledge black participation with concrete gains.

The executive order itself was a momentous prize, but perhaps even more important was the means by which it had been obtained. Instead of the methods used in previous years, such as sending letters and petitions, begging audiences with elected officials, or lobbying Congress to act against impregnable Southern filibusters, Randolph had hit on the idea of allowing the masses of black workers to speak for themselves by marching through the streets of the nation's capital. It is difficult to imagine today what apprehension this proposal stirred in the hearts of the men who sat in powerful places in the U.S. government. Washington, D.C., in 1941 was essentially still a segregated Southern city. Not only was the prospect of so many black people assembled anywhere daunting, and unprecedented, but the terrible Washington race riots of 1919 were, for many, not that remote a memory. With a war for democracy on the horizon, the country could ill afford the humiliation of tens of thousands of black citizens demonstrating in the shadow of the Capitol for their democratic rights, and perhaps rioting with soldiers and police.

"The most important and significant thing that has come out of this whole struggle is the lesson . . . that you possess power," Randolph told an NAACP gathering soon afterward. "The Negro has developed a mass movement and the mass movement has had the effect of arousing the government at Washington. We have been told . . . that Washington was never disturbed in all its history about anything as it has been disturbed about this March of Negroes on Washington."

The March on Washington movement reawakened a form of principled, nonviolent black protest that had been dormant for much of the twentieth century but that had surfaced throughout American history in slave work slowdowns, the Underground Railroad, Southern blacks "voting with their feet" by abandoning unfriendly Southern precincts to head North, and the protests against Jim Crow on the railroads by Ida Wells, Homer Plessy, and many others. It had the effect of relocating the impulse for change to within the black community itself. As Randolph asserted, American blacks could no longer wait for some "white angel" such as "Father" Abraham Lincoln or Herbert Hoover or FDR to save them. There was nothing more false than the belief in deliverance. Whites may join or abet the cause, Randolph noted, but the struggle for black equality must be led by black people.

Even before the war's end, the kind of nonviolent social action Randolph cited was applied by a new civil rights organization, the Congress of Racial Equality (CORE). Founded in Chicago in 1943 with an interracial membership, CORE pioneered the use of workshops and training to ready white and black "soldiers" for carefully targeted actions that nonviolently challenged segregation policies. CORE integrated restaurants and roller rinks in Chicago during the war years, and in 1947 courageously turned the method on the South. To test a recent federal ruling against segregation in interstate travel, CORE mounted the Journey of Reconciliation, an integrated bus trip through the upper South that culminated in the arrest of several members in Chapel Hill, North Carolina. One black participant, Bayard Rustin, wound up serving time on a chain gang.

Along with the actions of the March on Washington movement and CORE, several prominent literary events pointed to the changes the war had brought. Foremost among these was the publication of *An American*

Dilemma: The Negro Problem and American Democracy, the seminal 1944 book on U.S. race relations by the Swedish sociologist Gunnar Myrdal. America, Myrdal explained, would never be a truly great civilization unless it learned to confront its racial problems. He pointed out that the momentum for that ultimate reckoning had been sped up by the war, and reminded readers that in U.S. history wars had always preceded major advances in black progress. Myrdal also wrote the obituary for the kind of thinking that had long propped up segregation—the idea that blacks were intrinsically inferior human beings who should be content to remain second-class citizens. Such theories had steadily weakened since Franz Boas laid siege to them in the teens and '20s, and were now in more or less full retreat. "The gradual destruction of the popular theory behind race prejudice," Myrdal wrote, "is the most important of all social trends in the field of interracial relations. . . . The trend of psychology, education, anthropology, and social sciences is toward environmentalism in the explanation of group differences, which means that the racial beliefs which defended caste are being torn away." Recognizing that the challenge was monumental, Myrdal nonetheless predicted that the United States would ultimately, and probably soon, discover the means of tearing down the walls of legalized racial separation.

Critical to the coming upheaval over race was what Myrdal called the American Creed—the widely held adherence to the founding principles of the democracy. The Creed had guided Americans to produce the body of law that included the Thirteenth, Fourteenth, and Fifteenth Amendments and which contained, at least in skeletal form, the basic guarantees of black equality. Courts and legislative bodies at the state and federal levels had worked to weaken these rights, yet they had never been completely taken away. In the face of increased black pressure, Myrdal predicted, even those Americans who opposed black equality would ultimately have to surrender out of their own faith in the Creed. "The white man can humiliate the Negro; he can thwart his ambitions; he can starve him; he can press him down into vice and crime; he can occasionally beat him and even kill him," Myrdal concluded, "but he does not have the moral stamina to make the Negro's subjugation legal and approved by society."

Another important literary signpost was the popularity in summer 1945 of Richard Wright's *Black Boy,* a memoir of his Mississippi childhood and one of the first unsentimental autobiographical accounts of black life in the Jim Crow South. Particularly vivid were the book's descriptions of the numbing effect of daily racism, and the narrow line black Southerners walked, never sure which whites to trust, never completely at ease because physical harm or even death might lie in the next misunderstood encounter with the white world. Lynching, both in its literal form and as an abstract, brooding threat, is a motif in virtually all of Wright's work.

One of the most effective literary voices for Southern change was Lillian Smith, who with her partner Paula Snelling edited a liberal journal and ran a progressive girls' camp near Clayton, in the northeast corner of Georgia, on land once owned by her family. Smith was one of the first Southerners to make the point that segregation was not only unfair to black people but also destructive to everyone—that the maintenance of segregation and related hypocritical attitudes about race and sex, what she called "our twisted way of life," had impaired the emotional development of the Southern white. Her position was most famously expressed in her bestselling 1944 novel, *Strange Fruit,* the story of two families—one white, one black—in a small Southern town, and the doomed love affair between a young white man, Tracy Dean, and a young black woman, Nonnie Anderson. The book's characters, Smith explained, "were shaped and twisted in their learning as if their personalities had been placed in a steel frame within which they could grow, but only according to the limits defined by the rigid design of the frame." Dean returns from duty in the First World War sure of his love for Nonnie, but once home slowly accepts that he cannot overcome the strictures of family and community that prohibit his marrying her. When she becomes pregnant, Tracy pays a black man to wed Nonnie for appearances' sake, then is himself murdered by Nonnie's brother, who is enraged at the damage and injustice done to his sister.

The book does contain an account of a lynching, but Smith always maintained that the title—unlike the song written by Lewis Allan (Abel Meeropol) in 1939 and popularized by Billie Holiday ("*Southern trees bear a strange fruit / blood on the leaves and blood at the root / black bodies swinging in the Southern breeze / strange fruit hanging from the poplar trees*")—refers not to lynching victims but to all Southerners who are the "strange fruit" produced by the rotten tree of segregation and racial hypocrisy.

Strange Fruit was briefly banned in Boston and from the U.S. mails, and it made Lillian Smith a celebrity. It is the work with which her name is chiefly associated, although she was somewhat bitter over the fact that critics admired the book almost exclusively as a social-protest novel rather than a work of literature. In the late 1940s Smith returned to the issues of Southern sexual and racial mores in a provocative book of essays and recollections, *Killers of the Dream,* in which she described how the South had been poorly served by generations of "hotheaded, uninformed, defensive, greedy men, unwilling to accept criticism." As a result the entire region had, in one of the author's most memorable phrases, "walked backward into its future." She did not spare herself from blame, conceding that as one of the privileged white children of the South she had been raised on the "sugar-tit words" and "sugar-tit experiences" that had created for most Southerners a false sense of the racial reality—a pampered life of "cold lemonade, comfortable porches, and mammy's ample bosom." Smith was critical of Southern whites who still spoke in terms of "gradualism" and half-measures, who cautioned restraint and warned of violence if segregation was assaulted head-on. Even as the South protested vehemently against change it also desperately craved it, she believed, like a sick man who knows surgery is needed but can't find the courage to wield the scalpel himself.

What the Negro Wants (1944), edited by black scholar Rayford Logan and featuring articles by a spectrum of black thinkers including Roy Wilkins, W.E.B. Du Bois, Mary McLeod Bethune, Gordon Blaine Hancock, A. Philip Randolph, Langston Hughes, and Logan himself, was another noteworthy literary event of the immediate postwar era. The striking thing about the collected essays was their unanimity: what the Negro wanted was full equality. There was no talk of blacks casting down their buckets or accepting a role as the hewers of wood and the pickers of cotton. "The Negro soldiers are not fighting and dying to maintain the status quo for their race," one representative passage asserted:

> The young Negro fighter pilots . . . who were among those shooting down Nazi planes in the fierce fighting over the Anzio beachhead are not risking their lives to intrench further the way of life obtaining in their home towns. The Negro Marines in the South Pacific, the black engineers, the colored quartermaster units getting the supplies through the mud and heat and cold of the battle-fronts, are not working for the status quo. . . . Nor will they take kindly . . . to surly suggestions as to their "place."

The book's uniform message was so troubling that its publisher, the University of North Carolina Press, at first refused to release it, then did so only with a "Publisher's Introduction" that went to great lengths to belittle and highlight the impracticality of the writers' ideas. America's book critics, however, largely accepted the authors', not the publisher's, point of view. Blacks, one reviewer observed, "want the simple human things you and I want: To take part, without arbitrarily imposed handicaps, in the duties and the benefits of the society they live in."

The parallel between racial terrorism and the intolerance of fascism in the postwar era was made all the more apparent by the fact that many individuals targeted were returned veterans. Even before the soldiers had walked down the gangplanks of the returning troopships, Southern demagogues were warning of the dangers of having allowed 750,000 blacks to engage in a great war for democracy. Senator James O. Eastland of Mississippi claimed, ludicrously, that black soldiers in the Occupation Forces in Germany were routinely raping white women, five thousand in Stuttgart alone. Eastland's Mississippi Senate colleague, Theodore "The Man" Bilbo, maligned the troops' combat record, asserting that black soldiers in Europe and Asia had shown a lack of intelligence and initiative and had been a disgrace to the uniform (this despite public praise from U.S. generals George S. Patton and Dwight D. Eisenhower for the distinguished combat service of black troops). Meanwhile, William Lindley, head of the Florida Peace Officers Association, cautioned that black servicemen were coming home "pretending to be heroes" and "expecting to marry our girls."

There were numerous incidents of violence against returning black GIs. At the bus station in Freeport, Long Island, on February 5, 1946, Patrolman Joseph Romeika got into a confrontation with two black servicemen and their two brothers, who had been denied service at the station lunch counter. Witnesses said the brothers had not been disorderly, but Romeika claimed that one, Private Charles Ferguson, had threatened to shoot him and had made a move as if to draw a gun. Romeika drew his own revolver and fired, killing Charles Ferguson instantly and shooting Alfonzo Ferguson, who died later that day. Seaman Joseph Ferguson was struck in the shoulder, and he and the other surviving brother, Richard, were placed under arrest. Although a special investigation sponsored by New York's governor, Thomas E. Dewey, found that all four Ferguson brothers had been unarmed at the time of the shooting, Patrolman Romeika was completely exonerated.

A week after the Ferguson killings, Isaac Woodward, a black combat veteran who had seen action in the South Pacific, received his discharge at an army base in Georgia and boarded a bus headed north toward his parents' home in New York City. Just across the South Carolina border, Woodward and the bus driver quarreled because the soldier took longer using the bathroom at a rest stop than suited the driver's wishes. When Woodward was out of earshot, the driver radioed ahead to authorities at an upcoming stop in Batesburg that he had a troublesome Negro on board. At Batesburg, the GI was ordered off the bus and arrested by Police Chief Linwood Shull who, with the assistance of a deputy, took Woodward into an alley and beat him almost to death. The assault culminated with one of the whites driving a blunt instrument of some kind, probably a billy club, into Woodward's eyes, permanently blinding him. The NAACP threw itself into the case and, among other actions, circulated a photograph of Woodward, still wearing his uniform, but now with the dark glasses of a blind man, to the nation's press. Walter White, with the help of prominent liberals and celebrities including actor and film director Orson Welles, orchestrated a public campaign for a federal investigation, but Police Chief Shull, brought before a federal court in South Carolina, was ultimately acquitted of any wrongdoing.

A more complex and disruptive breakdown of law and order occurred in Columbia, Tennessee, later that month, when a fight between a black veteran and a white store owner set off a chain reaction that sent the town into turmoil. It began on February 24, 1946, when Mrs. Gladys Stephenson and her nineteen-year-old son, James, a recently discharged soldier, complained to Billy Fleming, the white owner of the Caster-Kott appliance store, that her radio was still broken despite his having charged her to fix it. Fleming, enraged at the accusation, argued with Mrs. Stephenson and slapped her across the face. James Stephenson pounced on Fleming and after a brief tussle struck the white man with such force the store owner fell backward through a plate-glass window and lay bleeding on the sidewalk. A stunned crowd of whites quickly formed. Sheriff J. J. Underwood appeared on the scene and, as an ambulance carried Fleming to a hospital, took both Stephensons into custody. Talk of the incident and Fleming's grave injuries quickly spread. On the lawn outside the courthouse jail where the black mother and son were being held, men gathered and spoke in urgent, conspiratorial tones; it was said someone had brought a rope.

Thirteen years earlier, in 1933, Columbia had been the site of a shameful lynching when a mob, finding itself in disagreement with a verdict of not guilty in the rape trial of a black teenager, seized the boy, dragged him screaming from the courthouse, and burned him at the stake. Eager to avoid the humiliation of another such affair, and noting the swelling crowd below his window, Sheriff Underwood called two prominent local black businessmen, barbershop owner Sol Blair and undertaker James

Morton, and arranged for them to bring a car around the back of the courthouse and sneak the Stephensons out of town.

When the mob learned the mother and son had escaped, anger turned against the black community as a whole, which resided in an area known as Mink Slide, not far from the courthouse. Mink Slide was now home to many black veterans who, like James Stephenson, had lost their former willingness to turn the other cheek. They also remembered the 1933 lynching, and were in no mood to sit still for such an outrage again. "We fought for freedom overseas and we'll fight for it here," Sheriff Underwood heard one black veteran say. Several of the GIs coached their neighbors on strategies for defending their homes, and that night, when a police patrol ventured into Mink Slide in an unmarked car, the defenders opened fire, wounding the officers.

During the night five hundred members of the Tennessee National Guard and one hundred state police arrived, joining a mob of citizens already gathered at the courthouse. "Niggers are shooting to kill!" people told one another in the darkness, as they loaded their weapons. "Let's clear them out!" Just before dawn this citizen-soldier army, under the command of State Commissioner of Safety Lynn Bomar, loosed an apocalyptic fury on the residents of Mink Slide. On the pretext of searching for weapons, they destroyed property, looted stores and smashed windows, pulled frightened black people from their homes, and fired tommy guns into the air. The mob brutalized anyone they apprehended—one man was dragged down the steps of the Masonic Hall and beaten so ferociously he lost an eye. Sol Blair's barbershop was targeted; vandals there stole money from the cash register and cut the felt on the pool tables. James Morton's undertaking establishment was trashed; the visitors squirted embalming fluid into several caskets, ruining them, and someone scrawled the initials "KKK" into the top of a casket.

Police and soldiers rounded up more than a hundred people—men, women, and children—who were forced at gunpoint to walk with their hands above their heads to the local lockup. Twenty-five men were charged with attempted murder for the shooting incident and detained. Two others—William Gordon and James Johnson, who the police were certain had fired on the unmarked police car—were later shot to death in jail while "trying to escape."

The NAACP acted swiftly to enter the case, rushing attorney Thurgood Marshall, the organization's special counsel, into the state to organize a defense for the arrested men. To the NAACP, the Columbia situation had some obvious parallels to the Ossian Sweet case of 1925, when a Detroit homeowner and his friends had fired into a white mob. In Columbia, it appeared, an entire community had been criminalized for having the audacity to defend itself.

Coming so soon after the war, the Columbia riot was readily seen by many as a frightening example of homegrown fascism. The raid on Mink Slide had resembled nothing if not the clearing out of a ghetto—uniformed soldiers and police working alongside local thugs to destroy property and randomly brutalize and arrest people, marching the inhabitants out at gunpoint with their hands over their heads, then summarily executing two men in their jail cells. It could have been a scene from Nazi-occupied Poland. The *New York Post* characterized Lynn Bomar's men as "storm troopers" who pursued "organized terror against not an individual but an entire minority group," and concluded, "The Columbia, Tennessee case goes beyond the ancient, bitter lynch story. It resembles the pattern of Nazi terror against the Jews which spearheaded Hitler's conquest of Germany." *The New York Times* headlined an editorial on the riot "Pogrom in Tennessee."

At the behest of the NAACP, the federal government investigated to determine if blacks' civil rights had been violated. The FBI interviewed 390 people in Columbia, but could find no witnesses who would give the names of any of the white men who had done the rioting in Mink Slide. A federal grand jury refused to indict any officials or alleged mob members, saying the level of force used to subdue the black community was "not unreasonable." The shooting of Johnson and Gordon in police custody was determined to be "justifiable homicide."

The NAACP was furious about the failure of the federal grand jury to hand down indictments in what seemed so obvious a case of officials acting under color of law to deprive citizens of their civil rights. Walter White worried in a letter to U.S. Attorney General Tom Clark that the grand jury's inaction would be seen as "a signal by state officials and the Ku Klux Klan throughout the South to terrorize Negro communities" during the coming primary elections in fall 1946, "without fear of federal interference." Eleanor Roosevelt, who served as cochair of a national committee organized by the NAACP to monitor the Columbia case, had also pursued Clark on the matter; in response, he assured her that the federal grand jury had "exhausted every possibility of disclosing a federal offense" and that despite a full FBI investigation, "No one is able to furnish the names of the perpetrators of the acts of vandalism. The grand jury had scores of witnesses before it to no avail." Clark knew that such a prosecution, no matter how well armed, would be futile: even if a strong case could be made that federal civil rights violations had occurred, the jury that would hear the case would still be made up of local men who would never vote to convict.

Pressure thus intensified on Thurgood Marshall to at least mount a successful defense for the two dozen men who had been arrested in the original rioting. Adding to his defense team black Nashville attorney Z. Alexander Looby and white labor lawyer Maurice Weaver from Chattanooga, Marshall sought and won a change of venue to move the case away from the Columbia courthouse. However, the local court trumped Marshall's strategy by transferring the trials to Lawrenceburg, a nearby community even less friendly to blacks than Columbia, a place where posted signs warned Negroes against tarrying overnight.

Marshall added the two Southern lawyers to his side both for their local expertise and to lessen the impression of outside intervention. The effort did little to diminish the hostility of local whites in the courtroom, who treated Marshall and Looby with a mixture of contempt and curiosity (they had rarely if ever seen or heard educated black people speak), and denigrated Weaver as a white "traitor" and worse. At one point in the proceedings, District Attorney Paul Bumpus warned the judge concerning Weaver, "If that son-of-a-bitch contradicts me again, I'm going to wrap a chair around his God Damned head." Later, Bumpus offered to resolve a procedural question that had arisen in the courtroom by stepping outside onto the lawn and settling things with Weaver "man-to-man."

In the trial, all the defendants but one were ultimately acquitted—largely through lack of evidence, partly because Lawrenceburg seemed to resent having to clean up another community's mess. The citizens of Columbia were not going to allow the NAACP to have the last word, however. Shortly after eight P.M. on the night of November 18, 1946, Marshall got into a car with Looby, Weaver, and white reporter Harry Raymond to return to their hotels in Nashville, as it was unsafe for them to remain overnight in the Columbia area. Out on the Nashville Highway, three state highway patrol cars intercepted the vehicle. "They approached us with right hands on their pistols and blinding us with flashlights carried in their left hands," Raymond recalled. "It looked like a lynching."

After some verbal intimidation, the troopers arrested Marshall on a charge of drunken driving and placed him in another vehicle, saying they would drive him back to Columbia. They waved the others ahead, telling them to continue on to Nashville. Fearing some harm was about to befall Marshall, his colleagues bravely ignored the cops' instructions and followed the police car, which headed down a dirt road to the secluded banks of the Duck River, where Marshall saw a group of white men gathered—presumably a lynch mob. The police, however, apparently spooked by the presence of the other car, which they knew contained the white newsman Raymond, aborted the plan and drove their captive back to town.

Luckily for Marshall, local magistrate C. Hayes Denton, who was suspected of having cooperated with lynch mobs in the past, was unavailable, so Marshall was sent before another magistrate, the elderly J. J. Pogue, on the drunk driving charge. Marshall, on a hunch, decided that instead of attempting a complicated legal argument about police harassment and violations of his civil rights, which might provoke Pogue, he'd simply refute the accusation. He told the judge he had not been drinking. "Boy, you want to take my test?" Pogue challenged. "I never had a drink in my life and I can smell a drink a mile off. . . . Blow your breath on me." Marshall accepted and blew into the smaller man's face "so hard he rocked." Pogue asked Marshall to exhale several more times, then told the arresting officers, "This man has not been drinking. I will not sign a warrant for his arrest."

While the NAACP's top lawyer was nearly getting himself lynched down in Tennessee, Walter White was serving as savior and mentor to a boy who had miraculously survived a lynching in Louisiana.

Corporal John C. Jones's "surliness" rubbed folks in Minden, Louisiana, the wrong way when he returned from overseas. He offended one local white man by refusing to sell him a German Luger he had brought back as a war souvenir, and troubled others by expressing his intent to recover a piece of land that had once belonged to his grandfather. On August 8, 1946, police charged Jones with "loitering" for having been discovered in a white woman's backyard, even though the woman, Mrs. Sam Maddry, Jr., refused to press charges, and it's not clear whether he had even been in the vicinity. Taken to jail with Jones was his seventeen-year-old cousin, Albert "Sonny Man" Harris, who was beaten and forced to say that Jones had been prowling in Maddry's backyard because he wished to molest her.

After being locked up all day, at about 8:30 P.M. the young men were told they were free to go. Jones, suspecting a trap had been laid to ambush them once they left the relative safety of the jail, insisted on remaining there until the next morning. Angered, Deputy Sheriff Oscar Haynes, Jr., informed Jones, "You've got to get out of this jail," and began pummeling him with his fists. Other deputies and whites then entered the jail, ganged up on the two blacks, and bodily carried them to waiting vehicles. They were driven three miles out of Minden to an isolated place called Dorcheat Bayou.

"They told me to hold my head down so I couldn't see where we was going," Albert Harris later recalled. "There wasn't much talking. . . . When we got out of the car they said they would beat us up. They said they ought to kill us. They threw me down on my stomach and put their feet on my head and on my feet so I couldn't move. Then they beat me with a strap. . . . They took John on the other side of a little creek. First, they'd beat me, then they'd beat him."

Jones was forced to endure a horrible death. Both of his hands were chopped off with a meat cleaver; then, as the mob held him down, his face and body were seared with the flame of a blowtorch. "The excessive heat and beatings caused his eyes to pop from their sockets," according to an NAACP account. "Jones was of light yellow complexion, but when his body was found his face was charred black."

Harris in turn was stripped of his clothes and beaten, then struck forcefully on the head with a pistol and left for dead. When he regained consciousness the mob was gone, and he heard Jones moaning in pain and begging for water. Harris dipped a shoe into the bayou and, cradling Jones's head, gave him a drink. Jones asked his cousin with his last breath to look after his wife and daughter.

White fishermen discovered Jones's body the next day. Coroner T. A. Richardson, summoned to the scene, announced that the man had died from multiple bruises and abrasions "sustained at the hands of a person or persons unknown." He also noted that Jones's wallet contained lewd photographs of white women and obscene poetry (a claim later disputed by the NAACP).

The whites who had killed Jones became apprehensive upon hearing Richardson's account, for the report of one black body in Dorcheat Bayou suggested that Harris had somehow survived. As an eyewitness to the murder, he conceivably held the whites' fate in his hands, unless he could be found and "reasoned with" as soon as possible. The next night whites came to Harris's house and roughed up his father in an effort to learn Sonny Man's whereabouts. The elder man feigned ignorance, although his son had come home the previous night and was in hiding nearby. After intentionally spreading a rumor in the black community that they were taking a bus to Texas, father and son then drove out of town in an automobile and disappeared in the opposite direction. For three weeks the lynch mob, the FBI, and the NAACP all worked to try to locate the two men, until finally the Harrises surfaced in Muskegon, Michigan, where they had found refuge in the home of some relatives.

Walter White knew that in Sonny Man Harris he had a unique resource—a viable and sympathetic witness to a lynching. The NAACP paid for both Harrises to come to New York City, and made Sonny Man available to reporters. The story he related of Corporal Jones's death gripped journalists and readers alike, as at that time there was still tremendous goodwill felt toward returning soldiers, and strong public dismay that one who had so recently served his country overseas had met an unjust death at home. Columnist Walter Winchell spoke out against the crime, and told White the Jones slaying was "one of the most unbelievable stories I have ever come across in 28 years of dealing with human cruelty," adding, "I shudder for America if it lets such cold-blooded savagery go unpunished."

In February 1947, the federal government brought charges against five of the lynchers, including two deputy sheriffs, accusing them of violating Jones's and Harris's civil rights by acting under color of law to deny them the right to due process under the Fourteenth Amendment. The members of the mob were identified secretly by a black café owner, who said the three deputies and six other men had relaxed in his establishment following the lynching, much as if they had come from their bowling league or a game of poker. Sonny Man Harris bravely returned to Shreveport to testify, and corroborated the café owner's identification of the mob members. Others testified they saw the mob abduct Harris and Jones from the Minden jail.

Despite such convincing elements in the prosecution's case, it had been apparent all along that gaining convictions would be nearly impossible. The defense threw up strongly worded objections that were blatant appeals to regional sentiment—that Harris himself had killed Jones, that the FBI had used "Gestapo tactics" to get evidence, that black witnesses had been coached by the NAACP, and that "this prosecution has been engineered by minority elements in the East." In the end, much to Walter White's angry disappointment, the jury cleared the defendants of all charges.

One consistent source of violence in the postwar South was the progress being made toward restoring the franchise to black citizens. The battle to reverse black disenfranchisement had seen its first landmark victory in 1915, when the NAACP helped aid a legal challenge to the constitutionality of the use of the "grandfather clause" in Oklahoma. In *Guinn v. United States,* the Supreme Court nullified a state law under the Fifteenth Amendment for the first time in forty-five years, invalidating the locally applied, transparently discriminatory grandfather regulation that a prospective voter must prove that an ancestor had been a registered voter. (The clause had allowed poor whites to avoid literacy and property qualifications.) Another significant breakthrough came in 1944, when the court invalidated the use of the white primary, the restricted form of election based on the premise that the Democratic party was a private organization and that its primary was a private affair and not a state function. Because after the 1890s any Republican opposition in a general election in the South tended to be nominal, the results of the Democratic primary were more or less certain to represent the final outcome of the general election, and excluding blacks from the Democratic primary was tantamount to excluding them entirely. A 1941 suit filed by a black voter in Texas who'd been turned away from the polls went all the way to the Supreme Court, and in April 1944 the court declared the white primary unconstitutional, ruling in *Smith v. Allwright* that primary elections are intrinsic to the nation's electoral process and therefore cannot be considered private.

The court's decision failed to touch other impediments to black voting still rampant in Southern districts, such as the poll tax, "citizenship" tests, and sheer physical intimidation, but with *Smith v. Allwright* important ground had been gained. By 1946, thanks in part to the Supreme Court's decision, as well as the surge in postwar liberal consciousness and the growth of black populations in cities, the number of registered black voters in the South climbed to 750,000, more than at any time since Reconstruction, after having plummeted to essentially zero at the turn of the century.

The reaction from whites was predictably bellicose, and contributed to a ghastly racial killing that same year—the quadruple lynching near Monroe, Georgia, of two black married couples in their twenties—Roger Malcolm, his wife, Dorothy, and George Dorsey and his wife, Mae Murray Dorsey. The July 1946 murders came about as the result of a fight between Roger Malcolm and his employer's son, but occurred in an atmosphere poisoned by the antiblack rhetoric of gubernatorial candidate Eugene Talmadge.

Talmadge, "Ol' Gene" as he was known, was in the midst of an emotional campaign that summer. Twice before he had been governor of Georgia, but he had had the office taken away from him in 1943 by Ellis Arnall, his own attorney general and onetime protégé. The 1946 election offered a spirited rematch with black voting rights a key issue, as Arnall had refused to defy the federal ruling on the white primary. Arnall was a Southern moderate, Talmadge an unrepentant white supremacist not above mentioning that he had once personally flogged a black man. He was beloved by rural Georgians, a popularity that was significant because of a detail of the state's electoral policies known as the "county unit system," which gave rural counties with small populations equal status with far more populous urban areas. This strongly diminished the concentrated electoral power of cities and, as a result, the advance and evolution of moderate political thought in Georgia. As "Ol' Gene" liked to boast, "I can carry any county that ain't got street cars."

The 1946 gubernatorial race would be the first election in which blacks could test the now open primary system. Talmadge aggressively warned them to stay away from voting places on July 17, the day of the primary. When he was declared the victor over Arnall, there occurred a celebratory outbreak of racist violence across the state. In one election district the only black man courageous enough to go to the polls was called from his home in the middle of the night and shot to death. In the town of Thomaston, the white editor of the local newspaper was dragged into the street by a mob and forced to apologize publicly for editorializing against Talmadge's victory.

The tense feeling of the Talmadge-Arnall primary formed the backdrop to the quadruple lynching in Monroe in the days surrounding the election. On July 14 Barney Hester, twenty-two, the son of a planter and local Talmadge supporter named Bob Hester, attempted to whip Roger Malcolm, who sharecropped on the Hesters' land. Barney later said he meant to punish the black man over reports that Malcolm was beating his wife, Dorothy, known as "Millie Kate," who was seven months pregnant. Local blacks would later contend that the fight actually began when Malcolm accused Barney of making sexual advances to Dorothy. Whatever the precise cause, in the midst of their brawl Malcolm stabbed Hester with a pocketknife. The wound was not serious, but the young white man required hospitalization, and his friends announced their intention to square accounts with Malcolm, at which point the sharecropper was arrested and taken away by Walton County sheriff E. S. Gordon.

After her husband's arrest, Dorothy left the Hester place and went to work at the farm of another white planter, J. Loy Harrison, where her brother George Dorsey, and his wife, Mae, lived and worked. George Dorsey was a decorated veteran who had seen action in Asia and North Africa. Walton and neighboring Oconee Counties were among the largest cotton-growing areas in Georgia, and Harrison was one of the most affluent cotton farmers in Oconee County. The Dorseys and Dorothy Malcolm approached their employer about helping to get Roger Malcolm out of jail, as they feared a mob might overwhelm deputies and jailers and carry him off to be lynched. Harrison at first refused, but finally, acknowledging that he "could use an extra hand," agreed to go Malcolm's bail and put him to work. On the afternoon of July 26 he drove into the town of Monroe with Dorothy, George, and Mae and paid six hundred dollars to bail Roger out.

"I made bond for Malcolm at the courthouse," Harrison later recalled. "I came outside and told the Negroes I'd pick them up later on. I made some purchases and then picked them up at a Negro joint. When I got them they were all lit [drunk]."

Leaving Monroe with the four blacks, Harrison came to a wooden bridge over the Appalachee River at a place known as Moore's Ford, the boundary of Walton and Oconee counties, where he found his way blocked by a car in the middle of the bridge. Suddenly another car came up from behind, ramming Harrison's bumper, and about twenty armed men on foot appeared from the woods.

"We came to the bridge across the river and I looked across and saw a car blocking the other end of the bridge," Harrison recalled. "I thought to myself: 'Federal men!' One of the men came out, put a shotgun against the back of my head and said 'all of you put 'em up'. . . . 'We want Roger.' Some of the men in the group then went to the two Negro men and slipped ropes around their hands—expert like, pretty like."

Malcolm and George Dorsey were taken from the car, one man sneering at Dorsey, "I bet you're one of those niggers who voted the other day." As the men were led away, Dorothy and Mae began "cussing like everything" out the car window at the mob, and one of them apparently called the name of a man who seemed to be in charge. Harrison later described him as "tall and dignified looking," like "a retired business man. He was about 65, wore a brown suit and had on a big broad brimmed hat. He looked like he had a good healthy Florida suntan." Hearing his name, the tall man turned and ordered, "Get those black bitches, too." The women did not go quietly. Deep scratches on the car doors made it clear they had attempted to fend off their abductors by clinging to the vehicle, but they were eventually overpowered and dragged into the woods. After a minute or two, Harrison, who was held at gunpoint back at the car, heard three volleys of shots from a woods near the river, then silence.

He was released unharmed after swearing that he did not recognize anyone, then drove to a country store a couple of miles away and phoned Sheriff Gordon. "The whole thing must have lasted three minutes," Harrison estimated.

The sheriff soon came speeding up the dusty road with Coroner W. T. Brown and, along with Harrison, investigated the appalling scene by the riverside. Even the pine and sweetgum trees were perforated with buckshot. The bodies, huddled together, had all been fired into numerous times; the tops of their heads had bullet wounds, indicating the mob had shot into them even after they'd fallen to the ground. Coroner Brown noted that the women's arms were broken and their elbows smashed, presumably as the result of being struck with gun butts as the mob fought to pry them from the car. Millie Kate's face had been almost completely blown off by a shotgun blast. Roger Malcolm, the mob's target, had been shot more than the others. By flashlight in the mounting darkness, Brown submitted his verdict to Sheriff Gordon: "Death at the hands of persons unknown."

Major W. E. Spence, head of the Georgia Bureau of Investigation, did not think the answer was as simple as that. To him, Loy Harrison was something of a question mark. There were rumors that he and George Dorsey had had a falling out recently over a crop settlement, and Spence felt the whole killing seemed too perfect. "It looks like it was a rehearsed affair," Spence told reporters. "It looks like it might have been planned since the Negro was first confined to jail."

Harrison had paid Malcolm's bail at two P.M., but it was almost five P.M. before he took Malcolm out of the lockup, while Dorsey and the two women relaxed and waited in a bar. The three-hour interval in which Harrison said he'd "made some purchases" would have been ample time for him to make phone calls alerting the mob that he'd be leaving Monroe with Roger Malcolm and the others, and for the lynch mob to assemble at Moore's Ford.

The murders quickly became a national news story, with the by-now-standard criticism of a Southern society that nurtured race hatred and allowed such things to occur, and special condemnation of the lynchers for killing a war veteran and two women. An editorial cartoon in the Louisville *Courier-Journal* showed a bound corpse labeled "Georgia Lynching" dangling from the limb of a tree labeled "Talmadge Campaign." The drawing was titled *The Fruit of the Tree*. The Methodist and Episcopal ministers of Atlanta issued a joint statement condemning the murders, noting, "We have just recently sent millions of the flower of our young manhood to Europe and to Asia to stamp out Nazism, whose habit has been to take the law into its own hands and murder helpless people. Now, in Georgia, something closely akin to Nazism in Europe and Asia has arisen, and in every sense it is just as brutal." An editorial in the Philadelphia *Record* was even more explicit. "The blood of these victims is on the head of grass-roots Fuhrer Talmadge," the paper commented, "and on some of the 'best people' who cynically backed him with their wealth for selfish, reactionary ends."

The Monroe killings drove influential *Atlanta Constitution* editor Ralph McGill, who'd repeatedly urged the region to move away from the prehistoric darkness of lynchings, to issue a forceful editorial indictment:

> We in the South cannot cry "let us alone." . . . We did that with slavery 85 years ago. We resented outside interference and we formed a new nation and stubbornly made slavery the keystone of our arch of government. From that moment on the moral weight of the nation and the world was against us. . . . We cannot make intolerance and murder the keystone of our society without destroying it. . . . We have said to let us alone and we would do the job. . . . We have not done that job. Shall we have the moral courage to do it or not? A lot of Americans want to know.

The *Constitution* received numerous letters of protest about the lynchings (including one from a concerned seventeen-year-old student at Morehouse College named Martin Luther King, Jr.). Protests and marches were staged in New York, Philadelphia, and San Francisco, where a group of black and white GIs marched together carrying a large sign that read "Guadalcanal '42; North Africa '43; Germany '44; Okinawa '45; Monroe, Ga., '46; We Veterans Are Still Being Killed by Racists." In Washington, fifteen thousand people gathered to remember the Malcolms and Dorseys before the Lincoln Memorial, while on Capitol Hill Senator William T. Knowland of California insisted that a news report about the Georgia case be inserted in the *Congressional Record*. (Senator Olin D. Johnston of South Carolina rose to criticize Knowland for making remarks reflecting on the integrity of another state, and advised him to pay more attention to "some of the things that happen in Hollywood.")

Rewards for information leading to a conviction of the lynch mob—from Governor Arnall, the NAACP, black celebrities Ossie Davis and Lena Horne, and several newspapers—amounted to almost $100,000. However, so great was the fear of the lynchers and what many people assumed was some kind of police conspiracy that even so staggering an amount of money would not produce a single person willing to identify the mob. It was well understood that anyone who spoke out would in essence be selling his own life.

In Walton County the threat of retaliation kept many blacks, even family members, from attending the victims' funerals. For two hours black morticians scoured the neighborhood, holding up the services in the hope some relatives might be induced to attend. One exasperated undertaker told a reporter, "They ain't home. They ain't nowhere. They hid out." Those blacks who did witness the burials were careful to make no allusion to the cause of death, but simply prayed and walked away in silence.

"The best people in town won't talk," Major Spence complained, frustrated after weeks of fruitless investigation into what he termed "the worst thing that ever happened in Georgia." "When I get back to [Atlanta], I'm going to ask the Governor to appeal to every Congressman to help pass federal legislation against mob violence."

Many shared his sense of outrage. President Harry Truman, a die-hard patriot who was enraged that a war veteran who had won medals for his bravery in combat had come home to be made a lynching victim, responded to Governor Arnall's request for federal help and ordered the Justice Department and the FBI into the case. "This crime is an affront to decent Americanism," Truman's attorney general, Tom Clark, announced. "Only due process of law sustains our claim to orderly self-government. I call upon all citizens to repudiate mob rule and to assist the authorities to bring these criminals to justice." Federal agents swarmed into Walton County with the aim of producing enough evidence for either a federal prosecution of civil rights violations (although this would almost certainly be futile before a Georgia jury) or, much more preferably, to enable Georgia authorities to prosecute the suspected parties.

But even for the highly skilled federal men, the going was tough. In a CIC tract written in the 1930s, Buck Kester had noted that as public attitudes changed and the fear of exposure had grown, spectacle lynching had become obsolete. In its place had arrived what he called the "underground lynching," one in which death was meted out to a victim in a swift, assured manner, by men who knew better than to call attention to their act, and who relied on the code of intimidation and silence in rural communities to evade prosecution. While the new form did away with the immolations and the more grotesque aspects of the crime, it substituted a new, frustrating degree of conspiracy and secretiveness.

In the end, the FBI interviewed 2,800 people in connection with the Monroe case, a large chunk of the population of Walton and Oconee counties. But like the state officials before them, the Bureau men soon realized there was no physical evidence linking any person to the crime and no one was willing to divulge information or identify any of the killers. "We were the most unpopular people who ever invaded Walton County," an FBI agent later said. One suspect, a tavern owner named Lester Little, was picked up because he resembled Harrison's description of the mob's leader, but Little had to be released when Harrison, the only witness, swore he had never seen him before. One hundred and six witnesses were paraded before a federal grand jury, and much testimony was heard, but in the end not a single person was indicted. The state also refused to go forward with any prosecution, given the paucity of information and the complete lack of collaborating evidence. It was left to President Truman himself to deliver the understated final "verdict" on what had occurred: "When the mob gangs can take four people out and shoot them in the back, and everybody in the country is acquainted with who did the shooting and nothing is done about it, that country is in a pretty bad fix from the law enforcement standpoint."

Harry Truman of Independence, Missouri, was a curious friend to black Americans. Vehemently anti-Red, conservative on issues regarding social equality between the races, Truman nonetheless allowed incidents like the Monroe killings and other violence toward black veterans to push him toward initiating some of the boldest federal civil rights initiatives since the Grant administration. Held in eternal contempt by W.E.B. Du Bois for having authorized the dropping of the atomic bombs on Hiroshima and Nagasaki, he was wooed by Walter White, who believed Truman uniquely equipped by circumstances and experience to take advantage of the postwar lessening of racial intolerance.

As early as his 1940 race for the Senate, Truman, grandson of a Confederate soldier, let it be known that he believed "in the brotherhood of man; not merely the brotherhood of white men, but the brotherhood of all men before the law." As president, he surprised many liberals and blacks with his willingness to sponsor forward-looking policies on race, including the first U.S. Commission on Civil Rights and the creation of a permanent Fair Employment Practices Commission (FEPC) to safeguard standards of equality in hiring, an effort he backed for years but that ultimately failed after it was fought tooth and nail by Southerners, who deemed it "communistic."

On June 29, 1947, he became the first president of the United States to address a gathering of the NAACP. With a beaming Walter White standing at his side at the Lincoln Memorial, Truman called for federal action against lynching, an end to the poll tax, and equality in employment and education. He told the black and white faces gathered before him, "Many of our people still suffer the indignity of insult, the narrowing fear of intimidation, and, I regret to say, the threat of physical and mob violence. . . . We cannot wait another decade or another generation to remedy these evils. We must work, as never before, to cure them now."

"The applause when he finished was hearty but not overwhelming," White later recalled. "I thought again of Lincoln—of the cool response which had been accorded the Gettysburg Address. I did not believe that Truman's speech possessed the literary quality of Lincoln's speech but in some respects it had been a more courageous one in its specific condemnation of evils based upon race prejudice which had too long disgraced America, and its call for immediate action against them."

One of the first indications of Truman's serious intent was his administration's October 1947 publication of *To Secure These Rights,* a series of findings and recommendations that called for the establishment of a permanent Commission on Civil Rights, new laws to address discrimination in voting, and a federal antilynching act. Above all, he admonished Americans to live and work together regardless of race. The book noted the detrimental effect of lynch law on the nation, saying, "Where the administration of justice is discriminatory, no man can be sure of security. . . . [Society] cannot permit human beings to be imprisoned or killed in the absence of due process of law without degrading its entire fabric." It also addressed the disastrous psychological impact of mob violence on the black community, observing that "The almost complete immunity from punishment enjoyed by lynchers is merely a striking form of the broad and general immunity from punishment enjoyed by whites in many communities for less extreme offenses against Negroes. Moreover, lynching is the ultimate threat by which his inferior status is driven home to the Negro."

To Secure These Rights was as strong a message against racial discrimination and race hatred as had ever come from the federal government. And Truman returned to these themes in a special civil rights message to Congress the following February, calling for an end to discrimination in jobs and labor unions, and in interstate travel. "If we wish to inspire the peoples of the world whose freedom is in jeopardy, if we wish to restore hope to those who have already lost their civil liberties, if we wish to fulfill the promise that is ours," Truman said, "we must correct the remaining imperfections in our practice of democracy."

The mandate *To Secure These Rights* handed down was poorly received by conservative elements, especially Southern Democrats. At the 1948 Democratic National Convention in Philadelphia, which nominated him for president, Truman tried to offer an olive branch to the Southerners by agreeing to revert to the far more tepid civil rights platform that had attended FDR's last run for office in 1944. But Truman's peace offering was hijacked by a group of young Democratic party activists, the liberal Americans for Democratic Action (ADA), led by Minneapolis mayor Hubert Humphrey. The Minnesotan appreciated better than Truman that liberals, many of whom were in 1948 flocking to former vice president Henry Wallace's Progressive party, expected dramatic action from the Democratic party on civil rights. In place of the 1944 platform the ADA forced the party to adopt a more vigorous civil rights platform that included the far-reaching items Truman had promised the NAACP at the Lincoln Memorial the previous summer. Humphrey, exuberantly taking command of the moment, told the convention delegates, "There are those who say to you—we are rushing this issue of civil rights. I say we are a hundred and seventy-two years too late. . . . The time has arrived for the Democratic Party to get out of the shadow of states' rights and walk forthrightly into the bright sunshine of human rights." His address was greeted with open disdain by the Southern delegations. When the convention, swept up by Humphrey's eloquence, narrowly voted its approval of the new platform, the Mississippi delegation and half of the Alabama delegation, led by Birmingham police commissioner Eugene "Bull" Connor, rose and walked out.

Almost directly from Philadelphia the disenchanted Southerners went to Birmingham, where in a rousing convention of their own breakaway party—the States Rights party, or, as it came to be known, the Dixiecrats—they denounced the Democrats' civil rights agenda and the mongrelization of the white race, and defied U.S. troops to enforce desegregation in their homeland. They nominated North Carolina senator Strom Thurmond for president and Fielding Wright, the governor of Mississippi, for vice president on the States Rights party ticket. Their own platform made it clear how far Southerners stood apart from the Humphrey brand of idealism. In a section devoted to defending the poll tax, it explained:

> The negro is a native of a tropical climate where fruits and nuts are plentiful and where clothing is not required for protection against the weather. . . . The essentials of society in the jungle are few and do not include the production, transportation and marketing of goods. [Thus] his racial constitution has been fashioned to exclude any idea of voluntary cooperation on his part.

After the business of the Dixiecrat convention was complete, enthusiastic delegates adjourned to Birmingham's Tutwiler Hotel where, partying late into the night amid rebel yells and free-flowing liquor, the guests constructed a dummy made to look like the president of the United States, put a sign around its neck that read TRUMAN KILLED BY CIVIL-RIGHT (sic) and symbolically "lynched" it from a balcony over Twentieth Street.

To the delight of the many Democrats who feared the Dixiecrat walkout would frighten Truman into downplaying action on civil rights, the president struck back courageously. In late July 1948 he signed two executive orders—one desegregating the U.S. armed forces, the other outlawing discrimination in federal employment—thus in one stroke stealing an issue from his Progressive competitor, former vice president Wallace, and kicking dirt in the eyes of the already livid Dixiecrats. Leslie Dunbar, head of the Southern Regional Council, characterized Truman's civil rights policies in the late 1940s as the repeal of the Compromise of 1877, the trade-off that ended Reconstruction and restored management of the nation's "Negro Problem" to the former slave states. It was this resumption—"presumption," most Southerners would call it—by the North of the role of protector of the country's black minority that had spurred the Dixiecrat exodus.

Ironically, Truman's "accidental" years as president, from 1945 to 1948, included his most impressive strides in civil rights. After being elected in his own right in the legendary election of 1948, when Truman squelched the Dixiecrat threat and narrowly defeated the presumed Republican victor, New York governor Thomas E. Dewey, he ran into greatly stiffening resistance in Congress from the Dixiecrat bloc, which had garnered only 1.5 million votes in the election but remained a potent force. The Dixiecrats torpedoed many of Truman's good works—the permanent FEPC, antilynching legislation, and measures to end the poll tax. The last effort at a federal antilynching bill, launched in 1948 by New Jersey Republican representative Clifford Case in the House and Democratic senators Robert Wagner of New York and Wayne Morse of Oregon in the Senate, was abandoned the next year after running head-on into the usual Southern filibuster. (A bill offered by New Yorkers Joseph Gavagan and Hamilton Fish in 1940 had met a similar fate.) And increasingly Truman was sidetracked by foreign affairs related to the war in Korea and mounting fears about communism after it was learned that Russia had the atomic bomb. As important as the desegregation orders, *To Secure These Rights,* and other advances were, perhaps most significant, Truman's biographer David McCullough suggests, was Truman's general contribution to the public mentality and discourse on the subject of racial equality. "He had," says McCullough, "done more than any President since Lincoln to awaken American conscience to the issues of civil rights."

In contrast, for the South the Dixiecrat revolt of 1948 proved a tragic misstep, as unfortunate as it probably was unavoidable. Born of obstinacy, it helped concretize a Southern defiance that would further divide the South from American life for the next generation, and necessitate a long and bloody struggle of protest, controversial court rulings, and race-related violence. The Dixiecrat retrenchment was a paramount failure of regional leadership at a time when courage and vision were most required. "It was not the multiplicity of Southern common folks who failed; rather it was their leaders, utterly and completely," historian John Egerton has observed. "They were the ones who defied Truman with so much vehemence, and stirred such a spirit of rebellion in the general population, and gave people outside the South evidence to reinforce their uninformed and stereotypical views about Southerners in general."

In the determined resistance the region would offer in the coming years, lynching would play its customary role as a form of terrorism to keep blacks in line. But because lynchings had become somewhat rare and were widely viewed as anachronistic, their occurrence now brought swift national denuciation, and helped to convince many Americans the South was once again carrying the country toward some form of cataclysm.

During the war, a novel about vigilantism caught the imagination of the American public. *The Ox-Bow Incident* by Walter van Tilburg Clark was the story of the lynching of three innocent men suspected as murderers and cattle rustlers in the Old West. The vigilante mob that takes their lives, the novel reveals, is driven by conformity and, ultimately, cowardice. "What I was most afraid of was not the German Nazis," the author explained, "but that ever-present element in any society which can always be led to act the same way. What I wanted to say was: It can happen here."

For many Americans, the disturbing parallel between European fascism and homegrown mobbism had perhaps its most literal manifestation in late summer 1949, when hundreds of American "patriots" assaulted concertgoers at two open-air performances featuring Paul Robeson outside Peekskill, New York. The fact that mob violence could occur within forty miles of the United Nations Building, far from its usual abode in Georgia or Mississippi, seemed to verify Clark's admonition. It *could* happen here.

Robeson, the renowned actor, baritone, human rights advocate, and expatriate (he had lived in London and in the Soviet Union for much of the late 1930s) had recently upset many of his countrymen with seemingly Moscow-friendly remarks he'd given at the Congress of World Partisans for Peace in Paris. Under the Smith Act, enacted in 1940, Congress had outlawed groups that advocated the overthrow of the U.S. government, and more recently Attorney General Tom Clark had placed the Communist party on a list of subversive organizations and authorized the arrest of numerous party leaders. There was anxiety among Americans that such global peace enterprises as the Paris meeting, however humanitarian the tone of their preachings, were actually Communist-inspired, and aimed at diminishing America's stature and resolve. Both Robeson and Du Bois, who was in attendance at the same conference, would suffer for the rest of their lives for their affiliation with such organizations.

Onstage at the conference, Robeson stated that his interest was in working for world peace; then, speaking of the "white workers from Europe" and the "millions of blacks" who had built America, he vowed: "And we shall not put up with any hysterical raving that urges us to make war on anyone. Our will to fight for peace is strong. We shall not make war on anyone. We shall not make war on the Soviet Union." His comments were garbled and misrepresented in the American press. He was incorrectly quoted as having compared the government of the United States to that of Hitler and Goebbels, and of recommending that black Americans never fight on behalf of the United States, a nation that oppressed them, against the Soviet Union, which treated blacks with fairness and dignity. At home, Robeson was vilified as a traitor.

The Peekskill area of Westchester County where Robeson's concert was to be held was rife for ideological conflict. It held a broad conservative working class whose lives and economy had faltered with the decline of the area's once-thriving Hudson River towns. However, because of its proximity to New York City and its river views, it had become a haven for artists, writers, and radicals, particularly during the summer, when Peekskill's year-round population of eighteen thousand residents blossomed to thirty thousand. Relations had been less than cordial recently between the townspeople and the seasonal visitors, whom the locals derided as "subway cowboys."

The concert scheduled for the Lakeland Acres picnic grounds outside Peekskill on August 27, 1949, was to be the fourth annual summer performance by Robeson, and was intended as a benefit for the Harlem chapter of the Civil Rights Congress (CRC), a legal-defense group formed in 1946 in a merger between the International Labor Defense and the National Federation for Constitutional Liberties. In 1948 William L. Patterson, a leading black Communist and former head of the ILD, as well as an old friend of Paul Robeson's, became executive secretary of the CRC and set out to make it, like the ILD, an activist force for racial justice.

Local officials and veterans' groups, most prominently the American Legion, gave notice they would stage a "patriotic demonstration" consisting of peaceful picketing outside the Robeson concert. The Peekskill *Evening Star* picked up the anti-Robeson chant that had been heard in the nation's papers that spring, making it clear that "the traitor and his followers" were not welcome. "Within the past several months, Robeson himself has turned violently and loudly pro-Russian," commented the *Star,* and quoted a former Communist who had stated at a HUAC hearing that Robeson "was ambitious to become 'the Black Stalin.' "

"The time for tolerant silence that signifies approval is running out," warned the *Star.* "Peekskill wants no rallies that support iron curtains . . . no matter how sweet the music."

On Saturday, August 27, right-wing demonstrators, many of whom had been drinking, stormed into the concert grounds and attacked the hundred or so people who had gathered to picnic before the concert, including numerous families. Caught with the picnickers were thirty-five or forty volunteers who had come early to set up the bandstand and folding chairs. Using rocks, clubs, and fists, the demonstrators staged several assaults on the crowd. A small number of police were on hand but stood by and made no effort to intervene as the mob cursed their adversaries as "Commies and Jews" and proclaimed: "We're Hitler's boys. We're going to get Robeson. Lynch Robeson! Give us Robeson!" At least three times concert workers braved the gauntlet to get out to a pay phone and place calls to the state police, but no help was forthcoming. A later investigation found that, despite the obvious threat of violence and preconcert requests from the Robeson forces for adequate police protection, only six officers had been detailed to the concert site.

The singer himself never showed up. Like many others attempting to get to the concert, Robeson arrived to find a mob blocking the road into the picnic grounds; intercepted by Patterson of the CRC, he was quickly escorted away to safety.

The writer Howard Fast, known for his novels about American history and "citizen heroes" such as Tom Paine, was among those defending the stage area. He recalled that "there were well over 500 of the fascists, and in the next half hour they attacked us twice without breaking our ranks. They had worked themselves into a screaming alcoholic frenzy, and they repeated their threats that no one would leave the picnic grounds alive." He remembered:

> Most of them were prosperous-appearing men, well set up, well-dressed, real estate men, grocery clerks, lunch counter attendants, filling station hands and more of the kind. . . . Throw in a couple of hundred "decent" citizens, one hundred teenagers whose heads were filled with anti-Communist sewage; add one hundred pillars of the local Catholic church, half a hundred college students home on vacation, half a hundred workers drawn along, and two or three hundred of the sweepings of filth of that whole Hudson River section, and you have a good idea of what we faced there that night.

Fast, who had only reluctantly agreed to assist with the concert in the first place, now found himself looked to as a "military" leader in charge of the defense because he "had written many books in which people did things in times like this." The predicament seemed as surreal as it did frightening. "It was still daylight; the world of the Hudson River Valley was still bathed in a golden glow; we were still people who had come to hear a concert."

When twilight fell, the floodlights illuminating the site were doused, and those trapped inside the grounds saw that several crosses were burning on the surrounding hills. It was never ascertained who was behind the cross-burnings; the CRC blamed the Ku Klux Klan, while Peekskill police said they had been the work of mischievous teenagers. Later, after a barrage of grapefruit-size rocks, the mob attacked again, backing the remaining defenders to the bandstand, where a vicious hand-to-hand skirmish ensued before the mob withdrew to build a huge bonfire, into which it hurled concert programs, pamphlets, and chairs. Eventually, at ten o'clock, after two hours of off-and-on assaults, the state police arrived and the mob dispersed.

The damage was significant. Numerous cars had been overturned and thirteen people required medical attention. Fast termed the physical attack he and the others had barely weathered "the most monstrous and inconceivable mass lynching ever attempted in the northern states of America, not simply a riot or a mob demonstration, but a calculated attack to kill two hundred people." Many who experienced the assaults cited the flaming crosses and the Hitleresque "book-burning" as particularly unsettling affronts, worse in a way for their awful symbolism than the hand-to-hand combat itself.

On Sunday morning, August 28, the riot was the talk of the New York City area. The local veterans' groups were all innocence, distancing themselves from those who had overturned the cars and pummeled concertgoers. Westchester County district attorney George Fanelli went on record as saying that the evidence indicated that this "most regrettable" incident had been provoked by Robeson's fans. In turn, outraged liberal supporters of the concert hastily organized as the Westchester Committee for Law and Order and drew up a resolution declaring: "We refuse to abandon any section of the United States to organized hoodlums. Our freedom and civil rights are at stake." Joined by many other Westchester residents, they immediately reextended the invitation to Robeson to come to Peekskill and sing.

On Tuesday, August 30, eight thousand people filled the Golden Gate Ballroom at 140th Street and Lenox Avenue in New York City to hear speaker after speaker denounce the mob violence. Leaflets entitled "The Ku Klux Klan held a LYNCHING PARTY in Peekskill Yesterday" were distributed. There was anger that a figure as beloved as Robeson had actually been in physical danger—had been targeted by a mob—and a thunderous roar of affirmation was heard when he mounted the stage. Robeson told his listeners that Peekskill was "a preview of American storm troopers in action" and vowed, "This means from now on out we take the offensive. *We* take it! We'll have our meetings and our concerts all over these United States. . . . I want my friends to know, in the South, in Mississippi, all over the United States, that I'll be there with my concerts, and I'll be in Peekskill, too." In retrospect it seems remarkable that, with the almost certain promise of further violence, the CRC and Robeson would choose to return to Peekskill. But as fervent as were postwar feelings about communism, they were matched by an equally strident anti-fascism, a deeply felt moral imperative to resist anything reminiscent of the European scourge.

Tensions quickly escalated, the American Legion readying itself for the Sunday, September 4, rescheduled concert with the boast that it had run "that nigger Robeson" out of town once and would do so again. Bumper stickers appeared bearing the message "Wake Up, America—Peekskill Did!," an expression of the community's pride at having drawn the line against "Commie infiltration." Vincent J. Boyle, head of the "Americanization Committee" of several Peekskill posts of the Legion, told reporters that as many as thirty thousand patriots would march in a peaceful demonstration outside the concert.

Of Boyle's thirty thousand "patriots," only about a thousand showed up, and they were easily overwhelmed by the twenty-five thousand concertgoers who streamed into Peekskill. Several hundred state troopers protected the entrance to the grounds where the patriotic demonstrators congregated, shouting racial and anti-Semitic epithets at people in arriving vehicles. Inside, the audience was treated to folk and light classical music offerings, then Robeson took the stage to a loud ovation, telling those assembled, "I am here to applaud *you!*" He sang "Let My People Go," "Old Man River," and a short program of spirituals and labor songs.

The concert proceeded virtually without incident, although trouble waited outside. The mob, unable to assault the patrons inside because of the tightened security, spread themselves along the country roads leading away from the site and, armed with rocks, bottles, and other missiles, bombarded cars and buses as they departed the concert.

"We saw children, women bleeding—blood all over the road," Robeson's son, Paul junior, later said. "The road was eventually slick with blood, just like a war." He recalled that entire families, "age ten to age seventy," appeared to have turned out to attack the concertgoers, "screaming epithets, throwing rocks, expressing that hate." Police and state troopers joined in the harassment. Some of the most disturbing news photographs of the violence are those showing fourteen- and fifteen-year-old girls standing side by side with uniformed lawmen as together they scream and spit at the Robeson fans. "It was a very tense atmosphere," veteran New York reporter Gabe Pressman admitted. "I'd been in the war, been in combat, and I was shocked. I didn't think there was that much hatred in the country."

The state police, visibly taxed by the situation and overwhelmed by the number of concertgoers, which had far exceeded expectations, refused to intervene in the rock-throwing attacks and instead conducted rather brutal and unnecessary "searches" of some of the cars leaving the grounds. Witnesses claimed the police at one point became so frenzied they began beating the automobiles as though they were living things. One recalled:

> A group of cops and deputies set upon me and the car occupants in the most violent and vicious manner that I have ever experienced. One grabbed me by the collar and throat at the same time and threw me to the ground face down in the dirt. . . . My shirt and suit were badly torn. Another cop dragged me to my feet and said, "Get in and get going, you red bastard!" Another, who was obviously a captain of police, said, "Go back to Jew town, and if we ever catch you up here again we'll kill you!"

Another person made it onto a departing bus, but then:

> A group of hoodlums came directly in front of the bus and threw a huge boulder in. This boulder struck my left hand and when I looked down I saw that the third joint of my middle finger was barely hanging by one tendon. Witnessing this whole incident were state troopers who were laughing. As the stones kept coming, all I could think of was: This is not America. This is Nazi Germany. I don't want to live like this.

Well after dark, cars and buses limped into the Bronx and Harlem to disgorge passengers with bloodied heads, hands, and arms cut by flying glass, and tales of narrow escapes from roadside mobs that had seemed intent on killing them.

In the riot's aftermath the two sides rendered far different verdicts as to where blame and responsibility should lie. District Attorney Fanelli submitted a report to Governor Dewey exonerating the state troopers and police, and the *Star* saluted the American Legion "patriots" and compared them to the brave vigilantes who had dumped English tea into Boston Harbor. Peekskill mayor John N. Schneider stated that culpability for the violence "rests solely on the Robesonites as they insisted on coming to a community where they weren't wanted." Dewey, after hearing from Westchester officials, concurred that "followers of Red totalitarianism, which teaches violence and the suppression of individual liberty," had been chiefly responsible for the melee. No one was ever prosecuted or punished for the violence.

The Peekskill affair quickly earned the opprobrium of the nation. "A mob of hoodlums has run wild," observed the *New York Post*. *The Christian Science Monitor* dubbed what had taken place "the Fascist pattern of violent suppression . . . the Ku Klux Klan pattern of lynch law." Many scored the local, county, and state police for allowing the rioting to occur, if not abetting it.

The intensity of the violence at Peekskill had caught Americans by surprise. Feelings of intense anxiety about encroaching communism had, it seemed, coalesced with fears of the growing black demands for advancement and equality, two strains that were uniquely combined in the person of Robeson. A Communist sympathizer, he was also a strong, unbowed black man with tremendous charisma who embodied the rising confidence of America's black minority. The obstinacy of the CRC crowd in resisting the Peekskill demonstrators was due in large measure to the intense loyalty people felt toward Robeson, who was seen as a kind of twentieth-century incarnation of Frederick Douglass. As Fast observed at the time, the fact that the "specific and stinking vileness which has sent the stench of American lynching into every corner of the earth . . . was directed against the one great man who had broken through their bonds and bondage, who would not be jimcrowed, who would not hang his head, who would not crawl and who would not be bought off," was completely unacceptable.

Sadly, though Robeson remained heroically defiant, he would be severely harassed and Red-baited for years to come, and his concert bookings after the Peekskill disturbance fell off dramatically. He went, as one account of the period notes, "from being the most popular black entertainer in the country to a singer who performed in church basements."

The battle by the Civil Rights Congress and other liberal organizations against Southern "lynch law" justice would center, in 1951, on two Southern states eager to put to death black men convicted of sexual crimes against white women. Advocates for the condemned would argue that rates of execution for black men far exceeded those for whites, and that capital punishment for rape, particularly if only black men were receiving such sentences, amounted to nothing less than an authorized lynching. In one of the cases, there was strong evidence that the sexual relationship had been consensual, heightening the sense that the courts were only mimicking the actions of a mob.

The first instance involved a group of defendants known as the Martinsville Seven and began on the afternoon of Saturday, January 8, 1949, when Ruby Floyd, a thirty-two-year-old white woman, entered a black neighborhood called Cherrywood in Martinsville, Virginia. Floyd was a familiar sight in Cherrywood, where she peddled used clothing, garden vegetables, and copies of *The Watchtower*, the publication of the Jehovah's Witnesses. At least one black friend who saw her that day advised her it was too close to dark for a lone white woman to be wandering the streets, but Floyd remained, seeking the home of a woman who owed her money for a dress. Several hours later Floyd was found staggering down the street, bleeding and disheveled, saying she had been gang-raped by several black men.

Investigating police arrested and obtained confessions from seven Cherrywood men—John Clabon Taylor, J. L. Hairston, Frank Hairston, Jr., Joe Henry Hampton, James Hairston, Booker T. Millner, and Francis Grayson. When all were quickly convicted of rape and sentenced to death, the CRC entered the case, appealing the convictions on procedural grounds. All the defendants had repudiated at trial the confessions wrung out of them by police, and defense counsel's request for a change of venue had been, in the CRC's view, improperly denied. Even if the confessions were taken at face value, there appeared to be enough inconsistency in the men's varying accounts of what had occurred to mitigate the severe sentences they'd received. For instance, only some of the defendants admitted to waylaying the victim, while others said they had come along as the rape was in progress; some had joined in, others had not. Two of the defendants said they had tried to have intercourse with Floyd but didn't because they could not "get hard." The jury, which by Virginia law was allowed to choose the punishment in addition to reaching a verdict, could sentence a convicted rapist to anywhere from five years imprisonment to death, and yet the jurymen, without apparently factoring in the varying degrees of guilt, had given the death penalty to all seven defendants.

In its appeal the CRC lawyers did not hesitate to introduce questions about Ruby Floyd's character. They said she had previously spent time in a mental asylum, had been deserted by her husband, and that after testifying against the Martinsville Seven had disappeared and was rumored to be institutionalized again in a neighboring state. But the effort led nowhere, probably because in court significant attention had been given to the defendants' due-process rights, the trial judge even stating at the outset that "this case must and will be tried in such a way as not to disturb the kindly feeling now locally existing between the races. It must be tried as though both parties were members of the same race."

Unable to get the case retried, CRC attorneys turned to an innovative strategy to win stays of execution for the condemned. Citing a long-existing pattern of racial bias, the CRC found that between 1908 and 1949 the state of Virginia had executed forty-five black men for rape, but not a single white. Two white Richmond policemen recently convicted of raping a black woman had been sentenced to only seven years in prison. Even people convicted of a crime, the attorneys reasoned, were entitled to be free of discrimination on racial grounds under the equal-protection clause of the Fourteenth Amendment, and Virginia's pattern of sentencing for rape was quite clearly biased and unjust.

The facts the CRC had uncovered were extremely disturbing, as their claim was groundbreaking. This was the first time to anyone's knowledge that attorneys anywhere in the United States had used this line of argument in seeking to obtain clemency. The Virginia Supreme Court, however, was unmoved, refusing to consider the request and deeming the statistical evidence worthless. Justices even accused the CRC lawyers of needlessly introducing race into the case. And the state's high court saw difficulty in invoking the equal-protection clause of the Fourteenth Amendment to repudiate the rights of local juries to choose punishment. On these grounds the U.S. Supreme Court also refused to hear the case.

Beyond its efforts in the legal realm, the CRC fought for the Martinsville Seven with the strategy known as "mass defense," the kind of all-fronts public crusade pioneered earlier by the ILD that included demonstrations, picketing, and public rallies. Editorials were written, rallies and candlelight vigils held, demonstrators circled the White House, and CRC lawyers appealed directly to Governor John S. Battle. These manifold efforts were fruitless in the end. In the first week of February 1951, all seven of the condemned were put to death in Virginia's electric chair. The CRC had not been able to save the Martinsville Seven, although the exposure of racial bias in the distribution of death sentences opened the eyes of legal rights crusaders to yet another way in which supposedly "fair and proper" court proceedings "lynched" minority defendants.

The injustice of the Martinsville executions—the electrocution of seven human beings following questionable judicial rulings—lingered heavily in the atmosphere that spring, as the CRC worked desperately to void yet another imminent death sentence, this one hanging over an innocent black man in Mississippi, Willie McGee.

McGee's nightmare had begun six years earlier, on November 3, 1945, when a Laurel woman, Mrs. Willametta Hawkins, gave the police a description of a man she said had raped her in her own house. She had been up most of the night with a new baby, and had finally gone to sleep with the infant next to her at four A.M. as her husband, Troy, and another child slept in a nearby room. It was then, she said, that a black intruder with kinky hair and wearing a white T-shirt entered through a window and raped her, threatening to cut her throat if she screamed. Neighbors said they had seen an unfamiliar truck parked outside the Hawkins house and Laurel police believed they had their man when, following up on information they had gathered about the vehicle, they arrested McGee, a delivery driver and father of four.

McGee was held incommunicado for a month, during which time police said he confessed to the assault on Mrs. Hawkins. At his first trial, in the Jones County courthouse in Laurel, the jury arrived at a verdict of guilty after deliberating for two and a half minutes. The CRC then entered the case, with attorneys Bella Abzug and John Coe able to convince the Mississippi Supreme Court to reverse the conviction on the grounds that McGee could not have had a fair trial in Jones County due to the strong public feeling over the crime. A second conviction in Hattiesburg in neighboring Forrest County was also reversed because the CRC showed that blacks were excluded from the jury pool. At a third trial, returned to Laurel, McGee was again convicted. This time the local hostility had shifted from the defendant to his out-of-town "commie" lawyers, and after threats on the life of CRC attorney John R. Poole, who left Mississippi before he had even delivered a summation, McGee, sitting alone at the defense table, was again convicted and sentenced to death.

The U.S. Supreme Court stayed McGee's execution three times so that the CRC could make appeals to the Mississippi Supreme Court. In July 1950, CRC lawyers Abzug and Emmanuel Bloch—inspired by the pleas of the Martinsville Seven's advocates in Virginia—pointed out to the court that there was no record that any white man had ever been executed for rape in Mississippi, and that of the 108 people executed for any reason between 1930 and 1948, only 18 had been white. As in Virginia, though, the argument did not take.

With McGee's fate seemingly fixed, CRC attorneys launched a decidedly risky appeal to the Mississippi high court, claiming the conviction could not stand because the state had not proven a rape had actually occurred. In effect, what McGee and his lawyers were saying was that the relationship between the defendant and Mrs. Hawkins had been consensual.

The justices reacted with vehement disfavor. Deeming the CRC appeal a "revolting insinuation," the chief justice assured McGee's representatives:

> If you believe, or are implying, that any white woman in the South, who was not completely down and out, degenerate, degraded and corrupt, could have anything to do with a Negro man, you not only do not know what you are talking about, but you are insulting us, the whole South. You do not know the South, and do not realize that we could not entertain such a proposition; that we could not even consider it in court.

McGee's predicament amounted to a strange inversion of the adage "the truth will set you free." The truth might well convince the world of his innocence, but in Mississippi it could only seal his fate more permanently. McGee had been well aware of the inherent irony of his situation all along, as had his lawyers. His defenders to greater and lesser degrees had been reluctant to attempt the strategy of telling the full truth until he had lost the third trial and all other legal remedies appeared exhausted. "I have given this account of the affair only in more detail and with additional circumstances to the lawyers who tried my case in the Court house before the jury," McGee stated in an affidavit the CRC submitted to the Mississippi Supreme Court. "But they told me to keep my mouth shut and not say anything about it because it would endanger me and hurt my case, and Mr. Poole told me if I said anything about it I'd get both him and myself killed."

One of McGee's best advocates proved to be his wife, Rosalee. She believed Willie had tried to break off with Mrs. Hawkins but that the white woman had blackmailed him by threatening to report him, knowing full well what consequences would result. According to Rosalee, McGee met Mrs. Hawkins when he and her husband had worked together at the Masonite Corporation in Laurel in the 1930s. Mr. and Mrs. Hawkins had hired him to do odd jobs around the house and in their yard. The clandestine relationship had begun in 1942, as he explained:

I became well acquainted with Mrs. Troy Hawkins and one day after I worked there on and off for about a year I was waxing floors with her in the house and she showed a willingness to be familiar and let me have intercourse with her in the back room. After that she frequently sent for me to do work which gave opportunities for intercourse which she accepted, and on occasions after dark she took me in her automobile out to a place near the graveyard where we had intercourse.

After their first sexual encounter, Mrs. Hawkins would visit McGee at a gas station where he worked and once left him a note stuck into the nozzle of a gas hose. She would also come to the McGees' house and inquire for him. Rosalee became suspicious after an incident in which Mrs. Hawkins drove up when they were walking home from a movie theater and attempted to coax him to go off with her in the car.

So all of a sudden Mrs. Hawkins come out of an alley and she says to Willie, "I got my car over here. Come on into my car with me." I got so mad I said, "What's that!" And I started to pull him away. And Willie himself he told her, "Go away. This is my wife. I'm with my wife." So she says to Willie out loud, "Don't fool with no Negro whores."

Rosalee, who had never been out of Mississippi before, went on a national speaking tour sponsored by the CRC. She confided to the writer Jessica Mitford, a CRC member who hosted her in Oakland, California, that if her husband was put to death he would be the third man in her family to be killed by Mississippi racists. She claimed to have watched her nephew lynched, and said one of her cousins had been executed in the state's portable electric chair. "People who don't know the South don't know what would have happened to Willie if he told her no," Rosalee told Mitford. "Down South, you tell a woman like that no, and she'll cry rape anyway. So what else could Willie do? That's why I never got angry at Willie." When Willie finally broke with Mrs. Hawkins in early 1945, Rosalee said, Troy Hawkins learned of the affair. After a ferocious spat between husband and wife that spilled out into the street in front of their house, Mrs. Hawkins called the police and said she had been raped by a black man with kinky hair.

The CRC fanned the McGee case into an international cause on the scale of Sacco and Vanzetti and the Scottsboro Boys, with rallies, leaflets, and imploring telegrams to high officials. As in the Scottsboro case, the CRC's legal appeal put Southern authorities in the embarrassing and cynical position of insisting on carrying out an execution of a black human being because consensual relationships between black men and white women did not officially exist in the state of Mississippi. To outsiders, such a position appeared not only hypocritical but inhumanely cruel.

Willie McGee's most colorful supporter was undoubtedly Josephine Baker, the American expatriate who had achieved world fame as a dancer, film star, and human rights advocate. She was a chief financial backer of Rosalee McGee's efforts to travel across the country to tell of her husband's plight while raising money for his legal defense. Baker, who as a child had survived the East St. Louis race riot of 1917, was deeply troubled by the plight of black Americans, as it contrasted so strongly with her own experiences in Europe. When Baker embarked on a U.S. performing tour in late 1950 she was warmly received by audiences. So great was her popularity that she was able to stipulate, in Southern auditoriums, that her audiences not have to sit segregated.

When, in early 1951, it became increasingly evident that Mississippi intended to carry out McGee's execution, Jessica Mitford and a handful of other West Coast CRC members traveled to Jackson with the idea to go door to door attempting to gauge and perhaps influence public opinion on the case. The plan was audacious but naive, given long-standing Southern views about discussing sensitive racial questions with outsiders, and the women found the door-to-door canvassing unrewarding. Even though many people with whom they spoke agreed that McGee should not be executed, almost all confided that they could not dare articulate such a thought. Jackson, with its massive phobias about sexually monstrous black men, Communists, and its complete stifling of contradictory opinion, struck Mitford as a "veritable concentration camp of the mind," where decent people became "prisoners" of the dominant attitudes. Mitford and her colleagues were themselves demonized by a Jackson newspaper article announcing that "150 women" had descended on the community, and offered that police would be only too glad to come to the aid of any citizen who felt put upon by these "troublemakers."

"Those Joe Stalin loving people are working all over the state of Mississippi trying to bribe people into thinking that the negro did not get a fair trial," a letter to the Jackson *Daily News* complained. "People the time is ripe for we as a peace loving people to bring this wooly negro to justice and then those who care to follow his beastly act."

On their way home in March, Mitford and her friends scored a coup when they stopped in Oxford, home of the University of Mississippi, and tracked down novelist William Faulkner, who had been awarded the 1950 Nobel Prize in Literature. Mitford, timidly knocking on Faulkner's door in hopes of obtaining a quick statement of support for Willie McGee, found herself invited in to listen to Faulkner expound on the case for nearly two hours. The author, whose novel *Light in August* involves a forbidden sexual relationship between a black man and a white woman, thought the McGee frame-up a complete outrage. In going on record against McGee's impending execution, Faulkner joined the many other prominent people who had spoken out against it, including Albert Einstein, but as Mississippi's best-known citizen his opinion was potentially more important. (When Mitford returned to California she discovered that while she'd been chatting with Faulkner, some of his fellow Mississippians had poured molasses into her car's gas tank.)

The people of Jackson, in particular, where most of the legal machinations on McGee's behalf took place, had long resented the publicity generated by the case and the seemingly endless delays. They were accustomed to "justice" moving much faster. When a group of CRC-organized protesters arrived in May 1951, the *Daily News* printed the headline: "Communists Coming Here," and remarked, "For sublimated gall, triple-plated audacity, bold insolence and downright arrogance, this proposed invasion of the Capitol City of our state by a gang of Communists truly passes all comprehension. These invaders are just as much enemies of the United States government as are soldiers fighting under the Communist banner in Korea." CRC attorney Emmanuel Bloch charged the newspaper with making unnecessarily inflammatory statements, but a colleague, CRC attorney Aubrey Grossman, fared worse. He was one of three CRC men "mussed up," as the local paper termed it, by white thugs who forced their way into Grossman's hotel room. "They Deserved It—And More," read the cheery headline of an editorial about the incident.

Indeed, many newspapers in the state had not hesitated to suggest over the years that, if the CRC continued to block the execution, Mississippi's citizens might have a swifter, surer way of exacting McGee's punishment. Noted the Jackson *Daily News* after the issuance of yet another stay: "Paul Robeson, Negro singer and notorious Communist, who declares he prefers Russia to the United States, blew off his loud bazoo to the effect that the next step should be to get Willie McGee out of jail. It could happen—but not in the way Robeson is thinking about."

In Jackson on May 5, 1951, a prayer meeting on McGee's behalf by white women and local blacks was broken up by police, who arrested forty-three people and charged them with "conspiracy." Veteran Southern activist Anne Braden of Louisville told reporters and police: "We are here because we are determined that no more innocent men shall die in the name of protecting Southern white womanhood. We have been made a party to this injustice too long." Those arrested were booked and released only after agreeing to leave the state at once. The blacks had shown almost suicidal nerve in daring to protest side by side with white women on the streets of Jackson, and had to be accompanied to the train station by Braden and her colleagues in order to ensure they would not be assaulted.

The hours leading up to McGee's scheduled execution on May 8, 1951, saw frenzied activity from the CRC. Abzug begged the federal district court in Jackson for another stay on the grounds that a newly filed CRC lawsuit against Mississippi officials brought up new questions about the due process McGee had been granted at trial, and should be heard. The lawsuit alleged that McGee's original confession had been coerced, and that the state had refused to allow testimony to the effect that McGee and Mrs. Hawkins had a consensual relationship. It also said that a black woman named Hattie Johnson, at whose house McGee had been playing cards with several other men from eleven P.M. to six A.M. the night of the alleged crime, had not been allowed to testify as an alibi witness. In addition, the suit alleged that the state had allowed Mr. and Mrs. Hawkins to give perjured testimony—for example, Troy Hawkins testified that he had never seen Willie McGee before his arrest—and that the state had failed to protect the defense counsel at the third trial in Laurel, forcing CRC lawyer Poole to leave for his own safety, thus stranding McGee without representation for the latter part of the trial.

When federal district judge Sidney C. Mize denied the stay application, Abzug and fellow CRC lawyer Ernest Goodman went to the governor's mansion in Jackson to beseech Governor Fielding Wright and Attorney General J. P. Coleman, who were there with their wives playing bridge. Abzug reminded the governor that there was still considerable doubt that McGee was guilty of rape, and that in any case no white person had been executed for rape in Mississippi in seventy-five years. Wright heard Abzug out but refused to intervene, and returned to his game of cards.

Josephine Baker, New York congressman Vito Marcantonio, and others spent the evening of May 7 frantically calling and telegramming Supreme Court justices, President Truman, and other officials—all to no avail.

In Laurel, officials were completing preparations for the execution which, by Mississippi custom and law, was designed to resemble a lynching as closely as possible. In response to popular demand, official executions were carried out not at a prison, as in most other states, but in the same county courtroom where the condemned had been sentenced to death. To support this method of conducting legal executions while satisfying the community's interest in taking part, the state used a portable electric chair that, by 1951, had taken the lives of ninety people.

Long before midnight, the hour when the switch would be thrown, upwards of five hundred men, women, and children gathered on the lawn of the Jones County courthouse. Some young men and boys climbed into trees from which they could see the portable electric chair situated in the center of the courtroom. Inside, a composed Willie McGee smoked a cigar while having his head shaved. Finally, he told a black minister who had visited with him, "I am ready to go," handed the clergyman $7.25 to give to Rosalee, and took a seat in the chair before a party of fifty witnesses that included Troy Hawkins. After two massive charges of current were sent through him, no sign of life was visible. Witnesses reported that McGee died with his fists clenched and a single tear halfway down one cheek.

Out on the lawn, when the portable generator stopped humming, indicating that the electrocution had taken place, the crowd burst into cheers, then crushed forward in an effort to glimpse the corpse as it was removed from the building. At that exact moment, at a street vigil more than a thousand miles away in Harlem, the CRC's William Patterson announced: "Willie McGee, an innocent man, has been executed only because he was a Negro." There were prayers spoken, then a speaker read an oath "to avenge the death of Willie McGee" and to "fight to the end the lynch law in the United States." At his request, the crowd repeated the oath word for word.

A few days earlier, the condemned man had written to his wife:

Dear Rosalee,
    They are planning here to kill me and I don't know if you and the people will be able to save me. If I have to die, I want you to say goodbye to my mother and the children, and all the people who know it is wrong to kill a man because of his color. You know I am innocent. Tell the people again

and again I did not commit this crime. Tell them the real reason they are going to take my life is to keep the Negro down in the South. They can't do this if you and the children keep on fighting. Never forget to tell them why they killed their daddy. I know you won't fail me. Tell the people to keep on fighting.

                                    Your truly husband, Willie McGee

Josephine Baker told an audience in Detroit the night after the execution, "When Willie McGee died, a part of all American Negroes died a little." Later, while on tour in South America, she told a reporter, "The United States is not a free country. They treat Negroes as though they were dogs." Baker would soon be made to pay for her candor; like Paul Robeson she would be scorned by U.S. concert promoters and investigated by the authorities, although the main focus of her humiliation was an incident at the Stork Club in New York City on the night of October 16, 1951.

Baker and three white friends had dropped by for dinner after seeing the Broadway musical *South Pacific*. The actress Grace Kelly and other notables, including columnist Walter Winchell, were dining at nearby tables. Waiters, apparently at the order of club owner Sherman Billingsley, were deliberately slow and inefficient in waiting on her party, "that hiatus," James Weldon Johnson once wrote, "of which every Negro in the United States knows the meaning." After enduring more than an hour of such treatment Baker threw a tantrum and stormed out, claiming racial discrimination. She filed a police complaint against Billingsley and, with even greater recklessness, publicly took to task the powerful Winchell for not intervening on her behalf. Her charges made news all over the country ("Stork Supplies Fork but Holds Steak on La Bake" said the Chicago *Defender*). Winchell, who was proud of his reputation as a progressive on civil rights issues and took as a matter of course the gratitude of black leaders and black celebrities, did not take kindly to being labeled a hypocrite, particularly by a woman most renowned for dancing in a loincloth.

Through his column and radio show, which together were said to reach 50 million people, an infuriated Winchell began savaging Baker, questioning her patriotism and calling her "Josephine Baker riot inciter" and other names. He also wrote privately to the FBI's J. Edgar Hoover to suggest she was likely a Communist and required investigating. As a result of Winchell's campaign, her bookings fell off and she ultimately left the United States to tour in other countries and then return to France.

She was far from alone in this kind of rough treatment. During the 1950s outspoken black leaders and entertainers—particularly those with international access—were routinely monitored and harassed by the State Department. Indeed, anti-Red paranoia was so pronounced in mid-1951, with U.S. troops engaged in combat with Communists in Korea, that to a remarkable degree Americans were convinced that Willie McGee's death could be blamed exclusively on the CRC intervention in his case. The CRC had left Mississippi no choice in the matter, went the argument, since to grant clemency to McGee in the face of the CRC legal assault would be to back down, before the eyes of the entire world, to Communist agitation. Not only the reactionary Southern press gave voice to this idea, but also such mainstream publications as *Life* and *Time* and even progressive ones such as *The Nation*. The CRC, after all, was seriously tainted by current standards: it had defended Communist party leaders indicted under the Smith antisedition act, and had been officially labeled "subversive" by the attorney general. Even Eleanor Roosevelt scolded Aubrey Grossman in the weeks before McGee's execution, "If your organization would leave these cases to the National Association for the Advancement of Colored People the men would not have added suspicions aroused against them."

Given the prevailing national mood there was, from a practical perspective, ample truth to the notion that the CRC had brought greater public contempt and scrutiny to an already volatile situation. But it's equally true that without the CRC's involvement, Willie McGee would probably have been executed or lynched years earlier, since the NAACP was more likely to hesitate to enter cases where the innocence of the defendant and/or the denial of due process were not more abundantly clear. The CRC had no such trouble, because its guiding philosophy was that the criminal justice system was fundamentally unfair to black defendants. The brilliance of the CRC's effort in the Martinsville Seven case in Virginia was to show how racially biased was the meting out of death sentences. In the McGee case the key "success" of the defense efforts, despite the death of their client, was to have ultimately made audible the whispered narrative of consensual interracial sex that had been the real story behind too many Southern lynchings. Mississippi Supreme Court justices, no less than other Southerners before them, had cupped their hands over their ears so as to be certain not to hear, but the words at last had been spoken.

CHAPTER 12

Under Color of Law

Since Ida Wells began her one-woman crusade in 1892, Americans had employed a succession of methods to combat lynching—public exposure, appeals to elected officials, legislative reform at the state and federal levels, even sociological analysis. In the era of internationalism that followed the Second World War, the effort would come to include an appeal to newly formed global organizations and world opinion.

By the late 1940s, lynching was nowhere near the cataclysm it had been when Wells had begun her work. The number of recorded annual lynchings had fallen steadily during the Second World War, from five in 1940 to only two in 1944, then climbed briefly in the immediate postwar years as violence was directed at returning vets and those Southern blacks involved in voting rights work—the latter a trend that would continue into the 1950s and early 1960s. The last well-known spectacle lynching may have been the 1937 blowtorch killings in Duck Hill, Mississippi, although the atmosphere surrounding the legal execution of Willie McGee in 1951 would have been hard to distinguish from those earlier festivals of blood passion. Largely replacing the spectacle lynching was the so-called underground lynching, which if anything harkened back to the Ku Klux Klan murders of the nineteenth century in that stealth, secrecy, and the complete anonymity of the perpetrators were emphasized—both for security purposes and as a means of striking permanent fear into blacks. As might be expected in an age of ever-growing communication and TV and radio news, individual lynchings had gained an even greater power to shock, and with lynching itself on the wane, civil rights organizations and human rights groups began to express greater concern for lynchlike abuses by the courts and the police, such as the killing of black men in police custody.

Foreign opinion had played an important role in the antilynching fight since Wells toured England and Scotland in the mid-1890s. As recently as the campaign to save Willie McGee, U.S. embassies abroad, particularly in France, had been inundated with letters and telegrams pleading that Southern justice be averted and McGee's life spared. The same year as the McGee debacle, 1951, European news organizations had dispatched correspondents all the way to rural North Carolina to cover the so-called Eyeball Case, in which a seventeen-year-old white woman, Willie Jean Boswell, accused sharecropper Mack Ingram of looking at her "peculiarly," or "eyeballing" her, as he slowed down while driving a truck by her father's tobacco farm. The Europeans were intrigued that merely staring at a woman could put a man in serious legal jeopardy. In court, where he stood charged with "assault with attempt to commit rape," the jury hung after Ingram explained that he had only been stopping to ask Boswell's father about the possibility of borrowing a trailer.

Black Americans had long been grateful that the foreign press took an interest in U.S. racial inequities, although efforts at placing the cause of black Americans on the agendas of official international conclaves had been far less successful. One of the most memorable attempts was William Monroe Trotter's quixotic trip to the Paris peace conference that ended the First World War. Denied an official invitation, as well as a visa, he finagled some seaman's papers under an assumed name, crossed the Atlantic as a cook's assistant on a Le Havre–bound freighter, and was in Paris during the lengthy negotiations in spring and summer 1919. He wanted President Wilson to add to the "Fourteen Points" of international peace and reconciliation a fifteenth—"the elimination of civil, political, and judicial distinctions based on race or color in all nations for the new era of freedom everywhere"—but he had little success even getting close to the conference delegates, let alone Wilson himself, who had never forgiven him for their rancorous exchange at the White House several years earlier.

In the late 1940s, however, in the aftermath of Hiroshima, Dresden, and Bergen-Belsen, the concept of international law and the necessity for global cooperation on human rights was given great impetus. The Nuremberg Trials, the war crimes hearings of 1945–49 at which former Nazi and German military leaders were held accountable by the victorious allies for "crimes against peace" and "crimes against humanity," served to establish the dual principles that individuals were responsible for their own actions even when acting under orders of their government, and that the social, military, or political policies a nation directed or allowed could potentially be viewed as criminal.

In 1946 the National Negro Congress submitted its "Petition to the United Nations on Behalf of 13 Million Oppressed Negro Citizens of the United States of America," which called upon the fledgling global body to "mobilize the influence of all organized mankind" to honor "the stated purpose of the United Nations to promote and encourage respect for human rights and for fundamental freedoms for all." The next year, the UN Commission on Human Rights, with Eleanor Roosevelt as chairman, drafted the Universal Declaration of Human Rights, after which the NAACP petitioned the United Nations with *An Appeal to the World,* a dense booklet citing statistics and laws and edited by W.E.B. Du Bois, who wrote that "a discrimination practiced in the United States against her own citizens and to a large extent a contravention of her own laws, cannot be persisted in, without infringing upon the rights of the peoples of the world and especially upon the ideals and the work of the United Nations." The dilemma of black Americans deserved and qualified for international scrutiny, *An Appeal* asserted, because the number of blacks in the United States—13 million—equaled or exceeded the population of many individual UN member countries.

An Appeal to the World made a strong case for international condemnation of U.S. racial policy, although its tone was genial in comparison with a far more scathing indictment, *We Charge Genocide: The Historic Petition to the United Nations for Relief from a Crime of the United States Government Against the Negro People,* which Civil Rights Congress chief William Patterson and Paul Robeson presented to the United Nations in December 1951.

What *An Appeal to the World* and *We Charge Genocide* had in common was their determination to put America's racial injustices into a global context. American blacks, brought to the New World in bondage, were victims of seventeenth- and eighteenth-century European imperialism no less than dark-skinned peoples in Africa and Asia now engaged in the struggle to throw off the last vestiges of colonial rule, and their continued suffering should be viewed in such terms. But as its shocking title implied, *We Charge Genocide* did not stop at asking for the world's acknowledgment of black Americans' fight for equality; it placed their lot with that of minority populations throughout human history who had been targeted for extinction.

"We maintain," the resolution read, "that the oppressed Negro citizens of the United States, segregated, discriminated against and long the target of violence, suffer from genocide as the result of the consistent, conscious, unified policies of every branch of government.... The genocide of which we complain is as much a fact as gravity. The whole world knows of it. In one form or another it has been practiced for more than 300 years.... Its very familiarity disguises its horror. It is a crime so embedded in law, so explained away by specious rationale ... that even the conscience of the tender minded is sometimes dulled." *We Charge Genocide* took special aim at the Supreme Court, which "[f]or generations ... has avoided the obvious intent, the plain, unambiguous words, the clear, self-evident meaning of the 14th and 15th Amendments."

The CRC indictment and the sensational use of the relatively new term *genocide* were in direct response to the creation in 1948 by the United Nations of the Convention on the Prevention and Punishment of the Crime of Genocide. The convention was the brainchild of a Polish Jewish attorney named Rafael Lemkin, who in the 1930s haunted international legal conferences promoting his idea for a global concord of some kind that would address what he called "the crime of barbarity." After narrowly evading the Nazis' onslaught against Polish Jewry, in which forty-nine family members and relatives lost their lives, Lemkin came to the West, wrote a book about the Axis powers, and later served as an adviser to the American legal team at the Nuremberg trials. Hearing Winston Churchill in a postwar radio address describe German wartime atrocities as "this crime without a name," Lemkin coined the term *genocide*, which was used for the first time at Nuremberg in the indictments against Rudolf Hess, Albert Speer, Hermann Goering, and other top Nazis.

Back in the United States, living alone in a New York Upper West Side residence hotel, Lemkin single-handedly crusaded for the nascent United Nations to establish a Genocide Convention, which he also wrote. He defined genocide as a condition that "can be effected by physical, political, social, cultural, biological, economic and religious and moral oppression." Although hailed as potentially the UN's most important achievement to date and quickly ratified by twenty countries, the effort to gain American ratification of the convention languished in the U.S. Congress, despite President Truman's having sent the document to Capitol Hill with his full approval in June 1949. Unlike the circumstances surrounding Congress's rejection of U.S. membership in the League of Nations after the First World War, Congress had been a supportive partner to the fledgling United Nations. Its goodwill, however, did not extend to the Genocide Convention, for domestic opponents feared it would be used as propaganda by foreign nations against the United States in protest of America's treatment of its black citizens.

There was no getting around the evidence that black Americans as a people were under daily assault in terms defined by Article II of the Convention, which designated genocide to mean killing members of a targeted group, causing serious bodily or mental harm to members of the group, or deliberately inflicting on the group conditions of life calculated to bring about its physical destruction in whole or in part. To qualify under this definition, *We Charge Genocide* offered records of high infant mortality rates among blacks, widespread disenfranchisement, malnutrition, a lack of medical and health services, denial of fair employment and educational opportunities, segregation in public accommodations, urban ghettos, mob violence and police brutality, as well as a tradition of bias in the courts and the prison system.

The lengthy "Evidence" section of *We Charge Genocide,* although limiting itself to incidents known to have occurred only during the years of the UN's existence, 1945–51, is a mind-numbing litany of killings and other largely unpunished abuses of blacks by whites—war veterans assaulted and lynched, black girls molested by white men, a man in Mississippi castrated by a mob, a successful black political candidate in Georgia committed by whites to an insane asylum, the manhandling and verbal abuse of the jazz singer Sarah Vaughan in a Greenwich Village subway station, black people dragged from their homes, beaten on buses, on trains, in front of their children, killed for refusing to sell a saddle, and so on. Of lynching the document complained:

> [B]y far the majority of Negro murders are never recorded, never known except to the perpetrators and the bereaved survivors of the victim. Negro men and women leave their homes and are never seen alive again. . . . This is a well-known pattern of American culture. . . .
>
> Mass murder on the basis of race is a powerful source of constant terror, as it is intended to be, to the whole Negro people. As a result of the pattern

of extra-legal violence in which they live out their lives, if they do live, the entire Negro people exists in a constant fear that cannot fail to cause serious bodily and mental harm. . . .

Perennial, hour by hour, moment by moment lynching of the Negro's soul in countless psychological, in myriad physical forms, that is the greatest and most enduring lynching of all. This is written into the spiritual hanging of all those millions, it is carved into their daily thinking, woven into their total living experience. They are lynched in the thousands of glances from white supremacists all over the land every day.

We Charge Genocide was signed by a total of ninety-four people, including W.E.B. Du Bois, Howard Fast, Paul Robeson, Mary Church Terrell, Jessica Mitford, Rosalee McGee, and Josephine Grayson, widow of one of the Martinsville Seven. Robeson and Fast headed the delegation that presented *We Charge Genocide* to the United Nations in New York on December 18, 1951. On the same day, Patterson presented the document to the organization's office in Paris, telling reporters, "If the power of evil men, caught in the act of murderous assault upon their own nationals, is not challenged by the United Nations, when and where shall hapless folk find redress for their grievances?"

With its ambitious thesis and its CRC provenance, *We Charge Genocide* could not help but be denounced as Communist propaganda, and excessive propaganda at that, since "genocide," it was commonly believed, could not possibly occur in a democratic society. By objective measure, after all, conditions for black Americans—though still far from perfect—were gradually improving, not getting worse. The document's publication was nonetheless something of a watershed. Whether what black Americans experienced actually "qualified" as genocide or not—and Eleanor Roosevelt and Rafael Lemkin himself, among many others, thought not—the petition scored a minor blow to America's postwar moral righteousness, raising painful questions about the country's commitment to the ideals for which the war had been fought.

On Christmas night 1951, as if to confirm the story told by *We Charge Genocide,* terrorists in Florida blew to bits the Orlando home of schoolteacher Harry T. Moore, head of the Florida NAACP. Moore died on the way to the hospital; his wife, Harriette, died nine days later. Shingles from the house, Christmas cards, Moore's extensive NAACP files and correspondence, and other fragments were strewn over a ten-block radius. Police investigators concluded that the destruction had been caused by an extremely powerful explosion, using either nitroglycerine or TNT. The press noted that by using high explosives, Moore's enemies had brought a new level of sophistication and intensity to Southern racial violence. The Moores' deaths are often cited as the first of the modern civil rights period.

"I tried to get him to quit the NAACP, thinking something might happen to him some day," Moore's mother lamented. "But he told me, 'I'm trying to do what I can to elevate the Negro race. Every advancement comes by the way of sacrifice.' " Not since the assault on John Shillady in Texas in 1919 had a high-ranking NAACP officer been targeted by violence, and the Moores were the first NAACP staff members to be killed in the line of duty.

The organization believed initially that the Moores had been murdered by white supremacists because of their voter-registration efforts in Florida's black communities. But a more sinister impetus for the killings soon came to light. Moore had recently angered Lake County sheriff Willis V. McCall by working to have the sheriff investigated for the unjustified shooting of two black prisoners, one of whom had died. The shooting stemmed from the 1949 rape of a seventeen-year-old white girl in the town of Groveland. When, in 1951, the two young black men convicted and sentenced to death for the rape—Samuel Shepherd and Walter Lee Irvin, both twenty-three—had their verdicts thrown out by a higher court on the grounds that no blacks had been in the jury that convicted them, the white community's resentment boiled over, and Sheriff McCall at one point was forced to hide the prisoners in his own home. In November, however, according to the sheriff, Shepherd and Irvin tried to escape when the squad car in which he was transporting them to a hearing had a tire blowout. He said he had no choice but to shoot them. Since both were handcuffed and unarmed, McCall's story seems dubious, and Irvin, who survived, told a coroner's jury that McCall had fabricated the story. But federal circuit court judge Truman Futch, turning aside Irvin's claim, declared McCall's actions justifiable.

No one was ever prosecuted for the Moores' deaths, despite the fact that several suspects were turned up by an NAACP investigation. Almost forty years later, in the late 1980s, a former Ku Klux Klansman troubled by his conscience admitted that he and others had conspired with various officials, including Sheriff Willis McCall, to rid the world of Harry T. Moore.

———

"We begin to see," W.E.B. Du Bois wrote in a prominent article in *The New York Times* Sunday magazine in November 1948, "that the Negro is fighting a slow, determined battle and is not going to give up. He proposes to reach full equality as an American citizen. And by equality he means abolition of separate schools, the disappearance of 'Jim Crow' travel; no segregation in public accommodations; the right to vote, the right to think and the right to speak, the right to work and to live in a decent home, and the right to marry any person who wishes to marry him. The Negro does not expect to reach these goals in a minute or in ten years. He is long-suffering and patient. But whether it takes thirty years or a thousand, equality is his goal and he will never stop until he reaches it." These assured words were at one with the consensus of *What the Negro Wants, To Secure These Rights,* the founding compact of the Southern Regional Council, and even the 1948 Democratic presidential platform. Coming from the eighty-year-old Du Bois they were particularly resonant, simultaneously evoking the distant eloquence of Justice Harlan's 1896 dissent in *Plessy*—"Our Constitution is color-blind, and neither knows nor tolerates classes among citizens"—and anticipating the difficult conflict over segregation many knew was drawing near.

The South, as the Dixiecrat rebellion had shown, was privy to the same set of indicators, and had made its own decision. "We shall fight this dastardly effort with all the strength and resources we have," Governor Herman Talmadge of Georgia vowed in 1949. "Hummun," as the younger Talmadge was known, had ascended to the highest office in Georgia upon the death of his father, the governor-elect, in December 1946. "We will fight them in the state courts. We will fight them in the federal courts. We will fight them in the counties and cities. We intend to fight hand to hand with our weapons and we will never submit to one inch of encroachment on our traditional pattern of segregation."

Some Southerners like Herman Talmadge swore complete defiance. Others stood as if struck dumb before the oncoming crash, frightened of the future but unsure how to deflect it. Even to the region's most wise and noble, integration still seemed a daunting concept. Southern moderates such as ex-governor Arnall of Georgia, Mayor William B. Hartsfield of Atlanta, and Ralph McGill of *The Atlanta Constitution* still spoke in terms of interracial tolerance, not an end to segregation.

One of the first dents in the South's mental armor came in 1947, when the American Heritage Foundation, in conjunction with the Truman administration and the National Archives, organized the Freedom Train, a traveling rail exhibit of the original copies of the Declaration of Independence, the Bill of Rights, and the Emancipation Proclamation. The train was likeable postwar patriotism, with an Irving Berlin song composed expressly for the occasion and thousands lining up at each station stop to pass through the exhibit. As Walter White said, it was "a ballyhoo stunt . . . but . . . it was good ballyhoo," for the Freedom Train could only help reawaken public feeling for the nation's founding ideals of equal rights and equal opportunity for all.

The train quickly took on more than symbolic meaning when Charles E. Wilson, president of the General Electric Corporation and chairman of Truman's Civil Rights Commission, announced that the Freedom Train would not visit any city that intended to segregate visitors to the exhibit. Memphis, Jackson, and Birmingham were among those Southern cities that refused to modify their customs, and the Freedom Train's scheduled visits at those locations were promptly canceled. What was revealing was that many citizens affected by the cancelations expressed immediate disappointment—not with the managers of the Freedom Train, but with the intransigence of their own civic leaders. Men were heard to grumble that they now would have to drive their families hundreds of miles to Nashville or St. Louis to see the show. Once it became apparent the exhibit's sponsors were serious about canceling the train's visits, many other Southern towns quietly fell into line, agreeing to disregard their segregation codes and allow integrated viewing of the exhibit. The nation's original "implements of freedom" had perhaps never before functioned quite so literally.

The year's most emotional breakthrough in civil rights, however, came not in a courthouse or at an exhibit, but on the baseball diamond, when on April 11, 1947, Jackie Robinson took the field at second base for the Brooklyn Dodgers. Robinson's debut and his outstanding success as a star player were significant in demonstrating to America that integration was imminent and suggesting, at least to those willing to be sympathetic to the idea, that it had a friendly face. Robinson had been chosen by Dodgers president Branch Rickey for his considerable athletic skill, his poise and good looks, but also because he believed Robinson possessed the strength of character not to react to racist provocation. His popularity—Robinson was the first black person ever pictured on the cover of *Life* magazine— helped guarantee the introduction to the majors of other quality black players such as Larry Doby, Leroy "Satchel" Paige, and Roy Campanella, making baseball the first national institution to become integrated.

The end of segregation in the nation's capital in spring 1953 was another promising sign. The final impetus for reform came from none other than Mary Church Terrell, the Memphis acquaintance of Ida Wells and now, at almost ninety, the grande dame of American black women's organizations. In January 1950, Terrell led a party of black men and women into Thompson's, a well-known downtown Washington restaurant that was strictly off limits to blacks. When they were refused service, the federal government brought suit against the establishment on Mrs. Terrell's behalf, based on an 1873 local antidiscrimination ordinance that stated that no public restaurant could refuse service to any "respectable" customer. The widow of an admired municipal judge, herself the recipient of honors and citations too numerous to mention, the matter of Mrs. Terrell's "respectability" was well beyond question. In June 1953, the case was decided by the Supreme Court in her favor. Overnight, segregation vanished from most of Washington, a victory cheered by a local black paper's jubilant headline: "EAT ANYWHERE!"

Evidence of the shifting tide was seen also in three important Supreme Court decisions. In *Henderson v. United States,* the high court prohibited Jim Crow seating arrangements in railroad dining cars; in *Sweatt v. Painter* it declared that a black applicant to the University of Texas Law School could not be made to attend a separate law school hastily created for blacks, because the latter institution would be inherently unequal to the real school in terms of quality and prestige; in *McLaurin v. Oklahoma State Regents* the court ruled that a black who had been admitted to the University of Oklahoma by a court order could not then be made to use segregated facilities at the school.

The lengths to which segregationists would go to enforce their code of separation were at times laughable. In the 1930s the state of Missouri hit upon the idea of offering fully paid out-of-state scholarships to blacks who applied to its university's law school; in *McLaurin,* the Oklahoma school tried to encase the black student it had been forced to accept in a "Negro bubble," sharing classrooms and cafeteria access yet always from behind carefully placed curtains and boundaries. The court, in its ruling, swept away all such artifice.

These latter two decisions formed the groundwork for the landmark 1954 ruling in *Brown v. Board of Education,* the case against segregation in public schools argued before the Supreme Court by Thurgood Marshall for the NAACP Legal Defense Fund. In its opinion the court at last repudiated the "separate but equal" doctrine set forth in *Plessy* that had long provided the legal buttress for segregation. Ruling that "separate" was inherently unequal, the *Brown* decision ended the federal government's sanction of a philosophy that had woefully influenced American race relations for fifty-eight years.

A more insurrectionary assault on Jim Crow came at Montgomery, Alabama, in late 1955 when a seamstress named Rosa Parks refused to relinquish her seat in the "white" section of a city bus when ordered to do so by the driver. Arrested for violating a local segregation ordinance that was blatantly unconstitutional, her case was appealed successfully all the way to the U.S. Supreme Court. While the legal motions went forward, the blacks of Montgomery staged a yearlong boycott of the city buses under the leadership of a charismatic twenty-six-year-old minister named Martin Luther King, Jr. The movement was noted worldwide for its cohesion and dedication to nonviolence; it also succeeded—as did many subsequent public accommodations battles—because economic reality was on its side. In Montgomery, black commuters constituted almost 75 percent of the total bus ridership.

The Montgomery movement was an inspirational story of American citizens deciding they would rather walk than ride as second-class citizens, a spontaneous but dignified mass uprising to end segregation. But it also represented the fruit of several long-established elements in the black struggle for social parity. Rosa Parks was a tired seamstress unwilling to give up her seat, but she was also an active NAACP member and a recent participant in a seminar on civil disobedience at the Highlander Folk School, an outpost of Southern radicalism in the foothills of Tennessee. E. D. Nixon, head of the Alabama NAACP, who encouraged Parks and orchestrated the early stages of the boycott, was a longtime member of the Brotherhood of Sleeping Car Porters; in the months prior to the boycott he had made a special effort to bring King, son of an influential Atlanta minister, to Montgomery as pastor of the Dexter Avenue Church.

The Montgomery boycott made it evident who would bring segregation to its knees in the South—not enlightened governors, not federal court decisions, but black Americans themselves. "The American Negro needs a Gandhi to lead him, and we need the American Negro to lead us," editor I. F. Stone had written prophetically only two months before Dr. King and the Montgomery Boycott emerged. "If he does not provide leadership against the sickness in the South, the time will come when we all will pay a terrible price for allowing a psychopathic racist brutality to flourish unchecked."

The killing of Harry and Harriet Moore was one of numerous lynchings and terrorist murders in the South during the 1950s as, in an echo of Reconstruction's violence, whites targeted blacks who sought to bring political change to the region—most notably in the areas of segregation and voting rights. At the same time, the FBI and the Justice Department were slowly expanding their efforts toward piercing the impenetrable shield that had long protected Ku Kluxism and lynchers from official reproof. One of the most significant tests would come in Mississippi, where deeply entrenched white supremacism and a fervent resistance to federal authority had over decades created a hermetically sealed environment, one that author and Ole Miss professor John Silver had famously dubbed "The Closed Society." (For his impudence, Silver was later run out of the state.) As Mississippi had only one functioning political party, politicians thrived not on compromise or deal-making with the opposition (for there was none), but with broad appeals to "the little man." The bashing of black people was a constant, as were theatrical harangues against mongrelization, federal courts, and the editors of Yankee newspapers, and its best-known elected officials tended to be fire-breathing fanatics such as Senator Theodore Bilbo and Representative John Rankin, as well as the more circumspect but equally dangerous Senator James Eastland.

The archetype of the modern white supremacist in Mississippi was James K. Vardaman, "The White Chief," a turn-of-the-century counterpart to South Carolina's Ben Tillman and Georgia's Tom Watson. Serving as governor between 1904 and 1908, Vardaman not only voiced the standard anti-Negro rhetoric, he advocated the intensification of Jim Crow laws and the abolition of all black education, and as a U.S. senator in the years 1913 to 1919, called for the repeal of the Fourteenth and Fifteenth Amendments. Vardaman was a man who was "haunted by Reconstruction," a phrase that probably contains the key to comprehending much of the Southern rancor of the early twentieth century. In varying degrees, the South's leaders struggled with the firm belief, concretized in the Reconstruction era, that having surrendered so basic an institution as slavery, and at such great cost, the region would indulge no further compromising of the racial status quo. If the South could not have slavery, it must at the least have complete control of the minority population slavery had left in its midst. This conviction, hallowed by the tremendous loss and humiliation of the Civil War and the mythic ravages of Reconstruction, became an article of faith to be rigorously defended, and this absolute refusal to accommodate further encroachments was itself seen as highly principled.

Theodore Bilbo, as governor of Mississippi from 1916 to 1920 and 1928 to 1932, compiled a middling record as a Vardaman protégé, but the strong rhetoric that had always been part of his approach turned nasty when he went to the U.S. Senate and suggested publicly that black Americans should be shipped back to Africa. His job, as he saw it, was to keep the 13 million blacks and 5 million Jews in the United States from "running roughshod over the rights and freedoms of the 120 million white American citizens." He was on record as saying that he'd rather see humanity destroyed quickly by the atom bomb than see it slowly degenerate through interbreeding. In the election of 1946, which came after the Supreme Court had kicked away the legal props for the all-white primary, Bilbo encouraged voting rights violations, telling Mississippians, "I call for every red-blooded white man to use any means to keep the nigger away from the polls. If you don't understand what that means you are just plain dumb." The best way to keep a black man from voting, Bilbo added, was "to see him the night before." In response to such flagrant denigration of the rule of law, the CRC in 1946 launched a "National Committee to Oust Bilbo"; at around the same time Bilbo came under suspicion for having sold influence to defense contractors; in January 1947, in an unusual step by Congress, he was barred from returning to the Senate despite having won reelection.

Other Mississippi politicians copied Bilbo's rancorous style. Longtime congressman John Rankin called for the closing of the United Nations but the opening of concentration camps for "disloyal minorities" in the United States. Jews, he noted, "have been run out of every civilized country on earth except this one, and they are headed for the same treatment here." Albert Einstein was "one of the greatest fakers the world ever knew," and merited immediate deportation for "communistic activities." Rankin was one of the original sponsors of HUAC and in 1945 succeeded in making it a standing committee with tremendous powers.

The question is perhaps not so much what motivated the Bilbos and Rankins or how much of their own babble they themselves really believed, but why their views were allowed to dominate for so long, particularly when their denial of reality was so clearly harmful to the region they professed to adore. "The people loved him not because they were deceived in him," Mississippi author William Alexander Percy wrote of Bilbo's followers in *Lanterns on the Levee,* "but because they understood him thoroughly; they said of him proudly, 'He's a slick little bastard.' He was one of them and he had risen from obscurity to the fame of glittering infamy—it was as if they themselves had crashed the headlines." Having, historically, had very little, perennially at the bottom of the nation's averages for literacy, education, paved roads, and other indicators of social development, perhaps Mississippians were simply loath to relinquish what they did have—their fierce independence from the mainstream of the onrushing world and their defiant and decidedly colorful cheerleaders.

The Mississippi syndrome reflected the South's most enduring enigma—the lack of development of moderate leadership and the tendency of the "best people," that oft-mentioned but seldom-heard-from group, to remain aloof from gritty politics, mobbism, and the atrocious behavior of public officials. One explanation is that the South, unlike the North, had no urban machine politicians to counter the antics of the reactionary state politicians, no large ethnic or religious minorities with strong liberal Democratic voting traditions, no powerful unions or labor brotherhoods. And while the New Deal had been popular with Southern farmers, by the time of the Cold War anxieties about race and ideology had supplanted Rooseveltian compassion. There were small groups of Southerners who stood somewhat outside the reactionary fold—businessmen, who resided chiefly in suburban areas of Atlanta or Miami; liberal intellectuals such as Lillian Smith; and hillbilly radicals such as Myles Horton at the Highlander Folk School—but they were, for the most part, marginalized in the South of the late 1940s and early 1950s, and often barely tolerated. Even moderates such as Albert Gore of Tennessee, Frank Smith of Mississippi, and J. William Fulbright of Arkansas could at times be cowed into silence on the issue that mattered most.

"As a Southern woman," Lillian Smith wrote in a letter to *The New York Times* on April 4, 1948, "I am deeply shocked that our liberals are putting up no real fight for human rights in the South. . . . We must remember that demagogues fatten on the poor man's vote and his loneliness, that they use the psychotic to do their dirty work, but they exist because we liberals let them exist. It is our caution, our lack of energy, our moral impotence and our awful if unconscious snobbery, that make demagoguery unafraid of liberalism."

To be sure, Mississippi differed not at all from the rest of the South in that it took poorly to news of the Supreme Court decision in *Brown v.*

Board of Education. It was a Mississippi judge, however, who named the day of the fateful decision—May 17, 1954—"Black Monday," and a former Ole Miss football star named Robert "Tut" Patterson who founded the White Citizens' Councils, with the aim of resisting *Brown* and other unwelcome changes. By 1956, the councils, often referred to as the "white collar Klan," claimed almost 150,000 members in Mississippi and Alabama. That same year Senator Eastland called for the creation in Mississippi of a State Sovereignty Commission to protect the state from encroachment by any agency of the federal government and to save it from race mongrelization. The Sovereignty Commission, based in Jackson, had an investigatory wing and used paid informers to gather intelligence about civil rights activity in the state; in a sense it mimicked, and was meant to counter, the efforts of the U.S. Justice Department's new Civil Rights Division (which officially came into being in 1957) and the FBI.

Meanwhile, on the national political stage, more than one hundred U.S. senators and representatives from the region signed a "Southern Manifesto" in March 1956 calling for a reversal of the *Brown* decision and warning that "the unwarranted decision of the Supreme Court in the public schools cases is now bearing the fruit always produced when men substitute naked power for established law." The solons were acting on their own beliefs, but were partly taking their cue from President Eisenhower, who was uncomfortable with civil rights issues and had expressed sympathy for how desegregation had been forced on the South.

Eastland, the owner of a sprawling cotton plantation in the Delta's Sunflower County, emerged as the leading Mississippi figure during the Eisenhower years, vowing to safeguard white supremacy at all costs. (His namesake, a relative also named James Eastland, had been killed in a shoot-out with a black farmhand in 1904; the alleged murderer and his wife were tortured with a corkscrew and then burned at the stake.) While the rest of the country may have capitulated to immigrants, communists, race mixers, and liberals, he contended, the South by virtue of its Anglo-Saxon purity and strength of character was the only genuine remnant of pioneer America, the nation's sole link to its ennobling past. This philosophy very closely anticipated the printed ravings distributed at county fairs by the Ku Klux Klan in the 1960s, but Eastland was no small-town vigilante—he was a powerful voice in the U.S. Senate, as chairman of the Judiciary Committee.

Historian Numan V. Bartley once described Eastland as "a simple man who found the past far more attractive than the future," and instead Eastland rose to the defense of the Lost Cause as if he could still smell the gunpowder. He managed to convince large numbers of people to share his delusion that the Supreme Court decision in *Brown* was not the shape of things to come but merely a tactical defeat, a temporary setback that could be reversed. And much as his Sovereignty Commission would balance the antics of the Justice Department, he encouraged the Citizens' Councils to take on the NAACP by becoming a competing national enterprise capable of propagandizing to America about the evils of desegregation. As Eastland told the Mississippi Association of Citizens' Councils in a much-reprinted address: "We must take the offense. We must carry the message to every section of the United States. Our position is righteous. The great majority of the rank and file of the people of the North believe exactly as we do. The law of nature is on our side. After all, the average American is not a racial pervert. We must place our case at the bar of public opinion."

Eastland also grew concerned about what he called the "Paper Curtain," the consistent pattern of condescending or disapproving stories about the South that appeared in Northern newspapers. This tissue of lies persisted, said the weekly *Poplarville Democrat* in Mississippi, "All because the South has not agreed to buckle under and accept the way of life that is detrimental to the strength of this nation and to the culture that has been developed through centuries."

In the convulsion that would occur in the South during the civil rights years, lynching would play a powerful role. By now, the question of lynching's rationale had become moot; whether lynch mobs functioned to punish civil rights advocates or to maintain sexual codes or to suppress black achievers, the most conspicuous aspect of the tradition was its utter backwardness, its anachronistic cruelty and disregard for law and order. Recorded in television broadcasts and weekly photo magazines, it came to represent the South's most desperate efforts to remain unchanged and at the same time reminded the rest of America of the righteousness of the civil rights cause itself. Three lynchings, all in Mississippi, of Emmett Till in 1955, Mack Charles Parker in 1959, and the integrated trio of civil rights workers Andrew Goodman, James Chaney, and Mickey Schwerner in 1964, all served to rivet the nation's attention on the Southern struggle, and each would prove a major stepping-stone in the law's effort to render lynching obsolete once and for all.

———

On an August morning in 1955, Mamie Till Bradley accompanied her fourteen-year-old son, Emmett, to the Illinois Central depot in Chicago to see him off on a two-week vacation with relatives in Leflore County in the Mississippi Delta. Emmett, who had just finished the seventh grade, was a native Chicagoan, but his mother had been born in Mississippi. The Delta had been the starting point for tens of thousands of black Americans who'd emigrated to Chicago over the years, including Mamie, and it was not uncommon in summertime to return home for a visit or send one's children there, as the countryside was seen to offer a respite from August in the city.

As Emmett boarded the train, his mother cautioned him one last time to mind his great-uncle Moses "Preacher" Wright and his wife, Elizabeth, with whom he'd be staying, and to be especially respectful of Mississippi whites, to say "yes, sir" and "no, sir," and to "kneel down if necessary," as things were "different" in Mississippi. But she wasn't overly concerned. Her son, who went by the nickname Bobo, stammered as the result of a childhood bout with polio, and due to his speech difficulties and his gentle nature he was not particularly loud or obstreperous. His great-uncle later remembered that, on a previous visit to the Delta, the boy had been most fond of quietly spending time by himself, petting and feeding the animals on the farm.

Once in Mississippi, Emmett quickly fell in with a large group of young relations and friends. For a city kid, the Delta's lush endless vistas and muddy streams, its huge twilight sky of early stars, was a kind of playland, a place to go barefoot and chase lightning bugs and catch toads. And Emmett didn't mind acting the city slicker, impressing his country cousins with his sophisticated ways, at one point even bragging that back in Chicago he had a white girlfriend. Not that anyone believed him. On August 24, when he rode with some friends and cousins into the hamlet of Money, where there was a cotton gin and a general store, they jokingly dared him to go inside and ask the white cashier for a date, "just to show us how much you Chicago cats know about white girls."

The Money grocery store, a modest one-story white building with a small porch area and a screen door, was operated by Ray and Carolyn Bryant. The afternoon Emmett visited, Ray was out of town on a truck-driving job in Texas and Carolyn was working alone in the store, her sister-in-law, Juanita Milam, having stopped by to keep her company. At twenty-one, Carolyn Bryant was something of a local attraction, a stunning brunette who had won two beauty pageants as a teenager. Of all the white women in the Delta for a black boy to "pretend" to express interest in, she may have been the worst possible choice.

There has never been an entirely satisfactory explanation of what transpired between Emmett Till and Carolyn Bryant. She later testified that when she gave him his change for some bubble gum he'd purchased, Till squeezed her hand and asked, "How about a date, baby?," and that when she pulled away he said, "Don't be afraid of me, baby, I ain't gonna hurt you. I been with white women before," and uttered "unprintable" words. At that point, she said, she ran to the back of the store and got a pistol, although when she returned with it she must not have appeared too threatening since her further testimony was that as Till exited the store he said, "Bye, baby," and wolf-whistled at her.

Most of this is difficult to believe. It seems unlikely a woman as conditioned as Carolyn Bryant was to fending off men's advances would take too seriously the overture of a moonfaced fourteen-year-old who'd just bought a handful of gum. It's possible that, so as not to lose face with his cousins, Till did make some mildly inappropriate or forward remark or in some way showed her less deference than she was accustomed to. Even had he simply allowed his gaze to rest a moment too long on her features, or made eye contact, he would have crossed the threshold of permissible conduct.

Emmett Till's mother always contended that on account of his speech impediment, Mrs. Bryant may have misunderstood a completely innocent statement Emmett made, or imagined she heard a wolf whistle. The Jackson *Daily News*'s simple explanation for Till's actions was that he was obviously insane, since no black boy in his right mind would dare come on to a white woman in Mississippi. Whatever occurred in the store, Till's cousins and friends knew that Carolyn Bryant was angry with him—one version of the incident has a cousin entering the store and pulling him out—and as Till and his friends departed Money, the young people became convinced they were being followed and, frightened, jumped out of the car to hide in a cornfield. His cousin Simeon also remembered that Emmett asked him not to tell his great-uncle about what had occurred.

For their part, Carolyn Bryant and Juanita Milam also decided it would be best not to tell their husbands of Till's forwardness. He was only a fresh colored boy, and they understood the calamitous results that would follow if their husbands knew. But upon his return from Texas, Ray Bryant learned of the incident from one of Till's young cousins, and once Bryant was aware his black customers knew his wife had been "bothered," he felt he had no choice but to act. Enlisting the help of his half-brother, J. W. "Big" Milam, they went to teach the young visitor a lesson.

Arriving at Moses and Elizabeth Wright's cabin outside Money at 2:30 A.M. on the morning of Sunday, August 27, Milam, holding a pistol in one hand and a flashlight in the other, demanded to see "the boy from Chicago who did the talking down at Money." Another white man, presumably Ray Bryant, stood by but did not speak. Moses, having heard of the encounter with Mrs. Bryant, tried to defuse the situation, telling Milam and Bryant he had already scolded the boy, adding, "He ain't got good sense. He was raised up yonder [in the North]." Elizabeth offered to pay the men "for damages." But Milam insisted on seeing Till, so Wright led the men to a back bedroom where Emmett was asleep. Milam shook the boy awake.

"Are you from Chicago?"

"Yes," Till answered.

"Did you say 'yes' to me? If you say 'yes' to me again, I'll knock your fucking brains out. Get up and put your clothes on."

Before leaving, Milam asked Wright if he knew him. Wright said no. Milam then asked his age, and when Wright replied "Sixty-four," Milam advised him that if he ever did recognize him, he "wouldn't live to be sixty-five."

"You niggers go back to sleep," Milam ordered. "I want to hear the springs squeak." But Moses and Elizabeth disobeyed, and watched Milam and Bryant as they led Emmett outside, where another person was waiting in the cab of a green Chevy pickup. When they reached the truck a man's voice inquired, "Is this the boy?" and a woman's voice answered, "Yes."

A few days later, on August 31, a fisherman was plying the Tallahatchie River just across the border from Leflore County. This late in the summer it was a common lament that the fish had "already seen all the bait there is to see," and would not take a hook. But as he sat waiting for his luck to change, something unusual bobbed to the surface against a rock. Staring closely and in astonishment, he recognized it as the mutilated body of a human being.

Authorities, quickly summoned, hauled the rotting corpse onto the shore. Tied around its neck, in an apparent attempt to keep it down at the river bottom, was a 125-pound cast-iron wheel from a cotton gin. Powder burns on the right temple suggested the victim, a teenage black boy, had been shot at close range, although the skull showed such massive blunt damage that one official concluded the boy had been struck and killed with an ax.

In Chicago, Mamie Till Bradley was incredulous at word of her son's murder. "He's never been in any trouble," she told a reporter. "He's been my lifesaver—did the washing, ironing, and housework so I could work. He has stood by me like a man. How could anyone do this terrible thing to him?"

A few days later Bradley received her son's remains at the Illinois Central Terminal, from which she'd sent him forth several days before. "Lord, take my soul," she cried upon seeing Emmett's casket at the door of the baggage car, and collapsed into the arms of her minister.

Many Southern race murders had ended there. Transgression, swift punishment, a lady's honor restored, the victim's family shamefully, quietly burying their dead. But Emmett Till's was destined to be a very unquiet death. Partly this was due to the victim's tender age, the innocence of his alleged offense, and the fact that he was a Northerner killed in the South—all elements that caught the attention of the press. Chiefly, however, it stemmed from his mother's resolve that the incident not be hushed up or brushed under the carpet. Refusing to become incapacitated by her grief, she began making plans for a public funeral for Emmett in Chicago so that others could "see what they did to my boy." She insisted, over the strong objections of the undertaker, on an open-casket service.

"Somebody is going to pay for this," she vowed. "The entire state of Mississippi is going to pay for this. Have you ever sent a loved son on vacation and had him returned to you in a pine box so horribly battered and waterlogged that someone needs to tell you this sickening sight is your son?"

An estimated ten thousand people filed by the casket in the days before Till's funeral. So great was the demand to view the corpse, the burial had to be postponed for two days, and a ghastly photograph of what people saw as they looked down at the lifeless form in the coffin, the murdered boy laid out in a tuxedo, his face barely recognizable as human, appeared in *Jet* magazine. People thousands of miles away wept upon seeing it. Mamie Till Bradley herself said of the photograph's disturbing power, "It just looked as though all the hatred and all the scorn [the world] ever had for a Negro was taken out on that child."

Bradley's decision to display the remains of her son and to denounce his murderers was both painful and courageous. It also made for powerful antilynching propaganda. For unlike most lynchings, where the accused was at least thought capable of having committed a crime, the murder of a fourteen-year-old boy for what appeared to be, at worst, an ill-considered prank could not help but reveal the cruel and sadistic strangeness of Southern custom. As a French newspaper wrote in condemning the murder: "[A] young Negro . . . whistled in admiration at a young white woman. In Europe this is an homage which provokes a smile. Here it was the equivalent of a death sentence."

The gruesomeness of sudden death stamped on the face of a child left a sickening taste even in the mouths of Mississippians, whose initial reaction to the case was sympathetic. Governor Hugh White denounced the killing and vowed a thorough investigation and prosecution, while the Jackson *Daily News* termed it "a brutal, senseless crime." But the mood turned to resentment once it became known that the NAACP and other outsiders intended to publicize Till's death as a lynching, not just a murder, and to link the incident to two other mob killings of Mississippi blacks that had occurred that year. On May 7, 1955, the Reverend George Lee had been ambushed in his car near the Delta town of Belzoni and shotgunned to death for registering to vote and encouraging other blacks to do likewise; on August 13, just before the Till murder, Lamar Smith, a sixty-three-year-old farmer also active in voter-registration work, was assassinated while climbing the steps of the courthouse in Brookhaven.

Coming on the heels of the NAACP's leading role in the hated *Brown* decision just the previous year, the association's entrance into the Till case solidified Mississippi's contempt for the "communistic" civil rights organization. Every Mississippi schoolchild already knew that the initials N-A-A-C-P stood for "Niggers, Alligators, Apes, Coons, and Possums." The animosity was returned in full, however. The Chicago branch of the NAACP called publicly for federal troops to occupy Mississippi, alleging that Till's demise and the other recent killings in the Delta represented such an extreme pattern of state-sanctioned terrorism that it weighed significantly "against the state's right to sovereignty among the states of this union."

"This is not a lynching," Governor White said, countering the NAACP accusations. "It is straight-out murder." The governor was correct in that no mob had invaded a jailhouse, no law officers had relinquished a prisoner, no one had been hanged or burned on a pyre. Yet a victim had been targeted for a perceived transgression of local custom, abducted and held without any official hearing or inquiry, then murdered secretly by at least two individuals acting in concert (Milam and Bryant had been arrested shortly after Till's body was found). To the NAACP and most Americans, this qualified as a lynching.

Soon Mississippi, with the world paying close attention, got down to the business of putting Milam and Bryant on trial. Expectations of a conviction were low. As Dr. T.R.M. Howard, a prominent black surgeon in the Delta town of Mound Bayou, pointed out to a visitor, whites in Mississippi generally received longer jail terms for killing deer out of season than for killing a Negro; yet no one knew what effect the presence of big-city reporters and television cameras might have. Money, where the abduction of Till had occurred, was in Leflore County, but the body had been discovered just inside neighboring Tallahatchie County, so the trial took place in Sumner, the Tallahatchie County seat.

Black people constituted 63 percent of Tallahatchie County's population of thirty thousand, but none was considered for service on the jury, and blacks wishing to attend the trial as spectators were made to sit in an upstairs alcove. Black reporters covering the event—as well as Mamie Till Bradley and black Michigan congressman Charles C. Diggs, Jr.—were allowed on the main floor, but were forced to sit at a card table off to one side with a poor view of the bench. As if these arrangements weren't unwelcoming enough, county sheriff H. C. Strider insisted on greeting the black newsmen and even Congressman Diggs each morning with a barbed "Good morning, niggers!," while Mamie Till Bradley was made to pass a gauntlet of small white boys who ran after her and snapped their cap guns at her each time she entered and left the building. Her determination to come to Sumner and suffer such indignities, not to mention the considerable risk that she herself would be harmed, only to have then to sit in the courtroom several feet away from the men who had so savagely destroyed her son, was a remarkable act of courage.

Milam and Bryant's defense team would probably have secured an acquittal from the local jury regardless of the evidence, but insomuch as the defense felt compelled to mount a case it hinged on the prosecution's lack of physical evidence. The murder weapon or weapons had never been discovered, and there was disagreement as to whether the disfigured corpse that had been found was actually Emmett Till. As a man who identified himself as a lifelong resident of Tallahatchie County insisted to a reporter from *The Nation,* "That river's full of niggers." If this was true, it was up to the prosecutors to convince the jury that they had found the right one.

Sheriff Strider was typical of those in Tallahatchie who had become increasingly bothered by the national scrutiny of the case. Originally, when Milam and Bryant were taken into custody, he vowed to see justice done. But he'd been angered by, among other things, an NAACP statement that "Mississippi has decided to maintain white supremacy by murdering children," and by the time of the trial Strider had sided with the defense. His testimony that the body removed from the water on August 31 was "in mighty bad shape" and had been dead at least eight days, whereas Till had been missing for only three, was considered extremely damaging to the prosecution. A doctor and an undertaker testified similarly that the body could not have been Till's because of the advanced state of decomposition. When the prosecution argued that Till's own mother had identified the body, and that a ring removed from a finger of the corpse was engraved with the letters "L.T.," for Till's father, Louis, who had been killed in the Second World War, the defense countered that the NAACP plot to defame Mississippi was so sophisticated, it was entirely feasible that the ring had been placed on the remains of an anonymous Negro and set adrift in the Tallahatchie. To an outsider, the details of such a defense were, of course, illogical, but the Tallahatchie jurymen appeared willing to consider that some sort of trickery might have occurred and to be confused about the identification issue. Throughout the trial the Jackson *Daily News* coverage lent itself wholeheartedly to this fraud, its reporter pondering the question of the body's identity and Emmett Till's present whereabouts as if these were unfathomable mysteries.

The defendants did not testify at the trial, although Leflore County sheriff George Smith told the court that Ray Bryant had admitted to him that he and Milam had abducted Till. He said Bryant claimed, however, that they had released the boy as soon as they were convinced he was not the person they were looking for.

The dramatic high point of the trial came with the testimony of Moses Wright, potentially the prosecution's most damaging witness. He had been warned by local whites not to dare take the witness stand, and he did so only after having made arrangements to leave town directly after testifying. New York columnist Murray Kempton termed the elderly man's courageous appearance "the hardest half hour in the hardest life possible for a human being in the United States."

The prosecution walked Wright through the middle-of-the-night abduction of Emmett Till. "Did you watch them leave?" he was asked.

"Yes. I stood on the porch about twenty minutes after they left."

"Have you ever seen Emmett Till alive since that night?"

"No."

"Did Bryant and Milam bring him back?"

"No."

"When was the next time you saw Emmett?"

"He was in a boat where they had taken him out of the river."

"Was he living or dead?"

"He was dead."

Wright was then asked if he could identify the man who had taken Emmett from the cabin. The old man stood erect before the room of Mississippi whites, extended a bony finger in the direction of "Big" Milam, and stated unequivocally, "Thar he." Wright also identified Ray Bryant as Milam's companion. Another black witness, eighteen-year-old Willis Reed, then testified that early in the morning after the abduction he had seen Milam take Till into a barn and that soon after he'd heard screams from within. And two other prosecution witnesses who worked on Milam's place—Henry Lee Loggin and Leroy "Too Tight" Collins—said they had been ordered to wash blood out of Milam's pickup truck.

The known facts that the jury took with them into the deliberation room might, anywhere else in the world, have pointed to a more or less automatic conviction. A boy named Emmett Till had vanished after insulting a pretty white woman. Bryant and Milam, her husband and brother-in-law, had admitted abducting him in the middle of the night. Although they claimed not to have harmed him, no one had ever seen him alive again. A body that then washed up in the river was identified as Till by his own mother and wore a singular piece of jewelry that could only have been in his possession. An eyewitness stated he'd seen a boy matching Till's general description being led into a barn by one of the defendants, who later ordered two of his employees to hose blood out of the back of his truck.

In its closing argument, however, the defense insisted the case was too confusing to resolve, and offered again the fundamental explanation that it was because the entire affair was a sham designed to discredit Mississippi. "There are people in the United States who want to destroy the way of life of Southern people," defense attorney John Whitten told the jury. "There are people . . . who will go as far as necessary to commit any crime known to man, to widen the gap between the white and colored people of the United States. They would not be above placing a rotting, stinking body in the river in the hope it would be identified as Emmett Till." In his turn, co–defense counsel J. W. Kellum reminded the jury that they were "custodians of American civilization" who had to "turn these boys [Milam and Bryant] loose" or "your forefathers will turn over in their graves."

The jury took a little over an hour to find Milam and Bryant not guilty. One juror told reporters later that the deliberations would not have taken so long if they "hadn't stopped to drink pop," while another confided that Sheriff Strider had told them to delay a bit "to make it look good." The wisecracking sheriff, expansive and relieved now that the ordeal had come to an end, assured newsmen he'd heard a rumor that Emmett Till was alive and well and living in Detroit.

Newspapers around the world carried photos of the happily reunited Bryant and Milam couples. At the suggestion of photographers, who throughout the trial had used any excuse they could dream up to photograph Carolyn Bryant, Juanita and Carolyn sat on their husbands' laps and kissed their men to celebrate the acquittal. "This is one way to make up for lost time," Mrs. Milam declared.

Although cleared of the murder charge, Milam and Bryant still faced possible indictment for kidnapping in Leflore County. But despite Bryant's direct admission to Sheriff Smith that he and Milam had abducted Till, the grand jury refused to hand down indictments on the kidnapping charge. The NAACP in frustration turned to the Justice Department, which rejected pleas to enter the case. The kidnapping did not fall under the Lindbergh Law because no state line had been crossed, and government lawyers in 1955 could not be at all sanguine about the likelihood of winning a civil rights conspiracy suit in Mississippi, particularly since no law officer appeared to be implicated. A telegram sent by Mamie Till Bradley to President Eisenhower asking for his personal intervention went unanswered.

Thurgood Marshall spoke out about the complete vulnerability of Delta blacks who, it was now clear, could not expect succor from either state or federal officials. "The country," Marshall said, "is in what may fairly be called a hell of a fix." Marshall did not exaggerate the total absence of protection. On November 25, Gus Courts, a grocer who was the head of the Belzoni NAACP and active in the Mississippi Regional Council of Negro Leadership, was shot and badly wounded; only a week later, on December 3, not far from the site of the Till murder, a black filling-station employee named Clinton Melton was gunned down after an argument with an inebriated white customer. Neither case was investigated or prosecuted.

The full facts in the Till case would ultimately be provided by none other than Bryant and Milam themselves. Now beyond the reach of the courts, they gave an extraordinary interview to writer William Bradford Huie in late 1955. Their lawyers arranged the meeting with Huie, who was doing an article for *Look* magazine, because Bryant and Milam needed the money (Huie had agreed to pay handsomely for the exclusive rights to their story), but also, according to their attorneys, because the former defendants wished to make a larger point. They believed that if the nation knew the truth of what had happened to Emmett Till—that he had been killed because he acted as though he stood on an equal footing with whites—the NAACP and other meddlers might at last see the folly of their ways and cease their efforts to force integration on the South. Their own experience provided a kind of cautionary tale, they believed, for they, after all, were not murderers; they were family men, husbands, much like everyone else. If regular guys such as Ray and "Big" could be driven to kill by a smart-mouthed black kid, then integration on a broader scale, allowing even greater contact between the races, was clearly impractical.

Huie, an Alabama novelist and nonfiction writer, was enough of a redneck himself to put Bryant and Milam at their ease. In his article, which appeared on January 24, 1956, Bryant and Milam confided that their original intention had been only to scare Till by pretending they were going to throw him off a cliff. In the dark, however, they couldn't find the river bluff they were searching for. After driving around with their captive for several hours, they decided to take him to a shed behind Milam's house. But even after roughing the boy up a bit, they explained, Till remained sassy and unrepentant, continuing to talk about his white girlfriend.

Like Carolyn Bryant's account of Till's behavior in the grocery, Milam and Bryant's version of events is also fairly improbable. Till was a fourteen-year-old child held captive by two armed, hostile white men, and it's highly doubtful he behaved insolently toward them. According to Elizabeth Wright, Emmett had been so afraid after his encounter with Carolyn Bryant at the store in Money that he had asked to be sent home to Chicago, but she had convinced him to stay so as not to ruin his vacation. Stephen Whitfield, author of a history of the case, thought that Milam and Bryant might not have originally intended to kill Emmett, but were angered upon finding a photograph of a white woman in his wallet (possibly a photo that came with the wallet when it was purchased). However, Olive A. Adams, who authored a booklet called *Time Bomb: Mississippi Exposed* for the Mississippi Regional Council of Negro Leadership in 1956, denigrated the "white girlfriend" story repeated by whites as "vicious propaganda, aimed at fitting Emmett Till into the 'sexually depraved' category among the stereotypes into which Negroes are so often cast. It was an obvious attempt to dream up a crime to fit the punishment."

By Milam and Bryant's explanation, it was Till's refusal to treat their injured feelings with respect, and his obstinate defiance, that ultimately cost him his life. As Milam told Huie: "Well, what else could we do? He was hopeless. I'm no bully; I never hurt a nigger in my life. I like niggers—in their place. . . . But I just decided it was time a few people got put on notice. . . . And when a nigger even gets close to mentioning sex with a white woman, he's tired o' livin'."

A year later, when Huie conducted a follow-up interview with Milam, the Mississippian repeated a version of the same story, adding, "I didn't intend to kill the nigger when we went and got him—just whip him and chase him back up yonder. But what the hell! He showed me the white gal's picture! Bragged of what he'd done to her. I counted pictures of three white girls in his pocketbook before I burned it. What else could I do? No use lettin' him get no bigger!"

Milam complained to Huie that although he and Bryant had evaded formal punishment, local blacks had boycotted and effectively ruined the business of several grocery stores in the Delta owned by the Milam and Bryant families, and that even whites in the business community to whom he'd turned for financial help had made it hard for him to start over as a cotton grower. The community had defended the two men inasmuch as they represented Mississippi white supremacist custom, but once the Till affair had ended people seemed uncomfortable having such well-known murderers in their midst, particularly after the two men confessed to the crime in the pages of a national magazine. One of the worst insults was the county's retraction of a special permit that had allowed Milam, a decorated war hero, to carry at all times his army .45 automatic, a weapon with which, friends liked to say, he could "knock off a turtle's head at fifty feet." The role of enforcer of the region's racial taboos, Milam seemed to be telling Huie, was no longer all it had been cracked up to be. "I got letters from all over the country congratulating me on my 'fine Americanism,' " Milam said wistfully; "but I don't get that kind of letters any more."

In late 1946, the NAACP's Thurgood Marshall wrote to Attorney General Tom Clark to complain that J. Edgar Hoover's FBI investigations of civil rights abuses, including lynchings, had been largely ineffective. He cited the fact that despite its exhaustive effort in the Monroe, Georgia, quadruple lynching, the FBI had not produced a single suspect. NAACP investigators, in contrast, had managed to come up with several leads in the same case; this had also been true in the blinding of Issac Woodward in South Carolina and the mob killing of John C. Jones in Minden, Louisiana. Marshall drew the only logical conclusion: the FBI was biased against black people.

"The FBI has established for itself an uncomparable [sic] record for ferreting out persons violating our federal laws," Marshall wrote the attorney general. "This great record extends from the prosecution of vicious spies and saboteurs, who are trained in the methods of evading identification and arrest, to nondescript hoodlums who steal cheap automobiles and drive them across state lines." Marshall, referring to Clark's known aim of fortifying federal civil rights statutes, wrote that "there would be very little use to strengthen these Civil Rights Statutes if the FBI continues its policy of being unable to produce the names of persons guilty of [lynchings]." In a separate memo to Walter White, Marshall confided: "I . . . have no faith in either Mr. Hoover or his investigators and there is no use in my saying I do."

When Clark forwarded a copy of Marshall's criticisms to Hoover, the FBI director wrote irritably to White, pointing out that the NAACP should not be taking complaints about the Bureau to the attorney general without coming to him first. He also reminded White that several FBI investigations of lynchings had failed to lead to convictions not due to any lack of diligence on the part of the Bureau, but because the federal statutes in place were too narrow to allow a grand jury to hand down an indictment. "As you realize," Hoover wrote, the FBI "has nothing whatsoever to do with the nature or context of Federal statutes which are initiated, approved and placed on the statute books by the Congress of the United States. If these statutes are defective or inadequate, the responsibility is that of Congress."

Marshall and Hoover were both, from different points of view, expressing the same basic concern—that the federal judiciary at the close of the Second World War was neither adequately equipped nor motivated to snuff out mob violence. This deficiency came to be addressed, however, as the Truman administration pivoted to deal with civil rights issues generally. *To Secure These Rights* in 1947 called for an expansion of the federal government's power to investigate and prosecute civil rights violations, a recommendation answered a decade later by the Civil Rights Act of 1957, the first substantive national civil rights legislation since the Civil Rights

Act of 1875. The 1957 act enlarged the potential federal role in the South by allowing the federal government to bring civil suits in its own name against those who violated others' voting rights. (Prior to this, an individual would have to bear the burden of bringing a case, usually too costly and intimidating an effort for private citizens.) Under the supervision of Attorney General Frank Murphy (who had presided over the Ossian Sweet case in Detroit), the Justice Department in 1939 had created a Civil Rights Section in its Criminal Division with the purpose of providing greater flexibility in investigating and prosecuting voting rights violations; the 1957 act elevated the Civil Rights Section to full division status, whose sole duty was to investigate civil rights complaints, and established a slot for a new assistant attorney general to run it.

President Eisenhower, who disliked the passionate nature of the civil rights cause, and had little knowledge of or empathy for blacks generally, nonetheless was sympathetic enough to the prevailing mood to back the act's passage. He also reluctantly sent U.S. troops to Little Rock in 1957 to halt violence directed at black children integrating Central High School when Arkansas's governor, Orval Faubus, refused to provide the National Guard for this purpose or to otherwise cooperate. Eisenhower became the first president to dispatch federal troops into the South to safeguard black rights since Ulysses S. Grant.

A lynching in southern Mississippi in 1959 would provide another crucial test of the government's new commitment to addressing racial injustice. This mob killing arose from the events of the night of February 23. Jimmy Walters, his pregnant wife, June, and their four-year-old daughter, Debbie, were driving toward their home in Petal, Mississippi, just outside Hattiesburg, after spending the day with relatives in Bogalusa, Louisiana. In the darkness, on an isolated stretch of Highway 11 between Poplarville and Lumberton, the Dodge sedan in which they were traveling suddenly broke down. Jimmy drew the car over to the side of the road and opened the hood, quickly confirming his suspicion that the car had thrown a rod. Admonishing his wife and daughter to remain in the car, he set out to walk the seven miles to Lumberton to get help.

After he had been gone a while, four young black men from nearby Poplarville driving home after a night of drinking and socializing slowed down to look inside the stalled car. According to later testimony from one of the passengers, the driver, M. C. "Mack" Parker, expressed interest in having sex with the white woman. His friends assumed he was only kidding, but after he had dropped them off at their homes, Parker apparently went to his own house, got a toy pistol, and went back alone to the stranded Dodge. A terrified June Walters wouldn't open the door for him, so he forced it open, telling her, "I am an escaped convict and have killed five people. Two more won't make any difference." He made June and Debbie get into his car, drove onto a nearby side road, and after evicting Debbie from the vehicle, raped June across the front seat as the little girl stood outside crying. When he was done he forced June out of the car and drove off.

The woman and her daughter found their way back to the highway, where June managed to flag down a trucker, telling him, "I've been raped by a nigger." He carried her and Debbie into Lumberton, where she saw Jimmy using the pay phone in a gas station.

Parker, who earned a living as a pulpwood truck driver, was picked up the next day by Pearl River County sheriff W. Osborne Moody and identified by June Walters in a lineup. Fearing a lynching, Moody removed Parker to the Hinds County jail in Jackson, where he was held until mid-April, when a grand jury in Poplarville, the seat of Pearl River County, indicted him for rape and kidnapping.

On April 17 Parker and his attorney appeared in the courthouse before Judge Sebe Dale, a former crony of Theodore Bilbo who, like Bilbo, was a staunch white supremacist. Parker's counsel, R. Jess Brown, associate counsel for the NAACP in Mississippi, had the distinction of having filed the first civil rights suit in the state seeking the enforcement of federal voting rights for blacks, and in 1948 had outraged the city of Jackson by seeking parity for black teachers who earned less than whites in the public school system. Probably the leading black attorney in the state, he had taken Parker's case only after the defendant's mother, Eliza Parker, contacted him and explained that no local lawyer in Poplarville, white or black, was willing to defend her son.

Parker and Brown managed immediately to annoy the court. Parker, it seemed to the whites present, acted disrespectful and cocksure, while Brown instantly hit Judge Dale with three separate motions challenging the procedural legitimacy of the trial: the grand jury that had indicted Parker had included no blacks; blacks were systematically kept from voting in Pearl River County, thus none could possibly be selected to serve on a petit jury that would hear Parker's case; and such intense local antagonism toward Parker existed that a fair trial could not possibly be held without a change of venue.

The motions relating to the absence of black people on juries were explosive ones at that time in Mississippi. Only a month earlier a federal appeals court had voided the 1954 conviction of a black murderer named Robert Lee Goldsby in Carroll County because there had been no blacks on the jury that had found him guilty. This was an alarming development because all Mississippians knew that there were few if any black people registered to vote anywhere in the state, meaning the possibility of blacks making their way onto a jury was virtually nil. If the federal courts could conceivably strike down any criminal conviction based on the lack of black representation in the jury pool, it would be hard to keep black criminals locked up.

Contrary to popular impression, Goldsby had not been released from prison because of the court's action, but the precedent fed the perennial anxiety that black rapists and murderers would evade punishment through courtroom manipulations and sentimental federal rulings. The federal government's victory in *Goldsby* had, in a sense, boxed Mississippi in by creating an unwanted consequence to the state's pattern of discrimination in voting rights. At the same time, it had made the region's most barbaric tradition appear newly attractive.

Another factor that may have contributed to a lynching mentality in Poplarsville was the involvement of attorney Brown. His reputation for tenacity was well known and, if the case came to trial, he—an insolent black—would be in a position to interrogate publicly a white woman about her having been raped. Considering that the prospect of even a white lawyer putting a dishonored woman through such an ordeal had long made people uncomfortable, the picture of a "puffed-up nigger in a suit and tie" performing such an act was cruelty itself. J. P. Walker, the former deputy sheriff who organized the Parker lynch mob, was heard to address this very point. Actually, after the lynching, June Walters herself said she believed Parker deserved a fair trial, and that she would not have minded testifying in open court about the assault or answering questions from a black attorney. In another departure from custom, Jimmy, the aggrieved husband, had refused to kill Parker when an opportunity—and a loaded gun—was handed him, preferring like his wife that the accused be tried in a court of law and duly punished.

On the night of April 25, 1959, J. P. Walker led a mob consisting of a local barber, an itinerant Baptist preacher, a farmer, and several others in abducting Parker from the jail. The jailer, Jewel Alford, allowed the mob access to the building. Mack Parker was a powerful man and put up a vicious resistance, at one point seizing a club from the hands of an attacker and crowning him over the head with it. He had to be dragged feet-first from his second-floor cell, his head crashing on each step, leaving a crimson trail all the way down to the first floor. The next morning his bloody handprints were found stamped all over the front of the courthouse, where he had desperately tried to cling to a railing before being dragged to the curb and stuffed into a waiting Oldsmobile.

In what must have seemed a bizarre turn of events, the lynch mob and its captive were forced to make their way slowly through a crowd of people leaving a dance at a local junior college, before speeding south to the bridge over the Pearl River at the Mississippi-Louisiana border. The mob intended to hang Parker from one of the arches of the bridge, but when they pulled him out of the car he made a sudden effort to flee and had to be knocked down and shot twice at close range. Just then an oncoming car approached, so the killers hurriedly threw Parker's body into the car and drove across the bridge into Louisiana before turning around and, on their way back across, hurling the body into the river on the downstream side.

By traditional standards the Mack Parker business was a quiet little Southern lynching, the kind that fifty years earlier would have garnered a one-paragraph account in Southern papers. In 1959, however, an incident anywhere in the United States in which a mob stormed a jail and hauled a prisoner away to his death was newsworthy. The Emmett Till case had demanded notice because of the tender age of the victim and the harmlessness of his alleged "crime"; the Parker case intrigued the nation's editors partly because it was, in an age of push-button hairspray and earth-orbiting satellites, such a blatant incongruity. The scenario of the classic lynching was complete nine days later when Parker's body washed ashore and a coroner's jury, after twelve minutes of deliberation, produced the inevitable verdict: "Death occurred at the hand of a person or persons unknown." The *Poplarville Democrat,* as if on cue, proceeded to report that "the general consensus . . . is that the abductors were from outside Pearl River County."

The FBI had entered the case almost immediately after Parker's abduction at the request of Governor J. P. Coleman of Mississippi. Under the Lindbergh Law, any kidnapping case unsolved after twenty-four hours could be presumed to contain the probability of interstate flight, and thus allowed federal involvement. The FBI investigation was massive and thorough, with up to sixty agents working in the Poplarville area. When Parker's corpse was found in the river several days after the lynching, the FBI identified him through his fingerprints, heading off any question of the body's identity, the technicality that had helped derail the Till case. As the *New York Times* reporter on the scene, Claude Sitton, reported, the "details of the lynching and the names of those involved are common knowledge" in Poplarville, and the FBI was able to piece together in minute detail how the lynching had occurred, and even obtained confessions from some members of the mob.

So intense was the FBI invasion of Poplarville and so ceaseless the questioning that one of the mob suspects died and two others were hospitalized. Arthur E. Smith was laid up with what his doctors diagnosed as a cerebral hemorrhage brought on by three solid days of interrogation, while C. C. "Crip" Reyer was admitted to a hospital after suffering a nervous breakdown. The Jackson *Daily News* reported that the wives of many Poplarville men were upset that, through its endless badgering, the FBI seemed intent on destroying their family life. But after viewing the FBI's final 378-page report on the case, U.S. attorney general William Rogers praised the Bureau's Mississippi effort as "one of the most complete investigations I've ever seen."

The federal government wanted Mississippi to prosecute the lynch mob. Federal kidnap laws, it turned out, had not been broken—Parker was already dead when carried across the state line into Louisiana—and the Justice Department was reluctant to pursue a difficult civil rights conspiracy prosecution in such hostile terrain. The most workable approach, one that would be practical and also sensitive to local feelings about federal interference, would be for the government to support Mississippi's prosecution with its comprehensive report and by making FBI agents available as witnesses.

In November 1959, Governor Coleman received the massive FBI report and its list of witnesses and handed both over to a Pearl River County grand jury. But to the consternation of the Justice Department, the local district attorney refused to present the report or call any FBI witnesses. The grand jury thus never saw or heard any of the damning information the federal government had gone to such trouble to procure, and as a result no indictments were handed down.

Despite the Justice Department's understandable incredulity, the actions of the district attorney and the grand jury were in keeping with widely held sentiments in Pearl River County. The competence and thoroughness of the FBI's work was meaningless next to the resentment locals felt for the "invasion" of FBI "spies" and news reporters they'd had to endure, all over the fate of a black drunkard who'd raped a white woman in front of her own daughter. The local American Legion had even uncovered the fact that Parker had been dishonorably discharged from the army, and went to the length of insisting that the U.S. flag that had draped his coffin be returned by the Parker family. Since everyone knew that potential Pearl River County jurors would never find their fellow Mississippians guilty of killing the likes of Parker—"You couldn't convict the guilty parties if you had a sound film of the lynching," one man told a reporter—ignoring the FBI report and short-circuiting any possible trial was simply the quickest way of putting the whole regrettable incident in the past and getting Poplarville out of the national spotlight.

The Justice Department, believing it had found the formula for accomplishing what had long been thought impossible—the cracking of a lynching case in a small Southern town with federal evidence and a local prosecution—reacted to the setback with visible annoyance. Attorney General Rogers termed the grand jury's behavior "as flagrant and calculated a miscarriage of justice as I know of," and immediately announced that the Justice Department would reenter the case. The federal charges would be brought under two Reconstruction-era statutes, Sections 51 and 52 (later, 241 and 242) of Title 18, the "Conspiracy Section," of the U.S. Criminal Code.

Bequeathed by the Republican Radicals of Charles Sumner's generation, these statutes were rather like old family heirlooms that wind up being moved back and forth between attic and basement numerous times, and that no one is ever quite sure what to do with. Originally part of the First Enforcement Act of 1870, Section 51 contained severe punishments for crimes in which "two or more persons conspire to injure, oppress, threaten, or intimidate any citizen in the exercise or enjoyment" of their constitutionally guaranteed rights, or in which "two or more people go in disguise on the highway" for such purpose. Section 52 initially belonged to the Civil Rights Act of 1866, and was aimed at those who acted "under color of law" to deny citizens of rights such as the right to due process. Both laws were created as means of enforcing the Thirteenth, Fourteenth, and Fifteenth Amendments against criminal encroachments, and passed in response to the Reconstruction terrorism aimed at freedmen in the South. The provisions of these acts were incorporated in the Civil Rights Act of 1875 but, like that act itself, drew the ire of states' rights advocates who saw them as part of an intolerable extension of federal power, and they were rejected by the Supreme Court's ruling in *United States v. Harris* in 1883. In 1909 some parts were adopted into the U.S. Criminal Code as ways of protecting citizens' right to exercise the franchise and other civil rights without harm or intimidation. A violation of Section 51 carried a maximum fine of five thousand dollars and ten years in prison, while those convicted under Section 52 were subject to a fine of one thousand dollars and one year's imprisonment.

Of course, the Supreme Court had greatly inhibited the use of these statutes with its late-nineteenth-century rulings that limited the application of the Fourteenth Amendment largely to protecting business interests, not the sanctity of persons, and kept the amendment's equal-protection guarantee from safeguarding people from acts of violence by private citizens. But slowly there had developed a willingness by federal civil rights attorneys to try to use these long-dormant laws to prosecute voting rights violations and acts of mobbism. Influencing this trend, in addition to the well-publicized lynchings of the 1930s, was the 1942 public immolation of Cleo Wright in Sikeston, Missouri. Wright, a black mill worker, charged with sexual assault and the shooting of a policeman, was removed from jail and dragged through the streets before being put to death—a distinct and embarrassing failure of America's wartime democracy.

Wright's was the first prominent lynching after Pearl Harbor, and when word arrived that the Japanese were citing the gruesome killing as the type of treatment East Indians could expect if the Allies won the war, Attorney General Francis Biddle ordered an FBI investigation and began exploring a prosecution in the Sikeston case under Sections 51 and 52. Biddle, as solicitor general, had been involved two years earlier when Justice Department lawyers Albert E. Arent and Irwin L. Langbein, working under the first head of the Civil Rights Section, Henry A. Schweinhaut, developed the idea of using the statutes as an antilynching law, since Congress appeared unable to enact a federal antilynching measure. Biddle failed to gain indictments in the Wright case, but the government's new strategy began to coalesce, particularly when, that same summer, President Roosevelt ordered the Justice Department to continue to look into all suspected lynchings of black Americans.

A breakthrough came in the famous *Screws* case of 1943. M. Claude Screws, sheriff of Baker County, Georgia, and two of his deputies were found guilty by a federal court of bludgeoning a black prisoner to death. The three policemen, after a night of drinking at a tavern, had gone to the home of Robert Hall and accused him of stealing a tire. He was handcuffed and taken by car to the courthouse, where he was attacked by his captors and pummeled with fists and a two-pound iron blackjack. Even after he had collapsed to the ground, Screws and the others continued to beat him for as long as half an hour. Hall never regained consciousness, and died after being taken by ambulance to a hospital. It was said Sheriff Screws had been out to get Hall because he considered him a "biggety Negro."

Although Screws and his colleagues were found guilty in federal court for violating Hall's civil rights, their convictions were overturned in 1945 by the U.S. Supreme Court. The court ruled that the sheriff and his deputies had not conspired or set out willfully to violate a specific federal right of the victim, such as the right to vote, and that without proof of such direct willful violation of a guaranteed right, the attack was a local offense that Georgia alone was responsible for prosecuting. Georgia, of course, did no such thing and Screws, having evaded punishment, went on to win election to the state senate.

While liberal observers were displeased by the Supreme Court's decision in *Screws,* they were at least heartened that a lower federal court had been willing to convict in a civil rights case based on Reconstruction-era law. Ultimately, it was believed, perhaps at the next opportunity, the Supreme Court would fall into line. According to a report issued by a 1947 legal conference organized by the NAACP, "the factors which swayed the Supreme Court more than 70 years ago to narrow the meaning and intent of the 14th Amendment should no longer bar the way to a proper and correct appraisal of the Amendment today. It is impossible to believe that the Supreme Court will continue to adhere to a view historically and legally unsound, that Congress is without power to prohibit individual action as well as State action where the deprivation of essential basic civil liberties by bands is involved." As Supreme Court Justice Frank Murphy wrote in a strongly worded dissent in *Screws:* "[W]here . . . the States are unwilling for some reason to prosecute such crimes, the federal government must step in unless constitutional guarantees are to become atrophied." Murphy questioned his colleagues' technical reasoning over the question of whether Screws and his fellow officers had "willfully" violated Hall's constitutional rights:

[T]he right not to be deprived of life without due process of law is distinctly and lucidly protected by the 14th Amendment. There is nothing vague or indefinite in these references to this most basic of all human rights. Knowledge of a comprehensive law library is unnecessary for offi-

cers of the law to know that the right to murder individuals in the course
of their duties is unrecognized in this nation.

In the years leading up to the Parker case, the Justice Department had
continued to pursue Sections 51 and 52 (now 241 and 242) cases, but of
the thousands of civil rights complaints the department received each
year, it had the resources to investigate and prosecute only a handful.
Many of the more prosecutable cases were voting rights violations, because of a 1941 Supreme Court ruling in *United States v. Classic,* which
supported the federal government's right to apply the conspiracy statutes
to ballot-box fraud when it was thought to be perpetrated by state officials.

The Justice Department's ability and willingness to pursue civil rights
cases had been abetted by the Civil Rights Act of 1957, which had added
manpower and greater administrative leeway to this area of potential
criminal prosecution. One obstacle that no amount of motivation in
Washington could ever completely get around, however, was the ingrained bias of some of the Southerners who sat on the federal bench.
Federal men from Washington down to observe Judge Sidney Mize, a native Mississippian, preside over the federal grand jury considering indictments in the Parker lynching in Biloxi in January 1960, could only
exchange knowing looks with their colleagues as Mize observed in his
opening remarks that "there is no place in the nation where the relation
between the two races is as good and as highly respected as in Mississippi."
Mize then proceeded to show intense hostility to the federal prosecution.
He informed jurors that to offer an indictment they would have to find
that there had been mob collaboration with a sheriff or other law officer,
in effect limiting the scope of the potential indictments to a lynching carried out "under color of law," a violation of Section 242 only. "The conduct of individuals forming a conspiracy and forcibly seizing a person
from a sheriff is not a violation of federal law," Mize told the grand jurors.
"Their conduct is a violation only of state laws and is punishable by state
laws."

Thirty-two witnesses appeared. Most were residents of Pearl River
County who uniformly pleaded the Fifth Amendment right against self-
incrimination. Several FBI agents testified, however, and named the participants in the lynching, including Jewel Alford, the jailer who had made
the keys needed to gain access to Parker's cell available to the mob, former
deputy J. P. Walker, "Crip" Reyer, and the others who'd abducted Parker
from the jail. (The jurors reserved their harshest questions for Parker's

victims, June and Jimmy Walters. One demanded of June, "You mean you let that nigger fuck you?" while Jimmy in turn was asked, "You mean to tell me that after that nigger fucked your wife you still lived with her?")

Perhaps most important, Mize ordered that the jurors would have to indict all or none of the alleged conspirators, a criterion that made it highly unlikely any indictments would be handed down, for while certain key figures in the conspiracy—Alford, Walker, Reyer—were deeply involved, others were more tangential, and the jurors would be hard-pressed to treat them all as equally culpable, even if they were disposed to punish the crime of lynching. As the hearings dragged on, Mize then made another peculiar move, canceling the appearances of fifteen prospective witnesses, including J. P. Walker, and declaring that he could not postpone a scheduled move of his court from Biloxi to Jackson, where a full docket of cases awaited him. Federal prosecutors were flabbergasted. For such a high-profile case, it was exceptional for a federal judge not to agree to extend a grand jury hearing.

In the end, of course, the Justice Department did not win the indictments for which it had so arduously worked. On January 14, 1960, the Mize grand jury announced it had found no basis for prosecution. After a brief national outcry of exasperation—one newspaper called the government's failure "a morally intolerable state of affairs"—and a few feeble calls for that venerable remedy, a federal antilynching statute, the case slipped into history, as cold and dead as Mack Charles Parker.

"Common sense, due process of law and the extension of voting rights among Negroes have their quiet and no doubt inevitably leisurely effect" on the progress of civil rights, a Northern newspaper editorial pondered on January 4, 1960. "The question is, how much patience does the situation require?"

The resounding answer came less than a month later when, on February 1, 1960, four young black college students staged a sit-in to protest segregation at a Woolworth's lunch counter in Greensboro, North Carolina. Their defiant act ignited first a regional, then a national movement, as tens of thousands of young people, black and white, joined to sit in and demonstrate their rejection of segregation in public accommodations. Because Woolworth's was a national chain, students at colleges all across the country could show their solidarity by picketing at the nearest store, thus placing enormous public pressure on the retailer. The demonstrations soon spread to other five-and-ten's such as McCrory's and Kresge's. The sit-in movement, which brought young blacks and whites to lunch counters in New York, Boston, Chicago, and other large Northern cities, as well as Atlanta, Nashville, and New Orleans, introduced many Northern students to the Southern civil rights struggle, a development formalized in April 1960 with the founding of the Student Nonviolent Coordinating Committee (SNCC). The following year, both CORE-led "freedom rides" into Alabama and Mississippi and the initiation of a SNCC voter-registration campaign in Mississippi established a beachhead for a small but dedicated group of Northern activists to begin to come south.

The rallying of young Americans to the civil rights cause helped dispel the bogeyman of McCarthyism that had hung over the heads of progressives during the 1950s. The charge that civil rights workers were Communists, or at the least misguided youth unwittingly "directed" by the Kremlin, would not vanish overnight, but it generally lost its potency in the face of so clearly indigenous a crusade as equal rights for black people. And the fact that most of the young people entering the movement were barely out of their teens made it difficult for anyone to taint them as purveyors of an alien ideology.

To Southerners, the sit-ins and the continuing pressure from civil rights workers arriving on freedom rides or venturing into backwater areas to develop voters' rights projects left no doubt that the region's worst nightmare had arrived—a "second Reconstruction" in which Northern do-gooders and the federal government would try once again to remake the South in the North's image. In 1955, the antics of "Martin Lucifer Coon" in Montgomery had won a federal ruling desegregating that city's buses; in 1957 Little Rock whites had seen the gleam of federal bayonets; and in 1959 Poplarville, Mississippi, a town trying to mind its own business, had been swamped by the FBI. But these encroachments would seem like minor skirmishes compared to what was to come.

In preparation, Ku Klux Klan chapters began to reappear in Georgia, Alabama, South Carolina, and Florida. In Mississippi, the combined efficiency of Eastland's Sovereignty Commission, the White Citizens' Councils, and the police in maintaining law and order—arriving freedom riders in 1961 had been promptly arrested at the Jackson depot and shipped off to the Parchman Prison Farm—delayed a Klan revival there. But that complacency was dashed in September 1962, when federal marshals were used to ensure the entry of a black student, James Meredith, into the University of Mississippi. Ole Miss was a traditional and much-gloried bastion of state and Confederate pride, and the federal government's willingness to use force against it came as a shock to whites who thought the Magnolia State impregnable. With a howl of indignation over the Meredith affair, many Mississippians turned to the newly formed White Knights of the Ku Klux Klan.

"Mississippi is a Sovereign State in a Federal Union, and insists upon being so regarded," declared Sam Holloway Bowers, the White Knights' founder and imperial wizard. "Communists are mongrelizers. They are out to destroy America and crush the American Spirit. Mississippi is their last great political obstacle. We stand almost alone between them and the Total Barbarism which is their goal."

Because of the constant threat of danger, black leaders of the Southern movement had always been cautious about the presence of white civil rights workers in the South, as it was believed this would only further incite local whites. By late 1963, however, civil rights efforts in Mississippi were proving difficult to advance. Voter registration and increased black voting offered the potential for needed social change in the region, but the going was slow, and many black citizens remained apathetic and afraid. It was extremely difficult to attempt overnight to inculcate a sense of democratic participation in people so long kept down and intimidated by whites, and resistance in the form of the beating and jailing of civil rights workers was taking a physical and psychological toll on the movement. Nonviolence was an inspiring ideal but a tough strategy to live with day after day when you were the one passively taking the blows. Movement leaders knew they were fighting not only Southern white extremists and the sovereign state of Mississippi, but the frustration and dwindling patience of their own troops.

The young black people who had nurtured the movement worried that the influx of whites would likely destroy its special germinal quality, and that the provocation of whites and blacks working together would prove too much for the local citizens and that some whites would be injured or killed. On the other hand, it seemed unthinkable to those who had worked so hard and at such great cost that their cause would falter short of its goals. In November 1963, Mississippi organizers of the Congress of Federated Organizations (COFO), a coalition of workers from SNCC, CORE, and other civil rights groups, made the fateful decision to heighten national recognition of what was taking place in Mississippi, and possibly topple the state's defenses in one final surge, by inviting a large number of white volunteers to come to Mississippi and assist the movement.

———

A representative Northern college student who eagerly responded to the call was twenty-year-old Andrew Goodman of New York City. Raised in a progressive New York Jewish family—his parents had belonged to various liberal and leftist causes—Goodman was a junior at Queens College and an amateur actor with a deep interest in civil rights issues. In early June 1964 he joined hundreds of other Mississippi-bound volunteers for a week of orientation at a college campus in Ohio for the Mississippi Summer Project, where he was teamed with twenty-four-year-old Mickey Schwerner, a white CORE worker who had been stationed in Meridian, Mississippi, since January with his wife, Rita, and James Chaney, twenty-one, a black CORE staffer from Meridian who worked closely with the Schwerners on voter registration and other efforts.

One special project of Schwerner and Chaney's that spring had been to initiate voting rights classes at a church in the small black community of Longdale, in rural Neshoba County, forty-five minutes northwest of Meridian. After Schwerner and Chaney had met with the local black leadership, however, whites—later revealed to be members of the White Knights of the Ku Klux Klan—burned the church to the ground and beat several of the members of the congregation.

Schwerner knew that Meridian whites did not care for him. They called him "Goatee" because of his facial hair, and routinely harassed the Meridian community center he and Rita had established. But aware as he was of the local resentment, he could not possibly have known that he had become the special target of the White Knights, that Sam Bowers had characterized him to Klansmen as "a thorn in the side of everyone living, especially white people," or that the Klan had engineered a conspiracy to eliminate him. The burning of the Longdale church was a warning to the blacks who worshiped there, but it had also been intended as a means of luring Schwerner back into Neshoba County, where the local White Knights klavern included Sheriff Lawrence Rainey and Deputy Cecil Ray Price.

Rainey, who had a reputation for brutality toward black people, had won the sheriff's office by vowing to keep civil rights trouble out of Neshoba. A big chaw of Red Man tobacco in his mouth, six-shooter on his hip, he comported himself like a Western lawman of old and appeared ready to live up to his election vow that he would be "the man who can cope with the situations that may arise." Price, his baby-faced deputy, was in a way even more frightening, for he was younger and more eager to prove himself, and possessed a violent streak belied by his genial appearance.

On Sunday, June 21, 1964, Goodman's first full day in Mississippi, the three civil rights workers drove to Longdale, viewed the ruined church, and visited those hurt in the Klan attack. Their presence was apparently reported by phone to Deputy Price, who a short time later arrested them on a trumped-up speeding charge and placed them in jail in the town of Philadelphia, the county seat. The imprisoned young men were denied their right to make a phone call and when, as part of a routine safety procedure, a volunteer at Schwerner's headquarters in Meridian phoned all jails in the vicinity to find out if the men had been arrested, the jailer's wife, Minnie Herring, lied and answered no. The Neshoba White Knights and a klavern from Meridian took advantage of the several hours Goodman, Schwerner, and Chaney were in the Neshoba jail to arrange an ambush upon their release. Word spread rapidly among the Klansmen that Deputy Price had three civil rights workers in jail who "needed their rear ends tore up," and that one of them was the hated Goatee.

By the time all the elements of the conspiracy were in place and Deputy Price came to release the young men, freeing them after they paid a fine for the speeding violation, it was pitch-dark. Schwerner and Chaney certainly knew better than to leave a rural jail at night—it was a cardinal rule for civil rights workers—and the fact that they did not immediately go to a pay phone to call in to their headquarters suggests that Price forced them to go directly to their car. He admitted later to the FBI that he followed them in his police cruiser to make sure they left town.

About ten miles south on the two-lane State Highway 19 leading back to Meridian, Chaney, who was driving the CORE station wagon, saw the headlights of vehicles coming on quickly in his rearview mirror. He accelerated and attempted to outrun the pursuing cars, and when that seemed futile took a sudden turn down a side road he knew. The pursuing vehicles managed to hang with him, though, and a moment later one of them turned on the flashing lights of a police car. Chaney, probably at Schwerner's instruction, pulled over.

"I thought you were going back to Meridian if we let you out of jail," Deputy Price said.

"We were going there," replied Chaney.

"Well, you sure were taking the long way around. Get out of the car."

Several men emerged from the other cars and helped place the civil rights workers in Deputy Price's car. A Klansman who later turned state's evidence, James Jordan, got behind the wheel of the station wagon. The caravan then drove for a few minutes to nearby Rock Cut Road, which was hidden from the highway and rarely traveled, where the three were removed from the police vehicle. "Are you that nigger lover?" Meridian White Knight Alton Wayne Roberts demanded, confronting Schwerner. While the Klansmen were accustomed to being disrespectful of black people—Roberts had played a leading role in beating the church members in Longdale—he and his cohorts may have been a bit awed to find themselves facing other white men, especially when Schwerner had the temerity to try and reason with the angry Roberts, telling him, "Sir, I know just how you feel." Roberts, unaccustomed to Schwerner's strange kind of bravado, immediately raised his gun and fired, killing the civil rights worker. He then pulled Goodman from the car, asking, "Are you that other nigger lover?," and shot and killed Goodman. Chaney backed away or perhaps ran several yards into a gully alongside the road before he was gunned down by James Jordan and Roberts. "Well," said Jordan, "you didn't leave me nothing but a nigger, but at least I killed me a nigger."

The murders of Goodman, Schwerner, and Chaney constituted one of the most sophisticated "underground" lynchings ever staged. The numerous elements—the fire at the Longdale church luring the workers into Neshoba, the arrest of the victims on a trumped-up charge, the detention of the men in jail, the chase, the executions, the burial of the bodies in an earthen dam being dug for a cattle pond on a nearby farm, and finally the disposal of their station wagon, which was driven into a swamp and burned, were all carefully synchronized. In fact, some of the conspirators were themselves so impressed with the plan's thoroughness they argued for releasing James Chaney, since it could appear demeaning to Mississippi whites to have gone to such elaborate lengths simply to take the life of a black man.

President Lyndon B. Johnson was a Southern moderate who, as a senator from Texas, had long had his eye on the presidency. He had stood apart from his Senate colleagues when they had signed the 1956 Southern Manifesto against *Brown,* and he'd worked to ease passage of the 1957 Civil Rights Act. After the death of President John F. Kennedy in 1963, he had made the passage of Kennedy's Civil Rights Act a personal crusade. Had Kennedy lived, his civil rights legislation would have undoubtedly had a difficult time making its way through Congress; as it was, the bill was passed as a kind of tribute to the slain leader, thanks in no small part to Johnson's considerable acumen as a legislative deal maker.

When Goodman, Schwerner, and Chaney disappeared in Mississippi seven months into Johnson's presidency, he had not yet been severely tested by Southern civil rights crises, as had Eisenhower at Little Rock in 1957 or Kennedy during the freedom rides in 1961 and the James Meredith standoff at Ole Miss the following year. Johnson reacted swiftly, authorizing the strongest measures ever taken by a president in response to an apparent lynching. As a Southerner, he no doubt felt the need to demonstrate clearly his abhorrence for what had occurred, and the fact that whites were among the presumed victims greatly magnified the national press coverage, placing immense pressure on him to act decisively. He immediately dispatched former CIA director Allen Dulles to Mississippi to confer with state officials about the case, received the parents of Goodman and Schwerner at the White House, and ordered an intensive FBI campaign to find the missing men and bring those responsible to justice.

If and when the federal government would deepen its involvement in the Southern struggle had long been an open question; Southerners had waited apprehensively, civil rights workers hopefully, for the answer. To many, the increased turmoil in the region since the mid-1950s was a direct result of the decision of the Supreme Court's ruling in *Brown,* and thus it followed that if the federal judiciary was willing to mandate radical change, it should bear the responsibility for policing it. Although their actions in the area of civil rights had increased as a steady number of complaints about voting rights and civil rights violations reached Washington from the movement's front lines, the Justice Department and the FBI clung through the early 1960s to the position that police responsibility belonged to the states. One obstacle may have been that, as Thurgood Marshall had complained, the FBI was not adequately motivated by Director Hoover to pursue civil rights investigations. He kept most of the Bureau's resources focused on Communists and organized crime, and was always quick to point out, as he had to Walter White in 1946, that his men could do little if Congress had not seen fit to create a system of federal protections that were prosecutable. His total lack of sympathy for the movement had never been more clear than in the fall of 1963, when he had refused to commit FBI resources and personnel to an investigation of the terror bombing of the black Sixteenth Street Church in Birmingham, Alabama, in which four adolescent girls, members of the church choir, had been killed.

By June 1964, however, much had changed. The Civil Rights Bill had been passed, and both Johnson and Hoover may have felt pressed to make a strong showing against lynching and lawlessness in general by the events of the previous November 22, when President Kennedy had been shot to death as he rode through the streets of Dallas. Hoover could have even felt guilty. He had never gotten on well with either John or Robert Kennedy, and the FBI had had Lee Harvey Oswald, the president's alleged assassin, under surveillance before the shooting. Hoover was also known to dislike the Klan. The FBI director had no affection for civil rights workers, and his disdain for Martin Luther King, Jr., was well known, but he even more vehemently opposed secret vigilante societies of any kind. Johnson played on this predilection by suggesting to Hoover that a Klan outfit was thought to be at the bottom of the Neshoba disappearance.

For forty-four days the disappearance of the missing three civil rights workers became a national obsession. There was daily coverage and commentary about the fate of an integrated trio of young men who had personified the most hopeful aims of the movement—a cause for which it now appeared they had given their lives. In the face of this outpouring of national concern, Mississippi remained obstinately unhelpful. State police, claiming to see no evidence of any crime, refused to even conduct an investigation, and many residents and officials, including Governor Paul Johnson, maintained that the disappearance of the three was probably some kind of hoax, meant to humiliate the South. It thus became of paramount importance for the FBI to locate the missing men—dead or alive.

Slowly the massive federal search achieved results. First the burned-out station wagon was found, then information provided by a black man who had once been abducted and threatened by Neshoba Klansmen helped the FBI get a sense of the probable location of the bodies. On August 4, with the help of a local informant, the Bureau unearthed the three men's remains on a farm southwest of Philadelphia. The unique interment of the murdered men had been the conspiracy's centerpiece as well as the source of the Klansmen's smugness, for the young men had been entombed so far beneath the innocent-looking landscape of a rustic cattle pond it seemed impossible that anyone would ever find them.

On December 4, 1964, FBI agents swept into Philadelphia and Meridian and arrested nineteen men, including Sheriff Rainey and Deputy Price, for federal conspiracy violations in the murders of Goodman,

Schwerner, and Chaney. At their arraignment hearing later that week, however, U.S. Commissioner for the Southern District of Mississippi Esther Carter refused to accept a signed, sworn confession from one of the government's informants, Klansman Horace Doyle Barnette, because only a single FBI agent had been in the room when the confession had taken place. Carter asserted his statement was "hearsay evidence" and thus inadmissible. The government's attorney angrily pointed out that Carter's ruling was unprecedented—a sworn statement witnessed by an FBI agent is ordinarily acceptable as evidence—but, sensing it had lost the day, the Justice Department chose to withdraw and regroup.

The turnabout served to embolden the suspects. If the federal government could be so easily rebuffed, the prospect of their spending even a single day in jail seemed remote. A photograph of the men, chortling and obviously enjoying their part in making a mockery of the federal effort, appeared as a double-page spread in *Life* magazine, Sheriff Rainey in the foreground in the act of stuffing a huge chaw of Red Man into his mouth. It is a famously disturbing image—modern America's first good look at a lynch mob and its police collaborators—and it had the effect of convicting the photographed men in the minds of most people who saw it.

The Justice Department tried again on January 11, 1965, at a grand jury hearing in Jackson before Judge William Harold Cox of the Southern District of Mississippi. Cox, an old friend of Senator Eastland and like him a native of the Delta's Sunflower County, had always made the lives of Justice Department lawyers in Mississippi difficult. In 1964, after it was reported that Cox, during a hearing in a voter discrimination suit, had said, "I don't know who is telling these Negroes they can push people around just by getting into a line and acting like a bunch of chimpanzees," Senators Jacob K. Javits of New York and Peter Rodino, Jr., of New Jersey initiated a movement in Congress to replace him. Cox kept his job but, chastened, appeared thereafter to be on slightly improved behavior.

The Cox grand jury met for four days before narrowly agreeing to indict the Neshoba mob under the federal conspiracy statutes, Sections 241 and 242 of the U.S. Criminal Code. A month later, however, Cox dismissed the 241 charges, pointing out that the statute was meant to protect federal rights, not rights ordinarily ascribed to the state such as the right to due process. In other words, Cox was refusing to allow the government to use 241 as a means to enforce the due-process clause of the Fourteenth Amendment. The Neshoba killings, Cox admitted, might constitute a "heinous crime against the State of Mississippi, but not a crime against the

United States." The judge also dismissed the 242 charges against everyone in the conspiracy but Rainey, Price, and Philadelphia police officer Richard Willis, explaining that the "color of law" statute could not be applied to ordinary citizens.

With a sigh, Justice Department attorneys recognized that the time for a legal showdown over the tactical usefulness of the Reconstruction statutes had arrived, and appealed Cox's ruling to the U.S. Supreme Court. Ever since the *Screws* case in the 1940s, in which the Court had insisted that the federal judiciary could protect the "exercise" of certain rights, such as voting, but not the "enjoyment" of others, such as the right to due process, the Justice Department and the Supreme Court had wrestled with the appropriateness of broadening the application of the 241 and 242 statutes so that they could be used to enforce the Fourteenth Amendment rights to due process and equal protection under the law. As Attorney General Tom Clark had once observed, potential federal action against mobs that attacked black people hung on "a very thin thread of law." With a more liberal Supreme Court, and civil rights–related violence on the rise, government lawyers were hopeful that the time had come for the high court to put teeth at last into the Fourteenth Amendment's historically bold and comprehensive guarantees.

Former NAACP counsel Thurgood Marshall, who was now U.S. solicitor general, argued the case for the government and characteristically did not mince words about what lay at the heart of the case: he urged the justices to give the federal government the ability to punish lynch mobs at long last. The court rose to the challenge. In its opinion in *United States v. Price, et al.,* written by Justice Abe Fortas and handed down on March 28, 1966, the court found that the indictment against Price and the others must stand because the mob had denied Goodman, Schwerner, and Chaney the right to due process as guaranteed under the Fourteenth Amendment. "The language of 241," Fortas wrote, "is plain and unlimited. . . . [It] embraces all of the rights and privileges secured to citizens by all of the Constitution and all of the laws of the United States." The Court affirmed that 241 addresses not only the interference with the exercising of a right, but can refer also to the deprivation of a right that one enjoys without exercising it, such as the right to due process. "The alleged conspiracy," Fortas concluded, had deprived the three young men of this fundamental right, for it "involved releasing the victims from jail at night; intercepting, assaulting and killing them; and disposing of their bodies. Its purpose was to punish the victims summarily."

The judges also concurred with Marshall and the Justice Department about the 242 issue. Marshall had argued that "when the private members of the mob knowingly linked hands with the officers to carry out a common plan to deprive Schwerner, Goodman and Chaney of their constitutional rights, they lost their claim to be treated as mere private citizens." In agreeing, Fortas described the crime as a "brutal joint adventure" between civilians and police, concluding:

> To act "under color" of law does not require that the accused be an officer of the State. It is enough that he is a willful participant in joint activity with the State or its agents. . . . State officers participated in every phase of the alleged venture: the release from jail, the interception, assault and murder. . . . Those who took advantage of participation by state officers in accomplishment of the foul purpose . . . were participants in official lawlessness, acting in willful concert with state officers and hence under color of law.

The Supreme Court's ruling in *Price* left no doubt that the court was now willing to give broad readings to Reconstruction-era civil rights statutes. To underscore the historic fact that it was at last, after ninety-six years, joining Section 241 with the kind of punitive and prosecutorial scope its 1870 authors had intended, the court attached as an appendix to its opinion remarks made in Congress during Reconstruction indicating that the original intention of the legislation was to help safeguard the freedmen in the South. Thus, in one fell swoop, the court abolished the long-standing restriction against holding private citizens accountable for violations of others' Fourteenth Amendment rights, and made it clear that private citizens could be held accountable for acts of conspiracy committed under color of law.

With this hurdle cleared, the Neshoba case finally came to trial before Judge Cox in federal district court in Meridian in fall 1967. Despite the Supreme Court's ruling, John Doar, the assistant attorney general for civil rights, who would prosecute the case, was aware his chances of victory were slim. Even though the Justice Department had, subsequent to *Price* (but before the Meridian trial opened), successfully prosecuted two other Section 241 cases—the 1964 shooting death of black army reservist Lemuel Penn in Georgia and the 1965 Klan assassination of white civil rights worker Viola Liuzzo in Alabama—this was the first prosecution of such a case in "Fortress Mississippi." Getting the kinks in the law worked out had been a necessary part of the job, but a monumental historical challenge remained, simple yet immense: Doar must convince the Mississippians who would sit on the jury that it was all right to cooperate with a federal criminal prosecution of white Mississippians in a civil rights case.

Doar was perhaps the Justice Department's best representative for the task—a slender, soft-spoken Midwesterner with a ruddy farmer's face, the polar opposite of the hated "New York lawyers" such as Samuel Leibowitz, who'd so antagonized Alabamans in the 1930s. Doar had a good reputation among civil rights workers as one of the more committed and sympathetic Justice Department lawyers, having entered the state along with some of the earliest SNCC arrivals in 1961, and he was respected if not admired by some white Mississippians. He was best known for an incident on the streets of Jackson in spring 1963 when, following the murder of NAACP leader Medgar Evers, he single-handedly defused a violent brick- and bottle-throwing confrontation between demonstrating black teenagers and Jackson's truncheon-happy police force, walking unarmed into the no-man's land between the two angry factions and appealing for calm.

He hoped the same kind of balanced, low-key approach would serve him in Judge Cox's courtroom, and that by selling the government's case in a firm but restrained manner, without appearing to lecture the jury or to bully witnesses, he would encourage a Mississippi judge and jury alike to understand the need for a guilty verdict.

The merit of this strategy was seen immediately. On the first day of the trial, one of the defense attorneys asked a black minister who was testifying about Schwerner's activities in Meridian during the spring of 1964 whether or not it was true that Schwerner had attempted to "get young Negro males to sign statements that they would rape one white woman a week during the hot summer of 1964 here in Mississippi." Judge Cox, visibly upset by the question, ascertained that it had originated with one of the Neshoba defendants, Edgar "Preacher" Killen. "I'm not going to allow a farce to be made of this trial," Cox warned, "and everybody might as well get that through their heads, including every one of these defendants."

Doar thought the exchange represented a breakthrough. The attitude of the defendants, from the time of their initial arrests in late 1964 until the present moment, had been one of impudence—three solid years of treating the legal proceedings against them as little more than a joke. Cox's warning signaled, for the first time, that just maybe Mississippi intended to treat the case seriously. As Doar later recalled, because Cox's complete fealty to Mississippi and his sentiments on black equality and the civil rights movement were well known, it struck the jury that if he was willing to behave this way, perhaps they might, too. "If there had been any feeling in the courtroom that the defendants were invulnerable to conviction in Mississippi, this incident dispelled it completely," Doar observed. And it was not lost on anyone that the defendants had been scolded for attempting crudely to raise lynching's most time-honored rationale.

Using a large number of witnesses and the testimony of informant James Jordan, who fainted twice before finally taking the stand in front of his former Klan brethren, Doar and his fellow prosecutors walked the jury through the events of June 21, 1964—the three civil rights workers' arrival in Longdale, the arrest by Deputy Price, the hours in jail until nightfall, then the release and ambush, the three murders on Rock Cut Road, and the midnight burial by bulldozer in the dam at a place called the Old Jolly Farm. The defense in response sought to taint the government's case by reminding the jury that the FBI had made payments to informants, that Mississippians had a right to be upset by a civil rights invasion from the North, and that on the night of the killings their clients had either been having dinner with their families (June 21, 1964, was Father's Day) or watching the popular family TV western drama *Bonanza.*

In his closing argument, Doar noted the importance the federal government attached to the case but stressed that the trial was taking place "in a Mississippi city, before a Mississippi federal judge, in a Mississippi courtroom, before twelve men and women from the state of Mississippi." He emphasized: "The sole responsibility of the determination of guilt or innocence of these men remains in the hands where it should remain, the hands of twelve citizens from the state of Mississippi."

The defense's closing response was ill prepared and far less serious, as attorney H. C. Watkins suggested that Goodman, Schwerner, and Chaney may well have been "sacrificed by their own kind for publicity," and that, in any case, they had broken the law by speeding. He also asserted, with complete inaccuracy, that the men had "violated the American Constitution by messing in local affairs in a local community," before closing with the observation that "Mississippians rightfully resent some hairy beatnik from another state visiting our state with hate and defying our people."

After the jury deliberated, it reported to the judge that it had split evenly and could attain no verdict. The jubilation of the defendants was cut short when Cox refused to order a mistrial. Instead he ordered the jury to go back to their deliberations and return with a verdict, a judicial directive known as the "Allen charge." In a marked departure from Judge Mize's action before the Mack Parker grand jury seven years earlier, Cox did not insist on an all-or-nothing verdict, and this made it easier for the jurors to resolve their differences by settling on convictions for some of the defendants, acquittals for others. Sheriff Rainey, "Preacher" Killen (both of whom had sound alibis), and several others went free, while convictions were returned against seven men, including the conspiracy's point man, Deputy Price; its author, Sam Bowers; and the triggerman, Alton Wayne Roberts. All were sentenced to federal penitentiaries for as much as ten years.

Americans of all colors and backgrounds had watched with interest as the trial proceeded, and cheered the verdicts. While most knew better than to claim it represented victory in the fight for equality and fair treatment under law, there was a sure sense of long-awaited vindication in the trial's conclusion: for the first time in as long as anyone cared to remember, a lynch mob had been tried, found guilty, and its members sentenced to prison. That this had happened in Mississippi, the self-described "last bastion of white supremacy," before a Mississippi judge and jury, with the federal government pressing the enforcement of long-neglected constitutional guarantees, made the moment especially meaningful. "A measure of the quiet revolution that is taking place in Southern attitudes," *The New York Times* hailed the verdict. "A slow, still faltering but inexorable conversion to the concept that a single standard of justice must cover whites and Negroes alike."

As John Doar had assured the jury before their deliberations, "What I say, what the other lawyers say here today . . . will soon be forgotten, but what you twelve people do here today will long be remembered." Time has proved him right.

Epilogue

One of the most frequently asked questions about lynching is: When did it stop? Even among students of the phenomenon there is no recognized end point in lynching history. My use of the 1964 murders of Goodman, Schwerner, and Chaney is somewhat arbitrary, although I would defend the choice by noting that the Neshoba case was probably the last lynching in which a mob acted in collaboration with police and intercepted its victims leaving a jail. It was also, as I've described, highly significant in that it represented the first time since Reconstruction that the federal government waded into a lynching case in the South and emerged with convictions and prison sentences, ending the long era in which lynch mobs operated with complete impunity.

Statistics, those of the Tuskegee Institute and others, generally show that the main U.S. lynching epoch was from about 1890 to the Red Summer of 1919, and that thereafter lynching totals began to decline. Some historians consider the end to have come in the mid-1930s, when the annual recorded lynchings of blacks decreased, for the first time, to single digits. Others cite a specific incident such as the Duck Hill, Mississippi, blowtorch lynching of 1937, probably the last spectacle lynching in which a crowd watched victims tortured and put to death, or the Claude Neal lynching of 1934, one of the last in which advance publicity was used to attract a throng to a lynching site—and even in that instance the mob did not produce their victim but did away with him in secret. The Claude Neal and Duck Hill lynchings are in a sense "old-fashioned" compared with the Monroe, Georgia, quadruple lynching of 1946 and the Emmett Till case of 1955, both of which were modern "underground" lynchings. By the 1950s, this version had largely stood traditional Southern lynchcraft on its head. The public lynching, with its elaborate and ritualized practices, had given way to the exact opposite: a meticulous effort to conceal all traces of the mob's handiwork from view. (According to William Bradford Huie, in the years after the Till case, which was considered by some a "lynching gone wrong" in that authorities had been allowed to locate the victim's corpse, the proper method of "venting" a body for permanent submersion in water, and other procedures of the underground lynching, were discussed and analyzed by Mississippians bracing for the anticipated pressures of the civil rights movement.)

As it turned out, assaults on civil rights workers more often resembled assassinations than lynchings. The Christmas 1951 bombing of the home of Florida NAACP director Harry Moore was the first of scores of dynamite attacks on individuals aligned with civil rights causes in the South during the next two decades, the most notorious being the Birmingham church bombing of September 1963 that killed Cynthia Wesley, Carol Robertson, and Addie Mae Collins, fourteen, and Denise McNair, eleven. This extended wave of violence also included many shooting deaths—of southern Mississippi voting rights activists Herbert Lee and Louis Allen, among others—and culminated in the assassinations of the NAACP's Medgar Evers in Jackson in 1963 and of Martin Luther King, Jr., in Memphis in 1968. The indeterminate rule of thumb that for every known lynching there were many others that went unreported was still functioning as late as 1964 during the well-publicized search for Goodman, Schwerner, and Chaney, when the bodies of at least three young black men, apparent lynching victims, only two of whom were identifiable, were found in the bayous and rivers in Mississippi by police and federal forces.

In 1981 a Klan organization in Alabama randomly selected and lynched a black teenager; that same year whites in Skidmore, Missouri, lynched the town's white bully; and as recently as June 1998 Americans were shocked by the Jasper, Texas, lynchlike murder of a black part-time musician named James Byrd, Jr., who was tied by his feet to the rear of a pickup truck and dragged to his death down a backwoods road by three white men.

Of course, although lynchings may belong as permanently to our nation's past as the whale-oil lamp and the Pony Express, the "tendency of the white majority to desire summary disposition of those they regard as marginal or powerless"—as Mary Frances Berry, chairman of the U.S. Civil Rights Commission, once termed it—has never entirely disappeared. Harsher prison sentences (blacks are incarcerated at seven times the rate that whites are, serve longer sentences, and have higher arrest and conviction rates), racially biased drug laws, illegal stops and searches of black youth, racial profiling on the nation's highways, and police brutality reveal that the presumption of black criminality is still very much alive. Although black Americans constitute 12 percent of the overall population, they make up half the country's prison population; and for every one black American who graduates from college, one hundred are arrested. A comprehensive review conducted in 2000 of the federal death penalty since its 1988 reinstatement found that 50 percent of those slated for execution were black, and that another 25 percent represented other racial or ethnic minorities.

Such statistics are by now familiar. Instances of police violence leading to summary punishment occur with such regularity as to rarely cause comment or outrage, except in certain flagrant instances such as the shooting of Amadou Diallo or the beating of Rodney King. Mob vigilantism driven by prejudice also clearly survives, as the deaths of black New Yorkers Michael Griffith and Yusef Hawkins, white homosexual Matthew Shepperd, and others plainly attest. And questions of how to balance constitutional guarantees of fairness and due process with the public's desire to control and feel secure from crime—the argument that has always formed part of the background to lynching and vigilantism—resonate in the ongoing debates over the death penalty, hate-crimes legislation, gun control, Megan's Law, shaming punishments, the scope of a detained person's Miranda rights, and the rights of crime victims and their families to influence the sentencing of convicted felons. It is also clear that, while lynch mobs are no longer active in New Orleans, Memphis, or Marietta, Georgia, their spirit survives elsewhere in the world, and the savagery that lynching represented remains fully part of the human repertoire.

What keeps us from being paralyzed by this limitless and apparently renewable capacity for evil is our knowledge that a powerful countervailing human impulse exists. "Torture and burning are forbidden not because the victim is not bad enough," Charles Sumner once observed, "but because we are too good." The South where the scenes of unspeakable brutality recounted in this book occurred is a place much changed, as was shown by the outpouring of sympathy from the Jasper, Texas, white community toward the family of James Byrd, Jr., in 1998, and the swift arrest and conviction of his killers. The fears that once fueled lynchings—that interracial sex would lead to mongrelization, that white women required protection, that blacks active in business or politics threatened white control—no longer engage much concern. Vast economic change, the coming of new industry, and the automation of farm labor have done much to diminish the South's racial caste system; if they hadn't known it before, regional business interests learned in the civil rights years that incidents of racial violence and expressions of intolerance were harmful to commerce; and the Lost Cause has been largely reduced to weekend battle reenactments and feeble controversies about whether the Confederate flag belongs on top of official buildings or somewhere else.

In Lake City, South Carolina, where a century ago whites murdered Frazier B. Baker rather than allow a black man to operate the local post office, banners advertise proudly the achievement of hometown hero Ronald McNair, the world's first black astronaut, who perished on the shuttle *Challenger* in 1986. The narrow streets of Abbeville, South Carolina, where Anthony Crawford fought for his life against a mob in 1916, now form a sort of unofficial regional "wedding capital," the town's picturesque cathedral and parklike town square the ideal backdrop for young couples from nearby Columbia and Atlanta. At Bascom, Florida, the farm hamlet where Lola Cannidy went for a fateful walk with Claude Neal on October 18, 1934, and where she is now buried, residents barely recall the events leading up to the lynching, but they warm to a discussion of another of the town's daughters, the actress Faye Dunaway, who drew on her Panhandle upbringing to portray the Depression-era moll Bonnie Parker in the acclaimed 1967 film *Bonnie and Clyde.* In Newnan, Georgia, local historians shy away from the subject of the long-ago lynching of Sam Hose, out of deference, they insist, to the descendants of Hose's victims, Alfred and Mattie Cranford, who still reside there. The scene of Hose's public immolation in a pine grove along what was then called the Palmetto Road, now Jackson Street, has for decades been the site of a popular family-owned barbecue restaurant.

As one might expect, such insufferable characters as "Pitchfork" Ben Tillman and Theodore Bilbo are distinctly out of favor these days, while Medgar Evers, Martin Luther King, Jr., civil rights heroine Fannie Lou Hamer, and bluesmen such as Sonny Boy Williamson and Robert Johnson—people who in their own lifetimes could barely walk without fear down streets that today bear their names in tribute—are discussed and celebrated. In Mississippi, books and concerts are dedicated to the memory of Emmett Till. A movement in Georgia seeks to remove the statue of Tom Watson from the grounds of the state capitol; and the names of most of the Knights of Mary Phagan who at Watson's urging lynched Leo Frank in 1915, and whose identities were long a guarded secret in Phagan's hometown of Marietta, are now at www.leofranklynchers.com.

The South that clung so adamantly to myth, and which refused so fiercely to confront its most painful secrets, has made and is making a new effort to understand the past. A massacre of black citizens in Tulsa in 1921 and the Elaine, Arkansas, sharecroppers' war of 1919, among other incidents of racial violence long omitted from the history books, are now the subjects of academic conferences and "truth commissions," and state attorneys general have begun to review old dog-eared investigation files of bombing, murder, and lynching cases once thought unprosecutable.

Lynching diminished for numerous reasons—changing ideas about women and their role in society, the sobering example of European barbarity during two world wars, the influence of white commerce and industry in the South, the due-process revolution in the courts that reflected a new concern for the sanctity of the person, the binding together of the nation by technology and ever-faster modes of transportation. Most indispensable to its demise was the steady pressure from the reformers and writers who never quit insisting that we were too good to be a nation of lynchers. Sadly, few lived to see the satisfying results of their lifework— Ida Wells-Barnett, after decades of public-service work in her adopted home, Chicago, died suddenly of uremic poisoning in 1931; William Monroe Trotter's great strength, his determination to brook no failure or excuse in the cause of civil rights, turned inward after financial reverses in the Depression, and he took his own life by leaping from the roof of his Boston apartment building in 1934; the eloquent James Weldon Johnson, who sought to save black America's body and white America's soul, died tragically in 1938 when his car collided with a train; Walter White, the confidant of presidents who perfected the art of public relations as a strategy for social change, passed away of a heart attack at age sixty-one in 1955, after thirty-seven years in the leadership of the NAACP. Even after White encountered severe heart problems, he refused to give up the helm of the organization or the cause in which he so ardently believed. In the end, his colleagues agreed, he simply worked himself to death.

"He could easily have joined the 12,000 Negroes who pass the color-line and disappear into the white majority every year in this country," *The New York Times* wrote in eulogy. "But he deliberately sacrificed his comfort to publicize himself as a Negro and to devote his entire adult life to completing the emancipation of his people."

Jessie Daniel Ames lived until 1972, and in the last decade of her life, much of which she spent in an Austin, Texas, nursing home, she watched as the South was transformed by the upheaval of the civil rights movement. To the young participants in that movement, with its sweeping demands for full citizenship rights and social equality in every sphere, the crusade she had guided against so medieval a custom as lynching would have seemed almost quaint. But among those who remembered her, and to an emerging generation of feminist historians in the 1980s and 1990s, the example of Ames and the Association of Southern Women for the Prevention of Lynching would appear ever more impressive, a creative grass-roots model of women assuming political responsibility for an issue and challenging it on their terms.

It is important to remember that the ASWPL and NAACP both performed extremely valuable services to the nation beyond their antilynching work. They helped compel a public dialogue, however rancorous, about the future of America's black minority, forged bonds between black reformers and white liberals, established outposts of reform in small Black Belt towns, and, by educating and inspiring so many otherwise isolated individuals around a common theme, helped lay the cornerstone of civil rights advocacy upon which the later Southern movement would build. There can perhaps be no better tribute to the antilynching and civil rights crusaders of the early twentieth century than to note that when youthful civil rights workers reached small towns in the Deep South in the 1960s, it was inevitably one of Jessie Daniel Ames's former members, a retired constituent of A. Philip Randolph's Brotherhood of Sleeping Car Porters, or someone who could recall being stirred by W.E.B. Du Bois's editorials in *The Crisis* who was there waiting, with a meal and a room and words of caution and encouragement.

Du Bois himself left the NAACP during the 1930s but returned in a diminished role a decade later. During the heated election of 1948, a memo he had written critical of the NAACP's endorsement of President Truman was leaked to the press and Du Bois was promptly fired by the board of directors. By 1950, as head of the Peace Information Center, he found himself at odds with the federal government over the issue of whether the center had to register under the Foreign Agents Registration Act. In February 1951 Du Bois and four colleagues were arraigned in federal court in Washington, during which procedure Du Bois had to submit to the indignity of being handcuffed. The case was ultimately dismissed, but Du Bois continued to have passport problems and was by then so thoroughly tainted by "un-Americanism" that the longtime editor of *The Crisis* and the author of *The Souls of Black Folk* found himself shunned even by many black people, his lectures and articles no longer in demand.

Du Bois ultimately accepted an invitation from Ghana's president Kwame Nkrumah to come to Ghana and work on the *Encyclopedia Africana,* a project Du Bois had made a start on as early as 1909 but had never managed to pursue. In October 1961 he sold off most of his possessions, gave his books and papers to the scholar Herbert Aptheker, and with his second wife, Shirley Graham, left the United States, never to return. The man born in the foothills of New England during Reconstruction, whose long life had been so passionately bound up with the life of his country, died in Africa, a citizen of Ghana, at age ninety-five on August 27, 1963.

By a strange coincidence his death came a day before the renowned 1963 March on Washington, best known for the historic "I Have a Dream" oration by Martin Luther King, Jr. NAACP executive secretary Roy Wilkins told the thousands of civil rights activists and other Americans gathered along the Reflecting Pool before the Lincoln Memorial, "Regardless of the fact that in his later years Dr. Du Bois chose another path, it is incontrovertible that at the dawn of the twentieth century his was the voice calling you to gather here today in this cause."

This grand occasion, with its talk of great measures accomplished and things left to achieve, its eloquent utterances about difficulties and dreams, might have struck a few of those present as a kind of fitting farewell to Du Bois—the professor who reversed his steps on Mitchell Street in Atlanta in 1899 because a man had been lynched in rural Georgia, and who walked home determined that his life henceforth would be one not only of words but of actions.

Acknowledgments

I wish to thank the archivists and staff at the Alabama State Archives, Montgomery; the Georgia State Archives, Atlanta; the University of Georgia Library, Athens (Georgia Newspaper Project; the Rebecca Felton Papers); Howard University Library, Washington, D.C.; the National Archives in Washington, D.C. (Freedmen's Bureau Records, Records Group 105), and Beltsville, Maryland (Department of Justice Records, Record Group 60); the Mississippi Department of Archives and History, Jackson; and the Southern Historical Collection, University of North Carolina, Chapel Hill.

I made extensive use of the resources at the Schomburg Center for Research in Black Culture in New York City, where I had access to the NAACP Papers, the Tuskegee Clippings Files, the International Labor Defense and Civil Rights Congress Papers, the Association of Southern Women to Prevent Lynching Papers, the Commission on Interracial Cooperation Papers, and the papers of W.E.B. Du Bois. The Schomburg also houses a complete collection of *The Crisis* as well as the papers of A. Phillip Randolph, Paul Robeson, and Jessie Daniel Ames. The stacks and microfilm collection of the main research library of the New York Public Library were also invaluable.

Research was also conducted at the South Caroliniana Library, University of South Carolina, Columbia; Clemson University Library; the Memphis Public Library; the Florida State Archives, Tallahassee; the Franklin D. Roosevelt Presidential Library, Hyde Park, New York; the Newnan Public Library, Georgia; the Peekskill Public Library, New York; the Beinecke Rare Book Collection at Yale University (the James Weldon Johnson Papers); the Chester County Historical Society, Pennsylvania; the New Hanover County Public Library, Wilmington, North Carolina; and the Phillips County Library, Helena, Arkansas.

A handful of books by other historians were particularly helpful. Richard Brown's *Strain of Violence: Historical Studies of Violence and Vigilantism* is a compendium of valuable data; John Egerton's *Speak Now Against the Day: The Generation Before the Civil Rights Movement in the South* was indispensable for gaining a sense of the South between the world wars; David Levering Lewis's *W.E.B. Du Bois: Biography of a Race, 1868–1919* is a masterful introduction to Du Bois and the world of the early NAACP; Herbert Shapiro's *White Violence and Black Response: From Reconstruction to Montgomery* provides a thoughtful chronology of the lynching era, as does Donald L. Grant in *The Development of the Anti-Lynching Reform Movement in the United States, 1883–1932.* Thomas F. Gossett's *Race: The History of an Idea in America* enabled my understanding of Social Darwinism and its relation to late-nineteenth-century views on race. Also useful were the articles collected in *Under Sentence of Death: Lynching in the South,* edited by W. Fitzhugh Brundage.

I wish to express my thanks and appreciation to Stephanie Steiker of New York City and Jerry Mitchell of the Jackson, Mississippi, *Clarion-Ledger,* for their friendship and assistance, and law professor Carol Steiker for valuable comments on the manuscript. Finally, this book would never have been undertaken if not for the encouragement of Elizabeth Sheinkman of the Elaine Markson Literary Agency, nor could it have been completed without the dedicated efforts of my editor at Random House, Scott Moyers.

Bibliography

Selected Books and Pamphlets

Akers, Monte. *Flames After Midnight: Murder, Vengeance, and Desolation in a Texas Community.* Austin, Tex.: University of Texas Press, 1999.

Allen, James. *Without Sanctuary: Lynching Photography in America.* Santa Fe, N.M.: Twin Palms, 2000.

Aptheker, Herbert. *American Negro Slave Revolts.* New York: International Publishers, 1963.

Ayers, Edward L. *Vengeance and Justice: Crime and Punishment in the 19th Century American South.* New York: Oxford University Press, 1984.

Baker, Lee. *From Savage to Negro: Anthropology and the Construction of Race, 1896–1954.* Berkeley: University of California Press, 1998.

Baldwin, James. *Nobody Knows My Name: More Notes of a Native Son.* Reprint. New York: Dell, 1961.

Bancroft, Hubert H. *Popular Tribunals,* vols. 36 and 37 of *The Works of Hubert Howe Bancroft.* 39 vols. San Francisco: A. L. Bancroft, 1888.

Bannister, Robert C. *Social Darwinism: Science and Myth in Anglo American Social Thought.* Philadelphia: Temple University Press, 1979.

Bartley, Numan V. *The Rise of Massive Resistance: Race and Politics in the South During the 1950s.* Baton Rouge: Louisiana State University Press, 1969.

Beard, Charles A. and Mary R. Beard. *The Rise of American Civilization.* New York: Macmillan, 1927.

Beck, E. M., and Stewart E. Tolnay. *A Festival of Violence: An Analysis of Southern Lynchings, 1882–1930.* Urbana, Ill.: University of Illinois Press, 1995.

Belford, Barbara. *Brilliant Bylines: A Biographical Anthology of Notable Newspaperwomen in America.* New York: Columbia University Press, 1986.

Belknap, Michael R. *Federal Law and Southern Order: Racial Violence and Constitutional Conflict in the Post-Brown South.* Athens, Ga.: University of Georgia Press, 1987.

Bernardi, Daniel, ed. *The Birth of Whiteness: Race and the Emergence of U.S. Cinema.* New Brunswick, N.J.: Rutgers University Press, 1996.

Berry, Mary Frances. *Black Resistance, White Law: A History of Constitutional Racism in America.* New York: Penguin ed., 1994.

Boas, Franz. *The Mind of Primitive Man.* New York: Macmillan, 1944.

Bowers, Claude G. *The Tragic Era: The Revolution After Lincoln.* Cambridge, Mass.: Houghton-Mifflin Co., 1929.

Brisbane, Robert H. *The Black Vanguard: Origins of the Negro Social Revolution 1900–1960.* Valley Forge, Pa.: Judson Press, 1970.

Brown, Richard. *Strain of Violence: Historical Studies of Violence and Vigilantism.* New York: Oxford University Press, 1975.

Brown, Sterling, ed. *The Negro Caravan.* New York: The Dryden Press, 1941.

Brownmiller, Susan. *Against Our Will: Men, Women and Rape.* New York: Simon & Schuster, 1975.

Bruce, Philip A. *The Plantation Negro as Freeman.* New York: G. P. Putnam's Sons, 1889.

Brundage, W. Fitzhugh. *Lynching in the New South: Georgia and Virginia, 1880–1930.* Urbana, Ill.: University of Illinois Press, 1993.

———, ed. *Under Sentence of Death: Lynching in the South.* Chapel Hill, N.C.: University of North Carolina Press, 1997.

Buck, Paul H. *The Road to Reunion, 1865–1900.* New York: Little, Brown & Co., 1937.

Cagin, Seth, and Philip Dray. *We Are Not Afraid: The Story of Goodman, Schwerner, and Chaney and the Civil Rights Campaign for Mississippi.* New York: Macmillan, 1988.

Capeci, Dominic J., Jr. *The Lynching of Cleo Wright.* Lexington: University Press of Kentucky, 1998.

Carroll, Charles. *The Negro a Beast, or "In the Image of God"* (1900) Reprint. Miami: Mnemosyne Publishing Company, 1969.

Carter, Dan T. *Scottsboro: A Tragedy of the American South.* Rev. ed. Baton Rouge: Louisiana State University Press, 1979.

Cash, W. J. *The Mind of the South.* New York: Knopf, 1941.

Cecelski, David S., and Timothy B. Tyson. *Democracy Betrayed: The Wilmington Race Riot of 1898 and Its Legacy.* Chapel Hill, N.C.: University of North Carolina Press, 1998.

Civil Rights Congress. *We Charge Genocide: The Historic Petition to the United Nations for Relief from a Crime of the United States Government Against the Negro People.* New York: Civil Rights Congress, 1951.

Clarke, John Henry, et al. *Black Titan: W.E.B. Du Bois.* Boston: Beacon Press, 1970.

Cole, David. *No Equal Justice: Race and Class in the American Criminal Justice System.* New York: The New Press, 1999.

Collins, Winfield H. *The Truth About Lynching and the Negro in the South.* New York: The Neale Publishing Company, 1918.

Cook, Raymond A. *Fire from the Flint: The Amazing Careers of Thomas Dixon.* Winston-Salem, N.C.: J. F. Blair, 1968.

Cortner, Richard C. *A Mob Intent on Death: The NAACP and the Arkansas Riot Cases.* Middletown, Conn.: Wesleyan University Press, 1988.

———. *A "Scottsboro" Case in Mississippi: The Supreme Court and Brown v. Mississippi.* Jackson, Miss.: University of Mississippi Press, 1986.

Current, Richard. *Three Carpetbag Governors.* Baton Rouge: Louisiana State University Press, 1967.

Curriden, Mark, and Leroy Phillips, Jr. *Contempt of Court: The Turn of the Century Lynching That Launched One Hundred Years of Federalism.* New York: Faber and Faber, 1999.

Cutler, James. *Lynch-Law: An Investigation into the History of Lynching in the United States.* New York: Longmans, Green, 1905.

Darrow, Clarence. *The Story of My Life.* New York: Charles Scribner's Sons, 1932.

DeCosta-Willis, Miriam, ed. *The Memphis Diary of Ida B. Wells: An Intimate Portrait of the Artist as a Young Woman.* Boston: Beacon Press, 1995.

Dimsdale, Thomas J. *The Vigilantes of Montana: Or Popular Justice in the Rocky Mountains.* 3rd ed. Butte, Mont.: W. F. Bartlett, 1915.

Dinnerstein, Leonard. *The Leo Frank Case.* Athens, Ga.: Georgia University Press, 1966.

Dollard, John. *Caste and Class in a Southern Town.* New Haven, Conn.: Oxford University Press, 1937.

Donald, David H. *Charles Sumner and the Coming of the Civil War.* Chicago: University of Chicago Press, 1960.

Douglass, Frederick. *The Life and Times of Frederick Douglass.* New York: Crowell, 1966.

Downey, Dennis B. *"No Crooked Death": Coatesville, Pa., and the Lynching of Zacharia Walker.* Urbana, Ill.: University of Illinois Press, 1991.

Duberman, Martin Bauml. *Paul Robeson.* New York: Knopf, 1989.

Du Bois, W.E.B. *The Autobiography of W.E.B. Du Bois: A Soliloquy on Viewing My Life from the Last Decade of Its First Century.* New York: International Publishers, 1968.

———. *Black Reconstruction.* New York: Harcourt, Brace and Company, 1935.

———. *Darkwater: Voices from Within the Veil.* New York: Harcourt, Brace and Howe, 1920.

———. *Dusk of Dawn: An Essay Toward an Autobiography of a Race Concept.* New York: Harcourt, Brace and Company, 1940.

———. *The Souls of Black Folk: Essays and Sketches.* Chicago: 1903; reprint, New York: Signet, 1982.

Duster, Alfreda M., ed. *Crusade for Justice: The Autobiography of Ida B. Wells.* Chicago: University of Chicago Press, 1970.

Dykeman, Wilma, and James Stokely. *Seeds of Southern Change: The Life of Will Alexander.* Chicago: University of Chicago Press, 1962.

Edmonds, Helen G. *The Negro and Fusion Politics in North Carolina, 1894–1901.* Chapel Hill, N.C.: University of North Carolina Press, 1951.

Egerton, John. *Speak Now Against the Day: The Generation Before the Civil Rights Movement in the South.* New York: Knopf, 1994.

Ellis, Mary Louise. *Rain Down Fire: The Lynching of Sam Hose.* Ph.D. diss. Florida State University, 1992.

Farr, Finis. *Black Champion: The Life and Times of Jack Johnson.* New York: Scribner, 1964.

Fast, Howard. *Peekskill USA: A Personal Experience.* New York: Civil Rights Congress, 1951.

Fedo, Michael. *The Lynchings in Duluth.* St. Paul, Minn.: Minnesota Historical Society Press, 2000.

Fine, Sidney. *Frank Murphy: The Detroit Years.* Ann Arbor, Mich.: University of Michigan Press, 1975.

Foner, Eric. *Reconstruction: America's Unfinished Revolution, 1863–1877.* New York: Harper & Row, 1988.

———. *A Short History of Reconstruction, 1863–1877.* New York: Harper Perennial, 1990.

Foster, Gaines M. *Ghosts of the Confederacy: Defeat, the Lost Cause, and the Emergence of the New South.* New York: Oxford University Press, 1987.

Fox, Stephen R. *The Guardian of Boston, William Monroe Trotter.* New York: Atheneum, 1970.

Franklin, John Hope. *Reconstruction After the Civil War.* Chicago: University of Chicago Press, 1961.

Friedman, Lawrence M. *Crime and Punishment in American History.* New York: Basic Books, 1993.

Fry, Gladys-Marie. *Night Riders in Black Folk History.* 2nd ed. Athens, Ga.: University of Georgia Press, 1991.

Gambino, Richard. *Vendetta.* Garden City, N.Y.: Doubleday, 1977.

Garrow, David J. *The FBI and Martin Luther King, Jr., from "Solo" to Memphis.* New York: W. W. Norton, 1981.

Gates, Henry Louis, Jr., and Cornel West. *The Future of the Race.* New York: Knopf, 1996.

Genovese, Eugene D. *Roll, Jordan, Roll: The World the Slaves Made.* New York: Pantheon Books, 1974.

Gilmore, Al-Tony. *Bad Nigger! The National Impact of Jack Johnson.* Port Washington, N.Y.: Kennikat Press, 1975.

Ginzberg, Ralph. *100 Years of Lynching.* New York: Lancer Books, 1962.

Gladney, Margaret Rose, ed. *How Am I to Be Heard? Letters of Lillian Smith.* Chapel Hill, N.C.: University of North Carolina Press, 1993.

Glueck, Sheldon, ed. *Roscoe Pound and Criminal Justice.* Dobbs Ferry, N.Y.: Oceana Publications, 1965.

Godshalk, David Fort. *In the Wake of Riot: Atlanta's Struggle for Order, 1899–1919.* Ph.D. diss. Yale University, 1992.

Goldman, Eric F. *Rendezvous with Destiny: A History of Modern American Reform.* New York: Knopf, 1952.

Goodwin, Doris Kearns. *No Ordinary Time—Franklin and Eleanor Roosevelt: The Home Front in World War II.* New York: Simon & Schuster, 1994.

Gossett, Thomas F. *Race: The History of an Idea in America.* New York: Oxford University Press, 1997.

Grant, Donald L. *The Development of the Anti-Lynching Reform Movement in the United States, 1883–1932.* Ph.D. diss. University of Missouri, 1972.

———. *The Way It Was in the South: The Black Experience in Georgia.* Secaucus, N.J.: Carol Publishing Group, 1993.

Greenbaum, Fred. *Fighting Progressive: A Biography of Edward P. Costigan.* Washington, D.C.: Public Affairs Press, 1971.

Hair, William Ivy. *Carnival of Fury: Robert Charles and the New Orleans Race Riot of 1900.* Baton Rouge: Louisiana State University Press, 1976.

Haldeman-Julius, Marcet. *Clarence Darrow's Two Great Trials.* Girard, Kans.: Haldeman-Julius, 1927.

Hale, Grace Elizabeth. *Making Whiteness: The Culture of Segregation in the South, 1890–1940.* New York: Pantheon Books, 1998.

Hall, Jacqueline Dowd. *Revolt Against Chivalry: Jessie Daniel Ames and the Women's Campaign Against Lynching.* New York: Columbia University Press, 1979.

Haney, Lynn. *Naked at the Feast: A Biography of Josephine Baker.* New York: Dodd, Mead, 1981.

Harlan, Louis. *Booker T. Washington: The Making of a Black Leader, 1856–1901.* New York: Oxford University Press, 1972.

———. *Booker T. Washington: The Wizard of Tuskegee, 1901–1915.* New York: Oxford University Press, 1983.

Harris, Trudier. *Exorcising Blackness: Historical and Literary Lynching and Burning Rituals.* Bloomington, Ind.: Indiana University Press, 1984.

Hawkins, Hugh, ed. *The Abolitionists: Means, Ends, and Motivations.* 2nd ed. Lexington, Mass.: Heath, 1972.

Helper, Hinton. *Nojoque. A Question for a Continent.* New York: G. W. Carleton and Co., 1867.

Hernton, Calvin C. *Sex and Racism in America.* New York: Grove Press, 1966.

Hixon, William B., Jr. *Moorfield Storey and the Abolitionist Tradition.* New York: Oxford University Press, 1972.

Hodes, Martha. *White Women, Black Men: Illicit Sex in the 19th Century South.* New Haven, Conn.: Yale University Press, 1997.

Hoffman, Frederick. *Race Traits and Tendencies of the American Negro.* New York: Macmillan, 1896.

Hofstadter, Richard. *The Age of Reform.* New York: Knopf, 1955.

Holmes, William. *The White Chief: James K. Vardaman.* Baton Rouge: Louisiana State University Press, 1970.

Hughes, Langston. *Fight for Freedom: The Story of the NAACP.* New York: Norton, 1962.

Huie, William Bradford. *Three Lives for Mississippi.* New York: WCC Books, 1965.

Humes, D. Joy. *Oswald Garrison Villard: Liberal of the 1920s.* Syracuse, N.Y.: Syracuse University Press, 1960.

Hunt, William R. *Front Page Detective: William J. Burns and the Detective Profession, 1880–1930.* Bowling Green, Ky.: Bowling Green State University Popular Press, 1990.

Hurst, James W. *The Growth of American Law: The Law Makers.* Boston: Little, Brown, 1950.

Hutchins, Fred L. *What Happened in Memphis.* Kingsport, Tenn.: Kingsport Press, 1965.

Jameson, Jack. *Night Riders in Sunny Florida: The KKK Murder of Joseph Shoemaker.* New York: Workers Library, 1936.

Johnson, James Weldon. *Along This Way: The Autobiography of James Weldon Johnson.* New York: Viking Press, 1933.

———. *Autobiography of an Ex-Colored Man.* Boston: Sherman, French & Co., 1912.

———. *Black Manhattan.* New York: Knopf, 1930.

Kellogg, Charles Flint. *NAACP: A History of the National Association for the Advancement of Colored People. Volume 1, 1909–1920.* Baltimore: Johns Hopkins Press, 1967.

Kennedy, Randall. *Race, Crime, and the Law.* New York: Random House, 1997.

Kennedy, Stetson. *Southern Exposure.* Garden City, N.Y.: Doubleday, 1946.

Kester, Howard. *Revolt Among the Sharecroppers.* New York: Covici Friede, 1936.

Knight, Alfred H. *The Life of the Law: The People and Cases That Have Shaped Our Society.* New York: Crown, 1996.

Larsen, Lawrence H., and Barbara Cottrell. *The Gate City: A History of Omaha.* Lincoln, Ne.: University of Nebraska Press, 1997.

Lemann, Nicholas. *The Promised Land: The Great Black Migration and How It Changed America.* New York: Knopf, 1991.

Lester, J. C., and D. L. Wilson. *Ku Klux Klan: Its Origins, Growth and Disbandment.* Nashville: Wheeler, Osborn & Duckworth Manufacturing Company, 1884.

Lewis, David Levering. *When Harlem Was in Vogue.* New York: Knopf, 1979.

———. *W.E.B. Du Bois: Biography of a Race, 1868–1919.* New York: Henry Holt, 1993.

Litwack, Leon. *Been in the Storm So Long: The Aftermath of Slavery.* New York: Knopf, 1979.

———. *Trouble in Mind: Black Southerners in the Age of Jim Crow.* New York: Knopf, 1998.

Logan, Rayford W. *The Betrayal of the Negro: From Rutherford B. Hayes to Woodrow Wilson.* New York: Da Capo Press, 1997.

Lommel, Cookie. *Robert Church: Entrepreneur.* Los Angeles: Melrose Square Publishing Company, 1995.

Loveland, Anne C. *Lillian Smith: A Southerner Confronting the South.* Baton Rouge: Louisiana State University Press, 1986.

Martin, Charles H. *The Angelo Herndon Case and Southern Justice.* Baton Rouge: Louisiana State University Press, 1976.

Mays, Benjamin E. *Born to Rebel: An Autobiography.* New York: Scribner, 1971.

McCullough, David. *Truman.* New York: Simon & Schuster, 1992.

McFeely, William S. *Frederick Douglass.* New York: W. W. Norton, 1991.

———. *Yankee Stepfather: General O. O. Howard and the Freedmen.* New Haven, Conn.: Yale University Press, 1968.

McGovern, James R. *Anatomy of a Lynching: The Killing of Claude Neal.* Baton Rouge: Louisiana State University Press, 1982.

McKay, Claude. *Selected Poems of Claude McKay.* New York: Harcourt, Brace & World, 1953.

McMurry, Linda O. *To Keep the Waters Troubled: The Life of Ida B. Wells.* New York: Oxford University Press, 1998.

Mitford, Jessica. *A Fine Old Conflict.* New York: Knopf, 1977.

Moses, Wilson J. *The Golden Age of Black Nationalism, 1850–1925.* New York: Oxford University Press, 1988.

Myrdal, Gunnar. *An American Dilemma: The Negro Problem and American Democracy.* New York: Harper & Brothers, 1944.

National Association for the Advancement of Colored People. *An Appeal to the World: A Statement on the Denial of Human Rights to Minorities in the Case of Citizens of Negro Descent in the United States of America and an Appeal to the United Nations for Redress.* New York: NAACP, 1947.

———. *Thirty Years of Lynching in the United States, 1889–1919.* New York: NAACP, 1919.

——— (Boston branch). *Fighting a Vicious Film: Protest Against "The Birth of a Nation."* Boston: NAACP, 1915.

Oshinsky, David M. *"Worse Than Slavery": Parchman Farm and the Experience of Jim Crow Justice.* New York: Free Press, 1996.

Ovington, Mary White. *Black and White Sat Down Together: Reminiscences of an NAACP Founder.* New York: Feminist Press at the City University of New York, 1995.

———. *The Walls Came Tumbling Down.* New York: Schocken Books, 1970.

Pach, Chester J., and Elmo Richardson. *The Presidency of Dwight D. Eisenhower.* Lawrence, Kans.: University Press of Kansas, 1991.

Page, Thomas Nelson. *The Negro: The Southerner's Problem.* New York: Scribner, 1904.

Palmer, Irenas J. *Black Man's Burden, or The Horror of Southern Lynchings.* Olean, N.Y.: Olean Evening Herald Print, 1902.

Patterson, Orlando. *Rituals of Blood: Consequences of Slavery in Two American Centuries.* New York: Basic Civitas, 1998.

Patterson, William L. *The Man Who Cried Genocide: An Autobiography.* New York: International Publishers, 1971.

Pike, James S. *The Prostrate State: South Carolina Under Negro Government.* New York: D. Appleton, 1874.

Pound, Roscoe. *Criminal Justice in America.* Cambridge, Mass.: Harvard University Press, 1945.

Prather, H. Leon, Sr. *We Have Taken a City: The Wilmington Racial Massacre and Coup of 1898.* Rutherford, N.J.: Fairleigh Dickinson University Press, 1984.

Rable, George C. *But There Was No Peace: The Role of Violence in the Politics of Reconstruction.* Athens, Ga.: University of Georgia Press, 1984.

Rampersad, Arnold. *The Art and Imagination of W.E.B. Du Bois.* Cambridge, Mass.: Harvard University Press, 1976.

Raper, Arthur. *The Tragedy of Lynching.* Chapel Hill, N.C.: University of North Carolina Press, 1933.

Redkey, Edwin S., ed. *Respect Black: The Writings and Speeches of Henry McNeal Turner.* New York: Arno Press, 1971.

Rise, Eric W. *The Martinsville Seven: Race, Rape and Capital Punishment.* Charlottesville, Va.: University Press of Virginia, 1995.

Roberts, Randy. *Papa Jack: Jack Johnson and the Era of White Hopes.* New York: Free Press, 1983.

Rudwick, Elliott M. *Race Riot at East St. Louis, July 2, 1917.* Carbondale, Ill.: Southern Illinois University Press, 1964.

———. *W.E.B. Du Bois: A Study in Minority Group Leadership.* Philadelphia: University of Pennsylvania Press, 1960.

Rydell, Robert W. *All the World's a Fair: Visions of Empire at American International Expositions, 1876–1916.* Chicago: University of Chicago Press, 1984.

Schurz, Carl. *Report on the Conditions of the South.* Reprint. New York: Arno Press, 1969.

Schwartz, Bernard, ed. *The Fourteenth Amendment Centennial Volume.* New York: New York University Press, 1970.

Senechel, Roberta. *The Sociogenesis of a Race Riot: Springfield, Illinois in 1908.* Urbana, Ill.: University of Illinois Press, 1990.

Shapiro, Herbert. *White Violence and Black Response: From Reconstruction to Montgomery.* Amherst, Mass.: University of Massachusetts Press, 1988.

Shufeldt, Robert W. *The Negro: A Menace to American Civilization.* Boston: R. G. Badger, 1907.

Silber, Nina. *The Romance of Reunion: Northerners and the South, 1865–1900.* Chapel Hill, N.C.: University of North Carolina Press, 1993.

Simkins, F. *Pitchfork Ben Tillman: South Carolinian.* Baton Rouge: Louisiana State University Press, 1944.

Simon, Paul. *Lovejoy: Martyr to Freedom.* St. Louis: Concordia, 1964.

Smead, Howard. *Blood Justice: The Lynching of Mack Charles Parker.* New York: Oxford University Press, 1986.

Smith, Lillian. *Killers of the Dream.* New York: W. W. Norton, 1949.

———. *Strange Fruit.* New York: Reynal & Hitchcock, 1944.

Southern Commission on the Study of Lynching. *Lynchings and What They Mean.* Atlanta: The Commission, 1931.

Starkey, Marion L. *The Devil in Massachusetts: A Modern Enquiry into the Salem Witch Trials.* New York: Knopf, 1949.

Sterling, Dorothy. *The Trouble They Seen: The Story of Reconstruction in the Words of African-Americans.* New York: Doubleday, 1976.

Talmadge, John. *Rebecca Latimer Felton: Nine Stormy Decades.* Athens, Ga.: University of Georgia Press, 1960.

Terrell, Mary Church. *A Colored Woman in a White World.* Washington, D.C.: Ransdell Inc., 1940.

Thompson, Mildred. *Ida B. Wells-Barnett: An Exploratory Study of an American Black Woman, 1893–1930.* Ph.D. diss. George Washington University, 1979.

Trelease, Allen W. *White Terror: The Ku Klux Klan Conspiracy and Southern Reconstruction.* Baton Rouge: Louisiana State University Press, 1971.

Tuttle, William M., Jr. *Race Riot: Chicago in the Red Summer of 1919.* New York: Atheneum, 1970.

Tygiel, Jules. *Baseball's Great Experiment.* New York: Oxford University Press, 1993.

U.S. Commission on Civil Rights. *Freedom to Be Free: A Century of Emancipation, 1863–1963.* Washington, D.C.: U.S. Government Printing Office, 1963.

U.S. 42nd Congress, 2nd Session, House Report 22. *Report of the Joint Select Committee to Inquire into the Condition of Affairs in the Late Insurrectionary States.* 13 vols. Washington, D.C.: Government Printing Office, 1872.

Wade, Wyn Craig. *The Fiery Cross: The Ku Klux Klan in America.* New York: Simon & Schuster, 1987.

Washington, Booker T. *Up from Slavery: An Autobiography.* New York: Doubleday, Page & Co., 1901.

Waskow, Arthur I. *From Race Riot to Sit-in, 1919 and the 1960s: A Study in the Connections Between Conflict and Violence.* Garden City, N.Y.: Doubleday, 1966.

———. *The 1919 Race Riots: A Study in the Connections Between Conflict and Violence.* Ph.D. diss. University of Wisconsin, 1963.

Weaver, John D. *The Brownsville Raid.* New York: W. W. Norton, 1970.

Wedin, Carolyn. *Inheritors of the Spirit: Mary White Ovington and the Founding of the NAACP.* New York: John Wiley & Sons, 1998.

Weiss, Nancy J. *Farewell to the Party of Lincoln: Black Politics in the Age of FDR.* Princeton, N.J.: Princeton University Press, 1983.

Wells, Ida B. *Mob Rule in New Orleans: Robert Charles and His Fight to the Death.* Chicago: Ida B. Wells-Barnett, 1900.

———. "The Reason Why the Colored American Is Not in the World's Columbian Exposition" (pamphlet). Chicago: Ida B. Wells, 1893.

———. *A Red Record: Tabulated Statistics and Alleged Causes of Lynchings in the United States, 1892–1893–1894.* Chicago: Donohue & Henneberry, 1895.

———. *Southern Horrors: Lynch Law in All Its Phases.* New York: New York Age Printing, 1892.

West, Cornel. *Race Matters.* Boston: Beacon Press, 1993.

Westchester Committee for a Fair Inquiry into the Peekskill Violence. *Eyewitness: Peekskill U.S.A. August 27–September 4, 1949.* White Plains, N.Y.: The Committee, 1949.

White, Walter. *The Fire in the Flint.* New York: Knopf, 1924.

———. *A Man Called White.* New York: Viking Press, 1948.

———. *Rope and Faggot: A Biography of Judge Lynch.* New York: Knopf, 1929.

Whitehead, Don. *Attack on Terror: The FBI Against the Ku Klux Klan in Mississippi.* New York: Funk & Wagnalls, 1970.

Whitfield, Stephen J. *A Death in the Delta: The Story of Emmett Till.* New York: Free Press, 1988.

Williams, Alfred B. *Hampton and His Red Shirts: South Carolina's Deliverance in 1876.* Freeport, N.Y.: Books for Libraries Press, 1970.

Williamson, Joel. *The Crucible of Race: Black-White Relations in the American South Since Emancipation.* New York: Oxford University Press, 1984.

———. *A Rage for Order: Black-White Relations in the American South Since Emancipation.* New York: Oxford University Press, 1986.

Woodward, C. Vann. *The Strange Career of Jim Crow.* 3rd rev. ed. New York: Oxford University Press, 1974.

———. *Tom Watson: Agrarian Rebel.* New York: The Macmillan Co., 1938.

Wright, George C. *Racial Violence in Kentucky, 1865–1940: Lynchings, Mob Rule, and "Legal Lynchings."* Baton Rouge: Louisiana State University Press, 1990.

Wright, Richard. *Black Boy: A Record of Childhood and Youth.* New York: Harper & Bros., 1945.

———. *Native Son.* New York: Harper & Bros., 1940.

———. *Uncle Tom's Children.* New York: Harper & Bros., 1938.

Wyatt-Brown, Bertram. *Southern Honor: Ethics and Behavior in the Old South.* New York: Oxford University Press, 1982.

Yarbrough, Tinsley E. *Judicial Enigma: The First Justice Harlan.* New York: Oxford University Press, 1995.

Zangrando, Robert L. *The NAACP Crusade Against Lynching, 1909–1950.* Philadelphia: Temple University Press, 1980.

Selected Articles

Adams, James Trustlow. "Our Lawless Heritage." *The Atlantic Monthly,* December 1928.

Ames, Jessie Daniel. "Can Newspapers Harmonize Their Editorial Policy on Lynching and Their News Stories on Lynching?" Reprinted in *Southern Newspaper Publishers' Association Bulletin* 65, July 1, 1936.

Aptheker, Bettina. "The Suppression of the *Free Speech:* Ida B. Wells and the Memphis Lynching, 1892." *San Jose Studies* 3, 1977.

Basso, Hamilton. "Five Days in Decatur." *The New Republic,* December 20, 1933.

Bernstein, Barton. "Plessy v. Ferguson: Conservative Sociological Jurisprudence." *Journal of Negro History,* July 1963.

Blumenthal, Henry. "Woodrow Wilson and the Race Question." *Journal of Negro History,* January 1963.

Boas, Franz. "The Real Race Problem." *The Crisis,* November 1910.

Bradley, Rose. "Back of the Maryland Lynching." *The Nation,* December 13, 1933.

Butts, J. W., and Dorothy James. "The Underlying Causes of the Elaine Riot of 1919." *Arkansas Historical Quarterly,* vol. XX, no. 1, Spring 1961.

Carl, Robert B. "Race Relations in the Agrarian Revolt: The Georgia Experience, 1889–1896." *Bulletin of the Atlanta Historical Society,* Winter 1977.

Carter, Dan T. "The Anatomy of Fear: The Christmas Day Insurrection Scare of 1865." *Journal of Southern History,* August 1976.

Cashin, Joan. "A Lynching in Wartime Carolina: The Death of Saxe Joiner," in Brundage, ed., *Under Sentence of Death: Lynching in the South.*

Chamlee, George W. "Is Lynching Ever Defensible?" *Forum,* February 1927.

Clark, Thomas D. "The Country Newspaper." *Journal of Southern History,* February 1948.

Cripps, Thomas. "The Birth of a Race: A Lost Film Rediscovered in Texas." *Texas Humanist* 5, 1983.

Crouthamel, James L. "The Springfield Race Riot of 1908." *Journal of Negro History,* July 1960.

Crowe, Charles. "Racial Massacre in Atlanta, September 22, 1906." *Journal of Negro History* 54, April 1969.

———. "Tom Watson, Populists, and Blacks Reconsidered." *Journal of Negro History,* April 1970.

Dabney, Virginius. "Dixie Rejects Lynching." *The Nation,* November 27, 1937.

Dudziak, Mary L. "Josephine Baker, Racial Protest, and the Cold War." *Journal of American History,* September 1994.

Fleming, Thomas J. "Take the Hatred Away, and You Have Nothing Left." *American Heritage,* December 1968.

Flower, B. O. "The Black Shadow in the South." *Forum,* vol. 16, October 1893.

———. "The Burning of Negroes in the South: A Protest and a Warning." *Arena,* April 1893.

Franklin, John Hope. "A Century of Civil War Observance." *Journal of Negro History,* October 1962.

Gatewood, Willard B. "Booker T. Washington and the Ulrich Affair." *Journal of Negro History,* January 1970.

Gilmore, Glenda E. "One of the Meanest Books: Thomas Dixon, Jr., and *The Leopard's Spots.*" *North Carolina Literary Review* (special edition on the Wilmington Race Riot of 1898), Spring 1994.

Hall, Jacqueline Dowd. "'The Mind That Burns in Each Body': Women, Rape, and Racial Violence." In *Powers of Desire: The Politics of Sexuality,* ed. Ann Sitlow, et al. New York Monthly Review Press, 1983.

Hixson, William B., Jr. "Moorfield Storey and the Struggle for Equality." *Journal of American History,* December 1968.

Howard, Walter. "A Blot on Tampa's History: The 1934 Lynching of Robert Johnson." *Tampa Bay History,* vol. 6, no. 2, Fall/Winter 1984.

Huie, William Bradford. "The Shocking Story of Approved Killing in Mississippi." *Look,* January 24, 1956.

———. "What's Happened to the Emmett Till Killers?" *Look,* January 22, 1957.

Hux, Roger K. "Lillian Clayton Jewett and the Rescue of the Baker Family, 1899–1900." *Historical Journal of Massachusetts,* Winter 1991.

Irwin, Will. "They Lynched the Wrong Man." *Liberty,* December 4, 1937.

Johnson, Charles S. "How Much Is the Migration a Flight from Persecution?" *Opportunity,* September 1923.

Johnson, Gerald W. "Maryland: Storm Warning." *The New Republic,* December 20, 1933.

Jordan, Joe. "Lynchers Don't Like Lead." *The Atlantic Monthly,* February 1946.

Kester, Howard. "The Marianna, Florida Lynching: A Report of an Investigation Made for the NAACP." NAACP Publication, November 30, 1934.

Klotman, Phyllis R. "Tearing a Hole in History: Lynching as Theme and Motif." *Black American Literature Forum,* Summer 1985.

Kountze, Mabe. "A History of the Early Colored Press in Massachusetts and a Second Sketch of the *Boston Guardian* Weekly." Unpublished paper, July 10, 1967.

Lilienthal, David E. "Has the Negro the Right of Self-Defense?" *The Nation,* December 23, 1925.

Lunardini, Christine A. "Confrontation at the White House: November 12, 1914." *Journal of Negro History,* Summer 1979.

MacLean, Nancy. "The Leo Frank Case Reconsidered: Gender and Sexual Politics in the Making of Reactionary Populism." *Journal of American History,* December 1991.

Martin, Charles H. "Black Protest, Anti-Communism and the Cold War: The Willie McGee Case." *Association for the Study of Afro-American Life and History,* 1980.

Meier, August, and John H. Bracey, Jr. "The NAACP as a Reform Movement, 1909–1965: To Reach the Conscience of America." *Journal of Southern History,* vol. LIX, no. 1, February 1993.

Mencken, H. L. "The Sahara of the Bozart," *Prejudices,* 2nd Series. New York, 1977.

Miles, Edwin A. "Mississippi Slave Insurrection Scare of 1835." *Journal of Negro History,* January 1957.

Nash, Roy. "The Lynching of Anthony Crawford." *Independent,* December 11, 1916.

National Lawyers Guild, the National Bar Association, and the NAACP Legal Committee, cosponsors. "Moderator's Report of Adequacy of Existing Anti-Lynching Legislation," prepared for a Legal Conference on Federal Power to Protect Civil Liberties, January 1947.

Nordyke, Lewis T. "Ladies and Lynching." *Survey Graphic,* November 1939.

Pound, Roscoe. "The Causes of Popular Dissatisfaction with the Administration of Justice." *Reports of the American Bar Association,* 29 (1906).

Prather, H. Leon, Sr. "The Red Shirt Movement in North Carolina, 1898–1900." *Journal of Negro History*, April 1977.

Puttkammer, Charles W., and Ruth Worthy. "William Monroe Trotter, 1872–1934." *Journal of Negro History*, October 1958.

Rogers, O. A. "The Elaine Race Riots of 1919." *Arkansas Historical Quarterly*, vol. XIX, no. 2, Summer 1960.

Rostar, James T. "Walter Hines Page: Editor, Publisher, and Enlightened Reformer." *North Carolina Literary Review* (special edition on the Wilmington Race Riot of 1898), Spring 1994.

Ryan, James Gilbert. "The Memphis Riots of 1866: Terror in a Black Community During Reconstruction." *Journal of Negro History*, July 1977.

Schecter, Patricia A. "Unsettled Business: Ida B. Wells Against Lynching, or, How Antilynching Got Its Gender," in Brundage, ed., *Under Sentence of Death: Lynching in the South.*

Scheiner, Seth M. "President Theodore Roosevelt and the Negro, 1901–1908." *Journal of Negro History*, October 1962.

Thornbrough, Emma Lou. "The National Afro-American League, 1887–1908." *Journal of Southern History*, November 1961.

Tucker, David M. "Miss Ida B. Wells and Memphis Lynching." *Phylon*, vol. XXXII, no. 2, Summer 1971.

Walling, William English. "The Race War in the North." *Independent*, September 3, 1908.

Wells-Barnett, Ida B. "How Enfranchisement Stops Lynchings." *Original Rights Magazine*, June 1910.

White, Walter. "I Investigate Lynchings." *American Mercury*, January 1929.

———. " 'Massacring Whites' in Arkansas." *The Nation*, December 6, 1919.

Williams, Melvin G. "Black Literature vs. Black Studies: Three Lynchings." *Black American Literature Forum*, Autumn 1977.

Williamson, Joel. "Wounds Not Scars: Lynching, the National Conscience, and the American Historian." *Journal of American History*, vol. 83, no. 4, March 1997.

Wolgemuth, Kathleen L. "Woodrow Wilson and Federal Segregation." *Journal of Negro History*, April 1959.

Wukovits, John F. "This Case Is Close to My Heart." *American History*, December 1998.

Ziglar, William. "Community on Trial: The Coatesville Lynching of 1911." *Southern Historical Quarterly*, April 1982.

Principal Cases Cited

Brown v. Board of Education, 347 US 483 (1954).

Brown v. Mississippi, 297 US 278 (1936).

Buchanan v. Warley, 245 US 60 (1917).

Civil Rights Cases, 109 US 3 (1883).

Corrigan v. Buckley, 271 US 323 (1926).

Frank v. Mangum, 237 US 309 (1915).

Gitlow v. New York, 268 US 652 (1925).

Gooch v. U.S., 297 US 124 (1936).

Guinn v. U.S., 238 US 347 (1915).

Herndon v. Lowry, 301 US 242 (1937).

McLaurin v. Oklahoma State Regents for Higher Education, 339 US 637 (1950).

Moore v. Dempsey, 261 US 86, 91 (1923).

Norris v. Alabama, 294 US 587 (1935).

Plessy v. Ferguson, 163 US 537 (1896).

Powell v. Alabama, 287 US 45 (1932).

Schenck v. U.S., 249 US 47 (1919).

Scott v. Sandford, 19 How. (60 US) 393 (1857).

Screws v. U.S., 325 US 91 (1945).

Shelley v. Kraemer, 334 US 1 (1948).
Slaughterhouse Cases, 16 Wall (83 US) 36 (1873).
Smith v. Allwright, 321 US 649 (1944).
Strauder v. West Virginia, 100 US 303 (1880).
Stromberg v. California, 283 US 359 (1931).
Sweatt v. Painter, 339 US 629 (1950).
U.S. v. Classic, 313 US 299 (1941).
U.S. v. Cruikshank, 92 US 214 (1876).
U.S. v. Price, 383 US 787 (1966).
U.S. v. Reese, 92 US 214 (1876).
U.S. v. Shipp, 214 US 386 (1909).

Notes

Epigraph

v   "So Quietly," by Leslie Pinckney Hill: *The Negro Caravan: Writings by American Negroes,* ed.
       Sterling Brown, Arthur P. Davis, and Ulysses Lee (New York City: The Dryden Press, 1941)
       pp. 338–39.

Preface

x   "reasons were actually wide-ranging": Richmond *Planet,* July 11, 1899.
xi   "I could not suppress the thought": Baldwin, "A Letter From the South," collected in *Nobody
       Knows My Name,* p. 87.

CHAPTER 1
"A Negro's Life Is a Very Cheap Thing in Georgia"

3   "It occurred to me": W.E.B. Du Bois Interview, 1960 Oral History Project, Columbia Uni-
       versity, p. 148.
4   "dethroned the reason": *Atlanta Constitution,* April 24, 1899. For a thorough account of the
       Hose case see Ellis, Mary Louise, *Rain Down Fire: The Lynching of Sam Hose;* there is also ex-
       tensive coverage in *The Atlanta Constitution,* mid-April to mid-May 1899.
4   "crept into that happy little home": From remarks by Georgia congressman James M. Griggs,
       quoted in Grant, *The Way It Was in the South,* p. 161.
4   Turn-of-the-century news accounts: The phrase *folk pornography* is used by historian Jacque-
       line Dowd Hall. See Hall, " 'The Mind That Burns in Each Body,' " p. 335.
5   "The black brute, whose carnival": Newnan *Herald and Advertiser,* April 14, 1899.
5   "be made summary enough": Ibid., April 19, 1899.
5   "No community in Georgia": Ibid., April 21, 1899.
6   "I very early got the idea": Du Bois Interview, Columbia University, pp. 22–23.
7   "trumped up to arouse": Ibid., pp. 147–48. Since it was inconceivable to whites that any but
       the most degraded white woman would give herself willingly to a Negro, and Victorian atti-
       tudes generally closed off the possibility that women might freely choose their sexual part-

ners, any amorous or suggestive encounter between a black man and a white woman might be considered rape. The commonly used term *outrage* meant chiefly rape, but could also serve to describe any insult or social transgression—inappropriate gazing at white women, touching them, writing notes to them, brushing by them on the street, and so on.

9   "hope that he will be compelled to seek rest": *New York Times,* April 15, 1899. The intensity of the search also produced several incorrect suspects. A posse brought one man to the Cranford home in Palmetto who resembled Hose, but a Cranford brother said he was not the criminal. The next day, a mob again came storming up the road to the Cranford farm, bullying another captive. It was soon determined that this suspect was the same man who had been captured the day before. Released a second time, he vowed to keep out of sight until the real Sam Hose was caught.

12   One later account even claimed: Alfred Cranford, noted a local news story, was interred next to an uncle, Zach Cranford, "who was murdered by a Negro about ten years ago in a manner somewhat similar." Mattie, the only person who could have cleared up the mystery of the alleged rape and perhaps explained the true circumstances of her husband's murder, maintained her silence until her death at age fifty in 1923. A descendant recalled years later that, after the events of 1899, "she never smiled again."

14   "Overtaken by the wrath": Newnan *Herald and Advertiser,* April 28, 1899.

14   "The excursionists returning": *Atlanta Constitution,* April 24, 1899.

14   "I did not meet Joel Chandler Harris": Lewis, *W.E.B. Du Bois,* p. 226.

15   "I was very much disappointed": Du Bois Interview, Columbia University, pp. 146–47.

15   In the days following: In the aftermath of the Hose lynching, local whites lynched an elderly black named Elijah Strickland, claiming that Hose had stated that Strickland had paid him to kill Alfred Cranford, presumably for Cranford's role in the January warehouse murders. But the connections remain too vague for this explanation to be substantiated; the mob may have put words in the mouth of a lynched man in order to have an excuse to taint Strickland.

CHAPTER 2
Judge Lynch's Law

17   For Melby Dotson: Hair, *Carnival of Fury,* pp. 184–85.

17   "The practice whereby mobs": Cutler, *Lynch-Law,* p. 1.

20   a vigilantes' war: Richard Brown, *Strain of Violence,* p. 41.

20   The Revolution helped foster: Localism and instrumentalism are ideas set forth by legal scholar James W. Hurst in *The Growth of American Law: The Law Makers,* pp. 39, 92–93.

21   "is like the light of the sun": Quoted in Richard Brown, *Strain of Violence,* p. 61.

24   "the revolution has been conducted here": In Vicksburg, a citizens' fund was created to erect a memorial to the heroism of Dr. Bodley—perhaps America's only public monument to the leader of a lynch mob. The obelisk, which still stands, bears the inscription: ERECTED BY A GRATEFUL COMMUNITY TO THE MEMORY OF HUGH BODLEY, MURDERED BY THE GAMBLERS.

25   "I am aware that many object": *Liberator,* January 1, 1831.

26   Scholar Herbert Aptheker estimates: Herbert Aptheker, *American Negro Slave Revolts,* p. 11.

26   "We are trying our best": Wyatt-Brown, *Southern Honor,* p. 418.

27   "this process of hanging": Abraham Lincoln, speech before the Young Men's Lyceum, Springfield, Illinois, January 27, 1837; quoted in Cutler, *Lynch-Law,* pp. 110–11.

28   "stunned a drunken people": Quoted in Simon, *Lovejoy,* p. 132.

29   "A Negro was suspected": Genovese, *Roll, Jordan, Roll,* p. 121.

31   "The mere fact that": Du Bois, *Black Reconstruction,* pp. 52–53.

31   "has chosen a mistress": Charles Sumner, "The Crime Against Kansas: Speech in the United States Senate, May 19, 1856," pamphlet published by the New York *Tribune,* p. 3. See also Donald, *Charles Sumner and the Coming of the Civil War,* pp. 278–311.

32   "a proper act": Hixon, *Moorfield Storey and the Abolitionist Tradition,* p. 137.

34   "the consummation of their deliverance": Schurz, *Report on the Conditions of the South,* p. 31.

35   "In addition to the property loss": Dollard, *Caste and Class in a Southern Town,* p. 186.

36   "The number of murders": Schurz, *Report,* p. 20.

37   "A great outrage": Record Group 105, Assistant Commissioners' Reports, Bureau of Refugees, Freedmen and Abandoned Lands (1865–1869), National Archives, Washington, D.C.

38   "grossly insulting proposals": Cashin, "A Lynching in Wartime Carolina," pp. 109–31.

40   This ridiculous passage: Bowers, *The Tragic Era*, p. 306.

41   The Klan's pointed phallic hats: Testimony given by men and women visited by night riders suggests that many knew full well who their callers really were, but went along with the ruse that they were visitors from another world in order not to further provoke the whites. Regardless of whether one believed in the Klan's hocus-pocus, of course, a visit from them in the middle of the night was terrifying.

41   "The incorrigibles": Schurz, *Report*, p. 5.

41   "They boast of Jeff. Davis": September 17, 1865, memo from Charles H. Gilchrist, Colonel, 50th U.S. Colored Infantry, Jackson, Miss., in ibid., p. 69.

42   "Dam Your Soul": Testimony, Joint Select Committee to Inquire into the Condition of Affairs in the Late Insurrectionary States, vol. 2, Washington, D.C., 1872; appears also in Shapiro, *White Violence and Black Response*, pp. 144–45.

43   "The habit is so inveterate": Schurz, *Report*, p. 20.

43   "It is all of them, mighty near": Many years later, whites who remembered the efficacy of Reconstruction-era whipping endorsed a return to the policy as a means of halting lynching. "Why kill out the race by lynching when subordinancy through fear of the lash will stop it all?" queried an editorial in the Newnan (Ga.) *Herald and Advertiser* at the turn of the century.

44   "There were a great many Northern men": Testimony of Nathan Bedford Forrest, Joint Committee to Inquire into the Condition of Affairs in the Late Insurrectionary States, Washington, D.C., 1872.

45   A bizarre manifestation: Fry, *Night Riders in Black Folk History*, p. 115; also Wyatt-Brown, *Southern Honor*, p. 456.

45   "Complaints are continually coming in": Tennessee House Journal Extra Session 1868, pp. 208–9, quoted in Trelease, *White Terror*, p. 42.

47   Wright points out: George C. Wright, *Racial Violence in Kentucky*, pp. 5–7.

48   "One was lynched in Bullock's grove": Ibid., p. 6.

48   Mass lynchings were not uncommon: Testimony, Joint Committee to Inquire into the Condition of Affairs in the Late Insurrectionary States, Washington, D.C., 1872.

48   "The butchery seems": *New National Era*, May 29, 1873.

48   One of the rare lynchings: *New York Times*, November 5, 1872.

49   Phil Sheridan calculated: Edgar T. Thompson, *Race Relations and the Race Problem* (Durham, N.C.: Duke University Press, 1939), p. 138.

50   "300,000 white people": Pike, *The Prostrate State*, p. xv.

50   "the most ignorant": Ibid., p. 12.

50   A similar trajectory: This point is made in Foner, *A Short History of Reconstruction, 1863–1877*, pp. 144–45.

51   Promoters of resorts in Virginia: The mood of sectional reunion would intensify in years to come. In the late 1880s Union and Confederate veterans held commemorative twenty-fifth-anniversary reunions of many of the Civil War's great battles. The 1888 commemoration of the Battle of Gettysburg, viewed by both sides as the war's most pivotal conflict, was a major news story and sent ripples of sentiment through America, captured in the *New York Times* headline above its lengthy coverage, "United at Gettysburg." Populists who convened in 1892 nominated a "reunion ticket" of one former Union general, James B. Weaver of Iowa, and a former Confederate general, James G. Field of Virginia. The theme of reunion dominated the convention, with extensive pageantry of former Yankees and Rebels dressed in their old uniforms, serenading one another, marching in tribute, and clasping hands in a "stampede to take fraternal grips." Bands alternately played "Dixie" and "Yankee Doodle" while the delegates kept time with their feet.

51   Reconstruction, clearly: What ultimately doomed the land-distribution plan was the federal unwillingness to abjure the property rights of the defeated Confederates, although Thaddeus Stevens and others attempted to show that the giving of small parcels of land to freedmen would have a negligible effect on large property holders.

CHAPTER 3

To Gather My Race in My Arms

55   "What is, or should be woman?": "Woman's Mission," published in New York *Freeman*, December 26, 1885, reprinted in DeCosta-Willis, *The Memphis Diary of Ida B. Wells*, pp. 179–82.

55   "It stops out beyond": Du Bois, *Darkwater*, p. 134.

56   The situation on the trains: The Civil Rights Act of 1875 declared that all persons in the United States should be entitled to "the full and equal enjoyment of the accommodations, facilities and privileges of inns, public conveyances on land or water, theaters, and other places of public amusement, subject only to the conditions and limitations established by law, and applicable alike to citizens of every race and color, regardless of any previous condition of servitude." Sumner told the Senate in 1873, "My desire . . . is to close forever this great question—so that hereafter in all our legislation there shall be no such words as 'black' or 'white,' but that we shall speak only of citizens and of men." After his death in 1874 the bill passed in honor of his memory, although in somewhat weakened form, notably omitting his original language calling for desegregated schools, and it was never really enforced.

56   "I had braced my feet": Duster, *Crusade for Justice*, p. 19.

57   "I feel so disappointed": Quoted in Belford, *Brilliant Bylines*, p. 89.

57   "From a mere, insignificant": *Washington Bee*, December 5, 1885.

57   "She has plenty of nerve": Quoted in McMurry, *To Keep the Waters Troubled*, p. 111.

58   "the universal and lamentable reign": Quoted in ibid., p. 121.

58   "the grandest idea": Quoted in Grant, *The Development of the Anti-Lynching Reform Movement*, p. 23.

58   "while T. Thomas Fortune": Quoted in ibid., p. 24.

59   "The old Southern voice": Memphis *Free Speech and Headlight*, quoted in Memphis *Avalanche*, July 13, 1889; also quoted in Tucker, "Miss Ida B. Wells."

59   "Those Georgetown, Ky. Negroes": Quoted in McMurry, pp. 128–29.

61   "March on like a soldier": Memphis *Appeal-Avalanche*, March 6, 1892, and Duster, *Crusade for Justice*, p. 49.

62   "Only in a community": Ibid., March 7, 1892.

62   "The affair was one": Ibid., March 9, 1892.

62   "There were four holes": Ibid., March 10, 1892.

62   "Tell my people to go": Duster, p. 51. The funerals for the slain men were said to be the largest public event in Memphis history. Race feelings in Memphis had never fully recovered from a race riot there in May 1866, the "Memphis Massacre," during which forty-six blacks and two whites were killed, and many homes and several schools and churches were torched.

62   The words of the martyred grocer: The idea of black migration to Oklahoma was much in the air even before the People's Grocery lynching. The Oklahoma Territory, opened for settlement in 1889, had figured in a determined black separatist movement. One of the architects of the scheme was Edwin P. McCabe, a former state auditor in Kansas, who founded Langston City, Oklahoma, in 1890 with the idea of making it an all-black community, the first in what would conceivably become a "black state." McCabe sent three hundred families from North Carolina and five hundred from South Carolina to Oklahoma, and made arrangements to send thousands more, but the idea of turning Oklahoma into the nation's black state foundered on the lack of federal support (although President Benjamin Harrison received McCabe and heard him out), as well as on a less than enthusiastic welcome from some of the whites and Indians already there.

63   "There is nothing": Belford, p. 90.

63   "unreasoning anger": Duster, p. 64.

63   For Ida Wells and other blacks: Wells's acquaintance Mollie Church (later the Washington, D.C., civil rights leader Mary Church Terrell) had been with child at the time of the lynching, and gave birth to a sickly baby who died after only a few days of life. Church always believed that her depression over the lynching of Tom Moss had detrimentally affected her pregnancy.

64   "When an unprotected woman": Memphis *Appeal-Avalanche*, May 30, 1892.

64   "Nobody in this section": Duster, pp. 65–66.

65   She knew she was courting: Quoted in McMurry, p. 120.

65   "The fact that a black scoundrel": Wells, *Southern Horrors*. Wells wrote that 728 blacks had been lynched in the South between 1884 and 1891, with 150 more just in 1892. Only one third, she said, were charged with rape. Wells herself later increased these figures, saying 1,119 had been lynched between 1884 and 1891, and 160 in 1892. In the year 1900 she would estimate, based on *Chicago Tribune* statistics, that 2,533 Negroes had been lynched in America between 1882 and 1899 (substantially higher than the Tuskegee calculation of 1,645).

66   "It may now be fairly doubted": *North American Review*, July 1892.

67   "All the presumptions": Ibid.

67   "I never believed I could speak in public": New York *Sun*, July 30, 1894.

68   "The miscegenation laws": Wells, *A Red Record*, p. 58.

69   "[The South's] police system": Du Bois, *The Souls of Black Folk*, pp. 200–201.

70   Wells applied this tactic: She once told Douglass, "I am only a mouthpiece through which to tell the story of lynching and I have told it so often that I know it by heart. I do not have to embellish; it makes its own way."

71   "[T]he sexual usefulness": Harris, *Exorcising Blackness*, p. 18.

71   "The more trails": Smith, *Killers of the Dream*, p. 121.

72   "In the Southern night": Baldwin, *Nobody Knows My Name*, pp. 93–94.

72   "If black men": Williamson, *The Crucible of Race*, p. 189.

72   "It would be as easy": Newnan *Herald and Advertiser*, April 28, 1899.

73   "[T]he difference between bad citizens": Ayers, *Vengeance and Justice*, p. 241.

73   "put sheet-iron lingerie": Grant, p. 9.

73   "Through it all I discerned": Johnson, *Along This Way*, p. 170.

75   "As we stand on the verge": Newnan *Herald and Advertiser*, April 7, 1899.

76   "At the present moment": Jane Addams, *A New Conscience and an Ancient Evil* (New York: Macmillan, 1912), p. 56.

77   "an outrage so terrible": Quoted in George C. Wright, *Racial Violence in Kentucky*, p. 95.

77   "outraged with demoniacal cruelty": Flower, "The Black Shadow in the South."

79   "The man died protesting his innocence": Duster, pp. 84–85.

80   "After the trauma of Appomatox": Orlando Patterson, *Rituals of Blood*, p. 215.

80   "It is exceedingly doubtful": White, *Rope and Faggot*, pp. 40–43.

80   "His Spirit in smoke ascended": McKay, *Selected Poems*, p. 37.

81   "Somewhere the Southland rears a tree": In *My Soul's High Song: The Collected Writings of Countee Cullen*, ed. Gerald Early (New York: Doubleday, 1991), pp. 207–36.

81   "A miserable negro beast": Diary of Henry Waring Ball, entry for June 5, 1903, Mississippi State Archives Manuscript Collection, Jackson, Miss.

82   It was an old belief: To attain this same goal, Southern prisons traditionally gave the cadavers of executed child killers and other sadistic criminals over to anatomists for immediate dissection.

83   "[A] crowd of white men": Mays, *Born to Rebel*, p. 1.

83   "I became conscious": Johnson, *Along This Way*, pp. 166–67.

84   "[N]o disinterested observer": Ayers, pp. 253–55.

85   "Our English press": McMurry, p. 187. Wells happened to be visiting Douglass when she learned of Impey and Mayo's invitation, and out of deference insisted that he accept in her place. Douglass demurred, saying, "You go, my child. You are the one to go, for you have the story to tell."

86   "A very interesting young lady": Duster, p. 90.

87   "The moral agencies at work": Duster, p. 100.

87   "very vivacious in manner": Quoted in the New York *Sun*, July 26, 1894.

87   "If her pleasant face": London *Sun* quote reprinted in Memphis *Appeal-Avalanche*, June 12, 1894.

88   "the most painful scene": Duster, pp. 103–5.

89   "Sixty-nine of them are here": Baker, *From Savage to Negro*, p. 58. Such displays were common at world's fairs into the early twentieth century. The 1904 St. Louis World's Fair featured the legendary Native American chieftain Geronimo, a federal prisoner of war, who sold bows and arrows and signed photographs of himself. An African Pygmy named Ota Benga, a member of another attraction at St. Louis, remained in the United States and was "sold" to the American Museum of Natural History in New York. Within two years he had

moved to the Bronx Zoo, where the director put him on exhibit in a cage with an orangutan. Vociferous protests from New York's black community—as well as Benga's own shenanigans such as undressing in front of visitors—forced the exhibit to close.

89   "an all-too-powerful metaphor": McFeely, *Frederick Douglass,* p. 368.

90   "a band of old-time plantation 'darkies' ": Rydell, *All the World's a Fair,* p. 28.

90   Arriving in Chicago to join Douglass: Douglass and Wells had a brief falling-out when a Colored People's Day at the fair was announced. Wells considered it an insult and refused to attend, but Douglass proceeded to cooperate with the event and to read a paper he'd written, "The Race Problem in America." He had gotten no further than the first few sentences when he began to be loudly jeered by some white men at the back of the crowd. The old man stumbled with his words for a moment, appearing frail and disoriented, but then suddenly stopped and angrily set aside his text. Tearing off his reading glasses, he embarked on an hour-long speech so full of his legendary eloquence and fire it was as if the great abolitionist orator who'd shaken the rafters of New England's churches half a century before had suddenly returned. "Men talk of the Negro problem," Douglass roared. "There is no Negro problem. The problem is whether the American people have loyalty enough, honor enough, patriotism enough, to live up to their own Constitution." Wells, learning of Douglass's courage and eloquence, immediately sought him out and apologized.

90   The initial suspect: Mayfield, Kentucky, *Monitor,* July 12, 1893.

92   "My name is C. J. Miller": Memphis *Appeal-Avalanche,* July 8, 1893.

93   "the Bardwell ravisher": Account of C. J. Miller lynching from Wells, *A Red Record,* and George C. Wright, *Racial Violence in Kentucky,* pp. 90–93.

94   "The head was in plain view": Wells, "The Reason Why . . .," p. 84.

96   One method was: Gossett, *Race,* p. 70.

97   "Not only is he cursed": Helper, *Nojoque,* p. 68.

98   "As Americans": Ibid., p. 472.

100   "the finest race": Quoted in Williamson, p. 90.

100   deportation as impractical: Nathaniel Southgate Shaler, "The Negro Problem," *The Atlantic Monthly,* November 1884.

100   "[The Negro] is not content": Bruce, *The Plantation Negro as Freeman,* p. 84.

100   "The protection of woman": Wyatt-Brown, *Southern Honor,* p. 439.

100   "the imperious voice of nature": Gossett, p. 166.

101   "It cannot be too often repeated": Quoted in Baker, p. 36.

101   "Woman," according to Carroll: Carroll, *The Negro a Beast,* pp. 186–87.

102   "All the facts brought together": Hoffman, *Race Traits and Tendencies of the American Negro,* p. 329.

103   "I sat under the shadow": Duster, p. 129.

104   "as if turned to stone": Ibid., p. 149.

104   "would lead a mob": Quoted in McMurry, p. 220.

105   "The Negroes in this country": Ibid., p. 245.

105   "Black Joan of Arc": Minutes of the first convention of the National Association of Colored Women, "Letter from the Women of Bethel Church (NY)," NACW Papers, Schomburg Center for Research in Black Culture, New York City, p. 20.

105   "Miss Ida B. Wells is a negress": London *Sun,* reprinted in Memphis *Appeal-Avalanche,* June 12, 1894; quoted in David M. Tucker, "Miss Ida B. Wells and the Memphis Lynching," *Phylon,* Summer 1971.

106   "Alien illiterates": Duster, pp. 151–52.

CHAPTER 4
The Compromise

110   "I am just as opposed": Quoted in Rudwick, *W.E.B. Du Bois,* p. 181.

111   "Our Constitution is color blind": The tragedy of the *Plessy* ruling was that the Court, believing it was acting in the interest of protecting "folkways," was actually ignoring them. As historian C. Vann Woodward would show in his landmark *The Strange Career of Jim Crow,* segregation laws in Southern states and towns at the time were of fairly recent vintage. Since Reconstruction, blacks and whites in the region had often eaten and slept in the same

establishments, traveled together in the same conveyances, gone to the same schools, and been tended to in the same hospitals. *Plessy*, by upholding state laws mandating a separation of the races, demonstrated that the federal judiciary believed stateways *could* make folkways.

111 The cumulative impact: Woodward, p. 85.

112 He had received his nickname: "He is an old bag of beef and I am going to Washington with a pitchfork and prod him in his old fat ribs." In Simkins, *Pitchfork Ben Tillman*, p. 315.

112 "We took the government away": *Congressional Record*, 57th Congress, 2d session, February 23, 1903.

113 "there was no middle ground": Quoted in Logan, *The Betrayal of the Negro*, p. 38.

113 "Time is the only cure": Ibid., p. 43.

114 "Many people have written": Rydell, *All the World's a Fair*, p. 85.

115 Washington began his Atlanta: Moses, *The Golden Age of Black Nationalism*, p. 96.

117 "authorities in Washington": Charleston *News and Courier*, February 23, 1898.

118 "was a federal matter, pure and simple": It wasn't Wells's first Washington experience; in 1894, she had lobbied for a bill sponsored by New Hampshire congressman Henry W. Blair to earmark $25,000 to create a federal commission to investigate lynching and mob violence. Blacks mobilized nationwide in support of the resolution, presenting the House with a petition signed by ten thousand persons, but the motion was voted down.

118 American troops quickly routed: The Treaty of Paris, negotiated in December 1898, saw Spain cede control of Cuba, Puerto Rico, and the Philippines to the United States, although the American public's appetite for foreign conquest waned when the country immediately found itself mired in a messy guerrilla war against Philippine insurrectionists.

119 "The men who are lynched": Quoted in Grant, *The Development of the Anti-Lynching Reform Movement*, pp. 38–39.

120 Lillian Clayton Jewett: This account is based largely on Hux, "Lillian Clayton Jewett and the Rescue of the Baker Family, 1899–1900."

123 "[t]he negro has proved": *Washington Post*, October 24, 1898.

123 Hamburg Massacre: The Hamburg Massacre was a noted incident in late-Reconstruction America, its infamy nearly on a par with Custer's Last Stand, which it followed by two weeks, and was seen to symbolize a growing posture of federal nonintervention in Southern affairs. Hamburg was a predominantly black community on the South Carolina side of the Savannah River across from Augusta, Georgia. On July 4, 1876, in what was probably a staged incident, two young white men driving a buggy demanded the right of way from a unit of black militiamen who were parading through town as part of the local celebration. The militiamen considered the incident unimportant until they learned the whites had brought suit against them for blocking the street. On July 8, South Carolina attorney and former Confederate general Matthew C. Butler arrived to prosecute the case, escorted by the Sweetwater Sabre Club, a notorious white vigilante gang from neighboring Edgefield County. When Butler demanded that the blacks give up their arms, the latter withdrew to a local armory and Butler's forces, joined by other whites, laid siege. A white man was killed, and when the blacks surrendered Butler's men began executing the captives. Four men—Dan Phillips, Albert Merritt, Hamp Stevens, and A. T. Attaway, a member of the South Carolina state legislature—were led away one at a time to a nearby field and shot in the back. A fifth, Pompey Curry, on hearing his name called, jumped up and ran away down the street, escaping with a leg wound. Led by the Sweetwater Sabre Club, whites then launched a general attack on the black community, destroying property and murdering numerous other people. Efforts to bring the vigilantes to justice failed.

124 In the middle of this: Felton's reform efforts in ending the convict-lease system in Georgia and promoting temperance and women's suffrage were laudable, but in 1892 the "race cause" came to preoccupy her. Appointed one of the "Lady Managers" of the 1893 Chicago world's fair, she became indignant when she discovered plans for an exhibit honoring Harriet Beecher Stowe, the author of the antislavery novel *Uncle Tom's Cabin*. In response, she quickly assembled her own exhibit, recruiting two elderly blacks to provide a living diorama of "real colored folks," in which "Uncle Jack" played the banjo and "Aunt Jinny" spun cotton.

125 "The black fiend": Quoted in Williamson, *A Rage for Order*, p. 95.

125 "Our experiences": Grant, p. 31.

125 "You set yourselves": *Atlanta Constitution,* November 10, 1898.

126 "Why should it be considered": *Atlanta Constitution,* November 2, 1898.

127 A white mob now ruled Wilmington: In the days leading up to the election, with violence at hand, Russell had tried to barter a compromise with the Democrats by negotiating away the votes of black Republicans, a move that in no way endeared him to those blacks who were attempting to stand firm.

128 "trapped by a problem": Hair, *Carnival of Fury,* p. 3. Hair's insightful account guided my understanding of the Robert Charles saga.

129 "Until we are free": Quoted in Grant, p. 27.

130 "we are on the threshold": Hair, pp. 141–42.

131 "When the law is powerless": Richard Brown, *Strain of Violence,* p. 153.

132 "If there is one thing more hateful": *North American Review,* May 1891.

133 "Under the dark, seething mass": Hair, pp. 148–49.

134 "attracted little notice from white people": Ibid., p. 201.

136 "The Archfiend of the Century": Ibid., p. 184.

136 In the wake of so: Boston's white antilynching crusader Lillian Clayton Jewett organized funds to be sent to those black families that had been victimized in the New Orleans violence. She appeared at a gathering in Boston on July 27 at which some black speakers praised Charles for defending himself. The Southern press was livid, accusing Jewett of riling up an army of blacks to invade New Orleans. A Louisiana white-supremacist club, the Green Turtles, publicly offered $1,000 for Jewett's scalp.

136 "knew nothing of grievances": Hair, p. 179.

136 "Men who knew him say": Wells, *Mob Rule in New Orleans,* p. 42.

137 "I once knew the Robert Charles song": Hair, p. 179.

CHAPTER 5
"Let the Eagle Scream!"

139 "a tool maintaining the caste system": Grant, *The Development of the Anti-Lynching Reform Movement,* p. 38.

139 "the chief onus": Du Bois, *The Autobiography of W.E.B. Du Bois,* p. 238.

139 "When Washington made": Du Bois Interview, Columbia University, p. 157.

140 "He was a man": Ibid., p. 150.

140 As Henry Louis Gates: Gates and West, *The Future of the Race,* p. 115.

141 "If Atlanta University": Quoted in Baker, *From Savage to Negro,* p. 122.

142 every inch a vehicle: Trotter and George W. Forbes opened *The Guardian* in 1901. At one point it occupied the same site used by William Lloyd Garrison in publishing *The Liberator.*

143 "We will not be satisfied": Clarke et al., *Black Titan,* p. 132. The group's name originated with the displacement of its first meeting. Scheduled to gather in Buffalo, New York, Du Bois and the others relocated to Fort Erie, Ontario, nearer to Niagara Falls, when they learned Buffalo's hotels were segregated.

144 "Why kill out the race": Newnan *Herald and Advertiser,* May 12, 1899.

145 "Negro police force": B. O. Flower, "The Black Shadow in the South," *Forum,* vol. 16, October 1893.

145 "There can be no doubt": Du Bois, *The Souls of Black Folk,* pp. 199–200.

146 Bob Davis was lynched: *Atlanta Constitution,* August 17, 1906.

146 "Society, as well as criminals": Jackson *Daily News,* May 6, 1951; amid the clemency campaign launched by Northerners and reformers in the case of convicted Mississippi rapist Willie McGee, the mayor of Laurel, Carroll Gartin, had sent his own appeal to Governor Fielding Wright—an appeal *not* to grant clemency.

147 "One is irresistibly impelled": *Southern Atlantic Quarterly,* October 1906.

147 Lizzie Borden: This point is made in Knight, *The Life of the Law,* pp. 185–86.

148 often acted like vigilantes: Legal scholar Herbert Packer, writing in 1964, suggested that instead of viewing some punishments as legal and good and others as extralegal and wrong, it would be more helpful to consider a "due process model" and a "crime control model" of law enforcement. Americans, Packer noted, had by their actions consistently demonstrated

greater support for the crime-control model, soundly rejecting many of the legal safeguards put in place to protect an individual suspect's rights in the due-process model. As such protections were obstacles to the control of crime, law enforcement could, in Packer's definition, straddle the nominal demarcations of "legal" and "illegal," and might include everything from a mob lynching to law officers behaving with vigilantelike determination to apprehend, interrogate, and obtain a confession from a suspect. See Herbert L. Packer, "Two Models of the Criminal Process," *University of Pennsylvania Law Review* 113 (1964); also Richard Brown, *Strain of Violence,* pp. 147–48.

148   "disrespect for law at the bottom": Pound, *Criminal Justice in America,* p. 64.

149   "liberty as contrasted with order": Ibid., p. 132.

149   "I can think of no threat": Quoted in Pound, "The Causes of Popular Dissatisfaction with the Administration of Justice," p. 62.

150   "working old worn-out animals": *Chattanooga Times,* July 28, 1905.

151   The local papers: *Chattanooga News,* January 24, 1906; *Chattanooga Times,* January 25, 1906.

153   "Thugs, thieves and sots": Curriden and Phillips, *Contempt of Court,* p. 100. My description of the Ed Johnson case is indebted to Curriden and Phillips's comprehensive account.

153   "Ed, there are two choices here": One of the most well-known incidents of this kind, and one that was no doubt on the minds of Johnson's attorneys, was the 1899 lynching of Richard Coleman in Maysville, Kentucky. Coleman, eighteen, was arrested for the rape and murder of his employer's wife. To head off a lynching, the sheriff removed him to the nearby city of Covington. Coleman readily confessed to the crime and agreed to forgo a trial, asking to be executed swiftly in Covington, for it was known the murdered woman's relatives had camped near the Covington jail to track his every movement. Authorities denied his request. Back in Maysville for trial, Coleman's nightmare came true: He was seized by a mob, beaten, mutilated, then burned slowly to death before an enthusiastic crowd. Aware that a lynching had been imminent, the national press was well represented ("Negro Boy Roasted Alive in Kentucky," proclaimed the New York *World*). Vivid descriptions of the tortures Coleman suffered, his pleas for mercy, and the meticulous care taken by the mob to prolong his agony were published in numerous city dailies.

154   acquainted with W.E.B. Du Bois: Parden was an ardent follower of Booker T. Washington and had been in the audience when the Wizard delivered his Atlanta Compromise address in 1895.

156   "People here are definitely anxious": *Chattanooga Times,* March 16, 1906.

156   "if by legal technicality": *Chattanooga News,* March 19, 1906.

158   "The mandate of the Supreme Court": *New York Times,* March 21, 1906.

158   "The Supreme Court of the United States": Richard Brown, *Strain of Violence,* p. 158.

158   "beseeching the men of the county": *New York Times,* August 3, 1906.

162   Roosevelt accepted Garlington's advice: Weaver, *The Brownsville Raid.* In a calculated move whose cynicism was not lost on anyone, Roosevelt waited to announce his decision in the Brownsville case until November 7, the day after important congressional elections in which the black vote helped the Republicans maintain their majority in the House. The president then brought further discredit on himself by authorizing secret investigations into the lives and conduct of the discharged men, apparently hoping to use damaging personal information to yet validate his own hasty order. The incident was not soon allowed to fade, thanks to the tenacity of Ohio Republican senator Joseph B. Foraker, who was convinced of the men's innocence and whose efforts led to extensive Senate hearings in 1907 and 1908. Despite Foraker's leadership and eloquence—"They ask no favor because they are Negroes, but only for justice because they are men"—the hearings did not substantially change Roosevelt's edict. Not until 1972, when only 1 of the 167 troopers remained alive, were the Brownsville soldiers officially exonerated.

163   The Decatur Street zone: Southern black men, not unlike their white counterparts, observed a powerful code of personal honor, although for different reasons: they were inclined to settle differences themselves because they knew they could not count on the police for help or the court system for justice.

163   In August 1906: Atlanta *Evening News,* August 26, 1906, quoted in Godshalk, *In the Wake of Riot.*

164   "To see a big black Negro": Atlanta *Evening News,* September 18, 1906.

164   "Political equality being preached": Quoted in Stetson Kennedy, *Southern Exposure,* p. 45.

165 "go home yourself, Jim": Charles Crowe, "Racial Massacre in Atlanta, September 22, 1906," *Journal of Negro History* 54, April 1969.

166 "The causes that led up to it": *Atlanta Constitution,* September 24, 1906.

168 Once again the militia restored: Senechel, *The Sociogenesis of a Race,* p. 42.

169 ALL NIGGERS ARE WARNED: *The Independent,* September 3, 1908.

169 "Either the spirit of the abolitionists": Ibid.

170 "If Mr. Lincoln could revisit": Quoted in Hughes, *Fight for Freedom.*

170 The organizers laid plans: The story of Mary White Ovington and the Cosmopolitan Club dinner is recounted in Wedin, *Inheritors of the Spirit,* pp. 97–98.

171 "Only under the Stars and Stripes": *New York Post,* June 1, 1909.

171 Trotter misbehaved: Trotter was concerned the new group would not assault Booker T. Washington with requisite vehemence. He had already started his own organization, the National Equal Rights League, which functioned intermittently from 1908 until 1921.

171 "I find myself still occasionally forgetting": Quoted in Rudwick, *Du Bois,* p. 127.

172 "White and Negroes Mix": Ibid., pp. 127–28.

172 "More Fool Negroes": Ibid.

173 "conclusive evidence of the failure": Quoted in McMurry, *To Keep the Waters Troubled,* p. 283.

175 "There were only a few signers present": Duster, *Crusade for Justice,* p. 316.

176 "has no place in Illinois": Illinois Executive Dept. *In the Matter of the Petition of Frank E. Davis for Reinstatement as Sheriff of Alexander County, Illinois, 1909.*

176 "If we only had a few men": *The Defender,* January 1, 1910.

176 When the charge came: Sheriff Nelis figured in another lynching drama involving Wells-Barnett during the summer of 1910. She had learned of the plight of Steve Green, a black sharecropper from Arkansas who had killed his boss in a labor dispute and was being extradited from Chicago to his home state. Knowing he would be lynched, Green had tried to commit suicide in his Chicago jail cell by eating a box of matches. By the time Wells-Barnett obtained permission from the Illinois attorney general to deny the extradition, a deputized posse from Arkansas had come to fetch Green and he was already en route home. Wells-Barnett frantically telephoned every county sheriff along the route of the Illinois Central, offering a hundred-dollar reward for the officer who would remove Green from the train. At Cairo, the last stop before the train left the state, Sheriff Nelis bounded aboard, put a heavy hand on Green's shoulder, and boomed, "I arrest this man in the name of the great state of Illinois."

176 In the history of the resistance: The Afro-American Council had attracted interest and support in recent years due to alarm among blacks about the marked increase in white violence and the assault on black voting rights, yet the group had seemed insufficiently activist, adept at passing resolutions against lynching and railroad segregation but unable to take the steps that many black leaders knew were necessary, such as building bridges to the black church or the Republican party, or mounting a black boycott of certain railroads.

177 "I can think of no more nauseating": Ovington, *The Walls Came Tumbling Down,* pp. 152–53. Around this time the organization was also successful at convincing the Associated Press to begin capitalizing the word *Negro* and, to a lesser degree, to refrain from using racial identifications in crime stories.

178 "In the residents of Livermore": *New York Times,* April 21 and 22, 1911.

178 All were rapidly acquitted: George C. Wright, *Racial Violence in Kentucky,* pp. 118–19.

180 In town there was talk of little else: From "Sidelights on the Bench and Bar of Chester County," a memoir by Wilmer W. McElree, Holton Collection of Coatesville History, Chester County Historical Society, Pennsylvania.

180 "You are God damned popular": Downey, *"No Crooked Death,"* p. 30.

181 "Everything was quiet": Coatesvile *Record,* August 14, 1911.

181 "Not in the history": West Chester *Daily Local News,* August 14, 1911.

182 "not pulling the South up": Boston *Guardian,* August 26, 1911.

182 "Let the eagle scream!": *The Crisis,* September 1911.

182 "What would her representative men have to say": *The Nation,* August 31, 1911.

184 "People are largely addicted": Albert Jay Nock, "What We All Stand For," *American Magazine,* February 1913.

184 "As the agitation which culminated": Emma Lou Thornbrough, "The National Afro-American League, 1887–1908."

185   One of the quiet miracles: Du Bois, in a sense, was simply being pragmatic to make the most of the opportunity the NAACP offered. Because of his criticisms of Washington he had become something of a liability to Atlanta University. Atlanta itself became an unhappy place for Du Bois and his wife, Nina, after their first child, Burghardt, age two, died suddenly on May 24, 1899, of nasopharyngeal diphtheria. Du Bois always felt somewhat guilty that he had not taken his son's symptoms seriously enough until it was too late, when there had been no white physician who would examine the boy. Du Bois always suspected that his son had become ill from the poor and unsanitary city sewage system that served the black part of town—racism in its most raw and putrid form.

185   "Once to every man and nation": Ovington, *Black and White Sat Down Together,* p. 67.

186   "In an era of rampant illiteracy": Lewis, *When Harlem Was in Vogue,* p. 7.

186   "the master builder": Wedin, *Inheritors of the Spirit,* p. 141.

187   "I am sick at heart over it": Quoted in Rudwick, *Du Bois,* pp. 167–68.

188   "It all goes to show that": *Atlanta Constitution,* March 23, 1911.

188   "Down here this woman's word": Quoted in *The Crisis,* May 1911.

CHAPTER 6
Writing History with Lightning

193   "unprecedented image of black power": Bernardi, *The Birth of Whiteness,* p. 176.

194   "obnoxious stunts": Quoted in Roberts, *Papa Jack,* p. 146.

194   "I want to say that I am not": Ibid., p. 149.

195   Convicted in the summer of 1913: Johnson returned to the United States in 1920 and was immediately arrested as a fugitive from justice. He was sentenced to a year and a day in a federal penitentiary.

196   What made the censorship: The U.S. Supreme Court codified the widespread anxiety about the power of film in its 1916 decision in *Mutual Film Corp. v. Ohio,* ruling that movies did not enjoy freedom of speech because filmmaking was "a business, pure and simple, originated and conducted for profit," and films were "capable of evil, having power for it, the greater because of their attractiveness and manner of exhibition." This interpretation was not substantially overturned until after the Second World War.

197   "not because it was the greatest": Quoted in Cook, *Fire from the Flint,* p. 170.

198   "like writing history with lightning": Ibid. Wilson, when the national controversy over the film became full-blown, would later deny making this endorsing remark. The only actual source for it was Thomas Dixon himself.

198   "Deserving white girls": Brisbane, *The Black Vanguard,* p. 54.

198   "I also worked": Quoted in Wolgemuth, "Woodrow Wilson and Federal Segregation."

198   "Mr. Wilson, do you know these things": *The Crisis,* September 1913.

199   "recent episode in which": *The Crisis,* February 1915.

200   "Trotter, by accident": Fox, *The Guardian of Boston,* p. 185.

200   only a few minor edits: Many of the historical tableaux shown in the film, such as Lincoln's assassination and the meeting between Grant and Lee at Appomatox, were faithful recreations of well-known lithographs or photographs, while the views of Southern legislatures taken over by apelike creatures were based on cartoonist Thomas Nast's crude caricatures.

201   Prior to *The Birth of a Nation*: In this movie, Griffith has turned minstrels into far less playful characters than on the stage. Ironically, the real black people in the film portray good characters, while the bad black people are portrayed by white men in blackface.

203   "It is a rebel play": Boston *Post,* April 18, 1915.

204   "We deplore this decision": NAACP "Vicious Film" pamphlet, 1915, NAACP Papers.

204   "surely the most vivid": Harlan, *Booker T. Washington,* pp. 379–404; Shapiro, *White Violence and Black Response,* p. 141.

205   "fitting themselves for high places": *Philadelphia Inquirer,* September 21, 1915.

206   "grotesque" and "tangled": A fragmentary print of *The Birth of a Race* was discovered in a Texas museum in the late 1970s.

207   "Frank is a small, wiry man": *Atlanta Constitution,* April 30, 1913. My account of Frank's arrest, trial, and lynching relies on Leonard Dinnerstein's authoritative *The Leo Frank Case.*

208   "I am not guilty": Ibid.
209   "Little Mary Phagan": Williamson, *A Rage for Order,* p. 244.
209   "Every woman in Atlanta": *Atlanta Constitution,* April 29, 1913.
209   "friend of the common man": The Populists, whom Watson led in the 1890s, distrusted the idea of a "New South" promoted by such figures as Henry W. Grady, publisher of *The Atlanta Constitution,* fearing it would only be a South better suited to serve the interests of Northern capitalists, railroads, and corporations, and would provide little practical good for the average Southerner who tilled his own soil. The Populists advocated free rural mail delivery, government ownership of railroads, the direct election of U.S. senators, women's suffrage, and the creation of a system that would allow farmers to store their products in order to market them in a more timely and profitable fashion. Watson saw that the black vote, which had so frightened Southern whites for so long, could and should be reclaimed by the South itself. He told Georgians of both races: "You are kept apart that you may be separately fleeced of your earnings. You are made to hate each other because upon that hatred is rested the keystone of the arch of financial despotism which enslaves you both." Watson acknowledged that blacks were vital to the region: "They are interwoven with our customs, our religion, our civilization. . . . They meet us at every turn—in the fields, shops, mines. They are a part of our system, and they are here to stay." In 1896 the bottom fell out of the Populist dream. There was a limit to how many whites would vote Populist because, despite the party's rhetoric about political equality *not* meaning social equality, that was the equation most whites understood and feared. There was talk, promoted by Democrats hoping to tear away the Populist mask of egalitarianism, that the Populists intended to "Africanize" the South. And blacks themselves began to distrust the concept when many white Populists fused with Democrats over national issues.
210   The Atlanta police had clearly botched: The Atlanta police force was not really trained or equipped to deal with the proper investigation of such a crime. Its hierarchy was structured largely on factors of nepotism and favoritism, and most officers had little expertise in the art of collecting forensic evidence. At the same time there was intense pressure to find and convict Phagan's killer. In the two years before her death, eighteen black women had been mysteriously murdered in Atlanta, their deaths unsolved. While the deaths of eighteen black women were not bound to unsettle the white public as much as the murder of one thirteen-year-old white girl, the police were aware that they were the targets of a local snickering campaign regarding their seeming incompetence to solve tough crimes.
210   "A HORRIBLE MISTAKE": *Atlanta Constitution,* May 1, 1914.
211   Ultimately, Burns departed: Burns later became head of the Justice Department's Bureau of Investigation, the precursor to the FBI, and had his exploits written up in dime novels and comic books.
213   "The minuteness of detail": *Atlanta Constitution,* August 18, 1915.
213   The Frank lynching: All quoted in *Jeffersonian,* September 2, 1915.
214   "The Voice of the People": Leo Frank was posthumously pardoned in 1982 when Alonzo Mann, an office boy in Frank's employ at the time of the killing of Mary Phagan, admitted he had seen Jim Conley carrying Phagan's body to the basement. Mann had kept his secret for nearly seventy years, he said, because Conley had threatened him. Conley died in 1962.

CHAPTER 7
The Wisest and Best Response

217   "We don't need no court!": Waco *Morning News,* May 16, 1916.
218   "Such a demonstration": *Waco Times-Herald,* May 15, 1916.
219   Freeman wrote a lengthy: With "The Waco Horror," the NAACP succeeded in acquainting Americans with the details of a specific and particularly gruesome lynching. Less well known, and coming directly on the heels of the Waco incident, was an August 1916 multiple lynching in Gainesville, Florida. On the morning of August 18, Constable C. G. Wynne accompanied Dr. L. G. Harris to the home of a black named Boisey Long and accused him of stealing a hog. Long argued, then drew a pistol from his pajamas and shot Wynne, who died later that day in

a Jacksonville hospital. A vehement search for the killer ensued. The posse, angry when it could not locate Long, seized five other blacks—Preacher Josh Baskins, Stella Young, Andrew McHenry, and Mary and Bert Dennis—and accused them of belonging to a hog-stealing ring with Long and of aiding his escape. All five were hanged from the same tree.

219   "The idea of *you* lynching": Mark Twain, *The Adventures of Huckleberry Finn* (New York: Oxford University Press, paperback, 1999), p. 133.

220   One of the first to come: *New York Times,* November 26, 1911.

221   Governor O'Neal ordered: Montgomery *Advertiser,* April 14, 1911.

221   "The Governor had given him": Ibid., May 26, 1911.

221   A week after Jinwright's downfall: *New York Times,* November 26, 1911.

222   "Here in our own Ohio": Cleveland *Advocate,* September 2, 1916.

223   "have sent from the South": Quoted in Grant, *The Way It Was in the South,* p. 291.

224   "At least, if trouble comes": Ibid., p. 290.

224   "After twenty years": Quoted in Litwack, *Trouble in Mind,* p. 490.

224   "I was just reading": Ibid., p. 491.

225   out-migration: The notion of a national out-migration of blacks was often entertained by both black and white Americans after the Civil War. But between 1865 and 1900 only about thirty thousand blacks left for Africa, the Caribbean, and Mexico. There was a movement out of the South in the late 1870s in reaction to the end of Reconstruction that saw about forty thousand blacks pick up and relocate to parts of Kansas, Indiana, and Nebraska, and a brief fling in the 1890s with the possibility that the Oklahoma Territory might serve as a "Negro state."

225   At times the slow trickle: The Hodges murders were thought to have resulted from a robbery gone awry. It was believed that Henry Hodges had surprised Cato and Reed in a stable, that the two blacks had killed him and, in a desperate attempt to leave no witnesses, had then murdered the Hodges's nine-year-old daughter, Kittie, by braining her with an iron bar. The little girl's screams brought the mother, Claudia, running with a lantern into the yard, where she, too, was killed. Cato and Reed then allegedly carried their victims' bodies into the house and set the structure on fire in an effort to disguise their crime. Two younger children who had hidden in the house were consumed in the blaze. "I hated to have to protect the negroes," said Sheriff Kendricks, who was a personal friend of the Hodges family, "but the duties of my office required it."

225   Such clearances often had: The triggering event was the rape and murder of a nineteen-year-old white woman. A hand mirror found near the rape scene was traced to Ernest Knox, an eighteen-year-old farmhand. Knox reportedly confessed to the crime and implicated several others. In the meantime, a black minister, Grant Smith, was horsewhipped on the courthouse square in the county seat of Cumming for making derisive comments about the character and morality of the rape victim. He was beaten almost to death and was about to be set afire by an infuriated mob of three hundred when sheriff's deputies intervened and carried him into the courthouse. Smith was safely removed to Atlanta, but another Forsyth black, Edward Roberts, was not so fortunate. He was in the Forsyth County jail in Cumming on another charge when, on September 10, whites broke in, shot him dead, mutilated him with a crowbar, then dragged his body outside and hung it from a telegraph pole. On October 3, Knox and an alleged accomplice, Oscar Daniel, were tried and executed before a crowd of ten thousand. As in Bulloch County eight years earlier, whites were not satisfied with vengeance having been exacted against a few men. Convinced that additional troublemakers remained, local planters initiated a series of clearances, dismissing large numbers of black workers and encouraging them to leave the area.

226   "He was getting rich": Charleston *News and Courier,* October 23, 1916.

227   "We are ALL responsible": Abbeville *Scimitar,* February 1, 1917.

228   "It does not matter": Ibid., February 27, 1817.

231   "At first I was afraid": Du Bois letter to James Weldon Johnson, November 1, 1916, in James Weldon Johnson Papers, Yale University.

231   "For weeks and months": Johnson, *Along This Way,* p. 170.

233   "Take this with our compliments": Account of Ell Persons lynching from "Memphis, May 22, A.D., 1917," a special supplement to *The Crisis,* July 1917.

233   "[T]hroughout the entire proceedings": Memphis *Commercial Appeal*, May 23, 1917.

234   "I reassembled the picture": Johnson, *Along This Way*, pp. 317–18.

235   "Just as America was speeding up": Quoted in *The Crisis*, October 1917.

235   "We have been inclined to disbelieve": Quoted in ibid.

235   to protest the Ell Persons killing: Johnson's horror at the lynching by the Macon Road Bridge
       was fully shared by a Memphis rabbi named William Fineshriber, who subsequently became
       a courageous antilynching reformer. Fineshriber played a key role in convincing the *Com-
       mercial Appeal* to adopt a more critical editorial perspective on mob violence.

236   "We march because": *New York Times*, July 29, 1917. The footsteps of the Negro Silent
       Protest Parade had barely echoed away when another orgy of racial violence erupted in late
       August at an army base outside Houston, Texas, where black members of the Twenty-fourth
       Infantry Division were stationed. The violence, much of which involved antagonism be-
       tween black soldiers and white police, may have been partly inspired by a recent Shreveport
       Journal article that had declared: "The swaggering of a Negro trooper in uniform is not a
       thing to be desired or to be suffered silently."

238   "[I]n that instant there opened up": White, *A Man Called White*, p. 11.

239   in the vicinity of Hoop Spur: Helena *Daily World*, October 2, 1919.

242   "But you're leaving, mister": Incident described in White, *A Man Called White*, pp. 49–51.
       Walter White's experience in Phillips County formed part of the basis for his first novel, *Fire
       in the Flint*, published in 1924, in which a young black doctor pays with his life for support-
       ing a rural black farmers' cooperative.

243   "But, Mr. President": Duster, *Crusade for Justice*, p. 397.

243   Taking advantage of the fact: Ibid., pp. 401–3.

244   "We have the whole community inflamed": *Moore v. Dempsey*.

244   The Supreme Court ruling in the case: See also Shapiro, *White Violence and Black Response*, pp.
       148–49.

246   "Fury of People": *Atlanta Constitution*, May 23, 1918.

246   "Mister, you ought to've heard": White, *Rope and Faggot*, p. 28. James Weldon Johnson was
       traveling in the South at this time, and John Shillady asked him to go to Quitman and inter-
       view a young black man who had driven the wagon carrying the remains of some of the per-
       sons lynched. The town was in an uproar over Walter White's published revelations. For
       Johnson, a strange black man in a small Southern town recently roiled by a monstrous lynch-
       ing, the situation was extremely dangerous. He found the young man who had driven the
       wagon, but the latter, admitting he knew who had been in the lynch mob, refused Johnson's
       offer to bring him to New York where he could be safe and reveal what he knew. Even if he
       got out of town alive, he insted, his mother and family left behind would surely be killed.

248   "There might be danger to someone else": Ovington, *Black and White Sat Down Together*, p. 91.

250   "Negro-loving white men": Kellogg, *NAACP*, p. 240.

250   "it was wrong to beat up a visitor": Ovington, *Black and White Sat Down Together*, pp. 92–93.

250   The chief reason: Ibid., p. 175; White, *A Man Called White*, pp. 46–47.

CHAPTER 8
The Shame of America

253   "It is, indeed, amazing": H. L. Mencken, "The Sahara of the Bozart," pp. 136–37. See also
       Egerton, *Speak Now Against the Day*.

254   "[I]f American intelligence": Hofstadter, *The Age of Reform*, p. 288.

256   "If we must die": *Liberator II*, July 1919, p. 21.

257   The centerpiece of this effort: New York *Sun*, May 6, 1919.

258   "The veil of self-satisfaction": Account of NAACP's May 1919 National Conference on
       Lynching in New York City, a two-day gathering at Carnegie Hall, in NAACP Papers.

258   "If the American people can stop": "Segregation and Anti-Lynching Hearing," House Judi-
       ciary Committee, January 12 and 29, 1920, H234 Pt. 2-1.

259   "Congress ought to wipe": *Congressional Record*, Sixty-seventh Congress, 1921, pp. 169–70.

261   "[I]t is bad enough": Washed up in elective politics, this charismatic individual later founded
       an all-black community in New Jersey named Whitesboro and went to work for the NAACP.

261 The world had changed much: The NAACP adroitly abandoned its resolution, drawn at its Carnegie Hall conference, asking Congress to "investigate" lynching, for fear such a process would become an excuse to stall on more concrete action. Its all-out emphasis would be on securing federal legislation that would punish lynchers and collaborating lawmen where states hesitated to prosecute such crimes.

263 "two horns of the dilemma": "Segregation and Anti-Lynching Hearing," House Judiciary Committee, January 12 and 29, 1920, H234 Pt. 2-1.

263 "It is the proud boast": Ibid.

264 "When men respond to that call": *Congressional Record,* Sixty-seventh Congress, 2nd Session, p. 799.

264 "a sod house on Fifth Avenue": Ibid., p. 1361.

264 "ignorant negroes": *New York Times,* December 3, 1922.

265 "sociological imbeciles": Macon *Daily News,* July 18, 1922.

265 "A cynic might deduce": *New York Times,* January 27, 1922.

265 "I am pouring into them": James Weldon Johnson to Walter White, January 6, 1922, JWJ Papers, Yale University Library.

266 "Sit down, niggers": *New York Times,* January 26, 1922.

267 The NAACP had a sympathizer: Political ambition may have also been a factor, for if Lodge suffered a humiliating legislative defeat on the lynching bill and lost reelection, Borah was in line to succeed him as chairman of the powerful Senate Foreign Relations Committee.

267 "The analogy between murder and lynching": Johnson, *Along This Way,* p. 369.

268 used the word *anarchy* deliberately: Walter White correspondence, fund-raising letter of December 1, 1922, NAACP Papers.

268 The Kirvin lynchings: See Akers, *Flames After Midnight.*

269 "My heart sank": The description of Senator Shortridge is in Johnson, *Along This Way,* p. 369.

270 Placing such highly visible notices: *New York Times,* November 23, 1922.

270 "It must be apparent": *The Crisis,* January 1923.

271 "We cannot pass the bill": *New York Times,* December 3, 1922.

271 "The Senate's Surrender": Ibid., December 4, 1922.

272 Once the Dyer Bill had been smothered: A news item Du Bois clipped and published soon after in *The Crisis* compared Senator Lodge to a small-town Southern sheriff and the Democrats to an unruly lynch mob: "The lynching bill was lynched. [A] mob assembled in the Senate chamber, and everybody knew it was forming and what they were going to do. The officers in charge made a slight pretense of defending their prisoner . . . [but] were truly delighted to have him forcibly taken . . . and put to death."

272 Lodge was incensed: Correspondence between Lodge and Johnson is in Anti-Lynching Campaign files (1922) in NAACP Papers.

272 "This outbreak of barbarism": James Weldon Johnson, "An Open Letter to Every Senator of the United States," December 13, 1922, JWJ Papers, Yale University Library.

273 "I know I do not deserve mercy": *Atlantic Monthly,* February 1946.

273 "Do as much as you have to do": *St. Louis Post-Dispatch,* February 15, 1920.

274 Kentucky had a harder time: *New York Times,* February 1, 1926.

276 "The mass production of the Model T": Wade, *The Fiery Cross,* pp. 171–72.

278 "Commerce has no social illusions": Walter Hines Page, "The Last Hold of the Southern Bully," *Forum,* 1893.

279 The public's disenchantment: The Klan was struck by scandal where it was at its most powerful, in Indiana. There, a Klan leader named D. C. Stephenson, known as "Steve," had achieved an almost Tammany-like control of the state's clergy, politicians, and lawmen. He was known for descending godlike in his private airplane to address rallies of the faithful gathered in farmers' fields, then, with a whir of the propeller, returning to the heavens as the masses watched in awed tribute from below. Steve had a romantic interest in a young woman named Madge Oberholzer. When she refused to accompany him on a business trip to Chicago, he had her abducted. She escaped, but in her desperation swallowed poison, and with her dying breaths managed to tell police a tale of kidnap and rape. That Steve, the beloved leader of a cult of avenging Christians, could be capable of such depravity came as a terrible shock to his followers. His conviction for Oberholzer's murder, accompanied by

revelations that many state officials were on his payroll, brought the Indiana Klan to a crashing halt, the state membership sinking from 350,000 to 15,000 within just a few months.

280 "biracial conference": "Louisville Lets Contract for Swimming Pool," press release in CIC Papers, Schomburg Center, New York City.

280 "Careful study has convinced us": Will Alexander to Governor H. L. Whitfield of Mississippi, May 4, 1926, in CIC Papers.

281 "If you come in here it will": Jackson *Clarion Ledger* and Memphis *Evening Appeal,* October 28, 1931; clippings in CIC Papers.

281 "by the wisdom and justice": Egerton, *Speak Now Against the Day,* p. 450.

281 "If we are to be even Christian": "America's Obligation to the Negro," CIC brochure, 1926, in CIC Papers.

282 "Here is a chance to vindicate": "It's Up to Us," CIC press release, January 1923, CIC Papers.

283 "The first negro family": Quoted in Walling, "The Race War in the North."

284 "A group of five thousand Nordic": Fine, *Frank Murphy,* p. 152.

285 "Had Turner stood firm": Walter White to James Weldon Johnson, September 16, 1925, Sweet case correspondence files, NAACP Papers.

285 But Darrow's legal strategy: Waskow, *The 1919 Race Riots,* p. 59.

286 Almost sixty-nine years old: Darrow first gained national prominence in 1924 when he saved the young Chicago "thrill killers" Nathan Leopold and Richard Loeb, who had wantonly murdered a child, from certain execution. In the just-concluded Tennessee case, Darrow's colorful adversary had been the former Populist and Democratic presidential candidate William Jennings Bryan, who had become a standard-bearer in the '20s fundamentalist revival. "The Great Commoner," as Bryan was known, had been instrumental in creating the Tennessee antievolution measure Darrow's client Scopes was accused of defying. The trial, a "battle royal" between two well-known giants of oratory, representing two major schools of thought in 1920s America, attracted reporters from across the country, who camped on the lawn of the Dayton courthouse and issued daily bulletins and photographs to the nation. The case was ultimately decided against Scopes, who was made to pay a hundred-dollar fine, although Darrow was, in the court of public opinion, considered the victor for the eloquence and strength of his arguments. With temperatures often hovering around a hundred degrees in the poorly ventilated courtroom, the trial was an endurance test for all involved—indeed, Bryan died a few days after its completion.

288 "We'll load this nigger's goods": Fine, p. 148.

289 Despite these accomplishments: Haldeman-Julius, *Clarence Darrow's Two Great Trials,* p. 32.

289 "When I opened the door": Ibid., p. 41.

290 *The Nation* described Darrow's questioning: *The Nation,* December 23, 1925. In the 1990s, commentators were heard to compare the 1925 Sweet case with the high-profile murder trial of O. J. Simpson. Among the parallels noted was that Simpson, like the Sweets, enjoyed the services of a "Dream Team" of attorneys who overwhelmed the talents of local prosecutors.

292 "the clatter of folding chairs": Haldeman-Julius, p. 73.

292 Unfortunately, the corresponding: Restrictive covenants would be not be outlawed until 1948; see *Shelley v. Kraemer.*

294 "roughneck men from out of Columbia": *New York Times,* April 30, 1923.

297 "If, therefore, it is claimed": "Commencement Address for Atlanta University" in *A Franz Boas Reader,* ed. G. Stocking (Chicago: The University of Chicago Press, 1974).

299 "It is possible": Gossett, *Race,* p. 418. Another development in which Boas figured was the entrance into the cause of black people of leading Jewish Americans. For Boas, his student Melville Herkovits, philanthropist Jacob Schiff, Joel and Arthur Spingarn of the NAACP, Julius Rosenwald of Sears Roebuck, settlement-house worker Lillian Wald, NAACP journalist Martha Gruening, and Paul Sachs and Edwin Seligman of the Urban League, just as for others in the antilynching and civil rights struggle, support for black rights was not only a humanitarian response to injustice, but also a way to confront the Anglo-Saxon hierarchy without fear of being labeled as radicals, since the black struggle for equality was undeniably American and homegrown.

302 "ANOTHER NEGRO LYNCHED IN GEORGIA": White, *Fire in the Flint,* p. 300.

CHAPTER 9

The Tragedy of Lynching

303   "It is hard to tell just what": Walter White to James Weldon Johnson, August 22, 1930, JWJ papers, Yale University Library.

306   "A strong wind was blowing": *Literary Digest,* January 31, 1931.

308   "a parody of due process": Randall Kennedy, *Race, Crime, and the Law,* p. 100. Another Scottsboro irregularity was that at one point a jury deliberating the fate of one defendant heard the courtroom explode in cheers when the guilty verdict of another two defendants was announced.

310   "Because my father was a slave": Duberman, *Paul Robeson,* p. 441.

311   "The only party that comes out squarely": Humes, *Oswald Garrison Villard,* pp. 82–83.

311   "It is perfectly apparent": *Powell v. Alabama.*

311   "The failure of the trial court": Ibid.

312   "touches no controversial": Carter, *Scottsboro,* p. 182.

313   "Show them that": *New York Times,* December 1, 1933. State attorney general Thomas Knight, who prosecuted the case, had inside information from one of the examining physicians that Bates had not been raped, information he kept to himself.

313   "might be a fallen woman": New York *Herald Tribune,* November 30, 1933.

314   "don't count a mite with the jury": Carter, p. 241.

314   "It is doubtful if a single person": *The Crisis,* January 1934.

315   The state's already weak position: *Norris v. Alabama.*

316   "Not too much for a negro": *Brown v. Mississippi,* quoted in Randall Kennedy, *Race, Crime, and the Law,* p. 104.

316   "a fictitious continuation": *Brown v. Mississippi,* quoted in ibid., p. 105.

317   "It would be difficult to conceive": *Brown v. Mississippi,* quoted in ibid., p. 106.

317   Though innocent: Another example of the Supreme Court's new willingness to interpret the Fourteenth Amendment as a federal protection against state excesses was the case of Angelo Herndon. In June 1932, Atlanta police stopped Herndon, a nineteen-year-old Communist, as he was leaving the city's main post office with a box of party recruitment materials. In his rented room more incriminating books and pamphlets were found. Charged with "an attempt to incite insurrection" against the state of Georgia, a Reconstruction-era law, Herndon was convicted and sentenced to twenty years in prison. His case became the focus of a national campaign, and the ILD hired prominent East Coast attorneys Walter Gellhorn and Whitney North Seymour to appeal the verdict to the U.S. Supreme Court. Gellhorn and Seymour referred the court to the famous "clear and present danger" doctrine first enunciated in 1919 by Justice Oliver Wendell Holmes in the case of *Schenk v. U.S.* Schenk, a Socialist, had been arrested under the Espionage Act of 1917 for distributing antidraft leaflets. "The question in every [such] case is whether the words used are used in such a nature as to create a clear and present danger that they will bring about the substantive evils that Congress has a right to prevent," Holmes wrote in a dissenting opinion in *Schenk.* "It is a question of proximity and degree." The issue surfaced again in *Gitlow v. New York,* in which Socialist Benjamin Gitlow appealed his conviction under a 1902 New York State law that made it a crime to advocate the overthrow of the government. Gitlow lost his appeal although Holmes again dissented, citing the same "clear and present danger" measure he had introduced in *Schenk.* Finally, in 1931, in *Stromberg v. California,* the court ruled that symbolic speech was not necessarily insurrectionary. *Stromberg* involved a California children's camp run by an alliance of leftist groups. A red flag had been flown over the camp by one of its directors, a woman named Yetta Stromberg. Invoking the "clear and present danger" concept, the justices ruled that the flying of a flag was an abstract doctrine at best and did not constitute a threat to the state of California. The Stromberg case was the first in which the high court used the Fourteenth Amendment's assurance that "no state shall make or enforce any law which shall abridge the privileges or immunities of citizens of the United States" to extend First Amendment rights to citizens of the states. In *Herndon,* the Supreme Court synchronized with its own decision in *Stromberg,* ruling that Herndon's activities—holding meetings to recruit members to the Communist party and asking for contributions for the party—did not amount to the

advocacy of forcible subversion, and in April 1937 the justices rejected Herndon's state conviction.

317   "I challenge any reputable": Senate Judiciary Hearing, "Punishment for the Crime of Lynching," Seventy-third Congress, 2d Session, 1934.

318   "A certain type of Negro": Letter from J. R. Steelman to Will Alexander, September 11, 1933, Correspondence Files, Association of Southern Women for the Prevention of Lynching Papers, Schomburg Center, New York.

319   "lantern-jawed morons": *New Republic,* June 20, 1934.

320   "All the emotion stirred": "Notes, Tuscaloosa Investigation," compiled by Arthur Raper, 1933, in ASWPL Papers.

320   A sham investigation: Department of Justice memo dated August 30, 1933, in File #158260, Record Group 60, National Archives.

321   had probably tried to rob Mrs. Denston: *The Nation,* December 13, 1933.

322   "the wildest lynching orgy": Washington *Herald,* October 19, 1933.

322   "I can't tell you how it made me feel": Baltimore *Sun,* October 20, 1933.

323   By daybreak: A bizarre accident occurred on October 20 when a black man taking part in an ILD protest at Baltimore City Hall put his head in a noose under an imitation gallows, which had been set up on a truck beneath a sign that read "Protest Lynching of George Armwood." When the truck moved unexpectedly the man lost his balance and "gave a realistic exhibition of a hanging" before he could be helped back to his feet.

323   It would be Ritchie's unhappy: The two Maryland cases had not done much for the ILD's reputation. When ILD attorney Bernard Ades and James Ford of the Legal Struggle for Negro Rights appeared by invitation at the Senate Judiciary Committee meeting considering points of view on the Wagner-Costigan antilynching bill in 1935, both men were promptly asked to step out of the witness chair after voicing "communistic" sentiments about lynching.

CHAPTER 10
States' Rights, States' Wrongs

324   "She was supposed to have ideals": Dykeman and Stokely, *Seeds of Southern Change,* p. 83.

325   "We have just emerged": Quoted in Hall, *Revolt Against Chivalry,* p. 89.

326   "the men might as well": Ibid.

327   "The continuance of lynching": "Recommendations of Colored Women," Memphis Conference, Women's Division of CIC, 1920, CIC Papers, Schomburg Center, New York.

327   "We all feel that you can control": Remarks at Memphis Conference in Jessie Daniel Ames Papers, Schomburg Center, New York.

327   "I am one of the Negroes": Remarks on October 1920 meeting recorded in October 1921 at Continuation Committee Meeting in Atlanta, CIC Papers.

328   "We are humiliated": Hall, p. 101.

328   "God-like pure snow white angelic": Ibid., p. 112.

330   "They had more power": Smith, *Killers of the Dream,* pp. 144–46.

330   Within months of its founding: Hall, p. 195.

333   "brought up on this theory": "Can Newspapers Harmonize Their Editorial Policy on Lynching and Their News Stories on Lynching," address by Jessie Daniel Ames at Southern Newspaper Publishers' Association meeting, Atlanta, May 18, 1936, in ASWPL Papers.

334   Crying and pleading for their lives: The kidnapping theme of the San Jose lynching, the use of a battering ram to gain entrance to the jail, and other details of the November 1933 incident would surface in the 1936 Fritz Lang film *Fury,* starring Spencer Tracy as a young man falsely accused of kidnapping. Another influence on the film was undoubtedly the 1930 killing of prisoner George Hughes in Sherman, Texas. Unable to get at Hughes, the mob simply torched the entire courthouse and burned Hughes alive along with the $60,000 edifice.

335   "The violence of the California mob": *New York Times,* November 29, 1933.

336   "This new generation": Ibid., December 7, 1933.

336   Lynching's persistence: Shapiro, *White Violence and Black Response,* p. 282.

337 Another influential change: *New York Times,* November 8, 1933. Another compelling reason, in the midst of the Depression, for the abolishment of Prohibition was the awareness on the part of virtually every town, county, and state government that the criminalization of liquor consumption meant an end to tax revenues from its consumption and a loss of related income and jobs, while expenditures for enforcement were high. It was estimated in 1933 that a walloping $36 billion worth of bootleg liquor had been sold since the early 1920s. In New York State alone, it was gauged, tax revenues from liquor would amount to $12 million, and thus allow for a reduction in income and sales taxes. In addition, it was thought a half-million new jobs would be created nationwide in agriculture and industry by the reinvigoration of the liquor business.

337 "National Disgrace No. 1": *Springfield Republican* quoted in Birmingham *Age-Herald,* November 1, 1934.

338 "how America can": Pittsburgh *Courier,* August 10, 1935.

338 "Not many persons": Quoted in Wade, *The Fiery Cross,* p. 257.

339 Party workers in Dallas: The Klan actively sought an alliance with Nazi sympathizers in the United States—the Swastika League, the Friends of Hitler, Teutonia—all of which later united as the Amerika-Deutscher Volksbund. (Curiously, the Klan was not the Volksbund's first choice of an American ally. Bund leader Julius Kuhn was convinced that the Nazis' natural partners in the United States would be Native Americans because they, like the Aryans, were a pure ethnic group that had been maligned and mistreated by history. But after slight contact with tribal officials it became clear that American Indians had little use for anti-Semitism, anti-Communism, and other fundamental tenets of the Nazi creed.) The American Nazis linked up with the Klan only for one joint rally, held in rural New Jersey, and the alliance was extremely short-lived. The rally site, a Nazi youth camp, was soon outlawed and closed by the U.S. government. The Volksbund's image in this country eroded quickly in response to German territorial aggression in Europe and upon the arrest and conviction of Julius Kuhn for embezzling his organization's funds, for which he was given a lengthy term in Sing Sing.

340 "The South," Du Bois wrote: *The Crisis,* January 1934.

342 "There are States' rights": Lynchburg *News,* January 9, 1934.

342 White's strategy: The NAACP also took great care to attack what Ida Wells-Barnett had once called "the old thread-bare lie"—the claim that black men instinctively and routinely assault white women, which had proved a major distraction during the Dyer Bill fight. To help defeat the rape myth even before the first Southern senator could raise it in floor debate, the NAACP published a lengthy list of the actual causes of some of the many lynchings it had investigated over the years. These included: "testifying against whites, making moonshine liquor, window peeping, criminal abortion, writing insulting letters, expressing satisfaction over the murder of a white man, slapping a child, vagrancy, prospective elopement, attempting to colonize Negroes, conjuring, incendiarism, proposing marriage to a white woman, introducing smallpox, stealing hogs, not turning out of road for a white boy in an automobile, being found under bed in white man's house, talking too much about the Chicago riot, being the relative of a lynched man, frightening children, escorting mother into town after her flogging by a mob, remaining in a town where Negroes not allowed, and seditious utterance."

343 "Twenty years ago": *The Nation,* November 27, 1937.

343 consistently attentive to his needs: White valued his good rapport with the Roosevelts in contrast with his dismal relationship with FDR's predecessor, Herbert Hoover, who held a grudge against White. As secretary of commerce in 1927, Hoover had directed federal relief efforts in the face of castastrophic floods in the Mississippi Valley, and White had publicly exposed the fact that National Guardsmen there were impressing blacks into work gangs to help control the flood damage, essentially reducing them to a state of peonage. (See Richard Wright's short story "Down by the Riverside" in *Uncle Tom's Children,* pp. 54–102.) During his presidency, Hoover consistently ignored White's requests for personal audiences, showing greater consideration even to the fiery Trotter, who was allowed to visit at the head of an antilynching delegation in 1930.

343 White was, in a sense: White had one adversary within the administration, an FDR aide named Steve Early, who reminded Eleanor that White had been arrested for attempting to

crash the color barrier at the Senate dining room. Eleanor assured Early, "I realize perfectly that he has an obsession on the lynching question and I do not doubt that he has been a great nuisance with his telegrams and letters," but, "If I were colored, I think I should have about the same obsession that he has. . . . If you ever talked to him, and knew him, I think you would feel as I do. He really is a very fine person with the sorrows of his people close to his heart." Eleanor Roosevelt to Steve Early, August 8, 1935, Eleanor Roosevelt Papers, FDR Presidential Library.

344   A popular rumor in the South: Also known as the "Daughters of Eleanor," their purported slogan was "A white woman in every kitchen." One thoroughly scandalized white woman in Washington, D.C., reported to the FBI that after telling her black maid to set the table for four because she and her husband were expecting another couple for dinner, she returned to find the table set for five. When she asked the maid why, she had answered that she was a member of an "Eleanor Club" and was going to eat with the guests that evening. See Eleanor Roosevelt FBI file in FDR Papers, FDR Library, Hyde Park.

344   "The President feels that lynching": Eleanor Roosevelt to Walter White, March 19, 1936, ER Correspondence, FDR Library.

344   "Here's Mr. Roosevelt's message": *Amsterdam News,* January 12, 1935.

345   The self-proclaimed Peanut Capital: There had been a particularly virulent Klan chapter here during Reconstruction that had induced many former slaves to depart, including the family of T. Thomas Fortune, who was born in Marianna in 1868. In the 1990s, a lone black resident of the town was trying without success to get a local post office named in Fortune's honor.

345   "There are too many": Howard "Buck" Kester, "Report on the Lynching of Claude Neal," 1934, NAACP Papers. For a comprehensive account see *Anatomy of a Lynching: The Killing of Claude Neal* by James R. McGovern.

347   "a prominent business man": Ibid.

347   "I got to thinking": Associated Press, October 26, 1934.

348   "Associated Press just informed us": Walter White telegram to Governor Sholtz, October 26, 1934, in Governors' Papers, Florida State Archives.

348   "wholly without legal authority": *Tampa Tribune,* February 2, 1934.

349   The mob had promised George: Marianna *Daily Times-Courier,* October 20, 1934.

349   There were a number of precedents: Ibid., October 27, 1934.

350   "The mob apparently started": Kester report, NAACP Papers.

351   Governor Sholtz, put on the spot: Sholtz would also later stress that, once Neal was in the mob's hands, even a large contingent of militia would have done little good, since troops were really only useful in guarding a stationary fixture such as a jail or courthouse. And even if soldiers could have managed to locate Neal and his abductors in the trackless marshlands and empty places of northwest Florida, the mob could always cross back over the border into Georgia or Alabama, out of reach of the Florida guardsmen. Considering how things turned out, Sholtz might have been better off disregarding Chambliss's assurances and sending troops anyway, for the sake of public relations if nothing else.

351   "I am not coming to Florida": Governors' Papers, Florida State Archives.

351   "a gory spectacle": *Tampa Tribune,* October 29, 1934.

352   "He described the scene": Letter from Howard Kester to Walter White, November 7, 1934, NAACP Papers.

352   "I have investigated": Walter White to Eleanor Roosevelt, November 20, 1934, ER Correspondence, FDR Library.

352   "Miss Lola Cannidy": Letter from Walter White to Governor David Sholtz, November 22, 1934. Report of Circuit Court of Jackson County, Florida, Fall Term 1934, in Governors' Papers, Florida State Archives.

353   "Otherwise" apparently meant: The NAACP renewed its plea for federal involvement in the Neal case two years later, when in early 1936 the Supreme Court ruled in the case of *Gooch v. United States.* Two outlaws, Gooch and Nix, had been accosted by policemen in Paris, Texas. Fearing arrest, Gooch and Nix disarmed the officers, kidnapped them, and took them by car into Oklahoma before setting them free. Eventually captured and convicted of kidnapping, Gooch appealed the legitimacy of the verdict under the Lindbergh statute. The high

court ruled against him, stating that the kidnapping of a police officer to avoid arrest could be prosecuted under the "otherwise" clause. Walter White was incensed that the federal judiciary would be willing to grant this reading of the law in *Gooch* while the Justice Department refused to consider it in the still-unsolved Neal case, and derided the Lindbergh Law as "an administrative policy to the effect that the Federal kidnapping law applies only to the kidnapping of wealthy white citizens and white peace officers."

353 "This, of course, seems and is morbid": Letter from Walter White to Mrs. Harry Payne Whitney, December 13, 1934, NAACP Papers; letter from Mrs. G. M. Trelease to Governor Sholtz, December 4, 1934, in Governors' Papers, Florida State Archives.

355 The CIC had come around: The CIC's work in the South had also waned considerably. With the departure of Will Alexander in 1935 to join the government as head of the Farm Security Administration under President Roosevelt, the CIC would never again be as fully active or effective.

355 the more autocratic Ames: Ames became isolated by her stubborn position that the states could handle lynching, an obstinacy that began to seem almost willfully forlorn as many of the groups associated with the ASWPL joined the call for federal intervention. Indeed, longtime ASWPL loyalists began to fear that a group once known for rigorous advocacy was, due to Ames's intransigence, being left behind by mainstream Southern opinion, and some of her top lieutenants, such as Florida's Jane Cornell, abandoned her. Ames, in her determination to go her own way, had even written to Texas senator Tom Connally, one of the Southerners known for filibustering antilynching bills to death, to assure him that the Gavagan–Wagner–Van Nuys bill's passage was not a matter of importance to either her or the ASWPL. When Connally made the letter public, Ames earned the harsh condemnation of many former allies, most notably W.E.B. Du Bois. "Instead now of your following up the excellent work which has been done by Southern people and upheld by leading Southern periodicals, utterly to stamp out lynching," he wrote angrily, "you begin by congratulating a Senator because he is about to win a fight to defeat the Anti-Lynching Bill, and you assume there is important far-reaching legislation which outweighs the effort to stop lynching. I am sorry and distressed that a person in your position should . . . think this." When, during the Second World War, a new Southern interracial organization, the Southern Regional Council, was raised in large part on the ruins of the CIC and the ASWPL, the headstrong, beleaguered Mrs. Ames was pointedly left out of its founding plans.

356 "National problems demand": *New York Times,* April 20, 1935.
356 "We'll be here until Christmas": Ibid., April 22, 1935.
356 "It shall not pass": Ibid., April 26, 1935.
357 "I did not choose": White, *A Man Called White,* pp. 169–70.
357 "It is a matter of great disappointment": Walter White to FDR, May 6, 1935, ER Correspondence, FDR Library.
360 "gang murder for which your state is known": *Atlanta Constitution,* April 14, 1937.
360 "Up North": New York *Daily News,* November 24, 1937.
360 To the chagrin of leading Southerners: *New York Post,* May 25, 1937.
361 "You certainly know my sentiments": James Weldon Johnson to Walter White, March 8, 1938, JWJ Papers, Yale University.

CHAPTER 11
It Can Happen Here

363 "The defense of our democracy": Quoted in Myrdal, *An American Dilemma,* p. 1009.
364 black participation with concrete gains: Randolph told Roosevelt that as many as 100,000 blacks would come to Washington on July 1 unless he issued an executive order opening work in the defense industries to black Americans. New York mayor Fiorello La Guardia helped break the impasse by suggesting that Randolph be allowed to work with government lawyer Joseph Rauh to see if they could not write out the draft of an executive order that FDR would be willing to sign. The result was Executive Order 8802, which banned discrimination on account of race, creed, color, or national origin in industries holding government contracts for war production. Keeping his end of the bargain, Randolph called off the march.

365   "The Negro has developed a mass movement": A. Phillip Randolph speech to NAACP meeting, Houston, Texas, June 25, 1941, A. Phillip Randolph Papers, Schomburg Center, New York.

366   "The gradual destruction of the popular theory": Myrdal, p. 1003.

366   "The white man can humiliate": Ibid., p. 1009.

366   Another important literary signpost: The precariousness of the world Southern blacks inhabited was also at the heart of Wright's 1937 story collection, *Uncle Tom's Children,* in which black children and adults strive for beauty, friendship, and love only to find their aspirations crushed by cruel, miscomprehending whites. As powerful as were these tales, Wright was concerned that the characters had been too likeable and one-dimensional. In his 1940 novel *Native Son,* Wright created a far more challenging and disturbing figure, the antihero Bigger Thomas, whose life in a white world is so thwarted he becomes a monster, albeit a recognizable one, a black murderer who is hard to like but whose humanity is impossible to deny.

368   "walked backward into its future": Smith, *Killers of the Dream,* p. 68.

368   "sugar-tit words": Ibid., p. 93.

369   "pretending to be heroes": Quoted in Civil Rights Congress, *We Charge Genocide,* p. 189.

371   "We fought for freedom overseas": Juan Williams, *Thurgood Marshall: American Revolutionary* (New York: Times Books, 1998), p. 133.

372   "storm troopers": *New York Post,* May 10, 1946.

372   "a signal by state officials": Walter White telegram to Tom Clark, June 15, 1946, NAACP Anti-Lynching Papers.

372   "exhausted every possibility": Tom Clark to Eleanor Roosevelt, July 9, 1946, NAACP Anti-Lynching Papers.

374   "Boy, you want to take my test?": NAACP Press Release, November 22, 1946, "Thurgood Marshall, NAACP Counsel, Nearly Jailed by Columbia Cops," in NAACP Papers; Juan Williams, interview with Thurgood Marshall, as posted on "Thurgood Marshall: American Revolutionary" website, www.thurgoodmarshall.com.

375   "They told me to hold my head down": *PM,* August 30, 1946.

375   "The excessive heat and beatings": *New York Post,* August 20, 1946.

376   "one of the most unbelievable": Walter Winchell to Walter White, September 3, 1946, NAACP Anti-Lynching Papers.

376   "Gestapo tactics": Telegram report filed with NAACP on February 26, 1947, NAACP Anti-Lynching Papers.

378   "I can carry any county": Arnall's break with Talmadge occurred when Talmadge brazenly removed several top academicians and administrators from Georgia state colleges for what he perceived to be their lax views on race, and called for the burning of all books favoring desegregation. As a result of these policies so clearly reminiscent of the early days of Nazism, all of Georgia's state schools lost their national accreditation. For his willingness to act on his belief that it was in Georgia's best interest to get in step with the rest of the United States, Arnall briefly became the darling of the national media and of many liberals. As governor, he introduced sweeping reforms in education, prosecuted the Ku Klux Klan, and oversaw the writing of a new state constitution.

380   "The whole thing must have lasted three minutes": Raleigh *News & Observer,* July 27, 1946.

381   *The Fruit of the Tree:* Louisville *Courier-Journal,* July 27, 1946.

381   "The blood of these victims": Philadelphia *Record,* July 29, 1946.

381   "We in the South cannot cry": *Atlanta Constitution,* August 3, 1946.

382   "This crime is an affront": Raleigh *News & Observer,* July 31, 1946.

383   "We were the most unpopular people": *Atlanta Constitution,* May 31, 1992.

383   "When the mob gangs can take": McCullough, *Truman,* p. 589. Unlike most long-ago lynchings, which are recounted only in brittle newspaper clippings and about which little new information ever comes to light, the Monroe killings of 1946 had an unusual reprise a half-century later. In 1992 Clinton Adams, a white man who claimed to have witnessed the shootings as a ten-year-old boy, came forward to tell the FBI that on July 26, 1946, he had been out "minding a cow" when he saw the mob gather at Moore's Ford and pull the victims from Loy Harrison's car. He said one of the cars in the ambush had been a state police car and that one of the men shooting the blacks had been Loy Harrison. He named several other

shooters, all local men who had since died. He told the FBI that he had been warned as a boy never to reveal what he knew.

384 "Many of our people still suffer": McCullough, pp. 569–70.

384 "The applause when he finished": White, *A Man Called White*, p. 348.

384 "Where the administration of justice is discriminatory": *To Secure These Rights, Report of the President's Committee on Civil Rights* (New York: Simon & Schuster, 1947), p. 6.

384 "The almost complete immunity": Ibid., p. 37.

385 "If we wish to inspire": U.S. Commission on Civil Rights, *Freedom to the Free*, p. 119.

385 "There are those who say to you": McCullough, p. 639.

386 "The negro is a native of a tropical climate": Civil Rights Congress, *We Charge Genocide*, p. 164.

387 "He had done more than any President": McCullough, p. 915.

387 "It was not the multiplicity": Egerton, *Speak Now Against the Day*, p. 510.

388 "What I was most afraid of": Walter Prescott Webb, afterword to *The Ox-Bow Incident* (New York: New American Library, 1960), pp. 223–24.

389 The concert scheduled: The CRC had already distinguished itself by assuming a leading role in defending the "Trenton Six"—six black men arrested in Trenton, New Jersey, in the summer of 1948 for the murder of a seventy-three-year-old white novelty-store owner. On largely circumstantial evidence all six were convicted and sentenced to death. In a series of trials, however, CRC attorneys succeeded in demonstrating that police had extracted confessions from the men using narcotics and threats, and ultimately all five surviving prisoners (one had died behind bars) were released.

389 "was ambitious to become": Peekskill *Evening Star*, August 23, 1949.

389 "The time for tolerant silence": Ibid., August 22, 1949.

390 "Most of them were prosperous-appearing": Fast, *Peekskill USA*, p. 24.

390 "had written many books": Ibid., p. 27.

390 "It was still daylight": Ibid., p. 26.

391 "the most monstrous": Ibid., pp. 46–47.

391 "a preview of American storm troopers": *New York Times*, August 31, 1949.

392 "We saw children": Westchester *Journal News*, August 27, 1999.

392 "It was a very tense atmosphere": Ibid.

393 "rests solely on the Robesonites": *New York Times*, September 6, 1949.

394 "specific and stinking vileness": Fast, pp. 62–67.

396 "this case must and will be tried": Quoted in *Hampton v. Commonwealth*, 58 s.e. 2d 288, 298 (Va. supt. ct. 1950).

398 "revolting insinuation": Charles H. Martin, "Black Protest, Anti-Communism and the Cold War: The Willie McGee Case," p. 8.

398 "I have given this account of the affair": Willie McGee, Affidavit to Mississippi Supreme Court, February 3, 1951, in Civil Rights Congress Papers, Schomburg Center, New York.

399 "So all of a sudden": Rosalee McGee statement, July 25, 1950, in CRC Papers.

399 "People who don't know the South": Mitford, *A Fine Old Conflict*, p. 164.

400 To outsiders, such a position: One of the inspirations for the outpouring of support for McGee from East Coast liberals may have been New York's own "Willie McGee" case of a decade before. On December 11, 1940, Mrs. Eleanor Strubing, a thirty-one-year-old white woman from Greenwich, Connecticut, accused her black chauffeur, Joseph Spell, also thirty-one, of sexually assaulting her. At Spell's trial in January 1941, a jury of six men and six women listened to both stories and ultimately believed Spell's explanation that Mrs. Strubing had enticed him into an adulterous relationship. Pivotal in the case was Mrs. Strubing's own admission that she had greeted Spell at the door of her bedroom wearing only a bath towel, and the testimony of Spell's wife, Vergis, who was also employed by the Strubings and had been in the house at the time of the alleged rape, and who claimed to have heard no struggle or outcry. In contrast to how such cases tended to play out in the South, the Strubing case was notably free of public demands that Spell be dealt with harshly because men of his race had a predilection to rape white women, and there were no suggestions that intimacy between a white woman and a black man implied force. "Spell was exonerated because justice triumphed over prejudice." *Amsterdam News*, February 8, 1941. See also *New York Times*, December 12, 1940, and February 1, 1941.

400   deeply troubled by the plight: The intrepid Baker pursued a daring project in 1948, traveling
        alone through the South under the name "Mrs. Brown" to report on segregation to the read-
        ers of *France Soir*. Baker the journalist was not content to observe local conditions, but con-
        ducted her own one-woman integration projects. "She was much tougher than all those
        sit-in cats you saw on TV," a friend said years later. "She used the drinking fountains, the
        lunch counters and the ladies' rooms. They threw her ass out in the street and she walked
        right back in." See Haney, *Naked at the Feast*, p. 247.

400   "Those Joe Stalin loving people": Letter from E. A. Ellis of Jackson, Jackson *Daily News*,
        March 28, 1951.

401   "For sublimated gall": Jackson *Daily News*, July 19, 1950.

401   "They Deserved It": Ibid., July 28, 1950.

401   "Paul Robeson": Quoted in Mitford, p. 179.

402   "We are here because we are determined": Jackson *Daily News*, May 6, 1951.

403   "Willie McGee, an innocent man": Ibid., May 9, 1951.

404   "When Willie McGee died": Pittsburgh *Courier*, May 19, 1951.

404   "The United States is not a free country": *Current Biography*, 1964.

404   "that hiatus": Johnson, *Along This Way*, p. 205.

405   She was far from alone: The McCarren Acts, named for their backer, Senator Patrick A.
        McCarren of Nevada, which became law in 1950 and 1952, respectively, authorized the reg-
        istration of all Communists and severely limited their freedom to travel in and out of the
        United States. Robeson, Du Bois, William Patterson of the CRC, authors Richard Wright
        and James Baldwin would all have difficulties. In contrast, well-known blacks who were
        more muted in their criticism of America, such as the NAACP's Walter White, or "accept-
        able" entertainers such as bandleader Louis "Satchmo" Armstrong, were allowed greater
        latitude, and were even encouraged to go abroad as "spokesmen" on State Department–
        sponsored trips (although in 1957 Armstrong would angrily drop out of a planned govern-
        ment-supported tour of the Soviet Union because of the desegregation fight taking place at
        Central High School in Little Rock, Arkansas).

405   "If your organization would leave": Eleanor Roosevelt to Aubrey Grossman, March 14, 1951,
        in CRC Papers, McGee Correspondence.

CHAPTER 12
Under Color of Law

408   "mobilize the influence": *Petition to the United Nations on Behalf of 13 Million Oppressed Negro
        Citizens of the United States of America*, 1946, in Civil Rights Congress Papers, p. 2.

408   "a discrimination practiced": W.E.B. Du Bois, ed., *An Appeal to the World*, NAACP Publica-
        tion (New York: NAACP, 1947).

409   "We maintain": Civil Rights Congress, *We Charge Genocide*, p. xi.

409   "The genocide of which we complain": Ibid., p. 4.

409   "[f]or generations . . . has avoided": Ibid., p. 183.

409   "can be effected by": Ibid., p. 46.

410   "[B]y far the majority": Ibid., p. 9.

410   "Mass murder": Ibid., p. 46.

411   "Perennial": Ibid., p. 78.

411   "If the power of evil men": William Patterson, statement to General Assembly of the United
        Nations in Paris, December 1951, in *We Charge Genocide* file, CRC Papers.

412   Almost forty years later: Egerton, p. 562.

413   "We begin to see": *New York Times Magazine*, November 21, 1948.

413   "We shall fight this dastardly effort": Quoted in *We Charge Genocide*, p. 187.

414   The train quickly took on: The Freedom Train generated several inspiring human-interest
        stories, such as that of the elderly black woman, born in slavery, who was escorted aboard the
        train in rural Maryland to see with her own eyes Abraham Lincoln's signature on the Eman-
        cipation Proclamation. But there were less happy reports. In Rochester, New York, on No-
        vember 6, 1947, a twenty-year-old black war veteran named Ronald L. Price, roused by his
        viewing of the Freedom Train documents, strode into the Royal Palm Restaurant and imme-

diately got into an argument with a white bartender over the latter's refusal to make change for him. Patrolman William Hamill arrived and forced the unarmed black man into the street, where he and five other policemen opened fire, killing Price instantly. Hamill and the other officers were cleared of any wrongdoing. See *New York Times,* December 25, 1947.

415 "EAT ANYWHERE!": U.S. Commission on Civil Rights, *Freedom to Be Free,* pp. 123–24.

415 "Negro bubble": The Supreme Court had been chipping away at segregation since at least 1948, when it moved to strike down restrictive covenants, the private agreements between seller and buyer that had long been used to maintain discrimination in housing. Restrictive covenants had survived an NAACP assault in the 1926 case of *Corrigan v. Buckley.* But in the 1948 case, *Shelley v. Kraemer,* the court ruled that although the covenants represented private behavior, those engaged in such contracts used the state apparatus to enforce them, and that therefore the covenants involved the state in upholding an action that was unconstitutional under the Fourteenth Amendment's equal-protection clause.

416 "The American Negro needs": I. F. Stone syndicated column, "The Murder of Emmett Till," October 3, 1955.

418 This conviction: John M. Cooper, Jr., "Racism and Reform: A Review Essay," *Wisconsin Magazine of History,* Winter 1971–1972.

418 "running roughshod": Egerton, p. 326.

418 "I call for every red-blooded": Memphis *Commercial Appeal,* May 30, 1946.

418 "to see him the night before": Quoted in *We Charge Genocide,* p. 188.

418 "disloyal minorities": Quoted in ibid., pp. 234–36.

418 "The people loved him": Quoted in Hattiesburg *American,* July 26, 1983.

419 "As a Southern woman": *New York Times,* April 4, 1948; in Gladney, ed., *How Am I to Be Heard,* pp. 119–22.

420 "unwarranted decision": "Southern Manifesto" reprinted in Joanne Grant, ed., *Black Protest: History, Documents, and Analyses, 1619 to the Present* (New York: Fawcett World Library, 1968), pp. 268–72.

421 "a simple man": Bartley, *The Rise of Massive Resistance,* p. 118.

421 "We must take the offense": Eastland speech to Mississippi Association of Citizens' Councils, printed in Jackson *Daily News,* December 1, 1955.

421 This tissue of lies: *Poplarville Weekly Democrat,* March 26, 1959.

422 "just to show us how much": W. B. Huie, "What's Happened to the Emmett Till Killers?" *Look,* January 22, 1957.

423 simple explanation: Mississippi officialdom would latch on to this same interpretation a few years later when a black history teacher named Clennon King applied to attend summer school at Ole Miss. For pursuing so absurd an objective, white authorities had him committed to a lunatic asylum.

423 hide in a cornfield: Jackson *Clarion Ledger,* August 25, 1985.

424 "Did you say 'yes' to me?": Olive A. Adams, *Time Bomb: Mississippi Exposed* (Mississippi Regional Council of Negro Leadership, 1956), p. 18.

425 "He's been my lifesaver": Baltimore *Afro-American,* September 18, 1955.

425 "Somebody is going to pay for this": Ibid., Tupelo *Daily Journal,* September 2, 1995.

425 "It just looked as though": Des Moines *Bystander,* October 27, 1955. In response to the national uproar over the photograph and the NAACP's efforts to collect money for Till's family, Jimmy Arrington, editor of a weekly newspaper in Collins, Mississippi, asked Senator Eastland to submit a bill in Congress "making it a federal offense for any person or organization to place on public exhibition a dead body for the purpose of raising funds." "Human decency demands such a law," Arrington wrote, "and civilized people are entitled to one."

426 "This is not a lynching": *New York Times,* September 2, 1955.

428 "the hardest half hour": Murray Kempton, "He Went All the Way," in *America Comes of Middle Age: Columns 1950–1962* (Boston: Little, Brown, 1962), p. 136. There is no known official transcript of the Emmett Till murder trail in existence, thus all references to testimony are derived from press accounts of the trial.

429 "There are people in the United States": Greenwood *Commonwealth,* September 23, 1955.

430 "custodians of American civilization": *New York Times,* September 24, 1955.

430 "a hell of a fix": Des Moines *Bystander,* September 15, 1955.

431   "white girlfriend" story: Adams, *Time Bomb,* p. 17.

432   "Well, what else could we do?": *Saturday Evening Post,* January 24, 1956.

432   "I didn't intend to": *Look,* January 22, 1957.

432   "I got letters from all over": Ibid.

433   "The FBI has established": Thurgood Marshall to Tom Clark, December 27, 1946, in NAACP Anti-Lynching Papers.

433   "I . . . have no faith": Memorandum, Thurgood Marshall to Walter White, January 23, 1947, in NAACP Anti-Lynching Papers.

433   "As you realize": J. Edgar Hoover to Walter White, January 13, 1947, in NAACP Anti-Lynching Papers.

437   a blatant incongruity: Smead, *Blood Justice,* p. 116. My discussion of the Parker lynching is indebted to Smead's insightful account.

437   "the general consensus": *Poplarville Democrat,* April 30, 1959.

439   "as flagrant and calculated": *New York Times,* January 4 and 17, 1960.

441   Georgia, of course, did no such thing: Randall Kennedy, *Race, Crime, and the Law,* pp. 52–53.

441   "[T]he right not to be deprived": "Moderator's Report of Adequacy of Existing Anti-Lynching Legislation," prepared for Legal Conference on Federal Power to Protect Civil Liberties, Washington, D.C., January 25, 1947, in Department of Justice Record Group 60, National Archives.

442   "The conduct of individuals": New Orleans *Times-Picayune,* January 5, 1960.

443   "You mean you let that": Smead, p. 187; also *New York Times,* January 5, 1960.

443   "Common sense": *New York Times,* January 4, 1960.

444   The rallying of young Americans: At the height of the sit-in movement in spring 1960, students and other young people challenged the witch-hunt apparatus head-on. On May 12, as HUAC conducted hearings at San Francisco City Hall, five thousand students from Berkeley and other Bay Area colleges demonstrated on the portico outside. Fire hoses trained on the demonstrators failed to disperse them, so police swooped in and, using billy clubs, chased the protestors down the steps of the building, beating them bloody and dragging them to the street, as news cameras captured the incredible drama. Film footage of the event proved an embarrassment for HUAC and a politically galvanizing experience for young Americans.

445   "Mississippi is a Sovereign State": "The Klan Ledger, Special Neshoba County Fair Edition, 1964," in Mississippi Sovereignty Commission File #6-37-3, Mississippi State Archives.

446   A representative Northern college student: A broader discussion of the 1964 Neshoba County murders of Goodman, Schwerner, and Chaney will be found in Cagin and Dray, *We Are Not Afraid.*

452   "a very thin thread of law": quoted in Shapiro, p. 353; also quoted in Milton Konvitz article on legal status of black Americans in *An Appeal to the World.*

453   "To act 'under color' of law does not require": *U.S. v. Price.*

453   With this hurdle cleared: Trial testimony and statements are in *U.S. v. Cecil Ray Price et al.,* Criminal Action No. 5291, heard in Federal District Court for the Southern District of Mississippi in Meridian, October 11–21, 1967 (trial transcript); see also Cagin and Dray, *We Are Not Afraid,* pp. 445–52.

Epilogue

459   "tendency of the white majority": Berry, *Black Resistance,* p. 240.

459   Harsher prison sentences: Cole, *No Equal Justice,* pp. 4–5.

462   "He could easily have joined": *New York Times,* March 22, 1955.

463   "Regardless of the fact": Quoted in Lewis, *W.E.B. Du Bois,* p. 2.

Index

ABOUT THE AUTHOR

PHILIP DRAY is the co-author of *We Are Not Afraid: The Story of Goodman, Schwerner, and Chaney and the Civil Rights Campaign for Mississippi,* a 1988 *New York Times* Notable Book. He lives in New York City.

ABOUT THE TYPE

This book was set in Bembo, a typeface based on an old-style Roman face that was used for Cardinal Bembo's tract *De Aetna* in 1495. Bembo was cut by Francisco Griffo in the early sixteenth century. The Lanston Monotype Machine Company of Philadelphia brought the well-proportioned letter forms of Bembo to the United States in the 1930s.

Printed in the United States
by Baker & Taylor Publisher Services